Texas Land Survey Maps
for
Young County

*With Roads, Railways, Waterways, Towns, Cemeteries &
Cross-referenced Indexes from the Texas Railroad Commission & General Land Office*

Texas Land Survey Maps
for
Young County

With Roads, Railways, Waterways, Towns, Cemeteries &
Cross-referenced Indexes from the Texas Railroad Commission & General Land Office

by Gregory A. Boyd, J.D.

Arphax Publishing Co.
www.arphax.com

Texas Land Survey Maps for Young County with Roads, Railways, Waterways, Towns, Cemeteries & Cross-referenced Indexes from the Texas Railroad Commission & General Land Office

by Gregory A. Boyd, J.D.

ISBN 1-4203-5058-7

Published by Arphax Publishing Co., 2210 Research Park Blvd., Norman, Oklahoma, USA 73069
www.arphax.com

First Edition

Editor: Vicki Boyd

This book is dedicated to Vicki's and my
many ancestors who have lived
and died in Texas and that
helped shape us into
who we are . . .

Arphaxad R. Dawson
Ephraim A. Dawson and Lucinda Parsons
James Cox and Mary M. Fox
Abraham George Washington Cox and Sarah F. Cox
James M. Cox and Nancy L. Dawson
Lindsey Hamilton Scoggin and Julia Ann Lawrence
James P. Scoggin and Nancy Jane Daugherty
John H. Daughtery, Jr.
Elijah Parsons
James M. Parsons & Elizabeth Jane Helem
Andrew J. Rayzor and Melissa Whitaker
Joseph "Joel" P. Frogge
John Potts and Nancy Best
Simeon A. Rayzor and Alice P. Frogge
James H. Potts and Mary Etta Rayzor
James E. Cox & Grace D. Scoggin
Glen W. Potts & Hazel M. Cox

Miles Bond and Rebecca W. Rennick
Andrew Jackson Kinard and Ama P. Bond
Logan Coffee and Mary E. Ragland
Robert Cessna Grundy and Mary Ann Overhults
Thomas Logan Coffee and Carrie L. Straughn
Glenn T. Coffee and Rosa A. English
Henry H. English and Eliva Harrell
Francis H. English and Laura Elizabeth Buchanan
Calvin Buchanan and Sarah Laura Hamilton
Joseph Allen Grundy and Lucinda F. Clack
William Henry Clack and Harriet Maria Morris
Isabella (Petty) Clack
Winsa Ann (Morgan) Kinard
John Bond and Lucinda Derryberry
William T. Harris and Katherine Frances Miller
Ira A. Harris and Nancy Jane Wilder
Alman A. Kinard and Emma P. Grundy
Virgil Glenn Coffee and Bertha Lou Harris

A Special Thank You

A special thank-you goes to the folks at
the Texas General Land Office whose hard work
has made this series possible and whose efforts
make Texas history research both a fun
and fruitful endeavor.

Contents

- Part I -

The Big Picture

- Part II -

Land Survey Maps

with Index including Abstract Number, and 1st & 2nd Survey Names

Foreword

It is with much excitement that we are at last able to release this series of Texas Land Survey Maps. It represents three years of hard work, much of it trial-and-error in seeking the best way to present a lot of data and a lot of maps, in the most comprehensive and simple way possible. I am very pleased with the results and think you will be too.

This series is the second I've produced. The first, the *Family Maps* series, maps original landowners among a number of the public-land states. That project began in 2003 and first came to market in June 2005 . That series continues to grow and promises to do so for a number of years—perhaps another decade.

This second series resembles our first in several ways, primarily in its essence—in presenting historical land-ownership-boundary maps in the context of modern roads and geographical features. The two primary goals being, first, to enable the analysis of "frontier neighborhoods", and the second, to allow field researchers to actually go and find particular parcels of land in the simplest manner possible.

This series differs from the first in perhaps more ways than it is similar. I will save that discussion for another place and time, but for those familiar with the *Family Maps* series, those differences will be evident to you fairly quickly.

One functional similarity in both series is the idea that researchers should move from the front to the back of the book as they seek their answers. The indexes are of primary importance here, so they are not relegated to the back of the book. I will withhold further discussion of the specifics on how to use this tool until the following chapter, which is designed for that purpose.

I will close by pointing out one imminently useful and unique feature that this series offers, and that lies in the nature of Texas's use of legal-descriptions of land. In most other states, after title passes from an original owner, that original owner's name is of no further legal consequence to later owners. In Texas, land will often pass from owner-to-owner and each conveyance will refer back to the "original survey." This system stops once an area is platted for city-use or perhaps for other reasons.

Why is that good news for historical and land researchers? I offer my own experience as an example. I am in the possession of dozens, if not hundreds of Texas deeds ranging in dates from the 1880s to the 1970s and every one of them refers to the original survey. Now I KNOW where that land is, and I can find it without going to the courthouse, or to the internet, or anywhere else. And now, YOU KNOW why this series exists. I cannot wait to hear how many of you come to enjoy the same benefits from this series that I intend to enjoy on my next research trek.

Good luck to you, and God bless,

Greg Boyd
May 2008

Key Terms Used in these Maps and Indexes

Abstract Number - in each County, a unique number has been assigned (by the State of Texas) to each Survey; that "abstract number" may apply to multiple parcels of land identified in the single survey.

GLO - the General Land Office for the State of Texas. A State agency.

G'ee - Grantee

Grantee - a grantee is that person originally given the right to purchase a particular parcel of land within the State of Texas (or if pre-Statehood, the Republic of Texas). The Grantee's name, as used herein, is provided by the Texas General Land Office. In many cases, the Grantee was willing and able to actually take title to the land and would ultimately become the "patentee" (see below). The short explanation is that a grantee had a right to take ownership, but the patentee actually did. How that came to be may have been by the grantee either forfeiting their rights or selling them to another. For MUCH more information, see the Texas General Land office's web-site at: http://www.glo.state.tx.us/archives/collections.html

P-Dt - Patent Date (seen in the Abstract Index); refers to patents obtained during Texas statehood.

Patentee - a patentee is that person who takes original title to a particular parcel of land within the State of Texas (or pre-Statehood), by virtue of a public grant which may or may not have originally been intended for the ultimate patentee. See the explanation of "Grantee", above and the Texas GLO web-site mentioned there.

P'ee - Patentee

Populated Places - may include incorporated and/or unincorporated towns, cities, neighborhoods, additions, or even sites of historical communities which no longer exist. Our source for most of these is the U.S.G.S. Geographic Name Service.

T-Dt - Title Date (seen in the Abstract Index); refers to title gained during before Texas statehood.

Railroad Commission - the Texas Railroad Commission, author of the survey boundary maps we rely upon.

S2 - see Survey 2.

Survey - in general, when the public lands of Texas were sold to its citizens, whether during pre-Statehood or Statehood, that sale was conditioned upon a survey of the land in question. That Survey became known by the name of the person originally authorized to purchase that land.

Survey 1 - refers to the name associated with the first survey of a property. This person may or may not have actually taken title to the property.

Survey 2 - refers to a subsequent name associated with a second survey of a property.

A Quick & Dirty Guide

It is anticipated that a more lengthy "How-to Use this Book" narrative will be made available to the public at a later-date, but it was decided not to stuff that lengthy discourse into all two-hundred-fifty-four volumes that will be produced in this series.

That being said, the following explanation should suffice to make you an expert in the use and understanding of what follows.

This book is meant to be utilized by moving from its front to the back. The indexes are of primary importance and so are not relegated to the back of the book.

I will essentially walk through the items listed in the Table of Contents, in order. This is how they are meant to be utilized in your own work within these pages. Of course, once you become conversant with all the parts of the book, you will find yourself bouncing among all the various indexes and maps in order to grasp all that is here. But that comes later. For now, let's work through the sections, in order.

The book is divided into two main parts, the first providing statewide and county-wide maps and indexes that ultimately mean to point you to the second part: the actual Land Survey Maps.

Part I - The Big Picture

Map A - Where the County Lies Within the State

This is self-explanatory, but for researchers not familiar with Texas, or at least with the subject county, it gives them a context of the county's location within the entire state of Texas.

Map B - The Subject County and Surrounding Counties

This zooms you into the subject county and allows you to more readily identify the surrounding counties, whether in Texas or one of the neighboring states.

Map C - Land Survey Maps (an Index Map)

This map simply shows you the grid used to break down the subject county into its various Land Survey Maps.

Map D - Cities & Towns

Building on the grid shown in Map C, this "index map" shows you which maps to turn to if you are seeking answers in the land surrounding a particular community. The accompanying index can help you locate hard-to-spot communities.

Map E - Cemeteries

Again, building on the grid shown in Map C, this "index map" shows you which maps to turn to if you are seeking answers in the land surrounding a particular cemetery. Use the accompanying index of cemeteries for help in locating which map a given cemetery is located. We encourage those of you who know of cemeteries not found in our maps, to copy relevant pages from among the survey maps, mark any cemeteries that you know are missing, and mail them to us for inclusion in future publications. Contact us via email at info@arphax.com or call us at 1-800-681-5298 for a current mailing address.

Every-Name Index With Abstract-Numbers

We call this the Every-Name/Abstract Index, for short. This represents every name associated with the surveys, grants, and patents used in the creation of this book. Multiple-persons who purchased land together have been broken out as individuals (or as simply last names, if that is all that is given).

A look at just three lines from an index in the Rusk County book will show you all you need to know:

ANDERSON, T: 55, 62

ANDERSON, THOMAS: 55, 62

ANDERSON, THOMAS J: 276, 827

From these three lines, it is clear that T. Anderson and Thomas Anderson are likely one and the same. The T. Anderson is what you would find in the typical land survey map for this individual. But by cross-referencing that data to newer GLO data, we learn that T. Anderson is Thomas Anderson. This will be more clear when you view the entries for the given abstracts in the next index—the *Abstract Listing*.

Abstract Listing (Extensive Data, including Land Survey Map Numbers)

This is the grandmother of all indexes, at least within the confines of this book. To build upon the sample lines from the just-described *Every-Name Index*, here is the entry for Abstract (which are numerially ordered) number 55, for Anderson, T.

```
Abstract # 55 - ANDERSON, T  <--- Survey Name
P'ee: BROWN, GEORGE W      <--- Patentee
G'ee: ANDERSON, THOMAS     <--- Grantee
T-Dt: -- --- -----          <--- Title-Date
P-Dt: 26 Aug 1848           <--- Patent-Date
Dist/Class: Rusk 3rd        <--- Surveying Authority (Law)
File#: 22
Patent#: 185                GLO File Information
Patent Vol.: 5
Certificate: 84
Acres: 320                  <--- Acres
Map(s) 10                   <--- MAPS to view in
                                this book
```

Each of these Abstract Listings tells a story. We learn from this case that the survey-name is T. Anderson, but that he was not the original patentee. That was a man named George W. Brown. Brown somehow

relinquished his right to the land and Anderson eventually became the grantee and the survey was given his name.

Apart from the other relevant data presented in these listings, the KEY line for purposes of moving forward in this book is that last one—the Map No(s). This points the way to Part II of this book and the relevant Survey Map(s) in which you will find the land referred to in the Abstract Listing.

- Part II -

Land Survey Maps

And so we finally come to the Land Survey Maps.

Before describing the maps specifically, a quick look at the accompanying index (on the right-hand page facing the map) is in order.

Again, I think an example will serve us best. Here is the item found in Map 10 in Rusk County that you would find for the aforementioned T. Anderson Survey:

ANDERSON, T
Abs # 55
26-Aug-1848

This index is meant mainly for two purposes: 1. to let you know that you have indeed arrived at the proper map for the person and parcel you are seeking, and, 2. to point you to any other maps which the given parcel may spill into.

When a parcel of land spills into more than one map, you will see an entry like this:

MCCLAIN, J
Abs # 19
12-Oct-1835
see also, Maps 6, 13, 14

So, now that all the major indexes have been described, let us take a look at a Survey Map, proper. A small portion of one will suffice for describing the elements that can be found throughout the actual maps in this book.

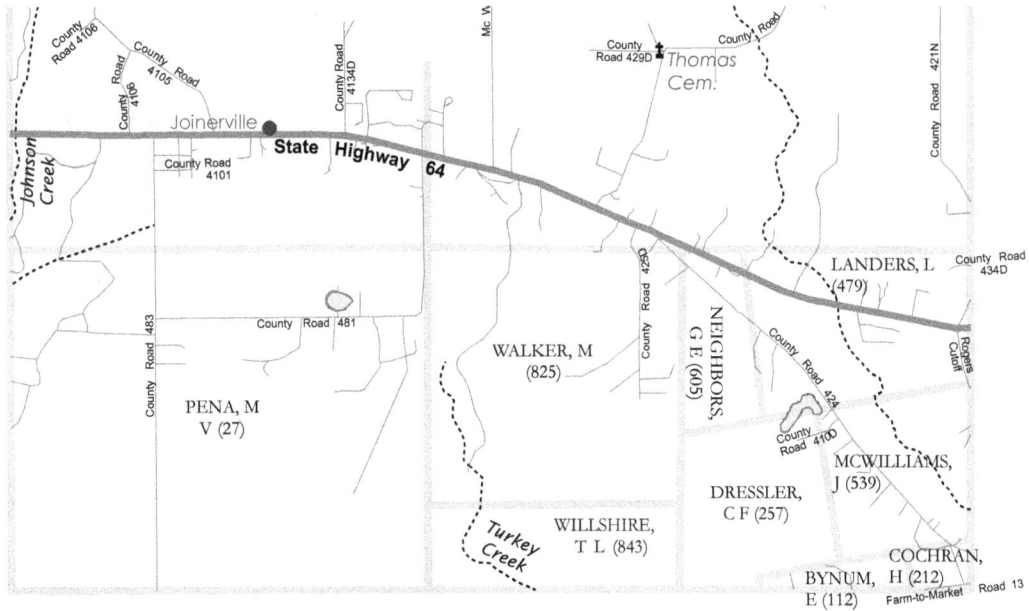

The partial map above is a sample from Rusk County, and apart from an interstate, a railrway, and a large body of water, it displays all the other elements you will find in maps throughout this series (note: a few counties show no railroads).

Surveys are always represented in the same typeface and are followed by the abstract number in parentheses.

You will note that in this small portion of a map, just how easy it is to see the relationship of one parcel to another, and how you can clearly view which creeks pass through the property, or which little county roads pass through or nearby, as well as major roads.

Cemeteries and Populated Places are also easy to spot.

Rather than repeat a Map Legend throughout the book, the Legend at right applies to all the maps in this series.

Finally, there is one last element that has not yet been mentioned. You will find in each Land Survey Map index-page, four small boxes that list significant features to be found in the accompanying map.

These are the Populated Places (center-points), Cemeteries, Large Bodies of Water, and Other Water (streams, creeks, etc.). A sample follows.

Scale: All maps are 6 miles tall x 4 miles wide

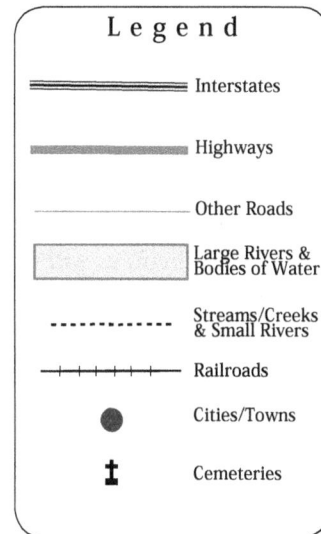

Legend
- ═══════ Interstates
- ━━━━━ Highways
- ───────── Other Roads
- ☐ Large Rivers & Bodies of Water
- - - - - - - Streams/Creeks & Small Rivers
- ┼┼┼┼┼┼ Railroads
- ● Cities/Towns
- ✝ Cemeteries

Populated Places
Friars
Joinerville
Cemeteries
Thomas Cemetery
Water (larger bodies)
Miller Lake
Other Water
Bromley Creek
Chambers Creek
Copper Creek
Johnson Creek
Mill Creek
Turkey Creek

The above sample feature-listings are actually from the same map shown on the previous page.

These listings not only let you know that these features do indeed appear in the accompanying map, but the "Other Water" listing will particularly come in handy. Becoming conversant with surrounding creeks can help you be a better land researcher. Many old deeds will refer to them, as will other historical documents and narratives.

One final bit of minutiae: in cross-referencing two sources of data (Texas Railroad Commission map-data with Texas General Land Office data), there is some fallout. You will find the details of what I am speaking in the final entries in each *Abstract Index*, and remnants of this data in the Survey maps, themselves

At the end of each Abstract Index, you will usually find entries like these:

Abstract # ?25 - WILSON, J
T-Dt: -- --- -----
P-Dt: -- --- -----

As of yet, we have not located GLO records that correspond to these references to parcels which are indeed in the maps. We suspect the underlying records were not at the GLO's disposal at the time indexes were created and hence the "?" (or "Q", in our case) was used to distinquish these parcels.

In the first printings of this series, some of these entries fail to list a map number. Luckily, they are few in number. If you cannot locate a parcel among these Abstracts containing a "?" in their number, please feel free to contact the publisher at info@arphax.com and a researcher will be happy to provide you an answer as soon as possible. We will later print an errata page and post it on our web-site.

– Part I –

The Big Picture

Map A - Where Young County, Texas Lies Within the State

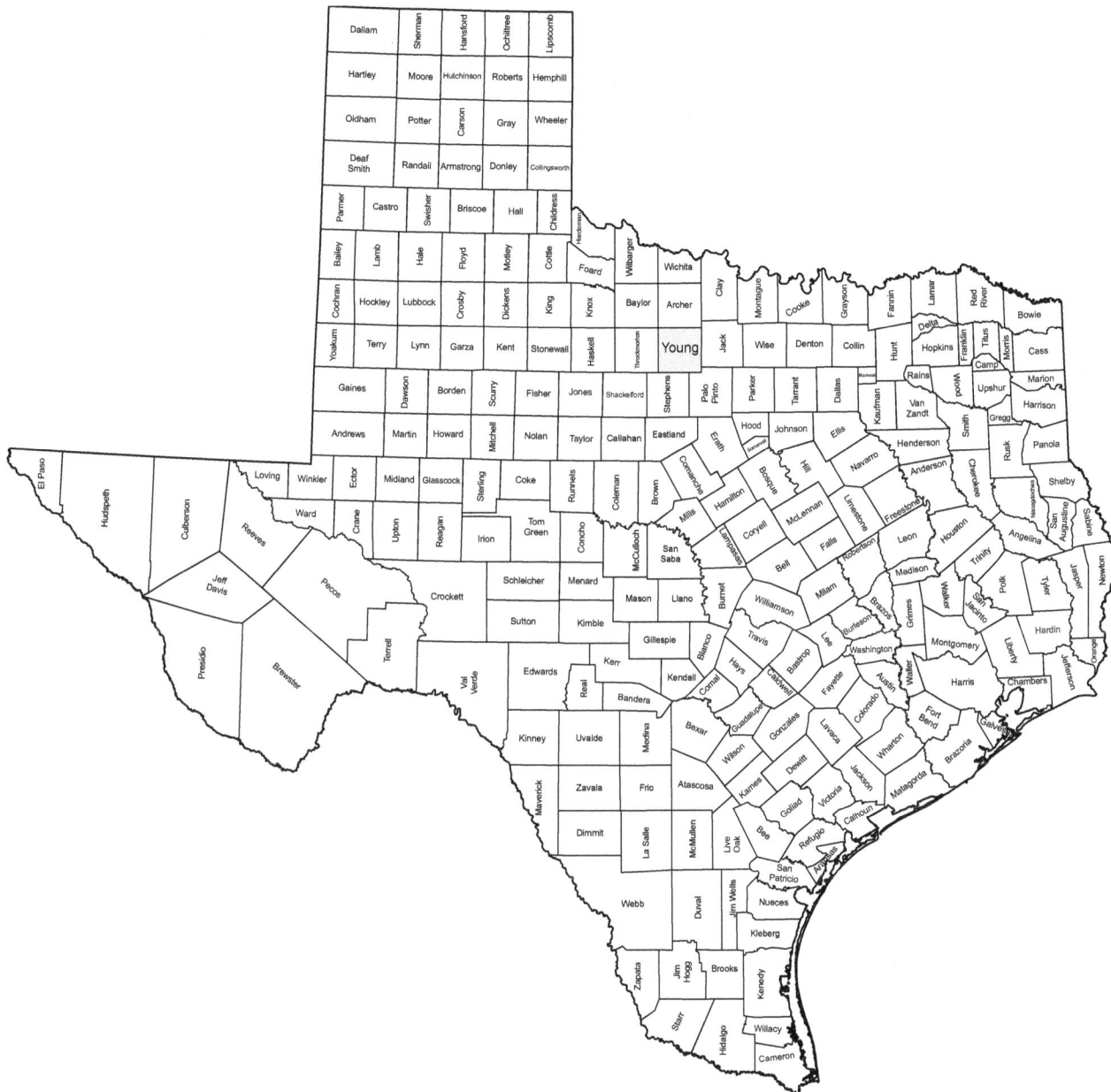

Legend

— State Boundary

— County Boundaries

☐ Young County, Texas

Helpful Hints

1 Map "A" simply shows you where within Texas this County lies.

2 Map "B" zooms in further to help you easily identify surrounding Counties.

3 Maps "C", "D", and "E" present an overview of the Land Survey Maps in this book.

Map B - Young County, Texas and Surrounding Counties

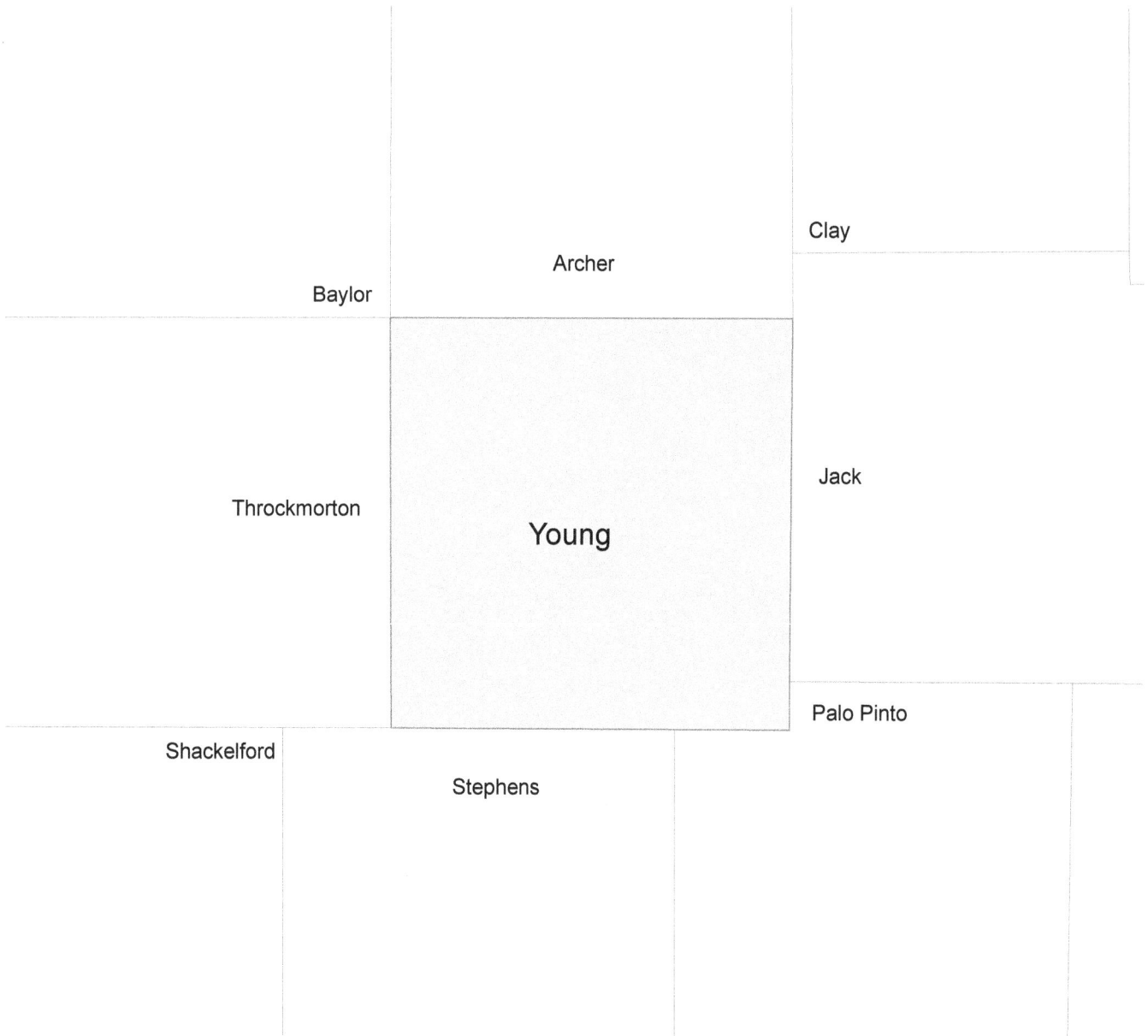

Clay

Archer

Baylor

Jack

Throckmorton

Young

Shackelford

Palo Pinto

Stephens

——— Legend ———

State Boundaries (when applicable)

—— County Boundaries

——— Helpful Hints ———

1 Many Patent-holders and their families purchased land in adjoining counties. It is always a good idea to check nearby counties for the subjects of your research.

2 Refer to Map "A" to see a broader view of where Young County lies within the State.

3 Maps C, D, and E will give you an overview of the various Land-Survey Maps in this book.

Land Survey Maps of Young County, Texas

1	2	3	4	5	6	7	8
9	10	11	12	13	14	15	16
17	18	19	20	21	22	23	24
25	26	27	28	29	30	31	32
33	34	35	36	37	38	39	40
41	42	43	44	45	46	47	48

——— Legend ———

☐ Young County, Texas

☐ Land-Survey Maps

——— Helpful Hints ———

1 Many Patent-holders purchased land across county lines. It is always a good idea to check nearby counties for the subjects of your research (See Map "B").

2 Refer to Map "A" to see a broader view of where Young County lies within the State, and Map "B" for a closer view of the surrounding counties.

Map D Index: Cities & Towns of Young County, Texas

The following represents the Cities and Towns of Young County, along with the corresponding Survey Map in which the center of each is found.

City/Town	Survey Map No.
Bunger	38
Eliasville	43
Farmer	6
Graham	30
Jean	13
Loving	15
Markley	8
Murray	25
Newcastle	20
Old Caseyville Crossing	37
Olney	3
Padgett	9
Proffitt	18
Proffitt Crossing	10
Red Top	14
South Bend	37
True	12
Twin Mountains	30

Map D - Cities & Towns of Young County, Texas

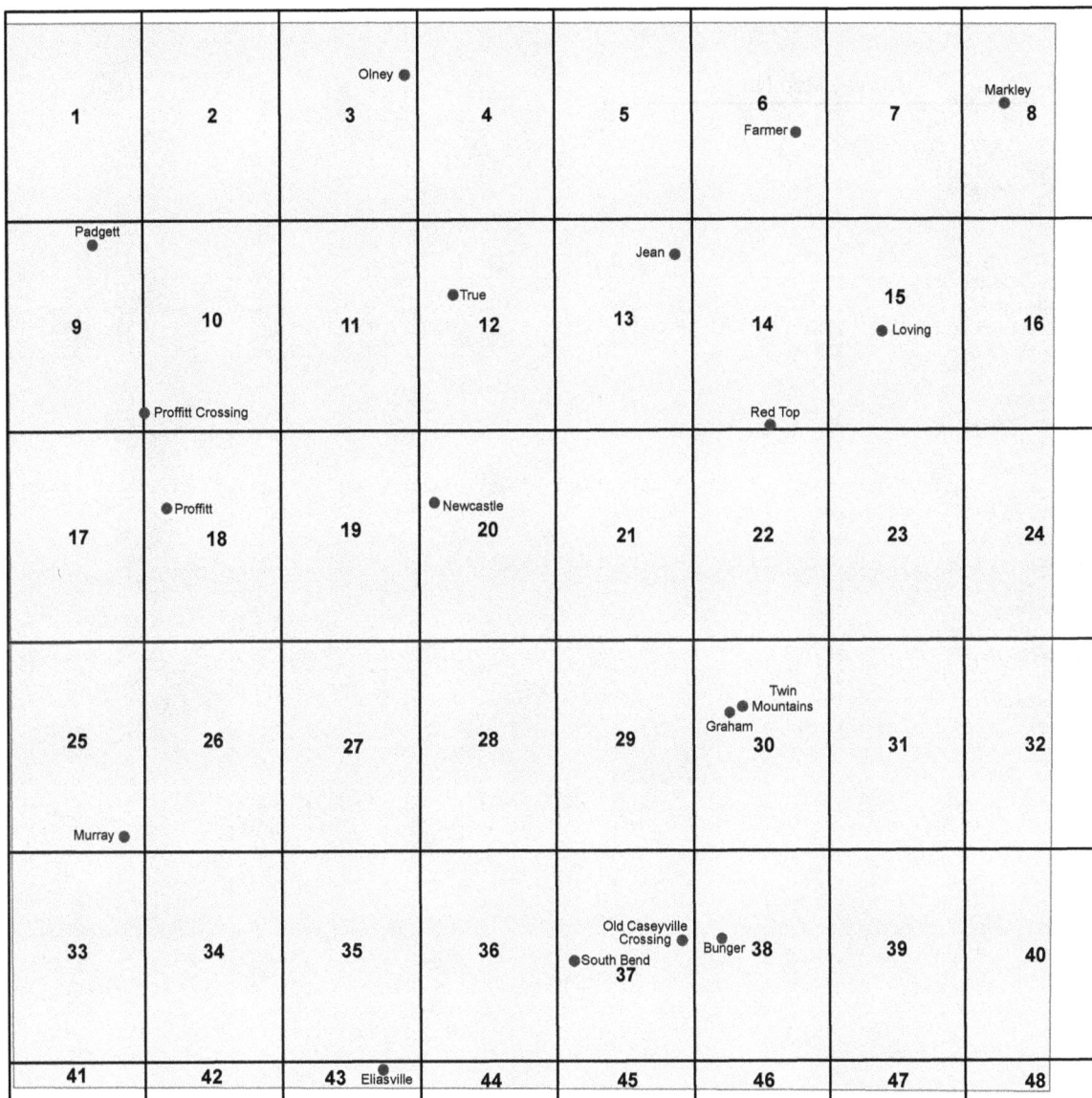

1	2	3 Olney ●	4	5	6 Farmer ●	7	Markley ● 8
Padgett ● 9	10 ● Proffitt Crossing	11	● True 12	Jean ● 13	14 Red Top ●	15 ● Loving	16
17	● Proffitt 18	19	● Newcastle 20	21	22	23	24
25	26	27	28	29	Twin ● Mountains Graham ● 30	31	32
Murray ●							
33	34	35	36	Old Caseyville Crossing ● ● South Bend 37	Bunger ● 38	39	40
41	42	43 Eliasville ●	44	45	46	47	48

────── Legend ──────

Young County, Texas

Land-Survey Maps

────── Helpful Hints ──────

1 Cities and towns are marked at their center-points as published by the USGS. This often enables us to more closely approximate where these might have existed when first settled.

2 To see more specifically where these Cities & Towns are located within the county, refer to the appropriate Land-Survey Map as indicated in the above map and/or the Index on the opposite page.

Map E Index: Cemeteries of Young County, Texas

The following represents many of the Cemeteries of Young County, along with the corresponding Land-Survey Map in which the center of each is located.

Cemetery	Survey Map No.
Belknap Cemetery	20
Brier Bend Cemetery	37
Brooks Cemetery	28
Center Ridge Cemetery	31
Donnell Cemetery	35
Farmer Cemetery	38
Gooseneck Cemetery	38
Hawkins Chapel Cemetery	15
Huffstuttle Cemetery	33
Indian Mound Cemetery	21
Loving Cemetery	15
Medlan Cemetery	36
Ming Bend Cemetery	39
Mountain Home Cemetery	38
Murray Cemetery	34
Oak Grove Cemetery	30
Orth Cemetery	11
Padgett Cemetery	9
Peveler Cemetery	44
Pioneer Cemetery	30
Proffitt Cemetery	18
Reynolds Cemetery	9
Saint Luke Cemetery	3
South Bend Cemetery	37
Tyra Cemetery	34
Woolfolk Cemetery	19
Wray Cemetery	20

Map E - Cemeteries of Young County, Texas

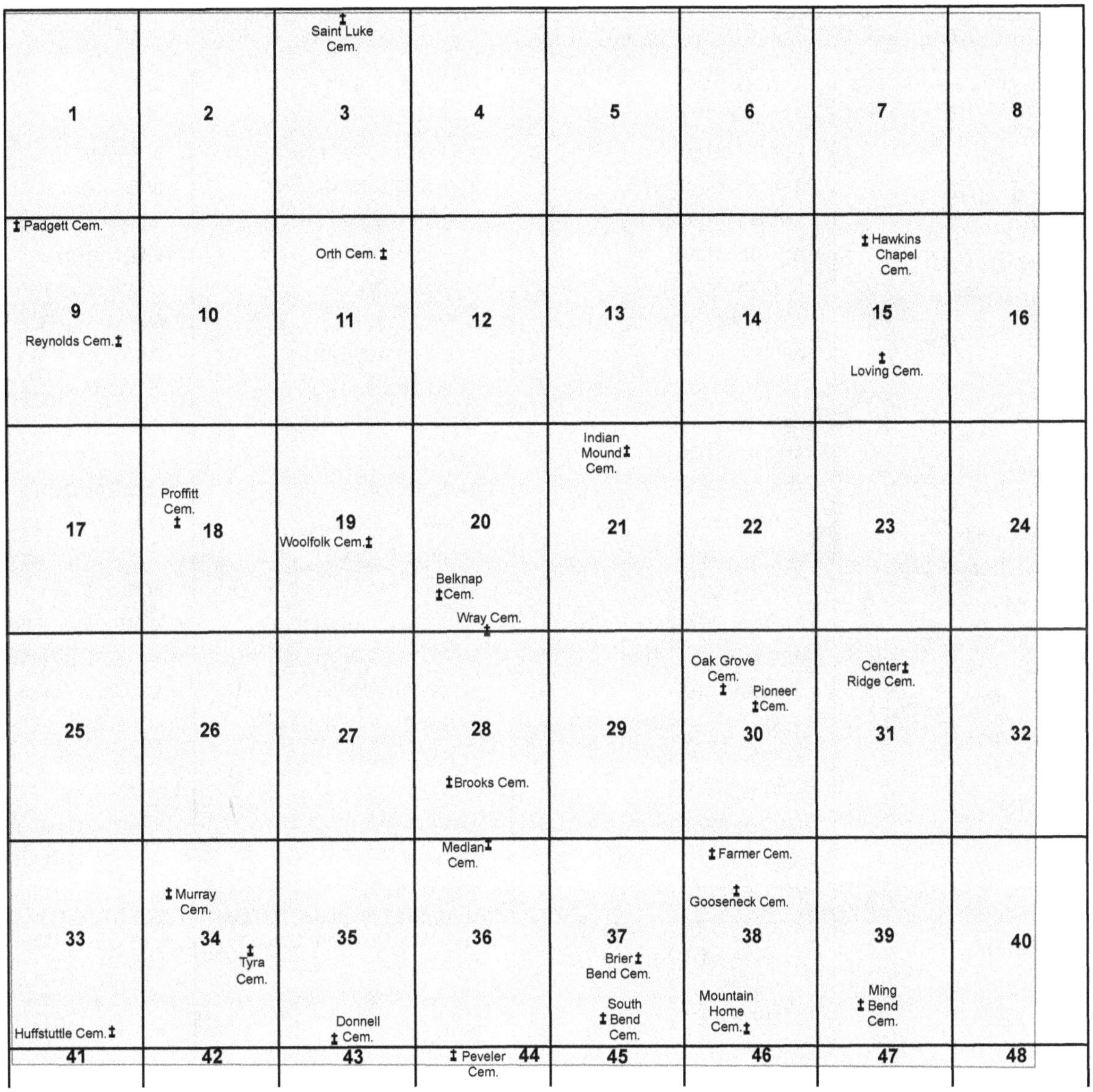

1	2	‡ Saint Luke Cem. 3	4	5	6	7	8
‡ Padgett Cem. 9 Reynolds Cem.‡	10	Orth Cem. ‡ 11	12	13	14	‡ Hawkins Chapel Cem. 15 ‡ Loving Cem.	16
17	Proffitt Cem. ‡ 18	19 Woolfolk Cem.‡	Indian Mound‡ Cem. 20 Belknap ‡Cem. Wray Cem. ‡	21	22	23	24
25	26	27	28 ‡Brooks Cem.	29	Oak Grove Cem. ‡ Pioneer ‡Cem. 30	Center‡ Ridge Cem. 31	32
33 Huffstuttle Cem. ‡	‡ Murray Cem. 34 ‡ Tyra Cem.	35 Donnell ‡ Cem.	Medlan‡ Cem. 36	37 Brier‡ Bend Cem. South ‡ Bend Cem.	‡ Farmer Cem. ‡ Gooseneck Cem. 38 Mountain Home Cem.‡	39 Ming ‡ Bend Cem.	40
41	42	43	‡ Peveler 44 Cem.	45	46	47	48

——— Legend ———

☐ Young County, Texas

☐ Land-Survey Maps

——— Helpful Hints ———

1 Cemeteries are marked at locations as published by the USGS.

2 To see more specifically where these Cemeteries are located, refer to the appropriate Land-Survey Map as indicated in the above map and/or the Index on the opposite page.

Every-Name Index With Abstract-Numbers

The following list represents every name we can find associated with the Land-Surveys of Young County. After each name, you are directed to one or more Abstract Numbers which are located in the Index just following this one. THAT index will guide you to one or more Maps where the underlying land is located AND will show you other names associated with the relevant parcel of land.

AB&M: 1369, 1370, 1418, 1684, 1734, 1748, 2131, 2168, 2169, 2170, 2246, 2298, 2336, 2350, 2482

ABBOTT: 196, 197

ABBOTT, EDWARD F: 1271

ABERNATHY, J: 1360, 1567

ABERNATHY, JESSE: 1567

ABERNATHY, M C: 1914

ADAMS: 1369, 1370, 2350

ADAMS, J M: 185

ADAMS, J P: 1362

ADAMS, M V B: 1368

ADAMS, MARTIN V B: 1368

ADAMS, W C: 1364

ADINGTON, I: 1947

ADINGTON, THOMAS: 1947

AHLERS, C: 1974

AHLERS, CHARLES: 1974

AINSWORTH, G L: 1948

AINSWORTH, J A: 2147, 2197

AKERS, N J: 1361

AKERS, W A J: 1363

AKERS, W J: 1361

AKIN, D R: 2233, 2234, 2235, 2236, 2237, 2238, 2239, 2240, 2241, 2249

AKIN, J W: 2234, 2235, 2236, 2237, 2238, 2239, 2240, 2241, 2249

AKIN, JO W: 2148

AKIN, O W: 2148

AKINS, J A: 1289, 2111

AKINS, JAMES A: 1289

AKLES, H B: 5

AKLES, HEZEKIAH B: 5

ALCORN, R: 1767

ALCORN, ROBERT: 1767

ALFORD, J L: 2211

ALLEN, CATHERINE (MRS): 1544

ALLEN, ISAAC: 1595, 1725

ALLEN, J: ?5, 1662

ALLEN, J B: 1367

ALLEN, JOSEPH: 1662

ANDERSON, A C: 2115

ANDERSON, CHARLES R: 226

ANDERSON, J: 6

ANDERSON, J E: 2311

ANDERSON, JOHN: 6

ANDERSON, R G: 1365

ANDERSON, R M: 1418

ANDERSON, S: 3

ANDERSON, SAMUEL: 3

ANDERSON, SAMUEL (HEIRS): 3

ARDIS, W H: 2198

ARNOLD, F T: 2272

ARNOLD, H: 2242

ARNOLD, H G: 2242

ASH, G H: 1366

ASKEW, J M: 1288

ATWOOD, W H: 2302, 2303

AUBURG, C E F: 1663

AUBURG, CHARLES E F: 1663

AUD, I L: 1

AUD, IGNATIUS L: 1

AUSTIN, ELLA V: 1826

AUSTIN, W W: 1826

AUTREY, T: 1716

AUTREY, THOMAS: 1716

AVERITT, P: 2

AVERITT, PHILLIP (DECEASED): 2

AVERITT, PHILLIP (HEIRS): 2

AYNESWORTH, G L: 1812, 1915, 1916, 1948

BACHEL, A: 1254

BACHELDOR, O B: 1592

BAHN, A: 38

BAILARD, P S: 1717

BAKER, G W: 1291

BAKER, J M: 1669

BAKER, J R: 56

BAKER, J W: 1377

BAKER, JOHN W: 1376

BAKER, M W: 52, 1572

BAKER, MARION W: 1572

BAKER, T J: 1377

BAKER, W A: 1293

BAKER, W H: 1376, 1514

BALL, THOMAS: 97, 98

BALLARD, P B: 1717

BARNARD, CHARLES E: 106, 1243

BARNARD, GEORGE: 188

BARNES, G L: 151

BARNES, M: 14

BARNES, MOSES: 14

BARNETT, D: 46

BARNETT, DUNCAN: 46

BARNETT, S: 45, 1580

BARNETT, W H: 2078

BARR, R: 9

BARR, ROBERT: 9

BARRETT, J M: 1612

BARRICK, S: 1975

BARRICK, SUSAN: 1975

BARRICK, SUSAN (MRS): 1975

BARRY, T H: 1668

BARRY, THOMAS: 1264

BARRY, THOMAS H: 1668

BARTEL, JOHN C: 121

BARTLETT, M: 55

BASS, A T: 1917

BASS, C F: 1571

BBB&C RR CO: 25, 26, 27, 28, 29, 30, 31, 32, 33, 34, 35, 36, 37, 1385, 1386, 1456, 1525, 1700, 1701, 1720, 1721, 1757, 1838, 1857, 2173, 2200, 2306

BEACKWOOD, J L: 1378

BEARD, F J: 1298

BEATY: 40, 41, 42, 43, 44, 1369, 1370, 2350

BECKHAM, CHARLES: 1375

BEEMAN, J S: 1379

BELLAH, GEORGE: 1573

BELLAMY, A F: 1290

BELLAMY, J N: 1574

BELLOMY, W: 2131

BELLOMY, W D: 1917, 2131

BELLUH, G: 1573

BEMUN, J S: 1379

BENNETT, J: 1577

BENNETT, T S: 2278

BENNETT, W A: 1832, 2122

BENSON, C P: 1569

BERNHARDT, WILLIAM: 1838

BICE, JAMES: 1651

BILLINGSLEY, J: 19

BILLINGSLEY, JESSIE: 19

BIRDWELL, J: 1768

BIRDWELL, J M: 1440, 1568

BIRDWELL, JOSEPH: 1768

BLACK, H M: 1260

BLACK, S: 1576

BLACK, SAMUEL: 1576

BLACKWOOD, J L: 1378

BLACKWOOD, L C: 2149

BLACKWOOD, L C (HEIRS): 2149

BLAINE, R A: 1382

BLAINE, R A (HEIRS): 1382

BLAKEY, C B: 1386

BLAKEY, W C: 1385

BLICK, W W: ?34

BOHN, A: 38

BOLTON, HRS J: 12

BOLTON, JAMES: 12

BOLTON, JAMES (HEIRS): 12

BONARD, CHARLES E: 1272

BOON, E: 31, 33, 34, 35

BOSKIN, JOHN C: 1664

BOTTORFF, JOHN F: 202

BOWERS, MARTIN V: 30

BOYD, RACHEL C: 1299

BRADDOCK, E M: 1879

BRADDOCK, T J: 1879

BRADLEY, HRS J: 1371

BRADLEY, HRS, J: 1972

BRADLEY, JAMES (HEIRS OF): 1371

BRADLEY, JAMES (HEIRS): 1371

BRADWELL, T M: 1664

BRAGG, B: 1769

BRAGG, BENJAMIN: 1769

BRAGG, FANNIE: 1489

BRAGG, G: 53

BRAGG, G B: 1380

BRAGG, GEORGE: 1380

BRAGG, GEORGE B: 53

BRAGG, J: 49

BRAGG, JESSIE: 49

BRAGG, W: 50

BRAGG, WILLIAM: 50, 1489

BRAY, J W: 1949

BRAY, S S: 1794

BRAY, W H: 1667

BRENIZER, N O: 2217

BRIDGES, J: 17

BRIDGES, JOHN: 17

BRIM, G P: 1347

BRIM, J F: 1771

BRIM, JOHN F: 1771

BRINKLEY, J W: 1978

BRINSON, MATHEW: 240

BRIR: 1347, 1366, 1367, 1374, 1383, 1410, 1416, 1417, 1430, 1440, 1452, 1453, 1455, 1471, 1500, 1519, 1534, 1541, 1542, 1556, 1557, 1564, 1579, 1580, 1585, 1590, 1604, 1613, 1623, 1632, 1637, 1640, 1646, 1655, 1658, 1672, 1685, 1689, 1694, 1709, 1730, 1738, 1771, 1773, 1781, 1795, 1812, 1818, 1837, 1840, 1848, 1860, 1866, 1873, 1896, 1898, 1900, 1915, 1916, 1935, 1938, 1948, 1955, 1980, 2011, 2071, 2073, 2119, 2135, 2136, 2142, 2144, 2147, 2148, 2150, 2154, 2179, 2180, 2183, 2185, 2189, 2197, 2201, 2202, 2203, 2204, 2205, 2208, 2209, 2212, 2215, 2216, 2217, 2218, 2219, 2221, 2222, 2225, 2228, 2230, 2231, 2233, 2234, 2235, 2236, 2237, 2239, 2240, 2241, 2243, 2244, 2245, 2247, 2248, 2249, 2250, 2251, 2253, 2255, 2261, 2290, 2304, 2329, 2341, 2360

BROGDEN, M: 2123

BROGDEN, P H: 2111

BROGDON, M: 2123

BROOKS, D C: 48, 1866

BROOKS, S A: 1887

BROWN, D: 16

BROWN, DOUGLASS: 16

BROWN, G F: 1670

BROWN, J C: 39, 1399

BROWN, JAMES C: 39

BROWN, JAMES H: 1604

BROWN, L A: 1399

BROWN, O T: 24

BROWN, OLIVER T: 24

BROWN, W H: 1865

BRYANT, A: 1950

BRYANT, ALEXANDER: 1950

BRYANT, R: 1794

BRYANT, W H: 1828

BS&F: 40, 41, 42, 43, 44, 1480, 1638, 1670, 1723, 1750, 1836, 1846, 2174, 2187, 2211, 2254, 2265

BUFFALO BAYOU, BRAZOS AND COLORADO RAILROAD COMPANY: 25, 26, 27, 28, 29, 30, 31, 32, 33, 34, 35, 36, 37

BUIE, L B: 1579

BULLARD, J D: 1718

BULLARD, L D: 1718

BULLARD, W A: 1951

BULLOCK, D: 10

BULLOCK, D M: 15

BULLOCK, DAVID: 10

BULLOCK, DAVID M: 15

BUNGER, S: 1292, 1375

BUNGER, SAMUEL: 1292

BUNGER, W T: 54, 1795

BUNGER, WILLIAM T: 1795

BURCH, A: 2150

BURCH, F P: 1578, 2243, 2251

BURCH, R: 2150

BURCH, T J: 1770, 1888

BURGER, SAMUEL: 1375

BURGESS, B E: 1329

BURK, J D: 2151, 2184

BURKETT, F M: 2276, 2279

BURNET, J W: 1381

BURNETT, J W: 1381

BURNS, W C: 2155, 2157

BURTON, E D: 2270

BURTON, R M: 8

BUSE, J: 1570

BUSE, JAMES: 1570

BUSSELL, B F: 1384

BUSSELL, C H: 1889

BUSSELL, J: 1575

BUSSELL, JAMES: 1575

BUSSEY, J F: 2152

BUSTILLO, J M: 7

BUSTILLO, JOSE MARIA: 7

BUTLER, B C: 233

BUTLER, E V: 1295

BUTLER, M: 1864

BUTLER, MOSES: 1864

BYERLY, W: 22, 23

BYERLY, WILLIAM: 22, 23

BYNUM, H C: 2304

BYNUM, H C JR: 2304

BYRD, R E: 47

BYRD, W A: 1383

BYRD, W B: 1374

BYRD, W E: 1374

BYRD, WILLIAM A: 1383

CADDLE, A: 61

CADDLE, ANDREW: 61

CAHILL, J: 59

CAHILL, JOHN: 59

CAIRNES, J A: 1296

CAIRNES, JOHN A: 1296

CALHOUN, J H: 1585

CALHOUN, J H (HEIRS): 1585

CALLEN, A N: 1977

CALLEN, S P: 1953

CAMPBELL, A J: 1918

CAMPBELL, ALEXANDER: 2258

CAMPBELL, JANE: 1777

CAMPBELL, L H: 1813

CAMPBELL, M: 2358

CAMPBELL, MARGUERITE: 2358

CAMPBELL, R: 2297

CAMPBELL, RUTHY: 2297

CAMPBELL, RUTHY (HEIRS): 2297

CANTWELL, A J: 2361

CANTWELL, J J: 1586

CANTWELL, JAMES J: 1586

CANTWELL, W: 1393

CANTWELL, WILLIAM: 1393

CAPPS, W T: 2212

CARMACK, A S: 1618

CARNAHAN, E: 164

CARROLL, JOSEPH A: 2085

CARSON, R: 69, 70, 71

CARSON, ROBERT: 69, 70, 71

CARSON, W J: 69

CARTER, W T: 62

CARTER, WILLIAM T: 62

CARTER, WILLIAM T (HEIRS): 62

CARTWRIGHT, MONROE: 1389

CASE, M (MRS): 1402

CASE, MRS M: 1402

CASEY, A C: 2026

CASEY, J W: 1541, 1672

CASSEL, HRS W: 67

CASSELL, WILLIAM: 67

CASTRO, M G: 60

CATES, J: 1398, 1673

CATES, J L: 1969

CATES, JOHN: 1398, 1673

CATLIN, R A: 1919

CAUFMAN, J: 63

CAUFMAN, JAMES: 63

CEPI&M CO: 2351

CHAMBERS, MATTIE (MRS): 2171

CHAMBERS, V M: 2172

CHEEK, W C: 1978

CHILDRESS, W: 1392, 1399

CHISM, E M: 1752

CHISM, M H: 2119

CHISM, MATT H: 2119

CHISUM, W C: 2312

CHISUM, W C JR: 2312

CHOATE, C S: 2280

CHOATE, E L: 2313

CI CO: 1300, 1301

CLARK, J F: 2200, 2201, 2202

CLARK, T B: 1796

CLELLEN, ROBERT: 1464

CLIFTON, G W: 1601

CLINGBERG, A: 1721

CLINGBERG, AUGUST: 1721

CLINGBERG, AUGUST (HEIRS): 1721

COCKRELL, T J: 1403

COE, J G: ?24

COFFMAN, A W: 72, 2185

COFFMAN, E M: 1404, 2011

COLE, J M: 2153, 2336

COLEMAN, THOMAS: 2178, 2194

COLSTON, J W: ?8, 1977

COLTHARP, E S: 1390

COLTHARP, H: 1582

COLTHARP, J: 1581

COLTHARP, JOHN: 1581

COLUMBUS TAP RAILROAD COMPANY: 68

COMBS, T J: 1298

COMPERE, W T: 1719, 1954

CONNELLY, W A: 1583

CONNER, J: 57

CONNER, JOHN: 57

CONSOLIDATED EL PASO IRRIGATION AND MANUFACTURING COMPANY: 2351

COOK, J R: 1405

COOK, L C: 1774

COOK, T M: 2274

COOK, W W: 2303

COOKE, EDWARD: 225

COOKE, J R: 1405

CORNELL, W L: 1890

CORNETT, W L: 73, 1890

COSBY, J: 1722, 1723

COSBY, JAMES: 1722, 1723

COSTELLO, CON: 2160, 2186, 2214

COSTELLO, E P: 2214

COSTELLO, E R: 2160, 2186

COTHRAN, G: 1401

COTHRAN, GEORGE: 1401

COTHRAN, J C: 1400

COTHRAN, JOHN: 1400

COTTLE, G W: 65, 66

COTTLE, G W (HEIRS): 65, 66

COTTLE, GEORGE W: 65, 66

COX, E E: 1920

COX, GEORGE: 64

COX, J: 1396

COX, JESSE: 1396

COY, G: 64

CRAIG, JONATHAN C: 142

CRAVENS, E P: 2337

CRAVENS, E P/SF 12559: 2337

CRAWFORD, V T: 2010

CRISELL, MRS M E: 1772

CRISWELL, C T: 1395

CRISWELL, MARY E (MRS): 1772

CRISWELL, O T: 1395

CRISWELL, O T (HEIRS): 1395

CRISWELL, S H: 1297

CRISWELL, T K: 2071

CROCKETT, E: 58

CROCKETT, ELIZABETH: 58

CROUCH, E H: 1405

CROUCH, J: 1299

CROUCH, J R: 1299

CROW, I G: 2116

CROW, J G: 2116

CROW, J T: 2298

CROW, JOHN G: 2298

CROW, T J: 2124

CRUMPTON, W A: 1391

CRYSP, G: 1397

CRYSP, GREEN: 1397

CT RR CO: 68, 2152, 2288

CUDDRILLA IRRIGATION COMPNAY: 1300, 1301

CULLERS, F M: 2166

CULP, A S: 1289

CUNNINGHAM, D: 74

CUNNINGHAM, DANIEL: 74

CUNNINGHAM, I H: 1955

CUNNINGHAM, J H: 1614, 1773, 1955

CUNNINGHAM, J T: 1720

CUNNINGHAM, R A: 1389

CUNNINGHAM, W H: 2154

CURTIS, V E: 1584, 1674

CUSENBARRY, D D: 2285

CUSENBARY, D D: 2285

DAILEY, MICHAEL: 82

DAILY, HRS J: 78

DAILY, JOHN (DECEASED): 78

DAILY, JOHN (HEIRS): 78

DAILY, M: 82

DANIEL, M L: 1415

DANIEL, S N: 1413

DANIEL, W H: 2299

DANIELS, CHARLES B (MRS): 2281

DANIELS, H C: 2264

DANIELS, MRS C E: 2281

DARDEN, J M: 1924

DAUGHERTY, W: 1410

DAUGHERTY, WILLIAM: 1410

DAVASHER, H W: 2261

DAVIDSON, J H: 85, 1418, 1592, 1599

DAVIDSON, J W: 1469, 1697

DAVIDSON, S: 84

DAVIDSON, SAMUEL: 84

DAVIS, A P: 1798

DAVIS, F M: 2213, 2214

DAVIS, H B L: 1891

DAVIS, H W: 1301

DAVIS, J J: 1979

DAVIS, R J: 96, 184, 219

DAVIS, S D: 1593

DAVIS, W: 1594, 1908

DAVIS, W J: 1303

DAVIS, WILLIAM: 1594

DAWS, J J: 1979

DAWSON, D: 76

DAWSON, DAVID: 76

DAWSON, DAVID (HEIRS): 76

DAWSON, J T: 1776

DE LONG, E: 1675

DECKER, J: 1302

DECKER, JOSEPH: 1302

DEDRICK, G: 75

DEDRICK, GEORGE: 75

DEDRICK, GEORGE (HEIRS): 75

DEE, A N: 1595

DEES, A N: 1595, 1725

DEISTER, J T: 1589

DELANEY, CAROLINA: 1507

DELANEY, T C: 1507

DELONG, ELIAS: 1675

DENISON, S: 77

DENISON, STEPHEN: 77

DENISON, STEPHEN (HEIRS): 77

DENTON, A L: 88

DEWITT, M: 1412

DEWITT, MATILDA: 1412

DICK, W J: 1786

DICKSON, J: 2282

DICKSON, J J: 2282

DIEW, F M: 1417

DOBBS, J L: 89

DOBBS, J M: 50

DOBBS, M: 1416

DONNELL, J M: 1594, 1922

DONNELL, W L: 1588, 1726, 1830

DOOLEY, F P (MRS): 1676

DOOLEY, MRS F P: 1676

DOUGLAS, J E: 1587

DOUGLASS, E L: 2155, 2156, 2157

DOWD, P: 79, 80

DOWD, PETER: 79, 80

DOWDLE, J E: 2215, 2250

DOWDLE, T E: 1646

DOZIER, H C: 1775

DOZIER, SEABORN: 1466

DRIVER, A I: 1948

DRIVER, A J: 1672

DRIVER, J: 1590

DRIVER, J A: 1948, 1980, 2073

DRIVER, JOHN: 1590

DRIVER, JOHN A: 1980, 2073

DRUM, W R: 1633

DUDNEY, B F: 1406

DUFF, J: 86

DUFF, JAMES: 86

DUNHAM, E: 1616

DUNLAP, JOHN Q: 1403

DUNN, M: 81

DUNN, MATTHEW: 81

DUNN, W: 83

DUNN, WILLIAM: 83

DURHAM, J: 1797

DURHAM, JAMES: 1797

DURHAM, JAMES (HEIRS): 1797

DUTY, J W: 1831

EADS, W A: 1833

EAST LINE AND RED RIVER RAILROAD COMPANY: 1307, 1424

EATON, A: 1483

EDDLEMAN, A B: 2347

EDDLEMAN, I F: 1587

EDDLEMAN, J: 1728

EDDLEMAN, JOHN: 1728

EDDLEMAN, R C: 1420

EDDLEMAN, W H: 1474, 1597

EDDLEMAN, W M: 1597

EDMONDS, M: 91

EDMONDS, MARGARET: 91

EDWARDS, H H: 60

EDWARDS, R: 97

EDWARDS, REBECCA: 90

EDWARDS, W W: 1422

EGGARS, C G: 1956

EGGERS, G: 1981, 2158

EGGERS, GUSTAV: 1981, 2158

EL&RR RR CO: 1307, 1424, 1814, 2207

ELDER, CHRISTIANA (MRS): 1419

ELDER, MRS C: 1419

ELKINS, W H: 1957

ELLIS, G W: 1769, 2028

ELMORE, J L: 1421

ERNEST, A J: 92

EVANS, S H: 1306

EVANS, SAMUEL H: 1306

EVANS, W P: 1832

EVERETT, J P: 1678, 2074

EWING, G: 1423

EWING, GRAFFUS: 1423

FAIR, G F: 1311

FARLEY, M: ?23

FARMER, ALEXANDER: 143

FARRIS, E: 94

FARRIS, EDWARD: 94

FERGUSON, H H: 1310

FERGUSON, J: 100

FERGUSON, J C: 1798

FERGUSON, JOHN C: 1798

FERGUSON, JOSEPH: 100

FERGUSON, S: 96

FERGUSON, SILAS: 96

FICKLIN, R G: 1834

FICKLIN, THOMAS F: 1791

FIELDS, J: 1431

FIELDS, JOSEPH: 1431

FINCH, W T: 1893

FINLAY, R: 2075

FINLEY, ROWLAND: 2075

FISHBAUGH, W: 93

FISHBAUGH, WILLIAM: 93

FISHBAUGH, WILLIAM (HEIRS): 93

FISHER, GEORGE W: 261, 262

FISHER, J H: 1598

FISHER, J S: 1340

FISHER, R J: 95

FISHER, REBECCA JANE: 95

FITCHETT, JOSEPH: 1581

FITCHETT, W H: 1430, 1432

FITCHETT, W W: 1432

FITE, W: 102

FITE, WILLIAM: 102

FLEMING, R F: 1691

FORD, B: 1679

FORD, DANIEL M: 7

FORE, G W: 103

FORE, J R: 1694

FORE, J S: 1309

FORE, JOHN S: 1309

FORTUNE, L: 1894

FORWOOD: 40, 41, 42, 43, 44

FOSTER, A E: 1833

FOSTER, D L: 2160, 2186

FOSTER, ELIZABETH (MRS): 1433

FOSTER, MRS E: 1433

FOSTER, S: 1308

FOUNTON, D F: 1644

FOWLER: 182

FOWLER, T: 1427

FOWLER, TONEY: 1427

FRANKLIN, D D: 1425, 1599

FRANKLIN, HIRAM: 1575, 1889

FRANKLIN, J B: 1429

FRAZIER, J S: 1985

FREEMAN, T F: 2262

FREEMAN, W H: 1428

FRISBIE, H S (MRS): 1321

FROIS, THEODORE: 149

FROST: 22, 23

FULKERSON, JAMES: 101

FULLER, M A: 1426

FULLERTON, J: 101

FULLERTON, W: 99

FULLERTON, WILLIAM: 99

G&BN CO: 84, 85, 114, 115, 116, 117, 118, 119, 120, 1686, 1714, 1719, 1852, 1862, 1920, 1947, 1954, 1963, 2023, 2224, 2299, 2344, 2364

GACHTER, J A: 2161

GALVESTON AND BRAZOS NAVIGA-TION COMPANY: 114, 115, 116, 117, 118, 119, 120

GAMBOA, F: 106

GAMBOA, FELICIANO: 106

GANT, A B: 63, 1307, 1326, 1370, 1458, 1459, 1547

GARDNER, J A: 1924

GARDNER, R H: 1984

GARMS, H: 104

GARMS, HENRY: 104

GARRETT, J: 107, 108

GARRETT, JACOB: 107, 108

GARRETT, S: 1982

GARRETT, SAMUEL: 1982

GASS, R B: 1440

GATES, J: 111

GATES, JAMES: 111

GATLIN, R A: 1919

GAY, A T: 1475

GEGG, NICHOLAS: 1526

GEORGE, H B: 110

GEORGE, HENRY B: 110

GEORGE, P S: 109

GEORGE, PHILLIP S: 109

GHOLSON, MORGAN A (MRS): 1983

GHOLSON, MRS M A: 1983

GIBSON, A J: 1835

GIBSON, A J JR: 1835

GIBSON, J W: 1821

GIBSON, P L: 2203

GILCHREST, C: 2084

GILCHRIST, CHARLES: 2084

GILFOIL, J: 1439

GILFOIL, JOHN SR: 1439

GILLESPIE, WILLIAM J (HEIRS): 83

GILLFOIL, J J: 1516

GILLIAM, R: 112

GILLIAM, RICHARD: 112

GILMORE, A C: 1313

GILMORE, J F: 2135, 2243, 2251

GILMORE, JAMES: 1615

GILMORE, JOHN F: 2251

GILMORE, W I: 2135

GILMORE, W J: 1730

GIVANS, JAMES: 1292

GLASGOW, G W: 1434

GLASGOW, GEORGE W: 1434

GLASS, H K: 1438

GLASS, T J: 1437

GLOVER, E D: 1310

GOLDEN, E: 1436

GOLDEN, P: 1312

GOLDEN, PHILIP: 1312

GOODE, W M: 1317

GOORL, H A: 1435

GORDON, GEORGE: 1532

GORRISSEN, V FREDRICK GUN-THER: 1600

GOSS, W N: 2156

GOSSETT, A E: 1799, 1800, 1801, 1802

GOUDY, F H: 1315, 1316

GOURLEY, HENRY A: 1435

GOWDY, E L: 1315

GOWDY, F H: 1316

GRAHAM, A A: 125

GRAHAM, E S: 1763, 1772, 1782, 1799, 1800, 1802, 1804, 1805, 1806, 1820

GRAHAM, G A: 70, 1460

GRAHAM, H T: 123

GRAHAM, J C C: 122

GRAHAM, S H: 124

GREEN, F L: 105

GREEN, J W: 2201

GREENWADE, J J: 2136, 2216, 2329

GREENWADE, R H: 1896

GREGORY, L M: 121

GRIFFIN, W W: 2131

GRIFFITH, B P: 1314

GRIMSHAW, AMOS: 2250

GUEST, M V: 1777

GUNTER: 40, 41, 42, 43, 114, 115, 116, 117, 118, 119, 157, 2350

GUTHRIE, J: 1959

GUTHRIE, JAMES: 1959

HALL, M: 1453

HALL, MARGARET (MRS): 1453

HALL, W R: 1452

HAMILTON, M: 138

HAMILTON, MARY: 138

HAMILTON, R: 1321

HAMILTON, ROBERT: 1321

HAMMONS, B W: 1320

HARDAWAY, S G: 136

HARDAWAY, SAM G: 136

HARDIN, AUGUSTIN B: 172

HARDIN, L E: 1682

HARDIN, L E (HEIRS): 1682

HARGRAVE, J B: 1871, 2190

HARKNESS, J A: 1442

HARMANSON, Z J: 165

HARMON, C: 1455

HARMON, CALVIN: 1455

HARMON, J: 1351

HARMON, M: 1446

HARMON, MARTIN: 1446

HARMONSON, P: 141

HARMONSON, PETER: 141

HARMONSON, WILLIAM P: 59

HARRINGTON, J: 1732

HARRINGTON, T: 152

HARRINGTON, THOMAS: 152

HARRIS, D: 1684, 1734, 2170

HARRIS, DAVID: 1412, 1684, 1734

HARRISON, S: 142

HARRISON, SAMUEL: 142

HARRISON, W A: 2187

HARROW, J P O: 1807

HART, GABRIEL: 1443

HART, R A: 1897

HART, S A: 1443, 1680

HART, S F: 1680

HART, STEPHEN A: 1443

HARVEY, H: 1606

HARVEY, HENRY: 1606

HATCHKISS, R: 147

HATFIELD, E R: 2071

HATLEY, TABLEY B: 10

HAWKINS, L B: 1386, 2306

HAWKINS, S J: 1836

HAYNES, J R: 2238

HEARNE, SAMUEL R: 128

HEART, HRS C P: 132

HEARTH, CHARLES P: 131, 132, 133

HEARTH, CHARLES P (HEIRS): 131, 132, 133

HEARTT, HRS C P: 131, 133

HEATH, GENEVA J (MRS): 1367

HEATH, THOMAS: 8

HEATH, THOMAS (HEIRS): 147, 220

HEDGCOX, O: 284

HEDGECOXE, HARRISON G: 257

HEDGECOXE, HENRY O: 824, 827, 830, 1044, 1045

HEDGECOXE, OLIVER: 606, 846, 1242

HEFNER, J L: 1783

HEIGHTON, J L: 2162

HENDERSON: 14

HENDERSON, H T: 1450

HENDERSON, M: 2141

HENDRICKS, GEORGE D: 17

HENRY, J R: 25, 26, 27, 28, 29

HENRY, JOHN R: 112, 217

HERRINGTON, JOHN: 1732

HERRON, F: 1898

HEWIT, ROBERT: 150

HEWITT, R: 150, 1454

HEWITT, ROBERT: 1454

HIGGINS, W J: 1927

HILL, A: 129

HILL, ALLEN: 129

HILL, B: 137, 144

HILL, BENJAMIN: 137, 144

HILL, BENJAMIN (HEIRS): 137, 144

HILL, G W: 151, 1444

HILL, GEORGE W: 64, 1444

HILL, H: 1890, 1899, 1910

HILL, I L: 126

HILL, ISAAC L: 126

HILL, J A: 127

HILL, J G: 1796, 1809

HILL, JOHN A: 127

HILL, W: 1985

HILL, WILLIAM: 1985

HINES, A: 135

HINES, ALLEN: 135

HITCHCOCK, A J: 128

HODGES, E L: 1577

HODGES, H: 134

HODGES, HENRY: 134

HODGES, S G: 2137, 2164

HODGES, W J: 1429, 1457

HOFFMAN: 143

HOFFMAN, JOHANN CARL: 143

HOLCOMB, V: 2348

HOLDERNESS, S M: 1804, 1805, 1806

HOLEMAN, ISAAC: 130

HOLEMAN, ISAAC (HEIRS): 130

HOLLEY, J L: 2165

HOLLEY, J W: 1637

HOLLY, B: 1608

HOLLY, J C: 1602

HOLLY, R S: 1503

HOLLY, T J: 1601

HOLMAN, I: 130

HOLMAN, JAMES S: 263

HOLMES, R: 1605

HOLMES, REBECCA: 1605

HOLT, B: 154

HOLT, BAZZEL: 154

HOLT, J A: 1385, 2265

HOPKINS, J A: 2086

HOPKINS, JAMES A: 2086

HOPKINS, JAMES A (HEIRS): 2086

HORNER, J W: 1319

HOTCHKISS, R: 147

HOUSTON AND GREAT NORTHERN RAILROAD COMPANY: 1324, 1325, 1326, 1458, 1459, 1460, 1461, 1462

HOWARD, H J: 1448

HOWARD, J W: 1600, 1604

HOWETH, F A: 1603

HUBER, B: 1323, 1445

HUBER, BENHARD: 1323

HUBER, BERNHARD: 1445

HUDGIN, B A: 1900

HUDGINS, B A: 1900

HUFFMACHER, A G: 1808

HUFFMASTER, A G: 1808

HUGHES, C: 139

HUGHES, CLAIBOURN: 139

HUGHES, W J: 1447, 1778

HULL, M: 1731

HULL, MAJOR: 1731

HUME, J P: 140

HUME, JAMES P: 140

HUMPHREY, JAMES: 239

HUMPHREYS, J A: 1413

HUMPHREYS, P J: 153

HUMPHRIES, CHARLES: 1360

HUNT, I: 1456

HUNT, IRA: 1456

HUNT, M: 149

HUNT, MARGARET S: 1496

HUNT, MEMUCAN: 149

HUNT, P B: 1901, 1991

HUNT, W C: 1622

HURT, W C: 2198

HYATT, J L E: 2166

I RR CO: 156, 2145, 2190, 2213

I&GN RR CO: 1324, 1325, 1326, 1458, 1459, 1460, 1461, 1462

INDIANOLA RAILROAD COMPANY: 156

IRVIN, A: 1779

IRVIN, ANDREW: 1779

JACKSON, J D: 1464

JACKSON, J I: 1828

JACKSON, J L: 1611

JACKSON, W C JR: 2333

JACOBI, ANSELM: 198

JAIME, F: 157

JAIME, FELIPE: 157

JAMES, J J: 1327

JAMES, J M: 1329

JAMES, JOHN: 1467

JAMES, JOHN J: 1327

JAMES, S H: 1465

JAMES, W F: 1610

JAMES, W W: 1812

JAMESON, A B: 1686

JAYNE, B H: 2016

JAYNE, B M: 2016

JEFFERY, S R: 1463, 1930

JEFFERY, SIDNEY R: 163

JEFFREY, SIDNEY R: 1463

JERRY, I: 1539

JOHNSON, A S: 2188

JOHNSON, C W: 1781, 2147, 2248, 2252, 2257, 2342

JOHNSON, E W: 2257

JOHNSON, J M: 161

JOHNSON, L A: 2260

JOHNSON, W: 159, 1685

JOHNSON, WILLIAM: 159, 175, 1685

JOHNSON, WILLIAM (HEIRS): 159

JOHNSTON, A SIDNEY: 2188

JOHNSTON, A W: 2339, 2340

JOHNSTON, J S: 160

JOHNSTON, JOSEPH S: 160

JOHNSTON, JOSEPH S (HEIRS): 160

JONES, A: 1735

JONES, ALBERT: 1735

JONES, H M: 1612, 1897

JONES, I H: 1471, 2185

JONES, J: 1467

JONES, J A: 264, 265, 266, 267, 268, 269

JONES, J C: 1811, 1961

JONES, J E: 164, 1328

JONES, J H B: 1468

JONES, J Y: 1902

JONES, MORGAN: 1461, 1462

JONES, R G: 1469

JONES, W P: 1431

JONES, W R: 1609

JOPLIN, G: 2302

JORDAN, F: ?19

JORDAN, T J: 1466

JORDAN, THOMAS J: 1466

JOWELL, J A: 1330

JOWELL, J R: 1331

JOWELL, J V: 1332

JOWELL, J V (HEIRS): 1332

KEARBY, W C: 1474

KEEN, W H: 1551, 1932

KELLEY, DAVID: 1476

KELLEY, WILLIAM: 1688

KELLUM, EMILY (MRS): 1782

KELLUM, MRS, E: 1782

KELLY, C A: 2167

KELLY, D: 1476

KELLY, E M: 1614

KELLY, H: 1814, 2167

KELLY, HENRY: 1814, 2167

KELLY, R J: 1813

KELLY, W: 1688

KELLY, W S: 2258

KEMBLE, J H: 1472

KENDALL, JOSIAH: 1722, 1723

KERBY, JOHN M: 1837

KILLION, D G: 2189, 2253

KILLION, D N: 163

KIMBREL, L H: 2190

KIMMEL, E C: 1473

KING, B C: 1470

KING, H G: 2217, 2218, 2219

KING, J H: 1648

KIRBY, J M: 1837, 1945

KIRK, J: 1613

KIRK, JAMES: 1613

KIRKPATRICK, R: 1471

KIRKPATRICK, REID: 1471

KISER, J A: 1736

KISINGER, G: 170

KISINGER, GEORGE: 170

KISINGER, JOHN: 2286

KISSINGER, J: 2286

KITCHINGS, D: 165

KITCHINGS, DANIEL: 165

KNIGHT, F M: 1457

KNIGHT, J F: 2204

KNOX, W: 32

KRAMER, B: 168

KRAMER, BENTON: 168

KRAMER, D: 1475

KRAMER, DAVID: 1475

KRIGBAUM, J H: 120

KUNKEL, H D: 1838

KUTCH, B F: 1333

KUTCH, R M: 169

KUYKENDALL, T P: 167

KUYKENDALL, THORNTON P: 167

KUYKENDALL, THORNTON P (HEIRS): 167

KUYKENDALL, W H: 1935

LAFFERTY, J A: 175

LAING, I: 2078

LAING, ISAAC: 2078

LAMAR, J T: 1335

LAMAR, JAMES T: 1335

LAMAR, R E: 1840

LAMB, WILLIAM G: 156

LARD, W T: 1336

LASSITER, M L: 1936

LASSITER, W S: 1964

LAUDERDALE, W: 174

LAUDERDALE, WILLIAM: 174

LAUDERDALE, WILLIAM (HEIRS): 174

LAYNE, J L: 1737

LAYNE, T A: 177

LEDBETTER, A B: 1689

LEDBETTER, F M: 1295

LEDBETTER, W H: 38

LEDRICK, H: 1337

LEDRICK, HENRY: 1337

LEE, J C: 1478

LEE, J S: 173

LEE, JONATHAN S: 173

LEE, M A: 1606

LEE, R W: 111

LEELIGSON, LEWIS: 79, 80

LEFFEL, J W: 1963, 2344

LEGRAND, G H: 2261

LEMONS, W H: 1477

LESLIE, JOHN T: 1698

LEWIS, T D: 69

LICHTE, FRITZ: 1720

LINDSEY, B F: 1839

LINDSEY, W P: 1962

LISLE, J N: 1938

LISLE, O D: 1896, 2221

LOGAN, W: 1690

LOGAN, W H: 1831, 2074

LOGAN, WILLIAM: 1690

LONG, W R: 2291

LOONEY, A: 1480

LOONEY, A (HEIRS): 1480

LORD, J W: ?2

LOVEJOY, J T: 178, 1738

LUCKEY, M W: ?37

LUCY, J E: 2317

LUCY, JAMES E: 2317

LYLES, R H: 1446

LYNCH, J M: 49

LYNCH, N: 171, 172

LYTLE, S: 1334

LYTLE, SARAH: 1334

LYTLE, W A: 176

LYTLE, W B: 176

MABRY, R E: 1738, 2287

MAGILL, GEORGE W: 1419

MAGILL, JOHN (HEIRS): 1303

MAHLER, H: 1345

MAHLER, HENRY: 1345

MAIMES, WILLIAM: 1740

MAINES, W: 1740

MANDEVILLE, A: 1966

MANDEVILLE, M: 1719, 1954

MANN, B F: 1391

MANNING, J W: 188

MANNING, JOHN W: 188

MARLIN, J: 199

MARLIN, JOHN: 199

MARLIN, W N P: 190

MARR, J W: 1905

MARR, JOHN W: 1905

MARSHALL, W H: 1339

MARSHALT, W H: 1339

MARTIN, G J: 1994

MARTIN, P A: 2274

MASSEY, E J: 1616

MATHEWS, A N: 210

MATHEWS, JACOB: 1572

MATHEWS, S M: 1845

MATHIS, L J: 1482

MATTHEWS, A N: 210

MATTHEWS, R H: 241, 1286

MATTHEWS, T E: 2162

MATTHEWS, W: 1484

MATTHEWS, W M: 1876

MATTHEWS, WILLIAM: 1484

MAUPIN, J G: 1483

MAYBEE, J: 186

MAYBEE, JACOB: 186

MAYBEE, JACOB (HEIRS): 186

MAYES, R K: 1493

MAYES, W W: 1494

MCADAMS, JOHN JR: 185

MCADAMS, W C: 2351

MCALINEY, FRANCIS: 1784

MCBRAYER, J M: 207

MCBRAYER, J W: 1848

MCBRAYER, J W (HEIRS): 1848

MCCALL, J L L: 1632

MCCALLISTER, G W: 1684, 1734

MCCAN, J S: 1398, 1994

MCCANN, A J: 1496

MCCARDEL, JAMES H: 171

MCCARDELL, J H: 36, 37

MCCARLY, W M: 1488

MCCARTY, WILLIAM M: 1488

MCCASLAND, A T: 1846

MCCLENDON, D F: 1623, 1629

MCCLURE, W: 183

MCCLURE, WILLIAM: 183

MCCOMBER, H A: 208, 1695, 2168

MCCONNELL, S M: 1842

MCCORKLE, R L: 1854, 2141

MCCOWAN, R: 182

MCCOWN, REBECCA: 182

MCCOY, E D: 187

MCCOY, EPHRAIM D: 187

MCCRAVEN, WILLIAM: 1287

MCDERMIT, G B: 1311, 1340

MCDERMITT, G B: 1340

MCDOWELL, W J: 1621

MCDOWELL, W J A: 1621

MCDOWELL, W M: 1486, 1620

MCFARLANE, A C: 193

MCFARLANE, ALEXANDER C: 193

MCFARLANE, ALEXANDER C (HEIRS): 193

MCGARY, M: 196, 197

MCGARY, MAXWELL: 196, 197

MCINTYRE, H C: 1280

MCKIMBS, SARAH: 2085

MCKIMBS,S: 2085

MCKINNEY: 202, 203, 204

MCKISSICK, S: 184

MCKISSICK, SARAH: 184

MCKNIGHT, W N: 2019, 2142

MCKNIGHT, WILLIAM: 2142

MCLAINE, J: 1344

MCLAINE, JAMES: 1344

MCLAREN: ?9

MCLAREN, F M: 211

MCLAREN, GEORGE H: 2276

MCLENNAN, A: 180, 194, 195

MCLENNAN, ALEXANDER: 180, 194, 195

MCLENNAN, ALEXANDER (HEIRS): 180, 194, 195

MCLEOND, W: 1481

MCLEOUD, WILLIAM: 1481

MCLYMAN, J B: 2109

MCMULLEN: 198

MCMULLEN, A: 198

MCNEILL, J B: ?6

MCNEW, ELI: 1783

MCNEW, W: 1783

MEADOR, M: 209

MEADOR, MARK: 209

MEADOR, R E: 1939

MEADORS, E: 1489

MEADORS, MARTHA E: 53

MEADOWS, A T: 1491

MEADOWS, E: 1489

MEADOWS, MRS S: 1492

MEADOWS, SARAH: 1492

MEADOWS, SARAH (MRS): 1492

MEDLAN, A B: 189

MEDLAN, E: 2283

MEDLAN, ELIZABETH: 2283

MELLINGER, D S: 1622

MENG, CHARLES J: 1234, 1235

MERCER, J L: 1343, 1873, 2360

MERCER, JAMES L: 1343

MERRY, CHARLES J: 1237

MESSENGER, D: 1841

MESSENGER, DANIEL: 1841

MEYER, J: 1693, 2348

MEYER, JACOB: 1693

MIERS, L: 1784

MIERS, LUCINDA: 1784

MILES, EDWARD: 201

MILLER, A K: 1347

MILLER, B B: 1619

MILLER, C J: 2246

MILLER, J T: 2197, 2290

MILLS, C H: 1369

MILSAP, FULLER: 1277

MITCHELL, H L: 2117

MITCHELL, MRS N A: 1785

MITCHELL, N A (MRS): 1785

MITCHELL, R F: 2205, 2244

MITCHENER, L: 205

MITCHENER, LUCETTA: 205

MONTGOMERY, J: 1485

MONTGOMERY, JOHN: 1485

MOONEY, J: 1744

MOONEY, JAMES: 1744

MOORE, A: 192

MOORE, A D: 1691

MOORE, ALFRED: 192

MOORE, ALFRED (HEIRS): 192

MOORE, J W: 2305

MORGAN, A: 1817

MORGAN, C: 200

MORGAN, CHARLES: 200

MORGAN, I A: 1817

MORGAN, J W: 1981, 2143

MORRIS, N: 1739

MORRIS, N B (MRS): 1739

MORRIS, W G: 1692

MORRIS, W M: 1495

MORRISON, C B: 1740

MORRISON, J E: 212, 1694

MORRISON, J P: 206

MORRISON, JESSE P: 206

MORRISON, JOHN A: 52

MORRISON, JOSHUA E: 212

MORROW, J G: 1904

MOSELEY, B G: 2222

MOSELEY, G W: 1355

MOSELEY, WILLIAM: 1352

MOSELY, BENJAMIN SR: 1338

MOSES, D: 179

MOSES, DAVID: 179

MOSES, DAVID (HEIRS): 179

MOSLEY, B J: 1338

MOSLEY, N S: 1741

MOSS, NANNIE: 1533

MOSS, S: 1615

MOSS, SAMUEL: 1615

MOSS, WILLIAM: 1533

MOULTON: 1369, 1370, 2350

MULANAX, J T M: 2044

MULLINS, J B: 1742

MUNDELL, J A: 234, 2263

MUNNERLYN, W B: 1341, 1818

MUNSON: 40, 41, 42, 43, 114, 115, 116, 117, 118, 119, 157, 2350

MURPHY, P: 191

MURPHY, PATRICK: 191

MURRAY, J J: 1618

NABERS, R W: 213

NABORS, ROBERT W: 213

NARRED, J L: 2318

NEELEY, A C: 1874

NEELY, A C: 1874

NEFF, A A: 1348

NEFF, J: 1696

NELSON, J A: 1624

NELSON, JOHN A: 1624

NELSON, P H: 1350, 1754

NEWBOLDS, W: 1502

NEWBOLDS, WILLIAM: 1502

NEWBY, J H: 1837

NEWBY, JOHN: 1500

NEWBY, JOHN H: 1417, 1556

NEWBY, L: 2293

NEWBY, LOWE: 2293

NEWBY, W L: 2209

NEWHAUS, C: 2206, 2207

NEWHOUS, CHARLES: 1814, 2206, 2207

NEWHOUSE, CONRAD: 173

NEWMAN, J H: 2306

NEWMAN, R D: 2110

NEWTON, S G: 214, 1498

NICHOLS, J: 1499

NICHOLS, JACOB: 1499

NICHOLSON, W A: 1697, 2224

NOBLE, J L: 1349

NORRIS, J B: 1580, 1742, 1840

NORTON, D A: 215

NORTON, D O: 215

O: 1504, 1505, 1807, 2356

O CONNER, P H: 1786

OCONNER, PATRICK H: 1786

ODLE, SAMUEL: 19

OHARROW, J H: 1505

OHARROW, W W: 1504

OLDHAM, M: 2208

OLDHAM, MASON: 2208

OLDHAM, S M: 2209

OLIVER, L F: 82

OLIVER, LOUIS F: 2084

OLIVER, W P: 1942

OLIVER, WILLIAM P: 1942

ONEAL, BEN G: 2356

ORR, E: 1507

ORR, ELISHA: 1507

ORRELL, MRS S: 1745

ORRELL, SARAH (MRS): 1745

ORRICK, W J: 217

OSBORN, V H: 2319

OSWALT, R D: 2320

OSWALT, ROBERT D: 2320

OTTS, P: 1941

OTTS, POSEY: 1941

OWEN, ALBERT: 1442

OWEN, R D: 2245

OWENS, A P: 1970

OXFORD, J G: 1503

OXFORD, JOHN G: 1503

OXFORD, W R: 216

PADDOCK, J W V: 1625

PADGETT, E C (MRS): 2169

PADGETT, I B: 1627

PADGETT, MRS E C: 2169

PALMER, J: 1510

PALMER, JOHN: 1510

PANKKONIN, L: 1701

PANKONIN, E: 1700

PANKONIN, L: 1701

PARHAM, ALLEN: 1519

PARHAM, J: 1748

PARHAM, JAMES: 1642, 1748, 2170

PARHAM, JAMES (HEIRS): 1748, 2170

PARHAN, A: 1519

PARKER, G W: 1513

PARKER, GEORGE W: 1513

PARROTT, R L: 1756

PARROTT, W G: 1486

PARSON, R W J: 2294

PARSONS, R W J: 2294

PARTRIDGE, J J: 234

PASSMORE, B: 1698

PASSMORE, BRYANT: 1698

PATILLO, T A: 2353, 2355

PATTER, H N: 224

PATTERSON, J B: 220

PATTERSON, JAMES B: 220

PAYNE, B H: 1569

PAYNE, E H: 1908

PAYNE, F G: 1515

PAYNE, I A: 1514

PAYNE, J A: 1514

PEACOCK, W: 1511

PEACOCK, WILLIAM: 1511

PEPPER, S T: ?38

PERRY: 114, 115, 116, 117, 118, 119

PERRY, C W: 274

PETERS, C: 1787

PETERS, CARL: 1787

PETRESWICK, F (DECEASED): 218

PETRESWICK, F (HEIRS): 218

PETRESWICK,HRS F: 218

PETTIT, CHARLES: 136

PEVELER, DAVID: 58

PEVELER, J M: 221, 222

PEVELER, W R: 223

PEVELER, WILLIAM R: 223

PHILLIPS, F T: 238

PHILLIPS, JOHN M: 1678

PIATT, HORACE A: 1325

PICKARD, E B: 2361

PIEARCY, J A: 1966

SMITH, I N: 1791, 1879

SMITH, J C: 1527

SMITH, J D: 1638

SMITH, J H: 1776

SMITH, J N: 1945

SMITH, JP: 1638

SMITH, L W: 1822

SMITH, M M: 1536

SMITH, T H: 2230

SMITH, THOMAS H: 2230

SMITH, W E: 1752

SMOOT, J: 1526

SMOOT, JOHN: 1526

SNEAD, R W: 272

SNODGRASS, J F: ?21

SOUTHERLIN, WILLIAM: 270

SOUTHERN PACIFIC RAILROAD COMPANY: 263, 264, 265, 266, 267, 268, 269, 2353, 2355

SP RR CO: 263, 264, 265, 266, 267, 268, 269, ?3, 1669, 1693, 1695, 1726, 1751, 1878, 2129, 2137, 2151, 2156, 2161, 2162, 2164, 2184, 2210, 2328, 2353, 2355

SPANE, P R: 259

SPIVEY, W D: 2254

SPIVY, W D: 2254

SPLANE, PEYTON R: 259

SPOTWOOD, M C: 1845

STAFFORD, MELVIN B: 1533

STAFFORD, MRS M B: 1533

STAFFORD, W E: 1410

STANTON, R R: ?22

STAPLES, R S: 1528

STAPP, ANDREW: 1267, 1268, 1269, 1270

STARR, JAMES H: 185

STATE OF TEXAS: ?29, ?31

STEADHAM, W T: 1548

STEEDMAN AND GUNTER: 68

STEEL, G W: 256

STEEN, J L: 1824

STEGALL, J H: 1637

STEINER, J M: 278

STELL, GEORGE W: 256

STEPHENSON: 196, 197

STEVENS, GEORGE B: 1473

STEWART, G D: 2308

STEWART, GRAHAM P: 2308

STEWART, J C: 1880

STEWART, SARAH A: 1361

STEWART, WILLIS: 1265

STINETT, J SR: 1753

STINNETT, G U: 2177

STINNETT, GEORGE U: 2177

STINNETT, J D: 1529

STINNETT, JAMES D: 1529

STINNETT, JAMES SR: 1753

STINNETT, W: 1531

STINNETT, W M: 1754, 1756

STINNETT, WILLIAM: 1531, 1754

STONEHAM, W: 250

STONHAM, WILLIAM: 250

STROUD, W W: 1707

SUMMERS, R M: 1384

SUTHERLIN, W: 270

SWINK, W T: 1774

T&NO RR CO: 1244, 1245, 1246, 1247, 1248, 1317, 1457, 1476, 1608, 1673, 1779, 1796, 1826, 1890, 1899, 1910, 1974, 2149, 2165, 2167, 2171, 2172, 2260, 2263, 2346

TACKETT, A C: 1260

TACKETT, W A: 1643

TACKILL, J G: 1358

TACKILL, P: 1255

TACKITT, A C: 1260

TACKITT, J G: 1358

TACKITT, PLEASANT: 1255

TANKERSLEY: ?9

TANKERSLEY, S: 278

TANKERSLEY, SARAH: 278

TANKERSLEY, W L: 1518, 1545

TANNER, J R: 276, 277

TANNER, JAMES R: 276, 277

TAYLOR, ANDREW: 1463

TAYLOR, B F: 1546, 1973

TAYLOR, J C: 1543

TAYLOR, J M: 1541

TAYLOR, J N: 1243

TAYLOR, JOHN N: 1243

TAYLOR, MARY: 1619

TAYLOR, R: 1542

TE&L CO: 282, 283, 284, 285, 286, 287, 288, 289, 290, 291, 292, 293, 294, 295, 296, 297, 298, 299, 300, 301, 302, 303, 304, 305, 306, 307, 308, 309, 310, 311, 312, 313, 314, 315, 316, 317, 318, 319, 320, 321, 322, 323, 324, 325, 326, 327, 328, 329, 330, 331, 332, 333, 334, 335, 336, 337, 338, 339, 340, 341, 342, 343, 344, 345, 346, 347, 348, 349, 350, 351, 352, 353, 354, 355, 356, 357, 358, 359, 360, 361, 362, 363, 364, 365, 366, 367, 368, 369, 370, 371, 372, 373, 374, 375, 376, 377, 378, 379, 380, 381, 382, 383, 384, 385, 386, 387, 388, 389, 390, 391, 392, 393, 394, 395, 396, 397, 398, 399, 400, 401, 402, 403, 404, 405, 406, 407, 408, 409, 410, 411, 412, 413, 414, 415, 416, 417, 418, 419, 420, 421, 422, 423, 424, 425, 426, 427, 428, 429, 430, 431, 432, 433, 434, 435, 436, 437, 438, 439, 440, 441, 442, 443, 444, 445, 446, 447, 448, 449, 450, 451, 452, 453, 454, 455, 456, 457, 458, 459, 460, 461, 462, 463, 464, 465, 466, 467, 468, 469, 470, 471, 472, 473, 474, 475, 476, 477, 478, 479, 480, 481, 482, 483, 484, 485, 486, 487, 488, 489, 490, 491, 492, 493, 494, 495, 496, 497, 498, 499, 500, 501, 502, 503, 504, 505, 506, 507, 508, 509, 510, 511, 512, 513, 514, 515, 516, 517, 518, 519, 520, 521, 522, 523, 524, 525, 526, 527, 528, 529, 530, 531, 532, 533, 534, 535, 536, 537, 538, 539, 540, 541, 542, 543, 544, 545, 546, 547, 548, 549, 550, 551, 552, 553, 554, 555, 556, 557, 558, 559, 560, 561, 562, 563, 564, 565, 566, 567, 568, 569, 570, 571, 572, 573, 574, 575, 576, 577, 578, 579, 580, 581, 582, 583, 584, 585, 586, 587, 588, 589, 590, 591, 592, 593, 594, 595, 596, 597, 598, 599, 600, 601, 602, 603, 604, 605, 606, 607, 608, 609, 610, 611, 612, 613, 614, 615, 616, 617, 618, 619, 620, 621, 622, 623, 624, 625, 626, 627, 628, 629, 630, 631, 632, 633, 634, 635, 636, 637, 638, 639, 640, 641, 642, 643, 644, 645, 646, 647, 648, 649, 650, 651, 652, 653, 654, 655, 656, 657, 658, 659, 660, 661, 662, 663, 664, 665, 666, 667, 668, 669, 670, 671, 672, 673, 674, 675, 676, 677, 678, 679, 680, 681, 682, 683, 684, 685, 686, 687, 688, 689, 690, 691, 692, 693, 694, 695, 696, 697, 698, 699, 700, 701, 702, 703, 704, 705, 706, 707, 708, 709, 710, 711, 712, 713, 714, 715, 716, 717, 718, 719, 720, 721, 722, 723, 724, 725, 726, 727, 728, 729, 730, 731, 732, 733, 734, 735, 736, 737, 738, 739, 740, 741, 742, 743, 744, 745, 746, 747, 748, 749, 750, 751, 752, 753, 754, 755, 756, 757, 758, 759, 760, 761, 762, 763, 764, 765, 766, 767, 768, 769, 770, 771, 772, 773, 774, 775, 776, 777, 778, 779, 780, 781, 782, 783, 784, 785, 786, 787, 788, 789, 790, 791, 792, 793, 794, 795, 796, 797, 798, 799, 800, 801, 802, 803, 804, 805, 806, 807, 808, 809, 810, 811, 812, 813, 814, 815, 816, 817, 818, 819, 820, 822, 823, 824, 825, 826, 827, 828, 829, 830, 831, 832, 833, 834, 835, 836, 837, 838, 839, 840, 841, 842, 843, 844, 845, 846, 847, 848, 849, 850, 851, 852, 853, 854, 855, 856, 857, 858, 859, 860, 861, 862, 863, 864, 865, 866, 867, 868, 869, 870, 871, 872, 873, 874, 875, 876, 877, 878, 879, 880, 881, 882, 883, 884, 885, 886, 887, 888, 889, 890, 891, 892, 893, 894, 895, 896, 897, 898, 899, 900, 901, 902, 903, 904, 905, 906, 907, 908, 909, 910, 911, 912, 913, 914, 915, 916, 917, 918, 919, 920, 921, 922, 923, 924, 925, 926, 927, 928, 929, 930, 931, 932, 933, 934, 935, 936, 937, 938, 939, 940, 941, 942, 943, 944, 945, 946, 947, 948, 949, 950, 951, 952, 953, 954, 955, 956, 957, 958, 959, 960, 961, 962, 963, 964, 965, 966, 967, 968, 969, 970, 971, 972, 973, 974, 975, 976, 977, 978, 979, 980, 981, 982, 983, 984, 985, 986, 987, 988, 989, 990, 991, 992, 993, 994, 995, 996, 997, 998, ?1, ?11, ?12, ?14, ?15, ?17, ?18, ?20, 999, 1000, 1001, 1002, 1003, 1004, 1005, 1006, 1007, 1008, 1009, 1010, 1011, 1012, 1013, 1014, 1015, 1016, 1017, 1018, 1019, 1020, 1021, 1022, 1023, 1024, 1025, 1026, 1027, 1028, 1029, 1030, 1031, 1032, 1033, 1034, 1035, 1036, 1037, 1038, 1039, 1040, 1041, 1042, 1043, 1044, 1045, 1046, 1047, 1048, 1049, 1050, 1051, 1052, 1053, 1054, 1055, 1056, 1057, 1058, 1059, 1060, 1061, 1062, 1063, 1064, 1065, 1066, 1067, 1068, 1069, 1070, 1071, 1072, 1073, 1074, 1075, 1076, 1077, 1078, 1079, 1080, 1081, 1082, 1083, 1084, 1085, 1086, 1087, 1088, 1089, 1090, 1091, 1092, 1093, 1094, 1095, 1096, 1097, 1098, 1099, 1100, 1101, 1102, 1103, 1104, 1105, 1106, 1107, 1108, 1109, 1110, 1111, 1112, 1113, 1114, 1115, 1116, 1117, 1118, 1119, 1120, 1121, 1122, 1123, 1124, 1125, 1126, 1127, 1128, 1129, 1130, 1131, 1132, 1133, 1134, 1135, 1136, 1137, 1138, 1139, 1140, 1141, 1142, 1143, 1144, 1145, 1146, 1147, 1148, 1149, 1150, 1151, 1152, 1153, 1154, 1155, 1156, 1157, 1158, 1159, 1160, 1161, 1162, 1163, 1164, 1165, 1166, 1167, 1168, 1169, 1170, 1171, 1172, 1173, 1174, 1175, 1176, 1177, 1178, 1179, 1180, 1181, 1182, 1183, 1184, 1185, 1186, 1187, 1188, 1189, 1190, 1191, 1192, 1193, 1194, 1195, 1196, 1197, 1198, 1199, 1200, 1201, 1202, 1203, 1204, 1205, 1206, 1207, 1208, 1209, 1210, 1211, 1212, 1213, 1214, 1215, 1216, 1217, 1218, 1219, 1220, 1221, 1222, 1223, 1224, 1225, 1226, 1227, 1228, 1229, 1230, 1231, 1232, 1233, 1234, 1235, 1236, 1237, 1239, 1240, 1241, 1242, 1357, 2021, 2049, 2050, 2051, 2052, 2053, 2055, 2056, 2057, 2058, 2059, 2060, 2065, 2066, 2067, 2068, 2087, 2088, 2089, 2090, 2091, 2092, 2093, 2094, 2095, 2096, 2097, 2098, 2099, 2100, 2101, 2102, 2103, 2104, 2105, 2106, 2107, 2178, 2194, 2349, 2361

TERRELL, JONATHAN W: 97, 98

TERRILL, J W: 90, 98

TERRY, ISAAC: 1539

TERRY, J W: 1544

TERRY, JAMES W: 1544

TERRY, M L: 1261

TEXAS AND NEW ORLEANS RAILROAD COMPANY: 1244, 1245, 1246,

1247, 1248

TEXAS AND PACIFIC RAILROAD COMPANY: 1254

TEXAS EMIGRATION AND LAND COMPANY: 282, 283, 284, 285, 286, 287, 288, 289, 290, 291, 292, 293, 294, 295, 296, 297, 298, 299, 300, 301, 302, 303, 304, 305, 306, 307, 308, 309, 310, 311, 312, 313, 314, 315, 316, 317, 318, 319, 320, 321, 322, 323, 324, 325, 326, 327, 328, 329, 330, 331, 332, 333, 334, 335, 336, 337, 338, 339, 340, 341, 342, 343, 344, 345, 346, 347, 348, 349, 350, 351, 352, 353, 354, 355, 356, 357, 358, 359, 360, 361, 362, 363, 364, 365, 366, 367, 368, 369, 370, 371, 372, 373, 374, 375, 376, 377, 378, 379, 380, 381, 382, 383, 384, 385, 386, 387, 388, 389, 390, 391, 392, 393, 394, 395, 396, 397, 398, 399, 400, 401, 402, 403, 404, 405, 406, 407, 408, 409, 410, 411, 412, 413, 414, 415, 416, 417, 418, 419, 420, 421, 422, 423, 424, 425, 426, 427, 428, 429, 430, 431, 432, 433, 434, 435, 436, 437, 438, 439, 440, 441, 442, 443, 444, 445, 446, 447, 448, 449, 450, 451, 452, 453, 454, 455, 456, 457, 458, 459, 460, 461, 462, 463, 464, 465, 466, 467, 468, 469, 470, 471, 472, 473, 474, 475, 476, 477, 478, 479, 480, 481, 482, 483, 484, 485, 486, 487, 488, 489, 490, 491, 492, 493, 494, 495, 496, 497, 498, 499, 500, 501, 502, 503, 504, 505, 506, 507, 508, 509, 510, 511, 512, 513, 514, 515, 516, 517, 518, 519, 520, 521, 522, 523, 524, 525, 526, 527, 528, 529, 530, 531, 532, 533, 534, 535, 536, 537, 538, 539, 540, 541, 542, 543, 544, 545, 546, 547, 548, 549, 550, 551, 552, 553, 554, 555, 556, 557, 558, 559, 560, 561, 562, 563, 564, 565, 566, 567, 568, 569, 570, 571, 572, 573, 574, 575, 576, 577, 578, 579, 580, 581, 582, 583, 584, 585, 586, 587, 588, 589, 590, 591, 592, 593, 594, 595, 596, 597, 598, 599, 600, 601, 602, 603, 604, 605, 606, 607, 608, 609, 610, 611, 612, 613, 614, 615, 616, 617, 618, 619, 620, 621, 622, 623, 624, 625, 626, 627, 628, 629, 630, 631, 632, 633, 634, 635, 636, 637, 638, 639, 640, 641, 642, 643, 644, 645, 646, 647, 648, 649, 650, 651, 652, 653, 654, 655, 656, 657, 658, 659, 660, 661, 662, 663, 664, 665, 666, 667, 668, 669, 670, 671, 672, 673, 674, 675, 676, 677, 678, 679, 680, 681, 682, 683, 684, 685, 686, 687, 688, 689, 690, 691, 692, 693, 694, 695, 696, 697, 698, 699, 700, 701, 702, 703, 704, 705, 706, 707, 708, 709, 710, 711, 712, 713, 714, 715, 716, 717, 718, 719, 720, 721, 722, 723, 724, 725, 726, 727, 728, 729, 730, 731, 732, 733, 734, 735, 736, 737, 738, 739, 740, 741, 742, 743, 744, 745, 746, 747, 748, 749, 750, 751, 752, 753, 754, 755, 756, 757, 758, 759, 760, 761, 762, 763, 764, 765, 766, 767, 768, 769, 770, 771, 772, 773, 774, 775, 776, 777, 778, 779, 780, 781, 782, 783, 784, 785, 786, 787, 788, 789, 790, 791, 792, 793, 794, 795, 796, 797, 798,

799, 800, 801, 802, 803, 804, 805, 806, 807, 808, 809, 810, 811, 812, 813, 814, 815, 816, 817, 818, 819, 820, 822, 823, 824, 825, 826, 827, 828, 829, 830, 831, 832, 833, 834, 835, 836, 837, 838, 839, 840, 841, 842, 843, 844, 845, 846, 847, 848, 849, 850, 851, 852, 853, 854, 855, 856, 857, 858, 859, 860, 861, 862, 863, 864, 865, 866, 867, 868, 869, 870, 871, 872, 873, 874, 875, 876, 877, 878, 879, 880, 881, 882, 883, 884, 885, 886, 887, 888, 889, 890, 891, 892, 893, 894, 895, 896, 897, 898, 899, 900, 901, 902, 903, 904, 905, 906, 907, 908, 909, 910, 911, 912, 913, 914, 915, 916, 917, 918, 919, 920, 921, 922, 923, 924, 925, 926, 927, 928, 929, 930, 931, 932, 933, 934, 935, 936, 937, 938, 939, 940, 941, 942, 943, 944, 945, 946, 947, 948, 949, 950, 951, 952, 953, 954, 955, 956, 957, 958, 959, 960, 961, 962, 963, 964, 965, 966, 967, 968, 969, 970, 971, 972, 973, 974, 975, 976, 977, 978, 979, 980, 981, 982, 983, 984, 985, 986, 987, 988, 989, 990, 991, 992, 993, 994, 995, 996, 997, 998, 999, 1000, 1001, 1002, 1003, 1004, 1005, 1006, 1007, 1008, 1009, 1010, 1011, 1012, 1013, 1014, 1015, 1016, 1017, 1018, 1019, 1020, 1021, 1022, 1023, 1024, 1025, 1026, 1027, 1028, 1029, 1030, 1031, 1032, 1033, 1034, 1035, 1036, 1037, 1038, 1039, 1040, 1041, 1042, 1043, 1044, 1045, 1046, 1047, 1048, 1049, 1050, 1051, 1052, 1053, 1054, 1055, 1056, 1057, 1058, 1059, 1060, 1061, 1062, 1063, 1064, 1065, 1066, 1067, 1068, 1069, 1070, 1071, 1072, 1073, 1074, 1075, 1076, 1077, 1078, 1079, 1080, 1081, 1082, 1083, 1084, 1085, 1086, 1087, 1088, 1089, 1090, 1091, 1092, 1093, 1094, 1095, 1096, 1097, 1098, 1099, 1100, 1101, 1102, 1103, 1104, 1105, 1106, 1107, 1108, 1109, 1110, 1111, 1112, 1113, 1114, 1115, 1116, 1117, 1118, 1119, 1120, 1121, 1122, 1123, 1124, 1125, 1126, 1127, 1128, 1129, 1130, 1131, 1132, 1133, 1134, 1135, 1136, 1137, 1138, 1139, 1140, 1141, 1142, 1143, 1144, 1145, 1146, 1147, 1148, 1149, 1150, 1151, 1152, 1153, 1154, 1155, 1156, 1157, 1158, 1159, 1160, 1161, 1162, 1163, 1164, 1165, 1166, 1167, 1168, 1169, 1170, 1171, 1172, 1173, 1174, 1175, 1176, 1177, 1178, 1179, 1180, 1181, 1182, 1183, 1184, 1185, 1186, 1187, 1188, 1189, 1190, 1191, 1192, 1193, 1194, 1195, 1196, 1197, 1198, 1199, 1200, 1201, 1202, 1203, 1204, 1205, 1206, 1207, 1208, 1209, 1210, 1211, 1212, 1213, 1214, 1215, 1216, 1217, 1218, 1219, 1220, 1221, 1222, 1223, 1224, 1225, 1226, 1227, 1228, 1229, 1230, 1231, 1232, 1233, 1234, 1235, 1236, 1237, 1239, 1240, 1241, 1242, 1357, 2021, 2049, 2050, 2051, 2052, 2053, 2055, 2056, 2057, 2058, 2059, 2060, 2065, 2066, 2067, 2068, 2087, 2088, 2089, 2090, 2091, 2092, 2093, 2094, 2095, 2096, 2097,

2098, 2099, 2100, 2101, 2102, 2103, 2104, 2105, 2106, 2107, 2178, 2194, 2349

THARP, D P: 1854

THOMAS, C H: 1984

THOMAS, D P: 1425

THOMAS, F L: 1259

THOMAS, FLOYD L: 1259

THOMAS, S A: 1646

THOMPSON, F A: 249

THOMPSON, J C: ?4

THOMPSON, W F: ?4

THORN: 22, 23

THORN, FROST: 60

THORN, FROST (HEIRS): 135

THROCKMORTON, J W: 280, 281

THROCKMORTON, JAMES W: 280, 281

TIDWELL, W F: 1621

TIDWELL, W I: 2022

TIDWELL, W J: 1402

TIMMONS, A: 1258

TIMMONS, A A: 2267

TIMMONS, J S: 1256, 1548, 2179

TIMMONS, N J: 1257

TIMMONS, W S: 2083

TOBIN, J: 279

TOBIN, JAMES (DECEASED): 279

TOBIN, JAMES (HEIRS): 279

TODD, CHARLES S: 183

TOWNSEND, C W: 1642, 1855, 2248

TOWNSEND, J C: 1363

TOWNSEND, J D: 1641

TOWNSEND, J O: 1641

TOWNSEND, J T: 1645

TRACY, N F: 1639

TREUE, J A: 1640

TREUE, JOHN A: 1640

TREUE, W C: 2180

TRIPLETT, C C: 2327, 2332

TRIPLETT, CHARLES C: 2327, 2332

TRYNDALE, W: 275

TT RR CO: 1547, 1711, 1766, 1886, 2122

TURNER, E C: 2200

TURNER, M F: 1857

TURNER, WILLIAM: 2146

TWILLEGEAR, Y H: 1883

TYLER TAP RAILROAD COMPANY: 1547

TYLER, J M: 2337

TYNDALE, WILLIAM: 275

TYNES, S: 274

TYNES, SYLPHIA: 274

TYSON, D B: 1644

UPHAM, C S: 1757

UPHAM, CHARLES: 1711

UPHAM, CHARLES S: 1757

UPHAM, E E: 1263

UPHAM, ED E: 1263

UPHAM, L E: 1264

URQUHART, ALLEN: 2226, 2227

VAN HOOSER, J C: 1648

VAN SICKLES, J H: 1549

VANHOOSER, JAKE: 1603

VANHOOSER, JOHN C: 1648

VAUGHN, JOSEPH: 1883

VICK, D G: 2161

VICK, JOHN H: 2174, 2187, 2254

VIREN, PHILIP: 1265

VIVEN, P: 1265

WADE, B J: 1912

WADE, L W: 1939

WADLEY, T C: 2231, 2309

WADLEY, T H: 2231

WALKER, A F: 1760

WALKER, J B: 1278, 1279

WALKER, W T: 2210, 2328

WALLACE, E M: 1893

WALLACE, M D: 1562

WALSH, G W: 1552

WALSH, GEORGE W: 1552

WALSH, J W: 1553

WALSH, JOHN W: 1553

WALSH, M F: 1554

WALSH, MARY F: 1554

WALTERS, J T: 1556

WALTERS, M: 1266

WALTERS, MOSES: 1266

WANN, S M: 1714

WARD, G: 1551

WARD, GEORGE: 1551

WARD, J M: 1515

WARD, SHELTON: 182

WASH, S A: 1267, 1268

WASH, SALLEY ANN: 1267, 1268

WASHINGTON COUNTY RAILROAD COMPANY: 1280

WATHAN, J R: 1281

WATHON, J R: 1281

WATSON, J E: 2260

WAYNE, T A: 1557

WC RR CO: 1280, 1323, 1981, 2143, 2158

WEBSTER, J S: 1745

WEEKLEY, G M: 1272

WEEKLEY, GEORGE M: 1272

WELCH, G T: 1564

WELCH, GEORGE T: 1564

WELCH, J A: 1512

WERTS, JACOB: 1557

WEST, A J: 1761

WHEELOCK, G R: 1277

WHEELOCK, GEORGE R: 1277

WHITE, A: 1269, 1270

WHITE, A C: 1534

WHITE, ARCHIBALD: 1269, 1270

WHITE, E: 1658

WHITE, GEORGE: 187

WHITE, N: 1858

WHITFIELD, J M: 2181

WHITTENBERG, R B: 2154

WHITTENBURG, J: 1860

WHITTENBURG, J A: 1359, 1651

WHITTENBURG, J B: 1282, 2255

WHITTENBURG, J B (HEIRS): 2255

WHITTENBURG, J C: 1359, 2319

WHITTENBURG, J N: 1651

WHITTENBURG, JACOB: 1860

WHITTENBURG, R B: 2310

WILCOX, ROBERT M: 1312

WILCOX, T A: 1550

WILCOX, THOMAS A: 1550

WILDER, JAMES B: 1236

WILHELM, J M: 1523

WILLESS, J: 1652

WILLESS, JAMES: 1652

WILLIAMS: 202, 203, 204

WILLIAMS, A: 2288

WILLIAMS, ALLEN: 2288

WILLIAMS, B F: 1781, 1808

WILLIAMS, H D: 1759

WILLIAMS, I E M: 1886

WILLIAMS, IRA E M: 1423, 1886

WILLIAMS, J H: 1555, 1713

WILLIAMS, JAMES H: 1855

WILLIAMS, L L: 1273

WILLIAMS, LUKE: 1424

WILLIAMS, NANCY: 1397

WILLIAMS, S D: 2482

WILLIAMS, W: 1758

WILLIAMS, WILLIAM: 1758

WILLIAMSON, C C (MRS): 200, 1300

WILLIS, H M: 2137, 2164

WILLIS, PRUDENCE: 1751, 2129

WILSON, J E: 1656, 2346

WILSON, JAMES T D: 1275, 1276

WILSON, M A: 1559

WILSON, R: 1275, 1276

WILSON, R M: 1653

WILSON, ROBERT: 1275, 1276

WINBORNE, E: 1558

WINBOURNE, E: 1558

WININGER, JAMES N: 1478

WITHEE, JOHN W: 1

WM CO: ?36

WOOD, A: 1274

WOOD, ANN: 1274

WOOD, B G: 1859

WOOD, F: 2146

WOOD, FRANKLIN: 2146

WOOD, G O: 1435

WOOD, J H: 1655, 2183, 2341

WOOD, JOHN H: 1655, 2183, 2341

WOOD, S: 1650

WOOD, SAMUEL: 1650

WOOD, Z F: 1763

WOODRUFF, R W: 1271

WOODS, B F: 1766

WOODS, B G: 1859

WOOLEY, THOMAS: 1582

WOOLEY, W: 1283

WOOLEY, WILLIAM: 1283

WOOLFOLK, R H: 1244, 1245, 1246, 1247, 1248

WOOLFORK, R O: 1278, 1279

WOOLLEY, T H: 1654

WRAY, H J: 2268

WRIGHT, A G: 2145

WRIGHT, W: 2256

WRIGHT, WILLIAM: 2256

YANCY, C D: 1448

YOUNG COUNTY SCHOOL COMMISSION: 1284, 1285

YOUNG COUNTY SCHOOL LAND: 1284, 1285

YOUNG CSL: 1284, 1285

YOUNG, H F: 1286

YOUNG, HUGH F: 1286

YOUNG, J: 2023

YOUNG, JOSEPH: 2023

YOUNG, P: 1287

YOUNG, PHILIP: 1287

ZINN, C M: 1565

ZINN, J A: 1661, 1862

ZINN, J A SR: 1862

Abstract Listing

This Index is really much more than an index. While its first purpose is to point you to the maps in which any given Abstract's land is found, it goes on to provide you with all names associated with this abstract: 1. the original Survey Name is on the first line of each entry after the abstract number, 2. if a 2nd Survey was conducted, it is preceded by the label of *S2*, 3. Grantee name (*G'ee*), and 4. Patentee (*P'ee*) names provided by the Texas GLO are also provided. Also, we have included relevant file information which enables further research at the Texas General Land Office.

Once you find one or more Map numbers here, proceed directly to those maps and see the parcel in the context of its neighboring survey-names. Also, remember to use the Big Picture Maps at the beginning of this section (*Maps C, D, and E*) to maintain perspective on where each Land-Survey Map is located within the county.

Abstract # 1 - AUD, I L
P'ee: WITHEE, JOHN W
G'ee: AUD, IGNATIUS L
T-Dt: -- --- -----
P-Dt: 16 Nov 1860
Dist/Class: Fannin 1st
File#: 1174
Patent#: 28
Patent Vol.: 14
Certificate: 812/911
Acres: 1155.09
Map(s) 21, 22, 29, 30

Abstract # 2 - AVERITT, P
P'ee: AVERITT, PHILLIP (HEIRS)
G'ee: AVERITT, PHILLIP (DECEASED)
T-Dt: -- --- -----
P-Dt: 17 Oct 1859
Dist/Class: Fannin 2nd
File#: 371
Patent#: 217
Patent Vol.: 6
Certificate: 202
Acres: 640
Map(s) 7

Abstract # 3 - ANDERSON, S
P'ee: ANDERSON, SAMUEL (HEIRS)
G'ee: ANDERSON, SAMUEL
T-Dt: -- --- -----
P-Dt: 07 Dec 1860
Dist/Class: Fannin 3rd
File#: 3600
Patent#: 135
Patent Vol.: 32
Acres: 426
Map(s) 26

Abstract # 5 - AKLES, H B
P'ee: AKLES, HEZEKIAH B
G'ee: AKLES, HEZEKIAH B
T-Dt: -- --- -----
P-Dt: 01 Jul 1859
Dist/Class: Fannin Bounty
File#: 805
Patent#: 19
Patent Vol.: 12
Certificate: 123
Acres: 240
Map(s) 4

Abstract # 6 - ANDERSON, J
P'ee: ANDERSON, JOHN
G'ee: ANDERSON, JOHN
T-Dt: -- --- -----
P-Dt: 02 Jul 1859
Dist/Class: Fannin Bounty

File#: 804
Patent#: 20
Patent Vol.: 12
Certificate: 121
Acres: 240
Map(s) 4

Abstract # 7 - BUSTILLO, J M
P'ee: FORD, DANIEL M
G'ee: BUSTILLO, JOSE MARIA
T-Dt: -- --- -----
P-Dt: 23 Aug 1876
Dist/Class: Fannin 1st
File#: 1598
Patent#: 624
Patent Vol.: 21
Certificate: 15/203
Acres: 267.78
Map(s) 33

Abstract # 8 - BURTON, R M
P'ee: HEATH, THOMAS
G'ee: BURTON, R M
T-Dt: -- --- -----
P-Dt: 05 Apr 1883
Dist/Class: Fannin 1st
File#: 1638
Patent#: 65
Patent Vol.: 24
Certificate: 32/76
Acres: 823.89
Map(s) 31, 32

Abstract # 9 - BARR, R
P'ee: BARR, ROBERT
G'ee: BARR, ROBERT
T-Dt: -- --- -----
P-Dt: 03 Aug 1875
Dist/Class: Fannin 1st
File#: 1778
Patent#: 209
Patent Vol.: 21
Certificate: 175
Acres: 624.95
Map(s) 39

Abstract # 10 - BULLOCK, D
P'ee: HATLEY, TABLEY B
G'ee: BULLOCK, DAVID
T-Dt: -- --- -----
P-Dt: 29 Apr 1861
Dist/Class: Fannin 3rd
File#: 3397
Patent#: 50
Patent Vol.: 33
Acres: 320
Map(s) 20

Abstract # 12 - BOLTON, HRS J
P'ee: BOLTON, JAMES (HEIRS)
G'ee: BOLTON, JAMES
T-Dt: -- --- -----
P-Dt: 31 Jul 1857
Dist/Class: Milam 3rd
File#: 1004
Patent#: 117
Patent Vol.: 16
Certificate: 1023
Acres: 320
Map(s) 36

Abstract # 14 - BARNES, M
P'ee: POWELL, C B AND HENDERSON
G'ee: BARNES, MOSES
T-Dt: -- --- -----
P-Dt: 27 Apr 1859
Dist/Class: Fannin Bounty
File#: 343
Patent#: 303
Patent Vol.: 7
Certificate: 1191
Acres: 1280
Map(s) 9

Abstract # 15 - BULLOCK, D M
P'ee: BULLOCK, DAVID M
G'ee: BULLOCK, DAVID M
T-Dt: -- --- -----
P-Dt: 28 Jan 1858
Dist/Class: Fannin Donation
File#: 441
Patent#: 575
Patent Vol.: 2
Certificate: 14
Acres: 187
Map(s) 19

Abstract # 16 - BROWN, D
P'ee: PRICE, JAMES M
G'ee: BROWN, DOUGLASS
T-Dt: -- --- -----
P-Dt: 22 Dec 1857
Dist/Class: Fannin Bounty
File#: 664
Patent#: 193
Patent Vol.: 7
Certificate: 1393
Acres: 640
Map(s) 22

Abstract # 17 - BRIDGES, J
P'ee: HENDRICKS, GEORGE D
G'ee: BRIDGES, JOHN
T-Dt: -- --- -----
P-Dt: 15 May 1857

Dist/Class: Fannin Bounty
File#: 731
Patent#: 134
Patent Vol.: 7
Certificate: 1867
Acres: 960
Map(s) 19, 27

Abstract # 19 - BILLINGSLEY, J
P'ee: ODLE, SAMUEL
G'ee: BILLINGSLEY, JESSIE
T-Dt: -- --- -----
P-Dt: 02 Apr 1861
Dist/Class: Fannin Bounty
File#: 923
Patent#: 422
Patent Vol.: 12
Certificate: 3054
Acres: 58
Map(s) 19

Abstract # 22 - BYERLY, W
P'ee: FROST AND THORN
G'ee: BYERLY, WILLIAM
T-Dt: -- --- -----
P-Dt: 09 Jul 1875
Dist/Class: Fannin Donation
File#: 1381
Patent#: 9
Patent Vol.: 4
Certificate: 159
Acres: 492
Map(s) 1

Abstract # 23 - BYERLY, W
P'ee: FROST AND THORN
G'ee: BYERLY, WILLIAM
T-Dt: -- --- -----
P-Dt: 09 Jul 1875
Dist/Class: Fannin Donation
File#: 1381
Patent#: 8
Patent Vol.: 4
Certificate: 159
Acres: 148
Map(s) 9

Abstract # 24 - BROWN, O T
P'ee: BROWN, OLIVER T
G'ee: BROWN, OLIVER T
T-Dt: -- --- -----
P-Dt: 15 Mar 1878
Dist/Class: Fannin Donation
File#: 1425 1/2
Patent#: 139
Patent Vol.: 4
Certificate: 101
Acres: 640
Map(s) 39, 40, 47, 48

Abstract # 25 - BBB&C RR CO
P'ee: HENRY, J R
G'ee: BUFFALO BAYOU, BRAZOS AND
COLORADO RAILROAD COMPANY
T-Dt: -- --- -----
P-Dt: 23 Mar 1859
Dist/Class: Fannin Scrip
File#: 250
Patent#: 156
Patent Vol.: 4
Certificate: 113
Survey/Blk/Twp: 1
Acres: 640
Map(s) 39, 40

Abstract # 26 - BBB&C RR CO
P'ee: HENRY, J R
G'ee: BUFFALO BAYOU, BRAZOS AND
COLORADO RAILROAD COMPANY
T-Dt: -- --- -----
P-Dt: 24 Mar 1859
Dist/Class: Fannin Scrip
File#: 251
Patent#: 157
Patent Vol.: 4
Certificate: 112
Survey/Blk/Twp: 2
Acres: 640
Map(s) 40

Abstract # 27 - BBB&C RR CO
P'ee: HENRY, J R
G'ee: BUFFALO BAYOU, BRAZOS AND
COLORADO RAILROAD COMPANY
T-Dt: -- --- -----
P-Dt: 24 Mar 1859
Dist/Class: Fannin Scrip
File#: 252
Patent#: 158
Patent Vol.: 4
Certificate: 116
Survey/Blk/Twp: 3
Acres: 640
Map(s) 39, 40

Abstract # 28 - BBB&C RR CO
P'ee: HENRY, J R
G'ee: BUFFALO BAYOU, BRAZOS AND
COLORADO RAILROAD COMPANY
T-Dt: -- --- -----
P-Dt: 24 Mar 1859
Dist/Class: Fannin Scrip
File#: 253
Patent#: 159
Patent Vol.: 4
Certificate: 114
Survey/Blk/Twp: 4
Acres: 640
Map(s) 40

Abstract # 29 - BBB&C RR CO
P'ee: HENRY, J R
G'ee: BUFFALO BAYOU, BRAZOS AND
COLORADO RAILROAD COMPANY
T-Dt: -- --- -----
P-Dt: 21 Mar 1859
Dist/Class: Fannin Scrip
File#: 255
Patent#: 161
Patent Vol.: 4
Certificate: 117
Survey/Blk/Twp: 6
Acres: 640
Map(s) 40

Abstract # 30 - BBB&C RR CO
P'ee: BOWERS, MARTIN V
G'ee: BUFFALO BAYOU, BRAZOS AND
COLORADO RAILROAD COMPANY
T-Dt: -- --- -----
P-Dt: 29 Oct 1861
Dist/Class: Fannin Scrip
File#: 1355
Patent#: 91
Patent Vol.: 14
Certificate: 349
Acres: 320
Map(s) 36

Abstract # 31 - BBB&C RR CO

P'ee: BOON, E
G'ee: BUFFALO BAYOU, BRAZOS AND
COLORADO RAILROAD COMPANY
T-Dt: -- --- -----
P-Dt: 28 Oct 1873
Dist/Class: Fannin Scrip
File#: 4655
Patent#: 100
Patent Vol.: 15
Certificate: 691
Survey/Blk/Twp: 1
Acres: 640
Map(s) 2, 3

Abstract # 32 - BBB&C RR CO
P'ee: KNOX, W
G'ee: BUFFALO BAYOU, BRAZOS AND
COLORADO RAILROAD COMPANY
T-Dt: -- --- -----
P-Dt: 21 May 1941
Dist/Class: Fannin Scrip
File#: 4657
Patent#: 472
Patent Vol.: 80A
Certificate: 681
Survey/Blk/Twp: 1
Acres: 640
Map(s) 31

Abstract # 33 - BBB&C RR CO
P'ee: BOON, E
G'ee: BUFFALO BAYOU, BRAZOS AND
COLORADO RAILROAD COMPANY
T-Dt: -- --- -----
P-Dt: 22 Oct 1873
Dist/Class: Fannin Scrip
File#: 5497 1/2
Patent#: 97
Patent Vol.: 15
Certificate: 682
Survey/Blk/Twp: 1
Acres: 640
Map(s) 15, 16

Abstract # 34 - BBB&C RR CO
P'ee: BOON, E
G'ee: BUFFALO BAYOU, BRAZOS AND
COLORADO RAILROAD COMPANY
T-Dt: -- --- -----
P-Dt: 21 Oct 1873
Dist/Class: Fannin Scrip
File#: 5498 1/2
Patent#: 93
Patent Vol.: 15
Certificate: 683
Survey/Blk/Twp: 1
Acres: 640
Map(s) 14, 15

Abstract # 35 - BBB&C RR CO
P'ee: BOON, E
G'ee: BUFFALO BAYOU, BRAZOS AND
COLORADO RAILROAD COMPANY
T-Dt: -- --- -----
P-Dt: 21 Oct 1873
Dist/Class: Fannin Scrip
File#: 5499 1/2
Patent#: 95
Patent Vol.: 15
Certificate: 686
Survey/Blk/Twp: 1
Acres: 640
Map(s) 6, 7

Abstract # 36 - BBB&C RR CO

P'ee: MCCARDELL, J H
G'ee: BUFFALO BAYOU, BRAZOS AND
COLORADO RAILROAD COMPANY
T-Dt: -- --- -----
P-Dt: 09 Oct 1876
Dist/Class: Fannin Scrip
File#: 6455
Patent#: 291
Patent Vol.: 15
Certificate: 748
Acres: 640
Map(s) 24

Abstract # 37 - BBB&C RR CO
P'ee: MCCARDELL, J H
G'ee: BUFFALO BAYOU, BRAZOS AND
COLORADO RAILROAD COMPANY
T-Dt: -- --- -----
P-Dt: 09 Oct 1876
Dist/Class: Fannin Scrip
File#: 6454
Patent#: 292
Patent Vol.: 15
Certificate: 746
Acres: 640
Map(s) 36

Abstract # 38 - BAHN, A
P'ee: LEDBETTER, W H
G'ee: BOHN, A
T-Dt: -- --- -----
P-Dt: 20 Nov 1875
Dist/Class: Fannin Scrip
File#: 8999
Patent#: 524
Patent Vol.: 21
Certificate: 19/703
Acres: 160
Map(s) 33, 41

Abstract # 39 - BROWN, J C
P'ee: BROWN, JAMES C
G'ee: BROWN, JAMES C
T-Dt: -- --- -----
P-Dt: 31 Jul 1875
Dist/Class: Fannin Scrip
File#: 9579
Patent#: 188
Patent Vol.: 21
Certificate: 30/111
Acres: 82
Map(s) 28, 29

Abstract # 40 - BS&F
P'ee: GUNTER AND MUNSON
G'ee: BEATY, SEALE AND FORWOOD
T-Dt: -- --- -----
P-Dt: 07 Jul 1875
Dist/Class: Fannin Scrip
File#: 9551
Patent#: 154
Patent Vol.: 21
Certificate: 1/264
Survey/Blk/Twp: 1
Acres: 640
Map(s) 14, 15

Abstract # 41 - BS&F
P'ee: GUNTER AND MUNSON
G'ee: BEATY, SEALE AND FORWOOD
T-Dt: -- --- -----
P-Dt: 07 Jul 1875
Dist/Class: Fannin Scrip
File#: 9553
Patent#: 156

Patent Vol.: 21
Certificate: 1/266
Survey/Blk/Twp: 3
Acres: 640
Map(s) 32, 40

Abstract # 42 - BS&F
P'ee: GUNTER AND MUNSON
G'ee: BEATY, SEALE AND FORWOOD
T-Dt: -- --- -----
P-Dt: 07 Jul 1875
Dist/Class: Fannin Scrip
File#: 9554
Patent#: 157
Patent Vol.: 21
Certificate: 1/268
Survey/Blk/Twp: 1
Acres: 640
Map(s) 32

Abstract # 43 - BS&F
P'ee: GUNTER AND MUNSON
G'ee: BEATY, SEALE AND FORWOOD
T-Dt: -- --- -----
P-Dt: 07 Jul 1875
Dist/Class: Fannin Scrip
File#: 9555
Patent#: 159
Patent Vol.: 21
Certificate: 1/269
Survey/Blk/Twp: 3
Acres: 640
Map(s) 35

Abstract # 44 - BS&F
P'ee: SHORT, J C
G'ee: BEATY, SEALE AND FORWOOD
T-Dt: -- --- -----
P-Dt: 01 Jul 1881
Dist/Class: Fannin Scrip
File#: 9556
Patent#: 182
Patent Vol.: 33
Certificate: 1/270
Survey/Blk/Twp: 1
Acres: 640
Map(s) 34, 35

Abstract # 45 - BARNETT, S
P'ee: BARNETT, S
G'ee: BARNETT, S
T-Dt: -- --- -----
P-Dt: 06 Jul 1877
Dist/Class: Fannin Preemption
File#: 1602
Patent#: 616
Patent Vol.: 5
Acres: 80
Map(s) 29, 30

Abstract # 46 - BARNETT, D
P'ee: BARNETT, DUNCAN
G'ee: BARNETT, DUNCAN
T-Dt: -- --- -----
P-Dt: 06 Jul 1877
Dist/Class: Fannin Preemption
File#: 1601
Patent#: 618
Patent Vol.: 5
Acres: 80
Map(s) 30

Abstract # 47 - BYRD, R E
P'ee: BYRD, R E
G'ee: BYRD, R E

T-Dt: -- --- -----
P-Dt: 02 Feb 1877
Dist/Class: Fannin Preemption
File#: 1307
Patent#: 270
Patent Vol.: 5
Acres: 160
Map(s) 38

Abstract # 48 - BROOKS, D C
P'ee: BROOKS, D C
G'ee: BROOKS, D C
T-Dt: -- --- -----
P-Dt: 07 Aug 1877
Dist/Class: Fannin Preemption
File#: 1300
Patent#: 51
Patent Vol.: 6
Acres: 160
Map(s) 39

Abstract # 49 - BRAGG, J
P'ee: LYNCH, J M
G'ee: BRAGG, JESSIE
T-Dt: -- --- -----
P-Dt: 07 May 1877
Dist/Class: Fannin Preemption
File#: 703
Patent#: 487
Patent Vol.: 5
Acres: 160
Map(s) 33

Abstract # 50 - BRAGG, W
P'ee: DOBBS, J M
G'ee: BRAGG, WILLIAM
T-Dt: -- --- -----
P-Dt: 01 Jun 1878
Dist/Class: Fannin Preemption
File#: 702
Patent#: 279
Patent Vol.: 7
Acres: 160
Map(s) 33, 34

Abstract # 52 - BAKER, M W
P'ee: MORRISON, JOHN A
G'ee: BAKER, M W
T-Dt: -- --- -----
P-Dt: 12 Apr 1877
Dist/Class: Fannin Preemption
File#: 1394
Patent#: 441
Patent Vol.: 5
Acres: 160
Map(s) 38

Abstract # 53 - BRAGG, G
P'ee: MEADORS, MARTHA E
G'ee: BRAGG, GEORGE B
T-Dt: -- --- -----
P-Dt: 08 Jan 1879
Dist/Class: Fannin Preemption
File#: 701
Patent#: 253
Patent Vol.: 8
Acres: 160
Map(s) 33, 34, 41, 42

Abstract # 54 - BUNGER, W T
P'ee: BUNGER, W T
G'ee: BUNGER, W T
T-Dt: -- --- -----
P-Dt: 15 Dec 1876
Dist/Class: Fannin Preemption

File#: 1302
Patent#: 149
Patent Vol.: 5
Acres: 160
Map(s) 37

Abstract # 55 - BARTLETT, M
P'ee: BARTLETT, M
G'ee: BARTLETT, M
T-Dt: -- --- -----
P-Dt: 23 Jun 1887
Dist/Class: Fannin Preemption
File#: 1294
Patent#: 594
Patent Vol.: 5
Acres: 80
Map(s) 37

Abstract # 56 - BAKER, J R
P'ee: BAKER, J R
G'ee: BAKER, J R
T-Dt: -- --- -----
P-Dt: 23 Jun 1877
Dist/Class: Fannin Preemption
File#: 1292
Patent#: 596
Patent Vol.: 5
Acres: 160
Map(s) 38

Abstract # 57 - CONNER, J
P'ee: CONNER, JOHN
G'ee: CONNER, JOHN
T-Dt: -- --- -----
P-Dt: 30 Oct 1857
Dist/Class: Fannin 1st
File#: 781
Patent#: 818
Patent Vol.: 12
Certificate: 2891/2992
Acres: 2683.60
Map(s) 39, 40

Abstract # 58 - CROCKETT, E
P'ee: PEVELER, DAVID
G'ee: CROCKETT, ELIZABETH
T-Dt: -- --- -----
P-Dt: 01 May 1861
Dist/Class: Fannin 1st
File#: 1121
Patent#: 41
Patent Vol.: 14
Certificate: 4/15
Acres: 505.34
Map(s) 19

Abstract # 59 - CAHILL, J
P'ee: HARMONSON, WILLIAM P
G'ee: CAHILL, JOHN
T-Dt: -- --- -----
P-Dt: 05 Feb 1862
Dist/Class: Fannin 1st
File#: 1257
Patent#: 577
Patent Vol.: 16
Certificate: 1366
Acres: 31.24
Map(s) 9

Abstract # 60 - CASTRO, M G
P'ee: THORN, FROST AND EDWARDS, H H
G'ee: CASTRO, M G
T-Dt: -- --- -----
P-Dt: 19 Nov 1875

Dist/Class: Fannin 1st
File#: 1645
Patent#: 360
Patent Vol.: 21
Certificate: 1622/1723
Acres: 177.10
Map(s) 1

Abstract # 61 - CADDLE, A
P'ee: CADDLE, ANDREW
G'ee: CADDLE, ANDREW
T-Dt: -- --- -----
P-Dt: 09 Mar 1861
Dist/Class: Milam 1st
File#: 1536
Patent#: 364
Patent Vol.: 16
Certificate: 423
Acres: 177
Map(s) 35

Abstract # 62 - CARTER, W T
P'ee: CARTER, WILLIAM T (HEIRS)
G'ee: CARTER, WILLIAM T
T-Dt: -- --- -----
P-Dt: 31 Jul 1857
Dist/Class: Milam 2nd
File#: 494
Patent#: 907
Patent Vol.: 3
Certificate: 1069
Acres: 640
Map(s) 36

Abstract # 63 - CAUFMAN, J
P'ee: GANT, A B
G'ee: CAUFMAN, JAMES
T-Dt: -- --- -----
P-Dt: 05 Jun 1875
Dist/Class: Fannin 3rd
File#: 4524
Patent#: 616
Patent Vol.: 42
Certificate: 15/141
Acres: 120
Map(s) 28, 29

Abstract # 64 - COY, G
P'ee: HILL, GEORGE W
G'ee: COX, GEORGE
T-Dt: -- --- -----
P-Dt: 21 Mar 1857
Dist/Class: Fannin Bounty
File#: 433
Patent#: 200
Patent Vol.: 8
Certificate: 838
Acres: 177
Map(s) 30

Abstract # 65 - COTTLE, G W
P'ee: COTTLE, G W (HEIRS)
G'ee: COTTLE, GEORGE W
T-Dt: -- --- -----
P-Dt: 05 Apr 1877
Dist/Class: Fannin Donation
File#: 851
Patent#: 107
Patent Vol.: 4
Certificate: 1024
Acres: 480
Map(s) 35, 36

Abstract # 66 - COTTLE, G W
P'ee: COTTLE, G W (HEIRS)

G'ee: COTTLE, GEORGE W
T-Dt: -- --- -----
P-Dt: 05 Apr 1877
Dist/Class: Fannin Donation
File#: 851
Patent#: 106
Patent Vol.: 4
Certificate: 1024
Acres: 160
Map(s) 35, 36

Abstract # 67 - CASSEL, HRS W
P'ee: CASSELL, WILLIAM
G'ee: CASSELL, WILLIAM
T-Dt: -- --- -----
P-Dt: 20 Dec 1876
Dist/Class: Fannin Bounty
File#: 1352
Patent#: 556
Patent Vol.: 15
Certificate: 29/152
Acres: 640
Map(s) 21

Abstract # 68 - CT RR CO
P'ee: STEEDMAN AND GUNTER
G'ee: COLUMBUS TAP RAILROAD COMPANY
T-Dt: -- --- -----
P-Dt: 01 Aug 1873
Dist/Class: Fannin Scrip
File#: 5511
Patent#: 16
Patent Vol.: 1
Certificate: 44
Survey/Blk/Twp: 1
Acres: 640
Map(s) 7, 8

Abstract # 69 - CARSON, R
P'ee: CARSON, W J AND LEWIS, T D
G'ee: CARSON, ROBERT
T-Dt: -- --- -----
P-Dt: 04 Aug 1875
Dist/Class: Fannin Scrip
File#: 9566
Patent#: 192
Patent Vol.: 21
Certificate: 19/277
Acres: 59.7
Map(s) 28

Abstract # 70 - CARSON, R
P'ee: GRAHAM, G A
G'ee: CARSON, ROBERT
T-Dt: -- --- -----
P-Dt: 25 Oct 1876
Dist/Class: Fannin Scrip
File#: 9563
Patent#: 303
Patent Vol.: 26
Certificate: 29/408
Acres: 160
Map(s) 29, 30

Abstract # 71 - CARSON, R
P'ee: CARSON, ROBERT
G'ee: CARSON, ROBERT
T-Dt: -- --- -----
P-Dt: 04 Aug 1875
Dist/Class: Fannin Scrip
File#: 9563
Patent#: 193
Patent Vol.: 21
Certificate: 19/777

Acres: 160
Map(s) 28

Abstract # 72 - COFFMAN, A W
P'ee: COFFMAN, A W
G'ee: COFFMAN, A W
T-Dt: -- --- -----
P-Dt: 08 Jan 1877
Dist/Class: Fannin Preemption
File#: 1310
Patent#: 192
Patent Vol.: 5
Acres: 160
Map(s) 37, 38

Abstract # 73 - CORNETT, W L
P'ee: CORNETT, W L
G'ee: CORNETT, W L
T-Dt: -- --- -----
P-Dt: 03 Aug 1877
Dist/Class: Fannin Preemption
File#: 1317
Patent#: 35
Patent Vol.: 6
Acres: 80
Map(s) 29

Abstract # 74 - CUNNINGHAM, D
P'ee: CUNNINGHAM, DANIEL
G'ee: CUNNINGHAM, DANIEL
T-Dt: -- --- -----
P-Dt: 06 Jul 1877
Dist/Class: Fannin Preemption
File#: 1321
Patent#: 619
Patent Vol.: 5
Acres: 80
Map(s) 30

Abstract # 75 - DEDRICK, G
P'ee: DEDRICK, GEORGE (HEIRS)
G'ee: DEDRICK, GEORGE
T-Dt: -- --- -----
P-Dt: 24 Sep 1860
Dist/Class: Fannin 1st
File#: 1117
Patent#: 284
Patent Vol.: 16
Certificate: 3/31
Acres: 1476
Map(s) 40

Abstract # 76 - DAWSON, D
P'ee: DAWSON, DAVID (HEIRS)
G'ee: DAWSON, DAVID
T-Dt: -- --- -----
P-Dt: 14 Dec 1874
Dist/Class: Fannin 1st
File#: 1502
Patent#: 474
Patent Vol.: 20
Certificate: 105
Acres: 1476.13
Map(s) 6

Abstract # 77 - DENISON, S
P'ee: DENISON, STEPHEN (HEIRS)
G'ee: DENISON, STEPHEN
T-Dt: -- --- -----
P-Dt: 04 Oct 1875
Dist/Class: Fannin 1st
File#: 1568
Patent#: 302
Patent Vol.: 21
Certificate: 211

Acres: 646.95
Map(s) 36

Abstract # 78 - DAILY, HRS J
P'ee: DAILY, JOHN (HEIRS)
G'ee: DAILY, JOHN (DECEASED)
T-Dt: -- --- -----
P-Dt: 15 Jul 1857
Dist/Class: Milam 3rd
File#: 911
Patent#: 592
Patent Vol.: 15
Certificate: 1025
Acres: 320
Map(s) 37

Abstract # 79 - DOWD, P
P'ee: LEELIGSON, LEWIS
G'ee: DOWD, PETER
T-Dt: -- --- -----
P-Dt: 24 Jul 1861
Dist/Class: Fannin 3rd
File#: 3770
Patent#: 284
Patent Vol.: 34
Certificate: 4896/4997
Acres: 187.50
Map(s) 19, 20, 28

Abstract # 80 - DOWD, P
P'ee: LEELIGSON, LEWIS
G'ee: DOWD, PETER
T-Dt: -- --- -----
P-Dt: 24 Jul 1861
Dist/Class: Fannin 3rd
File#: 3770
Patent#: 283
Patent Vol.: 34
Certificate: 4896/4997
Acres: 132.50
Map(s) 20

Abstract # 81 - DUNN, M
P'ee: DUNN, MATTHEW
G'ee: DUNN, MATTHEW
T-Dt: -- --- -----
P-Dt: 16 Jun 1868
Dist/Class: Fannin Donation
File#: 1060
Patent#: 294
Patent Vol.: 3
Certificate: 1200
Acres: 160
Map(s) 29, 30

Abstract # 82 - DAILY, M
P'ee: OLIVER, L F
G'ee: DAILEY, MICHAEL
T-Dt: -- --- -----
P-Dt: 23 Feb 1859
Dist/Class: Fannin Bounty
File#: 347
Patent#: 165
Patent Vol.: 9
Certificate: 1023
Acres: 320
Map(s) 1

Abstract # 83 - DUNN, W
P'ee: GILLESPIE, WILLIAM J (HEIRS)
G'ee: DUNN, WILLIAM
T-Dt: -- --- -----
P-Dt: 24 Nov 1871
Dist/Class: Fannin Bounty
File#: 449

Patent#: 67
Patent Vol.: 14
Certificate: 1363
Acres: 252
Map(s) 28, 36

Abstract # 84 - G&BN CO
S2: DAVIDSON, S
P'ee: DAVIDSON, SAMUEL
G'ee: DAVIDSON, SAMUEL
T-Dt: -- --- -----
P-Dt: 05 Oct 1885
Dist/Class: School
File#: 1000
Patent#: 95
Patent Vol.: 5
Survey/Blk/Twp: SE 1/4 1 G & BN CO.-
Acres: 160
Map(s) 6

Abstract # 85 - G&BN CO
S2: DAVIDSON, J H
P'ee: DAVIDSON, J H
G'ee: DAVIDSON, J H
T-Dt: -- --- -----
P-Dt: 13 Jan 1880
Dist/Class: School
File#: 1001
Patent#: 228
Patent Vol.: 1
Survey/Blk/Twp: NE 1/4 1 G & BN CO.-
Acres: 160
Map(s) 6

Abstract # 86 - DUFF, J
P'ee: DUFF, JAMES
G'ee: DUFF, JAMES
T-Dt: -- --- -----
P-Dt: 08 Oct 1917
Dist/Class: Fannin Scrip
File#: 1155
Patent#: 169
Patent Vol.: 39
Certificate: 11/1
Survey/Blk/Twp: 4
Acres: 160
Map(s) 37, 45

Abstract # 88 - DENTON, A L
P'ee: DENTON, A L
G'ee: DENTON, A L
T-Dt: -- --- -----
P-Dt: 10 Oct 1876
Dist/Class: Fannin Preemption
File#: 1324
Patent#: 606
Patent Vol.: 4
Acres: 160
Map(s) 39

Abstract # 89 - DOBBS, J L
P'ee: DOBBS, J L
G'ee: DOBBS, J L
T-Dt: -- --- -----
P-Dt: 12 Apr 1877
Dist/Class: Fannin Preemption
File#: 1050
Patent#: 439
Patent Vol.: 5
Acres: 160
Map(s) 35, 43

Abstract # 90 - TERRILL, J W
P'ee: EDWARDS, REBECCA
G'ee: EDWARDS, REBECCA

T-Dt: -- --- -----
P-Dt: 06 Apr 1858
Dist/Class: Fannin 1st
File#: 885
Patent#: 930
Patent Vol.: 12
Certificate: 3461/3562
Acres: 486.84
Map(s) 31, 32

Abstract # 91 - EDMONDS, M
P'ee: EDMONDS, MARGARET
G'ee: EDMONDS, MARGARET
T-Dt: -- --- -----
P-Dt: 21 Feb 1862
Dist/Class: Fannin 1st
File#: 1089
Patent#: 594
Patent Vol.: 16
Certificate: 369
Acres: 3227.34
Map(s) 26, 34

Abstract # 92 - ERNEST, A J
P'ee: ERNEST, A J
G'ee: ERNEST, A J
T-Dt: -- --- -----
P-Dt: 14 Oct 1876
Dist/Class: Fannin Preemption
File#: 1285
Patent#: 614
Patent Vol.: 4
Acres: 160
Map(s) 38

Abstract # 93 - FISHBAUGH, W
P'ee: FISHBAUGH, WILLIAM (HEIRS)
G'ee: FISHBAUGH, WILLIAM
T-Dt: -- --- -----
P-Dt: 25 Mar 1856
Dist/Class: Fannin 1st
File#: 462
Patent#: 25
Patent Vol.: 13
Certificate: 3055/3156
Acres: 546.16
Map(s) 9, 17

Abstract # 94 - FARRIS, E
P'ee: SLAUTER, FRANCIS (HEIRS)
G'ee: FARRIS, EDWARD
T-Dt: -- --- -----
P-Dt: 31 Oct 1857
Dist/Class: Fannin 2nd
File#: 350
Patent#: 990
Patent Vol.: 3
Certificate: 257/356
Acres: 177.10
Map(s) 39

Abstract # 95 - FISHER, R J
P'ee: FISHER, REBECCA JANE
G'ee: FISHER, REBECCA JANE
T-Dt: -- --- -----
P-Dt: 19 Sep 1855
Dist/Class: Fannin 3rd
File#: 1914
Patent#: 181
Patent Vol.: 12
Certificate: 3481/3582
Acres: 640
Map(s) 28

Abstract # 96 - FERGUSON, S

P'ee: DAVIS, R J
G'ee: FERGUSON, SILAS
T-Dt: -- --- -----
P-Dt: 16 Jun 1873
Dist/Class: Fannin 3rd
File#: 4303
Patent#: 176
Patent Vol.: 41
Certificate: 16/387
Acres: 511
Map(s) 30

Abstract # 97 - EDWARDS, R
P'ee: BALL, THOMAS
G'ee: TERRELL, JONATHAN W
T-Dt: -- --- -----
P-Dt: 21 Oct 1873
Dist/Class: Fannin 3rd
File#: 4359
Patent#: 410
Patent Vol.: 41
Certificate: 30/108
Acres: 160
Map(s) 19

Abstract # 98 - TERRILL, J W
P'ee: BALL, THOMAS
G'ee: TERRELL, JONATHAN W
T-Dt: -- --- -----
P-Dt: 22 Dec 1873
Dist/Class: Fannin 3rd
File#: 4359
Patent#: 511
Patent Vol.: 41
Certificate: 30/108
Acres: 517.5
Map(s) 23, 24, 31, 32

Abstract # 99 - FULLERTON, W
P'ee: FULLERTON, WILLIAM
G'ee: FULLERTON, WILLIAM
T-Dt: -- --- -----
P-Dt: 20 Feb 1861
Dist/Class: Fannin Bounty
File#: 919
Patent#: 392
Patent Vol.: 12
Acres: 320
Map(s) 37

Abstract # 100 - FERGUSON, J
P'ee: FERGUSON, JOSEPH
G'ee: FERGUSON, JOSEPH
T-Dt: -- --- -----
P-Dt: 10 Feb 1877
Dist/Class: Fannin Preemption
File#: 1330
Patent#: 286
Patent Vol.: 5
Acres: 160
Map(s) 38

Abstract # 101 - FULLERTON, J
P'ee: FULKERSON, JAMES
G'ee: FULKERSON, JAMES
T-Dt: -- --- -----
P-Dt: 20 Oct 1876
Dist/Class: Fannin Preemption
File#: 1340
Patent#: 627
Patent Vol.: 4
Acres: 160
Map(s) 38, 39

Abstract # 102 - FITE, W

P'ee: FITE, WILLIAM
G'ee: FITE, WILLIAM
T-Dt: -- --- -----
P-Dt: 09 Jul 1877
Dist/Class: Fannin Preemption
File#: 1335
Patent#: 629
Patent Vol.: 5
Acres: 160
Map(s) 37

Abstract # 103 - FORE, G W
P'ee: FORE, G W
G'ee: FORE, G W
T-Dt: -- --- -----
P-Dt: 09 Jul 1877
Dist/Class: Fannin Preemption
File#: 1338
Patent#: 625
Patent Vol.: 5
Acres: 160
Map(s) 38

Abstract # 104 - GARMS, H
P'ee: GARMS, HENRY
G'ee: GARMS, HENRY
T-Dt: -- --- -----
P-Dt: 20 Nov 1860
Dist/Class: Fannin 1st
File#: 1169
Patent#: 229
Patent Vol.: 15
Certificate: 157
Acres: 684
Map(s) 37

Abstract # 105 - GREEN, F L
P'ee: GREEN, F L
G'ee: GREEN, F L
T-Dt: -- --- -----
P-Dt: 27 Aug 1859
Dist/Class: Milam 1st
File#: 1421
Patent#: 44
Patent Vol.: 16
Certificate: 4212/4313
Acres: 3179.33
Map(s) 34

Abstract # 106 - GAMBOA, F
P'ee: BARNARD, CHARLES E
G'ee: GAMBOA, FELICIANO
T-Dt: -- --- -----
P-Dt: 26 May 1859
Dist/Class: Fannin 2nd
File#: 534
Patent#: 12
Patent Vol.: 7
Certificate: 427
Acres: 640
Map(s) 29

Abstract # 107 - GARRETT, J
P'ee: GARRETT, JACOB
G'ee: GARRETT, JACOB
T-Dt: -- --- -----
P-Dt: 01 Jun 1875
Dist/Class: Fannin 2nd
File#: 694
Patent#: 581
Patent Vol.: 8
Certificate: 29/354
Acres: 142
Map(s) 28

Abstract # 108 - GARRETT, J
P'ee: GARRETT, JACOB
G'ee: GARRETT, JACOB
T-Dt: -- --- -----
P-Dt: 29 Aug 1884
Dist/Class: Fannin 2nd
File#: 694
Patent#: 382
Patent Vol.: 9
Certificate: 29/354
Acres: 498
Map(s) 36, 37

Abstract # 109 - GEORGE, P S
P'ee: GEORGE, PHILLIP S
G'ee: GEORGE, PHILLIP S
T-Dt: -- --- -----
P-Dt: 15 May 1860
Dist/Class: Fannin 3rd
File#: 2664
Patent#: 443
Patent Vol.: 29
Acres: 320
Map(s) 28

Abstract # 110 - GEORGE, H B
P'ee: GEORGE, HENRY B
G'ee: GEORGE, HENRY B
T-Dt: -- --- -----
P-Dt: 24 Feb 1860
Dist/Class: Fannin 3rd
File#: 2886
Patent#: 547
Patent Vol.: 28
Acres: 160
Map(s) 36

Abstract # 111 - GATES, J
P'ee: LEE, R W
G'ee: GATES, JAMES
T-Dt: -- --- -----
P-Dt: 17 Mar 1876
Dist/Class: Fannin Bounty
File#: 1378
Patent#: 431
Patent Vol.: 15
Certificate: 18/111
Acres: 128
Map(s) 31

Abstract # 112 - GILLIAM, R
P'ee: HENRY, JOHN R
G'ee: GILLIAM, RICHARD
T-Dt: -- --- -----
P-Dt: 15 Mar 1878
Dist/Class: Fannin Bounty
File#: 1508
Patent#: 702
Patent Vol.: 15
Certificate: 1109
Acres: 463
Map(s) 39, 40

Abstract # 114 - G&BN CO
P'ee: GUNTER, MUNSON AND PERRY
G'ee: GALVESTON AND BRAZOS
NAVIGATION COMPANY
T-Dt: -- --- -----
P-Dt: 02 Aug 1873
Dist/Class: Fannin Scrip
File#: 5508
Patent#: 240
Patent Vol.: 20
Certificate: 36
Survey/Blk/Twp: 2

Acres: 640
Map(s) 24

Abstract # 115 - G&BN CO
P'ee: GUNTER, MUNSON AND PERRY
G'ee: GALVESTON AND BRAZOS
NAVIGATION COMPANY
T-Dt: -- --- -----
P-Dt: 05 Aug 1873
Dist/Class: Fannin Scrip
File#: 5506
Patent#: 244
Patent Vol.: 20
Certificate: 34
Survey/Blk/Twp: 6
Acres: 640
Map(s) 16, 24

Abstract # 116 - G&BN CO
P'ee: GUNTER, MUNSON AND PERRY
G'ee: GALVESTON AND BRAZOS
NAVIGATION COMPANY
T-Dt: -- --- -----
P-Dt: 01 Aug 1873
Dist/Class: Fannin Scrip
File#: 5505
Patent#: 238
Patent Vol.: 20
Certificate: 33
Survey/Blk/Twp: 8
Acres: 640
Map(s) 16, 24

Abstract # 117 - G&BN CO
P'ee: GUNTER, MUNSON AND PERRY
G'ee: GALVESTON AND BRAZOS
NAVIGATION COMPANY
T-Dt: -- --- -----
P-Dt: 31 Jul 1873
Dist/Class: Fannin Scrip
File#: 5504
Patent#: 237
Patent Vol.: 20
Certificate: 32
Survey/Blk/Twp: 10
Acres: 451.30
Map(s) 24

Abstract # 118 - G&BN CO
P'ee: GUNTER, MUNSON AND PERRY
G'ee: GALVESTON AND BRAZOS
NAVIGATION COMPANY
T-Dt: -- --- -----
P-Dt: 04 Aug 1873
Dist/Class: Fannin Scrip
File#: 5503
Patent#: 243
Patent Vol.: 20
Certificate: 31
Survey/Blk/Twp: 2
Acres: 640
Map(s) 6, 7

Abstract # 119 - G&BN CO
P'ee: GUNTER, MUNSON AND PERRY
G'ee: GALVESTON AND BRAZOS
NAVIGATION COMPANY
T-Dt: -- --- -----
P-Dt: 04 Aug 1873
Dist/Class: Fannin Scrip
File#: 5502
Patent#: 242
Patent Vol.: 20
Certificate: 29
Survey/Blk/Twp: 4

Acres: 640
Map(s) 6

Abstract # 120 - G&BN CO
P'ee: KRIGBAUM, J H
G'ee: GALVESTON AND BRAZOS
NAVIGATION COMPANY
T-Dt: -- --- -----
P-Dt: 07 Dec 1874
Dist/Class: Fannin Scrip
File#: 5603
Patent#: 596
Patent Vol.: 20
Certificate: 91
Survey/Blk/Twp: 2
Acres: 640
Map(s) 15

Abstract # 121 - GREGORY, L M
P'ee: BARTEL, JOHN C
G'ee: GREGORY, L M
T-Dt: -- --- -----
P-Dt: 27 Nov 1876
Dist/Class: Fannin Preemption
File#: 1345
Patent#: 101
Patent Vol.: 5
Acres: 160
Map(s) 30, 38

Abstract # 122 - GRAHAM, J C C
P'ee: GRAHAM, J C C
G'ee: GRAHAM, J C C
T-Dt: -- --- -----
P-Dt: 25 Sep 1876
Dist/Class: Fannin Preemption
File#: 1343
Patent#: 563
Patent Vol.: 4
Acres: 80
Map(s) 37

Abstract # 123 - GRAHAM, H T
P'ee: GRAHAM, H T
G'ee: GRAHAM, H T
T-Dt: -- --- -----
P-Dt: 11 Nov 1876
Dist/Class: Fannin Preemption
File#: 1342
Patent#: 67
Patent Vol.: 5
Acres: 80
Map(s) 37

Abstract # 124 - GRAHAM, S H
P'ee: GRAHAM, S H
G'ee: GRAHAM, S H
T-Dt: -- --- -----
P-Dt: 10 Oct 1876
Dist/Class: Fannin Preemption
File#: 1341
Patent#: 608
Patent Vol.: 4
Acres: 80
Map(s) 37

Abstract # 125 - GRAHAM, A A
P'ee: GRAHAM, A A
G'ee: GRAHAM, A A
T-Dt: -- --- -----
P-Dt: 10 Oct 1876
Dist/Class: Fannin Preemption
File#: 1503
Patent#: 610
Patent Vol.: 4

Acres: 80
Map(s) 37

Abstract # 126 - HILL, I L
P'ee: HILL, ISAAC L
G'ee: HILL, ISAAC L
T-Dt: -- --- -----
P-Dt: 19 Nov 1856
Dist/Class: Fannin 1st
File#: 556
Patent#: 612
Patent Vol.: 12
Acres: 1476.13
Map(s) 28

Abstract # 127 - HILL, J A
P'ee: HILL, JOHN A
G'ee: HILL, JOHN A
T-Dt: -- --- -----
P-Dt: 02 May 1859
Dist/Class: Fannin 1st
File#: 651 1/2
Patent#: 365
Patent Vol.: 13
Certificate: 2286/2387
Acres: 401.52
Map(s) 39

Abstract # 128 - HITCHCOCK, A J
P'ee: HEARNE, SAMUEL R
G'ee: HITCHCOCK, A J
T-Dt: -- --- -----
P-Dt: 22 Aug 1873
Dist/Class: Fannin 1st
File#: 1016
Patent#: 539
Patent Vol.: 19
Certificate: 372
Acres: 1156.12
Map(s) 21, 29

Abstract # 129 - HILL, A
P'ee: HILL, ALLEN
G'ee: HILL, ALLEN
T-Dt: -- --- -----
P-Dt: 09 Nov 1885
Dist/Class: Fannin 1st
File#: 1195
Patent#: 375
Patent Vol.: 24
Certificate: 31
Acres: 520.16
Map(s) 16

Abstract # 130 - HOLMAN, I
P'ee: HOLEMAN, ISAAC (HEIRS)
G'ee: HOLEMAN, ISAAC
T-Dt: -- --- -----
P-Dt: 15 Feb 1873
Dist/Class: Fannin 1st
File#: 1468
Patent#: 214
Patent Vol.: 19
Certificate: 672
Acres: 4605.50
Map(s) 2

Abstract # 131 - HEARTT, HRS C P
P'ee: HEARTH, CHARLES P (HEIRS)
G'ee: HEARTH, CHARLES P
T-Dt: -- --- -----
P-Dt: 20 Sep 1878
Dist/Class: Fannin 1st
File#: 1543
Patent#: 511

Patent Vol.: 22
Certificate: 3/49
Acres: 211.98
Map(s) 28

Abstract # 132 - HEART, HRS C P
P'ee: HEARTH, CHARLES P (HEIRS)
G'ee: HEARTH, CHARLES P
T-Dt: -- --- -----
P-Dt: 06 Oct 1880
Dist/Class: Fannin 1st
File#: 1543
Patent#: 340
Patent Vol.: 23
Certificate: 3/49
Acres: 263.69
Map(s) 29, 30

Abstract # 133 - HEARTT, HRS C P
P'ee: HEARTH, CHARLES P (HEIRS)
G'ee: HEARTH, CHARLES P
T-Dt: -- --- -----
P-Dt: 05 Nov 1889
Dist/Class: Fannin 1st
File#: 1543
Patent#: 46
Patent Vol.: 25
Certificate: 3/49
Acres: 1017.92
Map(s) 22, 30

Abstract # 134 - HODGES, H
P'ee: HODGES, HENRY
G'ee: HODGES, HENRY
T-Dt: -- --- -----
P-Dt: 24 May 1875
Dist/Class: Fannin 1st
File#: 1602
Patent#: 76
Patent Vol.: 21
Certificate: 30/203
Acres: 1933.13
Map(s) 33, 34

Abstract # 135 - HINES, A
P'ee: THORN, FROST (HEIRS)
G'ee: HINES, ALLEN
T-Dt: -- --- -----
P-Dt: 23 Nov 1866
Dist/Class: Milam 1st
File#: 1538
Patent#: 357
Patent Vol.: 17
Certificate: 5094/5095
Acres: 2151.50
Map(s) 26, 27

Abstract # 136 - HARDAWAY, S G
P'ee: PETTIT, CHARLES
G'ee: HARDAWAY, SAM G
T-Dt: -- --- -----
P-Dt: 20 Aug 1877
Dist/Class: Fannin 1st
File#: 1850
Patent#: 289
Patent Vol.: 22
Certificate: 18/169
Acres: 157.31
Map(s) 4

Abstract # 137 - HILL, B
P'ee: HILL, BENJAMIN (HEIRS)
G'ee: HILL, BENJAMIN
T-Dt: -- --- -----
P-Dt: 05 Sep 1860

Dist/Class: Fannin 2nd
File#: 339
Patent#: 155
Patent Vol.: 7
Certificate: 23
Acres: 1476.13
Map(s) 30

Abstract # 138 - HAMILTON, M
P'ee: HAMILTON, MARY
G'ee: HAMILTON, MARY
T-Dt: -- --- -----
P-Dt: 24 May 1860
Dist/Class: Fannin 2nd
File#: 400
Patent#: 109
Patent Vol.: 7
Certificate: 146
Acres: 640
Map(s) 20, 28

Abstract # 139 - HUGHES, C
P'ee: RUGGLES, DANIEL
G'ee: HUGHES, CLAIBOURN
T-Dt: -- --- -----
P-Dt: 15 May 1861
Dist/Class: Milam 3rd
File#: 1113
Patent#: 507
Patent Vol.: 32
Certificate: 3423
Acres: 290
Map(s) 28

Abstract # 140 - HUME, J P
P'ee: HUME, JAMES P
G'ee: HUME, JAMES P
T-Dt: -- --- -----
P-Dt: 23 Jul 1856
Dist/Class: Fannin 3rd
File#: 1900
Patent#: 1594
Patent Vol.: 12
Certificate: 282
Acres: 640
Map(s) 20, 28

Abstract # 141 - HARMONSON, P
P'ee: HARMONSON, PETER
G'ee: HARMONSON, PETER
T-Dt: -- --- -----
P-Dt: 07 Mar 1861
Dist/Class: Fannin 3rd
File#: 2885
Patent#: 43
Patent Vol.: 34
Acres: 160
Map(s) 20

Abstract # 142 - HARRISON, S
P'ee: CRAIG, JONATHAN C
G'ee: HARRISON, SAMUEL
T-Dt: -- --- -----
P-Dt: 30 Sep 1857
Dist/Class: Fannin 3rd
File#: 3185
Patent#: 308
Patent Vol.: 16
Acres: 320
Map(s) 20

Abstract # 143 - HOFFMAN
P'ee: FARMER, ALEXANDER
G'ee: HOFFMAN, JOHANN CARL
T-Dt: -- --- -----

P-Dt: 10 Jul 1873
Dist/Class: Fannin 3rd
File#: 4308
Patent#: 200
Patent Vol.: 41
Certificate: 552
Acres: 106.66
Map(s) 48

Abstract # 144 - HILL, B
P'ee: HILL, BENJAMIN (HEIRS)
G'ee: HILL, BENJAMIN
T-Dt: -- --- -----
P-Dt: 07 Sep 1860
Dist/Class: Fannin Bounty
File#: 412 1/2
Patent#: 274
Patent Vol.: 12
Certificate: 9385
Acres: 640
Map(s) 30

Abstract # 147 - HATCHKISS, R
P'ee: HEATH, THOMAS (HEIRS)
G'ee: HOTCHKISS, R
T-Dt: -- --- -----
P-Dt: 03 Jul 1875
Dist/Class: Fannin Bounty
File#: 1380
Patent#: 170
Patent Vol.: 15
Certificate: 20/59
Acres: 135
Map(s) 31, 32

Abstract # 149 - HUNT, M
P'ee: FROIS, THEODORE
G'ee: HUNT, MEMUCAN
T-Dt: -- --- -----
P-Dt: 12 Nov 1874
Dist/Class: Fannin Scrip
File#: 8890
Patent#: 566
Patent Vol.: 20
Certificate: 16/89
Acres: 320
Map(s) 34

Abstract # 150 - HEWITT, R
P'ee: HEWIT, ROBERT
G'ee: HEWIT, ROBERT
T-Dt: -- --- -----
P-Dt: 07 Aug 1876
Dist/Class: Fannin Preemption
File#: 722
Patent#: 446
Patent Vol.: 4
Acres: 80
Map(s) 41

Abstract # 151 - HILL, G W
P'ee: BARNES, G L
G'ee: HILL, G W
T-Dt: -- --- -----
P-Dt: 16 Sep 1876
Dist/Class: Fannin Preemption
File#: 978
Patent#: 549
Patent Vol.: 4
Acres: 160
Map(s) 35

Abstract # 152 - HARRINGTON, T
P'ee: HARRINGTON, THOMAS
G'ee: HARRINGTON, THOMAS

T-Dt: -- --- -----
P-Dt: 12 Sep 1876
Dist/Class: Fannin Preemption
File#: 1125
Patent#: 539
Patent Vol.: 4
Acres: 160
Map(s) 24

Abstract # 153 - HUMPHREYS, P J
P'ee: HUMPHREYS, P J
G'ee: HUMPHREYS, P J
T-Dt: -- --- -----
P-Dt: 23 Oct 1876
Dist/Class: Fannin Preemption
File#: 1359
Patent#: 8
Patent Vol.: 5
Acres: 160
Map(s) 39

Abstract # 154 - HOLT, B
P'ee: HOLT, BAZZEL
G'ee: HOLT, BAZZEL
T-Dt: -- --- -----
P-Dt: 17 Aug 1877
Dist/Class: Fannin Preemption
File#: 1555
Patent#: 83
Patent Vol.: 6
Acres: 160
Map(s) 37

Abstract # 156 - I RR CO
P'ee: LAMB, WILLIAM G
G'ee: INDIANOLA RAILROAD COM-
PANY
T-Dt: -- --- -----
P-Dt: 07 Jul 1875
Dist/Class: Fannin Scrip
File#: 9652
Patent#: 166
Patent Vol.: 22
Certificate: 16/161
Survey/Blk/Twp: 1
Acres: 640
Map(s) 32

Abstract # 157 - JAIME, F
P'ee: GUNTER AND MUNSON
G'ee: JAIME, FELIPE
T-Dt: -- --- -----
P-Dt: 20 Mar 1873
Dist/Class: Fannin 1st
File#: 1514
Patent#: 4
Patent Vol.: 20
Certificate: 13/342
Acres: 1288.41
Map(s) 22, 23

Abstract # 159 - JOHNSON, W
P'ee: JOHNSON, WILLIAM (HEIRS)
G'ee: JOHNSON, WILLIAM
T-Dt: -- --- -----
P-Dt: 31 Jul 1857
Dist/Class: Milam 2nd
File#: 497
Patent#: 906
Patent Vol.: 3
Certificate: 1067
Acres: 640
Map(s) 36, 37

Abstract # 160 - JOHNSTON, J S

P'ee: JOHNSTON, JOSEPH S (HEIRS)
G'ee: JOHNSTON, JOSEPH S
T-Dt: -- --- -----
P-Dt: 28 Jan 1858
Dist/Class: Fannin Bounty
File#: 665
Patent#: 431
Patent Vol.: 8
Certificate: 1382
Acres: 640
Map(s) 22, 23

Abstract # 161 - JOHNSON, J M
P'ee: JOHNSON, J M
G'ee: JOHNSON, J M
T-Dt: -- --- -----
P-Dt: 31 May 1862
Dist/Class: Fannin Bounty
File#: 997
Patent#: 204
Patent Vol.: 11
Certificate: 3019
Acres: 670
Map(s) 39, 40

Abstract # 163 - KILLION, D N
P'ee: KILLION, D N
G'ee: JEFFERY, SIDNEY R
T-Dt: -- --- -----
P-Dt: 31 May 1876
Dist/Class: Fannin Preemption
File#: 1240
Patent#: 289
Patent Vol.: 4
Acres: 160
Map(s) 29

Abstract # 164 - JONES, J E
P'ee: CARNAHAN, E
G'ee: JONES, J E
T-Dt: -- --- -----
P-Dt: 05 Jun 1875
Dist/Class: Fannin Preemption
File#: 913
Patent#: 570
Patent Vol.: 2
Acres: 160
Map(s) 30

Abstract # 165 - KITCHINGS, D
P'ee: HARMANSON, Z J
G'ee: KITCHINGS, DANIEL
T-Dt: -- --- -----
P-Dt: 05 Feb 1862
Dist/Class: Fannin 3rd
File#: 3885
Patent#: 67
Patent Vol.: 36
Certificate: 13/55
Acres: 160
Map(s) 9

Abstract # 167 - KUYKENDALL, T P
P'ee: KUYKENDALL, THORNTON P
(HEIRS)
G'ee: KUYKENDALL, THORNTON P
T-Dt: -- --- -----
P-Dt: 26 Feb 1890
Dist/Class: Fannin Donation
File#: 1470
Patent#: 239
Patent Vol.: 7
Certificate: 116 6/120
Acres: 221
Map(s) 28, 29

Abstract # 168 - KRAMER, B
P'ee: RICE, J P
G'ee: KRAMER, BENTON
T-Dt: -- --- -----
P-Dt: 22 Jan 1877
Dist/Class: Fannin Preemption
File#: 1415
Patent#: 223
Patent Vol.: 5
Acres: 80
Map(s) 37, 38

Abstract # 169 - KUTCH, R M
P'ee: KUTCH, R M
G'ee: KUTCH, R M
T-Dt: -- --- -----
P-Dt: 11 Nov 1876
Dist/Class: Fannin Preemption
File#: 1370
Patent#: 64
Patent Vol.: 5
Acres: 160
Map(s) 38

Abstract # 170 - KISINGER, G
P'ee: KISINGER, GEORGE
G'ee: KISINGER, GEORGE
T-Dt: -- --- -----
P-Dt: 11 Aug 1877
Dist/Class: Fannin Preemption
File#: 1501
Patent#: 66
Patent Vol.: 6
Acres: 80
Map(s) 39

Abstract # 171 - LYNCH, N
P'ee: MCCARDEL, JAMES H
G'ee: LYNCH, N
T-Dt: -- --- -----
P-Dt: 30 Mar 1875
Dist/Class: Fannin 1st
File#: 1608
Patent#: 605
Patent Vol.: 20
Certificate: 283
Acres: 639.95
Map(s) 30, 31

Abstract # 172 - LYNCH, N
P'ee: HARDIN, AUGUSTIN B
G'ee: LYNCH, N
T-Dt: -- --- -----
P-Dt: 30 Mar 1875
Dist/Class: Fannin 1st
File#: 1608
Patent#: 604
Patent Vol.: 20
Certificate: 283
Acres: 835.94
Map(s) 23, 31

Abstract # 173 - LEE, J S
P'ee: NEWHOUSE, CONRAD
G'ee: LEE, JONATHAN S
T-Dt: -- --- -----
P-Dt: 25 Oct 1860
Dist/Class: Fannin 3rd
File#: 3599
Patent#: 610
Patent Vol.: 30
Acres: 480
Map(s) 19, 20, 27, 28

Abstract # 174 - LAUDERDALE, W

P'ee: LAUDERDALE, WILLIAM (HEIRS)
G'ee: LAUDERDALE, WILLIAM
T-Dt: -- --- -----
P-Dt: 17 Jul 1874
Dist/Class: Fannin 3rd
File#: 4388
Patent#: 164
Patent Vol.: 42
Certificate: 13/3
Acres: 160
Map(s) 31

Abstract # 175 - LAFFERTY, J A
P'ee: JOHNSON, WILLIAM
G'ee: LAFFERTY, J A
T-Dt: -- --- -----
P-Dt: 28 Jul 1879
Dist/Class: Fannin Preemption
File#: 1371
Patent#: 256
Patent Vol.: 9
Acres: 160
Map(s) 38

Abstract # 176 - LYTLE, W A
P'ee: LYTLE, W B
G'ee: LYTLE, W B
T-Dt: -- --- -----
P-Dt: 25 Jan 1877
Dist/Class: Fannin Preemption
File#: 1379
Patent#: 232
Patent Vol.: 5
Acres: 160
Map(s) 38

Abstract # 177 - LAYNE, T A
P'ee: LAYNE, T A
G'ee: LAYNE, T A
T-Dt: -- --- -----
P-Dt: 26 Aug 1876
Dist/Class: Fannin Preemption
File#: 1374
Patent#: 501
Patent Vol.: 4
Acres: 160
Map(s) 29, 37

Abstract # 178 - LOVEJOY, J T
P'ee: LOVEJOY, J T
G'ee: LOVEJOY, J T
T-Dt: -- --- -----
P-Dt: 01 Dec 1876
Dist/Class: Fannin Preemption
File#: 1377
Patent#: 108
Patent Vol.: 5
Acres: 160
Map(s) 38

Abstract # 179 - MOSES, D
P'ee: MOSES, DAVID (HEIRS)
G'ee: MOSES, DAVID
T-Dt: -- --- -----
P-Dt: 16 Aug 1855
Dist/Class: Fannin 1st
File#: 565
Patent#: 412
Patent Vol.: 11
Certificate: 172
Acres: 640.03
Map(s) 28, 36

Abstract # 180 - MCLENNAN, A
P'ee: MCLENNAN, ALEXANDER

(HEIRS)
G'ee: MCLENNAN, ALEXANDER
T-Dt: -- --- -----
P-Dt: 12 Oct 1855
Dist/Class: Fannin 1st
File#: 567
Patent#: 263
Patent Vol.: 12
Certificate: 176
Acres: 1476.13
Map(s) 20, 28

Abstract # 182 - MCCOWAN, R
P'ee: WARD, SHELTON AND FOWLER
G'ee: MCCOWN, REBECCA
T-Dt: -- --- -----
P-Dt: 09 Oct 1874
Dist/Class: Fannin 1st
File#: 1101
Patent#: 372
Patent Vol.: 20
Certificate: 3674/3775
Acres: 905.85
Map(s) 33, 34

Abstract # 183 - MCCLURE, W
P'ee: TODD, CHARLES S
G'ee: MCCLURE, WILLIAM
T-Dt: -- --- -----
P-Dt: 02 Jun 1862
Dist/Class: Fannin 1st
File#: 1291
Patent#: 625
Patent Vol.: 16
Certificate: 445 6/460
Acres: 207.03
Map(s) 35

Abstract # 184 - MCKISSICK, S
P'ee: DAVIS, R J
G'ee: MCKISSICK, SARAH
T-Dt: -- --- -----
P-Dt: 16 Jun 1873
Dist/Class: Fannin 1st
File#: 1469
Patent#: 437
Patent Vol.: 19
Certificate: 16/76
Acres: 177.10
Map(s) 28, 29

Abstract # 185 - ADAMS, J M
P'ee: STARR, JAMES H
G'ee: MCADAMS, JOHN JR
T-Dt: -- --- -----
P-Dt: 03 May 1875
Dist/Class: Fannin 1st
File#: 1630
Patent#: 40
Patent Vol.: 21
Certificate: 16/245
Acres: 580.35
Map(s) 9

Abstract # 186 - MAYBEE, J
P'ee: MAYBEE, JACOB (HEIRS)
G'ee: MAYBEE, JACOB
T-Dt: -- --- -----
P-Dt: 08 Jul 1875
Dist/Class: Fannin 1st
File#: 1639
Patent#: 167
Patent Vol.: 21
Certificate: 29/92
Acres: 195.98

Map(s) 31

Abstract # 187 - MCCOY, E D
P'ee: WHITE, GEORGE
G'ee: MCCOY, EPHRAIM D
T-Dt: -- --- -----
P-Dt: 02 Feb 1856
Dist/Class: Fannin 3rd
File#: 997
Patent#: 783
Patent Vol.: 12
Certificate: 94
Acres: 312
Map(s) 19, 20

Abstract # 188 - MANNING, J W
P'ee: BARNARD, GEORGE
G'ee: MANNING, JOHN W
T-Dt: -- --- -----
P-Dt: 20 Feb 1860
Dist/Class: Fannin 3rd
File#: 2626
Patent#: 370
Patent Vol.: 25
Certificate: 3
Acres: 320
Map(s) 30

Abstract # 189 - MEDLAN, A B
P'ee: MEDLAN, A B
G'ee: MEDLAN, A B
T-Dt: -- --- -----
P-Dt: 25 Feb 1860
Dist/Class: Fannin 3rd
File#: 2887
Patent#: 186
Patent Vol.: 29
Acres: 160
Map(s) 28, 36

Abstract # 190 - MARLIN, W N P
P'ee: MARLIN, W N P
G'ee: MARLIN, W N P
T-Dt: -- --- -----
P-Dt: 15 Aug 1859
Dist/Class: Fannin 3rd
File#: 2909
Patent#: 600
Patent Vol.: 24
Acres: 320
Map(s) 28, 36

Abstract # 191 - MURPHY, P
P'ee: MURPHY, PATRICK
G'ee: MURPHY, PATRICK
T-Dt: -- --- -----
P-Dt: 02 Dec 1859
Dist/Class: Fannin 3rd
File#: 3023
Patent#: 273
Patent Vol.: 25
Acres: 160
Map(s) 20

Abstract # 192 - MOORE, A
P'ee: MOORE, ALFRED (HEIRS)
G'ee: MOORE, ALFRED
T-Dt: -- --- -----
P-Dt: 20 Sep 1872
Dist/Class: Fannin 3rd
File#: 3427
Patent#: 166
Patent Vol.: 40
Certificate: 207
Acres: 480

Map(s) 33

Abstract # 193 - MCFARLANE, A C
P'ee: MCFARLANE, ALEXANDER C
(HEIRS)
G'ee: MCFARLANE, ALEXANDER C
T-Dt: -- --- -----
P-Dt: 07 Mar 1878
Dist/Class: Fannin 3rd
File#: 3666
Patent#: 382
Patent Vol.: 44
Certificate: 2/3
Acres: 160
Map(s) 21

Abstract # 194 - MCLENNAN, A
P'ee: MCLENNAN, ALEXANDER
(HEIRS)
G'ee: MCLENNAN, ALEXANDER
T-Dt: -- --- -----
P-Dt: 10 Oct 1855
Dist/Class: Fannin Donation
File#: 447
Patent#: 449
Patent Vol.: 2
Certificate: 579
Acres: 446
Map(s) 28

Abstract # 195 - MCLENNAN, A
P'ee: MCLENNAN, ALEXANDER
(HEIRS)
G'ee: MCLENNAN, ALEXANDER
T-Dt: -- --- -----
P-Dt: 10 Oct 1855
Dist/Class: Fannin Donation
File#: 447
Patent#: 450
Patent Vol.: 2
Certificate: 579
Acres: 193
Map(s) 28

Abstract # 196 - MCGARY, M
P'ee: STEPHENSON AND ABBOTT
G'ee: MCGARY, MAXWELL
T-Dt: -- --- -----
P-Dt: 12 Sep 1857
Dist/Class: Fannin Bounty
File#: 680
Patent#: 360
Patent Vol.: 8
Certificate: 208
Acres: 200
Map(s) 29

Abstract # 197 - MCGARY, M
P'ee: STEPHENSON AND ABBOTT
G'ee: MCGARY, MAXWELL
T-Dt: -- --- -----
P-Dt: 12 Sep 1857
Dist/Class: Fannin Bounty
File#: 680
Patent#: 359
Patent Vol.: 8
Certificate: 208
Acres: 40
Map(s) 30

Abstract # 198 - MCMULLEN
P'ee: JACOBI, ANSELM
G'ee: MCMULLEN, A
T-Dt: -- --- -----
P-Dt: 15 May 1854

Dist/Class: Fannin Bounty
File#: 615
Patent#: 132
Patent Vol.: 7
Certificate: 4170
Acres: 854
Map(s) 7

Abstract # 199 - MARLIN, J
P'ee: MARLIN, JOHN
G'ee: MARLIN, JOHN
T-Dt: -- --- -----
P-Dt: 24 Oct 1857
Dist/Class: Fannin Bounty
File#: 869
Patent#: 178
Patent Vol.: 7
Certificate: 9446
Acres: 320
Map(s) 28, 29, 36, 37

Abstract # 200 - MORGAN, C
P'ee: WILLIAMSON, C C (MRS)
G'ee: MORGAN, CHARLES
T-Dt: -- --- -----
P-Dt: 28 May 1875
Dist/Class: Fannin Bounty
File#: 1310 1/2
Patent#: 148
Patent Vol.: 15
Certificate: 31/64
Acres: 320
Map(s) 38, 46

Abstract # 201 - SA&MG RR CO
G'ee: MILES, EDWARD
T-Dt: -- --- -----
P-Dt: -- --- -----
Dist/Class: Milam Bounty
File#: 962
Certificate: 4359
Acres: 281.50
Map(s) 19

Abstract # 202 - MCKINNEY & WIL-
LIAMS
P'ee: BOTTORFF, JOHN F
G'ee: MCKINNEY AND WILLIAMS
T-Dt: -- --- -----
P-Dt: 12 Mar 1861
Dist/Class: Fannin Scrip
File#: 1156
Patent#: 867
Patent Vol.: 4
Certificate: 2/4639
Acres: 320
Map(s) 36

Abstract # 203 - MCKINNEY & WIL-
LIAMS
P'ee: ROSS, S P
G'ee: MCKINNEY AND WILLIAMS
T-Dt: -- --- -----
P-Dt: 21 Feb 1873
Dist/Class: Fannin Scrip
File#: 4374 1/2
Patent#: 50
Patent Vol.: 20
Certificate: 17/101
Acres: 35
Map(s) 48

Abstract # 204 - MCKINNEY & WIL-
LIAMS
P'ee: ROSS, S P

G'ee: MCKINNEY AND WILLIAMS
T-Dt: -- --- -----
P-Dt: 28 Jan 1871
Dist/Class: Milam Scrip
File#: 298
Patent#: 306
Patent Vol.: 19
Certificate: 2/4670
Acres: 605
Map(s) 40, 48

Abstract # 205 - MITCHENER, L
P'ee: MITCHENER, LUCETTA
G'ee: MITCHENER, LUCETTA
T-Dt: -- --- -----
P-Dt: 21 Mar 1877
Dist/Class: Fannin Preemption
File#: 1392
Patent#: 364
Patent Vol.: 5
Acres: 160
Map(s) 37

Abstract # 206 - MORRISON, J P
P'ee: MORRISON, JESSE P
G'ee: MORRISON, JESSE P
T-Dt: -- --- -----
P-Dt: 23 Jun 1877
Dist/Class: Fannin Preemption
File#: 1396
Patent#: 597
Patent Vol.: 5
Acres: 160
Map(s) 38

Abstract # 207 - MCBRAYER, J M
P'ee: MCBRAYER, J M
G'ee: MCBRAYER, J M
T-Dt: -- --- -----
P-Dt: 22 Jan 1877
Dist/Class: Fannin Preemption
File#: 1386
Patent#: 222
Patent Vol.: 5
Acres: 160
Map(s) 37

Abstract # 208 - MCCOMBER, H A
P'ee: MCCOMBER, H A
G'ee: MCCOMBER, H A
T-Dt: -- --- -----
P-Dt: 05 Aug 1876
Dist/Class: Fannin Preemption
File#: 1177
Patent#: 444
Patent Vol.: 4
Acres: 160
Map(s) 32

Abstract # 209 - MEADOR, M
P'ee: MEADOR, MARK
G'ee: MEADOR, MARK
T-Dt: -- --- -----
P-Dt: 15 Dec 1876
Dist/Class: Fannin Preemption
File#: 1389
Patent#: 148
Patent Vol.: 5
Acres: 160
Map(s) 37

Abstract # 210 - MATHEWS, A N
P'ee: MATTHEWS, A N
G'ee: MATTHEWS, A N
T-Dt: -- --- -----

P-Dt: 13 Dec 1876
Dist/Class: Fannin Preemption
File#: 1383
Patent#: 132
Patent Vol.: 5
Acres: 80
Map(s) 37

Abstract # 211 - MCLAREN, F M
P'ee: MCLAREN, F M
G'ee: MCLAREN, F M
T-Dt: -- --- -----
P-Dt: 09 Aug 1877
Dist/Class: Fannin Preemption
File#: 1384
Patent#: 58
Patent Vol.: 6
Acres: 160
Map(s) 38

Abstract # 212 - MORRISON, J E
P'ee: MORRISON, JOSHUA E
G'ee: MORRISON, JOSHUA E
T-Dt: -- --- -----
P-Dt: 23 Jun 1877
Dist/Class: Fannin Preemption
File#: 1395
Patent#: 593
Patent Vol.: 5
Acres: 160
Map(s) 38

Abstract # 213 - NABERS, R W
P'ee: NABORS, ROBERT W
G'ee: NABORS, ROBERT W
T-Dt: -- --- -----
P-Dt: 31 Mar 1879
Dist/Class: Fannin 1st
File#: 1632
Patent#: 627
Patent Vol.: 22
Certificate: 31/255
Acres: 401.2
Map(s) 31, 32

Abstract # 214 - NEWTON, S G
P'ee: RUGGLES, DANIEL
G'ee: NEWTON, S G
T-Dt: -- --- -----
P-Dt: 23 Apr 1857
Dist/Class: Milam 3rd
File#: 1037
Patent#: 376
Patent Vol.: 15
Certificate: 12
Acres: 40
Map(s) 19, 27

Abstract # 215 - NORTON, D O
P'ee: NORTON, D A
G'ee: NORTON, D O
T-Dt: -- --- -----
P-Dt: 13 Jun 1873
Dist/Class: Fannin Scrip
File#: 4646
Patent#: 191
Patent Vol.: 20
Certificate: 18/195
Acres: 160
Map(s) 29

Abstract # 216 - OXFORD, W R
P'ee: OXFORD, W R
G'ee: OXFORD, W R
T-Dt: -- --- -----

P-Dt: 25 Apr 1877
Dist/Class: Fannin Preemption
File#: 1404
Patent#: 452
Patent Vol.: 5
Acres: 80
Map(s) 38

Abstract # 217 - ORRICK, W J
P'ee: HENRY, JOHN R
G'ee: ORRICK, W J
T-Dt: -- --- -----
P-Dt: 15 Mar 1878
Dist/Class: Fannin 3rd
File#: 4565
Patent#: 386
Patent Vol.: 44
Certificate: 32/145
Acres: 177
Map(s) 39, 40

Abstract # 218 - PETRESWICK,HRS F
P'ee: PETRESWICK, F (HEIRS)
G'ee: PETRESWICK, F (DECEASED)
T-Dt: -- --- -----
P-Dt: 02 Oct 1875
Dist/Class: Fannin 1st
File#: 1588
Patent#: 301
Patent Vol.: 21
Certificate: 31/38
Acres: 836
Map(s) 1, 9

Abstract # 219 - PIER, P
P'ee: DAVIS, R J
G'ee: PIER, PAUL (DECEASED)
T-Dt: -- --- -----
P-Dt: 11 Jun 1873
Dist/Class: Fannin 2nd
File#: 666
Patent#: 346
Patent Vol.: 8
Certificate: 1068
Acres: 640
Map(s) 30

Abstract # 220 - PATTERSON, J B
P'ee: HEATH, THOMAS (HEIRS)
G'ee: PATTERSON, JAMES B
T-Dt: -- --- -----
P-Dt: 05 Jul 1875
Dist/Class: Fannin 2nd
File#: 724
Patent#: 594
Patent Vol.: 8
Certificate: 20/53
Acres: 91.25
Map(s) 31

Abstract # 221 - PEVELER, J M
P'ee: PEVELER, J M
G'ee: PEVELER, J M
T-Dt: -- --- -----
P-Dt: 03 Nov 1859
Dist/Class: Fannin 3rd
File#: 2371
Patent#: 163
Patent Vol.: 28
Acres: 160
Map(s) 19

Abstract # 222 - PEVELER, J M
P'ee: PEVELER, J M
G'ee: PEVELER, J M

T-Dt: -- --- -----
P-Dt: 09 Dec 1859
Dist/Class: Fannin 3rd
File#: 3025
Patent#: 195
Patent Vol.: 28
Acres: 160
Map(s) 19

Abstract # 223 - PEVELER, W R
P'ee: PEVELER, WILLIAM R
G'ee: PEVELER, WILLIAM R
T-Dt: -- --- -----
P-Dt: 24 Apr 1860
Dist/Class: Fannin 3rd
File#: 3026
Patent#: 421
Patent Vol.: 25
Acres: 160
Map(s) 19

Abstract # 224 - PATTER, H N
P'ee: POTTER, HENRY N
G'ee: POTTER, HENRY N
T-Dt: -- --- -----
P-Dt: 14 Apr 1860
Dist/Class: Fannin 3rd
File#: 3679
Patent#: 366
Patent Vol.: 29
Certificate: 104
Acres: 320
Map(s) 39

Abstract # 225 - PORTER, W W
P'ee: COOKE, EDWARD
G'ee: PORTER, WILLIAM W
T-Dt: -- --- -----
P-Dt: 08 Jan 1862
Dist/Class: Fannin Scrip
File#: 1515
Patent#: 429
Patent Vol.: 9
Certificate: 72
Acres: 320
Map(s) 20, 21

Abstract # 226 - POITEVENT, J
P'ee: ANDERSON, CHARLES R
G'ee: POITEVENT, J
T-Dt: -- --- -----
P-Dt: 03 Mar 1875
Dist/Class: Fannin Scrip
File#: 8964
Patent#: 9
Patent Vol.: 21
Certificate: 1/129
Survey/Blk/Twp: 1
Acres: 640
Map(s) 3

Abstract # 227 - POITEVENT, J
P'ee: POITEVENT, J
G'ee: POITEVENT, J
T-Dt: -- --- -----
P-Dt: 21 Jan 1878
Dist/Class: Fannin Scrip
File#: 9917
Patent#: 417
Patent Vol.: 29
Certificate: 2/163
Survey/Blk/Twp: 1
Acres: 640
Map(s) 23, 24

Abstract # 228 - POITEVENT, J
P'ee: POITEVENT, J
G'ee: POITEVENT, J
T-Dt: -- --- -----
P-Dt: 22 Jan 1878
Dist/Class: Fannin Scrip
File#: 9918
Patent#: 415
Patent Vol.: 29
Certificate: 2/164
Survey/Blk/Twp: 3
Acres: 640
Map(s) 23, 24

Abstract # 229 - POITEVENT, J
P'ee: POITEVENT, J
G'ee: POITEVENT, J
T-Dt: -- --- -----
P-Dt: 22 Jan 1878
Dist/Class: Fannin Scrip
File#: 9922
Patent#: 416
Patent Vol.: 29
Certificate: 2/157
Survey/Blk/Twp: 1
Acres: 640
Map(s) 27, 28

Abstract # 230 - POITEVENT, J
P'ee: POITEVENT, J
G'ee: POITEVENT, J
T-Dt: -- --- -----
P-Dt: 22 Jan 1878
Dist/Class: Fannin Scrip
File#: 10573
Patent#: 410
Patent Vol.: 29
Certificate: 2/160
Survey/Blk/Twp: 1
Acres: 320
Map(s) 28

Abstract # 231 - POITEVENT, J
P'ee: POITEVENT, J
G'ee: POITEVENT, J
T-Dt: -- --- -----
P-Dt: 22 Jan 1878
Dist/Class: Fannin Scrip
File#: 10573
Patent#: 411
Patent Vol.: 29
Certificate: 2/160
Survey/Blk/Twp: 3
Acres: 320
Map(s) 35

Abstract # 232 - POITEVENT, J
P'ee: POITEVENT, J
G'ee: POITEVENT, J
T-Dt: -- --- -----
P-Dt: 19 Feb 1878
Dist/Class: Fannin Scrip
File#: 10871
Patent#: 510
Patent Vol.: 29
Certificate: 2/158
Survey/Blk/Twp: 1
Acres: 640
Map(s) 39, 40

Abstract # 233 - POITEVENT, J
P'ee: BUTLER, B C
G'ee: POITEVENT, J
T-Dt: -- --- -----
P-Dt: 04 Aug 1875

Dist/Class: Fannin Scrip
File#: 9580
Patent#: 194
Patent Vol.: 21
Certificate: 1/251
Survey/Blk/Twp: 1
Acres: 640
Map(s) 24

Abstract # 234 - PARTRIDGE, J J
P'ee: MUNDELL, J A
G'ee: PARTRIDGE, J J
T-Dt: -- --- -----
P-Dt: 28 Aug 1877
Dist/Class: Fannin Preemption
File#: 1406
Patent#: 113
Patent Vol.: 6
Acres: 160
Map(s) 29

Abstract # 236 - PIRTLE, G P
P'ee: PIRTLE, G P
G'ee: PIRTLE, G P
T-Dt: -- --- -----
P-Dt: 20 Oct 1876
Dist/Class: Fannin Preemption
File#: 1409
Patent#: 628
Patent Vol.: 4
Acres: 160
Map(s) 38

Abstract # 237 - PRICE, G
P'ee: PRICE, GEORGE
G'ee: PRICE, GEORGE
T-Dt: -- --- -----
P-Dt: 25 Aug 1877
Dist/Class: Fannin Preemption
File#: 1410
Patent#: 104
Patent Vol.: 6
Acres: 160
Map(s) 29

Abstract # 238 - QUERO, P
P'ee: PHILLIPS, F T
G'ee: QUERO, PEDRO
T-Dt: -- --- -----
P-Dt: 14 Jun 1875
Dist/Class: Fannin 1st
File#: 1656
Patent#: 113
Patent Vol.: 21
Certificate: 18/232
Acres: 177.10
Map(s) 46

Abstract # 239 - RECTOR, E G
P'ee: HUMPHREY, JAMES
G'ee: RECTOR, E G
T-Dt: -- --- -----
P-Dt: 19 Sep 1876
Dist/Class: Fannin 1st
File#: 1471
Patent#: 31
Patent Vol.: 22
Certificate: 17/239
Acres: 632.95
Map(s) 28

Abstract # 240 - ROHUS, A
P'ee: BRINSON, MATHEW
G'ee: ROHUS, A
T-Dt: -- --- -----

P-Dt: 03 Aug 1875
Dist/Class: Fannin 1st
File#: 1601
Patent#: 208
Patent Vol.: 21
Certificate: 325
Acres: 5046
Map(s) 6, 7, 8

Abstract # 241 - REMINGTON, D
P'ee: MATTHEWS, R H
G'ee: REMINGTON, DANIEL
T-Dt: -- --- -----
P-Dt: 07 Sep 1857
Dist/Class: Fannin 3rd
File#: 1896
Patent#: 783
Patent Vol.: 15
Certificate: 3491/3592
Acres: 491
Map(s) 19

Abstract # 242 - RAYNOR, C
P'ee: RAYNOR, CHARLES
G'ee: RAYNOR, CHARLES
T-Dt: -- --- -----
P-Dt: 02 Dec 1859
Dist/Class: Fannin 3rd
File#: 3024
Patent#: 274
Patent Vol.: 25
Acres: 160
Map(s) 20

Abstract # 243 - RHOTON, HRS E
P'ee: RHOTON, E D (HEIRS)
G'ee: RHOTON, E D (DECEASED)
T-Dt: -- --- -----
P-Dt: 15 Jul 1857
Dist/Class: Milam 3rd
File#: 1005
Patent#: 61
Patent Vol.: 16
Certificate: 1014
Acres: 320
Map(s) 36

Abstract # 244 - RATLIFF, A
P'ee: RATLIFF, ARCHILANS
G'ee: RATLIFF, ARCHILANS
T-Dt: -- --- -----
P-Dt: 24 Jul 1860
Dist/Class: Fannin 3rd
File#: 3254
Patent#: 58
Patent Vol.: 31
Acres: 160
Map(s) 28

Abstract # 245 - ROSE, HRS J
P'ee: ROSE, JAMES (HEIRS)
G'ee: ROSE, JAMES (HEIRS OF)
T-Dt: -- --- -----
P-Dt: 01 May 1862
Dist/Class: Fannin Bounty
File#: 998
Patent#: 77
Patent Vol.: 13
Certificate: 367
Acres: 1166
Map(s) 39, 40

Abstract # 246 - ROSS, MRS E H
P'ee: ROSS, E H (MRS)
G'ee: ROSS, E H (MRS)

T-Dt: -- --- -----
P-Dt: 15 Jun 1876
Dist/Class: Fannin Preemption
File#: 860
Patent#: 333
Patent Vol.: 4
Acres: 160
Map(s) 30, 31

Abstract # 247 - RICE, J M
P'ee: RICE, J M
G'ee: ROGERS, N C
T-Dt: -- --- -----
P-Dt: 03 Aug 1877
Dist/Class: Fannin Preemption
File#: 1416
Patent#: 34
Patent Vol.: 6
Acres: 80
Map(s) 37

Abstract # 248 - RIBBLE, W A
P'ee: RIBBLE, W A
G'ee: RIBBLE, W A
T-Dt: -- --- -----
P-Dt: 23 Jun 1877
Dist/Class: Fannin Preemption
File#: 1418
Patent#: 595
Patent Vol.: 5
Acres: 160
Map(s) 38

Abstract # 249 - SHELTON, J
P'ee: THOMPSON, F A
G'ee: SHELTON, JAMES
T-Dt: -- --- -----
P-Dt: 19 Sep 1855
Dist/Class: Fannin 1st
File#: 564
Patent#: 418
Patent Vol.: 11
Certificate: 1211/1310
Acres: 772.39
Map(s) 27, 28

Abstract # 250 - STONEHAM, W
P'ee: STONHAM, WILLIAM
G'ee: STONHAM, WILLIAM
T-Dt: -- --- -----
P-Dt: 08 Mar 1861
Dist/Class: Fannin 1st
File#: 1076
Patent#: 288
Patent Vol.: 15
Certificate: 35 6/40
Acres: 1343.40
Map(s) 7, 8

Abstract # 251 - SANDERS, J
P'ee: SANDERS, JOHN
G'ee: SANDERS, JOHN
T-Dt: -- --- -----
P-Dt: 05 Jul 1870
Dist/Class: Fannin 1st
File#: 1085
Patent#: 189
Patent Vol.: 18
Certificate: 146
Acres: 733.65
Map(s) 34, 35

Abstract # 252 - SALLIE, HRS S
P'ee: SALLIE, SUSAN (HEIRS)
G'ee: SALLIE, SUSAN (DECEASED)

T-Dt: -- --- -----
P-Dt: 31 Jul 1877
Dist/Class: Fannin 1st
File#: 1765
Patent#: 267
Patent Vol.: 22
Certificate: 5005/5006
Acres: 1535.17
Map(s) 7, 15

Abstract # 253 - SERGEANT, E W
P'ee: SERGENT, EDWARD W (HEIRS)
G'ee: SERGENT, EDWARD W
T-Dt: -- --- -----
P-Dt: 01 Jun 1859
Dist/Class: Fannin 2nd
File#: 569
Patent#: 17
Patent Vol.: 7
Certificate: 3058/3159
Acres: 1476.13
Map(s) 6, 7, 14, 15

Abstract # 254 - SMITH, G N
P'ee: SMITH, GEORGE N
G'ee: SMITH, GEORGE N
T-Dt: -- --- -----
P-Dt: 27 Sep 1860
Dist/Class: Fannin 2nd
File#: 555
Patent#: 170
Patent Vol.: 7
Certificate: 1253
Acres: 437
Map(s) 26

Abstract # 255 - SMITH, G N
P'ee: SMITH, GEORGE N
G'ee: SMITH, GEORGE N
T-Dt: -- --- -----
P-Dt: 27 Sep 1860
Dist/Class: Fannin 2nd
File#: 555
Patent#: 171
Patent Vol.: 7
Certificate: 1253
Acres: 203
Map(s) 35

Abstract # 256 - STEEL, G W
P'ee: STELL, GEORGE W
G'ee: STELL, GEORGE W
T-Dt: -- --- -----
P-Dt: 07 May 1875
Dist/Class: Fannin 2nd
File#: 738 1/2
Patent#: 574
Patent Vol.: 8
Certificate: 29/329
Acres: 694
Map(s) 3

Abstract # 257 - SCOTT, J P
P'ee: HEDGECOXE, HARRISON G
G'ee: SCOTT, JONATHAN P
T-Dt: -- --- -----
P-Dt: 08 Jun 1860
Dist/Class: Fannin 3rd
File#: 3742
Patent#: 523
Patent Vol.: 29
Certificate: 216
Acres: 320
Map(s) 14, 22

Abstract # 258 - SCOTT, R J
P'ee: SCOTT, ROBERT I (HEIRS)
G'ee: SCOTT, ROBERT I
T-Dt: -- --- -----
P-Dt: 08 Jun 1880
Dist/Class: Milam Donation
File#: 1295
Patent#: 203
Patent Vol.: 4
Certificate: 702
Survey/Blk/Twp: 3
Acres: 640
Map(s) 37

Abstract # 259 - SPANE, P R
P'ee: SPLANE, PEYTON R
G'ee: SPLANE, PEYTON R
T-Dt: -- --- -----
P-Dt: 19 Dec 1860
Dist/Class: Fannin Donation
File#: 883
Patent#: 49
Patent Vol.: 3
Certificate: 571
Acres: 640
Map(s) 7

Abstract # 261 - SA&MG RR CO
P'ee: FISHER, GEORGE W
G'ee: SAN ANTONIO AND MEXICAN
GULF RAILROAD COMPANY
T-Dt: -- --- -----
P-Dt: 11 Dec 1860
Dist/Class: Milam Scrip
File#: 380
Patent#: 6
Patent Vol.: 7
Certificate: 12
Survey/Blk/Twp: 1
Acres: 320
Map(s) 35, 36

Abstract # 262 - SA&MG RR CO
P'ee: FISHER, GEORGE W
G'ee: SAN ANTONIO AND MEXICAN
GULF RAILROAD COMPANY
T-Dt: -- --- -----
P-Dt: 11 Dec 1860
Dist/Class: Milam Scrip
File#: 458
Patent#: 7
Patent Vol.: 7
Certificate: 12
Acres: 320
Map(s) 20, 28

Abstract # 263 - SP RR CO
P'ee: HOLMAN, JAMES S
G'ee: SOUTHERN PACIFIC RAILROAD
COMPANY
T-Dt: -- --- -----
P-Dt: 29 May 1875
Dist/Class: Fannin Scrip
File#: 7735
Patent#: 575
Patent Vol.: 6
Certificate: 16/129
Survey/Blk/Twp: 9
Acres: 640
Map(s) 23

Abstract # 264 - SP RR CO
P'ee: JONES, J A
G'ee: SOUTHERN PACIFIC RAILROAD
COMPANY

T-Dt: -- --- -----
P-Dt: 01 Jun 1875
Dist/Class: Fannin Scrip
File#: 6456
Patent#: 578
Patent Vol.: 6
Certificate: 16/63
Survey/Blk/Twp: 1
Acres: 640
Map(s) 35

Abstract # 265 - SP RR CO
P'ee: JONES, J A
G'ee: SOUTHERN PACIFIC RAILROAD
COMPANY
T-Dt: -- --- -----
P-Dt: 31 Jul 1875
Dist/Class: Fannin Scrip
File#: 6458
Patent#: 586
Patent Vol.: 6
Certificate: 16/69
Survey/Blk/Twp: 5
Acres: 640
Map(s) 32

Abstract # 266 - SP RR CO
P'ee: JONES, J A
G'ee: SOUTHERN PACIFIC RAILROAD
COMPANY
T-Dt: -- --- -----
P-Dt: 01 Jun 1875
Dist/Class: Fannin Scrip
File#: 6459
Patent#: 577
Patent Vol.: 6
Certificate: 16/75
Survey/Blk/Twp: 3
Acres: 640
Map(s) 35

Abstract # 267 - SP RR CO
P'ee: JONES, J A
G'ee: SOUTHERN PACIFIC RAILROAD
COMPANY
T-Dt: -- --- -----
P-Dt: 29 Apr 1874
Dist/Class: Fannin Scrip
File#: 6460
Patent#: 451
Patent Vol.: 6
Certificate: 16/97
Survey/Blk/Twp: 1
Acres: 640
Map(s) 34, 35

Abstract # 268 - SP RR CO
P'ee: JONES, J A
G'ee: SOUTHERN PACIFIC RAILROAD
COMPANY
T-Dt: -- --- -----
P-Dt: 29 May 1875
Dist/Class: Fannin Scrip
File#: 6461
Patent#: 576
Patent Vol.: 6
Certificate: 16/115
Survey/Blk/Twp: 1
Acres: 640
Map(s) 31

Abstract # 269 - SP RR CO
P'ee: JONES, J A
G'ee: SOUTHERN PACIFIC RAILROAD
COMPANY

T-Dt: -- --- -----
P-Dt: 29 May 1875
Dist/Class: Fannin Scrip
File#: 6462
Patent#: 574
Patent Vol.: 6
Certificate: 16/181
Survey/Blk/Twp: 3
Acres: 640
Map(s) 32

Abstract # 270 - SUTHERLIN, W
P'ee: SOUTHERLIN, WILLIAM
G'ee: SOUTHERLIN, WILLIAM
T-Dt: -- --- -----
P-Dt: 08 Sep 1863
Dist/Class: Fannin Scrip
File#: 1354
Patent#: 163
Patent Vol.: 17
Acres: 160
Map(s) 26, 34

Abstract # 271 - SHERILL, E
P'ee: SHERRILL, ELI
G'ee: SHERRILL, ELI
T-Dt: -- --- -----
P-Dt: 07 Feb 1876
Dist/Class: Fannin Preemption
File#: 825
Patent#: 569
Patent Vol.: 3
Acres: 160
Map(s) 30

Abstract # 272 - SNEAD, R W
P'ee: SNEAD, R W
G'ee: SNEAD, R W
T-Dt: -- --- -----
P-Dt: 23 Oct 1876
Dist/Class: Fannin Preemption
File#: 1430
Patent#: 6
Patent Vol.: 5
Acres: 160
Map(s) 37, 38

Abstract # 273 - SEDDON, S T
P'ee: SEDDON, S T
G'ee: SEDDON, S T
T-Dt: -- --- -----
P-Dt: 28 Aug 1877
Dist/Class: Fannin Preemption
File#: 1424
Patent#: 110
Patent Vol.: 6
Acres: 160
Map(s) 29

Abstract # 274 - TYNES, S
P'ee: PERRY, C W
G'ee: TYNES, SYLPHIA
T-Dt: -- --- -----
P-Dt: 10 Mar 1879
Dist/Class: Fannin 1st
File#: 1072
Patent#: 611
Patent Vol.: 22
Certificate: 2876/2977
Acres: 3990
Map(s) 7, 8, 15, 16

Abstract # 275 - TRYNDALE, W
P'ee: TYNDALE, WILLIAM
G'ee: TYNDALE, WILLIAM

T-Dt: -- --- -----
P-Dt: 05 Feb 1862
Dist/Class: Fannin 1st
File#: 1287
Patent#: 580
Patent Vol.: 16
Certificate: 1032
Acres: 1149.36
Map(s) 1, 9

Abstract # 276 - TANNER, J R
P'ee: TANNER, JAMES R
G'ee: TANNER, JAMES R
T-Dt: -- --- -----
P-Dt: 21 Oct 1871
Dist/Class: Fannin 1st
File#: 1410
Patent#: 687
Patent Vol.: 18
Certificate: 73
Acres: 299.97
Map(s) 30

Abstract # 277 - TANNER, J R
P'ee: TANNER, JAMES R
G'ee: TANNER, JAMES R
T-Dt: -- --- -----
P-Dt: 08 Jun 1875
Dist/Class: Fannin 1st
File#: 1717
Patent#: 103
Patent Vol.: 21
Certificate: 20/199
Acres: 1175.91
Map(s) 33

Abstract # 278 - TANKERSLEY, S
P'ee: STEINER, J M
G'ee: TANKERSLEY, SARAH
T-Dt: -- --- -----
P-Dt: 19 Mar 1867
Dist/Class: Milam 1st
File#: 1494
Patent#: 388
Patent Vol.: 17
Acres: 717.55
Map(s) 36

Abstract # 279 - TOBIN, J
P'ee: TOBIN, JAMES (HEIRS)
G'ee: TOBIN, JAMES (DECEASED)
T-Dt: -- --- -----
P-Dt: 21 Jan 1858
Dist/Class: Milam 2nd
File#: 446
Patent#: 1046
Patent Vol.: 3
Certificate: 691
Acres: 1476
Map(s) 36, 37

Abstract # 280 - THROCKMORTON, J W
P'ee: THROCKMORTON, JAMES W
G'ee: THROCKMORTON, JAMES W
T-Dt: -- --- -----
P-Dt: 15 Apr 1857
Dist/Class: Fannin 3rd
File#: 998
Patent#: 1634
Patent Vol.: 9
Certificate: 3944/4045
Acres: 320
Map(s) 19

Abstract # 281 - THROCKMORTON, J W

P'ee: THROCKMORTON, JAMES W
G'ee: THROCKMORTON, JAMES W
T-Dt: -- --- -----
P-Dt: 15 Feb 1858
Dist/Class: Fannin 3rd
File#: 998
Patent#: 686
Patent Vol.: 16
Certificate: 3944/4045
Acres: 320
Map(s) 19

Abstract # 282 - TE&L CO
P'ee: TEXAS EMIGRATION AND LAND
COMPANY
G'ee: TEXAS EMIGRATION AND LAND
COMPANY
T-Dt: -- --- -----
P-Dt: 24 May 1859
Dist/Class: Texas Emmigration and Land
Company
File#: 5
Patent#: 513
Patent Vol.: 20
Certificate: 5
Survey/Blk/Twp: 1201
Acres: 320
Map(s) 35

Abstract # 283 - TE&L CO
P'ee: TEXAS EMIGRATION AND LAND
COMPANY
G'ee: TEXAS EMIGRATION AND LAND
COMPANY
T-Dt: -- --- -----
P-Dt: 26 May 1859
Dist/Class: Texas Emmigration and Land
Company
File#: 6
Patent#: 541
Patent Vol.: 20
Certificate: 6
Survey/Blk/Twp: 1202
Acres: 320
Map(s) 19, 20

Abstract # 284 - TE&L CO
P'ee: HEDGCOX, O
G'ee: TEXAS EMIGRATION AND LAND
COMPANY
T-Dt: -- --- -----
P-Dt: 24 Dec 1858
Dist/Class: Texas Emmigration and Land
Company
File#: 7
Patent#: 1109
Patent Vol.: 14
Certificate: 7
Survey/Blk/Twp: 1451
Acres: 265
Map(s) 5

Abstract # 285 - TE&L CO
P'ee: TEXAS EMIGRATION AND LAND
COMPANY
G'ee: TEXAS EMIGRATION AND LAND
COMPANY
T-Dt: -- --- -----
P-Dt: 11 Aug 1857
Dist/Class: Texas Emmigration and Land
Company
File#: 9
Patent#: 9
Patent Vol.: 14
Certificate: 9

Survey/Blk/Twp: 9
Acres: 320
Map(s) 20

Abstract # 286 - TE&L CO
P'ee: TEXAS EMIGRATION AND LAND
COMPANY
G'ee: TEXAS EMIGRATION AND LAND
COMPANY
T-Dt: -- --- -----
P-Dt: 11 Aug 1857
Dist/Class: Texas Emmigration and Land
Company
File#: 10
Patent#: 10
Patent Vol.: 14
Certificate: 10
Survey/Blk/Twp: 10
Acres: 320
Map(s) 20

Abstract # 287 - TE&L CO
P'ee: TEXAS EMIGRATION AND LAND
COMPANY
G'ee: TEXAS EMIGRATION AND LAND
COMPANY
T-Dt: -- --- -----
P-Dt: 11 Aug 1857
Dist/Class: Texas Emmigration and Land
Company
File#: 11
Patent#: 11
Patent Vol.: 14
Certificate: 11
Survey/Blk/Twp: 11
Acres: 320
Map(s) 20

Abstract # 288 - TE&L CO
P'ee: TEXAS EMIGRATION AND LAND
COMPANY
G'ee: TEXAS EMIGRATION AND LAND
COMPANY
T-Dt: -- --- -----
P-Dt: 28 Feb 1856
Dist/Class: Texas Emmigration and Land
Company
File#: 12
Patent#: 2
Patent Vol.: 14
Certificate: 12
Survey/Blk/Twp: 12
Acres: 320
Map(s) 19

Abstract # 289 - TE&L CO
P'ee: TEXAS EMIGRATION AND LAND
COMPANY
G'ee: TEXAS EMIGRATION AND LAND
COMPANY
T-Dt: -- --- -----
P-Dt: 01 Apr 1859
Dist/Class: Texas Emmigration and Land
Company
File#: 13
Patent#: 1132
Patent Vol.: 14
Certificate: 13
Survey/Blk/Twp: 13
Acres: 320
Map(s) 19

Abstract # 290 - TE&L CO
P'ee: TEXAS EMIGRATION AND LAND
COMPANY

G'ee: TEXAS EMIGRATION AND LAND
COMPANY
T-Dt: -- --- -----
P-Dt: 28 Feb 1856
Dist/Class: Texas Emmigration and Land
Company
File#: 14
Patent#: 3
Patent Vol.: 14
Certificate: 14
Survey/Blk/Twp: 14
Acres: 320
Map(s) 19

Abstract # 291 - TE&L CO
P'ee: TEXAS EMIGRATION AND LAND
COMPANY
G'ee: TEXAS EMIGRATION AND LAND
COMPANY
T-Dt: -- --- -----
P-Dt: 28 Feb 1856
Dist/Class: Texas Emmigration and Land
Company
File#: 15
Patent#: 4
Patent Vol.: 14
Certificate: 15
Survey/Blk/Twp: 15
Acres: 320
Map(s) 19

Abstract # 292 - TE&L CO
P'ee: TEXAS EMIGRATION AND LAND
COMPANY
G'ee: TEXAS EMIGRATION AND LAND
COMPANY
T-Dt: -- --- -----
P-Dt: 28 Feb 1856
Dist/Class: Texas Emmigration and Land
Company
File#: 16
Patent#: 5
Patent Vol.: 14
Certificate: 16
Survey/Blk/Twp: 16
Acres: 320
Map(s) 19

Abstract # 293 - TE&L CO
P'ee: TEXAS EMIGRATION AND LAND
COMPANY
G'ee: TEXAS EMIGRATION AND LAND
COMPANY
T-Dt: -- --- -----
P-Dt: 28 Feb 1856
Dist/Class: Texas Emmigration and Land
Company
File#: 17
Patent#: 1
Patent Vol.: 14
Certificate: 17
Survey/Blk/Twp: 17
Acres: 320
Map(s) 19

Abstract # 294 - TE&L CO
P'ee: TEXAS EMIGRATION AND LAND
COMPANY
G'ee: TEXAS EMIGRATION AND LAND
COMPANY
T-Dt: -- --- -----
P-Dt: 29 Feb 1856
Dist/Class: Texas Emmigration and Land
Company
File#: 18

Patent#: 6
Patent Vol.: 14
Certificate: 18
Survey/Blk/Twp: 18
Acres: 320
Map(s) 19

Abstract # 295 - TE&L CO
P'ee: TEXAS EMIGRATION AND LAND
COMPANY
G'ee: TEXAS EMIGRATION AND LAND
COMPANY
T-Dt: -- --- -----
P-Dt: 15 Aug 1857
Dist/Class: Texas Emmigration and Land
Company
File#: 19
Patent#: 19
Patent Vol.: 14
Certificate: 19
Survey/Blk/Twp: 19
Acres: 320
Map(s) 19

Abstract # 296 - TE&L CO
P'ee: TEXAS EMIGRATION AND LAND
COMPANY
G'ee: TEXAS EMIGRATION AND LAND
COMPANY
T-Dt: -- --- -----
P-Dt: 15 Aug 1857
Dist/Class: Texas Emmigration and Land
Company
File#: 20
Patent#: 20
Patent Vol.: 14
Certificate: 20
Survey/Blk/Twp: 20
Acres: 320
Map(s) 11, 19

Abstract # 297 - TE&L CO
P'ee: TEXAS EMIGRATION AND LAND
COMPANY
G'ee: TEXAS EMIGRATION AND LAND
COMPANY
T-Dt: -- --- -----
P-Dt: 15 Aug 1857
Dist/Class: Texas Emmigration and Land
Company
File#: 21
Patent#: 21
Patent Vol.: 14
Certificate: 21
Survey/Blk/Twp: 21
Acres: 320
Map(s) 11

Abstract # 298 - TE&L CO
P'ee: TEXAS EMIGRATION AND LAND
COMPANY
G'ee: TEXAS EMIGRATION AND LAND
COMPANY
T-Dt: -- --- -----
P-Dt: 15 Aug 1857
Dist/Class: Texas Emmigration and Land
Company
File#: 22
Patent#: 22
Patent Vol.: 14
Certificate: 22
Survey/Blk/Twp: 22
Acres: 320
Map(s) 11

Abstract # 299 - TE&L CO
P'ee: TEXAS EMIGRATION AND LAND
COMPANY
G'ee: TEXAS EMIGRATION AND LAND
COMPANY
T-Dt: -- --- -----
P-Dt: 15 Aug 1857
Dist/Class: Texas Emmigration and Land
Company
File#: 23
Patent#: 23
Patent Vol.: 14
Certificate: 23
Survey/Blk/Twp: 23
Acres: 320
Map(s) 11

Abstract # 300 - TE&L CO
P'ee: TEXAS EMIGRATION AND LAND
COMPANY
G'ee: TEXAS EMIGRATION AND LAND
COMPANY
T-Dt: -- --- -----
P-Dt: 17 Aug 1857
Dist/Class: Texas Emmigration and Land
Company
File#: 24
Patent#: 24
Patent Vol.: 14
Certificate: 24
Survey/Blk/Twp: 24
Acres: 320
Map(s) 11

Abstract # 301 - TE&L CO
P'ee: TEXAS EMIGRATION AND LAND
COMPANY
G'ee: TEXAS EMIGRATION AND LAND
COMPANY
T-Dt: -- --- -----
P-Dt: 17 Aug 1857
Dist/Class: Texas Emmigration and Land
Company
File#: 25
Patent#: 25
Patent Vol.: 14
Certificate: 25
Survey/Blk/Twp: 25
Acres: 320
Map(s) 11

Abstract # 302 - TE&L CO
P'ee: TEXAS EMIGRATION AND LAND
COMPANY
G'ee: TEXAS EMIGRATION AND LAND
COMPANY
T-Dt: -- --- -----
P-Dt: 17 Aug 1857
Dist/Class: Texas Emmigration and Land
Company
File#: 26
Patent#: 26
Patent Vol.: 14
Certificate: 26
Survey/Blk/Twp: 26
Acres: 320
Map(s) 11

Abstract # 303 - TE&L CO
P'ee: TEXAS EMIGRATION AND LAND
COMPANY
G'ee: TEXAS EMIGRATION AND LAND
COMPANY
T-Dt: -- --- -----
P-Dt: 17 Aug 1857

Dist/Class: Texas Emmigration and Land
Company
File#: 27
Patent#: 27
Patent Vol.: 14
Certificate: 27
Survey/Blk/Twp: 27
Acres: 320
Map(s) 11

Abstract # 304 - TE&L CO
P'ee: TEXAS EMIGRATION AND LAND
COMPANY
G'ee: TEXAS EMIGRATION AND LAND
COMPANY
T-Dt: -- --- -----
P-Dt: 17 Aug 1857
Dist/Class: Texas Emmigration and Land
Company
File#: 28
Patent#: 28
Patent Vol.: 14
Certificate: 28
Survey/Blk/Twp: 28
Acres: 320
Map(s) 11

Abstract # 305 - TE&L CO
P'ee: TEXAS EMIGRATION AND LAND
COMPANY
G'ee: TEXAS EMIGRATION AND LAND
COMPANY
T-Dt: -- --- -----
P-Dt: 17 Aug 1857
Dist/Class: Texas Emmigration and Land
Company
File#: 29
Patent#: 29
Patent Vol.: 14
Certificate: 29
Survey/Blk/Twp: 29
Acres: 320
Map(s) 11

Abstract # 306 - TE&L CO
P'ee: TEXAS EMIGRATION AND LAND
COMPANY
G'ee: TEXAS EMIGRATION AND LAND
COMPANY
T-Dt: -- --- -----
P-Dt: 17 Aug 1857
Dist/Class: Texas Emmigration and Land
Company
File#: 30
Patent#: 30
Patent Vol.: 14
Certificate: 30
Survey/Blk/Twp: 30
Acres: 320
Map(s) 11

Abstract # 307 - TE&L CO
P'ee: TEXAS EMIGRATION AND LAND
COMPANY
G'ee: TEXAS EMIGRATION AND LAND
COMPANY
T-Dt: -- --- -----
P-Dt: 18 Aug 1857
Dist/Class: Texas Emmigration and Land
Company
File#: 31
Patent#: 31
Patent Vol.: 14
Certificate: 31
Survey/Blk/Twp: 31

Acres: 320
Map(s) 11

Abstract # 308 - TE&L CO
P'ee: TEXAS EMIGRATION AND LAND
COMPANY
G'ee: TEXAS EMIGRATION AND LAND
COMPANY
T-Dt: -- --- -----
P-Dt: 18 Aug 1857
Dist/Class: Texas Emmigration and Land
Company
File#: 32
Patent#: 32
Patent Vol.: 14
Certificate: 32
Survey/Blk/Twp: 32
Acres: 320
Map(s) 11

Abstract # 309 - TE&L CO
P'ee: TEXAS EMIGRATION AND LAND
COMPANY
G'ee: TEXAS EMIGRATION AND LAND
COMPANY
T-Dt: -- --- -----
P-Dt: 18 Aug 1857
Dist/Class: Texas Emmigration and Land
Company
File#: 33
Patent#: 33
Patent Vol.: 14
Certificate: 33
Survey/Blk/Twp: 33
Acres: 320
Map(s) 11

Abstract # 310 - TE&L CO
P'ee: TEXAS EMIGRATION AND LAND
COMPANY
G'ee: TEXAS EMIGRATION AND LAND
COMPANY
T-Dt: -- --- -----
P-Dt: 18 Aug 1857
Dist/Class: Texas Emmigration and Land
Company
File#: 34
Patent#: 34
Patent Vol.: 14
Certificate: 34
Survey/Blk/Twp: 34
Acres: 320
Map(s) 11

Abstract # 311 - TE&L CO
P'ee: TEXAS EMIGRATION AND LAND
COMPANY
G'ee: TEXAS EMIGRATION AND LAND
COMPANY
T-Dt: -- --- -----
P-Dt: 18 Aug 1857
Dist/Class: Texas Emmigration and Land
Company
File#: 35
Patent#: 35
Patent Vol.: 14
Certificate: 35
Survey/Blk/Twp: 35
Acres: 320
Map(s) 10, 11

Abstract # 312 - TE&L CO
P'ee: TEXAS EMIGRATION AND LAND
COMPANY
G'ee: TEXAS EMIGRATION AND LAND

COMPANY
T-Dt: -- --- -----
P-Dt: 18 Aug 1857
Dist/Class: Texas Emmigration and Land
Company
File#: 36
Patent#: 36
Patent Vol.: 14
Certificate: 36
Survey/Blk/Twp: 36
Acres: 320
Map(s) 10, 11

Abstract # 313 - TE&L CO
P'ee: TEXAS EMIGRATION AND LAND
COMPANY
G'ee: TEXAS EMIGRATION AND LAND
COMPANY
T-Dt: -- --- -----
P-Dt: 19 Aug 1857
Dist/Class: Texas Emmigration and Land
Company
File#: 37
Patent#: 37
Patent Vol.: 14
Certificate: 37
Survey/Blk/Twp: 37
Acres: 320
Map(s) 11

Abstract # 314 - TE&L CO
P'ee: TEXAS EMIGRATION AND LAND
COMPANY
G'ee: TEXAS EMIGRATION AND LAND
COMPANY
T-Dt: -- --- -----
P-Dt: 25 Aug 1857
Dist/Class: Texas Emmigration and Land
Company
File#: 38
Patent#: 38
Patent Vol.: 14
Certificate: 38
Survey/Blk/Twp: 38
Acres: 320
Map(s) 11

Abstract # 315 - TE&L CO
P'ee: TEXAS EMIGRATION AND LAND
COMPANY
G'ee: TEXAS EMIGRATION AND LAND
COMPANY
T-Dt: -- --- -----
P-Dt: 19 Aug 1857
Dist/Class: Texas Emmigration and Land
Company
File#: 39
Patent#: 39
Patent Vol.: 14
Certificate: 39
Survey/Blk/Twp: 39
Acres: 320
Map(s) 11

Abstract # 316 - TE&L CO
P'ee: TEXAS EMIGRATION AND LAND
COMPANY
G'ee: TEXAS EMIGRATION AND LAND
COMPANY
T-Dt: -- --- -----
P-Dt: 25 Aug 1857
Dist/Class: Texas Emmigration and Land
Company
File#: 40
Patent#: 40

Patent Vol.: 14
Certificate: 40
Survey/Blk/Twp: 40
Acres: 320
Map(s) 11

Abstract # 317 - TE&L CO
P'ee: TEXAS EMIGRATION AND LAND COMPANY
G'ee: TEXAS EMIGRATION AND LAND COMPANY
T-Dt: -- --- -----
P-Dt: 07 Sep 1857
Dist/Class: Texas Emmigration and Land Company
File#: 41
Patent#: 41
Patent Vol.: 14
Certificate: 41
Survey/Blk/Twp: 41
Acres: 320
Map(s) 11

Abstract # 318 - TE&L CO
P'ee: TEXAS EMIGRATION AND LAND COMPANY
G'ee: TEXAS EMIGRATION AND LAND COMPANY
T-Dt: -- --- -----
P-Dt: 07 Sep 1857
Dist/Class: Texas Emmigration and Land Company
File#: 42
Patent#: 42
Patent Vol.: 14
Certificate: 42
Survey/Blk/Twp: 42
Acres: 320
Map(s) 11

Abstract # 319 - TE&L CO
P'ee: TEXAS EMIGRATION AND LAND COMPANY
G'ee: TEXAS EMIGRATION AND LAND COMPANY
T-Dt: -- --- -----
P-Dt: 07 Sep 1857
Dist/Class: Texas Emmigration and Land Company
File#: 43
Patent#: 43
Patent Vol.: 14
Certificate: 43
Survey/Blk/Twp: 43
Acres: 320
Map(s) 11

Abstract # 320 - TE&L CO
P'ee: TEXAS EMIGRATION AND LAND COMPANY
G'ee: TEXAS EMIGRATION AND LAND COMPANY
T-Dt: -- --- -----
P-Dt: 07 Sep 1857
Dist/Class: Texas Emmigration and Land Company
File#: 44
Patent#: 44
Patent Vol.: 14
Certificate: 44
Survey/Blk/Twp: 44
Acres: 320
Map(s) 11

Abstract # 321 - TE&L CO

P'ee: TEXAS EMIGRATION AND LAND COMPANY
G'ee: TEXAS EMIGRATION AND LAND COMPANY
T-Dt: -- --- -----
P-Dt: 07 Sep 1857
Dist/Class: Texas Emmigration and Land Company
File#: 45
Patent#: 45
Patent Vol.: 14
Certificate: 45
Survey/Blk/Twp: 45
Acres: 320
Map(s) 10, 11

Abstract # 322 - TE&L CO
P'ee: TEXAS EMIGRATION AND LAND COMPANY
G'ee: TEXAS EMIGRATION AND LAND COMPANY
T-Dt: -- --- -----
P-Dt: 07 Sep 1857
Dist/Class: Texas Emmigration and Land Company
File#: 46
Patent#: 46
Patent Vol.: 14
Certificate: 46
Survey/Blk/Twp: 46
Acres: 320
Map(s) 10, 11

Abstract # 323 - TE&L CO
P'ee: TEXAS EMIGRATION AND LAND COMPANY
G'ee: TEXAS EMIGRATION AND LAND COMPANY
T-Dt: -- --- -----
P-Dt: 07 Sep 1857
Dist/Class: Texas Emmigration and Land Company
File#: 47
Patent#: 47
Patent Vol.: 14
Certificate: 47
Survey/Blk/Twp: 47
Acres: 320
Map(s) 11

Abstract # 324 - TE&L CO
P'ee: TEXAS EMIGRATION AND LAND COMPANY
G'ee: TEXAS EMIGRATION AND LAND COMPANY
T-Dt: -- --- -----
P-Dt: 07 Sep 1857
Dist/Class: Texas Emmigration and Land Company
File#: 48
Patent#: 48
Patent Vol.: 14
Certificate: 48
Survey/Blk/Twp: 48
Acres: 320
Map(s) 11

Abstract # 325 - TE&L CO
P'ee: TEXAS EMIGRATION AND LAND COMPANY
G'ee: TEXAS EMIGRATION AND LAND COMPANY
T-Dt: -- --- -----
P-Dt: 07 Sep 1857
Dist/Class: Texas Emmigration and Land

Company
File#: 49
Patent#: 49
Patent Vol.: 14
Certificate: 49
Survey/Blk/Twp: 49
Acres: 320
Map(s) 11

Abstract # 326 - TE&L CO
P'ee: TEXAS EMIGRATION AND LAND COMPANY
G'ee: TEXAS EMIGRATION AND LAND COMPANY
T-Dt: -- --- -----
P-Dt: 08 Sep 1857
Dist/Class: Texas Emmigration and Land Company
File#: 50
Patent#: 50
Patent Vol.: 14
Certificate: 50
Survey/Blk/Twp: 50
Acres: 320
Map(s) 11

Abstract # 327 - TE&L CO
P'ee: TEXAS EMIGRATION AND LAND COMPANY
G'ee: TEXAS EMIGRATION AND LAND COMPANY
T-Dt: -- --- -----
P-Dt: 08 Sep 1857
Dist/Class: Texas Emmigration and Land Company
File#: 51
Patent#: 51
Patent Vol.: 14
Certificate: 51
Survey/Blk/Twp: 51
Acres: 320
Map(s) 11

Abstract # 328 - TE&L CO
P'ee: TEXAS EMIGRATION AND LAND COMPANY
G'ee: TEXAS EMIGRATION AND LAND COMPANY
T-Dt: -- --- -----
P-Dt: 09 Sep 1857
Dist/Class: Texas Emmigration and Land Company
File#: 52
Patent#: 52
Patent Vol.: 14
Certificate: 52
Survey/Blk/Twp: 52
Acres: 320
Map(s) 11

Abstract # 329 - TE&L CO
P'ee: TEXAS EMIGRATION AND LAND COMPANY
G'ee: TEXAS EMIGRATION AND LAND COMPANY
T-Dt: -- --- -----
P-Dt: 09 Sep 1857
Dist/Class: Texas Emmigration and Land Company
File#: 53
Patent#: 53
Patent Vol.: 14
Certificate: 53
Survey/Blk/Twp: 53
Acres: 320

Map(s) 11

Abstract # 330 - TE&L CO
P'ee: TEXAS EMIGRATION AND LAND COMPANY
G'ee: TEXAS EMIGRATION AND LAND COMPANY
T-Dt: -- --- -----
P-Dt: 09 Sep 1857
Dist/Class: Texas Emmigration and Land Company
File#: 54
Patent#: 54
Patent Vol.: 14
Certificate: 54
Survey/Blk/Twp: 54
Acres: 320
Map(s) 11

Abstract # 331 - TE&L CO
P'ee: TEXAS EMIGRATION AND LAND COMPANY
G'ee: TEXAS EMIGRATION AND LAND COMPANY
T-Dt: -- --- -----
P-Dt: 09 Sep 1857
Dist/Class: Texas Emmigration and Land Company
File#: 55
Patent#: 55
Patent Vol.: 14
Certificate: 55
Survey/Blk/Twp: 55
Acres: 320
Map(s) 10, 11

Abstract # 332 - TE&L CO
P'ee: TEXAS EMIGRATION AND LAND COMPANY
G'ee: TEXAS EMIGRATION AND LAND COMPANY
T-Dt: -- --- -----
P-Dt: 09 Sep 1857
Dist/Class: Texas Emmigration and Land Company
File#: 56
Patent#: 56
Patent Vol.: 14
Certificate: 56
Survey/Blk/Twp: 56
Acres: 320
Map(s) 10, 11

Abstract # 333 - TE&L CO
P'ee: TEXAS EMIGRATION AND LAND COMPANY
G'ee: TEXAS EMIGRATION AND LAND COMPANY
T-Dt: -- --- -----
P-Dt: 09 Sep 1857
Dist/Class: Texas Emmigration and Land Company
File#: 57
Patent#: 57
Patent Vol.: 14
Certificate: 57
Survey/Blk/Twp: 57
Acres: 320
Map(s) 11

Abstract # 334 - TE&L CO
P'ee: TEXAS EMIGRATION AND LAND COMPANY
G'ee: TEXAS EMIGRATION AND LAND COMPANY

T-Dt: -- --- -----
P-Dt: 09 Sep 1857
Dist/Class: Texas Emmigration and Land Company
File#: 58
Patent#: 58
Patent Vol.: 14
Certificate: 58
Survey/Blk/Twp: 58
Acres: 320
Map(s) 11

Abstract # 335 - TE&L CO
P'ee: TEXAS EMIGRATION AND LAND COMPANY
G'ee: TEXAS EMIGRATION AND LAND COMPANY
T-Dt: -- --- -----
P-Dt: 09 Sep 1857
Dist/Class: Texas Emmigration and Land Company
File#: 59
Patent#: 59
Patent Vol.: 14
Certificate: 59
Survey/Blk/Twp: 59
Acres: 320
Map(s) 11

Abstract # 336 - TE&L CO
P'ee: TEXAS EMIGRATION AND LAND COMPANY
G'ee: TEXAS EMIGRATION AND LAND COMPANY
T-Dt: -- --- -----
P-Dt: 10 Sep 1857
Dist/Class: Texas Emmigration and Land Company
File#: 60
Patent#: 60
Patent Vol.: 14
Certificate: 60
Survey/Blk/Twp: 60
Acres: 320
Map(s) 11

Abstract # 337 - TE&L CO
P'ee: TEXAS EMIGRATION AND LAND COMPANY
G'ee: TEXAS EMIGRATION AND LAND COMPANY
T-Dt: -- --- -----
P-Dt: 10 Sep 1857
Dist/Class: Texas Emmigration and Land Company
File#: 61
Patent#: 61
Patent Vol.: 14
Certificate: 61
Survey/Blk/Twp: 61
Acres: 320
Map(s) 10

Abstract # 338 - TE&L CO
P'ee: TEXAS EMIGRATION AND LAND COMPANY
G'ee: TEXAS EMIGRATION AND LAND COMPANY
T-Dt: -- --- -----
P-Dt: 10 Sep 1857
Dist/Class: Texas Emmigration and Land Company
File#: 62
Patent#: 62
Patent Vol.: 14

Certificate: 62
Survey/Blk/Twp: 62
Acres: 320
Map(s) 10

Abstract # 339 - TE&L CO
P'ee: TEXAS EMIGRATION AND LAND COMPANY
G'ee: TEXAS EMIGRATION AND LAND COMPANY
T-Dt: -- --- -----
P-Dt: 10 Sep 1857
Dist/Class: Texas Emmigration and Land Company
File#: 63
Patent#: 63
Patent Vol.: 14
Certificate: 63
Survey/Blk/Twp: 63
Acres: 320
Map(s) 10

Abstract # 340 - TE&L CO
P'ee: TEXAS EMIGRATION AND LAND COMPANY
G'ee: TEXAS EMIGRATION AND LAND COMPANY
T-Dt: -- --- -----
P-Dt: 11 Sep 1857
Dist/Class: Texas Emmigration and Land Company
File#: 64
Patent#: 64
Patent Vol.: 14
Certificate: 64
Survey/Blk/Twp: 64
Acres: 320
Map(s) 2, 10

Abstract # 341 - TE&L CO
P'ee: TEXAS EMIGRATION AND LAND COMPANY
G'ee: TEXAS EMIGRATION AND LAND COMPANY
T-Dt: -- --- -----
P-Dt: 12 Sep 1857
Dist/Class: Texas Emmigration and Land Company
File#: 65
Patent#: 65
Patent Vol.: 14
Certificate: 65
Survey/Blk/Twp: 65
Acres: 320
Map(s) 2

Abstract # 342 - TE&L CO
P'ee: TEXAS EMIGRATION AND LAND COMPANY
G'ee: TEXAS EMIGRATION AND LAND COMPANY
T-Dt: -- --- -----
P-Dt: 12 Sep 1857
Dist/Class: Texas Emmigration and Land Company
File#: 66
Patent#: 66
Patent Vol.: 14
Certificate: 66
Survey/Blk/Twp: 66
Acres: 320
Map(s) 2

Abstract # 343 - TE&L CO
P'ee: TEXAS EMIGRATION AND LAND

COMPANY
G'ee: TEXAS EMIGRATION AND LAND
COMPANY
T-Dt: -- --- -----
P-Dt: 12 Sep 1857
Dist/Class: Texas Emmigration and Land
Company
File#: 67
Patent#: 67
Patent Vol.: 14
Certificate: 67
Survey/Blk/Twp: 67
Acres: 320
Map(s) 2

Abstract # 344 - TE&L CO
P'ee: TEXAS EMIGRATION AND LAND
COMPANY
G'ee: TEXAS EMIGRATION AND LAND
COMPANY
T-Dt: -- --- -----
P-Dt: 12 Sep 1857
Dist/Class: Texas Emmigration and Land
Company
File#: 68
Patent#: 68
Patent Vol.: 14
Certificate: 68
Survey/Blk/Twp: 68
Acres: 320
Map(s) 2

Abstract # 345 - TE&L CO
P'ee: TEXAS EMIGRATION AND LAND
COMPANY
G'ee: TEXAS EMIGRATION AND LAND
COMPANY
T-Dt: -- --- -----
P-Dt: 12 Sep 1857
Dist/Class: Texas Emmigration and Land
Company
File#: 69
Patent#: 69
Patent Vol.: 14
Certificate: 69
Survey/Blk/Twp: 69
Acres: 320
Map(s) 2

Abstract # 346 - TE&L CO
P'ee: TEXAS EMIGRATION AND LAND
COMPANY
G'ee: TEXAS EMIGRATION AND LAND
COMPANY
T-Dt: -- --- -----
P-Dt: 14 Sep 1857
Dist/Class: Texas Emmigration and Land
Company
File#: 70
Patent#: 70
Patent Vol.: 14
Certificate: 70
Survey/Blk/Twp: 70
Acres: 320
Map(s) 2

Abstract # 347 - TE&L CO
P'ee: TEXAS EMIGRATION AND LAND
COMPANY
G'ee: TEXAS EMIGRATION AND LAND
COMPANY
T-Dt: -- --- -----
P-Dt: 14 Sep 1857
Dist/Class: Texas Emmigration and Land
Company

File#: 71
Patent#: 71
Patent Vol.: 14
Certificate: 71
Survey/Blk/Twp: 71
Acres: 320
Map(s) 2

Abstract # 348 - TE&L CO
P'ee: TEXAS EMIGRATION AND LAND
COMPANY
G'ee: TEXAS EMIGRATION AND LAND
COMPANY
T-Dt: -- --- -----
P-Dt: 14 Sep 1857
Dist/Class: Texas Emmigration and Land
Company
File#: 72
Patent#: 72
Patent Vol.: 14
Certificate: 72
Survey/Blk/Twp: 72
Acres: 320
Map(s) 2

Abstract # 349 - TE&L CO
P'ee: TEXAS EMIGRATION AND LAND
COMPANY
G'ee: TEXAS EMIGRATION AND LAND
COMPANY
T-Dt: -- --- -----
P-Dt: 14 Sep 1857
Dist/Class: Texas Emmigration and Land
Company
File#: 73
Patent#: 73
Patent Vol.: 14
Certificate: 73
Survey/Blk/Twp: 73
Acres: 320
Map(s) 2

Abstract # 350 - TE&L CO
P'ee: TEXAS EMIGRATION AND LAND
COMPANY
G'ee: TEXAS EMIGRATION AND LAND
COMPANY
T-Dt: -- --- -----
P-Dt: 14 Sep 1857
Dist/Class: Texas Emmigration and Land
Company
File#: 74
Patent#: 74
Patent Vol.: 14
Certificate: 74
Survey/Blk/Twp: 74
Acres: 320
Map(s) 2

Abstract # 351 - TE&L CO
P'ee: TEXAS EMIGRATION AND LAND
COMPANY
G'ee: TEXAS EMIGRATION AND LAND
COMPANY
T-Dt: -- --- -----
P-Dt: 14 Sep 1857
Dist/Class: Texas Emmigration and Land
Company
File#: 75
Patent#: 75
Patent Vol.: 14
Certificate: 75
Survey/Blk/Twp: 75
Acres: 320
Map(s) 2

Abstract # 352 - TE&L CO
P'ee: TEXAS EMIGRATION AND LAND
COMPANY
G'ee: TEXAS EMIGRATION AND LAND
COMPANY
T-Dt: -- --- -----
P-Dt: 14 Sep 1857
Dist/Class: Texas Emmigration and Land
Company
File#: 76
Patent#: 76
Patent Vol.: 14
Certificate: 76
Survey/Blk/Twp: 76
Acres: 320
Map(s) 2

Abstract # 353 - TE&L CO
P'ee: TEXAS EMIGRATION AND LAND
COMPANY
G'ee: TEXAS EMIGRATION AND LAND
COMPANY
T-Dt: -- --- -----
P-Dt: 14 Sep 1857
Dist/Class: Texas Emmigration and Land
Company
File#: 77
Patent#: 77
Patent Vol.: 14
Certificate: 77
Survey/Blk/Twp: 77
Acres: 320
Map(s) 1, 2

Abstract # 354 - TE&L CO
P'ee: TEXAS EMIGRATION AND LAND
COMPANY
G'ee: TEXAS EMIGRATION AND LAND
COMPANY
T-Dt: -- --- -----
P-Dt: 15 Sep 1857
Dist/Class: Texas Emmigration and Land
Company
File#: 78
Patent#: 78
Patent Vol.: 14
Certificate: 78
Survey/Blk/Twp: 78
Acres: 320
Map(s) 1, 2

Abstract # 355 - TE&L CO
P'ee: TEXAS EMIGRATION AND LAND
COMPANY
G'ee: TEXAS EMIGRATION AND LAND
COMPANY
T-Dt: -- --- -----
P-Dt: 15 Sep 1857
Dist/Class: Texas Emmigration and Land
Company
File#: 79
Patent#: 79
Patent Vol.: 14
Certificate: 79
Survey/Blk/Twp: 79
Acres: 320
Map(s) 1, 2

Abstract # 356 - TE&L CO
P'ee: TEXAS EMIGRATION AND LAND
COMPANY
G'ee: TEXAS EMIGRATION AND LAND
COMPANY
T-Dt: -- --- -----
P-Dt: 15 Sep 1857

Dist/Class: Texas Emmigration and Land
Company
File#: 80
Patent#: 80
Patent Vol.: 14
Certificate: 80
Survey/Blk/Twp: 80
Acres: 320
Map(s) 1, 2

Abstract # 357 - TE&L CO
P'ee: TEXAS EMIGRATION AND LAND
COMPANY
G'ee: TEXAS EMIGRATION AND LAND
COMPANY
T-Dt: -- --- -----
P-Dt: 15 Sep 1857
Dist/Class: Texas Emmigration and Land
Company
File#: 81
Patent#: 81
Patent Vol.: 14
Certificate: 81
Survey/Blk/Twp: 81
Acres: 320
Map(s) 1, 2

Abstract # 358 - TE&L CO
P'ee: TEXAS EMIGRATION AND LAND
COMPANY
G'ee: TEXAS EMIGRATION AND LAND
COMPANY
T-Dt: -- --- -----
P-Dt: 15 Sep 1857
Dist/Class: Texas Emmigration and Land
Company
File#: 82
Patent#: 82
Patent Vol.: 14
Certificate: 82
Survey/Blk/Twp: 82
Acres: 320
Map(s) 1, 2

Abstract # 359 - TE&L CO
P'ee: TEXAS EMIGRATION AND LAND
COMPANY
G'ee: TEXAS EMIGRATION AND LAND
COMPANY
T-Dt: -- --- -----
P-Dt: 15 Sep 1857
Dist/Class: Texas Emmigration and Land
Company
File#: 83
Patent#: 83
Patent Vol.: 14
Certificate: 83
Survey/Blk/Twp: 83
Acres: 320
Map(s) 1

Abstract # 360 - TE&L CO
P'ee: TEXAS EMIGRATION AND LAND
COMPANY
G'ee: TEXAS EMIGRATION AND LAND
COMPANY
T-Dt: -- --- -----
P-Dt: 15 Sep 1857
Dist/Class: Texas Emmigration and Land
Company
File#: 84
Patent#: 84
Patent Vol.: 14
Certificate: 84
Survey/Blk/Twp: 84

Acres: 320
Map(s) 1

Abstract # 361 - TE&L CO
P'ee: TEXAS EMIGRATION AND LAND
COMPANY
G'ee: TEXAS EMIGRATION AND LAND
COMPANY
T-Dt: -- --- -----
P-Dt: 15 Sep 1857
Dist/Class: Texas Emmigration and Land
Company
File#: 85
Patent#: 85
Patent Vol.: 14
Certificate: 85
Survey/Blk/Twp: 85
Acres: 320
Map(s) 1

Abstract # 362 - TE&L CO
P'ee: TEXAS EMIGRATION AND LAND
COMPANY
G'ee: TEXAS EMIGRATION AND LAND
COMPANY
T-Dt: -- --- -----
P-Dt: 15 Sep 1857
Dist/Class: Texas Emmigration and Land
Company
File#: 86
Patent#: 86
Patent Vol.: 14
Certificate: 86
Survey/Blk/Twp: 86
Acres: 320
Map(s) 1

Abstract # 363 - TE&L CO
P'ee: TEXAS EMIGRATION AND LAND
COMPANY
G'ee: TEXAS EMIGRATION AND LAND
COMPANY
T-Dt: -- --- -----
P-Dt: 16 Sep 1857
Dist/Class: Texas Emmigration and Land
Company
File#: 87
Patent#: 87
Patent Vol.: 14
Certificate: 87
Survey/Blk/Twp: 87
Acres: 320
Map(s) 1

Abstract # 364 - TE&L CO
P'ee: TEXAS EMIGRATION AND LAND
COMPANY
G'ee: TEXAS EMIGRATION AND LAND
COMPANY
T-Dt: -- --- -----
P-Dt: 16 Sep 1857
Dist/Class: Texas Emmigration and Land
Company
File#: 88
Patent#: 88
Patent Vol.: 14
Certificate: 88
Survey/Blk/Twp: 88
Acres: 320
Map(s) 1

Abstract # 365 - TE&L CO
P'ee: TEXAS EMIGRATION AND LAND
COMPANY
G'ee: TEXAS EMIGRATION AND LAND

COMPANY
T-Dt: -- --- -----
P-Dt: 16 Sep 1857
Dist/Class: Texas Emmigration and Land
Company
File#: 89
Patent#: 89
Patent Vol.: 14
Certificate: 89
Survey/Blk/Twp: 89
Acres: 320
Map(s) 1, 9

Abstract # 366 - TE&L CO
P'ee: TEXAS EMIGRATION AND LAND
COMPANY
G'ee: TEXAS EMIGRATION AND LAND
COMPANY
T-Dt: -- --- -----
P-Dt: 16 Sep 1857
Dist/Class: Texas Emmigration and Land
Company
File#: 90
Patent#: 90
Patent Vol.: 14
Certificate: 90
Survey/Blk/Twp: 90
Acres: 320
Map(s) 1, 9

Abstract # 367 - TE&L CO
P'ee: TEXAS EMIGRATION AND LAND
COMPANY
G'ee: TEXAS EMIGRATION AND LAND
COMPANY
T-Dt: -- --- -----
P-Dt: 16 Sep 1857
Dist/Class: Texas Emmigration and Land
Company
File#: 91
Patent#: 91
Patent Vol.: 14
Certificate: 91
Survey/Blk/Twp: 91
Acres: 320
Map(s) 1

Abstract # 368 - TE&L CO
P'ee: TEXAS EMIGRATION AND LAND
COMPANY
G'ee: TEXAS EMIGRATION AND LAND
COMPANY
T-Dt: -- --- -----
P-Dt: 17 Sep 1857
Dist/Class: Texas Emmigration and Land
Company
File#: 92
Patent#: 92
Patent Vol.: 14
Certificate: 92
Survey/Blk/Twp: 92
Acres: 320
Map(s) 1

Abstract # 369 - TE&L CO
P'ee: TEXAS EMIGRATION AND LAND
COMPANY
G'ee: TEXAS EMIGRATION AND LAND
COMPANY
T-Dt: -- --- -----
P-Dt: 17 Sep 1857
Dist/Class: Texas Emmigration and Land
Company
File#: 93
Patent#: 93

Patent Vol.: 14
Certificate: 93
Survey/Blk/Twp: 93
Acres: 320
Map(s) 1

Abstract # 370 - TE&L CO
P'ee: TEXAS EMIGRATION AND LAND COMPANY
G'ee: TEXAS EMIGRATION AND LAND COMPANY
T-Dt: -- --- -----
P-Dt: 17 Sep 1857
Dist/Class: Texas Emmigration and Land Company
File#: 94
Patent#: 94
Patent Vol.: 14
Certificate: 94
Survey/Blk/Twp: 94
Acres: 320
Map(s) 1

Abstract # 371 - TE&L CO
P'ee: TEXAS EMIGRATION AND LAND COMPANY
G'ee: TEXAS EMIGRATION AND LAND COMPANY
T-Dt: -- --- -----
P-Dt: 17 Sep 1857
Dist/Class: Texas Emmigration and Land Company
File#: 95
Patent#: 95
Patent Vol.: 14
Certificate: 95
Survey/Blk/Twp: 95
Acres: 320
Map(s) 1

Abstract # 372 - TE&L CO
P'ee: TEXAS EMIGRATION AND LAND COMPANY
G'ee: TEXAS EMIGRATION AND LAND COMPANY
T-Dt: -- --- -----
P-Dt: 17 Sep 1857
Dist/Class: Texas Emmigration and Land Company
File#: 96
Patent#: 96
Patent Vol.: 14
Certificate: 96
Survey/Blk/Twp: 96
Acres: 320
Map(s) 1

Abstract # 373 - TE&L CO
P'ee: TEXAS EMIGRATION AND LAND COMPANY
G'ee: TEXAS EMIGRATION AND LAND COMPANY
T-Dt: -- --- -----
P-Dt: 17 Sep 1857
Dist/Class: Texas Emmigration and Land Company
File#: 97
Patent#: 97
Patent Vol.: 14
Certificate: 97
Survey/Blk/Twp: 97
Acres: 320
Map(s) 1, 9

Abstract # 374 - TE&L CO

P'ee: TEXAS EMIGRATION AND LAND COMPANY
G'ee: TEXAS EMIGRATION AND LAND COMPANY
T-Dt: -- --- -----
P-Dt: 18 Sep 1857
Dist/Class: Texas Emmigration and Land Company
File#: 98
Patent#: 98
Patent Vol.: 14
Certificate: 98
Survey/Blk/Twp: 98
Acres: 320
Map(s) 1

Abstract # 375 - TE&L CO
P'ee: TEXAS EMIGRATION AND LAND COMPANY
G'ee: TEXAS EMIGRATION AND LAND COMPANY
T-Dt: -- --- -----
P-Dt: 18 Sep 1857
Dist/Class: Texas Emmigration and Land Company
File#: 99
Patent#: 99
Patent Vol.: 14
Certificate: 99
Survey/Blk/Twp: 99
Acres: 320
Map(s) 1

Abstract # 376 - TE&L CO
P'ee: TEXAS EMIGRATION AND LAND COMPANY
G'ee: TEXAS EMIGRATION AND LAND COMPANY
T-Dt: -- --- -----
P-Dt: 18 Sep 1857
Dist/Class: Texas Emmigration and Land Company
File#: 100
Patent#: 100
Patent Vol.: 14
Certificate: 100
Survey/Blk/Twp: 100
Acres: 320
Map(s) 1

Abstract # 377 - TE&L CO
P'ee: TEXAS EMIGRATION AND LAND COMPANY
G'ee: TEXAS EMIGRATION AND LAND COMPANY
T-Dt: -- --- -----
P-Dt: 21 Sep 1857
Dist/Class: Texas Emmigration and Land Company
File#: 101
Patent#: 101
Patent Vol.: 14
Certificate: 101
Survey/Blk/Twp: 101
Acres: 320
Map(s) 19

Abstract # 378 - TE&L CO
P'ee: TEXAS EMIGRATION AND LAND COMPANY
G'ee: TEXAS EMIGRATION AND LAND COMPANY
T-Dt: -- --- -----
P-Dt: 11 Mar 1859
Dist/Class: Texas Emmigration and Land

Company
File#: 102
Patent#: 1122
Patent Vol.: 14
Certificate: 102
Survey/Blk/Twp: 102
Acres: 320
Map(s) 19

Abstract # 379 - TE&L CO
P'ee: TEXAS EMIGRATION AND LAND COMPANY
G'ee: TEXAS EMIGRATION AND LAND COMPANY
T-Dt: -- --- -----
P-Dt: 11 Mar 1859
Dist/Class: Texas Emmigration and Land Company
File#: 103
Patent#: 1123
Patent Vol.: 14
Certificate: 103
Survey/Blk/Twp: 103
Acres: 320
Map(s) 19

Abstract # 380 - TE&L CO
P'ee: TEXAS EMIGRATION AND LAND COMPANY
G'ee: TEXAS EMIGRATION AND LAND COMPANY
T-Dt: -- --- -----
P-Dt: 23 Sep 1857
Dist/Class: Texas Emmigration and Land Company
File#: 104
Patent#: 104
Patent Vol.: 14
Certificate: 104
Survey/Blk/Twp: 104
Acres: 320
Map(s) 11, 19

Abstract # 381 - TE&L CO
P'ee: TEXAS EMIGRATION AND LAND COMPANY
G'ee: TEXAS EMIGRATION AND LAND COMPANY
T-Dt: -- --- -----
P-Dt: 23 Sep 1857
Dist/Class: Texas Emmigration and Land Company
File#: 105
Patent#: 105
Patent Vol.: 14
Certificate: 105
Survey/Blk/Twp: 105
Acres: 320
Map(s) 11, 19

Abstract # 382 - TE&L CO
P'ee: TEXAS EMIGRATION AND LAND COMPANY
G'ee: TEXAS EMIGRATION AND LAND COMPANY
T-Dt: -- --- -----
P-Dt: 23 Sep 1857
Dist/Class: Texas Emmigration and Land Company
File#: 106
Patent#: 106
Patent Vol.: 14
Certificate: 106
Survey/Blk/Twp: 106
Acres: 320

Map(s) 10, 11, 18, 19

Abstract # 383 - TE&L CO
P'ee: TEXAS EMIGRATION AND LAND
COMPANY
G'ee: TEXAS EMIGRATION AND LAND
COMPANY
T-Dt: -- --- -----
P-Dt: 23 Sep 1857
Dist/Class: Texas Emmigration and Land
Company
File#: 107
Patent#: 107
Patent Vol.: 14
Certificate: 107
Survey/Blk/Twp: 107
Acres: 320
Map(s) 10, 18

Abstract # 384 - TE&L CO
P'ee: TEXAS EMIGRATION AND LAND
COMPANY
G'ee: TEXAS EMIGRATION AND LAND
COMPANY
T-Dt: -- --- -----
P-Dt: 24 Sep 1857
Dist/Class: Texas Emmigration and Land
Company
File#: 108
Patent#: 108
Patent Vol.: 14
Certificate: 108
Survey/Blk/Twp: 108
Acres: 320
Map(s) 10, 18

Abstract # 385 - TE&L CO
P'ee: TEXAS EMIGRATION AND LAND
COMPANY
G'ee: TEXAS EMIGRATION AND LAND
COMPANY
T-Dt: -- --- -----
P-Dt: 24 Sep 1857
Dist/Class: Texas Emmigration and Land
Company
File#: 109
Patent#: 109
Patent Vol.: 14
Certificate: 109
Survey/Blk/Twp: 109
Acres: 320
Map(s) 10, 18

Abstract # 386 - TE&L CO
P'ee: TEXAS EMIGRATION AND LAND
COMPANY
G'ee: TEXAS EMIGRATION AND LAND
COMPANY
T-Dt: -- --- -----
P-Dt: 24 Sep 1857
Dist/Class: Texas Emmigration and Land
Company
File#: 110
Patent#: 110
Patent Vol.: 14
Certificate: 110
Survey/Blk/Twp: 110
Acres: 320
Map(s) 10, 18

Abstract # 387 - TE&L CO
P'ee: TEXAS EMIGRATION AND LAND
COMPANY
G'ee: TEXAS EMIGRATION AND LAND
COMPANY

T-Dt: -- --- -----
P-Dt: 24 Sep 1857
Dist/Class: Texas Emmigration and Land
Company
File#: 111
Patent#: 111
Patent Vol.: 14
Certificate: 111
Survey/Blk/Twp: 111
Acres: 320
Map(s) 10, 18

Abstract # 388 - TE&L CO
P'ee: TEXAS EMIGRATION AND LAND
COMPANY
G'ee: TEXAS EMIGRATION AND LAND
COMPANY
T-Dt: -- --- -----
P-Dt: 24 Sep 1857
Dist/Class: Texas Emmigration and Land
Company
File#: 112
Patent#: 112
Patent Vol.: 14
Certificate: 112
Survey/Blk/Twp: 112
Acres: 320
Map(s) 10, 18

Abstract # 389 - TE&L CO
P'ee: TEXAS EMIGRATION AND LAND
COMPANY
G'ee: TEXAS EMIGRATION AND LAND
COMPANY
T-Dt: -- --- -----
P-Dt: 05 Oct 1857
Dist/Class: Texas Emmigration and Land
Company
File#: 125
Patent#: 125
Patent Vol.: 14
Certificate: 125
Survey/Blk/Twp: 125
Acres: 320
Map(s) 10, 18

Abstract # 390 - TE&L CO
P'ee: TEXAS EMIGRATION AND LAND
COMPANY
G'ee: TEXAS EMIGRATION AND LAND
COMPANY
T-Dt: -- --- -----
P-Dt: 05 Oct 1857
Dist/Class: Texas Emmigration and Land
Company
File#: 126
Patent#: 126
Patent Vol.: 14
Certificate: 126
Survey/Blk/Twp: 126
Acres: 320
Map(s) 10, 18

Abstract # 391 - TE&L CO
P'ee: TEXAS EMIGRATION AND LAND
COMPANY
G'ee: TEXAS EMIGRATION AND LAND
COMPANY
T-Dt: -- --- -----
P-Dt: 06 Oct 1857
Dist/Class: Texas Emmigration and Land
Company
File#: 127
Patent#: 127
Patent Vol.: 14

Certificate: 127
Survey/Blk/Twp: 127
Acres: 320
Map(s) 10, 18

Abstract # 392 - TE&L CO
P'ee: TEXAS EMIGRATION AND LAND
COMPANY
G'ee: TEXAS EMIGRATION AND LAND
COMPANY
T-Dt: -- --- -----
P-Dt: 06 Oct 1857
Dist/Class: Texas Emmigration and Land
Company
File#: 128
Patent#: 128
Patent Vol.: 14
Certificate: 128
Survey/Blk/Twp: 128
Acres: 320
Map(s) 10

Abstract # 393 - TE&L CO
P'ee: TEXAS EMIGRATION AND LAND
COMPANY
G'ee: TEXAS EMIGRATION AND LAND
COMPANY
T-Dt: -- --- -----
P-Dt: 06 Oct 1857
Dist/Class: Texas Emmigration and Land
Company
File#: 129
Patent#: 129
Patent Vol.: 14
Certificate: 129
Survey/Blk/Twp: 129
Acres: 320
Map(s) 9, 10

Abstract # 394 - TE&L CO
P'ee: TEXAS EMIGRATION AND LAND
COMPANY
G'ee: TEXAS EMIGRATION AND LAND
COMPANY
T-Dt: -- --- -----
P-Dt: 06 Oct 1857
Dist/Class: Texas Emmigration and Land
Company
File#: 130
Patent#: 130
Patent Vol.: 14
Certificate: 130
Survey/Blk/Twp: 130
Acres: 320
Map(s) 9, 10

Abstract # 395 - TE&L CO
P'ee: TEXAS EMIGRATION AND LAND
COMPANY
G'ee: TEXAS EMIGRATION AND LAND
COMPANY
T-Dt: -- --- -----
P-Dt: 06 Oct 1857
Dist/Class: Texas Emmigration and Land
Company
File#: 131
Patent#: 131
Patent Vol.: 14
Certificate: 131
Survey/Blk/Twp: 131
Acres: 320
Map(s) 9

Abstract # 396 - TE&L CO
P'ee: TEXAS EMIGRATION AND LAND

COMPANY
G'ee: TEXAS EMIGRATION AND LAND
COMPANY
T-Dt: -- --- -----
P-Dt: 07 Oct 1857
Dist/Class: Texas Emmigration and Land
Company
File#: 132
Patent#: 132
Patent Vol.: 14
Certificate: 132
Survey/Blk/Twp: 132
Acres: 320
Map(s) 9

Abstract # 397 - TE&L CO
P'ee: TEXAS EMIGRATION AND LAND
COMPANY
G'ee: TEXAS EMIGRATION AND LAND
COMPANY
T-Dt: -- --- -----
P-Dt: 26 Oct 1857
Dist/Class: Texas Emmigration and Land
Company
File#: 150
Patent#: 150
Patent Vol.: 14
Certificate: 150
Survey/Blk/Twp: 150
Acres: 320
Map(s) 3, 11

Abstract # 398 - TE&L CO
P'ee: TEXAS EMIGRATION AND LAND
COMPANY
G'ee: TEXAS EMIGRATION AND LAND
COMPANY
T-Dt: -- --- -----
P-Dt: 26 Oct 1857
Dist/Class: Texas Emmigration and Land
Company
File#: 151
Patent#: 151
Patent Vol.: 14
Certificate: 151
Survey/Blk/Twp: 151
Acres: 320
Map(s) 3

Abstract # 399 - TE&L CO
P'ee: TEXAS EMIGRATION AND LAND
COMPANY
G'ee: TEXAS EMIGRATION AND LAND
COMPANY
T-Dt: -- --- -----
P-Dt: 27 Oct 1857
Dist/Class: Texas Emmigration and Land
Company
File#: 152
Patent#: 152
Patent Vol.: 14
Certificate: 152
Survey/Blk/Twp: 152
Acres: 320
Map(s) 3

Abstract # 400 - TE&L CO
P'ee: TEXAS EMIGRATION AND LAND
COMPANY
G'ee: TEXAS EMIGRATION AND LAND
COMPANY
T-Dt: -- --- -----
P-Dt: 27 Oct 1857
Dist/Class: Texas Emmigration and Land
Company

File#: 153
Patent#: 153
Patent Vol.: 14
Certificate: 153
Survey/Blk/Twp: 153
Acres: 320
Map(s) 3

Abstract # 401 - TE&L CO
P'ee: TEXAS EMIGRATION AND LAND
COMPANY
G'ee: TEXAS EMIGRATION AND LAND
COMPANY
T-Dt: -- --- -----
P-Dt: 27 Oct 1857
Dist/Class: Texas Emmigration and Land
Company
File#: 154
Patent#: 154
Patent Vol.: 14
Certificate: 154
Survey/Blk/Twp: 154
Acres: 320
Map(s) 3

Abstract # 402 - TE&L CO
P'ee: TEXAS EMIGRATION AND LAND
COMPANY
G'ee: TEXAS EMIGRATION AND LAND
COMPANY
T-Dt: -- --- -----
P-Dt: 27 Oct 1857
Dist/Class: Texas Emmigration and Land
Company
File#: 155
Patent#: 155
Patent Vol.: 14
Certificate: 155
Survey/Blk/Twp: 155
Acres: 320
Map(s) 3

Abstract # 403 - TE&L CO
P'ee: TEXAS EMIGRATION AND LAND
COMPANY
G'ee: TEXAS EMIGRATION AND LAND
COMPANY
T-Dt: -- --- -----
P-Dt: 27 Oct 1857
Dist/Class: Texas Emmigration and Land
Company
File#: 156
Patent#: 156
Patent Vol.: 14
Certificate: 156
Survey/Blk/Twp: 156
Acres: 320
Map(s) 3

Abstract # 404 - TE&L CO
P'ee: TEXAS EMIGRATION AND LAND
COMPANY
G'ee: TEXAS EMIGRATION AND LAND
COMPANY
T-Dt: -- --- -----
P-Dt: 27 Oct 1857
Dist/Class: Texas Emmigration and Land
Company
File#: 157
Patent#: 157
Patent Vol.: 14
Certificate: 157
Survey/Blk/Twp: 157
Acres: 320
Map(s) 3

Abstract # 405 - TE&L CO
P'ee: TEXAS EMIGRATION AND LAND
COMPANY
G'ee: TEXAS EMIGRATION AND LAND
COMPANY
T-Dt: -- --- -----
P-Dt: 27 Oct 1857
Dist/Class: Texas Emmigration and Land
Company
File#: 158
Patent#: 158
Patent Vol.: 14
Certificate: 158
Survey/Blk/Twp: 158
Acres: 320
Map(s) 3

Abstract # 406 - TE&L CO
P'ee: TEXAS EMIGRATION AND LAND
COMPANY
G'ee: TEXAS EMIGRATION AND LAND
COMPANY
T-Dt: -- --- -----
P-Dt: 28 Oct 1857
Dist/Class: Texas Emmigration and Land
Company
File#: 159
Patent#: 159
Patent Vol.: 14
Certificate: 159
Survey/Blk/Twp: 159
Acres: 320
Map(s) 3

Abstract # 407 - TE&L CO
P'ee: TEXAS EMIGRATION AND LAND
COMPANY
G'ee: TEXAS EMIGRATION AND LAND
COMPANY
T-Dt: -- --- -----
P-Dt: 28 Oct 1857
Dist/Class: Texas Emmigration and Land
Company
File#: 160
Patent#: 160
Patent Vol.: 14
Certificate: 160
Survey/Blk/Twp: 160
Acres: 320
Map(s) 3

Abstract # 408 - TE&L CO
P'ee: TEXAS EMIGRATION AND LAND
COMPANY
G'ee: TEXAS EMIGRATION AND LAND
COMPANY
T-Dt: -- --- -----
P-Dt: 28 Oct 1857
Dist/Class: Texas Emmigration and Land
Company
File#: 161
Patent#: 161
Patent Vol.: 14
Certificate: 161
Survey/Blk/Twp: 161
Acres: 320
Map(s) 3

Abstract # 409 - TE&L CO
P'ee: TEXAS EMIGRATION AND LAND
COMPANY
G'ee: TEXAS EMIGRATION AND LAND
COMPANY
T-Dt: -- --- -----
P-Dt: 28 Oct 1857

Dist/Class: Texas Emmigration and Land
Company
File#: 162
Patent#: 162
Patent Vol.: 14
Certificate: 162
Survey/Blk/Twp: 162
Acres: 320
Map(s) 3

Abstract # 410 - TE&L CO
P'ee: TEXAS EMIGRATION AND LAND
COMPANY
G'ee: TEXAS EMIGRATION AND LAND
COMPANY
T-Dt: -- --- -----
P-Dt: 28 Oct 1857
Dist/Class: Texas Emmigration and Land
Company
File#: 163
Patent#: 163
Patent Vol.: 14
Certificate: 163
Survey/Blk/Twp: 163
Acres: 320
Map(s) 3

Abstract # 411 - TE&L CO
P'ee: TEXAS EMIGRATION AND LAND
COMPANY
G'ee: TEXAS EMIGRATION AND LAND
COMPANY
T-Dt: -- --- -----
P-Dt: 28 Oct 1857
Dist/Class: Texas Emmigration and Land
Company
File#: 164
Patent#: 164
Patent Vol.: 14
Certificate: 164
Survey/Blk/Twp: 164
Acres: 320
Map(s) 3

Abstract # 412 - TE&L CO
P'ee: TEXAS EMIGRATION AND LAND
COMPANY
G'ee: TEXAS EMIGRATION AND LAND
COMPANY
T-Dt: -- --- -----
P-Dt: 28 Oct 1857
Dist/Class: Texas Emmigration and Land
Company
File#: 165
Patent#: 165
Patent Vol.: 14
Certificate: 165
Survey/Blk/Twp: 165
Acres: 320
Map(s) 3, 11

Abstract # 413 - TE&L CO
P'ee: TEXAS EMIGRATION AND LAND
COMPANY
G'ee: TEXAS EMIGRATION AND LAND
COMPANY
T-Dt: -- --- -----
P-Dt: 28 Oct 1857
Dist/Class: Texas Emmigration and Land
Company
File#: 166
Patent#: 166
Patent Vol.: 14
Certificate: 166
Survey/Blk/Twp: 166

Acres: 320
Map(s) 3, 11

Abstract # 414 - TE&L CO
P'ee: TEXAS EMIGRATION AND LAND
COMPANY
G'ee: TEXAS EMIGRATION AND LAND
COMPANY
T-Dt: -- --- -----
P-Dt: 28 Oct 1857
Dist/Class: Texas Emmigration and Land
Company
File#: 167
Patent#: 167
Patent Vol.: 14
Certificate: 167
Survey/Blk/Twp: 167
Acres: 320
Map(s) 3

Abstract # 415 - TE&L CO
P'ee: TEXAS EMIGRATION AND LAND
COMPANY
G'ee: TEXAS EMIGRATION AND LAND
COMPANY
T-Dt: -- --- -----
P-Dt: 31 Oct 1857
Dist/Class: Texas Emmigration and Land
Company
File#: 168
Patent#: 168
Patent Vol.: 14
Certificate: 168
Survey/Blk/Twp: 168
Acres: 320
Map(s) 3

Abstract # 416 - TE&L CO
P'ee: TEXAS EMIGRATION AND LAND
COMPANY
G'ee: TEXAS EMIGRATION AND LAND
COMPANY
T-Dt: -- --- -----
P-Dt: 31 Oct 1857
Dist/Class: Texas Emmigration and Land
Company
File#: 169
Patent#: 169
Patent Vol.: 14
Certificate: 169
Survey/Blk/Twp: 169
Acres: 320
Map(s) 3

Abstract # 417 - TE&L CO
P'ee: TEXAS EMIGRATION AND LAND
COMPANY
G'ee: TEXAS EMIGRATION AND LAND
COMPANY
T-Dt: -- --- -----
P-Dt: 31 Oct 1857
Dist/Class: Texas Emmigration and Land
Company
File#: 170
Patent#: 170
Patent Vol.: 14
Certificate: 170
Survey/Blk/Twp: 170
Acres: 320
Map(s) 3

Abstract # 418 - TE&L CO
P'ee: TEXAS EMIGRATION AND LAND
COMPANY
G'ee: TEXAS EMIGRATION AND LAND

COMPANY
T-Dt: -- --- -----
P-Dt: 31 Oct 1857
Dist/Class: Texas Emmigration and Land
Company
File#: 171
Patent#: 171
Patent Vol.: 14
Certificate: 171
Survey/Blk/Twp: 171
Acres: 320
Map(s) 3

Abstract # 419 - TE&L CO
P'ee: TEXAS EMIGRATION AND LAND
COMPANY
G'ee: TEXAS EMIGRATION AND LAND
COMPANY
T-Dt: -- --- -----
P-Dt: 31 Oct 1857
Dist/Class: Texas Emmigration and Land
Company
File#: 172
Patent#: 172
Patent Vol.: 14
Certificate: 172
Survey/Blk/Twp: 172
Acres: 320
Map(s) 3

Abstract # 420 - TE&L CO
P'ee: TEXAS EMIGRATION AND LAND
COMPANY
G'ee: TEXAS EMIGRATION AND LAND
COMPANY
T-Dt: -- --- -----
P-Dt: 20 Oct 1857
Dist/Class: Texas Emmigration and Land
Company
File#: 173
Patent#: 173
Patent Vol.: 14
Certificate: 173
Survey/Blk/Twp: 173
Acres: 320
Map(s) 3

Abstract # 421 - TE&L CO
P'ee: TEXAS EMIGRATION AND LAND
COMPANY
G'ee: TEXAS EMIGRATION AND LAND
COMPANY
T-Dt: -- --- -----
P-Dt: 31 Oct 1857
Dist/Class: Texas Emmigration and Land
Company
File#: 174
Patent#: 174
Patent Vol.: 14
Certificate: 174
Survey/Blk/Twp: 174
Acres: 320
Map(s) 3

Abstract # 422 - TE&L CO
P'ee: TEXAS EMIGRATION AND LAND
COMPANY
G'ee: TEXAS EMIGRATION AND LAND
COMPANY
T-Dt: -- --- -----
P-Dt: 31 Oct 1857
Dist/Class: Texas Emmigration and Land
Company
File#: 175
Patent#: 175

Patent Vol.: 14
Certificate: 175
Survey/Blk/Twp: 175
Acres: 320
Map(s) 3

Abstract # 423 - TE&L CO
P'ee: TEXAS EMIGRATION AND LAND
COMPANY
G'ee: TEXAS EMIGRATION AND LAND
COMPANY
T-Dt: -- --- -----
P-Dt: 31 Oct 1857
Dist/Class: Texas Emmigration and Land
Company
File#: 176
Patent#: 176
Patent Vol.: 14
Certificate: 176
Survey/Blk/Twp: 176
Acres: 320
Map(s) 3

Abstract # 424 - TE&L CO
P'ee: TEXAS EMIGRATION AND LAND
COMPANY
G'ee: TEXAS EMIGRATION AND LAND
COMPANY
T-Dt: -- --- -----
P-Dt: 31 Oct 1857
Dist/Class: Texas Emmigration and Land
Company
File#: 177
Patent#: 177
Patent Vol.: 14
Certificate: 177
Survey/Blk/Twp: 177
Acres: 320
Map(s) 3

Abstract # 425 - TE&L CO
P'ee: TEXAS EMIGRATION AND LAND
COMPANY
G'ee: TEXAS EMIGRATION AND LAND
COMPANY
T-Dt: -- --- -----
P-Dt: 31 Oct 1857
Dist/Class: Texas Emmigration and Land
Company
File#: 178
Patent#: 178
Patent Vol.: 14
Certificate: 178
Survey/Blk/Twp: 178
Acres: 320
Map(s) 3

Abstract # 426 - TE&L CO
P'ee: TEXAS EMIGRATION AND LAND
COMPANY
G'ee: TEXAS EMIGRATION AND LAND
COMPANY
T-Dt: -- --- -----
P-Dt: 31 Oct 1857
Dist/Class: Texas Emmigration and Land
Company
File#: 179
Patent#: 179
Patent Vol.: 14
Certificate: 179
Survey/Blk/Twp: 179
Acres: 320
Map(s) 3

Abstract # 427 - TE&L CO

P'ee: TEXAS EMIGRATION AND LAND
COMPANY
G'ee: TEXAS EMIGRATION AND LAND
COMPANY
T-Dt: -- --- -----
P-Dt: 10 Nov 1857
Dist/Class: Texas Emmigration and Land
Company
File#: 180
Patent#: 180
Patent Vol.: 14
Certificate: 180
Survey/Blk/Twp: 180
Acres: 320
Map(s) 3

Abstract # 428 - TE&L CO
P'ee: TEXAS EMIGRATION AND LAND
COMPANY
G'ee: TEXAS EMIGRATION AND LAND
COMPANY
T-Dt: -- --- -----
P-Dt: 11 Nov 1857
Dist/Class: Texas Emmigration and Land
Company
File#: 181
Patent#: 181
Patent Vol.: 14
Certificate: 181
Survey/Blk/Twp: 181
Acres: 320
Map(s) 3, 11

Abstract # 429 - TE&L CO
P'ee: TEXAS EMIGRATION AND LAND
COMPANY
G'ee: TEXAS EMIGRATION AND LAND
COMPANY
T-Dt: -- --- -----
P-Dt: 11 Nov 1857
Dist/Class: Texas Emmigration and Land
Company
File#: 182
Patent#: 182
Patent Vol.: 14
Certificate: 182
Survey/Blk/Twp: 182
Acres: 320
Map(s) 3, 11

Abstract # 430 - TE&L CO
P'ee: TEXAS EMIGRATION AND LAND
COMPANY
G'ee: TEXAS EMIGRATION AND LAND
COMPANY
T-Dt: -- --- -----
P-Dt: 11 Nov 1857
Dist/Class: Texas Emmigration and Land
Company
File#: 183
Patent#: 183
Patent Vol.: 14
Certificate: 183
Survey/Blk/Twp: 183
Acres: 320
Map(s) 3

Abstract # 431 - TE&L CO
P'ee: TEXAS EMIGRATION AND LAND
COMPANY
G'ee: TEXAS EMIGRATION AND LAND
COMPANY
T-Dt: -- --- -----
P-Dt: 11 Nov 1857
Dist/Class: Texas Emmigration and Land

Company
File#: 184
Patent#: 184
Patent Vol.: 14
Certificate: 184
Survey/Blk/Twp: 184
Acres: 320
Map(s) 3

Abstract # 432 - TE&L CO
P'ee: TEXAS EMIGRATION AND LAND
COMPANY
G'ee: TEXAS EMIGRATION AND LAND
COMPANY
T-Dt: -- --- -----
P-Dt: 17 Dec 1857
Dist/Class: Texas Emmigration and Land
Company
File#: 185
Patent#: 272
Patent Vol.: 14
Certificate: 185
Survey/Blk/Twp: 185
Acres: 320
Map(s) 3

Abstract # 433 - TE&L CO
P'ee: TEXAS EMIGRATION AND LAND
COMPANY
G'ee: TEXAS EMIGRATION AND LAND
COMPANY
T-Dt: -- --- -----
P-Dt: 18 Dec 1857
Dist/Class: Texas Emmigration and Land
Company
File#: 186
Patent#: 276
Patent Vol.: 14
Certificate: 186
Survey/Blk/Twp: 186
Acres: 320
Map(s) 3

Abstract # 434 - TE&L CO
P'ee: TEXAS EMIGRATION AND LAND
COMPANY
G'ee: TEXAS EMIGRATION AND LAND
COMPANY
T-Dt: -- --- -----
P-Dt: 18 Dec 1857
Dist/Class: Texas Emmigration and Land
Company
File#: 187
Patent#: 277
Patent Vol.: 14
Certificate: 187
Survey/Blk/Twp: 187
Acres: 320
Map(s) 3

Abstract # 435 - TE&L CO
P'ee: TEXAS EMIGRATION AND LAND
COMPANY
G'ee: TEXAS EMIGRATION AND LAND
COMPANY
T-Dt: -- --- -----
P-Dt: 12 Nov 1857
Dist/Class: Texas Emmigration and Land
Company
File#: 188
Patent#: 188
Patent Vol.: 14
Certificate: 188
Survey/Blk/Twp: 188
Acres: 320

Map(s) 3

Abstract # 436 - TE&L CO
P'ee: TEXAS EMIGRATION AND LAND COMPANY
G'ee: TEXAS EMIGRATION AND LAND COMPANY
T-Dt: -- --- -----
P-Dt: 13 Nov 1857
Dist/Class: Texas Emmigration and Land Company
File#: 189
Patent#: 189
Patent Vol.: 14
Certificate: 189
Survey/Blk/Twp: 189
Acres: 320
Map(s) 3

Abstract # 437 - TE&L CO
P'ee: TEXAS EMIGRATION AND LAND COMPANY
G'ee: TEXAS EMIGRATION AND LAND COMPANY
T-Dt: -- --- -----
P-Dt: 13 Nov 1857
Dist/Class: Texas Emmigration and Land Company
File#: 190
Patent#: 190
Patent Vol.: 14
Certificate: 190
Survey/Blk/Twp: 190
Acres: 320
Map(s) 2, 3

Abstract # 438 - TE&L CO
P'ee: TEXAS EMIGRATION AND LAND COMPANY
G'ee: TEXAS EMIGRATION AND LAND COMPANY
T-Dt: -- --- -----
P-Dt: 13 Nov 1857
Dist/Class: Texas Emmigration and Land Company
File#: 191
Patent#: 191
Patent Vol.: 14
Certificate: 191
Survey/Blk/Twp: 191
Acres: 320
Map(s) 2, 3

Abstract # 439 - TE&L CO
P'ee: TEXAS EMIGRATION AND LAND COMPANY
G'ee: TEXAS EMIGRATION AND LAND COMPANY
T-Dt: -- --- -----
P-Dt: 13 Nov 1857
Dist/Class: Texas Emmigration and Land Company
File#: 192
Patent#: 192
Patent Vol.: 14
Certificate: 192
Survey/Blk/Twp: 192
Acres: 320
Map(s) 2, 3

Abstract # 440 - TE&L CO
P'ee: TEXAS EMIGRATION AND LAND COMPANY
G'ee: TEXAS EMIGRATION AND LAND COMPANY

T-Dt: -- --- -----
P-Dt: 13 Nov 1857
Dist/Class: Texas Emmigration and Land Company
File#: 193
Patent#: 193
Patent Vol.: 14
Certificate: 193
Survey/Blk/Twp: 193
Acres: 320
Map(s) 2, 3

Abstract # 441 - TE&L CO
P'ee: TEXAS EMIGRATION AND LAND COMPANY
G'ee: TEXAS EMIGRATION AND LAND COMPANY
T-Dt: -- --- -----
P-Dt: 16 Nov 1857
Dist/Class: Texas Emmigration and Land Company
File#: 194
Patent#: 194
Patent Vol.: 14
Certificate: 194
Survey/Blk/Twp: 194
Acres: 320
Map(s) 2, 3

Abstract # 442 - TE&L CO
P'ee: TEXAS EMIGRATION AND LAND COMPANY
G'ee: TEXAS EMIGRATION AND LAND COMPANY
T-Dt: -- --- -----
P-Dt: 16 Nov 1857
Dist/Class: Texas Emmigration and Land Company
File#: 195
Patent#: 195
Patent Vol.: 14
Certificate: 195
Survey/Blk/Twp: 195
Acres: 320
Map(s) 2, 3

Abstract # 443 - TE&L CO
P'ee: TEXAS EMIGRATION AND LAND COMPANY
G'ee: TEXAS EMIGRATION AND LAND COMPANY
T-Dt: -- --- -----
P-Dt: 16 Nov 1857
Dist/Class: Texas Emmigration and Land Company
File#: 196
Patent#: 196
Patent Vol.: 14
Certificate: 196
Survey/Blk/Twp: 196
Acres: 320
Map(s) 2, 3

Abstract # 444 - TE&L CO
P'ee: TEXAS EMIGRATION AND LAND COMPANY
G'ee: TEXAS EMIGRATION AND LAND COMPANY
T-Dt: -- --- -----
P-Dt: 16 Nov 1857
Dist/Class: Texas Emmigration and Land Company
File#: 197
Patent#: 197
Patent Vol.: 14

Certificate: 197
Survey/Blk/Twp: 197
Acres: 320
Map(s) 2, 3, 10, 11

Abstract # 445 - TE&L CO
P'ee: TEXAS EMIGRATION AND LAND COMPANY
G'ee: TEXAS EMIGRATION AND LAND COMPANY
T-Dt: -- --- -----
P-Dt: 16 Nov 1857
Dist/Class: Texas Emmigration and Land Company
File#: 198
Patent#: 198
Patent Vol.: 14
Certificate: 198
Survey/Blk/Twp: 198
Acres: 320
Map(s) 2, 10

Abstract # 446 - TE&L CO
P'ee: TEXAS EMIGRATION AND LAND COMPANY
G'ee: TEXAS EMIGRATION AND LAND COMPANY
T-Dt: -- --- -----
P-Dt: 16 Nov 1857
Dist/Class: Texas Emmigration and Land Company
File#: 199
Patent#: 199
Patent Vol.: 14
Certificate: 199
Survey/Blk/Twp: 199
Acres: 320
Map(s) 2

Abstract # 447 - TE&L CO
P'ee: TEXAS EMIGRATION AND LAND COMPANY
G'ee: TEXAS EMIGRATION AND LAND COMPANY
T-Dt: -- --- -----
P-Dt: 16 Nov 1857
Dist/Class: Texas Emmigration and Land Company
File#: 200
Patent#: 200
Patent Vol.: 14
Certificate: 200
Survey/Blk/Twp: 200
Acres: 320
Map(s) 2

Abstract # 448 - TE&L CO
P'ee: TEXAS EMIGRATION AND LAND COMPANY
G'ee: TEXAS EMIGRATION AND LAND COMPANY
T-Dt: -- --- -----
P-Dt: 19 Nov 1857
Dist/Class: Texas Emmigration and Land Company
File#: 201
Patent#: 201
Patent Vol.: 14
Certificate: 201
Survey/Blk/Twp: 201
Acres: 320
Map(s) 3, 4, 11, 12

Abstract # 449 - TE&L CO
P'ee: TEXAS EMIGRATION AND LAND

COMPANY
G'ee: TEXAS EMIGRATION AND LAND
COMPANY
T-Dt: -- --- -----
P-Dt: 19 Nov 1857
Dist/Class: Texas Emmigration and Land
Company
File#: 202
Patent#: 202
Patent Vol.: 14
Certificate: 202
Survey/Blk/Twp: 202
Acres: 320
Map(s) 4, 12

Abstract # 450 - TE&L CO
P'ee: TEXAS EMIGRATION AND LAND
COMPANY
G'ee: TEXAS EMIGRATION AND LAND
COMPANY
T-Dt: -- --- -----
P-Dt: 19 Nov 1857
Dist/Class: Texas Emmigration and Land
Company
File#: 203
Patent#: 203
Patent Vol.: 14
Certificate: 203
Survey/Blk/Twp: 203
Acres: 320
Map(s) 4, 12

Abstract # 451 - TE&L CO
P'ee: TEXAS EMIGRATION AND LAND
COMPANY
G'ee: TEXAS EMIGRATION AND LAND
COMPANY
T-Dt: -- --- -----
P-Dt: 28 Sep 1953
Dist/Class: Texas Emmigration and Land
Company
File#: 204
Patent#: 98
Patent Vol.: 23-B
Certificate: 204
Survey/Blk/Twp: 204
Acres: 320
Map(s) 4, 12

Abstract # 452 - TE&L CO
P'ee: TEXAS EMIGRATION AND LAND
COMPANY
G'ee: TEXAS EMIGRATION AND LAND
COMPANY
T-Dt: -- --- -----
P-Dt: 23 Nov 1857
Dist/Class: Texas Emmigration and Land
Company
File#: 205
Patent#: 205
Patent Vol.: 14
Certificate: 205
Survey/Blk/Twp: 205
Acres: 320
Map(s) 4, 12

Abstract # 453 - TE&L CO
P'ee: TEXAS EMIGRATION AND LAND
COMPANY
G'ee: TEXAS EMIGRATION AND LAND
COMPANY
T-Dt: -- --- -----
P-Dt: 23 Nov 1857
Dist/Class: Texas Emmigration and Land
Company

File#: 206
Patent#: 206
Patent Vol.: 14
Certificate: 206
Survey/Blk/Twp: 206
Acres: 320
Map(s) 4

Abstract # 454 - TE&L CO
P'ee: TEXAS EMIGRATION AND LAND
COMPANY
G'ee: TEXAS EMIGRATION AND LAND
COMPANY
T-Dt: -- --- -----
P-Dt: 23 Nov 1857
Dist/Class: Texas Emmigration and Land
Company
File#: 207
Patent#: 207
Patent Vol.: 14
Certificate: 207
Survey/Blk/Twp: 207
Acres: 320
Map(s) 4

Abstract # 455 - TE&L CO
P'ee: TEXAS EMIGRATION AND LAND
COMPANY
G'ee: TEXAS EMIGRATION AND LAND
COMPANY
T-Dt: -- --- -----
P-Dt: 23 Nov 1857
Dist/Class: Texas Emmigration and Land
Company
File#: 208
Patent#: 208
Patent Vol.: 14
Certificate: 208
Survey/Blk/Twp: 208
Acres: 320
Map(s) 4

Abstract # 456 - TE&L CO
P'ee: TEXAS EMIGRATION AND LAND
COMPANY
G'ee: TEXAS EMIGRATION AND LAND
COMPANY
T-Dt: -- --- -----
P-Dt: 23 Nov 1857
Dist/Class: Texas Emmigration and Land
Company
File#: 209
Patent#: 209
Patent Vol.: 14
Certificate: 209
Survey/Blk/Twp: 209
Acres: 320
Map(s) 4

Abstract # 457 - TE&L CO
P'ee: TEXAS EMIGRATION AND LAND
COMPANY
G'ee: TEXAS EMIGRATION AND LAND
COMPANY
T-Dt: -- --- -----
P-Dt: 23 Nov 1857
Dist/Class: Texas Emmigration and Land
Company
File#: 210
Patent#: 210
Patent Vol.: 14
Certificate: 210
Survey/Blk/Twp: 210
Acres: 320
Map(s) 3, 4

Abstract # 458 - TE&L CO
P'ee: TEXAS EMIGRATION AND LAND
COMPANY
G'ee: TEXAS EMIGRATION AND LAND
COMPANY
T-Dt: -- --- -----
P-Dt: 23 Nov 1857
Dist/Class: Texas Emmigration and Land
Company
File#: 211
Patent#: 211
Patent Vol.: 14
Certificate: 211
Survey/Blk/Twp: 211
Acres: 320
Map(s) 3, 4

Abstract # 459 - TE&L CO
P'ee: TEXAS EMIGRATION AND LAND
COMPANY
G'ee: TEXAS EMIGRATION AND LAND
COMPANY
T-Dt: -- --- -----
P-Dt: 24 Nov 1857
Dist/Class: Texas Emmigration and Land
Company
File#: 212
Patent#: 212
Patent Vol.: 14
Certificate: 212
Survey/Blk/Twp: 212
Acres: 320
Map(s) 4

Abstract # 460 - TE&L CO
P'ee: TEXAS EMIGRATION AND LAND
COMPANY
G'ee: TEXAS EMIGRATION AND LAND
COMPANY
T-Dt: -- --- -----
P-Dt: 24 Nov 1857
Dist/Class: Texas Emmigration and Land
Company
File#: 213
Patent#: 213
Patent Vol.: 14
Certificate: 213
Survey/Blk/Twp: 213
Acres: 320
Map(s) 4

Abstract # 461 - TE&L CO
P'ee: TEXAS EMIGRATION AND LAND
COMPANY
G'ee: TEXAS EMIGRATION AND LAND
COMPANY
T-Dt: -- --- -----
P-Dt: 24 Nov 1857
Dist/Class: Texas Emmigration and Land
Company
File#: 214
Patent#: 214
Patent Vol.: 14
Certificate: 214
Survey/Blk/Twp: 214
Acres: 320
Map(s) 4

Abstract # 462 - TE&L CO
P'ee: TEXAS EMIGRATION AND LAND
COMPANY
G'ee: TEXAS EMIGRATION AND LAND
COMPANY
T-Dt: -- --- -----
P-Dt: 24 Nov 1857

Dist/Class: Texas Emmigration and Land
Company
File#: 215
Patent#: 215
Patent Vol.: 14
Certificate: 215
Survey/Blk/Twp: 215
Acres: 320
Map(s) 4

Abstract # 463 - TE&L CO
P'ee: TEXAS EMIGRATION AND LAND
COMPANY
G'ee: TEXAS EMIGRATION AND LAND
COMPANY
T-Dt: -- --- -----
P-Dt: 18 May 1858
Dist/Class: Texas Emmigration and Land
Company
File#: 216
Patent#: 646
Patent Vol.: 14
Certificate: 216
Survey/Blk/Twp: 216
Acres: 320
Map(s) 4

Abstract # 464 - TE&L CO
P'ee: TEXAS EMIGRATION AND LAND
COMPANY
G'ee: TEXAS EMIGRATION AND LAND
COMPANY
T-Dt: -- --- -----
P-Dt: 24 Nov 1857
Dist/Class: Texas Emmigration and Land
Company
File#: 217
Patent#: 217
Patent Vol.: 14
Certificate: 217
Survey/Blk/Twp: 217
Acres: 320
Map(s) 4

Abstract # 465 - TE&L CO
P'ee: TEXAS EMIGRATION AND LAND
COMPANY
G'ee: TEXAS EMIGRATION AND LAND
COMPANY
T-Dt: -- --- -----
P-Dt: 24 Nov 1857
Dist/Class: Texas Emmigration and Land
Company
File#: 218
Patent#: 218
Patent Vol.: 14
Certificate: 218
Survey/Blk/Twp: 218
Acres: 320
Map(s) 4

Abstract # 466 - TE&L CO
P'ee: TEXAS EMIGRATION AND LAND
COMPANY
G'ee: TEXAS EMIGRATION AND LAND
COMPANY
T-Dt: -- --- -----
P-Dt: 24 Nov 1857
Dist/Class: Texas Emmigration and Land
Company
File#: 219
Patent#: 219
Patent Vol.: 14
Certificate: 219
Survey/Blk/Twp: 219

Acres: 320
Map(s) 4

Abstract # 467 - TE&L CO
P'ee: TEXAS EMIGRATION AND LAND
COMPANY
G'ee: TEXAS EMIGRATION AND LAND
COMPANY
T-Dt: -- --- -----
P-Dt: 24 Nov 1857
Dist/Class: Texas Emmigration and Land
Company
File#: 220
Patent#: 220
Patent Vol.: 14
Certificate: 220
Survey/Blk/Twp: 220
Acres: 320
Map(s) 3, 4

Abstract # 468 - TE&L CO
P'ee: TEXAS EMIGRATION AND LAND
COMPANY
G'ee: TEXAS EMIGRATION AND LAND
COMPANY
T-Dt: -- --- -----
P-Dt: 25 Nov 1857
Dist/Class: Texas Emmigration and Land
Company
File#: 221
Patent#: 221
Patent Vol.: 14
Certificate: 221
Survey/Blk/Twp: 221
Acres: 320
Map(s) 3, 4

Abstract # 469 - TE&L CO
P'ee: TEXAS EMIGRATION AND LAND
COMPANY
G'ee: TEXAS EMIGRATION AND LAND
COMPANY
T-Dt: -- --- -----
P-Dt: 25 Nov 1857
Dist/Class: Texas Emmigration and Land
Company
File#: 222
Patent#: 222
Patent Vol.: 14
Certificate: 222
Survey/Blk/Twp: 222
Acres: 320
Map(s) 4

Abstract # 470 - TE&L CO
P'ee: TEXAS EMIGRATION AND LAND
COMPANY
G'ee: TEXAS EMIGRATION AND LAND
COMPANY
T-Dt: -- --- -----
P-Dt: 25 Nov 1857
Dist/Class: Texas Emmigration and Land
Company
File#: 223
Patent#: 223
Patent Vol.: 14
Certificate: 223
Survey/Blk/Twp: 223
Acres: 320
Map(s) 4

Abstract # 471 - TE&L CO
P'ee: TEXAS EMIGRATION AND LAND
COMPANY
G'ee: TEXAS EMIGRATION AND LAND

COMPANY
T-Dt: -- --- -----
P-Dt: 25 Nov 1857
Dist/Class: Texas Emmigration and Land
Company
File#: 224
Patent#: 224
Patent Vol.: 14
Certificate: 224
Survey/Blk/Twp: 224
Acres: 320
Map(s) 4

Abstract # 472 - TE&L CO
P'ee: TEXAS EMIGRATION AND LAND
COMPANY
G'ee: TEXAS EMIGRATION AND LAND
COMPANY
T-Dt: -- --- -----
P-Dt: 25 Nov 1857
Dist/Class: Texas Emmigration and Land
Company
File#: 225
Patent#: 225
Patent Vol.: 14
Certificate: 225
Survey/Blk/Twp: 225
Acres: 320
Map(s) 4

Abstract # 473 - TE&L CO
P'ee: TEXAS EMIGRATION AND LAND
COMPANY
G'ee: TEXAS EMIGRATION AND LAND
COMPANY
T-Dt: -- --- -----
P-Dt: 25 Nov 1857
Dist/Class: Texas Emmigration and Land
Company
File#: 226
Patent#: 226
Patent Vol.: 14
Certificate: 226
Survey/Blk/Twp: 226
Acres: 320
Map(s) 4

Abstract # 474 - TE&L CO
P'ee: TEXAS EMIGRATION AND LAND
COMPANY
G'ee: TEXAS EMIGRATION AND LAND
COMPANY
T-Dt: -- --- -----
P-Dt: 25 Nov 1857
Dist/Class: Texas Emmigration and Land
Company
File#: 227
Patent#: 227
Patent Vol.: 14
Certificate: 227
Survey/Blk/Twp: 227
Acres: 320
Map(s) 4

Abstract # 475 - TE&L CO
P'ee: TEXAS EMIGRATION AND LAND
COMPANY
G'ee: TEXAS EMIGRATION AND LAND
COMPANY
T-Dt: -- --- -----
P-Dt: 27 Nov 1857
Dist/Class: Texas Emmigration and Land
Company
File#: 228
Patent#: 228

Patent Vol.: 14
Certificate: 228
Survey/Blk/Twp: 228
Acres: 320
Map(s) 4

Abstract # 476 - TE&L CO
P'ee: TEXAS EMIGRATION AND LAND COMPANY
G'ee: TEXAS EMIGRATION AND LAND COMPANY
T-Dt: -- --- -----
P-Dt: 28 Nov 1857
Dist/Class: Texas Emmigration and Land Company
File#: 229
Patent#: 229
Patent Vol.: 14
Certificate: 229
Survey/Blk/Twp: 229
Acres: 320
Map(s) 4

Abstract # 477 - TE&L CO
P'ee: TEXAS EMIGRATION AND LAND COMPANY
G'ee: TEXAS EMIGRATION AND LAND COMPANY
T-Dt: -- --- -----
P-Dt: 28 Nov 1857
Dist/Class: Texas Emmigration and Land Company
File#: 230
Patent#: 230
Patent Vol.: 14
Certificate: 230
Survey/Blk/Twp: 230
Acres: 320
Map(s) 3, 4

Abstract # 478 - TE&L CO
P'ee: TEXAS EMIGRATION AND LAND COMPANY
G'ee: TEXAS EMIGRATION AND LAND COMPANY
T-Dt: -- --- -----
P-Dt: 28 Nov 1857
Dist/Class: Texas Emmigration and Land Company
File#: 231
Patent#: 231
Patent Vol.: 14
Certificate: 231
Survey/Blk/Twp: 231
Acres: 320
Map(s) 3, 4

Abstract # 479 - TE&L CO
P'ee: TEXAS EMIGRATION AND LAND COMPANY
G'ee: TEXAS EMIGRATION AND LAND COMPANY
T-Dt: -- --- -----
P-Dt: 30 Nov 1857
Dist/Class: Texas Emmigration and Land Company
File#: 232
Patent#: 232
Patent Vol.: 14
Certificate: 232
Survey/Blk/Twp: 232
Acres: 320
Map(s) 4

Abstract # 480 - TE&L CO

P'ee: TEXAS EMIGRATION AND LAND COMPANY
G'ee: TEXAS EMIGRATION AND LAND COMPANY
T-Dt: -- --- -----
P-Dt: 30 Nov 1857
Dist/Class: Texas Emmigration and Land Company
File#: 233
Patent#: 233
Patent Vol.: 14
Certificate: 233
Survey/Blk/Twp: 233
Acres: 320
Map(s) 4

Abstract # 481 - TE&L CO
P'ee: TEXAS EMIGRATION AND LAND COMPANY
G'ee: TEXAS EMIGRATION AND LAND COMPANY
T-Dt: -- --- -----
P-Dt: 30 Nov 1857
Dist/Class: Texas Emmigration and Land Company
File#: 234
Patent#: 234
Patent Vol.: 14
Certificate: 234
Survey/Blk/Twp: 234
Acres: 320
Map(s) 4

Abstract # 482 - TE&L CO
P'ee: TEXAS EMIGRATION AND LAND COMPANY
G'ee: TEXAS EMIGRATION AND LAND COMPANY
T-Dt: -- --- -----
P-Dt: 01 Dec 1857
Dist/Class: Texas Emmigration and Land Company
File#: 235
Patent#: 235
Patent Vol.: 14
Certificate: 235
Survey/Blk/Twp: 235
Acres: 320
Map(s) 4

Abstract # 483 - TE&L CO
P'ee: TEXAS EMIGRATION AND LAND COMPANY
G'ee: TEXAS EMIGRATION AND LAND COMPANY
T-Dt: -- --- -----
P-Dt: 01 Dec 1857
Dist/Class: Texas Emmigration and Land Company
File#: 236
Patent#: 236
Patent Vol.: 14
Certificate: 236
Survey/Blk/Twp: 236
Acres: 320
Map(s) 4

Abstract # 484 - TE&L CO
P'ee: TEXAS EMIGRATION AND LAND COMPANY
G'ee: TEXAS EMIGRATION AND LAND COMPANY
T-Dt: -- --- -----
P-Dt: 01 Dec 1857
Dist/Class: Texas Emmigration and Land

Company
File#: 237
Patent#: 237
Patent Vol.: 14
Certificate: 237
Survey/Blk/Twp: 237
Acres: 320
Map(s) 4

Abstract # 485 - TE&L CO
P'ee: TEXAS EMIGRATION AND LAND COMPANY
G'ee: TEXAS EMIGRATION AND LAND COMPANY
T-Dt: -- --- -----
P-Dt: 01 Dec 1857
Dist/Class: Texas Emmigration and Land Company
File#: 238
Patent#: 238
Patent Vol.: 14
Certificate: 238
Survey/Blk/Twp: 238
Acres: 320
Map(s) 4

Abstract # 486 - TE&L CO
P'ee: TEXAS EMIGRATION AND LAND COMPANY
G'ee: TEXAS EMIGRATION AND LAND COMPANY
T-Dt: -- --- -----
P-Dt: 01 Dec 1857
Dist/Class: Texas Emmigration and Land Company
File#: 239
Patent#: 239
Patent Vol.: 14
Certificate: 239
Survey/Blk/Twp: 239
Acres: 320
Map(s) 4

Abstract # 487 - TE&L CO
P'ee: TEXAS EMIGRATION AND LAND COMPANY
G'ee: TEXAS EMIGRATION AND LAND COMPANY
T-Dt: -- --- -----
P-Dt: 01 Dec 1857
Dist/Class: Texas Emmigration and Land Company
File#: 240
Patent#: 240
Patent Vol.: 14
Certificate: 240
Survey/Blk/Twp: 240
Acres: 320
Map(s) 3, 4

Abstract # 488 - TE&L CO
P'ee: TEXAS EMIGRATION AND LAND COMPANY
G'ee: TEXAS EMIGRATION AND LAND COMPANY
T-Dt: -- --- -----
P-Dt: 02 Dec 1857
Dist/Class: Texas Emmigration and Land Company
File#: 241
Patent#: 241
Patent Vol.: 14
Certificate: 241
Survey/Blk/Twp: 241
Acres: 320

Map(s) 11, 12

Abstract # 489 - TE&L CO
P'ee: TEXAS EMIGRATION AND LAND COMPANY
G'ee: TEXAS EMIGRATION AND LAND COMPANY
T-Dt: -- --- -----
P-Dt: 02 Dec 1857
Dist/Class: Texas Emmigration and Land Company
File#: 242
Patent#: 242
Patent Vol.: 14
Certificate: 242
Survey/Blk/Twp: 242
Acres: 320
Map(s) 12

Abstract # 490 - TE&L CO
P'ee: TEXAS EMIGRATION AND LAND COMPANY
G'ee: TEXAS EMIGRATION AND LAND COMPANY
T-Dt: -- --- -----
P-Dt: 03 Dec 1857
Dist/Class: Texas Emmigration and Land Company
File#: 243
Patent#: 243
Patent Vol.: 14
Certificate: 243
Survey/Blk/Twp: 243
Acres: 320
Map(s) 12

Abstract # 491 - TE&L CO
P'ee: TEXAS EMIGRATION AND LAND COMPANY
G'ee: TEXAS EMIGRATION AND LAND COMPANY
T-Dt: -- --- -----
P-Dt: 03 Dec 1857
Dist/Class: Texas Emmigration and Land Company
File#: 244
Patent#: 244
Patent Vol.: 14
Certificate: 244
Survey/Blk/Twp: 244
Acres: 320
Map(s) 12

Abstract # 492 - TE&L CO
P'ee: TEXAS EMIGRATION AND LAND COMPANY
G'ee: TEXAS EMIGRATION AND LAND COMPANY
T-Dt: -- --- -----
P-Dt: 03 Dec 1857
Dist/Class: Texas Emmigration and Land Company
File#: 245
Patent#: 245
Patent Vol.: 14
Certificate: 245
Survey/Blk/Twp: 245
Acres: 320
Map(s) 12

Abstract # 493 - TE&L CO
P'ee: TEXAS EMIGRATION AND LAND COMPANY
G'ee: TEXAS EMIGRATION AND LAND COMPANY

T-Dt: -- --- -----
P-Dt: 03 Dec 1857
Dist/Class: Texas Emmigration and Land Company
File#: 246
Patent#: 246
Patent Vol.: 14
Certificate: 246
Survey/Blk/Twp: 246
Acres: 320
Map(s) 12

Abstract # 494 - TE&L CO
P'ee: TEXAS EMIGRATION AND LAND COMPANY
G'ee: TEXAS EMIGRATION AND LAND COMPANY
T-Dt: -- --- -----
P-Dt: 03 Dec 1857
Dist/Class: Texas Emmigration and Land Company
File#: 247
Patent#: 247
Patent Vol.: 14
Certificate: 247
Survey/Blk/Twp: 247
Acres: 320
Map(s) 4, 12

Abstract # 495 - TE&L CO
P'ee: TEXAS EMIGRATION AND LAND COMPANY
G'ee: TEXAS EMIGRATION AND LAND COMPANY
T-Dt: -- --- -----
P-Dt: 03 Dec 1857
Dist/Class: Texas Emmigration and Land Company
File#: 248
Patent#: 248
Patent Vol.: 14
Certificate: 248
Survey/Blk/Twp: 248
Acres: 320
Map(s) 12

Abstract # 496 - TE&L CO
P'ee: TEXAS EMIGRATION AND LAND COMPANY
G'ee: TEXAS EMIGRATION AND LAND COMPANY
T-Dt: -- --- -----
P-Dt: 04 Dec 1857
Dist/Class: Texas Emmigration and Land Company
File#: 249
Patent#: 249
Patent Vol.: 14
Certificate: 249
Survey/Blk/Twp: 249
Acres: 320
Map(s) 12

Abstract # 497 - TE&L CO
P'ee: TEXAS EMIGRATION AND LAND COMPANY
G'ee: TEXAS EMIGRATION AND LAND COMPANY
T-Dt: -- --- -----
P-Dt: 04 Dec 1857
Dist/Class: Texas Emmigration and Land Company
File#: 250
Patent#: 250
Patent Vol.: 14

Certificate: 250
Survey/Blk/Twp: 250
Acres: 320
Map(s) 12

Abstract # 498 - TE&L CO
P'ee: TEXAS EMIGRATION AND LAND COMPANY
G'ee: TEXAS EMIGRATION AND LAND COMPANY
T-Dt: -- --- -----
P-Dt: 04 Dec 1857
Dist/Class: Texas Emmigration and Land Company
File#: 251
Patent#: 251
Patent Vol.: 14
Certificate: 251
Survey/Blk/Twp: 251
Acres: 320
Map(s) 12

Abstract # 499 - TE&L CO
P'ee: TEXAS EMIGRATION AND LAND COMPANY
G'ee: TEXAS EMIGRATION AND LAND COMPANY
T-Dt: -- --- -----
P-Dt: 04 Dec 1857
Dist/Class: Texas Emmigration and Land Company
File#: 252
Patent#: 252
Patent Vol.: 14
Certificate: 252
Survey/Blk/Twp: 252
Acres: 320
Map(s) 12

Abstract # 500 - TE&L CO
P'ee: TEXAS EMIGRATION AND LAND COMPANY
G'ee: TEXAS EMIGRATION AND LAND COMPANY
T-Dt: -- --- -----
P-Dt: 04 Dec 1857
Dist/Class: Texas Emmigration and Land Company
File#: 253
Patent#: 253
Patent Vol.: 14
Certificate: 253
Survey/Blk/Twp: 253
Acres: 320
Map(s) 12

Abstract # 501 - TE&L CO
P'ee: TEXAS EMIGRATION AND LAND COMPANY
G'ee: TEXAS EMIGRATION AND LAND COMPANY
T-Dt: -- --- -----
P-Dt: 04 Dec 1857
Dist/Class: Texas Emmigration and Land Company
File#: 254
Patent#: 254
Patent Vol.: 14
Certificate: 254
Survey/Blk/Twp: 254
Acres: 320
Map(s) 12

Abstract # 502 - TE&L CO
P'ee: TEXAS EMIGRATION AND LAND

COMPANY
G'ee: TEXAS EMIGRATION AND LAND
COMPANY
T-Dt: -- --- -----
P-Dt: 07 Dec 1857
Dist/Class: Texas Emmigration and Land
Company
File#: 255
Patent#: 255
Patent Vol.: 14
Certificate: 255
Survey/Blk/Twp: 255
Acres: 320
Map(s) 12

Abstract # 503 - TE&L CO
P'ee: TEXAS EMIGRATION AND LAND
COMPANY
G'ee: TEXAS EMIGRATION AND LAND
COMPANY
T-Dt: -- --- -----
P-Dt: 09 Dec 1857
Dist/Class: Texas Emmigration and Land
Company
File#: 256
Patent#: 256
Patent Vol.: 14
Certificate: 256
Survey/Blk/Twp: 256
Acres: 320
Map(s) 12

Abstract # 504 - TE&L CO
P'ee: TEXAS EMIGRATION AND LAND
COMPANY
G'ee: TEXAS EMIGRATION AND LAND
COMPANY
T-Dt: -- --- -----
P-Dt: 09 Dec 1857
Dist/Class: Texas Emmigration and Land
Company
File#: 257
Patent#: 257
Patent Vol.: 14
Certificate: 257
Survey/Blk/Twp: 257
Acres: 320
Map(s) 12

Abstract # 505 - TE&L CO
P'ee: TEXAS EMIGRATION AND LAND
COMPANY
G'ee: TEXAS EMIGRATION AND LAND
COMPANY
T-Dt: -- --- -----
P-Dt: 10 Dec 1857
Dist/Class: Texas Emmigration and Land
Company
File#: 258
Patent#: 258
Patent Vol.: 14
Certificate: 258
Survey/Blk/Twp: 258
Acres: 320
Map(s) 12

Abstract # 506 - TE&L CO
P'ee: TEXAS EMIGRATION AND LAND
COMPANY
G'ee: TEXAS EMIGRATION AND LAND
COMPANY
T-Dt: -- --- -----
P-Dt: 10 Dec 1857
Dist/Class: Texas Emmigration and Land
Company

File#: 259
Patent#: 259
Patent Vol.: 14
Certificate: 259
Survey/Blk/Twp: 259
Acres: 320
Map(s) 12

Abstract # 507 - TE&L CO
P'ee: TEXAS EMIGRATION AND LAND
COMPANY
G'ee: TEXAS EMIGRATION AND LAND
COMPANY
T-Dt: -- --- -----
P-Dt: 10 Dec 1857
Dist/Class: Texas Emmigration and Land
Company
File#: 260
Patent#: 260
Patent Vol.: 14
Certificate: 260
Survey/Blk/Twp: 260
Acres: 320
Map(s) 12

Abstract # 508 - TE&L CO
P'ee: TEXAS EMIGRATION AND LAND
COMPANY
G'ee: TEXAS EMIGRATION AND LAND
COMPANY
T-Dt: -- --- -----
P-Dt: 11 Dec 1857
Dist/Class: Texas Emmigration and Land
Company
File#: 261
Patent#: 261
Patent Vol.: 14
Certificate: 261
Survey/Blk/Twp: 261
Acres: 320
Map(s) 12

Abstract # 509 - TE&L CO
P'ee: TEXAS EMIGRATION AND LAND
COMPANY
G'ee: TEXAS EMIGRATION AND LAND
COMPANY
T-Dt: -- --- -----
P-Dt: 12 Dec 1857
Dist/Class: Texas Emmigration and Land
Company
File#: 262
Patent#: 262
Patent Vol.: 14
Certificate: 262
Survey/Blk/Twp: 262
Acres: 320
Map(s) 12, 20

Abstract # 510 - TE&L CO
P'ee: TEXAS EMIGRATION AND LAND
COMPANY
G'ee: TEXAS EMIGRATION AND LAND
COMPANY
T-Dt: -- --- -----
P-Dt: 12 Dec 1857
Dist/Class: Texas Emmigration and Land
Company
File#: 263
Patent#: 263
Patent Vol.: 14
Certificate: 263
Survey/Blk/Twp: 263
Acres: 320
Map(s) 12

Abstract # 511 - TE&L CO
P'ee: TEXAS EMIGRATION AND LAND
COMPANY
G'ee: TEXAS EMIGRATION AND LAND
COMPANY
T-Dt: -- --- -----
P-Dt: 12 Dec 1857
Dist/Class: Texas Emmigration and Land
Company
File#: 264
Patent#: 264
Patent Vol.: 14
Certificate: 264
Survey/Blk/Twp: 264
Acres: 320
Map(s) 12

Abstract # 512 - TE&L CO
P'ee: TEXAS EMIGRATION AND LAND
COMPANY
G'ee: TEXAS EMIGRATION AND LAND
COMPANY
T-Dt: -- --- -----
P-Dt: 12 Dec 1857
Dist/Class: Texas Emmigration and Land
Company
File#: 265
Patent#: 265
Patent Vol.: 14
Certificate: 265
Survey/Blk/Twp: 265
Acres: 320
Map(s) 12

Abstract # 513 - TE&L CO
P'ee: TEXAS EMIGRATION AND LAND
COMPANY
G'ee: TEXAS EMIGRATION AND LAND
COMPANY
T-Dt: -- --- -----
P-Dt: 15 Dec 1857
Dist/Class: Texas Emmigration and Land
Company
File#: 266
Patent#: 266
Patent Vol.: 14
Certificate: 266
Survey/Blk/Twp: 266
Acres: 320
Map(s) 11, 12

Abstract # 514 - TE&L CO
P'ee: TEXAS EMIGRATION AND LAND
COMPANY
G'ee: TEXAS EMIGRATION AND LAND
COMPANY
T-Dt: -- --- -----
P-Dt: 15 Dec 1857
Dist/Class: Texas Emmigration and Land
Company
File#: 267
Patent#: 267
Patent Vol.: 14
Certificate: 267
Survey/Blk/Twp: 267
Acres: 320
Map(s) 11, 12

Abstract # 515 - TE&L CO
P'ee: TEXAS EMIGRATION AND LAND
COMPANY
G'ee: TEXAS EMIGRATION AND LAND
COMPANY
T-Dt: -- --- -----
P-Dt: 15 Dec 1857

Dist/Class: Texas Emmigration and Land
Company
File#: 268
Patent#: 268
Patent Vol.: 14
Certificate: 268
Survey/Blk/Twp: 268
Acres: 320
Map(s) 11, 12

Abstract # 516 - TE&L CO
P'ee: TEXAS EMIGRATION AND LAND
COMPANY
G'ee: TEXAS EMIGRATION AND LAND
COMPANY
T-Dt: -- --- -----
P-Dt: 15 Dec 1857
Dist/Class: Texas Emmigration and Land
Company
File#: 269
Patent#: 269
Patent Vol.: 14
Certificate: 269
Survey/Blk/Twp: 269
Acres: 320
Map(s) 20

Abstract # 517 - TE&L CO
P'ee: TEXAS EMIGRATION AND LAND
COMPANY
G'ee: TEXAS EMIGRATION AND LAND
COMPANY
T-Dt: -- --- -----
P-Dt: 15 Dec 1857
Dist/Class: Texas Emmigration and Land
Company
File#: 270
Patent#: 270
Patent Vol.: 14
Certificate: 270
Survey/Blk/Twp: 270
Acres: 320
Map(s) 12

Abstract # 518 - TE&L CO
P'ee: TEXAS EMIGRATION AND LAND
COMPANY
G'ee: TEXAS EMIGRATION AND LAND
COMPANY
T-Dt: -- --- -----
P-Dt: 17 Dec 1857
Dist/Class: Texas Emmigration and Land
Company
File#: 271
Patent#: 271
Patent Vol.: 14
Certificate: 271
Survey/Blk/Twp: 271
Acres: 320
Map(s) 12

Abstract # 519 - TE&L CO
P'ee: TEXAS EMIGRATION AND LAND
COMPANY
G'ee: TEXAS EMIGRATION AND LAND
COMPANY
T-Dt: -- --- -----
P-Dt: 27 May 1858
Dist/Class: Texas Emmigration and Land
Company
File#: 272
Patent#: 691
Patent Vol.: 14
Certificate: 272
Survey/Blk/Twp: 272

Acres: 320
Map(s) 12

Abstract # 520 - TE&L CO
P'ee: TEXAS EMIGRATION AND LAND
COMPANY
G'ee: TEXAS EMIGRATION AND LAND
COMPANY
T-Dt: -- --- -----
P-Dt: 17 Dec 1857
Dist/Class: Texas Emmigration and Land
Company
File#: 273
Patent#: 273
Patent Vol.: 14
Certificate: 273
Survey/Blk/Twp: 273
Acres: 320
Map(s) 12

Abstract # 521 - TE&L CO
P'ee: TEXAS EMIGRATION AND LAND
COMPANY
G'ee: TEXAS EMIGRATION AND LAND
COMPANY
T-Dt: -- --- -----
P-Dt: 17 Dec 1857
Dist/Class: Texas Emmigration and Land
Company
File#: 274
Patent#: 274
Patent Vol.: 14
Certificate: 274
Survey/Blk/Twp: 274
Acres: 320
Map(s) 12

Abstract # 522 - TE&L CO
P'ee: TEXAS EMIGRATION AND LAND
COMPANY
G'ee: TEXAS EMIGRATION AND LAND
COMPANY
T-Dt: -- --- -----
P-Dt: 17 Dec 1857
Dist/Class: Texas Emmigration and Land
Company
File#: 275
Patent#: 275
Patent Vol.: 14
Certificate: 275
Survey/Blk/Twp: 275
Acres: 320
Map(s) 12

Abstract # 523 - TE&L CO
P'ee: TEXAS EMIGRATION AND LAND
COMPANY
G'ee: TEXAS EMIGRATION AND LAND
COMPANY
T-Dt: -- --- -----
P-Dt: 18 Dec 1857
Dist/Class: Texas Emmigration and Land
Company
File#: 276
Patent#: 280
Patent Vol.: 14
Certificate: 276
Survey/Blk/Twp: 276
Acres: 320
Map(s) 12

Abstract # 524 - TE&L CO
P'ee: TEXAS EMIGRATION AND LAND
COMPANY
G'ee: TEXAS EMIGRATION AND LAND

COMPANY
T-Dt: -- --- -----
P-Dt: 18 Dec 1857
Dist/Class: Texas Emmigration and Land
Company
File#: 277
Patent#: 281
Patent Vol.: 14
Certificate: 277
Survey/Blk/Twp: 277
Acres: 320
Map(s) 12

Abstract # 525 - TE&L CO
P'ee: TEXAS EMIGRATION AND LAND
COMPANY
G'ee: TEXAS EMIGRATION AND LAND
COMPANY
T-Dt: -- --- -----
P-Dt: 19 Dec 1857
Dist/Class: Texas Emmigration and Land
Company
File#: 278
Patent#: 278
Patent Vol.: 14
Certificate: 278
Survey/Blk/Twp: 278
Acres: 320
Map(s) 12

Abstract # 526 - TE&L CO
P'ee: TEXAS EMIGRATION AND LAND
COMPANY
G'ee: TEXAS EMIGRATION AND LAND
COMPANY
T-Dt: -- --- -----
P-Dt: 19 Dec 1857
Dist/Class: Texas Emmigration and Land
Company
File#: 279
Patent#: 279
Patent Vol.: 14
Certificate: 279
Survey/Blk/Twp: 279
Acres: 320
Map(s) 12

Abstract # 527 - TE&L CO
P'ee: TEXAS EMIGRATION AND LAND
COMPANY
G'ee: TEXAS EMIGRATION AND LAND
COMPANY
T-Dt: -- --- -----
P-Dt: 03 Apr 1858
Dist/Class: Texas Emmigration and Land
Company
File#: 280
Patent#: 485
Patent Vol.: 14
Certificate: 280
Survey/Blk/Twp: 280
Acres: 320
Map(s) 12, 20

Abstract # 528 - TE&L CO
P'ee: TEXAS EMIGRATION AND LAND
COMPANY
G'ee: TEXAS EMIGRATION AND LAND
COMPANY
T-Dt: -- --- -----
P-Dt: 05 Apr 1858
Dist/Class: Texas Emmigration and Land
Company
File#: 281
Patent#: 487

Patent Vol.: 14
Certificate: 281
Survey/Blk/Twp: 281
Acres: 320
Map(s) 12, 20

Abstract # 529 - TE&L CO
P'ee: TEXAS EMIGRATION AND LAND COMPANY
G'ee: TEXAS EMIGRATION AND LAND COMPANY
T-Dt: -- --- -----
P-Dt: 29 Dec 1857
Dist/Class: Texas Emmigration and Land Company
File#: 282
Patent#: 282
Patent Vol.: 14
Certificate: 282
Survey/Blk/Twp: 282
Acres: 320
Map(s) 12, 20

Abstract # 530 - TE&L CO
P'ee: TEXAS EMIGRATION AND LAND COMPANY
G'ee: TEXAS EMIGRATION AND LAND COMPANY
T-Dt: -- --- -----
P-Dt: 29 Dec 1857
Dist/Class: Texas Emmigration and Land Company
File#: 283
Patent#: 283
Patent Vol.: 14
Certificate: 283
Survey/Blk/Twp: 283
Acres: 320
Map(s) 12, 13

Abstract # 531 - TE&L CO
P'ee: TEXAS EMIGRATION AND LAND COMPANY
G'ee: TEXAS EMIGRATION AND LAND COMPANY
T-Dt: -- --- -----
P-Dt: 29 Dec 1857
Dist/Class: Texas Emmigration and Land Company
File#: 284
Patent#: 284
Patent Vol.: 14
Certificate: 284
Survey/Blk/Twp: 284
Acres: 320
Map(s) 13

Abstract # 532 - TE&L CO
P'ee: TEXAS EMIGRATION AND LAND COMPANY
G'ee: TEXAS EMIGRATION AND LAND COMPANY
T-Dt: -- --- -----
P-Dt: 30 Dec 1857
Dist/Class: Texas Emmigration and Land Company
File#: 285
Patent#: 285
Patent Vol.: 14
Certificate: 285
Survey/Blk/Twp: 285
Acres: 320
Map(s) 13

Abstract # 533 - TE&L CO

P'ee: TEXAS EMIGRATION AND LAND COMPANY
G'ee: TEXAS EMIGRATION AND LAND COMPANY
T-Dt: -- --- -----
P-Dt: 31 Dec 1857
Dist/Class: Texas Emmigration and Land Company
File#: 286
Patent#: 286
Patent Vol.: 14
Certificate: 286
Survey/Blk/Twp: 286
Acres: 320
Map(s) 13

Abstract # 534 - TE&L CO
P'ee: TEXAS EMIGRATION AND LAND COMPANY
G'ee: TEXAS EMIGRATION AND LAND COMPANY
T-Dt: -- --- -----
P-Dt: 31 Dec 1857
Dist/Class: Texas Emmigration and Land Company
File#: 287
Patent#: 287
Patent Vol.: 14
Certificate: 287
Survey/Blk/Twp: 287
Acres: 320
Map(s) 13

Abstract # 535 - TE&L CO
P'ee: TEXAS EMIGRATION AND LAND COMPANY
G'ee: TEXAS EMIGRATION AND LAND COMPANY
T-Dt: -- --- -----
P-Dt: 31 Dec 1857
Dist/Class: Texas Emmigration and Land Company
File#: 288
Patent#: 288
Patent Vol.: 14
Certificate: 288
Survey/Blk/Twp: 288
Acres: 320
Map(s) 13

Abstract # 536 - TE&L CO
P'ee: TEXAS EMIGRATION AND LAND COMPANY
G'ee: TEXAS EMIGRATION AND LAND COMPANY
T-Dt: -- --- -----
P-Dt: 31 Dec 1857
Dist/Class: Texas Emmigration and Land Company
File#: 289
Patent#: 289
Patent Vol.: 14
Certificate: 289
Survey/Blk/Twp: 289
Acres: 320
Map(s) 13

Abstract # 537 - TE&L CO
P'ee: TEXAS EMIGRATION AND LAND COMPANY
G'ee: TEXAS EMIGRATION AND LAND COMPANY
T-Dt: -- --- -----
P-Dt: 31 Dec 1857
Dist/Class: Texas Emmigration and Land

Company
File#: 290
Patent#: 290
Patent Vol.: 14
Certificate: 290
Survey/Blk/Twp: 290
Acres: 320
Map(s) 12, 13

Abstract # 538 - TE&L CO
P'ee: TEXAS EMIGRATION AND LAND COMPANY
G'ee: TEXAS EMIGRATION AND LAND COMPANY
T-Dt: -- --- -----
P-Dt: 31 Dec 1857
Dist/Class: Texas Emmigration and Land Company
File#: 291
Patent#: 291
Patent Vol.: 14
Certificate: 291
Survey/Blk/Twp: 291
Acres: 320
Map(s) 12, 13

Abstract # 539 - TE&L CO
P'ee: TEXAS EMIGRATION AND LAND COMPANY
G'ee: TEXAS EMIGRATION AND LAND COMPANY
T-Dt: -- --- -----
P-Dt: 31 Dec 1857
Dist/Class: Texas Emmigration and Land Company
File#: 292
Patent#: 292
Patent Vol.: 14
Certificate: 292
Survey/Blk/Twp: 292
Acres: 320
Map(s) 13

Abstract # 540 - TE&L CO
P'ee: TEXAS EMIGRATION AND LAND COMPANY
G'ee: TEXAS EMIGRATION AND LAND COMPANY
T-Dt: -- --- -----
P-Dt: 01 Jan 1858
Dist/Class: Texas Emmigration and Land Company
File#: 293
Patent#: 293
Patent Vol.: 14
Certificate: 293
Survey/Blk/Twp: 293
Acres: 320
Map(s) 13

Abstract # 541 - TE&L CO
P'ee: TEXAS EMIGRATION AND LAND COMPANY
G'ee: TEXAS EMIGRATION AND LAND COMPANY
T-Dt: -- --- -----
P-Dt: 02 Jan 1858
Dist/Class: Texas Emmigration and Land Company
File#: 294
Patent#: 294
Patent Vol.: 14
Certificate: 294
Survey/Blk/Twp: 294
Acres: 320

Map(s) 13

Abstract # 542 - TE&L CO
P'ee: TEXAS EMIGRATION AND LAND COMPANY
G'ee: TEXAS EMIGRATION AND LAND COMPANY
T-Dt: -- --- -----
P-Dt: 02 Jan 1858
Dist/Class: Texas Emmigration and Land Company
File#: 295
Patent#: 295
Patent Vol.: 14
Certificate: 295
Survey/Blk/Twp: 295
Acres: 320
Map(s) 5, 13

Abstract # 543 - TE&L CO
P'ee: TEXAS EMIGRATION AND LAND COMPANY
G'ee: TEXAS EMIGRATION AND LAND COMPANY
T-Dt: -- --- -----
P-Dt: 02 Jan 1858
Dist/Class: Texas Emmigration and Land Company
File#: 296
Patent#: 296
Patent Vol.: 14
Certificate: 296
Survey/Blk/Twp: 296
Acres: 320
Map(s) 5, 13

Abstract # 544 - TE&L CO
P'ee: TEXAS EMIGRATION AND LAND COMPANY
G'ee: TEXAS EMIGRATION AND LAND COMPANY
T-Dt: -- --- -----
P-Dt: 02 Jan 1858
Dist/Class: Texas Emmigration and Land Company
File#: 297
Patent#: 297
Patent Vol.: 14
Certificate: 297
Survey/Blk/Twp: 297
Acres: 320
Map(s) 4, 5, 12, 13

Abstract # 545 - TE&L CO
P'ee: TEXAS EMIGRATION AND LAND COMPANY
G'ee: TEXAS EMIGRATION AND LAND COMPANY
T-Dt: -- --- -----
P-Dt: 02 Jan 1858
Dist/Class: Texas Emmigration and Land Company
File#: 298
Patent#: 298
Patent Vol.: 14
Certificate: 298
Survey/Blk/Twp: 298
Acres: 320
Map(s) 13

Abstract # 546 - TE&L CO
P'ee: TEXAS EMIGRATION AND LAND COMPANY
G'ee: TEXAS EMIGRATION AND LAND COMPANY

T-Dt: -- --- -----
P-Dt: 04 Jan 1858
Dist/Class: Texas Emmigration and Land Company
File#: 299
Patent#: 299
Patent Vol.: 14
Certificate: 299
Survey/Blk/Twp: 299
Acres: 320
Map(s) 13

Abstract # 547 - TE&L CO
P'ee: TEXAS EMIGRATION AND LAND COMPANY
G'ee: TEXAS EMIGRATION AND LAND COMPANY
T-Dt: -- --- -----
P-Dt: 04 Jan 1858
Dist/Class: Texas Emmigration and Land Company
File#: 300
Patent#: 300
Patent Vol.: 14
Certificate: 300
Survey/Blk/Twp: 300
Acres: 320
Map(s) 13

Abstract # 548 - TE&L CO
P'ee: TEXAS EMIGRATION AND LAND COMPANY
G'ee: TEXAS EMIGRATION AND LAND COMPANY
T-Dt: -- --- -----
P-Dt: 09 Jan 1858
Dist/Class: Texas Emmigration and Land Company
File#: 301
Patent#: 301
Patent Vol.: 14
Certificate: 301
Survey/Blk/Twp: 301
Acres: 320
Map(s) 1

Abstract # 549 - TE&L CO
P'ee: TEXAS EMIGRATION AND LAND COMPANY
G'ee: TEXAS EMIGRATION AND LAND COMPANY
T-Dt: -- --- -----
P-Dt: 09 Jan 1858
Dist/Class: Texas Emmigration and Land Company
File#: 302
Patent#: 302
Patent Vol.: 14
Certificate: 302
Survey/Blk/Twp: 302
Acres: 320
Map(s) 1

Abstract # 550 - TE&L CO
P'ee: TEXAS EMIGRATION AND LAND COMPANY
G'ee: TEXAS EMIGRATION AND LAND COMPANY
T-Dt: -- --- -----
P-Dt: 09 Jan 1858
Dist/Class: Texas Emmigration and Land Company
File#: 303
Patent#: 303
Patent Vol.: 14

Certificate: 303
Survey/Blk/Twp: 303
Acres: 320
Map(s) 1

Abstract # 551 - TE&L CO
P'ee: TEXAS EMIGRATION AND LAND COMPANY
G'ee: TEXAS EMIGRATION AND LAND COMPANY
T-Dt: -- --- -----
P-Dt: 11 Jan 1858
Dist/Class: Texas Emmigration and Land Company
File#: 304
Patent#: 304
Patent Vol.: 14
Certificate: 304
Survey/Blk/Twp: 304
Acres: 320
Map(s) 1

Abstract # 552 - TE&L CO
P'ee: TEXAS EMIGRATION AND LAND COMPANY
G'ee: TEXAS EMIGRATION AND LAND COMPANY
T-Dt: -- --- -----
P-Dt: 11 Jan 1858
Dist/Class: Texas Emmigration and Land Company
File#: 305
Patent#: 305
Patent Vol.: 14
Certificate: 305
Survey/Blk/Twp: 305
Acres: 320
Map(s) 1

Abstract # 553 - TE&L CO
P'ee: TEXAS EMIGRATION AND LAND COMPANY
G'ee: TEXAS EMIGRATION AND LAND COMPANY
T-Dt: -- --- -----
P-Dt: 11 Jan 1858
Dist/Class: Texas Emmigration and Land Company
File#: 306
Patent#: 306
Patent Vol.: 14
Certificate: 306
Survey/Blk/Twp: 306
Acres: 320
Map(s) 1

Abstract # 554 - TE&L CO
P'ee: TEXAS EMIGRATION AND LAND COMPANY
G'ee: TEXAS EMIGRATION AND LAND COMPANY
T-Dt: -- --- -----
P-Dt: 12 Jan 1858
Dist/Class: Texas Emmigration and Land Company
File#: 307
Patent#: 307
Patent Vol.: 14
Certificate: 307
Survey/Blk/Twp: 307
Acres: 320
Map(s) 1

Abstract # 555 - TE&L CO
P'ee: TEXAS EMIGRATION AND LAND

COMPANY
G'ee: TEXAS EMIGRATION AND LAND
COMPANY
T-Dt: -- --- -----
P-Dt: 12 Jan 1858
Dist/Class: Texas Emmigration and Land
Company
File#: 308
Patent#: 308
Patent Vol.: 14
Certificate: 308
Survey/Blk/Twp: 308
Acres: 320
Map(s) 1

Abstract # 556 - TE&L CO
P'ee: TEXAS EMIGRATION AND LAND
COMPANY
G'ee: TEXAS EMIGRATION AND LAND
COMPANY
T-Dt: -- --- -----
P-Dt: 12 Jan 1858
Dist/Class: Texas Emmigration and Land
Company
File#: 309
Patent#: 309
Patent Vol.: 14
Certificate: 309
Survey/Blk/Twp: 309
Acres: 320
Map(s) 1

Abstract # 557 - TE&L CO
P'ee: TEXAS EMIGRATION AND LAND
COMPANY
G'ee: TEXAS EMIGRATION AND LAND
COMPANY
T-Dt: -- --- -----
P-Dt: 12 Jan 1858
Dist/Class: Texas Emmigration and Land
Company
File#: 310
Patent#: 310
Patent Vol.: 14
Certificate: 310
Survey/Blk/Twp: 310
Acres: 320
Map(s) 1

Abstract # 558 - TE&L CO
P'ee: TEXAS EMIGRATION AND LAND
COMPANY
G'ee: TEXAS EMIGRATION AND LAND
COMPANY
T-Dt: -- --- -----
P-Dt: 13 Jan 1858
Dist/Class: Texas Emmigration and Land
Company
File#: 311
Patent#: 311
Patent Vol.: 14
Certificate: 311
Survey/Blk/Twp: 311
Acres: 320
Map(s) 1

Abstract # 559 - TE&L CO
P'ee: TEXAS EMIGRATION AND LAND
COMPANY
G'ee: TEXAS EMIGRATION AND LAND
COMPANY
T-Dt: -- --- -----
P-Dt: 13 Jan 1858
Dist/Class: Texas Emmigration and Land
Company

File#: 312
Patent#: 312
Patent Vol.: 14
Certificate: 312
Survey/Blk/Twp: 312
Acres: 320
Map(s) 1

Abstract # 560 - TE&L CO
P'ee: TEXAS EMIGRATION AND LAND
COMPANY
G'ee: TEXAS EMIGRATION AND LAND
COMPANY
T-Dt: -- --- -----
P-Dt: 13 Jan 1858
Dist/Class: Texas Emmigration and Land
Company
File#: 313
Patent#: 313
Patent Vol.: 14
Certificate: 313
Survey/Blk/Twp: 313
Acres: 320
Map(s) 2, 10

Abstract # 561 - TE&L CO
P'ee: TEXAS EMIGRATION AND LAND
COMPANY
G'ee: TEXAS EMIGRATION AND LAND
COMPANY
T-Dt: -- --- -----
P-Dt: 13 Jan 1858
Dist/Class: Texas Emmigration and Land
Company
File#: 314
Patent#: 314
Patent Vol.: 14
Certificate: 314
Survey/Blk/Twp: 314
Acres: 320
Map(s) 1, 2, 9, 10

Abstract # 562 - TE&L CO
P'ee: TEXAS EMIGRATION AND LAND
COMPANY
G'ee: TEXAS EMIGRATION AND LAND
COMPANY
T-Dt: -- --- -----
P-Dt: 13 Jan 1858
Dist/Class: Texas Emmigration and Land
Company
File#: 315
Patent#: 315
Patent Vol.: 14
Certificate: 315
Survey/Blk/Twp: 315
Acres: 320
Map(s) 10

Abstract # 563 - TE&L CO
P'ee: TEXAS EMIGRATION AND LAND
COMPANY
G'ee: TEXAS EMIGRATION AND LAND
COMPANY
T-Dt: -- --- -----
P-Dt: 14 Jan 1858
Dist/Class: Texas Emmigration and Land
Company
File#: 316
Patent#: 316
Patent Vol.: 14
Certificate: 316
Survey/Blk/Twp: 316
Acres: 320
Map(s) 10

Abstract # 564 - TE&L CO
P'ee: TEXAS EMIGRATION AND LAND
COMPANY
G'ee: TEXAS EMIGRATION AND LAND
COMPANY
T-Dt: -- --- -----
P-Dt: 15 Jan 1858
Dist/Class: Texas Emmigration and Land
Company
File#: 317
Patent#: 317
Patent Vol.: 14
Certificate: 317
Survey/Blk/Twp: 317
Acres: 320
Map(s) 10

Abstract # 565 - TE&L CO
P'ee: TEXAS EMIGRATION AND LAND
COMPANY
G'ee: TEXAS EMIGRATION AND LAND
COMPANY
T-Dt: -- --- -----
P-Dt: 15 Jan 1858
Dist/Class: Texas Emmigration and Land
Company
File#: 318
Patent#: 318
Patent Vol.: 14
Certificate: 318
Survey/Blk/Twp: 318
Acres: 320
Map(s) 9, 10

Abstract # 566 - TE&L CO
P'ee: TEXAS EMIGRATION AND LAND
COMPANY
G'ee: TEXAS EMIGRATION AND LAND
COMPANY
T-Dt: -- --- -----
P-Dt: 15 Jan 1858
Dist/Class: Texas Emmigration and Land
Company
File#: 319
Patent#: 319
Patent Vol.: 14
Certificate: 319
Survey/Blk/Twp: 319
Acres: 320
Map(s) 9

Abstract # 567 - TE&L CO
P'ee: TEXAS EMIGRATION AND LAND
COMPANY
G'ee: TEXAS EMIGRATION AND LAND
COMPANY
T-Dt: -- --- -----
P-Dt: 15 Jan 1858
Dist/Class: Texas Emmigration and Land
Company
File#: 320
Patent#: 320
Patent Vol.: 14
Certificate: 320
Survey/Blk/Twp: 320
Acres: 320
Map(s) 9

Abstract # 568 - TE&L CO
P'ee: TEXAS EMIGRATION AND LAND
COMPANY
G'ee: TEXAS EMIGRATION AND LAND
COMPANY
T-Dt: -- --- -----
P-Dt: 15 Jan 1858

Dist/Class: Texas Emmigration and Land
Company
File#: 321
Patent#: 321
Patent Vol.: 14
Certificate: 321
Survey/Blk/Twp: 321
Acres: 320
Map(s) 9

Abstract # 569 - TE&L CO
P'ee: TEXAS EMIGRATION AND LAND
COMPANY
G'ee: TEXAS EMIGRATION AND LAND
COMPANY
T-Dt: -- --- -----
P-Dt: 15 Jan 1858
Dist/Class: Texas Emmigration and Land
Company
File#: 322
Patent#: 322
Patent Vol.: 14
Certificate: 322
Survey/Blk/Twp: 322
Acres: 320
Map(s) 9

Abstract # 570 - TE&L CO
P'ee: TEXAS EMIGRATION AND LAND
COMPANY
G'ee: TEXAS EMIGRATION AND LAND
COMPANY
T-Dt: -- --- -----
P-Dt: 15 Jan 1858
Dist/Class: Texas Emmigration and Land
Company
File#: 323
Patent#: 323
Patent Vol.: 14
Certificate: 323
Survey/Blk/Twp: 323
Acres: 320
Map(s) 9

Abstract # 571 - TE&L CO
P'ee: TEXAS EMIGRATION AND LAND
COMPANY
G'ee: TEXAS EMIGRATION AND LAND
COMPANY
T-Dt: -- --- -----
P-Dt: 16 Jan 1858
Dist/Class: Texas Emmigration and Land
Company
File#: 324
Patent#: 324
Patent Vol.: 14
Certificate: 324
Survey/Blk/Twp: 324
Acres: 320
Map(s) 9

Abstract # 572 - TE&L CO
P'ee: TEXAS EMIGRATION AND LAND
COMPANY
G'ee: TEXAS EMIGRATION AND LAND
COMPANY
T-Dt: -- --- -----
P-Dt: 16 Jan 1858
Dist/Class: Texas Emmigration and Land
Company
File#: 325
Patent#: 325
Patent Vol.: 14
Certificate: 325
Survey/Blk/Twp: 325

Acres: 320
Map(s) 9, 10

Abstract # 573 - TE&L CO
P'ee: TEXAS EMIGRATION AND LAND
COMPANY
G'ee: TEXAS EMIGRATION AND LAND
COMPANY
T-Dt: -- --- -----
P-Dt: 22 Jan 1858
Dist/Class: Texas Emmigration and Land
Company
File#: 326
Patent#: 326
Patent Vol.: 14
Certificate: 326
Survey/Blk/Twp: 326
Acres: 320
Map(s) 10

Abstract # 574 - TE&L CO
P'ee: TEXAS EMIGRATION AND LAND
COMPANY
G'ee: TEXAS EMIGRATION AND LAND
COMPANY
T-Dt: -- --- -----
P-Dt: 22 Jan 1858
Dist/Class: Texas Emmigration and Land
Company
File#: 327
Patent#: 327
Patent Vol.: 14
Certificate: 327
Survey/Blk/Twp: 327
Acres: 320
Map(s) 10

Abstract # 575 - TE&L CO
P'ee: TEXAS EMIGRATION AND LAND
COMPANY
G'ee: TEXAS EMIGRATION AND LAND
COMPANY
T-Dt: -- --- -----
P-Dt: 22 Jan 1858
Dist/Class: Texas Emmigration and Land
Company
File#: 328
Patent#: 328
Patent Vol.: 14
Certificate: 328
Survey/Blk/Twp: 328
Acres: 320
Map(s) 9

Abstract # 576 - TE&L CO
P'ee: TEXAS EMIGRATION AND LAND
COMPANY
G'ee: TEXAS EMIGRATION AND LAND
COMPANY
T-Dt: -- --- -----
P-Dt: 22 Jan 1858
Dist/Class: Texas Emmigration and Land
Company
File#: 329
Patent#: 329
Patent Vol.: 14
Certificate: 329
Survey/Blk/Twp: 329
Acres: 320
Map(s) 9

Abstract # 577 - TE&L CO
P'ee: TEXAS EMIGRATION AND LAND
COMPANY
G'ee: TEXAS EMIGRATION AND LAND

COMPANY
T-Dt: -- --- -----
P-Dt: 22 Jan 1858
Dist/Class: Texas Emmigration and Land
Company
File#: 330
Patent#: 330
Patent Vol.: 14
Certificate: 330
Survey/Blk/Twp: 330
Acres: 320
Map(s) 9, 10

Abstract # 578 - TE&L CO
P'ee: TEXAS EMIGRATION AND LAND
COMPANY
G'ee: TEXAS EMIGRATION AND LAND
COMPANY
T-Dt: -- --- -----
P-Dt: 22 Jan 1858
Dist/Class: Texas Emmigration and Land
Company
File#: 331
Patent#: 331
Patent Vol.: 14
Certificate: 331
Survey/Blk/Twp: 331
Acres: 320
Map(s) 10

Abstract # 579 - TE&L CO
P'ee: TEXAS EMIGRATION AND LAND
COMPANY
G'ee: TEXAS EMIGRATION AND LAND
COMPANY
T-Dt: -- --- -----
P-Dt: 22 Jan 1858
Dist/Class: Texas Emmigration and Land
Company
File#: 332
Patent#: 332
Patent Vol.: 14
Certificate: 332
Survey/Blk/Twp: 332
Acres: 320
Map(s) 10

Abstract # 580 - TE&L CO
P'ee: TEXAS EMIGRATION AND LAND
COMPANY
G'ee: TEXAS EMIGRATION AND LAND
COMPANY
T-Dt: -- --- -----
P-Dt: 23 Jan 1858
Dist/Class: Texas Emmigration and Land
Company
File#: 333
Patent#: 333
Patent Vol.: 14
Certificate: 333
Survey/Blk/Twp: 333
Acres: 320
Map(s) 10

Abstract # 581 - TE&L CO
P'ee: TEXAS EMIGRATION AND LAND
COMPANY
G'ee: TEXAS EMIGRATION AND LAND
COMPANY
T-Dt: -- --- -----
P-Dt: 25 Jan 1858
Dist/Class: Texas Emmigration and Land
Company
File#: 334
Patent#: 334

Patent Vol.: 14
Certificate: 334
Survey/Blk/Twp: 334
Acres: 320
Map(s) 10

Abstract # 582 - TE&L CO
P'ee: TEXAS EMIGRATION AND LAND
COMPANY
G'ee: TEXAS EMIGRATION AND LAND
COMPANY
T-Dt: -- --- -----
P-Dt: 23 Jan 1858
Dist/Class: Texas Emmigration and Land
Company
File#: 335
Patent#: 335
Patent Vol.: 14
Certificate: 335
Survey/Blk/Twp: 335
Acres: 320
Map(s) 10

Abstract # 583 - TE&L CO
P'ee: TEXAS EMIGRATION AND LAND
COMPANY
G'ee: TEXAS EMIGRATION AND LAND
COMPANY
T-Dt: -- --- -----
P-Dt: 25 Jan 1858
Dist/Class: Texas Emmigration and Land
Company
File#: 336
Patent#: 336
Patent Vol.: 14
Certificate: 336
Survey/Blk/Twp: 336
Acres: 320
Map(s) 10

Abstract # 584 - TE&L CO
P'ee: TEXAS EMIGRATION AND LAND
COMPANY
G'ee: TEXAS EMIGRATION AND LAND
COMPANY
T-Dt: -- --- -----
P-Dt: 25 Jan 1858
Dist/Class: Texas Emmigration and Land
Company
File#: 337
Patent#: 337
Patent Vol.: 14
Certificate: 337
Survey/Blk/Twp: 337
Acres: 320
Map(s) 10

Abstract # 585 - TE&L CO
P'ee: TEXAS EMIGRATION AND LAND
COMPANY
G'ee: TEXAS EMIGRATION AND LAND
COMPANY
T-Dt: -- --- -----
P-Dt: 25 Jan 1858
Dist/Class: Texas Emmigration and Land
Company
File#: 338
Patent#: 338
Patent Vol.: 14
Certificate: 338
Survey/Blk/Twp: 338
Acres: 320
Map(s) 9, 10

Abstract # 586 - TE&L CO

P'ee: TEXAS EMIGRATION AND LAND
COMPANY
G'ee: TEXAS EMIGRATION AND LAND
COMPANY
T-Dt: -- --- -----
P-Dt: 25 Jan 1858
Dist/Class: Texas Emmigration and Land
Company
File#: 339
Patent#: 339
Patent Vol.: 14
Certificate: 339
Survey/Blk/Twp: 339
Acres: 320
Map(s) 9

Abstract # 587 - TE&L CO
P'ee: TEXAS EMIGRATION AND LAND
COMPANY
G'ee: TEXAS EMIGRATION AND LAND
COMPANY
T-Dt: -- --- -----
P-Dt: 25 Jan 1858
Dist/Class: Texas Emmigration and Land
Company
File#: 340
Patent#: 340
Patent Vol.: 14
Certificate: 340
Survey/Blk/Twp: 340
Acres: 320
Map(s) 9

Abstract # 588 - TE&L CO
P'ee: TEXAS EMIGRATION AND LAND
COMPANY
G'ee: TEXAS EMIGRATION AND LAND
COMPANY
T-Dt: -- --- -----
P-Dt: 27 Jan 1858
Dist/Class: Texas Emmigration and Land
Company
File#: 341
Patent#: 341
Patent Vol.: 14
Certificate: 341
Survey/Blk/Twp: 341
Acres: 320
Map(s) 9

Abstract # 589 - TE&L CO
P'ee: TEXAS EMIGRATION AND LAND
COMPANY
G'ee: TEXAS EMIGRATION AND LAND
COMPANY
T-Dt: -- --- -----
P-Dt: 27 Jan 1858
Dist/Class: Texas Emmigration and Land
Company
File#: 342
Patent#: 342
Patent Vol.: 14
Certificate: 342
Survey/Blk/Twp: 342
Acres: 320
Map(s) 9, 10

Abstract # 590 - TE&L CO
P'ee: TEXAS EMIGRATION AND LAND
COMPANY
G'ee: TEXAS EMIGRATION AND LAND
COMPANY
T-Dt: -- --- -----
P-Dt: 27 Jan 1858
Dist/Class: Texas Emmigration and Land

Company
File#: 343
Patent#: 343
Patent Vol.: 14
Certificate: 343
Survey/Blk/Twp: 343
Acres: 320
Map(s) 10

Abstract # 591 - TE&L CO
P'ee: TEXAS EMIGRATION AND LAND
COMPANY
G'ee: TEXAS EMIGRATION AND LAND
COMPANY
T-Dt: -- --- -----
P-Dt: 27 Jan 1858
Dist/Class: Texas Emmigration and Land
Company
File#: 344
Patent#: 344
Patent Vol.: 14
Certificate: 344
Survey/Blk/Twp: 344
Acres: 320
Map(s) 10

Abstract # 592 - TE&L CO
P'ee: TEXAS EMIGRATION AND LAND
COMPANY
G'ee: TEXAS EMIGRATION AND LAND
COMPANY
T-Dt: -- --- -----
P-Dt: 28 Jan 1858
Dist/Class: Texas Emmigration and Land
Company
File#: 345
Patent#: 345
Patent Vol.: 14
Certificate: 345
Survey/Blk/Twp: 345
Acres: 320
Map(s) 10

Abstract # 593 - TE&L CO
P'ee: TEXAS EMIGRATION AND LAND
COMPANY
G'ee: TEXAS EMIGRATION AND LAND
COMPANY
T-Dt: -- --- -----
P-Dt: 28 Jan 1858
Dist/Class: Texas Emmigration and Land
Company
File#: 346
Patent#: 346
Patent Vol.: 14
Certificate: 346
Survey/Blk/Twp: 346
Acres: 320
Map(s) 10

Abstract # 594 - TE&L CO
P'ee: TEXAS EMIGRATION AND LAND
COMPANY
G'ee: TEXAS EMIGRATION AND LAND
COMPANY
T-Dt: -- --- -----
P-Dt: 28 Jan 1858
Dist/Class: Texas Emmigration and Land
Company
File#: 347
Patent#: 347
Patent Vol.: 14
Certificate: 347
Survey/Blk/Twp: 347
Acres: 320

Map(s) 10

Abstract # 595 - TE&L CO
P'ee: TEXAS EMIGRATION AND LAND COMPANY
G'ee: TEXAS EMIGRATION AND LAND COMPANY
T-Dt: -- --- -----
P-Dt: 28 Jan 1858
Dist/Class: Texas Emmigration and Land Company
File#: 348
Patent#: 348
Patent Vol.: 14
Certificate: 348
Survey/Blk/Twp: 348
Acres: 320
Map(s) 10

Abstract # 596 - TE&L CO
P'ee: TEXAS EMIGRATION AND LAND COMPANY
G'ee: TEXAS EMIGRATION AND LAND COMPANY
T-Dt: -- --- -----
P-Dt: 28 Jan 1858
Dist/Class: Texas Emmigration and Land Company
File#: 349
Patent#: 349
Patent Vol.: 14
Certificate: 349
Survey/Blk/Twp: 349
Acres: 320
Map(s) 10

Abstract # 597 - TE&L CO
P'ee: TEXAS EMIGRATION AND LAND COMPANY
G'ee: TEXAS EMIGRATION AND LAND COMPANY
T-Dt: -- --- -----
P-Dt: 28 Jan 1858
Dist/Class: Texas Emmigration and Land Company
File#: 350
Patent#: 350
Patent Vol.: 14
Certificate: 350
Survey/Blk/Twp: 350
Acres: 320
Map(s) 10

Abstract # 598 - TE&L CO
P'ee: TEXAS EMIGRATION AND LAND COMPANY
G'ee: TEXAS EMIGRATION AND LAND COMPANY
T-Dt: -- --- -----
P-Dt: 19 Feb 1858
Dist/Class: Texas Emmigration and Land Company
File#: 351
Patent#: 351
Patent Vol.: 14
Certificate: 351
Survey/Blk/Twp: 351
Acres: 320
Map(s) 10

Abstract # 599 - TE&L CO
P'ee: TEXAS EMIGRATION AND LAND COMPANY
G'ee: TEXAS EMIGRATION AND LAND COMPANY

T-Dt: -- --- -----
P-Dt: 19 Feb 1858
Dist/Class: Texas Emmigration and Land Company
File#: 352
Patent#: 352
Patent Vol.: 14
Certificate: 352
Survey/Blk/Twp: 252
Acres: 320
Map(s) 10, 11

Abstract # 600 - TE&L CO
P'ee: TEXAS EMIGRATION AND LAND COMPANY
G'ee: TEXAS EMIGRATION AND LAND COMPANY
T-Dt: -- --- -----
P-Dt: 19 Feb 1858
Dist/Class: Texas Emmigration and Land Company
File#: 353
Patent#: 353
Patent Vol.: 14
Certificate: 353
Survey/Blk/Twp: 353
Acres: 320
Map(s) 11, 19

Abstract # 601 - TE&L CO
P'ee: TEXAS EMIGRATION AND LAND COMPANY
G'ee: TEXAS EMIGRATION AND LAND COMPANY
T-Dt: -- --- -----
P-Dt: 19 Feb 1858
Dist/Class: Texas Emmigration and Land Company
File#: 354
Patent#: 354
Patent Vol.: 14
Certificate: 354
Survey/Blk/Twp: 354
Acres: 320
Map(s) 11, 19

Abstract # 602 - TE&L CO
P'ee: TEXAS EMIGRATION AND LAND COMPANY
G'ee: TEXAS EMIGRATION AND LAND COMPANY
T-Dt: -- --- -----
P-Dt: 19 Feb 1858
Dist/Class: Texas Emmigration and Land Company
File#: 355
Patent#: 355
Patent Vol.: 14
Certificate: 355
Survey/Blk/Twp: 355
Acres: 320
Map(s) 19

Abstract # 603 - TE&L CO
P'ee: TEXAS EMIGRATION AND LAND COMPANY
G'ee: TEXAS EMIGRATION AND LAND COMPANY
T-Dt: -- --- -----
P-Dt: 20 Feb 1858
Dist/Class: Texas Emmigration and Land Company
File#: 356
Patent#: 356
Patent Vol.: 14

Certificate: 356
Survey/Blk/Twp: 356
Acres: 320
Map(s) 11, 19

Abstract # 604 - TE&L CO
P'ee: TEXAS EMIGRATION AND LAND COMPANY
G'ee: TEXAS EMIGRATION AND LAND COMPANY
T-Dt: -- --- -----
P-Dt: 23 Feb 1858
Dist/Class: Texas Emmigration and Land Company
File#: 357
Patent#: 357
Patent Vol.: 14
Certificate: 357
Survey/Blk/Twp: 357
Acres: 320
Map(s) 19, 27

Abstract # 605 - TE&L CO
P'ee: TEXAS EMIGRATION AND LAND COMPANY
G'ee: TEXAS EMIGRATION AND LAND COMPANY
T-Dt: -- --- -----
P-Dt: 23 Feb 1858
Dist/Class: Texas Emmigration and Land Company
File#: 358
Patent#: 358
Patent Vol.: 14
Certificate: 358
Survey/Blk/Twp: 358
Acres: 320
Map(s) 19, 27

Abstract # 606 - TE&L CO
P'ee: HEDGECOXE, OLIVER
G'ee: TEXAS EMIGRATION AND LAND COMPANY
T-Dt: -- --- -----
P-Dt: 11 Jan 1858
Dist/Class: Texas Emmigration and Land Company
File#: 359
Patent#: 305
Patent Vol.: 14
Certificate: 3
Survey/Blk/Twp: 359
Acres: 320
Map(s) 19, 27

Abstract # 607 - TE&L CO
P'ee: TEXAS EMIGRATION AND LAND COMPANY
G'ee: TEXAS EMIGRATION AND LAND COMPANY
T-Dt: -- --- -----
P-Dt: 24 Feb 1858
Dist/Class: Texas Emmigration and Land Company
File#: 361
Patent#: 361
Patent Vol.: 14
Certificate: 361
Survey/Blk/Twp: 361
Acres: 320
Map(s) 20, 28

Abstract # 608 - TE&L CO
P'ee: TEXAS EMIGRATION AND LAND COMPANY

G'ee: TEXAS EMIGRATION AND LAND
COMPANY
T-Dt: -- --- -----
P-Dt: 19 Mar 1858
Dist/Class: Texas Emmigration and Land
Company
File#: 401
Patent#: 401
Patent Vol.: 14
Certificate: 401
Survey/Blk/Twp: 401
Acres: 320
Map(s) 2

Abstract # 609 - TE&L CO
P'ee: TEXAS EMIGRATION AND LAND
COMPANY
G'ee: TEXAS EMIGRATION AND LAND
COMPANY
T-Dt: -- --- -----
P-Dt: 19 Mar 1858
Dist/Class: Texas Emmigration and Land
Company
File#: 402
Patent#: 402
Patent Vol.: 14
Certificate: 402
Survey/Blk/Twp: 402
Acres: 320
Map(s) 2

Abstract # 610 - TE&L CO
P'ee: TEXAS EMIGRATION AND LAND
COMPANY
G'ee: TEXAS EMIGRATION AND LAND
COMPANY
T-Dt: -- --- -----
P-Dt: 19 Mar 1858
Dist/Class: Texas Emmigration and Land
Company
File#: 403
Patent#: 403
Patent Vol.: 14
Certificate: 403
Survey/Blk/Twp: 403
Acres: 320
Map(s) 2

Abstract # 611 - TE&L CO
P'ee: TEXAS EMIGRATION AND LAND
COMPANY
G'ee: TEXAS EMIGRATION AND LAND
COMPANY
T-Dt: -- --- -----
P-Dt: 19 Mar 1858
Dist/Class: Texas Emmigration and Land
Company
File#: 404
Patent#: 404
Patent Vol.: 14
Certificate: 404
Survey/Blk/Twp: 404
Acres: 320
Map(s) 2

Abstract # 612 - TE&L CO
P'ee: TEXAS EMIGRATION AND LAND
COMPANY
G'ee: TEXAS EMIGRATION AND LAND
COMPANY
T-Dt: -- --- -----
P-Dt: 19 Mar 1858
Dist/Class: Texas Emmigration and Land
Company
File#: 405

Patent#: 405
Patent Vol.: 14
Certificate: 405
Survey/Blk/Twp: 405
Acres: 320
Map(s) 2

Abstract # 613 - TE&L CO
P'ee: TEXAS EMIGRATION AND LAND
COMPANY
G'ee: TEXAS EMIGRATION AND LAND
COMPANY
T-Dt: -- --- -----
P-Dt: 19 Mar 1858
Dist/Class: Texas Emmigration and Land
Company
File#: 406
Patent#: 406
Patent Vol.: 14
Certificate: 406
Survey/Blk/Twp: 406
Acres: 320
Map(s) 2

Abstract # 614 - TE&L CO
P'ee: TEXAS EMIGRATION AND LAND
COMPANY
G'ee: TEXAS EMIGRATION AND LAND
COMPANY
T-Dt: -- --- -----
P-Dt: 20 Mar 1858
Dist/Class: Texas Emmigration and Land
Company
File#: 407
Patent#: 407
Patent Vol.: 14
Certificate: 407
Survey/Blk/Twp: 407
Acres: 320
Map(s) 2

Abstract # 615 - TE&L CO
P'ee: TEXAS EMIGRATION AND LAND
COMPANY
G'ee: TEXAS EMIGRATION AND LAND
COMPANY
T-Dt: -- --- -----
P-Dt: 20 Mar 1858
Dist/Class: Texas Emmigration and Land
Company
File#: 408
Patent#: 408
Patent Vol.: 14
Certificate: 408
Survey/Blk/Twp: 408
Acres: 320
Map(s) 2

Abstract # 616 - TE&L CO
P'ee: TEXAS EMIGRATION AND LAND
COMPANY
G'ee: TEXAS EMIGRATION AND LAND
COMPANY
T-Dt: -- --- -----
P-Dt: 20 Mar 1858
Dist/Class: Texas Emmigration and Land
Company
File#: 409
Patent#: 409
Patent Vol.: 14
Certificate: 409
Survey/Blk/Twp: 409
Acres: 320
Map(s) 2

Abstract # 617 - TE&L CO
P'ee: TEXAS EMIGRATION AND LAND
COMPANY
G'ee: TEXAS EMIGRATION AND LAND
COMPANY
T-Dt: -- --- -----
P-Dt: 20 Mar 1858
Dist/Class: Texas Emmigration and Land
Company
File#: 410
Patent#: 410
Patent Vol.: 14
Certificate: 410
Survey/Blk/Twp: 410
Acres: 320
Map(s) 2

Abstract # 618 - TE&L CO
P'ee: TEXAS EMIGRATION AND LAND
COMPANY
G'ee: TEXAS EMIGRATION AND LAND
COMPANY
T-Dt: -- --- -----
P-Dt: 20 Mar 1858
Dist/Class: Texas Emmigration and Land
Company
File#: 411
Patent#: 411
Patent Vol.: 14
Certificate: 411
Survey/Blk/Twp: 411
Acres: 320
Map(s) 2

Abstract # 619 - TE&L CO
P'ee: TEXAS EMIGRATION AND LAND
COMPANY
G'ee: TEXAS EMIGRATION AND LAND
COMPANY
T-Dt: -- --- -----
P-Dt: 22 Mar 1858
Dist/Class: Texas Emmigration and Land
Company
File#: 412
Patent#: 412
Patent Vol.: 14
Certificate: 412
Survey/Blk/Twp: 412
Acres: 320
Map(s) 2

Abstract # 620 - TE&L CO
P'ee: TEXAS EMIGRATION AND LAND
COMPANY
G'ee: TEXAS EMIGRATION AND LAND
COMPANY
T-Dt: -- --- -----
P-Dt: 22 Mar 1858
Dist/Class: Texas Emmigration and Land
Company
File#: 413
Patent#: 413
Patent Vol.: 14
Certificate: 413
Survey/Blk/Twp: 413
Acres: 320
Map(s) 2, 10

Abstract # 621 - TE&L CO
P'ee: TEXAS EMIGRATION AND LAND
COMPANY
G'ee: TEXAS EMIGRATION AND LAND
COMPANY
T-Dt: -- --- -----
P-Dt: 22 Mar 1858

Dist/Class: Texas Emmigration and Land
Company
File#: 414
Patent#: 414
Patent Vol.: 14
Certificate: 414
Survey/Blk/Twp: 414
Acres: 320
Map(s) 20

Abstract # 622 - TE&L CO
P'ee: TEXAS EMIGRATION AND LAND
COMPANY
G'ee: TEXAS EMIGRATION AND LAND
COMPANY
T-Dt: -- --- -----
P-Dt: 22 Mar 1858
Dist/Class: Texas Emmigration and Land
Company
File#: 415
Patent#: 415
Patent Vol.: 14
Certificate: 415
Survey/Blk/Twp: 415
Acres: 320
Map(s) 20

Abstract # 623 - TE&L CO
P'ee: TEXAS EMIGRATION AND LAND
COMPANY
G'ee: TEXAS EMIGRATION AND LAND
COMPANY
T-Dt: -- --- -----
P-Dt: 22 Mar 1858
Dist/Class: Texas Emmigration and Land
Company
File#: 416
Patent#: 416
Patent Vol.: 14
Certificate: 416
Survey/Blk/Twp: 416
Acres: 320
Map(s) 20

Abstract # 624 - TE&L CO
P'ee: TEXAS EMIGRATION AND LAND
COMPANY
G'ee: TEXAS EMIGRATION AND LAND
COMPANY
T-Dt: -- --- -----
P-Dt: 22 Mar 1858
Dist/Class: Texas Emmigration and Land
Company
File#: 417
Patent#: 417
Patent Vol.: 14
Certificate: 417
Survey/Blk/Twp: 417
Acres: 320
Map(s) 20

Abstract # 625 - TE&L CO
P'ee: TEXAS EMIGRATION AND LAND
COMPANY
G'ee: TEXAS EMIGRATION AND LAND
COMPANY
T-Dt: -- --- -----
P-Dt: 22 Mar 1858
Dist/Class: Texas Emmigration and Land
Company
File#: 418
Patent#: 418
Patent Vol.: 14
Certificate: 418
Survey/Blk/Twp: 418

Acres: 320
Map(s) 20

Abstract # 626 - TE&L CO
P'ee: TEXAS EMIGRATION AND LAND
COMPANY
G'ee: TEXAS EMIGRATION AND LAND
COMPANY
T-Dt: -- --- -----
P-Dt: 22 Mar 1858
Dist/Class: Texas Emmigration and Land
Company
File#: 419
Patent#: 419
Patent Vol.: 14
Certificate: 419
Survey/Blk/Twp: 419
Acres: 320
Map(s) 20

Abstract # 627 - TE&L CO
P'ee: TEXAS EMIGRATION AND LAND
COMPANY
G'ee: TEXAS EMIGRATION AND LAND
COMPANY
T-Dt: -- --- -----
P-Dt: 22 Mar 1858
Dist/Class: Texas Emmigration and Land
Company
File#: 420
Patent#: 420
Patent Vol.: 14
Certificate: 420
Survey/Blk/Twp: 420
Acres: 320
Map(s) 20

Abstract # 628 - TE&L CO
P'ee: TEXAS EMIGRATION AND LAND
COMPANY
G'ee: TEXAS EMIGRATION AND LAND
COMPANY
T-Dt: -- --- -----
P-Dt: 23 Mar 1858
Dist/Class: Texas Emmigration and Land
Company
File#: 421
Patent#: 421
Patent Vol.: 14
Certificate: 421
Survey/Blk/Twp: 421
Acres: 320
Map(s) 20

Abstract # 629 - TE&L CO
P'ee: TEXAS EMIGRATION AND LAND
COMPANY
G'ee: TEXAS EMIGRATION AND LAND
COMPANY
T-Dt: -- --- -----
P-Dt: 23 Mar 1858
Dist/Class: Texas Emmigration and Land
Company
File#: 422
Patent#: 422
Patent Vol.: 14
Certificate: 422
Survey/Blk/Twp: 422
Acres: 320
Map(s) 20

Abstract # 630 - TE&L CO
P'ee: TEXAS EMIGRATION AND LAND
COMPANY
G'ee: TEXAS EMIGRATION AND LAND

COMPANY
T-Dt: -- --- -----
P-Dt: 23 Mar 1858
Dist/Class: Texas Emmigration and Land
Company
File#: 423
Patent#: 423
Patent Vol.: 14
Certificate: 423
Survey/Blk/Twp: 423
Acres: 320
Map(s) 20

Abstract # 631 - TE&L CO
P'ee: TEXAS EMIGRATION AND LAND
COMPANY
G'ee: TEXAS EMIGRATION AND LAND
COMPANY
T-Dt: -- --- -----
P-Dt: 23 Mar 1858
Dist/Class: Texas Emmigration and Land
Company
File#: 424
Patent#: 424
Patent Vol.: 14
Certificate: 424
Survey/Blk/Twp: 424
Acres: 320
Map(s) 20

Abstract # 632 - TE&L CO
P'ee: TEXAS EMIGRATION AND LAND
COMPANY
G'ee: TEXAS EMIGRATION AND LAND
COMPANY
T-Dt: -- --- -----
P-Dt: 23 Mar 1858
Dist/Class: Texas Emmigration and Land
Company
File#: 425
Patent#: 425
Patent Vol.: 14
Certificate: 425
Survey/Blk/Twp: 425
Acres: 320
Map(s) 20, 21

Abstract # 633 - TE&L CO
P'ee: SHIRLEY, ZACHARIAH
G'ee: TEXAS EMIGRATION AND LAND
COMPANY
T-Dt: -- --- -----
P-Dt: 24 Sep 1857
Dist/Class: Texas Emmigration and Land
Company
File#: 426
Patent#: 113
Patent Vol.: 14
Certificate: 426
Survey/Blk/Twp: 426
Acres: 320
Map(s) 21

Abstract # 634 - TE&L CO
P'ee: SHIRLEY, ZACHARIAH
G'ee: TEXAS EMIGRATION AND LAND
COMPANY
T-Dt: -- --- -----
P-Dt: 24 Sep 1857
Dist/Class: Texas Emmigration and Land
Company
File#: 427
Patent#: 114
Patent Vol.: 14
Certificate: 427

Survey/Blk/Twp: 427
Acres: 320
Map(s) 21

Abstract # 635 - TE&L CO
P'ee: TEXAS EMIGRATION AND LAND COMPANY
G'ee: TEXAS EMIGRATION AND LAND COMPANY
T-Dt: -- --- -----
P-Dt: 24 Mar 1858
Dist/Class: Texas Emmigration and Land Company
File#: 428
Patent#: 428
Patent Vol.: 14
Certificate: 428
Survey/Blk/Twp: 428
Acres: 320
Map(s) 20

Abstract # 636 - TE&L CO
P'ee: TEXAS EMIGRATION AND LAND COMPANY
G'ee: TEXAS EMIGRATION AND LAND COMPANY
T-Dt: -- --- -----
P-Dt: 24 Mar 1858
Dist/Class: Texas Emmigration and Land Company
File#: 429
Patent#: 429
Patent Vol.: 14
Certificate: 429
Survey/Blk/Twp: 429
Acres: 320
Map(s) 20, 21

Abstract # 637 - TE&L CO
P'ee: SHIRLEY, ZACHARIAH
G'ee: TEXAS EMIGRATION AND LAND COMPANY
T-Dt: -- --- -----
P-Dt: 25 Sep 1857
Dist/Class: Texas Emmigration and Land Company
File#: 430
Patent#: 115
Patent Vol.: 14
Certificate: 430
Survey/Blk/Twp: 430
Acres: 320
Map(s) 21

Abstract # 638 - TE&L CO
P'ee: SHIRLEY, ZACHARIAH
G'ee: TEXAS EMIGRATION AND LAND COMPANY
T-Dt: -- --- -----
P-Dt: 25 Sep 1857
Dist/Class: Texas Emmigration and Land Company
File#: 431
Patent#: 116
Patent Vol.: 14
Certificate: 431
Survey/Blk/Twp: 431
Acres: 320
Map(s) 21

Abstract # 639 - TE&L CO
P'ee: TEXAS EMIGRATION AND LAND COMPANY
G'ee: TEXAS EMIGRATION AND LAND COMPANY

T-Dt: -- --- -----
P-Dt: 24 Mar 1858
Dist/Class: Texas Emmigration and Land Company
File#: 432
Patent#: 432
Patent Vol.: 14
Certificate: 432
Survey/Blk/Twp: 432
Acres: 320
Map(s) 21

Abstract # 640 - TE&L CO
P'ee: TEXAS EMIGRATION AND LAND COMPANY
G'ee: TEXAS EMIGRATION AND LAND COMPANY
T-Dt: -- --- -----
P-Dt: 24 Mar 1858
Dist/Class: Texas Emmigration and Land Company
File#: 433
Patent#: 433
Patent Vol.: 14
Certificate: 433
Survey/Blk/Twp: 433
Acres: 320
Map(s) 21

Abstract # 641 - TE&L CO
P'ee: TEXAS EMIGRATION AND LAND COMPANY
G'ee: TEXAS EMIGRATION AND LAND COMPANY
T-Dt: -- --- -----
P-Dt: 24 Mar 1858
Dist/Class: Texas Emmigration and Land Company
File#: 434
Patent#: 434
Patent Vol.: 14
Certificate: 434
Survey/Blk/Twp: 434
Acres: 320
Map(s) 20, 21

Abstract # 642 - TE&L CO
P'ee: TEXAS EMIGRATION AND LAND COMPANY
G'ee: TEXAS EMIGRATION AND LAND COMPANY
T-Dt: -- --- -----
P-Dt: 24 Mar 1858
Dist/Class: Texas Emmigration and Land Company
File#: 435
Patent#: 435
Patent Vol.: 14
Certificate: 435
Survey/Blk/Twp: 435
Acres: 320
Map(s) 20

Abstract # 643 - TE&L CO
P'ee: TEXAS EMIGRATION AND LAND COMPANY
G'ee: TEXAS EMIGRATION AND LAND COMPANY
T-Dt: -- --- -----
P-Dt: 24 Mar 1858
Dist/Class: Texas Emmigration and Land Company
File#: 436
Patent#: 436
Patent Vol.: 14

Certificate: 436
Survey/Blk/Twp: 436
Acres: 320
Map(s) 20

Abstract # 644 - TE&L CO
P'ee: TEXAS EMIGRATION AND LAND COMPANY
G'ee: TEXAS EMIGRATION AND LAND COMPANY
T-Dt: -- --- -----
P-Dt: 27 Jun 1951
Dist/Class: Texas Emmigration and Land Company
File#: 437
Patent#: 35
Patent Vol.: 18-B
Certificate: 437
Survey/Blk/Twp: 437
Acres: 320
Map(s) 20, 21

Abstract # 645 - TE&L CO
P'ee: TEXAS EMIGRATION AND LAND COMPANY
G'ee: TEXAS EMIGRATION AND LAND COMPANY
T-Dt: -- --- -----
P-Dt: 25 Mar 1858
Dist/Class: Texas Emmigration and Land Company
File#: 438
Patent#: 438
Patent Vol.: 14
Certificate: 438
Survey/Blk/Twp: 438
Acres: 320
Map(s) 21

Abstract # 646 - TE&L CO
P'ee: TEXAS EMIGRATION AND LAND COMPANY
G'ee: TEXAS EMIGRATION AND LAND COMPANY
T-Dt: -- --- -----
P-Dt: 25 Mar 1858
Dist/Class: Texas Emmigration and Land Company
File#: 439
Patent#: 439
Patent Vol.: 14
Certificate: 439
Survey/Blk/Twp: 439
Acres: 320
Map(s) 21

Abstract # 647 - TE&L CO
P'ee: TEXAS EMIGRATION AND LAND COMPANY
G'ee: TEXAS EMIGRATION AND LAND COMPANY
T-Dt: -- --- -----
P-Dt: 25 Mar 1858
Dist/Class: Texas Emmigration and Land Company
File#: 440
Patent#: 440
Patent Vol.: 14
Certificate: 440
Survey/Blk/Twp: 440
Acres: 320
Map(s) 21

Abstract # 648 - TE&L CO
P'ee: TEXAS EMIGRATION AND LAND

COMPANY
G'ee: TEXAS EMIGRATION AND LAND
COMPANY
T-Dt: -- --- -----
P-Dt: 25 Mar 1858
Dist/Class: Texas Emmigration and Land
Company
File#: 441
Patent#: 441
Patent Vol.: 14
Certificate: 441
Survey/Blk/Twp: 441
Acres: 320
Map(s) 21

Abstract # 649 - TE&L CO
P'ee: TEXAS EMIGRATION AND LAND
COMPANY
G'ee: TEXAS EMIGRATION AND LAND
COMPANY
T-Dt: -- --- -----
P-Dt: 25 Mar 1858
Dist/Class: Texas Emmigration and Land
Company
File#: 442
Patent#: 442
Patent Vol.: 14
Certificate: 442
Survey/Blk/Twp: 442
Acres: 320
Map(s) 20, 21

Abstract # 650 - TE&L CO
P'ee: TEXAS EMIGRATION AND LAND
COMPANY
G'ee: TEXAS EMIGRATION AND LAND
COMPANY
T-Dt: -- --- -----
P-Dt: 25 Mar 1858
Dist/Class: Texas Emmigration and Land
Company
File#: 443
Patent#: 443
Patent Vol.: 14
Certificate: 443
Survey/Blk/Twp: 443
Acres: 320
Map(s) 20

Abstract # 651 - TE&L CO
P'ee: TEXAS EMIGRATION AND LAND
COMPANY
G'ee: TEXAS EMIGRATION AND LAND
COMPANY
T-Dt: -- --- -----
P-Dt: 25 Mar 1858
Dist/Class: Texas Emmigration and Land
Company
File#: 444
Patent#: 444
Patent Vol.: 14
Certificate: 444
Survey/Blk/Twp: 444
Acres: 320
Map(s) 21

Abstract # 652 - TE&L CO
P'ee: TEXAS EMIGRATION AND LAND
COMPANY
G'ee: TEXAS EMIGRATION AND LAND
COMPANY
T-Dt: -- --- -----
P-Dt: 25 Mar 1858
Dist/Class: Texas Emmigration and Land
Company

File#: 445
Patent#: 445
Patent Vol.: 14
Certificate: 445
Survey/Blk/Twp: 445
Acres: 320
Map(s) 21

Abstract # 653 - TE&L CO
P'ee: SHIRLEY, ZACHARIAH
G'ee: TEXAS EMIGRATION AND LAND
COMPANY
T-Dt: -- --- -----
P-Dt: 25 Sep 1857
Dist/Class: Texas Emmigration and Land
Company
File#: 446
Patent#: 117
Patent Vol.: 14
Certificate: 446
Survey/Blk/Twp: 446
Acres: 320
Map(s) 21, 22

Abstract # 654 - TE&L CO
P'ee: SHIRLEY, ZACHARIAH
G'ee: TEXAS EMIGRATION AND LAND
COMPANY
T-Dt: -- --- -----
P-Dt: 21 Sep 1857
Dist/Class: Texas Emmigration and Land
Company
File#: 447
Patent#: 103
Patent Vol.: 14
Certificate: 447
Survey/Blk/Twp: 447
Acres: 320
Map(s) 22

Abstract # 655 - TE&L CO
P'ee: TEXAS EMIGRATION AND LAND
COMPANY
G'ee: TEXAS EMIGRATION AND LAND
COMPANY
T-Dt: -- --- -----
P-Dt: 26 Mar 1858
Dist/Class: Texas Emmigration and Land
Company
File#: 448
Patent#: 448
Patent Vol.: 14
Certificate: 448
Survey/Blk/Twp: 448
Acres: 320
Map(s) 22

Abstract # 656 - TE&L CO
P'ee: TEXAS EMIGRATION AND LAND
COMPANY
G'ee: TEXAS EMIGRATION AND LAND
COMPANY
T-Dt: -- --- -----
P-Dt: 26 Mar 1858
Dist/Class: Texas Emmigration and Land
Company
File#: 449
Patent#: 449
Patent Vol.: 14
Certificate: 449
Survey/Blk/Twp: 449
Acres: 320
Map(s) 22

Abstract # 657 - TE&L CO

P'ee: TEXAS EMIGRATION AND LAND
COMPANY
G'ee: TEXAS EMIGRATION AND LAND
COMPANY
T-Dt: -- --- -----
P-Dt: 26 Mar 1858
Dist/Class: Texas Emmigration and Land
Company
File#: 450
Patent#: 450
Patent Vol.: 14
Certificate: 450
Survey/Blk/Twp: 450
Acres: 320
Map(s) 22

Abstract # 658 - TE&L CO
P'ee: TEXAS EMIGRATION AND LAND
COMPANY
G'ee: TEXAS EMIGRATION AND LAND
COMPANY
T-Dt: -- --- -----
P-Dt: 29 Mar 1858
Dist/Class: Texas Emmigration and Land
Company
File#: 451
Patent#: 451
Patent Vol.: 14
Certificate: 451
Survey/Blk/Twp: 451
Acres: 320
Map(s) 22

Abstract # 659 - TE&L CO
P'ee: TEXAS EMIGRATION AND LAND
COMPANY
G'ee: TEXAS EMIGRATION AND LAND
COMPANY
T-Dt: -- --- -----
P-Dt: 29 Mar 1858
Dist/Class: Texas Emmigration and Land
Company
File#: 452
Patent#: 452
Patent Vol.: 14
Certificate: 452
Survey/Blk/Twp: 452
Acres: 320
Map(s) 22

Abstract # 660 - TE&L CO
P'ee: TEXAS EMIGRATION AND LAND
COMPANY
G'ee: TEXAS EMIGRATION AND LAND
COMPANY
T-Dt: -- --- -----
P-Dt: 29 Mar 1858
Dist/Class: Texas Emmigration and Land
Company
File#: 453
Patent#: 453
Patent Vol.: 14
Certificate: 453
Survey/Blk/Twp: 453
Acres: 320
Map(s) 22

Abstract # 661 - TE&L CO
P'ee: TEXAS EMIGRATION AND LAND
COMPANY
G'ee: TEXAS EMIGRATION AND LAND
COMPANY
T-Dt: -- --- -----
P-Dt: 29 Mar 1858
Dist/Class: Texas Emmigration and Land

Company
File#: 454
Patent#: 454
Patent Vol.: 14
Certificate: 454
Survey/Blk/Twp: 454
Acres: 320
Map(s) 22

Abstract # 662 - TE&L CO
P'ee: TEXAS EMIGRATION AND LAND
COMPANY
G'ee: TEXAS EMIGRATION AND LAND
COMPANY
T-Dt: -- --- -----
P-Dt: 29 Mar 1858
Dist/Class: Texas Emmigration and Land
Company
File#: 455
Patent#: 455
Patent Vol.: 14
Certificate: 455
Survey/Blk/Twp: 455
Acres: 320
Map(s) 21, 22

Abstract # 663 - TE&L CO
P'ee: TEXAS EMIGRATION AND LAND
COMPANY
G'ee: TEXAS EMIGRATION AND LAND
COMPANY
T-Dt: -- --- -----
P-Dt: 29 Mar 1858
Dist/Class: Texas Emmigration and Land
Company
File#: 456
Patent#: 456
Patent Vol.: 14
Certificate: 456
Survey/Blk/Twp: 456
Acres: 320
Map(s) 21

Abstract # 664 - TE&L CO
P'ee: TEXAS EMIGRATION AND LAND
COMPANY
G'ee: TEXAS EMIGRATION AND LAND
COMPANY
T-Dt: -- --- -----
P-Dt: 29 Mar 1858
Dist/Class: Texas Emmigration and Land
Company
File#: 457
Patent#: 457
Patent Vol.: 14
Certificate: 457
Survey/Blk/Twp: 457
Acres: 320
Map(s) 21

Abstract # 665 - TE&L CO
P'ee: TEXAS EMIGRATION AND LAND
COMPANY
G'ee: TEXAS EMIGRATION AND LAND
COMPANY
T-Dt: -- --- -----
P-Dt: 30 Mar 1858
Dist/Class: Texas Emmigration and Land
Company
File#: 458
Patent#: 458
Patent Vol.: 14
Certificate: 458
Survey/Blk/Twp: 458
Acres: 320

Map(s) 21

Abstract # 666 - TE&L CO
P'ee: TEXAS EMIGRATION AND LAND
COMPANY
G'ee: TEXAS EMIGRATION AND LAND
COMPANY
T-Dt: -- --- -----
P-Dt: 30 Mar 1858
Dist/Class: Texas Emmigration and Land
Company
File#: 459
Patent#: 459
Patent Vol.: 14
Certificate: 459
Survey/Blk/Twp: 459
Acres: 320
Map(s) 21

Abstract # 667 - TE&L CO
P'ee: TEXAS EMIGRATION AND LAND
COMPANY
G'ee: TEXAS EMIGRATION AND LAND
COMPANY
T-Dt: -- --- -----
P-Dt: 30 Mar 1858
Dist/Class: Texas Emmigration and Land
Company
File#: 460
Patent#: 460
Patent Vol.: 14
Certificate: 460
Survey/Blk/Twp: 460
Acres: 320
Map(s) 21, 22

Abstract # 668 - TE&L CO
P'ee: TEXAS EMIGRATION AND LAND
COMPANY
G'ee: TEXAS EMIGRATION AND LAND
COMPANY
T-Dt: -- --- -----
P-Dt: 30 Mar 1858
Dist/Class: Texas Emmigration and Land
Company
File#: 461
Patent#: 461
Patent Vol.: 14
Certificate: 461
Survey/Blk/Twp: 461
Acres: 320
Map(s) 22

Abstract # 669 - TE&L CO
P'ee: TEXAS EMIGRATION AND LAND
COMPANY
G'ee: TEXAS EMIGRATION AND LAND
COMPANY
T-Dt: -- --- -----
P-Dt: 30 Mar 1858
Dist/Class: Texas Emmigration and Land
Company
File#: 462
Patent#: 462
Patent Vol.: 14
Certificate: 462
Survey/Blk/Twp: 462
Acres: 320
Map(s) 22

Abstract # 670 - TE&L CO
P'ee: TEXAS EMIGRATION AND LAND
COMPANY
G'ee: TEXAS EMIGRATION AND LAND
COMPANY

T-Dt: -- --- -----
P-Dt: 30 Mar 1858
Dist/Class: Texas Emmigration and Land
Company
File#: 463
Patent#: 463
Patent Vol.: 14
Certificate: 463
Survey/Blk/Twp: 463
Acres: 320
Map(s) 22

Abstract # 671 - TE&L CO
P'ee: TEXAS EMIGRATION AND LAND
COMPANY
G'ee: TEXAS EMIGRATION AND LAND
COMPANY
T-Dt: -- --- -----
P-Dt: 30 Mar 1858
Dist/Class: Texas Emmigration and Land
Company
File#: 464
Patent#: 464
Patent Vol.: 14
Certificate: 464
Survey/Blk/Twp: 464
Acres: 320
Map(s) 22

Abstract # 672 - TE&L CO
P'ee: TEXAS EMIGRATION AND LAND
COMPANY
G'ee: TEXAS EMIGRATION AND LAND
COMPANY
T-Dt: -- --- -----
P-Dt: 30 Mar 1858
Dist/Class: Texas Emmigration and Land
Company
File#: 465
Patent#: 465
Patent Vol.: 14
Certificate: 465
Survey/Blk/Twp: 465
Acres: 320
Map(s) 21

Abstract # 673 - TE&L CO
P'ee: TEXAS EMIGRATION AND LAND
COMPANY
G'ee: TEXAS EMIGRATION AND LAND
COMPANY
T-Dt: -- --- -----
P-Dt: 31 Mar 1858
Dist/Class: Texas Emmigration and Land
Company
File#: 466
Patent#: 466
Patent Vol.: 14
Certificate: 466
Survey/Blk/Twp: 466
Acres: 320
Map(s) 21

Abstract # 674 - TE&L CO
P'ee: TEXAS EMIGRATION AND LAND
COMPANY
G'ee: TEXAS EMIGRATION AND LAND
COMPANY
T-Dt: -- --- -----
P-Dt: 31 Mar 1858
Dist/Class: Texas Emmigration and Land
Company
File#: 467
Patent#: 467
Patent Vol.: 14

Certificate: 467
Survey/Blk/Twp: 467
Acres: 320
Map(s) 22

Abstract # 675 - TE&L CO
P'ee: TEXAS EMIGRATION AND LAND
COMPANY
G'ee: TEXAS EMIGRATION AND LAND
COMPANY
T-Dt: -- --- -----
P-Dt: 31 Mar 1858
Dist/Class: Texas Emmigration and Land
Company
File#: 468
Patent#: 468
Patent Vol.: 14
Certificate: 468
Survey/Blk/Twp: 468
Acres: 320
Map(s) 22

Abstract # 676 - TE&L CO
P'ee: TEXAS EMIGRATION AND LAND
COMPANY
G'ee: TEXAS EMIGRATION AND LAND
COMPANY
T-Dt: -- --- -----
P-Dt: 31 Mar 1858
Dist/Class: Texas Emmigration and Land
Company
File#: 469
Patent#: 469
Patent Vol.: 14
Certificate: 469
Survey/Blk/Twp: 469
Acres: 320
Map(s) 21, 22

Abstract # 677 - TE&L CO
P'ee: TEXAS EMIGRATION AND LAND
COMPANY
G'ee: TEXAS EMIGRATION AND LAND
COMPANY
T-Dt: -- --- -----
P-Dt: 31 Mar 1858
Dist/Class: Texas Emmigration and Land
Company
File#: 470
Patent#: 470
Patent Vol.: 14
Certificate: 470
Survey/Blk/Twp: 470
Acres: 320
Map(s) 21

Abstract # 678 - TE&L CO
P'ee: TEXAS EMIGRATION AND LAND
COMPANY
G'ee: TEXAS EMIGRATION AND LAND
COMPANY
T-Dt: -- --- -----
P-Dt: 31 Mar 1858
Dist/Class: Texas Emmigration and Land
Company
File#: 471
Patent#: 471
Patent Vol.: 14
Certificate: 471
Survey/Blk/Twp: 471
Acres: 320
Map(s) 21

Abstract # 679 - TE&L CO
P'ee: TEXAS EMIGRATION AND LAND

COMPANY
G'ee: TEXAS EMIGRATION AND LAND
COMPANY
T-Dt: -- --- -----
P-Dt: 31 Mar 1858
Dist/Class: Texas Emmigration and Land
Company
File#: 472
Patent#: 472
Patent Vol.: 14
Certificate: 472
Survey/Blk/Twp: 472
Acres: 320
Map(s) 21

Abstract # 680 - TE&L CO
P'ee: TEXAS EMIGRATION AND LAND
COMPANY
G'ee: TEXAS EMIGRATION AND LAND
COMPANY
T-Dt: -- --- -----
P-Dt: 01 Apr 1858
Dist/Class: Texas Emmigration and Land
Company
File#: 473
Patent#: 473
Patent Vol.: 14
Certificate: 473
Survey/Blk/Twp: 473
Acres: 320
Map(s) 21

Abstract # 681 - TE&L CO
P'ee: TEXAS EMIGRATION AND LAND
COMPANY
G'ee: TEXAS EMIGRATION AND LAND
COMPANY
T-Dt: -- --- -----
P-Dt: 01 Apr 1858
Dist/Class: Texas Emmigration and Land
Company
File#: 474
Patent#: 474
Patent Vol.: 14
Certificate: 474
Survey/Blk/Twp: 474
Acres: 320
Map(s) 21, 22

Abstract # 682 - TE&L CO
P'ee: TEXAS EMIGRATION AND LAND
COMPANY
G'ee: TEXAS EMIGRATION AND LAND
COMPANY
T-Dt: -- --- -----
P-Dt: 01 Apr 1858
Dist/Class: Texas Emmigration and Land
Company
File#: 475
Patent#: 475
Patent Vol.: 14
Certificate: 475
Survey/Blk/Twp: 475
Acres: 320
Map(s) 22

Abstract # 683 - TE&L CO
P'ee: TEXAS EMIGRATION AND LAND
COMPANY
G'ee: TEXAS EMIGRATION AND LAND
COMPANY
T-Dt: -- --- -----
P-Dt: 01 Apr 1858
Dist/Class: Texas Emmigration and Land
Company

File#: 476
Patent#: 476
Patent Vol.: 14
Certificate: 476
Survey/Blk/Twp: 476
Acres: 320
Map(s) 22

Abstract # 684 - TE&L CO
P'ee: TEXAS EMIGRATION AND LAND
COMPANY
G'ee: TEXAS EMIGRATION AND LAND
COMPANY
T-Dt: -- --- -----
P-Dt: 01 Apr 1858
Dist/Class: Texas Emmigration and Land
Company
File#: 477
Patent#: 477
Patent Vol.: 14
Certificate: 477
Survey/Blk/Twp: 477
Acres: 320
Map(s) 21, 29

Abstract # 685 - TE&L CO
P'ee: TEXAS EMIGRATION AND LAND
COMPANY
G'ee: TEXAS EMIGRATION AND LAND
COMPANY
T-Dt: -- --- -----
P-Dt: 06 Apr 1858
Dist/Class: Texas Emmigration and Land
Company
File#: 494
Patent#: 494
Patent Vol.: 14
Certificate: 494
Survey/Blk/Twp: 494
Acres: 320
Map(s) 19

Abstract # 686 - TE&L CO
P'ee: TEXAS EMIGRATION AND LAND
COMPANY
G'ee: TEXAS EMIGRATION AND LAND
COMPANY
T-Dt: -- --- -----
P-Dt: 10 Apr 1858
Dist/Class: Texas Emmigration and Land
Company
File#: 495
Patent#: 495
Patent Vol.: 14
Certificate: 495
Survey/Blk/Twp: 495
Acres: 320
Map(s) 18, 19

Abstract # 687 - TE&L CO
P'ee: TEXAS EMIGRATION AND LAND
COMPANY
G'ee: TEXAS EMIGRATION AND LAND
COMPANY
T-Dt: -- --- -----
P-Dt: 10 Apr 1858
Dist/Class: Texas Emmigration and Land
Company
File#: 496
Patent#: 496
Patent Vol.: 14
Certificate: 496
Survey/Blk/Twp: 496
Acres: 320
Map(s) 18

Abstract # 688 - TE&L CO
P'ee: TEXAS EMIGRATION AND LAND
COMPANY
G'ee: TEXAS EMIGRATION AND LAND
COMPANY
T-Dt: -- --- -----
P-Dt: 19 Mar 1859
Dist/Class: Texas Emmigration and Land
Company
File#: 497
Patent#: 1131
Patent Vol.: 14
Certificate: 497
Survey/Blk/Twp: 497
Acres: 320
Map(s) 18

Abstract # 689 - TE&L CO
P'ee: TEXAS EMIGRATION AND LAND
COMPANY
G'ee: TEXAS EMIGRATION AND LAND
COMPANY
T-Dt: -- --- -----
P-Dt: 10 Apr 1858
Dist/Class: Texas Emmigration and Land
Company
File#: 498
Patent#: 498
Patent Vol.: 14
Certificate: 498
Survey/Blk/Twp: 498
Acres: 320
Map(s) 18

Abstract # 690 - TE&L CO
P'ee: TEXAS EMIGRATION AND LAND
COMPANY
G'ee: TEXAS EMIGRATION AND LAND
COMPANY
T-Dt: -- --- -----
P-Dt: 12 Apr 1858
Dist/Class: Texas Emmigration and Land
Company
File#: 499
Patent#: 499
Patent Vol.: 14
Certificate: 499
Survey/Blk/Twp: 499
Acres: 320
Map(s) 18

Abstract # 691 - TE&L CO
P'ee: TEXAS EMIGRATION AND LAND
COMPANY
G'ee: TEXAS EMIGRATION AND LAND
COMPANY
T-Dt: -- --- -----
P-Dt: 13 Apr 1858
Dist/Class: Texas Emmigration and Land
Company
File#: 500
Patent#: 500
Patent Vol.: 14
Certificate: 500
Survey/Blk/Twp: 500
Acres: 320
Map(s) 18

Abstract # 692 - TE&L CO
P'ee: TEXAS EMIGRATION AND LAND
COMPANY
G'ee: TEXAS EMIGRATION AND LAND
COMPANY
T-Dt: -- --- -----
P-Dt: 10 May 1858

Dist/Class: Texas Emmigration and Land
Company
File#: 601
Patent#: 601
Patent Vol.: 14
Certificate: 601
Survey/Blk/Twp: 601
Acres: 320
Map(s) 13

Abstract # 693 - TE&L CO
P'ee: TEXAS EMIGRATION AND LAND
COMPANY
G'ee: TEXAS EMIGRATION AND LAND
COMPANY
T-Dt: -- --- -----
P-Dt: 10 May 1858
Dist/Class: Texas Emmigration and Land
Company
File#: 602
Patent#: 602
Patent Vol.: 14
Certificate: 602
Survey/Blk/Twp: 602
Acres: 320
Map(s) 13

Abstract # 694 - TE&L CO
P'ee: TEXAS EMIGRATION AND LAND
COMPANY
G'ee: TEXAS EMIGRATION AND LAND
COMPANY
T-Dt: -- --- -----
P-Dt: 10 May 1858
Dist/Class: Texas Emmigration and Land
Company
File#: 603
Patent#: 603
Patent Vol.: 14
Certificate: 603
Survey/Blk/Twp: 603
Acres: 320
Map(s) 13

Abstract # 695 - TE&L CO
P'ee: TEXAS EMIGRATION AND LAND
COMPANY
G'ee: TEXAS EMIGRATION AND LAND
COMPANY
T-Dt: -- --- -----
P-Dt: 10 May 1858
Dist/Class: Texas Emmigration and Land
Company
File#: 604
Patent#: 604
Patent Vol.: 14
Certificate: 604
Survey/Blk/Twp: 604
Acres: 320
Map(s) 13

Abstract # 696 - TE&L CO
P'ee: TEXAS EMIGRATION AND LAND
COMPANY
G'ee: TEXAS EMIGRATION AND LAND
COMPANY
T-Dt: -- --- -----
P-Dt: 10 May 1858
Dist/Class: Texas Emmigration and Land
Company
File#: 605
Patent#: 605
Patent Vol.: 14
Certificate: 605
Survey/Blk/Twp: 605

Acres: 320
Map(s) 13, 21

Abstract # 697 - TE&L CO
P'ee: TEXAS EMIGRATION AND LAND
COMPANY
G'ee: TEXAS EMIGRATION AND LAND
COMPANY
T-Dt: -- --- -----
P-Dt: 11 May 1858
Dist/Class: Texas Emmigration and Land
Company
File#: 606
Patent#: 606
Patent Vol.: 14
Certificate: 606
Survey/Blk/Twp: 606
Acres: 320
Map(s) 13, 21

Abstract # 698 - TE&L CO
P'ee: TEXAS EMIGRATION AND LAND
COMPANY
G'ee: TEXAS EMIGRATION AND LAND
COMPANY
T-Dt: -- --- -----
P-Dt: 11 May 1858
Dist/Class: Texas Emmigration and Land
Company
File#: 607
Patent#: 607
Patent Vol.: 14
Certificate: 607
Survey/Blk/Twp: 607
Acres: 320
Map(s) 13

Abstract # 699 - TE&L CO
P'ee: TEXAS EMIGRATION AND LAND
COMPANY
G'ee: TEXAS EMIGRATION AND LAND
COMPANY
T-Dt: -- --- -----
P-Dt: 11 May 1858
Dist/Class: Texas Emmigration and Land
Company
File#: 608
Patent#: 608
Patent Vol.: 14
Certificate: 608
Survey/Blk/Twp: 608
Acres: 320
Map(s) 13

Abstract # 700 - TE&L CO
P'ee: TEXAS EMIGRATION AND LAND
COMPANY
G'ee: TEXAS EMIGRATION AND LAND
COMPANY
T-Dt: -- --- -----
P-Dt: 11 May 1858
Dist/Class: Texas Emmigration and Land
Company
File#: 609
Patent#: 609
Patent Vol.: 14
Certificate: 609
Survey/Blk/Twp: 609
Acres: 320
Map(s) 13

Abstract # 701 - TE&L CO
P'ee: TEXAS EMIGRATION AND LAND
COMPANY
G'ee: TEXAS EMIGRATION AND LAND

COMPANY
T-Dt: -- --- -----
P-Dt: 28 May 1858
Dist/Class: Texas Emmigration and Land Company
File#: 610
Patent#: 610
Patent Vol.: 14
Certificate: 610
Survey/Blk/Twp: 610
Acres: 320
Map(s) 13

Abstract # 702 - TE&L CO
P'ee: TEXAS EMIGRATION AND LAND COMPANY
G'ee: TEXAS EMIGRATION AND LAND COMPANY
T-Dt: -- --- -----
P-Dt: 11 May 1858
Dist/Class: Texas Emmigration and Land Company
File#: 611
Patent#: 611
Patent Vol.: 14
Certificate: 611
Survey/Blk/Twp: 611
Acres: 320
Map(s) 13

Abstract # 703 - TE&L CO
P'ee: TEXAS EMIGRATION AND LAND COMPANY
G'ee: TEXAS EMIGRATION AND LAND COMPANY
T-Dt: -- --- -----
P-Dt: 12 May 1858
Dist/Class: Texas Emmigration and Land Company
File#: 612
Patent#: 612
Patent Vol.: 14
Certificate: 612
Survey/Blk/Twp: 612
Acres: 320
Map(s) 13

Abstract # 704 - TE&L CO
P'ee: TEXAS EMIGRATION AND LAND COMPANY
G'ee: TEXAS EMIGRATION AND LAND COMPANY
T-Dt: -- --- -----
P-Dt: 12 May 1858
Dist/Class: Texas Emmigration and Land Company
File#: 613
Patent#: 613
Patent Vol.: 14
Certificate: 613
Survey/Blk/Twp: 613
Acres: 320
Map(s) 13

Abstract # 705 - TE&L CO
P'ee: TEXAS EMIGRATION AND LAND COMPANY
G'ee: TEXAS EMIGRATION AND LAND COMPANY
T-Dt: -- --- -----
P-Dt: 12 May 1858
Dist/Class: Texas Emmigration and Land Company
File#: 614
Patent#: 614

Patent Vol.: 14
Certificate: 614
Survey/Blk/Twp: 614
Acres: 320
Map(s) 13

Abstract # 706 - TE&L CO
P'ee: TEXAS EMIGRATION AND LAND COMPANY
G'ee: TEXAS EMIGRATION AND LAND COMPANY
T-Dt: -- --- -----
P-Dt: 12 May 1858
Dist/Class: Texas Emmigration and Land Company
File#: 615
Patent#: 615
Patent Vol.: 14
Certificate: 615
Survey/Blk/Twp: 615
Acres: 320
Map(s) 13, 21

Abstract # 707 - TE&L CO
P'ee: TEXAS EMIGRATION AND LAND COMPANY
G'ee: TEXAS EMIGRATION AND LAND COMPANY
T-Dt: -- --- -----
P-Dt: 12 May 1858
Dist/Class: Texas Emmigration and Land Company
File#: 616
Patent#: 616
Patent Vol.: 14
Certificate: 616
Survey/Blk/Twp: 616
Acres: 320
Map(s) 12, 13, 20, 21

Abstract # 708 - TE&L CO
P'ee: TEXAS EMIGRATION AND LAND COMPANY
G'ee: TEXAS EMIGRATION AND LAND COMPANY
T-Dt: -- --- -----
P-Dt: 13 May 1858
Dist/Class: Texas Emmigration and Land Company
File#: 617
Patent#: 617
Patent Vol.: 14
Certificate: 617
Survey/Blk/Twp: 617
Acres: 320
Map(s) 12, 13

Abstract # 709 - TE&L CO
P'ee: TEXAS EMIGRATION AND LAND COMPANY
G'ee: TEXAS EMIGRATION AND LAND COMPANY
T-Dt: -- --- -----
P-Dt: 13 May 1858
Dist/Class: Texas Emmigration and Land Company
File#: 618
Patent#: 618
Patent Vol.: 14
Certificate: 618
Survey/Blk/Twp: 618
Acres: 320
Map(s) 12, 13

Abstract # 710 - TE&L CO

P'ee: TEXAS EMIGRATION AND LAND COMPANY
G'ee: TEXAS EMIGRATION AND LAND COMPANY
T-Dt: -- --- -----
P-Dt: 13 May 1858
Dist/Class: Texas Emmigration and Land Company
File#: 619
Patent#: 619
Patent Vol.: 14
Certificate: 619
Survey/Blk/Twp: 619
Acres: 320
Map(s) 12, 13

Abstract # 711 - TE&L CO
P'ee: TEXAS EMIGRATION AND LAND COMPANY
G'ee: TEXAS EMIGRATION AND LAND COMPANY
T-Dt: -- --- -----
P-Dt: 31 May 1858
Dist/Class: Texas Emmigration and Land Company
File#: 706
Patent#: 706
Patent Vol.: 14
Certificate: 706
Survey/Blk/Twp: 706
Acres: 320
Map(s) 9, 10, 17, 18

Abstract # 712 - TE&L CO
P'ee: TEXAS EMIGRATION AND LAND COMPANY
G'ee: TEXAS EMIGRATION AND LAND COMPANY
T-Dt: -- --- -----
P-Dt: 31 May 1858
Dist/Class: Texas Emmigration and Land Company
File#: 707
Patent#: 707
Patent Vol.: 14
Certificate: 707
Survey/Blk/Twp: 707
Acres: 320
Map(s) 9, 17

Abstract # 713 - TE&L CO
P'ee: TEXAS EMIGRATION AND LAND COMPANY
G'ee: TEXAS EMIGRATION AND LAND COMPANY
T-Dt: -- --- -----
P-Dt: 31 May 1858
Dist/Class: Texas Emmigration and Land Company
File#: 708
Patent#: 708
Patent Vol.: 14
Certificate: 708
Survey/Blk/Twp: 708
Acres: 320
Map(s) 9, 17

Abstract # 714 - TE&L CO
P'ee: TEXAS EMIGRATION AND LAND COMPANY
G'ee: TEXAS EMIGRATION AND LAND COMPANY
T-Dt: -- --- -----
P-Dt: 01 Jun 1858
Dist/Class: Texas Emmigration and Land

Company
File#: 709
Patent#: 709
Patent Vol.: 14
Certificate: 709
Survey/Blk/Twp: 709
Acres: 385
Map(s) 9, 17

Abstract # 715 - TE&L CO
P'ee: TEXAS EMIGRATION AND LAND
COMPANY
G'ee: TEXAS EMIGRATION AND LAND
COMPANY
T-Dt: -- --- -----
P-Dt: 01 Jun 1858
Dist/Class: Texas Emmigration and Land
Company
File#: 710
Patent#: 710
Patent Vol.: 14
Certificate: 710
Survey/Blk/Twp: 710
Acres: 320
Map(s) 18

Abstract # 716 - TE&L CO
P'ee: TEXAS EMIGRATION AND LAND
COMPANY
G'ee: TEXAS EMIGRATION AND LAND
COMPANY
T-Dt: -- --- -----
P-Dt: 01 Jun 1858
Dist/Class: Texas Emmigration and Land
Company
File#: 711
Patent#: 711
Patent Vol.: 14
Certificate: 711
Survey/Blk/Twp: 711
Acres: 320
Map(s) 18

Abstract # 717 - TE&L CO
P'ee: TEXAS EMIGRATION AND LAND
COMPANY
G'ee: TEXAS EMIGRATION AND LAND
COMPANY
T-Dt: -- --- -----
P-Dt: 01 Jun 1858
Dist/Class: Texas Emmigration and Land
Company
File#: 712
Patent#: 712
Patent Vol.: 14
Certificate: 712
Survey/Blk/Twp: 712
Acres: 320
Map(s) 18

Abstract # 718 - TE&L CO
P'ee: TEXAS EMIGRATION AND LAND
COMPANY
G'ee: TEXAS EMIGRATION AND LAND
COMPANY
T-Dt: -- --- -----
P-Dt: 01 Jun 1858
Dist/Class: Texas Emmigration and Land
Company
File#: 713
Patent#: 713
Patent Vol.: 14
Certificate: 713
Survey/Blk/Twp: 713
Acres: 320

Map(s) 18

Abstract # 719 - TE&L CO
P'ee: TEXAS EMIGRATION AND LAND
COMPANY
G'ee: TEXAS EMIGRATION AND LAND
COMPANY
T-Dt: -- --- -----
P-Dt: 01 Jun 1858
Dist/Class: Texas Emmigration and Land
Company
File#: 714
Patent#: 714
Patent Vol.: 14
Certificate: 714
Survey/Blk/Twp: 714
Acres: 320
Map(s) 18

Abstract # 720 - TE&L CO
P'ee: TEXAS EMIGRATION AND LAND
COMPANY
G'ee: TEXAS EMIGRATION AND LAND
COMPANY
T-Dt: -- --- -----
P-Dt: 02 Jun 1858
Dist/Class: Texas Emmigration and Land
Company
File#: 715
Patent#: 715
Patent Vol.: 14
Certificate: 715
Survey/Blk/Twp: 715
Acres: 320
Map(s) 18

Abstract # 721 - TE&L CO
P'ee: TEXAS EMIGRATION AND LAND
COMPANY
G'ee: TEXAS EMIGRATION AND LAND
COMPANY
T-Dt: -- --- -----
P-Dt: 02 Jun 1858
Dist/Class: Texas Emmigration and Land
Company
File#: 716
Patent#: 716
Patent Vol.: 14
Certificate: 716
Survey/Blk/Twp: 716
Acres: 320
Map(s) 18

Abstract # 722 - TE&L CO
P'ee: TEXAS EMIGRATION AND LAND
COMPANY
G'ee: TEXAS EMIGRATION AND LAND
COMPANY
T-Dt: -- --- -----
P-Dt: 02 Jun 1858
Dist/Class: Texas Emmigration and Land
Company
File#: 717
Patent#: 717
Patent Vol.: 14
Certificate: 717
Survey/Blk/Twp: 717
Acres: 320
Map(s) 18

Abstract # 723 - TE&L CO
P'ee: TEXAS EMIGRATION AND LAND
COMPANY
G'ee: TEXAS EMIGRATION AND LAND
COMPANY

T-Dt: -- --- -----
P-Dt: 02 Jun 1858
Dist/Class: Texas Emmigration and Land
Company
File#: 718
Patent#: 718
Patent Vol.: 14
Certificate: 718
Survey/Blk/Twp: 718
Acres: 320
Map(s) 18

Abstract # 724 - TE&L CO
P'ee: TEXAS EMIGRATION AND LAND
COMPANY
G'ee: TEXAS EMIGRATION AND LAND
COMPANY
T-Dt: -- --- -----
P-Dt: 02 Jun 1858
Dist/Class: Texas Emmigration and Land
Company
File#: 719
Patent#: 719
Patent Vol.: 14
Certificate: 719
Survey/Blk/Twp: 719
Acres: 320
Map(s) 17, 18

Abstract # 725 - TE&L CO
P'ee: TEXAS EMIGRATION AND LAND
COMPANY
G'ee: TEXAS EMIGRATION AND LAND
COMPANY
T-Dt: -- --- -----
P-Dt: 02 Jun 1858
Dist/Class: Texas Emmigration and Land
Company
File#: 720
Patent#: 720
Patent Vol.: 14
Certificate: 720
Survey/Blk/Twp: 720
Acres: 320
Map(s) 17

Abstract # 726 - TE&L CO
P'ee: TEXAS EMIGRATION AND LAND
COMPANY
G'ee: TEXAS EMIGRATION AND LAND
COMPANY
T-Dt: -- --- -----
P-Dt: 02 Jun 1858
Dist/Class: Texas Emmigration and Land
Company
File#: 721
Patent#: 721
Patent Vol.: 14
Certificate: 721
Survey/Blk/Twp: 721
Acres: 320
Map(s) 17

Abstract # 727 - TE&L CO
P'ee: TEXAS EMIGRATION AND LAND
COMPANY
G'ee: TEXAS EMIGRATION AND LAND
COMPANY
T-Dt: -- --- -----
P-Dt: 03 Jun 1858
Dist/Class: Texas Emmigration and Land
Company
File#: 722
Patent#: 722
Patent Vol.: 14

Certificate: 722
Survey/Blk/Twp: 722
Acres: 320
Map(s) 17

Abstract # 728 - TE&L CO
P'ee: TEXAS EMIGRATION AND LAND
COMPANY
G'ee: TEXAS EMIGRATION AND LAND
COMPANY
T-Dt: -- --- -----
P-Dt: 03 Jun 1858
Dist/Class: Texas Emmigration and Land
Company
File#: 723
Patent#: 723
Patent Vol.: 14
Certificate: 723
Survey/Blk/Twp: 723
Acres: 320
Map(s) 17

Abstract # 729 - TE&L CO
P'ee: TEXAS EMIGRATION AND LAND
COMPANY
G'ee: TEXAS EMIGRATION AND LAND
COMPANY
T-Dt: -- --- -----
P-Dt: 03 Jun 1858
Dist/Class: Texas Emmigration and Land
Company
File#: 724
Patent#: 724
Patent Vol.: 14
Certificate: 724
Survey/Blk/Twp: 724
Acres: 320
Map(s) 17

Abstract # 730 - TE&L CO
P'ee: TEXAS EMIGRATION AND LAND
COMPANY
G'ee: TEXAS EMIGRATION AND LAND
COMPANY
T-Dt: -- --- -----
P-Dt: 03 Jun 1858
Dist/Class: Texas Emmigration and Land
Company
File#: 725
Patent#: 725
Patent Vol.: 14
Certificate: 725
Survey/Blk/Twp: 725
Acres: 320
Map(s) 17

Abstract # 731 - TE&L CO
P'ee: TEXAS EMIGRATION AND LAND
COMPANY
G'ee: TEXAS EMIGRATION AND LAND
COMPANY
T-Dt: -- --- -----
P-Dt: 03 Jun 1858
Dist/Class: Texas Emmigration and Land
Company
File#: 726
Patent#: 726
Patent Vol.: 14
Certificate: 726
Survey/Blk/Twp: 726
Acres: 320
Map(s) 17

Abstract # 732 - TE&L CO
P'ee: TEXAS EMIGRATION AND LAND

COMPANY
G'ee: TEXAS EMIGRATION AND LAND
COMPANY
T-Dt: -- --- -----
P-Dt: 04 Jun 1858
Dist/Class: Texas Emmigration and Land
Company
File#: 727
Patent#: 727
Patent Vol.: 14
Certificate: 727
Survey/Blk/Twp: 727
Acres: 320
Map(s) 17

Abstract # 733 - TE&L CO
P'ee: TEXAS EMIGRATION AND LAND
COMPANY
G'ee: TEXAS EMIGRATION AND LAND
COMPANY
T-Dt: -- --- -----
P-Dt: 04 Jun 1858
Dist/Class: Texas Emmigration and Land
Company
File#: 728
Patent#: 728
Patent Vol.: 14
Certificate: 728
Survey/Blk/Twp: 728
Acres: 320
Map(s) 17, 18

Abstract # 734 - TE&L CO
P'ee: TEXAS EMIGRATION AND LAND
COMPANY
G'ee: TEXAS EMIGRATION AND LAND
COMPANY
T-Dt: -- --- -----
P-Dt: 04 Jun 1858
Dist/Class: Texas Emmigration and Land
Company
File#: 729
Patent#: 729
Patent Vol.: 14
Certificate: 729
Survey/Blk/Twp: 729
Acres: 320
Map(s) 18

Abstract # 735 - TE&L CO
P'ee: TEXAS EMIGRATION AND LAND
COMPANY
G'ee: TEXAS EMIGRATION AND LAND
COMPANY
T-Dt: -- --- -----
P-Dt: 04 Jun 1858
Dist/Class: Texas Emmigration and Land
Company
File#: 730
Patent#: 730
Patent Vol.: 14
Certificate: 730
Survey/Blk/Twp: 730
Acres: 320
Map(s) 18

Abstract # 736 - TE&L CO
P'ee: TEXAS EMIGRATION AND LAND
COMPANY
G'ee: TEXAS EMIGRATION AND LAND
COMPANY
T-Dt: -- --- -----
P-Dt: 04 Jun 1858
Dist/Class: Texas Emmigration and Land
Company

File#: 731
Patent#: 731
Patent Vol.: 14
Certificate: 731
Survey/Blk/Twp: 731
Acres: 320
Map(s) 18

Abstract # 737 - TE&L CO
P'ee: TEXAS EMIGRATION AND LAND
COMPANY
G'ee: TEXAS EMIGRATION AND LAND
COMPANY
T-Dt: -- --- -----
P-Dt: 04 Jun 1858
Dist/Class: Texas Emmigration and Land
Company
File#: 732
Patent#: 732
Patent Vol.: 14
Certificate: 732
Survey/Blk/Twp: 732
Acres: 320
Map(s) 18

Abstract # 738 - TE&L CO
P'ee: TEXAS EMIGRATION AND LAND
COMPANY
G'ee: TEXAS EMIGRATION AND LAND
COMPANY
T-Dt: -- --- -----
P-Dt: 04 Jun 1858
Dist/Class: Texas Emmigration and Land
Company
File#: 733
Patent#: 733
Patent Vol.: 14
Certificate: 733
Survey/Blk/Twp: 733
Acres: 320
Map(s) 18

Abstract # 739 - TE&L CO
P'ee: TEXAS EMIGRATION AND LAND
COMPANY
G'ee: TEXAS EMIGRATION AND LAND
COMPANY
T-Dt: -- --- -----
P-Dt: 05 Jun 1858
Dist/Class: Texas Emmigration and Land
Company
File#: 734
Patent#: 734
Patent Vol.: 14
Certificate: 734
Survey/Blk/Twp: 734
Acres: 320
Map(s) 18

Abstract # 740 - TE&L CO
P'ee: TEXAS EMIGRATION AND LAND
COMPANY
G'ee: TEXAS EMIGRATION AND LAND
COMPANY
T-Dt: -- --- -----
P-Dt: 05 Jun 1858
Dist/Class: Texas Emmigration and Land
Company
File#: 735
Patent#: 735
Patent Vol.: 14
Certificate: 735
Survey/Blk/Twp: 735
Acres: 320
Map(s) 18

Abstract # 741 - TE&L CO
P'ee: TEXAS EMIGRATION AND LAND COMPANY
G'ee: TEXAS EMIGRATION AND LAND COMPANY
T-Dt: -- --- -----
P-Dt: 05 Jun 1858
Dist/Class: Texas Emmigration and Land Company
File#: 736
Patent#: 736
Patent Vol.: 14
Certificate: 736
Survey/Blk/Twp: 736
Acres: 320
Map(s) 18

Abstract # 742 - TE&L CO
P'ee: TEXAS EMIGRATION AND LAND COMPANY
G'ee: TEXAS EMIGRATION AND LAND COMPANY
T-Dt: -- --- -----
P-Dt: 05 Jun 1858
Dist/Class: Texas Emmigration and Land Company
File#: 737
Patent#: 737
Patent Vol.: 14
Certificate: 737
Survey/Blk/Twp: 737
Acres: 320
Map(s) 18, 26

Abstract # 743 - TE&L CO
P'ee: TEXAS EMIGRATION AND LAND COMPANY
G'ee: TEXAS EMIGRATION AND LAND COMPANY
T-Dt: -- --- -----
P-Dt: 05 Jun 1858
Dist/Class: Texas Emmigration and Land Company
File#: 738
Patent#: 738
Patent Vol.: 14
Certificate: 738
Survey/Blk/Twp: 738
Acres: 320
Map(s) 18

Abstract # 744 - TE&L CO
P'ee: TEXAS EMIGRATION AND LAND COMPANY
G'ee: TEXAS EMIGRATION AND LAND COMPANY
T-Dt: -- --- -----
P-Dt: 07 Jun 1858
Dist/Class: Texas Emmigration and Land Company
File#: 739
Patent#: 739
Patent Vol.: 14
Certificate: 739
Survey/Blk/Twp: 739
Acres: 320
Map(s) 18

Abstract # 745 - TE&L CO
P'ee: TEXAS EMIGRATION AND LAND COMPANY
G'ee: TEXAS EMIGRATION AND LAND COMPANY
T-Dt: -- --- -----
P-Dt: 07 Jun 1858

Dist/Class: Texas Emmigration and Land Company
File#: 740
Patent#: 740
Patent Vol.: 14
Certificate: 740
Survey/Blk/Twp: 740
Acres: 320
Map(s) 18, 26

Abstract # 746 - TE&L CO
P'ee: TEXAS EMIGRATION AND LAND COMPANY
G'ee: TEXAS EMIGRATION AND LAND COMPANY
T-Dt: -- --- -----
P-Dt: 13 Mar 1911
Dist/Class: Texas Emmigration and Land Company
File#: 741
Patent#: 102
Patent Vol.: 47
Certificate: 741
Survey/Blk/Twp: 741
Acres: 320
Map(s) 17, 18, 25, 26

Abstract # 747 - TE&L CO
P'ee: TEXAS EMIGRATION AND LAND COMPANY
G'ee: TEXAS EMIGRATION AND LAND COMPANY
T-Dt: -- --- -----
P-Dt: 07 Jun 1858
Dist/Class: Texas Emmigration and Land Company
File#: 742
Patent#: 742
Patent Vol.: 14
Certificate: 742
Survey/Blk/Twp: 742
Acres: 320
Map(s) 17, 18

Abstract # 748 - TE&L CO
P'ee: TEXAS EMIGRATION AND LAND COMPANY
G'ee: TEXAS EMIGRATION AND LAND COMPANY
T-Dt: -- --- -----
P-Dt: 07 Jun 1858
Dist/Class: Texas Emmigration and Land Company
File#: 743
Patent#: 743
Patent Vol.: 14
Certificate: 743
Survey/Blk/Twp: 743
Acres: 320
Map(s) 17, 18

Abstract # 749 - TE&L CO
P'ee: TEXAS EMIGRATION AND LAND COMPANY
G'ee: TEXAS EMIGRATION AND LAND COMPANY
T-Dt: -- --- -----
P-Dt: 07 Jun 1858
Dist/Class: Texas Emmigration and Land Company
File#: 744
Patent#: 744
Patent Vol.: 14
Certificate: 744
Survey/Blk/Twp: 744

Acres: 320
Map(s) 17

Abstract # 750 - TE&L CO
P'ee: TEXAS EMIGRATION AND LAND COMPANY
G'ee: TEXAS EMIGRATION AND LAND COMPANY
T-Dt: -- --- -----
P-Dt: 08 Jun 1858
Dist/Class: Texas Emmigration and Land Company
File#: 745
Patent#: 745
Patent Vol.: 14
Certificate: 745
Survey/Blk/Twp: 745
Acres: 320
Map(s) 17

Abstract # 751 - TE&L CO
P'ee: TEXAS EMIGRATION AND LAND COMPANY
G'ee: TEXAS EMIGRATION AND LAND COMPANY
T-Dt: -- --- -----
P-Dt: 08 Jun 1858
Dist/Class: Texas Emmigration and Land Company
File#: 746
Patent#: 746
Patent Vol.: 14
Certificate: 746
Survey/Blk/Twp: 746
Acres: 320
Map(s) 17, 25

Abstract # 752 - TE&L CO
P'ee: TEXAS EMIGRATION AND LAND COMPANY
G'ee: TEXAS EMIGRATION AND LAND COMPANY
T-Dt: -- --- -----
P-Dt: 08 Jun 1858
Dist/Class: Texas Emmigration and Land Company
File#: 747
Patent#: 747
Patent Vol.: 14
Certificate: 747
Survey/Blk/Twp: 747
Acres: 320
Map(s) 17, 25

Abstract # 753 - TE&L CO
P'ee: TEXAS EMIGRATION AND LAND COMPANY
G'ee: TEXAS EMIGRATION AND LAND COMPANY
T-Dt: -- --- -----
P-Dt: 08 Jun 1858
Dist/Class: Texas Emmigration and Land Company
File#: 748
Patent#: 748
Patent Vol.: 14
Certificate: 748
Survey/Blk/Twp: 748
Acres: 320
Map(s) 17

Abstract # 754 - TE&L CO
P'ee: TEXAS EMIGRATION AND LAND COMPANY
G'ee: TEXAS EMIGRATION AND LAND

COMPANY
T-Dt: -- --- -----
P-Dt: 08 Jun 1858
Dist/Class: Texas Emmigration and Land Company
File#: 749
Patent#: 749
Patent Vol.: 14
Certificate: 749
Survey/Blk/Twp: 749
Acres: 320
Map(s) 17

Abstract # 755 - TE&L CO
P'ee: TEXAS EMIGRATION AND LAND COMPANY
G'ee: TEXAS EMIGRATION AND LAND COMPANY
T-Dt: -- --- -----
P-Dt: 08 Jun 1858
Dist/Class: Texas Emmigration and Land Company
File#: 750
Patent#: 750
Patent Vol.: 14
Certificate: 750
Survey/Blk/Twp: 750
Acres: 320
Map(s) 17

Abstract # 756 - TE&L CO
P'ee: TEXAS EMIGRATION AND LAND COMPANY
G'ee: TEXAS EMIGRATION AND LAND COMPANY
T-Dt: -- --- -----
P-Dt: 08 Jun 1858
Dist/Class: Texas Emmigration and Land Company
File#: 751
Patent#: 751
Patent Vol.: 14
Certificate: 751
Survey/Blk/Twp: 751
Acres: 320
Map(s) 17

Abstract # 757 - TE&L CO
P'ee: TEXAS EMIGRATION AND LAND COMPANY
G'ee: TEXAS EMIGRATION AND LAND COMPANY
T-Dt: -- --- -----
P-Dt: 09 Jun 1858
Dist/Class: Texas Emmigration and Land Company
File#: 752
Patent#: 752
Patent Vol.: 14
Certificate: 752
Survey/Blk/Twp: 752
Acres: 320
Map(s) 17, 25

Abstract # 758 - TE&L CO
P'ee: TEXAS EMIGRATION AND LAND COMPANY
G'ee: TEXAS EMIGRATION AND LAND COMPANY
T-Dt: -- --- -----
P-Dt: 09 Jun 1858
Dist/Class: Texas Emmigration and Land Company
File#: 753
Patent#: 753

Patent Vol.: 14
Certificate: 753
Survey/Blk/Twp: 753
Acres: 320
Map(s) 17

Abstract # 759 - TE&L CO
P'ee: TEXAS EMIGRATION AND LAND COMPANY
G'ee: TEXAS EMIGRATION AND LAND COMPANY
T-Dt: -- --- -----
P-Dt: 09 Jun 1858
Dist/Class: Texas Emmigration and Land Company
File#: 754
Patent#: 754
Patent Vol.: 14
Certificate: 754
Survey/Blk/Twp: 754
Acres: 320
Map(s) 17

Abstract # 760 - TE&L CO
P'ee: TEXAS EMIGRATION AND LAND COMPANY
G'ee: TEXAS EMIGRATION AND LAND COMPANY
T-Dt: -- --- -----
P-Dt: 09 Jun 1858
Dist/Class: Texas Emmigration and Land Company
File#: 755
Patent#: 755
Patent Vol.: 14
Certificate: 755
Survey/Blk/Twp: 755
Acres: 320
Map(s) 17

Abstract # 761 - TE&L CO
P'ee: TEXAS EMIGRATION AND LAND COMPANY
G'ee: TEXAS EMIGRATION AND LAND COMPANY
T-Dt: -- --- -----
P-Dt: 09 May 1858
Dist/Class: Texas Emmigration and Land Company
File#: 756
Patent#: 756
Patent Vol.: 14
Certificate: 756
Survey/Blk/Twp: 756
Acres: 320
Map(s) 17

Abstract # 762 - TE&L CO
P'ee: TEXAS EMIGRATION AND LAND COMPANY
G'ee: TEXAS EMIGRATION AND LAND COMPANY
T-Dt: -- --- -----
P-Dt: 09 Jun 1858
Dist/Class: Texas Emmigration and Land Company
File#: 757
Patent#: 757
Patent Vol.: 14
Certificate: 757
Survey/Blk/Twp: 757
Acres: 320
Map(s) 17

Abstract # 763 - TE&L CO

P'ee: TEXAS EMIGRATION AND LAND COMPANY
G'ee: TEXAS EMIGRATION AND LAND COMPANY
T-Dt: -- --- -----
P-Dt: 09 Jun 1858
Dist/Class: Texas Emmigration and Land Company
File#: 758
Patent#: 758
Patent Vol.: 14
Certificate: 758
Survey/Blk/Twp: 758
Acres: 320
Map(s) 17, 18

Abstract # 764 - TE&L CO
P'ee: TEXAS EMIGRATION AND LAND COMPANY
G'ee: TEXAS EMIGRATION AND LAND COMPANY
T-Dt: -- --- -----
P-Dt: 10 Jun 1858
Dist/Class: Texas Emmigration and Land Company
File#: 759
Patent#: 759
Patent Vol.: 14
Certificate: 759
Survey/Blk/Twp: 759
Acres: 320
Map(s) 17

Abstract # 765 - TE&L CO
P'ee: TEXAS EMIGRATION AND LAND COMPANY
G'ee: TEXAS EMIGRATION AND LAND COMPANY
T-Dt: -- --- -----
P-Dt: 10 Jun 1858
Dist/Class: Texas Emmigration and Land Company
File#: 760
Patent#: 760
Patent Vol.: 14
Certificate: 760
Survey/Blk/Twp: 760
Acres: 320
Map(s) 17

Abstract # 766 - TE&L CO
P'ee: TEXAS EMIGRATION AND LAND COMPANY
G'ee: TEXAS EMIGRATION AND LAND COMPANY
T-Dt: -- --- -----
P-Dt: 10 Jun 1858
Dist/Class: Texas Emmigration and Land Company
File#: 761
Patent#: 761
Patent Vol.: 14
Certificate: 761
Survey/Blk/Twp: 761
Acres: 320
Map(s) 17

Abstract # 767 - TE&L CO
P'ee: TEXAS EMIGRATION AND LAND COMPANY
G'ee: TEXAS EMIGRATION AND LAND COMPANY
T-Dt: -- --- -----
P-Dt: 10 Jun 1858
Dist/Class: Texas Emmigration and Land

Company
File#: 762
Patent#: 762
Patent Vol.: 14
Certificate: 762
Survey/Blk/Twp: 762
Acres: 320
Map(s) 17

Abstract # 768 - TE&L CO
P'ee: TEXAS EMIGRATION AND LAND COMPANY
G'ee: TEXAS EMIGRATION AND LAND COMPANY
T-Dt: -- --- -----
P-Dt: 10 Jun 1858
Dist/Class: Texas Emmigration and Land Company
File#: 763
Patent#: 763
Patent Vol.: 14
Certificate: 763
Survey/Blk/Twp: 763
Acres: 320
Map(s) 17

Abstract # 769 - TE&L CO
P'ee: TEXAS EMIGRATION AND LAND COMPANY
G'ee: TEXAS EMIGRATION AND LAND COMPANY
T-Dt: -- --- -----
P-Dt: 10 Jun 1858
Dist/Class: Texas Emmigration and Land Company
File#: 764
Patent#: 764
Patent Vol.: 14
Certificate: 764
Survey/Blk/Twp: 764
Acres: 320
Map(s) 17

Abstract # 770 - TE&L CO
P'ee: TEXAS EMIGRATION AND LAND COMPANY
G'ee: TEXAS EMIGRATION AND LAND COMPANY
T-Dt: -- --- -----
P-Dt: 10 Jun 1858
Dist/Class: Texas Emmigration and Land Company
File#: 765
Patent#: 765
Patent Vol.: 14
Certificate: 765
Survey/Blk/Twp: 765
Acres: 320
Map(s) 17

Abstract # 771 - TE&L CO
P'ee: TEXAS EMIGRATION AND LAND COMPANY
G'ee: TEXAS EMIGRATION AND LAND COMPANY
T-Dt: -- --- -----
P-Dt: 10 Jun 1858
Dist/Class: Texas Emmigration and Land Company
File#: 766
Patent#: 766
Patent Vol.: 14
Certificate: 766
Survey/Blk/Twp: 766
Acres: 320

Map(s) 17

Abstract # 772 - TE&L CO
P'ee: TEXAS EMIGRATION AND LAND COMPANY
G'ee: TEXAS EMIGRATION AND LAND COMPANY
T-Dt: -- --- -----
P-Dt: 11 Jun 1858
Dist/Class: Texas Emmigration and Land Company
File#: 767
Patent#: 767
Patent Vol.: 14
Certificate: 767
Survey/Blk/Twp: 767
Acres: 320
Map(s) 17

Abstract # 773 - TE&L CO
P'ee: TEXAS EMIGRATION AND LAND COMPANY
G'ee: TEXAS EMIGRATION AND LAND COMPANY
T-Dt: -- --- -----
P-Dt: 11 Jun 1858
Dist/Class: Texas Emmigration and Land Company
File#: 768
Patent#: 768
Patent Vol.: 14
Certificate: 768
Survey/Blk/Twp: 768
Acres: 320
Map(s) 17

Abstract # 774 - TE&L CO
P'ee: TEXAS EMIGRATION AND LAND COMPANY
G'ee: TEXAS EMIGRATION AND LAND COMPANY
T-Dt: -- --- -----
P-Dt: 11 Jun 1858
Dist/Class: Texas Emmigration and Land Company
File#: 769
Patent#: 769
Patent Vol.: 14
Certificate: 769
Survey/Blk/Twp: 769
Acres: 320
Map(s) 17

Abstract # 775 - TE&L CO
P'ee: TEXAS EMIGRATION AND LAND COMPANY
G'ee: TEXAS EMIGRATION AND LAND COMPANY
T-Dt: -- --- -----
P-Dt: 11 Jun 1858
Dist/Class: Texas Emmigration and Land Company
File#: 770
Patent#: 770
Patent Vol.: 14
Certificate: 770
Survey/Blk/Twp: 770
Acres: 320
Map(s) 17

Abstract # 776 - TE&L CO
P'ee: TEXAS EMIGRATION AND LAND COMPANY
G'ee: TEXAS EMIGRATION AND LAND COMPANY

T-Dt: -- --- -----
P-Dt: 11 Jun 1858
Dist/Class: Texas Emmigration and Land Company
File#: 771
Patent#: 771
Patent Vol.: 14
Certificate: 771
Survey/Blk/Twp: 771
Acres: 320
Map(s) 17

Abstract # 777 - TE&L CO
P'ee: TEXAS EMIGRATION AND LAND COMPANY
G'ee: TEXAS EMIGRATION AND LAND COMPANY
T-Dt: -- --- -----
P-Dt: 12 Jun 1858
Dist/Class: Texas Emmigration and Land Company
File#: 777
Patent#: 777
Patent Vol.: 14
Certificate: 777
Survey/Blk/Twp: 777
Acres: 320
Map(s) 9, 17

Abstract # 778 - TE&L CO
P'ee: TEXAS EMIGRATION AND LAND COMPANY
G'ee: TEXAS EMIGRATION AND LAND COMPANY
T-Dt: -- --- -----
P-Dt: 13 May 1858
Dist/Class: Texas Emmigration and Land Company
File#: 620
Patent#: 620
Patent Vol.: 14
Certificate: 620
Survey/Blk/Twp: 620
Acres: 320
Map(s) 12, 13

Abstract # 779 - TE&L CO
P'ee: TEXAS EMIGRATION AND LAND COMPANY
G'ee: TEXAS EMIGRATION AND LAND COMPANY
T-Dt: -- --- -----
P-Dt: 13 May 1858
Dist/Class: Texas Emmigration and Land Company
File#: 621
Patent#: 621
Patent Vol.: 14
Certificate: 621
Survey/Blk/Twp: 621
Acres: 320
Map(s) 13

Abstract # 780 - TE&L CO
P'ee: TEXAS EMIGRATION AND LAND COMPANY
G'ee: TEXAS EMIGRATION AND LAND COMPANY
T-Dt: -- --- -----
P-Dt: 13 May 1858
Dist/Class: Texas Emmigration and Land Company
File#: 622
Patent#: 622
Patent Vol.: 14

Certificate: 622
Survey/Blk/Twp: 622
Acres: 320
Map(s) 13

Abstract # 781 - TE&L CO
P'ee: TEXAS EMIGRATION AND LAND
COMPANY
G'ee: TEXAS EMIGRATION AND LAND
COMPANY
T-Dt: -- --- -----
P-Dt: 13 May 1858
Dist/Class: Texas Emmigration and Land
Company
File#: 623
Patent#: 623
Patent Vol.: 14
Certificate: 623
Survey/Blk/Twp: 623
Acres: 320
Map(s) 13

Abstract # 782 - TE&L CO
P'ee: TEXAS EMIGRATION AND LAND
COMPANY
G'ee: TEXAS EMIGRATION AND LAND
COMPANY
T-Dt: -- --- -----
P-Dt: 13 May 1858
Dist/Class: Texas Emmigration and Land
Company
File#: 624
Patent#: 624
Patent Vol.: 14
Certificate: 624
Survey/Blk/Twp: 624
Acres: 320
Map(s) 13, 21

Abstract # 783 - TE&L CO
P'ee: TEXAS EMIGRATION AND LAND
COMPANY
G'ee: TEXAS EMIGRATION AND LAND
COMPANY
T-Dt: -- --- -----
P-Dt: 14 May 1858
Dist/Class: Texas Emmigration and Land
Company
File#: 625
Patent#: 625
Patent Vol.: 14
Certificate: 625
Survey/Blk/Twp: 625
Acres: 320
Map(s) 13, 14

Abstract # 784 - TE&L CO
P'ee: TEXAS EMIGRATION AND LAND
COMPANY
G'ee: TEXAS EMIGRATION AND LAND
COMPANY
T-Dt: -- --- -----
P-Dt: 14 May 1858
Dist/Class: Texas Emmigration and Land
Company
File#: 626
Patent#: 626
Patent Vol.: 14
Certificate: 626
Survey/Blk/Twp: 626
Acres: 320
Map(s) 14

Abstract # 785 - TE&L CO
P'ee: TEXAS EMIGRATION AND LAND

COMPANY
G'ee: TEXAS EMIGRATION AND LAND
COMPANY
T-Dt: -- --- -----
P-Dt: 14 May 1858
Dist/Class: Texas Emmigration and Land
Company
File#: 627
Patent#: 627
Patent Vol.: 14
Certificate: 627
Survey/Blk/Twp: 627
Acres: 320
Map(s) 14

Abstract # 786 - TE&L CO
P'ee: TEXAS EMIGRATION AND LAND
COMPANY
G'ee: TEXAS EMIGRATION AND LAND
COMPANY
T-Dt: -- --- -----
P-Dt: 14 May 1858
Dist/Class: Texas Emmigration and Land
Company
File#: 628
Patent#: 628
Patent Vol.: 14
Certificate: 628
Survey/Blk/Twp: 628
Acres: 320
Map(s) 13, 14

Abstract # 787 - TE&L CO
P'ee: TEXAS EMIGRATION AND LAND
COMPANY
G'ee: TEXAS EMIGRATION AND LAND
COMPANY
T-Dt: -- --- -----
P-Dt: 14 May 1858
Dist/Class: Texas Emmigration and Land
Company
File#: 629
Patent#: 629
Patent Vol.: 14
Certificate: 629
Survey/Blk/Twp: 629
Acres: 320
Map(s) 13

Abstract # 788 - TE&L CO
P'ee: TEXAS EMIGRATION AND LAND
COMPANY
G'ee: TEXAS EMIGRATION AND LAND
COMPANY
T-Dt: -- --- -----
P-Dt: 14 May 1858
Dist/Class: Texas Emmigration and Land
Company
File#: 630
Patent#: 630
Patent Vol.: 14
Certificate: 630
Survey/Blk/Twp: 630
Acres: 320
Map(s) 13, 14

Abstract # 789 - TE&L CO
P'ee: TEXAS EMIGRATION AND LAND
COMPANY
G'ee: TEXAS EMIGRATION AND LAND
COMPANY
T-Dt: -- --- -----
P-Dt: 15 May 1858
Dist/Class: Texas Emmigration and Land
Company

File#: 631
Patent#: 631
Patent Vol.: 14
Certificate: 631
Survey/Blk/Twp: 631
Acres: 320
Map(s) 14

Abstract # 790 - TE&L CO
P'ee: TEXAS EMIGRATION AND LAND
COMPANY
G'ee: TEXAS EMIGRATION AND LAND
COMPANY
T-Dt: -- --- -----
P-Dt: 15 May 1858
Dist/Class: Texas Emmigration and Land
Company
File#: 632
Patent#: 632
Patent Vol.: 14
Certificate: 632
Survey/Blk/Twp: 632
Acres: 320
Map(s) 14

Abstract # 791 - TE&L CO
P'ee: TEXAS EMIGRATION AND LAND
COMPANY
G'ee: TEXAS EMIGRATION AND LAND
COMPANY
T-Dt: -- --- -----
P-Dt: 15 Apr 1858
Dist/Class: Texas Emmigration and Land
Company
File#: 633
Patent#: 633
Patent Vol.: 14
Certificate: 633
Survey/Blk/Twp: 633
Acres: 320
Map(s) 14

Abstract # 792 - TE&L CO
P'ee: TEXAS EMIGRATION AND LAND
COMPANY
G'ee: TEXAS EMIGRATION AND LAND
COMPANY
T-Dt: -- --- -----
P-Dt: 15 Apr 1858
Dist/Class: Texas Emmigration and Land
Company
File#: 634
Patent#: 634
Patent Vol.: 14
Certificate: 634
Survey/Blk/Twp: 634
Acres: 320
Map(s) 14

Abstract # 793 - TE&L CO
P'ee: TEXAS EMIGRATION AND LAND
COMPANY
G'ee: TEXAS EMIGRATION AND LAND
COMPANY
T-Dt: -- --- -----
P-Dt: 15 May 1858
Dist/Class: Texas Emmigration and Land
Company
File#: 635
Patent#: 635
Patent Vol.: 14
Certificate: 635
Survey/Blk/Twp: 635
Acres: 320
Map(s) 13, 14

Abstract # 794 - TE&L CO
P'ee: TEXAS EMIGRATION AND LAND
COMPANY
G'ee: TEXAS EMIGRATION AND LAND
COMPANY
T-Dt: -- --- -----
P-Dt: 17 May 1858
Dist/Class: Texas Emmigration and Land
Company
File#: 636
Patent#: 636
Patent Vol.: 14
Certificate: 636
Survey/Blk/Twp: 636
Acres: 320
Map(s) 13, 14

Abstract # 795 - TE&L CO
P'ee: TEXAS EMIGRATION AND LAND
COMPANY
G'ee: TEXAS EMIGRATION AND LAND
COMPANY
T-Dt: -- --- -----
P-Dt: 17 May 1858
Dist/Class: Texas Emmigration and Land
Company
File#: 637
Patent#: 637
Patent Vol.: 14
Certificate: 637
Survey/Blk/Twp: 637
Acres: 320
Map(s) 13, 14

Abstract # 796 - TE&L CO
P'ee: TEXAS EMIGRATION AND LAND
COMPANY
G'ee: TEXAS EMIGRATION AND LAND
COMPANY
T-Dt: -- --- -----
P-Dt: 17 May 1858
Dist/Class: Texas Emmigration and Land
Company
File#: 638
Patent#: 638
Patent Vol.: 14
Certificate: 638
Survey/Blk/Twp: 638
Acres: 320
Map(s) 13, 14

Abstract # 797 - TE&L CO
P'ee: TEXAS EMIGRATION AND LAND
COMPANY
G'ee: TEXAS EMIGRATION AND LAND
COMPANY
T-Dt: -- --- -----
P-Dt: 17 May 1858
Dist/Class: Texas Emmigration and Land
Company
File#: 639
Patent#: 639
Patent Vol.: 14
Certificate: 639
Survey/Blk/Twp: 639
Acres: 320
Map(s) 14

Abstract # 798 - TE&L CO
P'ee: TEXAS EMIGRATION AND LAND
COMPANY
G'ee: TEXAS EMIGRATION AND LAND
COMPANY
T-Dt: -- --- -----
P-Dt: 17 May 1858

Dist/Class: Texas Emmigration and Land
Company
File#: 640
Patent#: 640
Patent Vol.: 14
Certificate: 640
Survey/Blk/Twp: 640
Acres: 320
Map(s) 14

Abstract # 799 - TE&L CO
P'ee: TEXAS EMIGRATION AND LAND
COMPANY
G'ee: TEXAS EMIGRATION AND LAND
COMPANY
T-Dt: -- --- -----
P-Dt: 17 May 1858
Dist/Class: Texas Emmigration and Land
Company
File#: 641
Patent#: 641
Patent Vol.: 14
Certificate: 641
Survey/Blk/Twp: 641
Acres: 320
Map(s) 14

Abstract # 800 - TE&L CO
P'ee: TEXAS EMIGRATION AND LAND
COMPANY
G'ee: TEXAS EMIGRATION AND LAND
COMPANY
T-Dt: -- --- -----
P-Dt: 17 May 1858
Dist/Class: Texas Emmigration and Land
Company
File#: 642
Patent#: 642
Patent Vol.: 14
Certificate: 642
Survey/Blk/Twp: 642
Acres: 320
Map(s) 14

Abstract # 801 - TE&L CO
P'ee: TEXAS EMIGRATION AND LAND
COMPANY
G'ee: TEXAS EMIGRATION AND LAND
COMPANY
T-Dt: -- --- -----
P-Dt: 17 May 1858
Dist/Class: Texas Emmigration and Land
Company
File#: 643
Patent#: 643
Patent Vol.: 14
Certificate: 643
Survey/Blk/Twp: 643
Acres: 320
Map(s) 14

Abstract # 802 - TE&L CO
P'ee: TEXAS EMIGRATION AND LAND
COMPANY
G'ee: TEXAS EMIGRATION AND LAND
COMPANY
T-Dt: -- --- -----
P-Dt: 18 May 1858
Dist/Class: Texas Emmigration and Land
Company
File#: 644
Patent#: 644
Patent Vol.: 14
Certificate: 644
Survey/Blk/Twp: 644

Acres: 320
Map(s) 14, 22

Abstract # 803 - TE&L CO
P'ee: TEXAS EMIGRATION AND LAND
COMPANY
G'ee: TEXAS EMIGRATION AND LAND
COMPANY
T-Dt: -- --- -----
P-Dt: 18 May 1858
Dist/Class: Texas Emmigration and Land
Company
File#: 645
Patent#: 645
Patent Vol.: 14
Certificate: 645
Survey/Blk/Twp: 645
Acres: 320
Map(s) 14, 22

Abstract # 804 - TE&L CO
P'ee: SHIRLEY, ZACHARIAH
G'ee: TEXAS EMIGRATION AND LAND
COMPANY
T-Dt: -- --- -----
P-Dt: 21 Sep 1857
Dist/Class: Texas Emmigration and Land
Company
File#: 646
Patent#: 102
Patent Vol.: 14
Certificate: 646
Survey/Blk/Twp: 646
Acres: 320
Map(s) 14, 22

Abstract # 805 - TE&L CO
P'ee: TEXAS EMIGRATION AND LAND
COMPANY
G'ee: TEXAS EMIGRATION AND LAND
COMPANY
T-Dt: -- --- -----
P-Dt: 18 May 1858
Dist/Class: Texas Emmigration and Land
Company
File#: 647
Patent#: 647
Patent Vol.: 14
Certificate: 647
Survey/Blk/Twp: 647
Acres: 320
Map(s) 13, 14, 21, 22

Abstract # 806 - TE&L CO
P'ee: TEXAS EMIGRATION AND LAND
COMPANY
G'ee: TEXAS EMIGRATION AND LAND
COMPANY
T-Dt: -- --- -----
P-Dt: 28 May 1858
Dist/Class: Texas Emmigration and Land
Company
File#: 701
Patent#: 701
Patent Vol.: 14
Certificate: 701
Survey/Blk/Twp: 701
Acres: 320
Map(s) 18

Abstract # 807 - TE&L CO
P'ee: TEXAS EMIGRATION AND LAND
COMPANY
G'ee: TEXAS EMIGRATION AND LAND
COMPANY

T-Dt: -- --- -----
P-Dt: 31 May 1858
Dist/Class: Texas Emmigration and Land Company
File#: 702
Patent#: 702
Patent Vol.: 14
Certificate: 702
Survey/Blk/Twp: 702
Acres: 320
Map(s) 18

Abstract # 808 - TE&L CO
P'ee: TEXAS EMIGRATION AND LAND COMPANY
G'ee: TEXAS EMIGRATION AND LAND COMPANY
T-Dt: -- --- -----
P-Dt: 31 May 1858
Dist/Class: Texas Emmigration and Land Company
File#: 703
Patent#: 703
Patent Vol.: 14
Certificate: 703
Survey/Blk/Twp: 703
Acres: 320
Map(s) 18

Abstract # 809 - TE&L CO
P'ee: TEXAS EMIGRATION AND LAND COMPANY
G'ee: TEXAS EMIGRATION AND LAND COMPANY
T-Dt: -- --- -----
P-Dt: 31 May 1858
Dist/Class: Texas Emmigration and Land Company
File#: 704
Patent#: 704
Patent Vol.: 14
Certificate: 704
Survey/Blk/Twp: 704
Acres: 320
Map(s) 18

Abstract # 810 - TE&L CO
P'ee: TEXAS EMIGRATION AND LAND COMPANY
G'ee: TEXAS EMIGRATION AND LAND COMPANY
T-Dt: -- --- -----
P-Dt: 31 May 1858
Dist/Class: Texas Emmigration and Land Company
File#: 705
Patent#: 705
Patent Vol.: 14
Certificate: 705
Survey/Blk/Twp: 705
Acres: 320
Map(s) 10, 18

Abstract # 811 - TE&L CO
P'ee: TEXAS EMIGRATION AND LAND COMPANY
G'ee: TEXAS EMIGRATION AND LAND COMPANY
T-Dt: -- --- -----
P-Dt: 14 Jun 1858
Dist/Class: Texas Emmigration and Land Company
File#: 778
Patent#: 778
Patent Vol.: 14

Certificate: 778
Survey/Blk/Twp: 778
Acres: 320
Map(s) 9, 17

Abstract # 812 - TE&L CO
P'ee: TEXAS EMIGRATION AND LAND COMPANY
G'ee: TEXAS EMIGRATION AND LAND COMPANY
T-Dt: -- --- -----
P-Dt: 14 Jun 1858
Dist/Class: Texas Emmigration and Land Company
File#: 779
Patent#: 779
Patent Vol.: 14
Certificate: 779
Survey/Blk/Twp: 779
Acres: 320
Map(s) 9, 17

Abstract # 813 - TE&L CO
P'ee: TEXAS EMIGRATION AND LAND COMPANY
G'ee: TEXAS EMIGRATION AND LAND COMPANY
T-Dt: -- --- -----
P-Dt: 14 Jun 1858
Dist/Class: Texas Emmigration and Land Company
File#: 780
Patent#: 780
Patent Vol.: 14
Certificate: 780
Survey/Blk/Twp: 780
Acres: 320
Map(s) 9

Abstract # 814 - TE&L CO
P'ee: TEXAS EMIGRATION AND LAND COMPANY
G'ee: TEXAS EMIGRATION AND LAND COMPANY
T-Dt: -- --- -----
P-Dt: 14 Jun 1858
Dist/Class: Texas Emmigration and Land Company
File#: 781
Patent#: 781
Patent Vol.: 14
Certificate: 781
Survey/Blk/Twp: 781
Acres: 320
Map(s) 9

Abstract # 815 - TE&L CO
P'ee: TEXAS EMIGRATION AND LAND COMPANY
G'ee: TEXAS EMIGRATION AND LAND COMPANY
T-Dt: -- --- -----
P-Dt: 15 Jun 1858
Dist/Class: Texas Emmigration and Land Company
File#: 786
Patent#: 786
Patent Vol.: 14
Certificate: 786
Survey/Blk/Twp: 786
Acres: 320
Map(s) 9

Abstract # 816 - TE&L CO
P'ee: TEXAS EMIGRATION AND LAND

COMPANY
G'ee: TEXAS EMIGRATION AND LAND COMPANY
T-Dt: -- --- -----
P-Dt: 15 Jun 1858
Dist/Class: Texas Emmigration and Land Company
File#: 789
Patent#: 789
Patent Vol.: 14
Certificate: 789
Survey/Blk/Twp: 789
Acres: 320
Map(s) 9

Abstract # 817 - TE&L CO
P'ee: TEXAS EMIGRATION AND LAND COMPANY
G'ee: TEXAS EMIGRATION AND LAND COMPANY
T-Dt: -- --- -----
P-Dt: 15 Jun 1858
Dist/Class: Texas Emmigration and Land Company
File#: 790
Patent#: 790
Patent Vol.: 14
Certificate: 790
Survey/Blk/Twp: 790
Acres: 320
Map(s) 9

Abstract # 818 - TE&L CO
P'ee: TEXAS EMIGRATION AND LAND COMPANY
G'ee: TEXAS EMIGRATION AND LAND COMPANY
T-Dt: -- --- -----
P-Dt: 17 Jun 1858
Dist/Class: Texas Emmigration and Land Company
File#: 791
Patent#: 791
Patent Vol.: 14
Certificate: 791
Survey/Blk/Twp: 791
Acres: 320
Map(s) 9

Abstract # 819 - TE&L CO
P'ee: TEXAS EMIGRATION AND LAND COMPANY
G'ee: TEXAS EMIGRATION AND LAND COMPANY
T-Dt: -- --- -----
P-Dt: 16 Jun 1858
Dist/Class: Texas Emmigration and Land Company
File#: 792
Patent#: 792
Patent Vol.: 14
Certificate: 792
Survey/Blk/Twp: 792
Acres: 320
Map(s) 9

Abstract # 820 - TE&L CO
P'ee: TEXAS EMIGRATION AND LAND COMPANY
G'ee: TEXAS EMIGRATION AND LAND COMPANY
T-Dt: -- --- -----
P-Dt: 14 Jun 1858
Dist/Class: Texas Emmigration and Land Company

File#: 782
Patent#: 782
Patent Vol.: 14
Certificate: 782
Survey/Blk/Twp: 782
Acres: 320
Map(s) 9

Abstract # 822 - TE&L CO
P'ee: TEXAS EMIGRATION AND LAND
COMPANY
G'ee: TEXAS EMIGRATION AND LAND
COMPANY
T-Dt: -- --- -----
P-Dt: 03 Aug 1858
Dist/Class: Texas Emmigration and Land
Company
File#: 1004
Patent#: 1000
Patent Vol.: 14
Certificate: 1004
Survey/Blk/Twp: 3
Acres: 320
Map(s) 19, 20

Abstract # 823 - TE&L CO
P'ee: TEXAS EMIGRATION AND LAND
COMPANY
G'ee: TEXAS EMIGRATION AND LAND
COMPANY
T-Dt: -- --- -----
P-Dt: 14 Mar 1859
Dist/Class: Texas Emmigration and Land
Company
File#: 1013
Patent#: 1125
Patent Vol.: 14
Certificate: 1013
Survey/Blk/Twp: 1013
Acres: 320
Map(s) 36

Abstract # 824 - TE&L CO
P'ee: HEDGECOXE, HENRY O
G'ee: TEXAS EMIGRATION AND LAND
COMPANY
T-Dt: -- --- -----
P-Dt: 01 Feb 1860
Dist/Class: Texas Emmigration and Land
Company
File#: 1015
Patent#: 1139
Patent Vol.: 14
Certificate: 1015
Survey/Blk/Twp: 1015
Acres: 320
Map(s) 37

Abstract # 825 - TE&L CO
P'ee: TEXAS EMIGRATION AND LAND
COMPANY
G'ee: TEXAS EMIGRATION AND LAND
COMPANY
T-Dt: -- --- -----
P-Dt: 26 Aug 1858
Dist/Class: Texas Emmigration and Land
Company
File#: 1019
Patent#: 1052
Patent Vol.: 14
Certificate: 1019
Survey/Blk/Twp: 1019
Acres: 320
Map(s) 35, 36, 43, 44

Abstract # 826 - TE&L CO
P'ee: TEXAS EMIGRATION AND LAND
COMPANY
G'ee: TEXAS EMIGRATION AND LAND
COMPANY
T-Dt: -- --- -----
P-Dt: 26 Aug 1858
Dist/Class: Texas Emmigration and Land
Company
File#: 1020
Patent#: 1053
Patent Vol.: 14
Certificate: 1020
Survey/Blk/Twp: 1020
Acres: 320
Map(s) 35, 43, 44

Abstract # 827 - TE&L CO
P'ee: HEDGECOXE, HENRY O
G'ee: TEXAS EMIGRATION AND LAND
COMPANY
T-Dt: -- --- -----
P-Dt: 01 Feb 1860
Dist/Class: Texas Emmigration and Land
Company
File#: 1104
Patent#: 1138
Patent Vol.: 14
Certificate: 1104
Survey/Blk/Twp: 1104
Acres: 288
Map(s) 37

Abstract # 828 - TE&L CO
P'ee: TEXAS EMIGRATION AND LAND
COMPANY
G'ee: TEXAS EMIGRATION AND LAND
COMPANY
T-Dt: -- --- -----
P-Dt: 25 May 1859
Dist/Class: Texas Emmigration and Land
Company
File#: 1107
Patent#: 523
Patent Vol.: 20
Certificate: 1107
Survey/Blk/Twp: 1107
Acres: 320
Map(s) 36

Abstract # 829 - TE&L CO
P'ee: TEXAS EMIGRATION AND LAND
COMPANY
G'ee: TEXAS EMIGRATION AND LAND
COMPANY
T-Dt: -- --- -----
P-Dt: 25 May 1859
Dist/Class: Texas Emmigration and Land
Company
File#: 1108
Patent#: 524
Patent Vol.: 20
Certificate: 1108
Survey/Blk/Twp: 1108
Acres: 320
Map(s) 36

Abstract # 830 - TE&L CO
P'ee: HEDGECOXE, HENRY O
G'ee: TEXAS EMIGRATION AND LAND
COMPANY
T-Dt: -- --- -----
P-Dt: 24 Oct 1895
Dist/Class: Texas Emmigration and Land
Company

File#: 1110
Patent#: 509
Patent Vol.: 46
Certificate: 1110
Survey/Blk/Twp: 1110
Acres: 320
Map(s) 36

Abstract # 831 - TE&L CO
P'ee: TEXAS EMIGRATION AND LAND
COMPANY
G'ee: TEXAS EMIGRATION AND LAND
COMPANY
T-Dt: -- --- -----
P-Dt: 29 Jul 1858
Dist/Class: Texas Emmigration and Land
Company
File#: 1111
Patent#: 79
Patent Vol.: 20
Certificate: 1111
Survey/Blk/Twp: 1111
Acres: 320
Map(s) 36, 44

Abstract # 832 - TE&L CO
P'ee: TEXAS EMIGRATION AND LAND
COMPANY
G'ee: TEXAS EMIGRATION AND LAND
COMPANY
T-Dt: -- --- -----
P-Dt: 29 Jul 1858
Dist/Class: Texas Emmigration and Land
Company
File#: 1112
Patent#: 80
Patent Vol.: 20
Certificate: 1112
Survey/Blk/Twp: 1112
Acres: 320
Map(s) 36, 44

Abstract # 833 - TE&L CO
P'ee: TEXAS EMIGRATION AND LAND
COMPANY
G'ee: TEXAS EMIGRATION AND LAND
COMPANY
T-Dt: -- --- -----
P-Dt: 26 May 1859
Dist/Class: Texas Emmigration and Land
Company
File#: 1113
Patent#: 525
Patent Vol.: 20
Certificate: 1113
Survey/Blk/Twp: 1113
Acres: 320
Map(s) 36, 44

Abstract # 834 - TE&L CO
P'ee: TEXAS EMIGRATION AND LAND
COMPANY
G'ee: TEXAS EMIGRATION AND LAND
COMPANY
T-Dt: -- --- -----
P-Dt: 29 Jul 1858
Dist/Class: Texas Emmigration and Land
Company
File#: 1114
Patent#: 81
Patent Vol.: 20
Certificate: 1114
Survey/Blk/Twp: 1114
Acres: 320
Map(s) 36, 44

Abstract # 835 - TE&L CO
P'ee: TEXAS EMIGRATION AND LAND COMPANY
G'ee: TEXAS EMIGRATION AND LAND COMPANY
T-Dt: -- --- -----
P-Dt: 18 Mar 1859
Dist/Class: Texas Emmigration and Land Company
File#: 1115
Patent#: 507
Patent Vol.: 20
Certificate: 1115
Survey/Blk/Twp: 1115
Acres: 256
Map(s) 36, 44

Abstract # 836 - TE&L CO
P'ee: TEXAS EMIGRATION AND LAND COMPANY
G'ee: TEXAS EMIGRATION AND LAND COMPANY
T-Dt: -- --- -----
P-Dt: 29 Jul 1858
Dist/Class: Texas Emmigration and Land Company
File#: 1117
Patent#: 82
Patent Vol.: 20
Certificate: 1117
Survey/Blk/Twp: 1117
Acres: 320
Map(s) 35, 36, 44

Abstract # 837 - TE&L CO
P'ee: TEXAS EMIGRATION AND LAND COMPANY
G'ee: TEXAS EMIGRATION AND LAND COMPANY
T-Dt: -- --- -----
P-Dt: 29 Jul 1858
Dist/Class: Texas Emmigration and Land Company
File#: 1119
Patent#: 83
Patent Vol.: 20
Certificate: 1119
Survey/Blk/Twp: 1119
Acres: 320
Map(s) 36, 44

Abstract # 838 - TE&L CO
P'ee: TEXAS EMIGRATION AND LAND COMPANY
G'ee: TEXAS EMIGRATION AND LAND COMPANY
T-Dt: -- --- -----
P-Dt: 14 Jul 1858
Dist/Class: Texas Emmigration and Land Company
File#: 1182
Patent#: 70
Patent Vol.: 20
Certificate: 1182
Survey/Blk/Twp: 1182
Acres: 320
Map(s) 33

Abstract # 839 - TE&L CO
P'ee: TEXAS EMIGRATION AND LAND COMPANY
G'ee: TEXAS EMIGRATION AND LAND COMPANY
T-Dt: -- --- -----
P-Dt: 14 Jul 1858

Dist/Class: Texas Emmigration and Land Company
File#: 1183
Patent#: 71
Patent Vol.: 20
Certificate: 1183
Survey/Blk/Twp: 1183
Acres: 320
Map(s) 33

Abstract # 840 - TE&L CO
P'ee: TEXAS EMIGRATION AND LAND COMPANY
G'ee: TEXAS EMIGRATION AND LAND COMPANY
T-Dt: -- --- -----
P-Dt: 15 Jul 1858
Dist/Class: Texas Emmigration and Land Company
File#: 1184
Patent#: 72
Patent Vol.: 20
Certificate: 1184
Survey/Blk/Twp: 1184
Acres: 320
Map(s) 33

Abstract # 841 - TE&L CO
P'ee: TEXAS EMIGRATION AND LAND COMPANY
G'ee: TEXAS EMIGRATION AND LAND COMPANY
T-Dt: -- --- -----
P-Dt: 15 Jul 1858
Dist/Class: Texas Emmigration and Land Company
File#: 1185
Patent#: 73
Patent Vol.: 20
Certificate: 1185
Survey/Blk/Twp: 1185
Acres: 370
Map(s) 33

Abstract # 842 - TE&L CO
P'ee: TEXAS EMIGRATION AND LAND COMPANY
G'ee: TEXAS EMIGRATION AND LAND COMPANY
T-Dt: -- --- -----
P-Dt: 15 Jul 1858
Dist/Class: Texas Emmigration and Land Company
File#: 1186
Patent#: 74
Patent Vol.: 20
Certificate: 1186
Survey/Blk/Twp: 1186
Acres: 320
Map(s) 33

Abstract # 843 - TE&L CO
P'ee: TEXAS EMIGRATION AND LAND COMPANY
G'ee: TEXAS EMIGRATION AND LAND COMPANY
T-Dt: -- --- -----
P-Dt: 16 Jul 1858
Dist/Class: Texas Emmigration and Land Company
File#: 1187
Patent#: 75
Patent Vol.: 20
Certificate: 1187
Survey/Blk/Twp: 1187

Acres: 320
Map(s) 33

Abstract # 844 - TE&L CO
P'ee: TEXAS EMIGRATION AND LAND COMPANY
G'ee: TEXAS EMIGRATION AND LAND COMPANY
T-Dt: -- --- -----
P-Dt: 16 Jul 1858
Dist/Class: Texas Emmigration and Land Company
File#: 1188
Patent#: 76
Patent Vol.: 20
Certificate: 1188
Survey/Blk/Twp: 1188
Acres: 320
Map(s) 33

Abstract # 845 - TE&L CO
P'ee: TEXAS EMIGRATION AND LAND COMPANY
G'ee: TEXAS EMIGRATION AND LAND COMPANY
T-Dt: -- --- -----
P-Dt: 16 Jul 1858
Dist/Class: Texas Emmigration and Land Company
File#: 1189
Patent#: 77
Patent Vol.: 20
Certificate: 1189
Survey/Blk/Twp: 1189
Acres: 320
Map(s) 33

Abstract # 846 - TE&L CO
P'ee: HEDGECOXE, OLIVER
G'ee: TEXAS EMIGRATION AND LAND COMPANY
T-Dt: -- --- -----
P-Dt: 03 Aug 1858
Dist/Class: Texas Emmigration and Land Company
File#: 1201
Patent#: 303
Patent Vol.: 14
Certificate: 2
Survey/Blk/Twp: 1201
Acres: 320
Map(s) 20

Abstract # 847 - TE&L CO
P'ee: TEXAS EMIGRATION AND LAND COMPANY
G'ee: TEXAS EMIGRATION AND LAND COMPANY
T-Dt: -- --- -----
P-Dt: 03 Aug 1858
Dist/Class: Texas Emmigration and Land Company
File#: 1202
Patent#: 114
Patent Vol.: 20
Certificate: 1202
Survey/Blk/Twp: 1202
Acres: 320
Map(s) 35

Abstract # 848 - TE&L CO
P'ee: TEXAS EMIGRATION AND LAND COMPANY
G'ee: TEXAS EMIGRATION AND LAND COMPANY

T-Dt: -- --- -----
P-Dt: 31 May 1859
Dist/Class: Texas Emmigration and Land
Company
File#: 1203
Patent#: 544
Patent Vol.: 20
Certificate: 1203
Survey/Blk/Twp: 1203
Acres: 320
Map(s) 35

Abstract # 849 - TE&L CO
P'ee: TEXAS EMIGRATION AND LAND
COMPANY
G'ee: TEXAS EMIGRATION AND LAND
COMPANY
T-Dt: -- --- -----
P-Dt: 31 May 1859
Dist/Class: Texas Emmigration and Land
Company
File#: 1204
Patent#: 545
Patent Vol.: 20
Certificate: 1204
Survey/Blk/Twp: 1204
Acres: 320
Map(s) 35

Abstract # 850 - TE&L CO
P'ee: TEXAS EMIGRATION AND LAND
COMPANY
G'ee: TEXAS EMIGRATION AND LAND
COMPANY
T-Dt: -- --- -----
P-Dt: 11 Jun 1858
Dist/Class: Texas Emmigration and Land
Company
File#: 1205
Patent#: 1
Patent Vol.: 20
Certificate: 1205
Survey/Blk/Twp: 1205
Acres: 320
Map(s) 35, 43

Abstract # 851 - TE&L CO
P'ee: TEXAS EMIGRATION AND LAND
COMPANY
G'ee: TEXAS EMIGRATION AND LAND
COMPANY
T-Dt: -- --- -----
P-Dt: 03 Aug 1858
Dist/Class: Texas Emmigration and Land
Company
File#: 1206
Patent#: 115
Patent Vol.: 20
Certificate: 1206
Survey/Blk/Twp: 1206
Acres: 320
Map(s) 35, 43

Abstract # 852 - TE&L CO
P'ee: TEXAS EMIGRATION AND LAND
COMPANY
G'ee: TEXAS EMIGRATION AND LAND
COMPANY
T-Dt: -- --- -----
P-Dt: 18 Aug 1858
Dist/Class: Texas Emmigration and Land
Company
File#: 1394
Patent#: 241
Patent Vol.: 20

Certificate: 1394
Survey/Blk/Twp: 1394
Acres: 332.6
Map(s) 6

Abstract # 853 - TE&L CO
P'ee: TEXAS EMIGRATION AND LAND
COMPANY
G'ee: TEXAS EMIGRATION AND LAND
COMPANY
T-Dt: -- --- -----
P-Dt: 19 Aug 1858
Dist/Class: Texas Emmigration and Land
Company
File#: 1395
Patent#: 242
Patent Vol.: 20
Certificate: 1395
Survey/Blk/Twp: 1395
Acres: 320
Map(s) 6

Abstract # 854 - TE&L CO
P'ee: TEXAS EMIGRATION AND LAND
COMPANY
G'ee: TEXAS EMIGRATION AND LAND
COMPANY
T-Dt: -- --- -----
P-Dt: 19 Aug 1858
Dist/Class: Texas Emmigration and Land
Company
File#: 1396
Patent#: 243
Patent Vol.: 20
Certificate: 1396
Survey/Blk/Twp: 1396
Acres: 320
Map(s) 6

Abstract # 855 - TE&L CO
P'ee: TEXAS EMIGRATION AND LAND
COMPANY
G'ee: TEXAS EMIGRATION AND LAND
COMPANY
T-Dt: -- --- -----
P-Dt: 13 Aug 1858
Dist/Class: Texas Emmigration and Land
Company
File#: 1365
Patent#: 213
Patent Vol.: 20
Certificate: 1365
Survey/Blk/Twp: 1365
Acres: 320
Map(s) 4

Abstract # 856 - TE&L CO
P'ee: TEXAS EMIGRATION AND LAND
COMPANY
G'ee: TEXAS EMIGRATION AND LAND
COMPANY
T-Dt: -- --- -----
P-Dt: 13 Aug 1858
Dist/Class: Texas Emmigration and Land
Company
File#: 1366
Patent#: 214
Patent Vol.: 20
Certificate: 1366
Survey/Blk/Twp: 1366
Acres: 320
Map(s) 4

Abstract # 857 - TE&L CO
P'ee: TEXAS EMIGRATION AND LAND

COMPANY
G'ee: TEXAS EMIGRATION AND LAND
COMPANY
T-Dt: -- --- -----
P-Dt: 13 Aug 1858
Dist/Class: Texas Emmigration and Land
Company
File#: 1367
Patent#: 215
Patent Vol.: 20
Certificate: 1367
Survey/Blk/Twp: 1367
Acres: 320
Map(s) 4

Abstract # 858 - TE&L CO
P'ee: TEXAS EMIGRATION AND LAND
COMPANY
G'ee: TEXAS EMIGRATION AND LAND
COMPANY
T-Dt: -- --- -----
P-Dt: 13 Aug 1858
Dist/Class: Texas Emmigration and Land
Company
File#: 1368
Patent#: 216
Patent Vol.: 20
Certificate: 1368
Survey/Blk/Twp: 1368
Acres: 320
Map(s) 4

Abstract # 859 - TE&L CO
P'ee: TEXAS EMIGRATION AND LAND
COMPANY
G'ee: TEXAS EMIGRATION AND LAND
COMPANY
T-Dt: -- --- -----
P-Dt: 13 Aug 1858
Dist/Class: Texas Emmigration and Land
Company
File#: 1369
Patent#: 217
Patent Vol.: 20
Certificate: 1369
Survey/Blk/Twp: 1369
Acres: 320
Map(s) 4

Abstract # 860 - TE&L CO
P'ee: TEXAS EMIGRATION AND LAND
COMPANY
G'ee: TEXAS EMIGRATION AND LAND
COMPANY
T-Dt: -- --- -----
P-Dt: 13 Aug 1858
Dist/Class: Texas Emmigration and Land
Company
File#: 1370
Patent#: 218
Patent Vol.: 20
Certificate: 1370
Survey/Blk/Twp: 1370
Acres: 320
Map(s) 4

Abstract # 861 - TE&L CO
P'ee: TEXAS EMIGRATION AND LAND
COMPANY
G'ee: TEXAS EMIGRATION AND LAND
COMPANY
T-Dt: -- --- -----
P-Dt: 13 Aug 1858
Dist/Class: Texas Emmigration and Land
Company

File#: 1371
Patent#: 219
Patent Vol.: 20
Certificate: 1371
Survey/Blk/Twp: 1371
Acres: 320
Map(s) 4

Abstract # 862 - TE&L CO
P'ee: TEXAS EMIGRATION AND LAND
COMPANY
G'ee: TEXAS EMIGRATION AND LAND
COMPANY
T-Dt: -- --- -----
P-Dt: 13 Aug 1858
Dist/Class: Texas Emmigration and Land
Company
File#: 1372
Patent#: 220
Patent Vol.: 20
Certificate: 1372
Survey/Blk/Twp: 1372
Acres: 320
Map(s) 4

Abstract # 863 - TE&L CO
P'ee: TEXAS EMIGRATION AND LAND
COMPANY
G'ee: TEXAS EMIGRATION AND LAND
COMPANY
T-Dt: -- --- -----
P-Dt: 17 Aug 1858
Dist/Class: Texas Emmigration and Land
Company
File#: 1375
Patent#: 223
Patent Vol.: 20
Certificate: 1375
Survey/Blk/Twp: 1375
Acres: 320
Map(s) 4, 5

Abstract # 864 - TE&L CO
P'ee: TEXAS EMIGRATION AND LAND
COMPANY
G'ee: TEXAS EMIGRATION AND LAND
COMPANY
T-Dt: -- --- -----
P-Dt: 17 Aug 1858
Dist/Class: Texas Emmigration and Land
Company
File#: 1376
Patent#: 224
Patent Vol.: 20
Certificate: 1376
Survey/Blk/Twp: 1376
Acres: 320
Map(s) 5

Abstract # 865 - TE&L CO
P'ee: TEXAS EMIGRATION AND LAND
COMPANY
G'ee: TEXAS EMIGRATION AND LAND
COMPANY
T-Dt: -- --- -----
P-Dt: 18 Aug 1858
Dist/Class: Texas Emmigration and Land
Company
File#: 1390
Patent#: 237
Patent Vol.: 20
Certificate: 1390
Survey/Blk/Twp: 1390
Acres: 320
Map(s) 5

Abstract # 866 - TE&L CO
P'ee: TEXAS EMIGRATION AND LAND
COMPANY
G'ee: TEXAS EMIGRATION AND LAND
COMPANY
T-Dt: -- --- -----
P-Dt: 18 Aug 1858
Dist/Class: Texas Emmigration and Land
Company
File#: 1391
Patent#: 238
Patent Vol.: 20
Certificate: 1391
Survey/Blk/Twp: 1391
Acres: 320
Map(s) 5

Abstract # 867 - TE&L CO
P'ee: TEXAS EMIGRATION AND LAND
COMPANY
G'ee: TEXAS EMIGRATION AND LAND
COMPANY
T-Dt: -- --- -----
P-Dt: 18 Aug 1858
Dist/Class: Texas Emmigration and Land
Company
File#: 1392
Patent#: 239
Patent Vol.: 20
Certificate: 1392
Survey/Blk/Twp: 1392
Acres: 320
Map(s) 5

Abstract # 868 - TE&L CO
P'ee: TEXAS EMIGRATION AND LAND
COMPANY
G'ee: TEXAS EMIGRATION AND LAND
COMPANY
T-Dt: -- --- -----
P-Dt: 24 Jan 1859
Dist/Class: Texas Emmigration and Land
Company
File#: 1442
Patent#: 484
Patent Vol.: 20
Certificate: 1442
Survey/Blk/Twp: 1442
Acres: 265
Map(s) 13, 14

Abstract # 869 - TE&L CO
P'ee: TEXAS EMIGRATION AND LAND
COMPANY
G'ee: TEXAS EMIGRATION AND LAND
COMPANY
T-Dt: -- --- -----
P-Dt: 25 Jan 1859
Dist/Class: Texas Emmigration and Land
Company
File#: 1443
Patent#: 488
Patent Vol.: 20
Certificate: 1443
Survey/Blk/Twp: 1443
Acres: 265
Map(s) 13

Abstract # 870 - TE&L CO
P'ee: TEXAS EMIGRATION AND LAND
COMPANY
G'ee: TEXAS EMIGRATION AND LAND
COMPANY
T-Dt: -- --- -----
P-Dt: 17 Jan 1859

Dist/Class: Texas Emmigration and Land
Company
File#: 1444
Patent#: 413
Patent Vol.: 20
Certificate: 1444
Survey/Blk/Twp: 1444
Acres: 265
Map(s) 13

Abstract # 871 - TE&L CO
P'ee: TEXAS EMIGRATION AND LAND
COMPANY
G'ee: TEXAS EMIGRATION AND LAND
COMPANY
T-Dt: -- --- -----
P-Dt: 17 Jan 1859
Dist/Class: Texas Emmigration and Land
Company
File#: 1445
Patent#: 417
Patent Vol.: 20
Certificate: 1445
Survey/Blk/Twp: 1445
Acres: 247
Map(s) 5, 13

Abstract # 872 - TE&L CO
P'ee: TEXAS EMIGRATION AND LAND
COMPANY
G'ee: TEXAS EMIGRATION AND LAND
COMPANY
T-Dt: -- --- -----
P-Dt: 25 Jan 1859
Dist/Class: Texas Emmigration and Land
Company
File#: 1446
Patent#: 490
Patent Vol.: 20
Certificate: 1446
Survey/Blk/Twp: 1446
Acres: 265
Map(s) 5

Abstract # 873 - TE&L CO
P'ee: TEXAS EMIGRATION AND LAND
COMPANY
G'ee: TEXAS EMIGRATION AND LAND
COMPANY
T-Dt: -- --- -----
P-Dt: 26 Jan 1859
Dist/Class: Texas Emmigration and Land
Company
File#: 1447
Patent#: 493
Patent Vol.: 20
Certificate: 1447
Survey/Blk/Twp: 1447
Acres: 265
Map(s) 5

Abstract # 874 - TE&L CO
P'ee: TEXAS EMIGRATION AND LAND
COMPANY
G'ee: TEXAS EMIGRATION AND LAND
COMPANY
T-Dt: -- --- -----
P-Dt: 26 Jan 1859
Dist/Class: Texas Emmigration and Land
Company
File#: 1448
Patent#: 494
Patent Vol.: 20
Certificate: 1448
Survey/Blk/Twp: 1448

Acres: 265
Map(s) 5

Abstract # 875 - TE&L CO
P'ee: TEXAS EMIGRATION AND LAND
COMPANY
G'ee: TEXAS EMIGRATION AND LAND
COMPANY
T-Dt: -- --- -----
P-Dt: 26 Jan 1859
Dist/Class: Texas Emmigration and Land
Company
File#: 1449
Patent#: 495
Patent Vol.: 20
Certificate: 1449
Survey/Blk/Twp: 1449
Acres: 265
Map(s) 5

Abstract # 876 - TE&L CO
P'ee: TEXAS EMIGRATION AND LAND
COMPANY
G'ee: TEXAS EMIGRATION AND LAND
COMPANY
T-Dt: -- --- -----
P-Dt: 21 Oct 1858
Dist/Class: Texas Emmigration and Land
Company
File#: 1451
Patent#: 403
Patent Vol.: 20
Certificate: 1451
Survey/Blk/Twp: 7
Acres: 320
Map(s) 19, 20

Abstract # 877 - TE&L CO
P'ee: TEXAS EMIGRATION AND LAND
COMPANY
G'ee: TEXAS EMIGRATION AND LAND
COMPANY
T-Dt: -- --- -----
P-Dt: 23 Oct 1858
Dist/Class: Texas Emmigration and Land
Company
File#: 7
Patent#: 404
Patent Vol.: 20
Certificate: 1450
Survey/Blk/Twp: 1450
Acres: 265
Map(s) 5

Abstract # 878 - TE&L CO
P'ee: TEXAS EMIGRATION AND LAND
COMPANY
G'ee: TEXAS EMIGRATION AND LAND
COMPANY
T-Dt: -- --- -----
P-Dt: 17 Jan 1859
Dist/Class: Texas Emmigration and Land
Company
File#: 1452
Patent#: 418
Patent Vol.: 20
Certificate: 1452
Survey/Blk/Twp: 1452
Acres: 265
Map(s) 5

Abstract # 879 - TE&L CO
P'ee: TEXAS EMIGRATION AND LAND
COMPANY
G'ee: TEXAS EMIGRATION AND LAND

COMPANY
T-Dt: -- --- -----
P-Dt: 18 Jan 1859
Dist/Class: Texas Emmigration and Land
Company
File#: 1453
Patent#: 427
Patent Vol.: 20
Certificate: 1453
Survey/Blk/Twp: 1453
Acres: 265
Map(s) 5

Abstract # 880 - TE&L CO
P'ee: TEXAS EMIGRATION AND LAND
COMPANY
G'ee: TEXAS EMIGRATION AND LAND
COMPANY
T-Dt: -- --- -----
P-Dt: 20 Jan 1859
Dist/Class: Texas Emmigration and Land
Company
File#: 1454
Patent#: 458
Patent Vol.: 20
Certificate: 1454
Survey/Blk/Twp: 1454
Acres: 265
Map(s) 5

Abstract # 881 - TE&L CO
P'ee: TEXAS EMIGRATION AND LAND
COMPANY
G'ee: TEXAS EMIGRATION AND LAND
COMPANY
T-Dt: -- --- -----
P-Dt: 20 Jan 1859
Dist/Class: Texas Emmigration and Land
Company
File#: 1455
Patent#: 459
Patent Vol.: 20
Certificate: 1455
Survey/Blk/Twp: 1455
Acres: 265
Map(s) 5

Abstract # 882 - TE&L CO
P'ee: TEXAS EMIGRATION AND LAND
COMPANY
G'ee: TEXAS EMIGRATION AND LAND
COMPANY
T-Dt: -- --- -----
P-Dt: 20 Jan 1859
Dist/Class: Texas Emmigration and Land
Company
File#: 1456
Patent#: 456
Patent Vol.: 20
Certificate: 1456
Survey/Blk/Twp: 1456
Acres: 265
Map(s) 5

Abstract # 883 - TE&L CO
P'ee: TEXAS EMIGRATION AND LAND
COMPANY
G'ee: TEXAS EMIGRATION AND LAND
COMPANY
T-Dt: -- --- -----
P-Dt: 20 Jan 1859
Dist/Class: Texas Emmigration and Land
Company
File#: 1457
Patent#: 457

Patent Vol.: 20
Certificate: 1457
Survey/Blk/Twp: 1457
Acres: 240
Map(s) 5

Abstract # 884 - TE&L CO
P'ee: TEXAS EMIGRATION AND LAND
COMPANY
G'ee: TEXAS EMIGRATION AND LAND
COMPANY
T-Dt: -- --- -----
P-Dt: 20 Jan 1859
Dist/Class: Texas Emmigration and Land
Company
File#: 1458
Patent#: 452
Patent Vol.: 20
Certificate: 1458
Survey/Blk/Twp: 1458
Acres: 240
Map(s) 5

Abstract # 885 - TE&L CO
P'ee: TEXAS EMIGRATION AND LAND
COMPANY
G'ee: TEXAS EMIGRATION AND LAND
COMPANY
T-Dt: -- --- -----
P-Dt: 20 Jan 1859
Dist/Class: Texas Emmigration and Land
Company
File#: 1459
Patent#: 453
Patent Vol.: 20
Certificate: 1459
Survey/Blk/Twp: 1459
Acres: 265
Map(s) 5

Abstract # 886 - TE&L CO
P'ee: TEXAS EMIGRATION AND LAND
COMPANY
G'ee: TEXAS EMIGRATION AND LAND
COMPANY
T-Dt: -- --- -----
P-Dt: 19 Jan 1859
Dist/Class: Texas Emmigration and Land
Company
File#: 1460
Patent#: 447
Patent Vol.: 20
Certificate: 1460
Survey/Blk/Twp: 1460
Acres: 265
Map(s) 5

Abstract # 887 - TE&L CO
P'ee: TEXAS EMIGRATION AND LAND
COMPANY
G'ee: TEXAS EMIGRATION AND LAND
COMPANY
T-Dt: -- --- -----
P-Dt: 19 Jan 1859
Dist/Class: Texas Emmigration and Land
Company
File#: 1461
Patent#: 446
Patent Vol.: 20
Certificate: 1461
Survey/Blk/Twp: 1461
Acres: 265
Map(s) 5

Abstract # 888 - TE&L CO

P'ee: TEXAS EMIGRATION AND LAND
COMPANY
G'ee: TEXAS EMIGRATION AND LAND
COMPANY
T-Dt: -- --- -----
P-Dt: 19 Jan 1859
Dist/Class: Texas Emmigration and Land
Company
File#: 1462
Patent#: 441
Patent Vol.: 20
Certificate: 1462
Survey/Blk/Twp: 1462
Acres: 265
Map(s) 5

Abstract # 889 - TE&L CO
P'ee: TEXAS EMIGRATION AND LAND
COMPANY
G'ee: TEXAS EMIGRATION AND LAND
COMPANY
T-Dt: -- --- -----
P-Dt: 19 Jan 1859
Dist/Class: Texas Emmigration and Land
Company
File#: 1463
Patent#: 442
Patent Vol.: 20
Certificate: 1463
Survey/Blk/Twp: 1463
Acres: 265
Map(s) 5

Abstract # 890 - TE&L CO
P'ee: TEXAS EMIGRATION AND LAND
COMPANY
G'ee: TEXAS EMIGRATION AND LAND
COMPANY
T-Dt: -- --- -----
P-Dt: 19 Jan 1859
Dist/Class: Texas Emmigration and Land
Company
File#: 1464
Patent#: 438
Patent Vol.: 20
Certificate: 1464
Survey/Blk/Twp: 1464
Acres: 265
Map(s) 5

Abstract # 891 - TE&L CO
P'ee: TEXAS EMIGRATION AND LAND
COMPANY
G'ee: TEXAS EMIGRATION AND LAND
COMPANY
T-Dt: -- --- -----
P-Dt: 19 Jan 1859
Dist/Class: Texas Emmigration and Land
Company
File#: 1465
Patent#: 439
Patent Vol.: 20
Certificate: 1465
Survey/Blk/Twp: 1465
Acres: 265
Map(s) 5

Abstract # 892 - TE&L CO
P'ee: TEXAS EMIGRATION AND LAND
COMPANY
G'ee: TEXAS EMIGRATION AND LAND
COMPANY
T-Dt: -- --- -----
P-Dt: 19 Jan 1859
Dist/Class: Texas Emmigration and Land

Company
File#: 1466
Patent#: 435
Patent Vol.: 20
Certificate: 1466
Survey/Blk/Twp: 1466
Acres: 265
Map(s) 5, 6

Abstract # 893 - TE&L CO
P'ee: TEXAS EMIGRATION AND LAND
COMPANY
G'ee: TEXAS EMIGRATION AND LAND
COMPANY
T-Dt: -- --- -----
P-Dt: 19 Jan 1859
Dist/Class: Texas Emmigration and Land
Company
File#: 1467
Patent#: 436
Patent Vol.: 20
Certificate: 1467
Survey/Blk/Twp: 1467
Acres: 265
Map(s) 5, 6, 13, 14

Abstract # 894 - TE&L CO
P'ee: TEXAS EMIGRATION AND LAND
COMPANY
G'ee: TEXAS EMIGRATION AND LAND
COMPANY
T-Dt: -- --- -----
P-Dt: 18 Jan 1859
Dist/Class: Texas Emmigration and Land
Company
File#: 1468
Patent#: 434
Patent Vol.: 20
Certificate: 1468
Survey/Blk/Twp: 1468
Acres: 265
Map(s) 5, 6

Abstract # 895 - TE&L CO
P'ee: TEXAS EMIGRATION AND LAND
COMPANY
G'ee: TEXAS EMIGRATION AND LAND
COMPANY
T-Dt: -- --- -----
P-Dt: 19 Jan 1859
Dist/Class: Texas Emmigration and Land
Company
File#: 1469
Patent#: 437
Patent Vol.: 20
Certificate: 1469
Survey/Blk/Twp: 1469
Acres: 265
Map(s) 5

Abstract # 896 - TE&L CO
P'ee: TEXAS EMIGRATION AND LAND
COMPANY
G'ee: TEXAS EMIGRATION AND LAND
COMPANY
T-Dt: -- --- -----
P-Dt: 19 Jan 1859
Dist/Class: Texas Emmigration and Land
Company
File#: 1470
Patent#: 440
Patent Vol.: 20
Certificate: 1470
Survey/Blk/Twp: 1470
Acres: 265

Map(s) 5

Abstract # 897 - TE&L CO
P'ee: TEXAS EMIGRATION AND LAND
COMPANY
G'ee: TEXAS EMIGRATION AND LAND
COMPANY
T-Dt: -- --- -----
P-Dt: 19 Jan 1859
Dist/Class: Texas Emmigration and Land
Company
File#: 1471
Patent#: 443
Patent Vol.: 20
Certificate: 1471
Survey/Blk/Twp: 1471
Acres: 265
Map(s) 5

Abstract # 898 - TE&L CO
P'ee: TEXAS EMIGRATION AND LAND
COMPANY
G'ee: TEXAS EMIGRATION AND LAND
COMPANY
T-Dt: -- --- -----
P-Dt: 20 Jan 1859
Dist/Class: Texas Emmigration and Land
Company
File#: 1472
Patent#: 454
Patent Vol.: 20
Certificate: 1472
Survey/Blk/Twp: 1472
Acres: 265
Map(s) 5

Abstract # 899 - TE&L CO
P'ee: TEXAS EMIGRATION AND LAND
COMPANY
G'ee: TEXAS EMIGRATION AND LAND
COMPANY
T-Dt: -- --- -----
P-Dt: 20 Jan 1859
Dist/Class: Texas Emmigration and Land
Company
File#: 1473
Patent#: 455
Patent Vol.: 20
Certificate: 1473
Survey/Blk/Twp: 1473
Acres: 265
Map(s) 5, 6

Abstract # 900 - TE&L CO
P'ee: TEXAS EMIGRATION AND LAND
COMPANY
G'ee: TEXAS EMIGRATION AND LAND
COMPANY
T-Dt: -- --- -----
P-Dt: 18 Jan 1859
Dist/Class: Texas Emmigration and Land
Company
File#: 1474
Patent#: 430
Patent Vol.: 20
Certificate: 1474
Survey/Blk/Twp: 1474
Acres: 265
Map(s) 5, 6

Abstract # 901 - TE&L CO
P'ee: TEXAS EMIGRATION AND LAND
COMPANY
G'ee: TEXAS EMIGRATION AND LAND
COMPANY

T-Dt: -- --- -----
P-Dt: 18 Jan 1859
Dist/Class: Texas Emmigration and Land
Company
File#: 1475
Patent#: 431
Patent Vol.: 20
Certificate: 1475
Survey/Blk/Twp: 1475
Acres: 265
Map(s) 5

Abstract # 902 - TE&L CO
P'ee: TEXAS EMIGRATION AND LAND
COMPANY
G'ee: TEXAS EMIGRATION AND LAND
COMPANY
T-Dt: -- --- -----
P-Dt: 19 Jan 1859
Dist/Class: Texas Emmigration and Land
Company
File#: 1476
Patent#: 448
Patent Vol.: 20
Certificate: 1476
Survey/Blk/Twp: 1476
Acres: 265
Map(s) 5

Abstract # 903 - TE&L CO
P'ee: TEXAS EMIGRATION AND LAND
COMPANY
G'ee: TEXAS EMIGRATION AND LAND
COMPANY
T-Dt: -- --- -----
P-Dt: 20 Jan 1859
Dist/Class: Texas Emmigration and Land
Company
File#: 1477
Patent#: 449
Patent Vol.: 20
Certificate: 1477
Survey/Blk/Twp: 1477
Acres: 265
Map(s) 5

Abstract # 904 - TE&L CO
P'ee: TEXAS EMIGRATION AND LAND
COMPANY
G'ee: TEXAS EMIGRATION AND LAND
COMPANY
T-Dt: -- --- -----
P-Dt: 19 Jan 1859
Dist/Class: Texas Emmigration and Land
Company
File#: 1478
Patent#: 444
Patent Vol.: 20
Certificate: 1478
Survey/Blk/Twp: 1478
Acres: 265
Map(s) 5

Abstract # 905 - TE&L CO
P'ee: TEXAS EMIGRATION AND LAND
COMPANY
G'ee: TEXAS EMIGRATION AND LAND
COMPANY
T-Dt: -- --- -----
P-Dt: 19 Jan 1859
Dist/Class: Texas Emmigration and Land
Company
File#: 1479
Patent#: 445
Patent Vol.: 20

Certificate: 1479
Survey/Blk/Twp: 1479
Acres: 265
Map(s) 5, 6

Abstract # 906 - TE&L CO
P'ee: TEXAS EMIGRATION AND LAND
COMPANY
G'ee: TEXAS EMIGRATION AND LAND
COMPANY
T-Dt: -- --- -----
P-Dt: 17 Jan 1859
Dist/Class: Texas Emmigration and Land
Company
File#: 1480
Patent#: 412
Patent Vol.: 20
Certificate: 1480
Survey/Blk/Twp: 1480
Acres: 265
Map(s) 5, 6

Abstract # 907 - TE&L CO
P'ee: TEXAS EMIGRATION AND LAND
COMPANY
G'ee: TEXAS EMIGRATION AND LAND
COMPANY
T-Dt: -- --- -----
P-Dt: 17 Jan 1859
Dist/Class: Texas Emmigration and Land
Company
File#: 1481
Patent#: 414
Patent Vol.: 20
Certificate: 1481
Survey/Blk/Twp: 1481
Acres: 265
Map(s) 5

Abstract # 908 - TE&L CO
P'ee: TEXAS EMIGRATION AND LAND
COMPANY
G'ee: TEXAS EMIGRATION AND LAND
COMPANY
T-Dt: -- --- -----
P-Dt: 17 Jan 1859
Dist/Class: Texas Emmigration and Land
Company
File#: 1482
Patent#: 415
Patent Vol.: 20
Certificate: 1482
Survey/Blk/Twp: 1482
Acres: 265
Map(s) 5

Abstract # 909 - TE&L CO
P'ee: TEXAS EMIGRATION AND LAND
COMPANY
G'ee: TEXAS EMIGRATION AND LAND
COMPANY
T-Dt: -- --- -----
P-Dt: 17 Jan 1859
Dist/Class: Texas Emmigration and Land
Company
File#: 1483
Patent#: 416
Patent Vol.: 20
Certificate: 1483
Survey/Blk/Twp: 1483
Acres: 265
Map(s) 5

Abstract # 910 - TE&L CO
P'ee: TEXAS EMIGRATION AND LAND

COMPANY
G'ee: TEXAS EMIGRATION AND LAND
COMPANY
T-Dt: -- --- -----
P-Dt: 17 Jan 1859
Dist/Class: Texas Emmigration and Land
Company
File#: 1484
Patent#: 419
Patent Vol.: 20
Certificate: 1484
Survey/Blk/Twp: 1484
Acres: 265
Map(s) 5

Abstract # 911 - TE&L CO
P'ee: TEXAS EMIGRATION AND LAND
COMPANY
G'ee: TEXAS EMIGRATION AND LAND
COMPANY
T-Dt: -- --- -----
P-Dt: 17 Jan 1859
Dist/Class: Texas Emmigration and Land
Company
File#: 1485
Patent#: 420
Patent Vol.: 20
Certificate: 1485
Survey/Blk/Twp: 1485
Acres: 265
Map(s) 14

Abstract # 912 - TE&L CO
P'ee: TEXAS EMIGRATION AND LAND
COMPANY
G'ee: TEXAS EMIGRATION AND LAND
COMPANY
T-Dt: -- --- -----
P-Dt: 18 Jan 1859
Dist/Class: Texas Emmigration and Land
Company
File#: 1486
Patent#: 421
Patent Vol.: 20
Certificate: 1486
Survey/Blk/Twp: 1486
Acres: 265
Map(s) 6, 14

Abstract # 913 - TE&L CO
P'ee: TEXAS EMIGRATION AND LAND
COMPANY
G'ee: TEXAS EMIGRATION AND LAND
COMPANY
T-Dt: -- --- -----
P-Dt: 18 Jan 1859
Dist/Class: Texas Emmigration and Land
Company
File#: 1487
Patent#: 422
Patent Vol.: 20
Certificate: 1487
Survey/Blk/Twp: 1487
Acres: 265
Map(s) 6, 14

Abstract # 914 - TE&L CO
P'ee: TEXAS EMIGRATION AND LAND
COMPANY
G'ee: TEXAS EMIGRATION AND LAND
COMPANY
T-Dt: -- --- -----
P-Dt: 18 Jan 1859
Dist/Class: Texas Emmigration and Land
Company

File#: 1488
Patent#: 423
Patent Vol.: 20
Certificate: 1488
Survey/Blk/Twp: 1488
Acres: 265
Map(s) 14

Abstract # 915 - TE&L CO
P'ee: TEXAS EMIGRATION AND LAND COMPANY
G'ee: TEXAS EMIGRATION AND LAND COMPANY
T-Dt: -- --- -----
P-Dt: 18 Jan 1859
Dist/Class: Texas Emmigration and Land Company
File#: 1489
Patent#: 424
Patent Vol.: 20
Certificate: 1489
Survey/Blk/Twp: 1489
Acres: 265
Map(s) 14

Abstract # 916 - TE&L CO
P'ee: TEXAS EMIGRATION AND LAND COMPANY
G'ee: TEXAS EMIGRATION AND LAND COMPANY
T-Dt: -- --- -----
P-Dt: 18 Jan 1859
Dist/Class: Texas Emmigration and Land Company
File#: 1490
Patent#: 425
Patent Vol.: 20
Certificate: 1490
Survey/Blk/Twp: 1490
Acres: 265
Map(s) 6, 14

Abstract # 917 - TE&L CO
P'ee: TEXAS EMIGRATION AND LAND COMPANY
G'ee: TEXAS EMIGRATION AND LAND COMPANY
T-Dt: -- --- -----
P-Dt: 18 Jan 1859
Dist/Class: Texas Emmigration and Land Company
File#: 1491
Patent#: 426
Patent Vol.: 20
Certificate: 1491
Survey/Blk/Twp: 1491
Acres: 265
Map(s) 6

Abstract # 918 - TE&L CO
P'ee: TEXAS EMIGRATION AND LAND COMPANY
G'ee: TEXAS EMIGRATION AND LAND COMPANY
T-Dt: -- --- -----
P-Dt: 14 Jan 1859
Dist/Class: Texas Emmigration and Land Company
File#: 1492
Patent#: 406
Patent Vol.: 20
Certificate: 1492
Survey/Blk/Twp: 1492
Acres: 265
Map(s) 6

Abstract # 919 - TE&L CO
P'ee: TEXAS EMIGRATION AND LAND COMPANY
G'ee: TEXAS EMIGRATION AND LAND COMPANY
T-Dt: -- --- -----
P-Dt: 14 Jan 1859
Dist/Class: Texas Emmigration and Land Company
File#: 1493
Patent#: 407
Patent Vol.: 20
Certificate: 1493
Survey/Blk/Twp: 1493
Acres: 265
Map(s) 6

Abstract # 920 - TE&L CO
P'ee: TEXAS EMIGRATION AND LAND COMPANY
G'ee: TEXAS EMIGRATION AND LAND COMPANY
T-Dt: -- --- -----
P-Dt: 14 Jan 1859
Dist/Class: Texas Emmigration and Land Company
File#: 1494
Patent#: 408
Patent Vol.: 20
Certificate: 1494
Survey/Blk/Twp: 1494
Acres: 265
Map(s) 6

Abstract # 921 - TE&L CO
P'ee: TEXAS EMIGRATION AND LAND COMPANY
G'ee: TEXAS EMIGRATION AND LAND COMPANY
T-Dt: -- --- -----
P-Dt: 14 Jan 1859
Dist/Class: Texas Emmigration and Land Company
File#: 1495
Patent#: 409
Patent Vol.: 20
Certificate: 1495
Survey/Blk/Twp: 1495
Acres: 265
Map(s) 6

Abstract # 922 - TE&L CO
P'ee: TEXAS EMIGRATION AND LAND COMPANY
G'ee: TEXAS EMIGRATION AND LAND COMPANY
T-Dt: -- --- -----
P-Dt: 18 Jan 1859
Dist/Class: Texas Emmigration and Land Company
File#: 1496
Patent#: 428
Patent Vol.: 20
Certificate: 1496
Survey/Blk/Twp: 1496
Acres: 265
Map(s) 6

Abstract # 923 - TE&L CO
P'ee: TEXAS EMIGRATION AND LAND COMPANY
G'ee: TEXAS EMIGRATION AND LAND COMPANY
T-Dt: -- --- -----
P-Dt: 18 Jan 1859

Dist/Class: Texas Emmigration and Land Company
File#: 1497
Patent#: 429
Patent Vol.: 20
Certificate: 1497
Survey/Blk/Twp: 1497
Acres: 265
Map(s) 6

Abstract # 924 - TE&L CO
P'ee: TEXAS EMIGRATION AND LAND COMPANY
G'ee: TEXAS EMIGRATION AND LAND COMPANY
T-Dt: -- --- -----
P-Dt: 17 Jan 1859
Dist/Class: Texas Emmigration and Land Company
File#: 1498
Patent#: 410
Patent Vol.: 20
Certificate: 1498
Survey/Blk/Twp: 1498
Acres: 265
Map(s) 6

Abstract # 925 - TE&L CO
P'ee: TEXAS EMIGRATION AND LAND COMPANY
G'ee: TEXAS EMIGRATION AND LAND COMPANY
T-Dt: -- --- -----
P-Dt: 17 Jan 1859
Dist/Class: Texas Emmigration and Land Company
File#: 1499
Patent#: 411
Patent Vol.: 20
Certificate: 1499
Survey/Blk/Twp: 1499
Acres: 265
Map(s) 6

Abstract # 926 - TE&L CO
P'ee: TEXAS EMIGRATION AND LAND COMPANY
G'ee: TEXAS EMIGRATION AND LAND COMPANY
T-Dt: -- --- -----
P-Dt: 26 Jan 1859
Dist/Class: Texas Emmigration and Land Company
File#: 1500
Patent#: 496
Patent Vol.: 20
Certificate: 1500
Survey/Blk/Twp: 1500
Acres: 265
Map(s) 6

Abstract # 927 - TE&L CO
P'ee: TEXAS EMIGRATION AND LAND COMPANY
G'ee: TEXAS EMIGRATION AND LAND COMPANY
T-Dt: -- --- -----
P-Dt: 07 Sep 1858
Dist/Class: Texas Emmigration and Land Company
File#: 1577
Patent#: 321
Patent Vol.: 20
Certificate: 1577
Survey/Blk/Twp: 1577

Acres: 320
Map(s) 22, 23, 30, 31

Abstract # 928 - TE&L CO
P'ee: TEXAS EMIGRATION AND LAND COMPANY
G'ee: TEXAS EMIGRATION AND LAND COMPANY
T-Dt: -- --- -----
P-Dt: 08 Sep 1858
Dist/Class: Texas Emmigration and Land Company
File#: 1585
Patent#: 329
Patent Vol.: 20
Certificate: 1585
Survey/Blk/Twp: 1585
Acres: 320
Map(s) 1

Abstract # 929 - TE&L CO
P'ee: TEXAS EMIGRATION AND LAND COMPANY
G'ee: TEXAS EMIGRATION AND LAND COMPANY
T-Dt: -- --- -----
P-Dt: 08 Sep 1858
Dist/Class: Texas Emmigration and Land Company
File#: 1586
Patent#: 330
Patent Vol.: 20
Certificate: 1586
Survey/Blk/Twp: 1586
Acres: 320
Map(s) 1

Abstract # 930 - TE&L CO
P'ee: TEXAS EMIGRATION AND LAND COMPANY
G'ee: TEXAS EMIGRATION AND LAND COMPANY
T-Dt: -- --- -----
P-Dt: 08 Sep 1858
Dist/Class: Texas Emmigration and Land Company
File#: 1588
Patent#: 332
Patent Vol.: 20
Certificate: 1588
Survey/Blk/Twp: 1588
Acres: 320
Map(s) 1

Abstract # 931 - TE&L CO
P'ee: TEXAS EMIGRATION AND LAND COMPANY
G'ee: TEXAS EMIGRATION AND LAND COMPANY
T-Dt: -- --- -----
P-Dt: 08 Sep 1858
Dist/Class: Texas Emmigration and Land Company
File#: 1589
Patent#: 333
Patent Vol.: 20
Certificate: 1589
Survey/Blk/Twp: 1589
Acres: 320
Map(s) 1

Abstract # 932 - TE&L CO
P'ee: TEXAS EMIGRATION AND LAND COMPANY
G'ee: TEXAS EMIGRATION AND LAND COMPANY
T-Dt: -- --- -----
P-Dt: 08 Sep 1858
Dist/Class: Texas Emmigration and Land Company
File#: 1590
Patent#: 334
Patent Vol.: 20
Certificate: 1590
Survey/Blk/Twp: 1590
Acres: 320
Map(s) 1

Abstract # 933 - TE&L CO
P'ee: TEXAS EMIGRATION AND LAND COMPANY
G'ee: TEXAS EMIGRATION AND LAND COMPANY
T-Dt: -- --- -----
P-Dt: 08 Sep 1858
Dist/Class: Texas Emmigration and Land Company
File#: 1591
Patent#: 335
Patent Vol.: 20
Certificate: 1591
Survey/Blk/Twp: 1591
Acres: 320
Map(s) 1, 2

Abstract # 934 - TE&L CO
P'ee: TEXAS EMIGRATION AND LAND COMPANY
G'ee: TEXAS EMIGRATION AND LAND COMPANY
T-Dt: -- --- -----
P-Dt: 08 Sep 1858
Dist/Class: Texas Emmigration and Land Company
File#: 1592
Patent#: 336
Patent Vol.: 20
Certificate: 1592
Survey/Blk/Twp: 1592
Acres: 320
Map(s) 2

Abstract # 935 - TE&L CO
P'ee: TEXAS EMIGRATION AND LAND COMPANY
G'ee: TEXAS EMIGRATION AND LAND COMPANY
T-Dt: -- --- -----
P-Dt: 23 Sep 1858
Dist/Class: Texas Emmigration and Land Company
File#: 1648
Patent#: 388
Patent Vol.: 20
Certificate: 1648
Survey/Blk/Twp: 1648
Acres: 320
Map(s) 25

Abstract # 936 - TE&L CO
P'ee: TEXAS EMIGRATION AND LAND COMPANY
G'ee: TEXAS EMIGRATION AND LAND COMPANY
T-Dt: -- --- -----
P-Dt: 23 Sep 1858
Dist/Class: Texas Emmigration and Land Company
File#: 1649
Patent#: 389
Patent Vol.: 20
Certificate: 1649
Survey/Blk/Twp: 1649
Acres: 320
Map(s) 25, 33

Abstract # 937 - TE&L CO
P'ee: TEXAS EMIGRATION AND LAND COMPANY
G'ee: TEXAS EMIGRATION AND LAND COMPANY
T-Dt: -- --- -----
P-Dt: 10 Jul 1858
Dist/Class: Texas Emmigration and Land Company
File#: 1650
Patent#: 103
Patent Vol.: 21
Certificate: 1650
Survey/Blk/Twp: 1650
Acres: 320
Map(s) 33

Abstract # 938 - TE&L CO
P'ee: TEXAS EMIGRATION AND LAND COMPANY
G'ee: TEXAS EMIGRATION AND LAND COMPANY
T-Dt: -- --- -----
P-Dt: 12 Jul 1858
Dist/Class: Texas Emmigration and Land Company
File#: 1651
Patent#: 104
Patent Vol.: 21
Certificate: 1651
Survey/Blk/Twp: 1651
Acres: 320
Map(s) 33

Abstract # 939 - TE&L CO
P'ee: TEXAS EMIGRATION AND LAND COMPANY
G'ee: TEXAS EMIGRATION AND LAND COMPANY
T-Dt: -- --- -----
P-Dt: 12 Jul 1858
Dist/Class: Texas Emmigration and Land Company
File#: 1652
Patent#: 105
Patent Vol.: 21
Certificate: 1652
Survey/Blk/Twp: 1652
Acres: 320
Map(s) 33

Abstract # 940 - TE&L CO
P'ee: TEXAS EMIGRATION AND LAND COMPANY
G'ee: TEXAS EMIGRATION AND LAND COMPANY
T-Dt: -- --- -----
P-Dt: 12 Jul 1858
Dist/Class: Texas Emmigration and Land Company
File#: 1653
Patent#: 106
Patent Vol.: 21
Certificate: 1653
Survey/Blk/Twp: 1653
Acres: 320
Map(s) 33

Abstract # 941 - TE&L CO

P'ee: TEXAS EMIGRATION AND LAND
COMPANY
G'ee: TEXAS EMIGRATION AND LAND
COMPANY
T-Dt: -- --- -----
P-Dt: 13 Jul 1858
Dist/Class: Texas Emmigration and Land
Company
File#: 1654
Patent#: 107
Patent Vol.: 21
Certificate: 1654
Survey/Blk/Twp: 1654
Acres: 320
Map(s) 33

Abstract # 942 - TE&L CO
P'ee: TEXAS EMIGRATION AND LAND
COMPANY
G'ee: TEXAS EMIGRATION AND LAND
COMPANY
T-Dt: -- --- -----
P-Dt: 13 Jul 1858
Dist/Class: Texas Emmigration and Land
Company
File#: 1655
Patent#: 108
Patent Vol.: 21
Certificate: 1655
Survey/Blk/Twp: 1655
Acres: 320
Map(s) 33

Abstract # 943 - TE&L CO
P'ee: TEXAS EMIGRATION AND LAND
COMPANY
G'ee: TEXAS EMIGRATION AND LAND
COMPANY
T-Dt: -- --- -----
P-Dt: 12 Jun 1858
Dist/Class: Texas Emmigration and Land
Company
File#: 1656
Patent#: 26
Patent Vol.: 21
Certificate: 1656
Survey/Blk/Twp: 1656
Acres: 320
Map(s) 25, 33

Abstract # 944 - TE&L CO
P'ee: TEXAS EMIGRATION AND LAND
COMPANY
G'ee: TEXAS EMIGRATION AND LAND
COMPANY
T-Dt: -- --- -----
P-Dt: 12 Jun 1858
Dist/Class: Texas Emmigration and Land
Company
File#: 1657
Patent#: 27
Patent Vol.: 21
Certificate: 1657
Survey/Blk/Twp: 1657
Acres: 320
Map(s) 25

Abstract # 945 - TE&L CO
P'ee: TEXAS EMIGRATION AND LAND
COMPANY
G'ee: TEXAS EMIGRATION AND LAND
COMPANY
T-Dt: -- --- -----
P-Dt: 13 Jul 1858
Dist/Class: Texas Emmigration and Land

Company
File#: 1658
Patent#: 109
Patent Vol.: 21
Certificate: 1658
Survey/Blk/Twp: 1658
Acres: 320
Map(s) 25

Abstract # 946 - TE&L CO
P'ee: TEXAS EMIGRATION AND LAND
COMPANY
G'ee: TEXAS EMIGRATION AND LAND
COMPANY
T-Dt: -- --- -----
P-Dt: 13 Jul 1858
Dist/Class: Texas Emmigration and Land
Company
File#: 1659
Patent#: 110
Patent Vol.: 21
Certificate: 1659
Survey/Blk/Twp: 1659
Acres: 320
Map(s) 25, 33

Abstract # 947 - TE&L CO
P'ee: TEXAS EMIGRATION AND LAND
COMPANY
G'ee: TEXAS EMIGRATION AND LAND
COMPANY
T-Dt: -- --- -----
P-Dt: 13 Jul 1858
Dist/Class: Texas Emmigration and Land
Company
File#: 1660
Patent#: 111
Patent Vol.: 21
Certificate: 1660
Survey/Blk/Twp: 1660
Acres: 320
Map(s) 33

Abstract # 948 - TE&L CO
P'ee: TEXAS EMIGRATION AND LAND
COMPANY
G'ee: TEXAS EMIGRATION AND LAND
COMPANY
T-Dt: -- --- -----
P-Dt: 13 Jul 1858
Dist/Class: Texas Emmigration and Land
Company
File#: 1661
Patent#: 112
Patent Vol.: 21
Certificate: 1661
Survey/Blk/Twp: 1661
Acres: 320
Map(s) 33

Abstract # 949 - TE&L CO
P'ee: TEXAS EMIGRATION AND LAND
COMPANY
G'ee: TEXAS EMIGRATION AND LAND
COMPANY
T-Dt: -- --- -----
P-Dt: 14 Jul 1858
Dist/Class: Texas Emmigration and Land
Company
File#: 1662
Patent#: 113
Patent Vol.: 21
Certificate: 1662
Survey/Blk/Twp: 1662
Acres: 320

Map(s) 33

Abstract # 950 - TE&L CO
P'ee: TEXAS EMIGRATION AND LAND
COMPANY
G'ee: TEXAS EMIGRATION AND LAND
COMPANY
T-Dt: -- --- -----
P-Dt: 14 Jul 1858
Dist/Class: Texas Emmigration and Land
Company
File#: 1663
Patent#: 114
Patent Vol.: 21
Certificate: 1663
Survey/Blk/Twp: 1663
Acres: 320
Map(s) 33

Abstract # 951 - TE&L CO
P'ee: TEXAS EMIGRATION AND LAND
COMPANY
G'ee: TEXAS EMIGRATION AND LAND
COMPANY
T-Dt: -- --- -----
P-Dt: 14 Jul 1858
Dist/Class: Texas Emmigration and Land
Company
File#: 1664
Patent#: 115
Patent Vol.: 21
Certificate: 1664
Survey/Blk/Twp: 1664
Acres: 320
Map(s) 33

Abstract # 952 - TE&L CO
P'ee: TEXAS EMIGRATION AND LAND
COMPANY
G'ee: TEXAS EMIGRATION AND LAND
COMPANY
T-Dt: -- --- -----
P-Dt: 14 Jul 1858
Dist/Class: Texas Emmigration and Land
Company
File#: 1665
Patent#: 116
Patent Vol.: 21
Certificate: 1665
Survey/Blk/Twp: 1665
Acres: 320
Map(s) 33

Abstract # 953 - TE&L CO
P'ee: TEXAS EMIGRATION AND LAND
COMPANY
G'ee: TEXAS EMIGRATION AND LAND
COMPANY
T-Dt: -- --- -----
P-Dt: 14 Jul 1858
Dist/Class: Texas Emmigration and Land
Company
File#: 1666
Patent#: 117
Patent Vol.: 21
Certificate: 1666
Survey/Blk/Twp: 1666
Acres: 320
Map(s) 33

Abstract # 954 - TE&L CO
P'ee: TEXAS EMIGRATION AND LAND
COMPANY
G'ee: TEXAS EMIGRATION AND LAND
COMPANY

T-Dt: -- --- -----
P-Dt: 14 Jul 1858
Dist/Class: Texas Emmigration and Land Company
File#: 1667
Patent#: 118
Patent Vol.: 21
Certificate: 1667
Survey/Blk/Twp: 1667
Acres: 320
Map(s) 33

Abstract # 955 - TE&L CO
P'ee: TEXAS EMIGRATION AND LAND COMPANY
G'ee: TEXAS EMIGRATION AND LAND COMPANY
T-Dt: -- --- -----
P-Dt: 15 Jul 1858
Dist/Class: Texas Emmigration and Land Company
File#: 1668
Patent#: 119
Patent Vol.: 21
Certificate: 1668
Survey/Blk/Twp: 1668
Acres: 320
Map(s) 33

Abstract # 956 - TE&L CO
P'ee: TEXAS EMIGRATION AND LAND COMPANY
G'ee: TEXAS EMIGRATION AND LAND COMPANY
T-Dt: -- --- -----
P-Dt: 15 Jul 1858
Dist/Class: Texas Emmigration and Land Company
File#: 1669
Patent#: 120
Patent Vol.: 21
Certificate: 1669
Survey/Blk/Twp: 1669
Acres: 320
Map(s) 33

Abstract # 957 - TE&L CO
P'ee: TEXAS EMIGRATION AND LAND COMPANY
G'ee: TEXAS EMIGRATION AND LAND COMPANY
T-Dt: -- --- -----
P-Dt: 15 Jul 1858
Dist/Class: Texas Emmigration and Land Company
File#: 1670
Patent#: 121
Patent Vol.: 21
Certificate: 1670
Survey/Blk/Twp: 1670
Acres: 320
Map(s) 33

Abstract # 958 - TE&L CO
P'ee: TEXAS EMIGRATION AND LAND COMPANY
G'ee: TEXAS EMIGRATION AND LAND COMPANY
T-Dt: -- --- -----
P-Dt: 15 Jul 1858
Dist/Class: Texas Emmigration and Land Company
File#: 1671
Patent#: 122
Patent Vol.: 21

Certificate: 1671
Survey/Blk/Twp: 1671
Acres: 320
Map(s) 33

Abstract # 959 - TE&L CO
P'ee: TEXAS EMIGRATION AND LAND COMPANY
G'ee: TEXAS EMIGRATION AND LAND COMPANY
T-Dt: -- --- -----
P-Dt: 15 Jul 1858
Dist/Class: Texas Emmigration and Land Company
File#: 1672
Patent#: 123
Patent Vol.: 21
Certificate: 1672
Survey/Blk/Twp: 1672
Acres: 320
Map(s) 33

Abstract # 960 - TE&L CO
P'ee: TEXAS EMIGRATION AND LAND COMPANY
G'ee: TEXAS EMIGRATION AND LAND COMPANY
T-Dt: -- --- -----
P-Dt: 15 Jul 1858
Dist/Class: Texas Emmigration and Land Company
File#: 1673
Patent#: 124
Patent Vol.: 21
Certificate: 1673
Survey/Blk/Twp: 1673
Acres: 320
Map(s) 33

Abstract # 961 - TE&L CO
P'ee: TEXAS EMIGRATION AND LAND COMPANY
G'ee: TEXAS EMIGRATION AND LAND COMPANY
T-Dt: -- --- -----
P-Dt: 16 Jul 1858
Dist/Class: Texas Emmigration and Land Company
File#: 1674
Patent#: 125
Patent Vol.: 21
Certificate: 1674
Survey/Blk/Twp: 1674
Acres: 320
Map(s) 25, 33

Abstract # 962 - TE&L CO
P'ee: TEXAS EMIGRATION AND LAND COMPANY
G'ee: TEXAS EMIGRATION AND LAND COMPANY
T-Dt: -- --- -----
P-Dt: 16 Jul 1858
Dist/Class: Texas Emmigration and Land Company
File#: 1675
Patent#: 126
Patent Vol.: 21
Certificate: 1675
Survey/Blk/Twp: 1675
Acres: 320
Map(s) 25

Abstract # 963 - TE&L CO
P'ee: TEXAS EMIGRATION AND LAND

COMPANY
G'ee: TEXAS EMIGRATION AND LAND COMPANY
T-Dt: -- --- -----
P-Dt: 12 Jun 1858
Dist/Class: Texas Emmigration and Land Company
File#: 1676
Patent#: 28
Patent Vol.: 21
Certificate: 1676
Survey/Blk/Twp: 1676
Acres: 320
Map(s) 17

Abstract # 964 - TE&L CO
P'ee: TEXAS EMIGRATION AND LAND COMPANY
G'ee: TEXAS EMIGRATION AND LAND COMPANY
T-Dt: -- --- -----
P-Dt: 12 Jun 1858
Dist/Class: Texas Emmigration and Land Company
File#: 1677
Patent#: 29
Patent Vol.: 21
Certificate: 1677
Survey/Blk/Twp: 1677
Acres: 320
Map(s) 17, 25

Abstract # 965 - TE&L CO
P'ee: TEXAS EMIGRATION AND LAND COMPANY
G'ee: TEXAS EMIGRATION AND LAND COMPANY
T-Dt: -- --- -----
P-Dt: 16 Jul 1858
Dist/Class: Texas Emmigration and Land Company
File#: 1678
Patent#: 127
Patent Vol.: 21
Certificate: 1678
Survey/Blk/Twp: 1678
Acres: 320
Map(s) 25

Abstract # 966 - TE&L CO
P'ee: TEXAS EMIGRATION AND LAND COMPANY
G'ee: TEXAS EMIGRATION AND LAND COMPANY
T-Dt: -- --- -----
P-Dt: 16 Jul 1858
Dist/Class: Texas Emmigration and Land Company
File#: 1679
Patent#: 128
Patent Vol.: 21
Certificate: 1679
Survey/Blk/Twp: 1679
Acres: 320
Map(s) 25

Abstract # 967 - TE&L CO
P'ee: TEXAS EMIGRATION AND LAND COMPANY
G'ee: TEXAS EMIGRATION AND LAND COMPANY
T-Dt: -- --- -----
P-Dt: 16 Jul 1858
Dist/Class: Texas Emmigration and Land Company

File#: 1680
Patent#: 129
Patent Vol.: 21
Certificate: 1680
Survey/Blk/Twp: 1680
Acres: 320
Map(s) 25

Abstract # 968 - TE&L CO
P'ee: TEXAS EMIGRATION AND LAND
COMPANY
G'ee: TEXAS EMIGRATION AND LAND
COMPANY
T-Dt: -- --- -----
P-Dt: 16 Jul 1858
Dist/Class: Texas Emmigration and Land
Company
File#: 1681
Patent#: 130
Patent Vol.: 21
Certificate: 1681
Survey/Blk/Twp: 1681
Acres: 320
Map(s) 25

Abstract # 969 - TE&L CO
P'ee: TEXAS EMIGRATION AND LAND
COMPANY
G'ee: TEXAS EMIGRATION AND LAND
COMPANY
T-Dt: -- --- -----
P-Dt: 17 Jul 1858
Dist/Class: Texas Emmigration and Land
Company
File#: 1682
Patent#: 131
Patent Vol.: 21
Certificate: 1682
Survey/Blk/Twp: 1682
Acres: 320
Map(s) 17, 25

Abstract # 970 - TE&L CO
P'ee: TEXAS EMIGRATION AND LAND
COMPANY
G'ee: TEXAS EMIGRATION AND LAND
COMPANY
T-Dt: -- --- -----
P-Dt: 17 Jul 1858
Dist/Class: Texas Emmigration and Land
Company
File#: 1683
Patent#: 132
Patent Vol.: 21
Certificate: 1683
Survey/Blk/Twp: 1683
Acres: 320
Map(s) 17

Abstract # 971 - TE&L CO
P'ee: TEXAS EMIGRATION AND LAND
COMPANY
G'ee: TEXAS EMIGRATION AND LAND
COMPANY
T-Dt: -- --- -----
P-Dt: 05 Aug 1858
Dist/Class: Texas Emmigration and Land
Company
File#: 1809
Patent#: 222
Patent Vol.: 21
Certificate: 1809
Survey/Blk/Twp: 1809
Acres: 320
Map(s) 4

Abstract # 972 - TE&L CO
P'ee: TEXAS EMIGRATION AND LAND
COMPANY
G'ee: TEXAS EMIGRATION AND LAND
COMPANY
T-Dt: -- --- -----
P-Dt: 11 Aug 1858
Dist/Class: Texas Emmigration and Land
Company
File#: 1857
Patent#: 274
Patent Vol.: 21
Certificate: 1857
Survey/Blk/Twp: 1857
Acres: 320
Map(s) 6

Abstract # 973 - TE&L CO
P'ee: TEXAS EMIGRATION AND LAND
COMPANY
G'ee: TEXAS EMIGRATION AND LAND
COMPANY
T-Dt: -- --- -----
P-Dt: 11 Aug 1858
Dist/Class: Texas Emmigration and Land
Company
File#: 1858
Patent#: 275
Patent Vol.: 21
Certificate: 1858
Survey/Blk/Twp: 1858
Acres: 320
Map(s) 6

Abstract # 974 - TE&L CO
P'ee: TEXAS EMIGRATION AND LAND
COMPANY
G'ee: TEXAS EMIGRATION AND LAND
COMPANY
T-Dt: -- --- -----
P-Dt: 12 Aug 1858
Dist/Class: Texas Emmigration and Land
Company
File#: 1877
Patent#: 293
Patent Vol.: 21
Certificate: 1877
Survey/Blk/Twp: 8
Acres: 320
Map(s) 20

Abstract # 975 - TE&L CO
P'ee: TEXAS EMIGRATION AND LAND
COMPANY
G'ee: TEXAS EMIGRATION AND LAND
COMPANY
T-Dt: -- --- -----
P-Dt: 25 Jan 1859
Dist/Class: Texas Emmigration and Land
Company
File#: 1901
Patent#: 510
Patent Vol.: 21
Certificate: 1901
Survey/Blk/Twp: 1901
Acres: 265
Map(s) 6

Abstract # 976 - TE&L CO
P'ee: TEXAS EMIGRATION AND LAND
COMPANY
G'ee: TEXAS EMIGRATION AND LAND
COMPANY
T-Dt: -- --- -----
P-Dt: 25 Jan 1859

Dist/Class: Texas Emmigration and Land
Company
File#: 1902
Patent#: 511
Patent Vol.: 21
Certificate: 1902
Survey/Blk/Twp: 1902
Acres: 265
Map(s) 6

Abstract # 977 - TE&L CO
P'ee: TEXAS EMIGRATION AND LAND
COMPANY
G'ee: TEXAS EMIGRATION AND LAND
COMPANY
T-Dt: -- --- -----
P-Dt: 25 Jan 1859
Dist/Class: Texas Emmigration and Land
Company
File#: 1903
Patent#: 512
Patent Vol.: 21
Certificate: 1903
Survey/Blk/Twp: 1903
Acres: 265
Map(s) 6

Abstract # 978 - TE&L CO
P'ee: TEXAS EMIGRATION AND LAND
COMPANY
G'ee: TEXAS EMIGRATION AND LAND
COMPANY
T-Dt: -- --- -----
P-Dt: 29 Jan 1859
Dist/Class: Texas Emmigration and Land
Company
File#: 1904
Patent#: 543
Patent Vol.: 21
Certificate: 1904
Survey/Blk/Twp: 1904
Acres: 265
Map(s) 6

Abstract # 979 - TE&L CO
P'ee: TEXAS EMIGRATION AND LAND
COMPANY
G'ee: TEXAS EMIGRATION AND LAND
COMPANY
T-Dt: -- --- -----
P-Dt: 29 Jan 1859
Dist/Class: Texas Emmigration and Land
Company
File#: 1905
Patent#: 544
Patent Vol.: 21
Certificate: 1905
Survey/Blk/Twp: 1905
Acres: 265
Map(s) 6

Abstract # 980 - TE&L CO
P'ee: TEXAS EMIGRATION AND LAND
COMPANY
G'ee: TEXAS EMIGRATION AND LAND
COMPANY
T-Dt: -- --- -----
P-Dt: 27 Jan 1859
Dist/Class: Texas Emmigration and Land
Company
File#: 1906
Patent#: 521
Patent Vol.: 21
Certificate: 1906
Survey/Blk/Twp: 1906

Acres: 265
Map(s) 6, 14

Abstract # 981 - TE&L CO
P'ee: TEXAS EMIGRATION AND LAND
COMPANY
G'ee: TEXAS EMIGRATION AND LAND
COMPANY
T-Dt: -- --- -----
P-Dt: 27 Jan 1859
Dist/Class: Texas Emmigration and Land
Company
File#: 1907
Patent#: 522
Patent Vol.: 21
Certificate: 1907
Survey/Blk/Twp: 1907
Acres: 265
Map(s) 6, 14

Abstract # 982 - TE&L CO
P'ee: TEXAS EMIGRATION AND LAND
COMPANY
G'ee: TEXAS EMIGRATION AND LAND
COMPANY
T-Dt: -- --- -----
P-Dt: 28 Jan 1859
Dist/Class: Texas Emmigration and Land
Company
File#: 1908
Patent#: 523
Patent Vol.: 21
Certificate: 1908
Survey/Blk/Twp: 1908
Acres: 265
Map(s) 6, 14

Abstract # 983 - TE&L CO
P'ee: TEXAS EMIGRATION AND LAND
COMPANY
G'ee: TEXAS EMIGRATION AND LAND
COMPANY
T-Dt: -- --- -----
P-Dt: 28 Jan 1859
Dist/Class: Texas Emmigration and Land
Company
File#: 1909
Patent#: 524
Patent Vol.: 21
Certificate: 1909
Survey/Blk/Twp: 1909
Acres: 265
Map(s) 14

Abstract # 984 - TE&L CO
P'ee: TEXAS EMIGRATION AND LAND
COMPANY
G'ee: TEXAS EMIGRATION AND LAND
COMPANY
T-Dt: -- --- -----
P-Dt: 28 Jan 1859
Dist/Class: Texas Emmigration and Land
Company
File#: 1910
Patent#: 525
Patent Vol.: 21
Certificate: 1910
Survey/Blk/Twp: 1910
Acres: 265
Map(s) 14

Abstract # 985 - TE&L CO
P'ee: TEXAS EMIGRATION AND LAND
COMPANY
G'ee: TEXAS EMIGRATION AND LAND

COMPANY
T-Dt: -- --- -----
P-Dt: 28 Jan 1859
Dist/Class: Texas Emmigration and Land
Company
File#: 1911
Patent#: 526
Patent Vol.: 21
Certificate: 1911
Survey/Blk/Twp: 1911
Acres: 265
Map(s) 14

Abstract # 986 - TE&L CO
P'ee: TEXAS EMIGRATION AND LAND
COMPANY
G'ee: TEXAS EMIGRATION AND LAND
COMPANY
T-Dt: -- --- -----
P-Dt: 28 Jan 1859
Dist/Class: Texas Emmigration and Land
Company
File#: 1912
Patent#: 527
Patent Vol.: 21
Certificate: 1912
Survey/Blk/Twp: 1912
Acres: 265
Map(s) 14

Abstract # 987 - TE&L CO
P'ee: TEXAS EMIGRATION AND LAND
COMPANY
G'ee: TEXAS EMIGRATION AND LAND
COMPANY
T-Dt: -- --- -----
P-Dt: 28 Jan 1859
Dist/Class: Texas Emmigration and Land
Company
File#: 1913
Patent#: 528
Patent Vol.: 21
Certificate: 1913
Survey/Blk/Twp: 1913
Acres: 265
Map(s) 14

Abstract # 988 - TE&L CO
P'ee: TEXAS EMIGRATION AND LAND
COMPANY
G'ee: TEXAS EMIGRATION AND LAND
COMPANY
T-Dt: -- --- -----
P-Dt: 26 Jan 1859
Dist/Class: Texas Emmigration and Land
Company
File#: 1914
Patent#: 513
Patent Vol.: 21
Certificate: 1914
Survey/Blk/Twp: 1914
Acres: 265
Map(s) 14

Abstract # 989 - TE&L CO
P'ee: TEXAS EMIGRATION AND LAND
COMPANY
G'ee: TEXAS EMIGRATION AND LAND
COMPANY
T-Dt: -- --- -----
P-Dt: 26 Jan 1859
Dist/Class: Texas Emmigration and Land
Company
File#: 1915
Patent#: 514

Patent Vol.: 21
Certificate: 1915
Survey/Blk/Twp: 1915
Acres: 265
Map(s) 14

Abstract # 990 - TE&L CO
P'ee: TEXAS EMIGRATION AND LAND
COMPANY
G'ee: TEXAS EMIGRATION AND LAND
COMPANY
T-Dt: -- --- -----
P-Dt: 26 Jan 1859
Dist/Class: Texas Emmigration and Land
Company
File#: 1916
Patent#: 515
Patent Vol.: 21
Certificate: 1916
Survey/Blk/Twp: 1916
Acres: 265
Map(s) 14

Abstract # 991 - TE&L CO
P'ee: TEXAS EMIGRATION AND LAND
COMPANY
G'ee: TEXAS EMIGRATION AND LAND
COMPANY
T-Dt: -- --- -----
P-Dt: 26 Jan 1859
Dist/Class: Texas Emmigration and Land
Company
File#: 1917
Patent#: 516
Patent Vol.: 21
Certificate: 1917
Survey/Blk/Twp: 1917
Acres: 265
Map(s) 14

Abstract # 992 - TE&L CO
P'ee: TEXAS EMIGRATION AND LAND
COMPANY
G'ee: TEXAS EMIGRATION AND LAND
COMPANY
T-Dt: -- --- -----
P-Dt: 26 Jan 1859
Dist/Class: Texas Emmigration and Land
Company
File#: 1918
Patent#: 517
Patent Vol.: 21
Certificate: 1918
Survey/Blk/Twp: 1918
Acres: 265
Map(s) 14

Abstract # 993 - TE&L CO
P'ee: TEXAS EMIGRATION AND LAND
COMPANY
G'ee: TEXAS EMIGRATION AND LAND
COMPANY
T-Dt: -- --- -----
P-Dt: 26 Jan 1859
Dist/Class: Texas Emmigration and Land
Company
File#: 1919
Patent#: 518
Patent Vol.: 21
Certificate: 1919
Survey/Blk/Twp: 1919
Acres: 235
Map(s) 14

Abstract # 994 - TE&L CO

P'ee: TEXAS EMIGRATION AND LAND
COMPANY
G'ee: TEXAS EMIGRATION AND LAND
COMPANY
T-Dt: -- --- -----
P-Dt: 27 Jan 1859
Dist/Class: Texas Emmigration and Land
Company
File#: 1920
Patent#: 519
Patent Vol.: 21
Certificate: 1920
Survey/Blk/Twp: 1920
Acres: 232
Map(s) 14

Abstract # 995 - TE&L CO
P'ee: TEXAS EMIGRATION AND LAND
COMPANY
G'ee: TEXAS EMIGRATION AND LAND
COMPANY
T-Dt: -- --- -----
P-Dt: 27 Jan 1859
Dist/Class: Texas Emmigration and Land
Company
File#: 1921
Patent#: 520
Patent Vol.: 21
Certificate: 1921
Survey/Blk/Twp: 1921
Acres: 265
Map(s) 14

Abstract # 996 - TE&L CO
P'ee: TEXAS EMIGRATION AND LAND
COMPANY
G'ee: TEXAS EMIGRATION AND LAND
COMPANY
T-Dt: -- --- -----
P-Dt: 28 Jan 1859
Dist/Class: Texas Emmigration and Land
Company
File#: 1922
Patent#: 529
Patent Vol.: 21
Certificate: 1922
Survey/Blk/Twp: 1922
Acres: 265
Map(s) 14

Abstract # 997 - TE&L CO
P'ee: TEXAS EMIGRATION AND LAND
COMPANY
G'ee: TEXAS EMIGRATION AND LAND
COMPANY
T-Dt: -- --- -----
P-Dt: 28 Jan 1859
Dist/Class: Texas Emmigration and Land
Company
File#: 1923
Patent#: 530
Patent Vol.: 21
Certificate: 1923
Survey/Blk/Twp: 1923
Acres: 265
Map(s) 14

Abstract # 998 - TE&L CO
P'ee: TEXAS EMIGRATION AND LAND
COMPANY
G'ee: TEXAS EMIGRATION AND LAND
COMPANY
T-Dt: -- --- -----
P-Dt: 28 Jan 1859
Dist/Class: Texas Emmigration and Land

Company
File#: 1924
Patent#: 531
Patent Vol.: 21
Certificate: 1924
Survey/Blk/Twp: 1924
Acres: 265
Map(s) 14

Abstract # 999 - TE&L CO
P'ee: TEXAS EMIGRATION AND LAND
COMPANY
G'ee: TEXAS EMIGRATION AND LAND
COMPANY
T-Dt: -- --- -----
P-Dt: 28 Jan 1859
Dist/Class: Texas Emmigration and Land
Company
File#: 1925
Patent#: 532
Patent Vol.: 21
Certificate: 1925
Survey/Blk/Twp: 1925
Acres: 265
Map(s) 14

Abstract # 1000 - TE&L CO
P'ee: TEXAS EMIGRATION AND LAND
COMPANY
G'ee: TEXAS EMIGRATION AND LAND
COMPANY
T-Dt: -- --- -----
P-Dt: 28 Jan 1859
Dist/Class: Texas Emmigration and Land
Company
File#: 1926
Patent#: 533
Patent Vol.: 21
Certificate: 1926
Survey/Blk/Twp: 1926
Acres: 265
Map(s) 14

Abstract # 1001 - TE&L CO
P'ee: TEXAS EMIGRATION AND LAND
COMPANY
G'ee: TEXAS EMIGRATION AND LAND
COMPANY
T-Dt: -- --- -----
P-Dt: 28 Jan 1859
Dist/Class: Texas Emmigration and Land
Company
File#: 1927
Patent#: 534
Patent Vol.: 21
Certificate: 1927
Survey/Blk/Twp: 1927
Acres: 265
Map(s) 14

Abstract # 1002 - TE&L CO
P'ee: TEXAS EMIGRATION AND LAND
COMPANY
G'ee: TEXAS EMIGRATION AND LAND
COMPANY
T-Dt: -- --- -----
P-Dt: 28 Jan 1859
Dist/Class: Texas Emmigration and Land
Company
File#: 1928
Patent#: 535
Patent Vol.: 21
Certificate: 1928
Survey/Blk/Twp: 1928
Acres: 265

Map(s) 14

Abstract # 1003 - TE&L CO
P'ee: TEXAS EMIGRATION AND LAND
COMPANY
G'ee: TEXAS EMIGRATION AND LAND
COMPANY
T-Dt: -- --- -----
P-Dt: 29 Jan 1859
Dist/Class: Texas Emmigration and Land
Company
File#: 1929
Patent#: 536
Patent Vol.: 21
Certificate: 1929
Survey/Blk/Twp: 1929
Acres: 228
Map(s) 14

Abstract # 1004 - TE&L CO
P'ee: TEXAS EMIGRATION AND LAND
COMPANY
G'ee: TEXAS EMIGRATION AND LAND
COMPANY
T-Dt: -- --- -----
P-Dt: 29 Jan 1859
Dist/Class: Texas Emmigration and Land
Company
File#: 1930
Patent#: 537
Patent Vol.: 21
Certificate: 1930
Survey/Blk/Twp: 1930
Acres: 225
Map(s) 14

Abstract # 1005 - TE&L CO
P'ee: TEXAS EMIGRATION AND LAND
COMPANY
G'ee: TEXAS EMIGRATION AND LAND
COMPANY
T-Dt: -- --- -----
P-Dt: 29 Jan 1859
Dist/Class: Texas Emmigration and Land
Company
File#: 1931
Patent#: 538
Patent Vol.: 21
Certificate: 1931
Survey/Blk/Twp: 1931
Acres: 265
Map(s) 14

Abstract # 1006 - TE&L CO
P'ee: TEXAS EMIGRATION AND LAND
COMPANY
G'ee: TEXAS EMIGRATION AND LAND
COMPANY
T-Dt: -- --- -----
P-Dt: 29 Jan 1859
Dist/Class: Texas Emmigration and Land
Company
File#: 1932
Patent#: 539
Patent Vol.: 21
Certificate: 1932
Survey/Blk/Twp: 1932
Acres: 265
Map(s) 14

Abstract # 1007 - TE&L CO
P'ee: TEXAS EMIGRATION AND LAND
COMPANY
G'ee: TEXAS EMIGRATION AND LAND
COMPANY

T-Dt: -- --- -----
P-Dt: 29 Jan 1859
Dist/Class: Texas Emmigration and Land Company
File#: 1933
Patent#: 540
Patent Vol.: 21
Certificate: 1933
Survey/Blk/Twp: 1933
Acres: 265
Map(s) 14

Abstract # 1008 - TE&L CO
P'ee: TEXAS EMIGRATION AND LAND COMPANY
G'ee: TEXAS EMIGRATION AND LAND COMPANY
T-Dt: -- --- -----
P-Dt: 29 Jan 1859
Dist/Class: Texas Emmigration and Land Company
File#: 1934
Patent#: 541
Patent Vol.: 21
Certificate: 1934
Survey/Blk/Twp: 1934
Acres: 265
Map(s) 14

Abstract # 1009 - TE&L CO
P'ee: TEXAS EMIGRATION AND LAND COMPANY
G'ee: TEXAS EMIGRATION AND LAND COMPANY
T-Dt: -- --- -----
P-Dt: 29 Jan 1859
Dist/Class: Texas Emmigration and Land Company
File#: 1935
Patent#: 542
Patent Vol.: 21
Certificate: 1935
Survey/Blk/Twp: 1935
Acres: 265
Map(s) 14, 15

Abstract # 1010 - TE&L CO
P'ee: TEXAS EMIGRATION AND LAND COMPANY
G'ee: TEXAS EMIGRATION AND LAND COMPANY
T-Dt: -- --- -----
P-Dt: 31 Jan 1859
Dist/Class: Texas Emmigration and Land Company
File#: 1936
Patent#: 545
Patent Vol.: 21
Certificate: 1936
Survey/Blk/Twp: 1936
Acres: 265
Map(s) 15

Abstract # 1011 - TE&L CO
P'ee: TEXAS EMIGRATION AND LAND COMPANY
G'ee: TEXAS EMIGRATION AND LAND COMPANY
T-Dt: -- --- -----
P-Dt: 31 Jan 1859
Dist/Class: Texas Emmigration and Land Company
File#: 1937
Patent#: 546
Patent Vol.: 21

Certificate: 1937
Survey/Blk/Twp: 1937
Acres: 265
Map(s) 15

Abstract # 1012 - TE&L CO
P'ee: TEXAS EMIGRATION AND LAND COMPANY
G'ee: TEXAS EMIGRATION AND LAND COMPANY
T-Dt: -- --- -----
P-Dt: 31 Jan 1859
Dist/Class: Texas Emmigration and Land Company
File#: 1938
Patent#: 547
Patent Vol.: 21
Certificate: 1938
Survey/Blk/Twp: 1938
Acres: 265
Map(s) 15

Abstract # 1013 - TE&L CO
P'ee: TEXAS EMIGRATION AND LAND COMPANY
G'ee: TEXAS EMIGRATION AND LAND COMPANY
T-Dt: -- --- -----
P-Dt: 31 Jan 1859
Dist/Class: Texas Emmigration and Land Company
File#: 1939
Patent#: 548
Patent Vol.: 21
Certificate: 1939
Survey/Blk/Twp: 1939
Acres: 265
Map(s) 15

Abstract # 1014 - TE&L CO
P'ee: TEXAS EMIGRATION AND LAND COMPANY
G'ee: TEXAS EMIGRATION AND LAND COMPANY
T-Dt: -- --- -----
P-Dt: 31 Jan 1859
Dist/Class: Texas Emmigration and Land Company
File#: 1940
Patent#: 549
Patent Vol.: 21
Certificate: 1940
Survey/Blk/Twp: 1940
Acres: 265
Map(s) 15

Abstract # 1015 - TE&L CO
P'ee: TEXAS EMIGRATION AND LAND COMPANY
G'ee: TEXAS EMIGRATION AND LAND COMPANY
T-Dt: -- --- -----
P-Dt: 31 Jan 1859
Dist/Class: Texas Emmigration and Land Company
File#: 1941
Patent#: 550
Patent Vol.: 21
Certificate: 1941
Survey/Blk/Twp: 1941
Acres: 265
Map(s) 15

Abstract # 1016 - TE&L CO
P'ee: TEXAS EMIGRATION AND LAND

COMPANY
G'ee: TEXAS EMIGRATION AND LAND COMPANY
T-Dt: -- --- -----
P-Dt: 31 Jan 1859
Dist/Class: Texas Emmigration and Land Company
File#: 1942
Patent#: 551
Patent Vol.: 21
Certificate: 1942
Survey/Blk/Twp: 1942
Acres: 265
Map(s) 14, 15

Abstract # 1017 - TE&L CO
P'ee: TEXAS EMIGRATION AND LAND COMPANY
G'ee: TEXAS EMIGRATION AND LAND COMPANY
T-Dt: -- --- -----
P-Dt: 31 Jan 1859
Dist/Class: Texas Emmigration and Land Company
File#: 1943
Patent#: 552
Patent Vol.: 21
Certificate: 1943
Survey/Blk/Twp: 1943
Acres: 265
Map(s) 14

Abstract # 1018 - TE&L CO
P'ee: TEXAS EMIGRATION AND LAND COMPANY
G'ee: TEXAS EMIGRATION AND LAND COMPANY
T-Dt: -- --- -----
P-Dt: 31 Jan 1859
Dist/Class: Texas Emmigration and Land Company
File#: 1944
Patent#: 553
Patent Vol.: 21
Certificate: 1944
Survey/Blk/Twp: 1944
Acres: 265
Map(s) 14

Abstract # 1019 - TE&L CO
P'ee: TEXAS EMIGRATION AND LAND COMPANY
G'ee: TEXAS EMIGRATION AND LAND COMPANY
T-Dt: -- --- -----
P-Dt: 31 Jan 1859
Dist/Class: Texas Emmigration and Land Company
File#: 1945
Patent#: 554
Patent Vol.: 21
Certificate: 1945
Survey/Blk/Twp: 1945
Acres: 265
Map(s) 14

Abstract # 1020 - TE&L CO
P'ee: TEXAS EMIGRATION AND LAND COMPANY
G'ee: TEXAS EMIGRATION AND LAND COMPANY
T-Dt: -- --- -----
P-Dt: 31 Jan 1859
Dist/Class: Texas Emmigration and Land Company

File#: 1946
Patent#: 555
Patent Vol.: 21
Certificate: 1946
Survey/Blk/Twp: 1946
Acres: 265
Map(s) 14

Abstract # 1021 - TE&L CO
P'ee: TEXAS EMIGRATION AND LAND COMPANY
G'ee: TEXAS EMIGRATION AND LAND COMPANY
T-Dt: -- --- -----
P-Dt: 31 Jan 1859
Dist/Class: Texas Emmigration and Land Company
File#: 1947
Patent#: 556
Patent Vol.: 21
Certificate: 1947
Survey/Blk/Twp: 1947
Acres: 265
Map(s) 14, 15

Abstract # 1022 - TE&L CO
P'ee: TEXAS EMIGRATION AND LAND COMPANY
G'ee: TEXAS EMIGRATION AND LAND COMPANY
T-Dt: -- --- -----
P-Dt: 31 Jan 1859
Dist/Class: Texas Emmigration and Land Company
File#: 1948
Patent#: 557
Patent Vol.: 21
Certificate: 1948
Survey/Blk/Twp: 1948
Acres: 265
Map(s) 15

Abstract # 1023 - TE&L CO
P'ee: TEXAS EMIGRATION AND LAND COMPANY
G'ee: TEXAS EMIGRATION AND LAND COMPANY
T-Dt: -- --- -----
P-Dt: 31 Jan 1859
Dist/Class: Texas Emmigration and Land Company
File#: 1949
Patent#: 558
Patent Vol.: 21
Certificate: 1949
Survey/Blk/Twp: 1949
Acres: 265
Map(s) 15

Abstract # 1024 - TE&L CO
P'ee: TEXAS EMIGRATION AND LAND COMPANY
G'ee: TEXAS EMIGRATION AND LAND COMPANY
T-Dt: -- --- -----
P-Dt: 01 Feb 1859
Dist/Class: Texas Emmigration and Land Company
File#: 1950
Patent#: 559
Patent Vol.: 21
Certificate: 1950
Survey/Blk/Twp: 1950
Acres: 265
Map(s) 15

Abstract # 1025 - TE&L CO
P'ee: TEXAS EMIGRATION AND LAND COMPANY
G'ee: TEXAS EMIGRATION AND LAND COMPANY
T-Dt: -- --- -----
P-Dt: 01 Feb 1859
Dist/Class: Texas Emmigration and Land Company
File#: 1951
Patent#: 560
Patent Vol.: 21
Certificate: 1951
Survey/Blk/Twp: 1951
Acres: 265
Map(s) 15

Abstract # 1026 - TE&L CO
P'ee: TEXAS EMIGRATION AND LAND COMPANY
G'ee: TEXAS EMIGRATION AND LAND COMPANY
T-Dt: -- --- -----
P-Dt: 01 Feb 1859
Dist/Class: Texas Emmigration and Land Company
File#: 1952
Patent#: 561
Patent Vol.: 21
Certificate: 1952
Survey/Blk/Twp: 1952
Acres: 265
Map(s) 15

Abstract # 1027 - TE&L CO
P'ee: TEXAS EMIGRATION AND LAND COMPANY
G'ee: TEXAS EMIGRATION AND LAND COMPANY
T-Dt: -- --- -----
P-Dt: 01 Feb 1859
Dist/Class: Texas Emmigration and Land Company
File#: 1953
Patent#: 562
Patent Vol.: 21
Certificate: 1953
Survey/Blk/Twp: 1953
Acres: 265
Map(s) 15

Abstract # 1028 - TE&L CO
P'ee: TEXAS EMIGRATION AND LAND COMPANY
G'ee: TEXAS EMIGRATION AND LAND COMPANY
T-Dt: -- --- -----
P-Dt: 01 Feb 1859
Dist/Class: Texas Emmigration and Land Company
File#: 1954
Patent#: 563
Patent Vol.: 21
Certificate: 1954
Survey/Blk/Twp: 1954
Acres: 265
Map(s) 14, 15

Abstract # 1029 - TE&L CO
P'ee: TEXAS EMIGRATION AND LAND COMPANY
G'ee: TEXAS EMIGRATION AND LAND COMPANY
T-Dt: -- --- -----
P-Dt: 01 Feb 1859

Dist/Class: Texas Emmigration and Land Company
File#: 1955
Patent#: 564
Patent Vol.: 21
Certificate: 1955
Survey/Blk/Twp: 1955
Acres: 265
Map(s) 14

Abstract # 1030 - TE&L CO
P'ee: TEXAS EMIGRATION AND LAND COMPANY
G'ee: TEXAS EMIGRATION AND LAND COMPANY
T-Dt: -- --- -----
P-Dt: 01 Feb 1859
Dist/Class: Texas Emmigration and Land Company
File#: 1956
Patent#: 565
Patent Vol.: 21
Certificate: 1956
Survey/Blk/Twp: 1956
Acres: 265
Map(s) 14

Abstract # 1031 - TE&L CO
P'ee: TEXAS EMIGRATION AND LAND COMPANY
G'ee: TEXAS EMIGRATION AND LAND COMPANY
T-Dt: -- --- -----
P-Dt: 01 Feb 1859
Dist/Class: Texas Emmigration and Land Company
File#: 1957
Patent#: 566
Patent Vol.: 21
Certificate: 1957
Survey/Blk/Twp: 1957
Acres: 245
Map(s) 14, 22

Abstract # 1032 - TE&L CO
P'ee: TEXAS EMIGRATION AND LAND COMPANY
G'ee: TEXAS EMIGRATION AND LAND COMPANY
T-Dt: -- --- -----
P-Dt: 01 Feb 1859
Dist/Class: Texas Emmigration and Land Company
File#: 1958
Patent#: 567
Patent Vol.: 21
Certificate: 1958
Survey/Blk/Twp: 1958
Acres: 265
Map(s) 14, 22

Abstract # 1033 - TE&L CO
P'ee: TEXAS EMIGRATION AND LAND COMPANY
G'ee: TEXAS EMIGRATION AND LAND COMPANY
T-Dt: -- --- -----
P-Dt: 01 Feb 1859
Dist/Class: Texas Emmigration and Land Company
File#: 1959
Patent#: 568
Patent Vol.: 21
Certificate: 1959
Survey/Blk/Twp: 1959

Acres: 265
Map(s) 14, 15, 22, 23

Abstract # 1034 - TE&L CO
P'ee: TEXAS EMIGRATION AND LAND
COMPANY
G'ee: TEXAS EMIGRATION AND LAND
COMPANY
T-Dt: -- --- -----
P-Dt: 01 Feb 1859
Dist/Class: Texas Emmigration and Land
Company
File#: 1960
Patent#: 569
Patent Vol.: 21
Certificate: 1960
Survey/Blk/Twp: 1960
Acres: 265
Map(s) 15, 23

Abstract # 1035 - TE&L CO
P'ee: TEXAS EMIGRATION AND LAND
COMPANY
G'ee: TEXAS EMIGRATION AND LAND
COMPANY
T-Dt: -- --- -----
P-Dt: 01 Feb 1859
Dist/Class: Texas Emmigration and Land
Company
File#: 1961
Patent#: 570
Patent Vol.: 21
Certificate: 1961
Survey/Blk/Twp: 1961
Acres: 265
Map(s) 15, 23

Abstract # 1036 - TE&L CO
P'ee: TEXAS EMIGRATION AND LAND
COMPANY
G'ee: TEXAS EMIGRATION AND LAND
COMPANY
T-Dt: -- --- -----
P-Dt: 01 Feb 1859
Dist/Class: Texas Emmigration and Land
Company
File#: 1962
Patent#: 571
Patent Vol.: 21
Certificate: 1962
Survey/Blk/Twp: 1962
Acres: 265
Map(s) 15, 23

Abstract # 1037 - TE&L CO
P'ee: TEXAS EMIGRATION AND LAND
COMPANY
G'ee: TEXAS EMIGRATION AND LAND
COMPANY
T-Dt: -- --- -----
P-Dt: 02 Feb 1859
Dist/Class: Texas Emmigration and Land
Company
File#: 1963
Patent#: 572
Patent Vol.: 21
Certificate: 1963
Survey/Blk/Twp: 1963
Acres: 265
Map(s) 23

Abstract # 1038 - TE&L CO
P'ee: TEXAS EMIGRATION AND LAND
COMPANY
G'ee: TEXAS EMIGRATION AND LAND

COMPANY
T-Dt: -- --- -----
P-Dt: 02 Feb 1859
Dist/Class: Texas Emmigration and Land
Company
File#: 1964
Patent#: 573
Patent Vol.: 21
Certificate: 1964
Survey/Blk/Twp: 1964
Acres: 265
Map(s) 23

Abstract # 1039 - TE&L CO
P'ee: TEXAS EMIGRATION AND LAND
COMPANY
G'ee: TEXAS EMIGRATION AND LAND
COMPANY
T-Dt: -- --- -----
P-Dt: 02 Feb 1859
Dist/Class: Texas Emmigration and Land
Company
File#: 1965
Patent#: 574
Patent Vol.: 21
Certificate: 1965
Survey/Blk/Twp: 1965
Acres: 265
Map(s) 23

Abstract # 1040 - TE&L CO
P'ee: TEXAS EMIGRATION AND LAND
COMPANY
G'ee: TEXAS EMIGRATION AND LAND
COMPANY
T-Dt: -- --- -----
P-Dt: 02 Feb 1859
Dist/Class: Texas Emmigration and Land
Company
File#: 1966
Patent#: 575
Patent Vol.: 21
Certificate: 1966
Survey/Blk/Twp: 1966
Acres: 265
Map(s) 22, 23

Abstract # 1041 - TE&L CO
P'ee: TEXAS EMIGRATION AND LAND
COMPANY
G'ee: TEXAS EMIGRATION AND LAND
COMPANY
T-Dt: -- --- -----
P-Dt: 02 Feb 1859
Dist/Class: Texas Emmigration and Land
Company
File#: 1967
Patent#: 576
Patent Vol.: 21
Certificate: 1967
Survey/Blk/Twp: 1967
Acres: 265
Map(s) 22

Abstract # 1042 - TE&L CO
P'ee: TEXAS EMIGRATION AND LAND
COMPANY
G'ee: TEXAS EMIGRATION AND LAND
COMPANY
T-Dt: -- --- -----
P-Dt: 02 Feb 1859
Dist/Class: Texas Emmigration and Land
Company
File#: 1968
Patent#: 577

Patent Vol.: 21
Certificate: 1968
Survey/Blk/Twp: 1968
Acres: 265
Map(s) 22

Abstract # 1043 - TE&L CO
P'ee: TEXAS EMIGRATION AND LAND
COMPANY
G'ee: TEXAS EMIGRATION AND LAND
COMPANY
T-Dt: -- --- -----
P-Dt: 02 Feb 1859
Dist/Class: Texas Emmigration and Land
Company
File#: 1969
Patent#: 578
Patent Vol.: 21
Certificate: 1969
Survey/Blk/Twp: 1969
Acres: 265
Map(s) 22, 23

Abstract # 1044 - TE&L CO
P'ee: HEDGECOXE, HENRY O
G'ee: TEXAS EMIGRATION AND LAND
COMPANY
T-Dt: -- --- -----
P-Dt: 01 Feb 1860
Dist/Class: Texas Emmigration and Land
Company
File#: 1970
Patent#: 1140
Patent Vol.: 14
Certificate: 1970
Survey/Blk/Twp: 1970
Acres: 265
Map(s) 23

Abstract # 1045 - TE&L CO
P'ee: HEDGECOXE, HENRY O
G'ee: TEXAS EMIGRATION AND LAND
COMPANY
T-Dt: -- --- -----
P-Dt: 02 Feb 1860
Dist/Class: Texas Emmigration and Land
Company
File#: 1971
Patent#: 1141
Patent Vol.: 14
Certificate: 1971
Survey/Blk/Twp: 1971
Acres: 265
Map(s) 23

Abstract # 1046 - TE&L CO
P'ee: TEXAS EMIGRATION AND LAND
COMPANY
G'ee: TEXAS EMIGRATION AND LAND
COMPANY
T-Dt: -- --- -----
P-Dt: 02 Feb 1859
Dist/Class: Texas Emmigration and Land
Company
File#: 1972
Patent#: 579
Patent Vol.: 21
Certificate: 1972
Survey/Blk/Twp: 1972
Acres: 265
Map(s) 23

Abstract # 1047 - TE&L CO
P'ee: TEXAS EMIGRATION AND LAND
COMPANY

G'ee: TEXAS EMIGRATION AND LAND
COMPANY
T-Dt: -- --- -----
P-Dt: 02 Feb 1859
Dist/Class: Texas Emmigration and Land
Company
File#: 1973
Patent#: 580
Patent Vol.: 21
Certificate: 1973
Survey/Blk/Twp: 1973
Acres: 265
Map(s) 23

Abstract # 1048 - TE&L CO
P'ee: TEXAS EMIGRATION AND LAND
COMPANY
G'ee: TEXAS EMIGRATION AND LAND
COMPANY
T-Dt: -- --- -----
P-Dt: 21 Mar 1859
Dist/Class: Texas Emmigration and Land
Company
File#: 1974
Patent#: 579
Patent Vol.: 22
Certificate: 1974
Survey/Blk/Twp: 1974
Acres: 265
Map(s) 23

Abstract # 1049 - TE&L CO
P'ee: TEXAS EMIGRATION AND LAND
COMPANY
G'ee: TEXAS EMIGRATION AND LAND
COMPANY
T-Dt: -- --- -----
P-Dt: 24 Jan 1859
Dist/Class: Texas Emmigration and Land
Company
File#: 1975
Patent#: 509
Patent Vol.: 21
Certificate: 1975
Survey/Blk/Twp: 1975
Acres: 265
Map(s) 23

Abstract # 1050 - TE&L CO
P'ee: TEXAS EMIGRATION AND LAND
COMPANY
G'ee: TEXAS EMIGRATION AND LAND
COMPANY
T-Dt: -- --- -----
P-Dt: 02 Feb 1859
Dist/Class: Texas Emmigration and Land
Company
File#: 1976
Patent#: 581
Patent Vol.: 21
Certificate: 1976
Survey/Blk/Twp: 1976
Acres: 265
Map(s) 22, 23

Abstract # 1051 - TE&L CO
P'ee: TEXAS EMIGRATION AND LAND
COMPANY
G'ee: TEXAS EMIGRATION AND LAND
COMPANY
T-Dt: -- --- -----
P-Dt: 02 Feb 1859
Dist/Class: Texas Emmigration and Land
Company
File#: 1977

Patent#: 582
Patent Vol.: 21
Certificate: 1977
Survey/Blk/Twp: 1977
Acres: 265
Map(s) 22

Abstract # 1052 - TE&L CO
P'ee: TEXAS EMIGRATION AND LAND
COMPANY
G'ee: TEXAS EMIGRATION AND LAND
COMPANY
T-Dt: -- --- -----
P-Dt: 02 Feb 1859
Dist/Class: Texas Emmigration and Land
Company
File#: 1978
Patent#: 583
Patent Vol.: 21
Certificate: 1978
Survey/Blk/Twp: 1978
Acres: 265
Map(s) 15

Abstract # 1053 - TE&L CO
P'ee: TEXAS EMIGRATION AND LAND
COMPANY
G'ee: TEXAS EMIGRATION AND LAND
COMPANY
T-Dt: -- --- -----
P-Dt: 02 Feb 1859
Dist/Class: Texas Emmigration and Land
Company
File#: 1979
Patent#: 584
Patent Vol.: 21
Certificate: 1979
Survey/Blk/Twp: 1979
Acres: 265
Map(s) 15

Abstract # 1054 - TE&L CO
P'ee: TEXAS EMIGRATION AND LAND
COMPANY
G'ee: TEXAS EMIGRATION AND LAND
COMPANY
T-Dt: -- --- -----
P-Dt: 02 Feb 1859
Dist/Class: Texas Emmigration and Land
Company
File#: 1980
Patent#: 585
Patent Vol.: 21
Certificate: 1980
Survey/Blk/Twp: 1980
Acres: 265
Map(s) 15

Abstract # 1055 - TE&L CO
P'ee: TEXAS EMIGRATION AND LAND
COMPANY
G'ee: TEXAS EMIGRATION AND LAND
COMPANY
T-Dt: -- --- -----
P-Dt: 02 Feb 1859
Dist/Class: Texas Emmigration and Land
Company
File#: 1981
Patent#: 586
Patent Vol.: 21
Certificate: 1981
Survey/Blk/Twp: 1981
Acres: 265
Map(s) 15

Abstract # 1056 - TE&L CO
P'ee: TEXAS EMIGRATION AND LAND
COMPANY
G'ee: TEXAS EMIGRATION AND LAND
COMPANY
T-Dt: -- --- -----
P-Dt: 03 Feb 1859
Dist/Class: Texas Emmigration and Land
Company
File#: 1982
Patent#: 587
Patent Vol.: 21
Certificate: 1982
Survey/Blk/Twp: 1982
Acres: 265
Map(s) 15, 23

Abstract # 1057 - TE&L CO
P'ee: TEXAS EMIGRATION AND LAND
COMPANY
G'ee: TEXAS EMIGRATION AND LAND
COMPANY
T-Dt: -- --- -----
P-Dt: 03 Feb 1859
Dist/Class: Texas Emmigration and Land
Company
File#: 1983
Patent#: 588
Patent Vol.: 21
Certificate: 1983
Survey/Blk/Twp: 1983
Acres: 265
Map(s) 23

Abstract # 1058 - TE&L CO
P'ee: TEXAS EMIGRATION AND LAND
COMPANY
G'ee: TEXAS EMIGRATION AND LAND
COMPANY
T-Dt: -- --- -----
P-Dt: 12 Feb 1859
Dist/Class: Texas Emmigration and Land
Company
File#: 1984
Patent#: 559
Patent Vol.: 22
Certificate: 1984
Survey/Blk/Twp: 1984
Acres: 265
Map(s) 23

Abstract # 1059 - TE&L CO
P'ee: TEXAS EMIGRATION AND LAND
COMPANY
G'ee: TEXAS EMIGRATION AND LAND
COMPANY
T-Dt: -- --- -----
P-Dt: 12 Feb 1859
Dist/Class: Texas Emmigration and Land
Company
File#: 1985
Patent#: 560
Patent Vol.: 22
Certificate: 1985
Survey/Blk/Twp: 1985
Acres: 265
Map(s) 23

Abstract # 1060 - TE&L CO
P'ee: TEXAS EMIGRATION AND LAND
COMPANY
G'ee: TEXAS EMIGRATION AND LAND
COMPANY
T-Dt: -- --- -----
P-Dt: 12 Feb 1859

Dist/Class: Texas Emmigration and Land
Company
File#: 1986
Patent#: 561
Patent Vol.: 22
Certificate: 1986
Survey/Blk/Twp: 1986
Acres: 265
Map(s) 23

Abstract # 1061 - TE&L CO
P'ee: TEXAS EMIGRATION AND LAND
COMPANY
G'ee: TEXAS EMIGRATION AND LAND
COMPANY
T-Dt: -- --- -----
P-Dt: 12 Feb 1859
Dist/Class: Texas Emmigration and Land
Company
File#: 1987
Patent#: 562
Patent Vol.: 22
Certificate: 1987
Survey/Blk/Twp: 1987
Acres: 265
Map(s) 23

Abstract # 1062 - TE&L CO
P'ee: TEXAS EMIGRATION AND LAND
COMPANY
G'ee: TEXAS EMIGRATION AND LAND
COMPANY
T-Dt: -- --- -----
P-Dt: 12 Feb 1859
Dist/Class: Texas Emmigration and Land
Company
File#: 1988
Patent#: 563
Patent Vol.: 22
Certificate: 1988
Survey/Blk/Twp: 1988
Acres: 265
Map(s) 23

Abstract # 1063 - TE&L CO
P'ee: TEXAS EMIGRATION AND LAND
COMPANY
G'ee: TEXAS EMIGRATION AND LAND
COMPANY
T-Dt: -- --- -----
P-Dt: 12 Feb 1859
Dist/Class: Texas Emmigration and Land
Company
File#: 1989
Patent#: 564
Patent Vol.: 22
Certificate: 1989
Survey/Blk/Twp: 1989
Acres: 265
Map(s) 15, 23

Abstract # 1064 - TE&L CO
P'ee: TEXAS EMIGRATION AND LAND
COMPANY
G'ee: TEXAS EMIGRATION AND LAND
COMPANY
T-Dt: -- --- -----
P-Dt: 14 Feb 1859
Dist/Class: Texas Emmigration and Land
Company
File#: 1990
Patent#: 565
Patent Vol.: 22
Certificate: 1990
Survey/Blk/Twp: 1990

Acres: 265
Map(s) 15

Abstract # 1065 - TE&L CO
P'ee: TEXAS EMIGRATION AND LAND
COMPANY
G'ee: TEXAS EMIGRATION AND LAND
COMPANY
T-Dt: -- --- -----
P-Dt: 14 Feb 1859
Dist/Class: Texas Emmigration and Land
Company
File#: 1991
Patent#: 566
Patent Vol.: 22
Certificate: 1991
Survey/Blk/Twp: 1991
Acres: 265
Map(s) 15

Abstract # 1066 - TE&L CO
P'ee: TEXAS EMIGRATION AND LAND
COMPANY
G'ee: TEXAS EMIGRATION AND LAND
COMPANY
T-Dt: -- --- -----
P-Dt: 14 Feb 1859
Dist/Class: Texas Emmigration and Land
Company
File#: 1992
Patent#: 567
Patent Vol.: 22
Certificate: 1992
Survey/Blk/Twp: 1992
Acres: 265
Map(s) 15

Abstract # 1067 - TE&L CO
P'ee: TEXAS EMIGRATION AND LAND
COMPANY
G'ee: TEXAS EMIGRATION AND LAND
COMPANY
T-Dt: -- --- -----
P-Dt: 14 Feb 1859
Dist/Class: Texas Emmigration and Land
Company
File#: 1993
Patent#: 568
Patent Vol.: 22
Certificate: 1993
Survey/Blk/Twp: 1993
Acres: 265
Map(s) 15

Abstract # 1068 - TE&L CO
P'ee: TEXAS EMIGRATION AND LAND
COMPANY
G'ee: TEXAS EMIGRATION AND LAND
COMPANY
T-Dt: -- --- -----
P-Dt: 14 Feb 1859
Dist/Class: Texas Emmigration and Land
Company
File#: 1994
Patent#: 569
Patent Vol.: 22
Certificate: 1994
Survey/Blk/Twp: 1994
Acres: 265
Map(s) 15

Abstract # 1069 - TE&L CO
P'ee: TEXAS EMIGRATION AND LAND
COMPANY
G'ee: TEXAS EMIGRATION AND LAND

COMPANY
T-Dt: -- --- -----
P-Dt: 14 Feb 1859
Dist/Class: Texas Emmigration and Land
Company
File#: 1995
Patent#: 570
Patent Vol.: 22
Certificate: 1995
Survey/Blk/Twp: 1995
Acres: 265
Map(s) 15

Abstract # 1070 - TE&L CO
P'ee: TEXAS EMIGRATION AND LAND
COMPANY
G'ee: TEXAS EMIGRATION AND LAND
COMPANY
T-Dt: -- --- -----
P-Dt: 14 Feb 1859
Dist/Class: Texas Emmigration and Land
Company
File#: 1996
Patent#: 571
Patent Vol.: 22
Certificate: 1996
Survey/Blk/Twp: 1996
Acres: 265
Map(s) 15

Abstract # 1071 - TE&L CO
P'ee: TEXAS EMIGRATION AND LAND
COMPANY
G'ee: TEXAS EMIGRATION AND LAND
COMPANY
T-Dt: -- --- -----
P-Dt: 14 Feb 1859
Dist/Class: Texas Emmigration and Land
Company
File#: 1997
Patent#: 572
Patent Vol.: 22
Certificate: 1997
Survey/Blk/Twp: 1997
Acres: 265
Map(s) 15

Abstract # 1072 - TE&L CO
P'ee: TEXAS EMIGRATION AND LAND
COMPANY
G'ee: TEXAS EMIGRATION AND LAND
COMPANY
T-Dt: -- --- -----
P-Dt: 14 Feb 1859
Dist/Class: Texas Emmigration and Land
Company
File#: 1998
Patent#: 573
Patent Vol.: 22
Certificate: 1998
Survey/Blk/Twp: 1998
Acres: 265
Map(s) 14, 15

Abstract # 1073 - TE&L CO
P'ee: TEXAS EMIGRATION AND LAND
COMPANY
G'ee: TEXAS EMIGRATION AND LAND
COMPANY
T-Dt: -- --- -----
P-Dt: 14 Feb 1859
Dist/Class: Texas Emmigration and Land
Company
File#: 1999
Patent#: 574

Patent Vol.: 22
Certificate: 1999
Survey/Blk/Twp: 1999
Acres: 265
Map(s) 15

Abstract # 1074 - TE&L CO
P'ee: TEXAS EMIGRATION AND LAND
COMPANY
G'ee: TEXAS EMIGRATION AND LAND
COMPANY
T-Dt: -- --- -----
P-Dt: 14 Feb 1859
Dist/Class: Texas Emmigration and Land
Company
File#: 2000
Patent#: 575
Patent Vol.: 22
Certificate: 2000
Survey/Blk/Twp: 2000
Acres: 265
Map(s) 15, 16

Abstract # 1075 - TE&L CO
P'ee: TEXAS EMIGRATION AND LAND
COMPANY
G'ee: TEXAS EMIGRATION AND LAND
COMPANY
T-Dt: -- --- -----
P-Dt: 25 Aug 1858
Dist/Class: Texas Emmigration and Land
Company
File#: 2047
Patent#: 353
Patent Vol.: 21
Certificate: 2047
Survey/Blk/Twp: 2047
Acres: 320
Map(s) 22

Abstract # 1076 - TE&L CO
P'ee: TEXAS EMIGRATION AND LAND
COMPANY
G'ee: TEXAS EMIGRATION AND LAND
COMPANY
T-Dt: -- --- -----
P-Dt: 31 Aug 1858
Dist/Class: Texas Emmigration and Land
Company
File#: 2057
Patent#: 363
Patent Vol.: 21
Certificate: 2057
Survey/Blk/Twp: 2057
Acres: 320
Map(s) 22

Abstract # 1077 - TE&L CO
P'ee: TEXAS EMIGRATION AND LAND
COMPANY
G'ee: TEXAS EMIGRATION AND LAND
COMPANY
T-Dt: -- --- -----
P-Dt: 04 Oct 1858
Dist/Class: Texas Emmigration and Land
Company
File#: 2244
Patent#: 43
Patent Vol.: 22
Certificate: 2244
Survey/Blk/Twp: 2244
Acres: 320
Map(s) 12

Abstract # 1078 - TE&L CO

P'ee: TEXAS EMIGRATION AND LAND
COMPANY
G'ee: TEXAS EMIGRATION AND LAND
COMPANY
T-Dt: -- --- -----
P-Dt: 04 Oct 1858
Dist/Class: Texas Emmigration and Land
Company
File#: 2245
Patent#: 44
Patent Vol.: 22
Certificate: 2245
Survey/Blk/Twp: 2245
Acres: 320
Map(s) 11, 12

Abstract # 1079 - TE&L CO
P'ee: TEXAS EMIGRATION AND LAND
COMPANY
G'ee: TEXAS EMIGRATION AND LAND
COMPANY
T-Dt: -- --- -----
P-Dt: 04 Oct 1858
Dist/Class: Texas Emmigration and Land
Company
File#: 2246
Patent#: 45
Patent Vol.: 22
Certificate: 2246
Survey/Blk/Twp: 2246
Acres: 320
Map(s) 11, 12

Abstract # 1080 - TE&L CO
P'ee: TEXAS EMIGRATION AND LAND
COMPANY
G'ee: TEXAS EMIGRATION AND LAND
COMPANY
T-Dt: -- --- -----
P-Dt: 04 Oct 1858
Dist/Class: Texas Emmigration and Land
Company
File#: 2247
Patent#: 46
Patent Vol.: 22
Certificate: 2247
Survey/Blk/Twp: 2247
Acres: 320
Map(s) 12

Abstract # 1081 - TE&L CO
P'ee: TEXAS EMIGRATION AND LAND
COMPANY
G'ee: TEXAS EMIGRATION AND LAND
COMPANY
T-Dt: -- --- -----
P-Dt: 04 Oct 1858
Dist/Class: Texas Emmigration and Land
Company
File#: 2248
Patent#: 47
Patent Vol.: 22
Certificate: 2248
Survey/Blk/Twp: 2248
Acres: 320
Map(s) 12

Abstract # 1082 - TE&L CO
P'ee: TEXAS EMIGRATION AND LAND
COMPANY
G'ee: TEXAS EMIGRATION AND LAND
COMPANY
T-Dt: -- --- -----
P-Dt: 04 Oct 1858
Dist/Class: Texas Emmigration and Land

Company
File#: 2249
Patent#: 48
Patent Vol.: 22
Certificate: 2249
Survey/Blk/Twp: 2249
Acres: 320
Map(s) 11, 12

Abstract # 1083 - TE&L CO
P'ee: TEXAS EMIGRATION AND LAND
COMPANY
G'ee: TEXAS EMIGRATION AND LAND
COMPANY
T-Dt: -- --- -----
P-Dt: 05 Mar 1859
Dist/Class: Texas Emmigration and Land
Company
File#: 2250
Patent#: 578
Patent Vol.: 22
Certificate: 2250
Survey/Blk/Twp: 4
Acres: 292.75
Map(s) 19, 20

Abstract # 1084 - TE&L CO
P'ee: TEXAS EMIGRATION AND LAND
COMPANY
G'ee: TEXAS EMIGRATION AND LAND
COMPANY
T-Dt: -- --- -----
P-Dt: 18 Mar 1858
Dist/Class: Texas Emmigration and Land
Company
File#: 2251
Patent#: 390
Patent Vol.: 14
Certificate: 2251
Survey/Blk/Twp: 2251
Acres: 320
Map(s) 12, 20

Abstract # 1085 - TE&L CO
P'ee: TEXAS EMIGRATION AND LAND
COMPANY
G'ee: TEXAS EMIGRATION AND LAND
COMPANY
T-Dt: -- --- -----
P-Dt: 15 Oct 1858
Dist/Class: Texas Emmigration and Land
Company
File#: 2368
Patent#: 156
Patent Vol.: 22
Certificate: 2368
Survey/Blk/Twp: 2368
Acres: 320
Map(s) 25

Abstract # 1086 - TE&L CO
P'ee: TEXAS EMIGRATION AND LAND
COMPANY
G'ee: TEXAS EMIGRATION AND LAND
COMPANY
T-Dt: -- --- -----
P-Dt: 15 Oct 1858
Dist/Class: Texas Emmigration and Land
Company
File#: 2369
Patent#: 157
Patent Vol.: 22
Certificate: 2369
Survey/Blk/Twp: 2369
Acres: 320

Map(s) 25

Abstract # 1087 - TE&L CO
P'ee: TEXAS EMIGRATION AND LAND
COMPANY
G'ee: TEXAS EMIGRATION AND LAND
COMPANY
T-Dt: -- --- -----
P-Dt: 16 Oct 1858
Dist/Class: Texas Emmigration and Land
Company
File#: 2370
Patent#: 158
Patent Vol.: 22
Certificate: 2370
Survey/Blk/Twp: 2370
Acres: 320
Map(s) 25

Abstract # 1088 - TE&L CO
P'ee: TEXAS EMIGRATION AND LAND
COMPANY
G'ee: TEXAS EMIGRATION AND LAND
COMPANY
T-Dt: -- --- -----
P-Dt: 16 Oct 1858
Dist/Class: Texas Emmigration and Land
Company
File#: 2371
Patent#: 159
Patent Vol.: 22
Certificate: 2371
Survey/Blk/Twp: 2371
Acres: 320
Map(s) 25

Abstract # 1089 - TE&L CO
P'ee: TEXAS EMIGRATION AND LAND
COMPANY
G'ee: TEXAS EMIGRATION AND LAND
COMPANY
T-Dt: -- --- -----
P-Dt: 16 Oct 1858
Dist/Class: Texas Emmigration and Land
Company
File#: 2372
Patent#: 160
Patent Vol.: 22
Certificate: 2372
Survey/Blk/Twp: 2372
Acres: 320
Map(s) 25

Abstract # 1090 - TE&L CO
P'ee: TEXAS EMIGRATION AND LAND
COMPANY
G'ee: TEXAS EMIGRATION AND LAND
COMPANY
T-Dt: -- --- -----
P-Dt: 16 Oct 1858
Dist/Class: Texas Emmigration and Land
Company
File#: 2373
Patent#: 161
Patent Vol.: 22
Certificate: 2373
Survey/Blk/Twp: 2373
Acres: 320
Map(s) 25

Abstract # 1091 - TE&L CO
P'ee: TEXAS EMIGRATION AND LAND
COMPANY
G'ee: TEXAS EMIGRATION AND LAND
COMPANY

T-Dt: -- --- -----
P-Dt: 16 Oct 1858
Dist/Class: Texas Emmigration and Land
Company
File#: 2374
Patent#: 162
Patent Vol.: 22
Certificate: 2374
Survey/Blk/Twp: 2374
Acres: 320
Map(s) 25

Abstract # 1092 - TE&L CO
P'ee: TEXAS EMIGRATION AND LAND
COMPANY
G'ee: TEXAS EMIGRATION AND LAND
COMPANY
T-Dt: -- --- -----
P-Dt: 16 Oct 1858
Dist/Class: Texas Emmigration and Land
Company
File#: 2375
Patent#: 163
Patent Vol.: 22
Certificate: 2375
Survey/Blk/Twp: 2375
Acres: 320
Map(s) 25

Abstract # 1093 - TE&L CO
P'ee: TEXAS EMIGRATION AND LAND
COMPANY
G'ee: TEXAS EMIGRATION AND LAND
COMPANY
T-Dt: -- --- -----
P-Dt: 16 Oct 1858
Dist/Class: Texas Emmigration and Land
Company
File#: 2376
Patent#: 164
Patent Vol.: 22
Certificate: 2376
Survey/Blk/Twp: 2376
Acres: 320
Map(s) 25

Abstract # 1094 - TE&L CO
P'ee: TEXAS EMIGRATION AND LAND
COMPANY
G'ee: TEXAS EMIGRATION AND LAND
COMPANY
T-Dt: -- --- -----
P-Dt: 16 Oct 1858
Dist/Class: Texas Emmigration and Land
Company
File#: 2377
Patent#: 165
Patent Vol.: 22
Certificate: 2377
Survey/Blk/Twp: 2377
Acres: 320
Map(s) 25

Abstract # 1095 - TE&L CO
P'ee: TEXAS EMIGRATION AND LAND
COMPANY
G'ee: TEXAS EMIGRATION AND LAND
COMPANY
T-Dt: -- --- -----
P-Dt: 16 Oct 1858
Dist/Class: Texas Emmigration and Land
Company
File#: 2378
Patent#: 166
Patent Vol.: 22

Certificate: 2378
Survey/Blk/Twp: 2378
Acres: 320
Map(s) 25

Abstract # 1096 - TE&L CO
P'ee: TEXAS EMIGRATION AND LAND
COMPANY
G'ee: TEXAS EMIGRATION AND LAND
COMPANY
T-Dt: -- --- -----
P-Dt: 18 Oct 1858
Dist/Class: Texas Emmigration and Land
Company
File#: 2379
Patent#: 167
Patent Vol.: 22
Certificate: 2379
Survey/Blk/Twp: 2379
Acres: 320
Map(s) 25

Abstract # 1097 - TE&L CO
P'ee: TEXAS EMIGRATION AND LAND
COMPANY
G'ee: TEXAS EMIGRATION AND LAND
COMPANY
T-Dt: -- --- -----
P-Dt: 18 Oct 1858
Dist/Class: Texas Emmigration and Land
Company
File#: 2380
Patent#: 168
Patent Vol.: 22
Certificate: 2380
Survey/Blk/Twp: 2380
Acres: 320
Map(s) 25

Abstract # 1098 - TE&L CO
P'ee: TEXAS EMIGRATION AND LAND
COMPANY
G'ee: TEXAS EMIGRATION AND LAND
COMPANY
T-Dt: -- --- -----
P-Dt: 18 Oct 1858
Dist/Class: Texas Emmigration and Land
Company
File#: 2381
Patent#: 169
Patent Vol.: 22
Certificate: 2381
Survey/Blk/Twp: 2381
Acres: 320
Map(s) 25

Abstract # 1099 - TE&L CO
P'ee: TEXAS EMIGRATION AND LAND
COMPANY
G'ee: TEXAS EMIGRATION AND LAND
COMPANY
T-Dt: -- --- -----
P-Dt: 18 Oct 1858
Dist/Class: Texas Emmigration and Land
Company
File#: 2382
Patent#: 170
Patent Vol.: 22
Certificate: 2382
Survey/Blk/Twp: 2382
Acres: 320
Map(s) 25

Abstract # 1100 - TE&L CO
P'ee: TEXAS EMIGRATION AND LAND

COMPANY
G'ee: TEXAS EMIGRATION AND LAND
COMPANY
T-Dt: -- --- -----
P-Dt: 18 Oct 1858
Dist/Class: Texas Emmigration and Land
Company
File#: 2383
Patent#: 171
Patent Vol.: 22
Certificate: 2383
Survey/Blk/Twp: 2383
Acres: 320
Map(s) 25

Abstract # 1101 - TE&L CO
P'ee: TEXAS EMIGRATION AND LAND
COMPANY
G'ee: TEXAS EMIGRATION AND LAND
COMPANY
T-Dt: -- --- -----
P-Dt: 18 Oct 1858
Dist/Class: Texas Emmigration and Land
Company
File#: 2384
Patent#: 172
Patent Vol.: 22
Certificate: 2384
Survey/Blk/Twp: 2384
Acres: 320
Map(s) 25

Abstract # 1102 - TE&L CO
P'ee: TEXAS EMIGRATION AND LAND
COMPANY
G'ee: TEXAS EMIGRATION AND LAND
COMPANY
T-Dt: -- --- -----
P-Dt: 18 Oct 1858
Dist/Class: Texas Emmigration and Land
Company
File#: 2385
Patent#: 173
Patent Vol.: 22
Certificate: 2385
Survey/Blk/Twp: 2385
Acres: 320
Map(s) 25

Abstract # 1103 - TE&L CO
P'ee: TEXAS EMIGRATION AND LAND
COMPANY
G'ee: TEXAS EMIGRATION AND LAND
COMPANY
T-Dt: -- --- -----
P-Dt: 18 Oct 1858
Dist/Class: Texas Emmigration and Land
Company
File#: 2386
Patent#: 174
Patent Vol.: 22
Certificate: 2386
Survey/Blk/Twp: 2386
Acres: 320
Map(s) 25

Abstract # 1104 - TE&L CO
P'ee: TEXAS EMIGRATION AND LAND
COMPANY
G'ee: TEXAS EMIGRATION AND LAND
COMPANY
T-Dt: -- --- -----
P-Dt: 18 Oct 1858
Dist/Class: Texas Emmigration and Land
Company

File#: 2387
Patent#: 175
Patent Vol.: 22
Certificate: 2387
Survey/Blk/Twp: 2387
Acres: 320
Map(s) 25

Abstract # 1105 - TE&L CO
P'ee: TEXAS EMIGRATION AND LAND
COMPANY
G'ee: TEXAS EMIGRATION AND LAND
COMPANY
T-Dt: -- --- -----
P-Dt: 18 Oct 1858
Dist/Class: Texas Emmigration and Land
Company
File#: 2388
Patent#: 176
Patent Vol.: 22
Certificate: 2388
Survey/Blk/Twp: 2388
Acres: 320
Map(s) 25

Abstract # 1106 - TE&L CO
P'ee: TEXAS EMIGRATION AND LAND
COMPANY
G'ee: TEXAS EMIGRATION AND LAND
COMPANY
T-Dt: -- --- -----
P-Dt: 18 Oct 1858
Dist/Class: Texas Emmigration and Land
Company
File#: 2389
Patent#: 177
Patent Vol.: 22
Certificate: 2389
Survey/Blk/Twp: 2389
Acres: 320
Map(s) 25

Abstract # 1107 - TE&L CO
P'ee: TEXAS EMIGRATION AND LAND
COMPANY
G'ee: TEXAS EMIGRATION AND LAND
COMPANY
T-Dt: -- --- -----
P-Dt: 18 Oct 1858
Dist/Class: Texas Emmigration and Land
Company
File#: 2390
Patent#: 178
Patent Vol.: 22
Certificate: 2390
Survey/Blk/Twp: 2390
Acres: 320
Map(s) 25

Abstract # 1108 - TE&L CO
P'ee: TEXAS EMIGRATION AND LAND
COMPANY
G'ee: TEXAS EMIGRATION AND LAND
COMPANY
T-Dt: -- --- -----
P-Dt: 18 Oct 1858
Dist/Class: Texas Emmigration and Land
Company
File#: 2391
Patent#: 179
Patent Vol.: 22
Certificate: 2391
Survey/Blk/Twp: 2391
Acres: 320
Map(s) 25

Abstract # 1109 - TE&L CO
P'ee: TEXAS EMIGRATION AND LAND
COMPANY
G'ee: TEXAS EMIGRATION AND LAND
COMPANY
T-Dt: -- --- -----
P-Dt: 18 Oct 1858
Dist/Class: Texas Emmigration and Land
Company
File#: 2392
Patent#: 180
Patent Vol.: 22
Certificate: 2392
Survey/Blk/Twp: 2392
Acres: 320
Map(s) 25

Abstract # 1110 - TE&L CO
P'ee: TEXAS EMIGRATION AND LAND
COMPANY
G'ee: TEXAS EMIGRATION AND LAND
COMPANY
T-Dt: -- --- -----
P-Dt: 18 Oct 1858
Dist/Class: Texas Emmigration and Land
Company
File#: 2393
Patent#: 181
Patent Vol.: 22
Certificate: 2393
Survey/Blk/Twp: 2393
Acres: 320
Map(s) 25

Abstract # 1111 - TE&L CO
P'ee: TEXAS EMIGRATION AND LAND
COMPANY
G'ee: TEXAS EMIGRATION AND LAND
COMPANY
T-Dt: -- --- -----
P-Dt: 19 Oct 1858
Dist/Class: Texas Emmigration and Land
Company
File#: 2394
Patent#: 182
Patent Vol.: 22
Certificate: 2394
Survey/Blk/Twp: 2394
Acres: 320
Map(s) 25

Abstract # 1112 - TE&L CO
P'ee: TEXAS EMIGRATION AND LAND
COMPANY
G'ee: TEXAS EMIGRATION AND LAND
COMPANY
T-Dt: -- --- -----
P-Dt: 19 Oct 1858
Dist/Class: Texas Emmigration and Land
Company
File#: 2395
Patent#: 183
Patent Vol.: 22
Certificate: 2395
Survey/Blk/Twp: 2395
Acres: 320
Map(s) 25

Abstract # 1113 - TE&L CO
P'ee: TEXAS EMIGRATION AND LAND
COMPANY
G'ee: TEXAS EMIGRATION AND LAND
COMPANY
T-Dt: -- --- -----
P-Dt: 19 Oct 1858

Dist/Class: Texas Emmigration and Land
Company
File#: 2396
Patent#: 184
Patent Vol.: 22
Certificate: 2396
Survey/Blk/Twp: 2396
Acres: 320
Map(s) 25, 26

Abstract # 1114 - TE&L CO
P'ee: TEXAS EMIGRATION AND LAND
COMPANY
G'ee: TEXAS EMIGRATION AND LAND
COMPANY
T-Dt: -- --- -----
P-Dt: 19 Oct 1858
Dist/Class: Texas Emmigration and Land
Company
File#: 2397
Patent#: 185
Patent Vol.: 22
Certificate: 2397
Survey/Blk/Twp: 2397
Acres: 320
Map(s) 25, 26

Abstract # 1115 - TE&L CO
P'ee: TEXAS EMIGRATION AND LAND
COMPANY
G'ee: TEXAS EMIGRATION AND LAND
COMPANY
T-Dt: -- --- -----
P-Dt: 19 Oct 1858
Dist/Class: Texas Emmigration and Land
Company
File#: 2398
Patent#: 186
Patent Vol.: 22
Certificate: 2398
Survey/Blk/Twp: 2398
Acres: 320
Map(s) 25, 26

Abstract # 1116 - TE&L CO
P'ee: TEXAS EMIGRATION AND LAND
COMPANY
G'ee: TEXAS EMIGRATION AND LAND
COMPANY
T-Dt: -- --- -----
P-Dt: 19 Oct 1858
Dist/Class: Texas Emmigration and Land
Company
File#: 2399
Patent#: 187
Patent Vol.: 22
Certificate: 2399
Survey/Blk/Twp: 2399
Acres: 320
Map(s) 25, 26

Abstract # 1117 - TE&L CO
P'ee: TEXAS EMIGRATION AND LAND
COMPANY
G'ee: TEXAS EMIGRATION AND LAND
COMPANY
T-Dt: -- --- -----
P-Dt: 22 Oct 1858
Dist/Class: Texas Emmigration and Land
Company
File#: 2439
Patent#: 226
Patent Vol.: 22
Certificate: 2439
Survey/Blk/Twp: 2439

Acres: 320
Map(s) 1

Abstract # 1118 - TE&L CO
P'ee: TEXAS EMIGRATION AND LAND
COMPANY
G'ee: TEXAS EMIGRATION AND LAND
COMPANY
T-Dt: -- --- -----
P-Dt: 22 Oct 1858
Dist/Class: Texas Emmigration and Land
Company
File#: 2440
Patent#: 227
Patent Vol.: 22
Certificate: 2440
Survey/Blk/Twp: 2440
Acres: 320
Map(s) 1

Abstract # 1119 - TE&L CO
P'ee: TEXAS EMIGRATION AND LAND
COMPANY
G'ee: TEXAS EMIGRATION AND LAND
COMPANY
T-Dt: -- --- -----
P-Dt: 21 Oct 1858
Dist/Class: Texas Emmigration and Land
Company
File#: 2441
Patent#: 228
Patent Vol.: 22
Certificate: 2441
Survey/Blk/Twp: 2441
Acres: 320
Map(s) 1

Abstract # 1120 - TE&L CO
P'ee: TEXAS EMIGRATION AND LAND
COMPANY
G'ee: TEXAS EMIGRATION AND LAND
COMPANY
T-Dt: -- --- -----
P-Dt: 21 Oct 1858
Dist/Class: Texas Emmigration and Land
Company
File#: 2442
Patent#: 229
Patent Vol.: 22
Certificate: 2442
Survey/Blk/Twp: 2442
Acres: 320
Map(s) 1

Abstract # 1121 - TE&L CO
P'ee: TEXAS EMIGRATION AND LAND
COMPANY
G'ee: TEXAS EMIGRATION AND LAND
COMPANY
T-Dt: -- --- -----
P-Dt: 21 Oct 1858
Dist/Class: Texas Emmigration and Land
Company
File#: 2443
Patent#: 230
Patent Vol.: 22
Certificate: 2443
Survey/Blk/Twp: 2443
Acres: 320
Map(s) 1

Abstract # 1122 - TE&L CO
P'ee: TEXAS EMIGRATION AND LAND
COMPANY
G'ee: TEXAS EMIGRATION AND LAND

COMPANY
T-Dt: -- --- -----
P-Dt: 21 Oct 1858
Dist/Class: Texas Emmigration and Land
Company
File#: 2444
Patent#: 231
Patent Vol.: 22
Certificate: 2444
Survey/Blk/Twp: 2444
Acres: 320
Map(s) 1

Abstract # 1123 - TE&L CO
P'ee: TEXAS EMIGRATION AND LAND
COMPANY
G'ee: TEXAS EMIGRATION AND LAND
COMPANY
T-Dt: -- --- -----
P-Dt: 21 Oct 1858
Dist/Class: Texas Emmigration and Land
Company
File#: 2445
Patent#: 232
Patent Vol.: 22
Certificate: 2445
Survey/Blk/Twp: 2445
Acres: 320
Map(s) 1

Abstract # 1124 - TE&L CO
P'ee: TEXAS EMIGRATION AND LAND
COMPANY
G'ee: TEXAS EMIGRATION AND LAND
COMPANY
T-Dt: -- --- -----
P-Dt: 21 May 1858
Dist/Class: Texas Emmigration and Land
Company
File#: 2446
Patent#: 46
Patent Vol.: 21
Certificate: 2446
Survey/Blk/Twp: 2446
Acres: 320
Map(s) 1, 2

Abstract # 1125 - TE&L CO
P'ee: TEXAS EMIGRATION AND LAND
COMPANY
G'ee: TEXAS EMIGRATION AND LAND
COMPANY
T-Dt: -- --- -----
P-Dt: 21 May 1858
Dist/Class: Texas Emmigration and Land
Company
File#: 2447
Patent#: 47
Patent Vol.: 21
Certificate: 2447
Survey/Blk/Twp: 2447
Acres: 320
Map(s) 2

Abstract # 1126 - TE&L CO
P'ee: TEXAS EMIGRATION AND LAND
COMPANY
G'ee: TEXAS EMIGRATION AND LAND
COMPANY
T-Dt: -- --- -----
P-Dt: 22 Oct 1858
Dist/Class: Texas Emmigration and Land
Company
File#: 2448
Patent#: 233

Patent Vol.: 22
Certificate: 2448
Survey/Blk/Twp: 2448
Acres: 320
Map(s) 2

Abstract # 1127 - TE&L CO
P'ee: TEXAS EMIGRATION AND LAND
COMPANY
G'ee: TEXAS EMIGRATION AND LAND
COMPANY
T-Dt: -- --- -----
P-Dt: 22 Oct 1858
Dist/Class: Texas Emmigration and Land
Company
File#: 2449
Patent#: 234
Patent Vol.: 22
Certificate: 2449
Survey/Blk/Twp: 2449
Acres: 320
Map(s) 1

Abstract # 1128 - TE&L CO
P'ee: TEXAS EMIGRATION AND LAND
COMPANY
G'ee: TEXAS EMIGRATION AND LAND
COMPANY
T-Dt: -- --- -----
P-Dt: 18 Nov 1858
Dist/Class: Texas Emmigration and Land
Company
File#: 2675
Patent#: 435
Patent Vol.: 22
Certificate: 2675
Survey/Blk/Twp: 2675
Acres: 320
Map(s) 31

Abstract # 1129 - TE&L CO
P'ee: TEXAS EMIGRATION AND LAND
COMPANY
G'ee: TEXAS EMIGRATION AND LAND
COMPANY
T-Dt: -- --- -----
P-Dt: 18 Nov 1858
Dist/Class: Texas Emmigration and Land
Company
File#: 2676
Patent#: 436
Patent Vol.: 22
Certificate: 2676
Survey/Blk/Twp: 2676
Acres: 320
Map(s) 23, 31

Abstract # 1130 - TE&L CO
P'ee: TEXAS EMIGRATION AND LAND
COMPANY
G'ee: TEXAS EMIGRATION AND LAND
COMPANY
T-Dt: -- --- -----
P-Dt: 19 Nov 1858
Dist/Class: Texas Emmigration and Land
Company
File#: 2691
Patent#: 451
Patent Vol.: 22
Certificate: 2691
Survey/Blk/Twp: 2691
Acres: 320
Map(s) 22, 30, 31

Abstract # 1131 - TE&L CO

P'ee: TEXAS EMIGRATION AND LAND
COMPANY
G'ee: TEXAS EMIGRATION AND LAND
COMPANY
T-Dt: -- --- -----
P-Dt: 19 Nov 1858
Dist/Class: Texas Emmigration and Land
Company
File#: 2692
Patent#: 452
Patent Vol.: 22
Certificate: 2692
Survey/Blk/Twp: 2692
Acres: 320
Map(s) 30, 31

Abstract # 1132 - TE&L CO
P'ee: TEXAS EMIGRATION AND LAND
COMPANY
G'ee: TEXAS EMIGRATION AND LAND
COMPANY
T-Dt: -- --- -----
P-Dt: 20 Nov 1858
Dist/Class: Texas Emmigration and Land
Company
File#: 2693
Patent#: 453
Patent Vol.: 22
Certificate: 2693
Survey/Blk/Twp: 2693
Acres: 320
Map(s) 30

Abstract # 1133 - TE&L CO
P'ee: TEXAS EMIGRATION AND LAND
COMPANY
G'ee: TEXAS EMIGRATION AND LAND
COMPANY
T-Dt: -- --- -----
P-Dt: 04 Feb 1859
Dist/Class: Texas Emmigration and Land
Company
File#: 2701
Patent#: 459
Patent Vol.: 22
Certificate: 2701
Survey/Blk/Twp: 2701
Acres: 265
Map(s) 15, 16

Abstract # 1134 - TE&L CO
P'ee: TEXAS EMIGRATION AND LAND
COMPANY
G'ee: TEXAS EMIGRATION AND LAND
COMPANY
T-Dt: -- --- -----
P-Dt: 04 Feb 1859
Dist/Class: Texas Emmigration and Land
Company
File#: 2702
Patent#: 460
Patent Vol.: 22
Certificate: 2702
Survey/Blk/Twp: 2702
Acres: 265
Map(s) 15, 16

Abstract # 1135 - TE&L CO
P'ee: TEXAS EMIGRATION AND LAND
COMPANY
G'ee: TEXAS EMIGRATION AND LAND
COMPANY
T-Dt: -- --- -----
P-Dt: 04 Feb 1859
Dist/Class: Texas Emmigration and Land

Company
File#: 2703
Patent#: 461
Patent Vol.: 22
Certificate: 2703
Survey/Blk/Twp: 2703
Acres: 265
Map(s) 15, 16

Abstract # 1136 - TE&L CO
P'ee: TEXAS EMIGRATION AND LAND
COMPANY
G'ee: TEXAS EMIGRATION AND LAND
COMPANY
T-Dt: -- --- -----
P-Dt: 04 Feb 1859
Dist/Class: Texas Emmigration and Land
Company
File#: 2704
Patent#: 462
Patent Vol.: 22
Certificate: 2704
Survey/Blk/Twp: 2704
Acres: 265
Map(s) 15, 16

Abstract # 1137 - TE&L CO
P'ee: TEXAS EMIGRATION AND LAND
COMPANY
G'ee: TEXAS EMIGRATION AND LAND
COMPANY
T-Dt: -- --- -----
P-Dt: 04 Feb 1859
Dist/Class: Texas Emmigration and Land
Company
File#: 2705
Patent#: 463
Patent Vol.: 22
Certificate: 2705
Survey/Blk/Twp: 2705
Acres: 265
Map(s) 15, 16, 23, 24

Abstract # 1138 - TE&L CO
P'ee: TEXAS EMIGRATION AND LAND
COMPANY
G'ee: TEXAS EMIGRATION AND LAND
COMPANY
T-Dt: -- --- -----
P-Dt: 04 Feb 1859
Dist/Class: Texas Emmigration and Land
Company
File#: 2706
Patent#: 464
Patent Vol.: 22
Certificate: 2706
Survey/Blk/Twp: 2706
Acres: 265
Map(s) 23, 24

Abstract # 1139 - TE&L CO
P'ee: TEXAS EMIGRATION AND LAND
COMPANY
G'ee: TEXAS EMIGRATION AND LAND
COMPANY
T-Dt: -- --- -----
P-Dt: 04 Feb 1859
Dist/Class: Texas Emmigration and Land
Company
File#: 2707
Patent#: 465
Patent Vol.: 22
Certificate: 2707
Survey/Blk/Twp: 2707
Acres: 265

Map(s) 23, 24

Abstract # 1140 - TE&L CO
P'ee: TEXAS EMIGRATION AND LAND
COMPANY
G'ee: TEXAS EMIGRATION AND LAND
COMPANY
T-Dt: -- --- -----
P-Dt: 04 Feb 1859
Dist/Class: Texas Emmigration and Land
Company
File#: 2708
Patent#: 466
Patent Vol.: 22
Certificate: 2708
Survey/Blk/Twp: 2708
Acres: 265
Map(s) 23, 24

Abstract # 1141 - TE&L CO
P'ee: TEXAS EMIGRATION AND LAND
COMPANY
G'ee: TEXAS EMIGRATION AND LAND
COMPANY
T-Dt: -- --- -----
P-Dt: 04 Feb 1859
Dist/Class: Texas Emmigration and Land
Company
File#: 2709
Patent#: 467
Patent Vol.: 22
Certificate: 2709
Survey/Blk/Twp: 2709
Acres: 265
Map(s) 24

Abstract # 1142 - TE&L CO
P'ee: TEXAS EMIGRATION AND LAND
COMPANY
G'ee: TEXAS EMIGRATION AND LAND
COMPANY
T-Dt: -- --- -----
P-Dt: 05 Feb 1859
Dist/Class: Texas Emmigration and Land
Company
File#: 2710
Patent#: 468
Patent Vol.: 22
Certificate: 2710
Survey/Blk/Twp: 2710
Acres: 265
Map(s) 24

Abstract # 1143 - TE&L CO
P'ee: TEXAS EMIGRATION AND LAND
COMPANY
G'ee: TEXAS EMIGRATION AND LAND
COMPANY
T-Dt: -- --- -----
P-Dt: 05 Feb 1859
Dist/Class: Texas Emmigration and Land
Company
File#: 2711
Patent#: 469
Patent Vol.: 22
Certificate: 2711
Survey/Blk/Twp: 2711
Acres: 265
Map(s) 24

Abstract # 1144 - TE&L CO
P'ee: TEXAS EMIGRATION AND LAND
COMPANY
G'ee: TEXAS EMIGRATION AND LAND
COMPANY

T-Dt: -- --- -----
P-Dt: 05 Feb 1859
Dist/Class: Texas Emmigration and Land
Company
File#: 2712
Patent#: 470
Patent Vol.: 22
Certificate: 2712
Survey/Blk/Twp: 2712
Acres: 265
Map(s) 16, 24

Abstract # 1145 - TE&L CO
P'ee: TEXAS EMIGRATION AND LAND
COMPANY
G'ee: TEXAS EMIGRATION AND LAND
COMPANY
T-Dt: -- --- -----
P-Dt: 05 Feb 1859
Dist/Class: Texas Emmigration and Land
Company
File#: 2713
Patent#: 471
Patent Vol.: 22
Certificate: 2713
Survey/Blk/Twp: 2713
Acres: 265
Map(s) 16

Abstract # 1146 - TE&L CO
P'ee: TEXAS EMIGRATION AND LAND
COMPANY
G'ee: TEXAS EMIGRATION AND LAND
COMPANY
T-Dt: -- --- -----
P-Dt: 05 Feb 1859
Dist/Class: Texas Emmigration and Land
Company
File#: 2714
Patent#: 472
Patent Vol.: 22
Certificate: 2714
Survey/Blk/Twp: 2714
Acres: 265
Map(s) 16

Abstract # 1147 - TE&L CO
P'ee: TEXAS EMIGRATION AND LAND
COMPANY
G'ee: TEXAS EMIGRATION AND LAND
COMPANY
T-Dt: -- --- -----
P-Dt: 05 Feb 1859
Dist/Class: Texas Emmigration and Land
Company
File#: 2715
Patent#: 473
Patent Vol.: 22
Certificate: 2715
Survey/Blk/Twp: 2715
Acres: 265
Map(s) 16

Abstract # 1148 - TE&L CO
P'ee: TEXAS EMIGRATION AND LAND
COMPANY
G'ee: TEXAS EMIGRATION AND LAND
COMPANY
T-Dt: -- --- -----
P-Dt: 05 Feb 1859
Dist/Class: Texas Emmigration and Land
Company
File#: 2716
Patent#: 474
Patent Vol.: 22

Certificate: 2716
Survey/Blk/Twp: 2716
Acres: 265
Map(s) 16

Abstract # 1149 - TE&L CO
P'ee: TEXAS EMIGRATION AND LAND
COMPANY
G'ee: TEXAS EMIGRATION AND LAND
COMPANY
T-Dt: -- --- -----
P-Dt: 05 Feb 1859
Dist/Class: Texas Emmigration and Land
Company
File#: 2717
Patent#: 475
Patent Vol.: 22
Certificate: 2717
Survey/Blk/Twp: 2717
Acres: 265
Map(s) 16

Abstract # 1150 - TE&L CO
P'ee: TEXAS EMIGRATION AND LAND
COMPANY
G'ee: TEXAS EMIGRATION AND LAND
COMPANY
T-Dt: -- --- -----
P-Dt: 05 Feb 1859
Dist/Class: Texas Emmigration and Land
Company
File#: 2718
Patent#: 476
Patent Vol.: 22
Certificate: 2718
Survey/Blk/Twp: 2718
Acres: 265
Map(s) 16

Abstract # 1151 - TE&L CO
P'ee: TEXAS EMIGRATION AND LAND
COMPANY
G'ee: TEXAS EMIGRATION AND LAND
COMPANY
T-Dt: -- --- -----
P-Dt: 07 Feb 1859
Dist/Class: Texas Emmigration and Land
Company
File#: 2719
Patent#: 477
Patent Vol.: 22
Certificate: 2719
Survey/Blk/Twp: 2719
Acres: 265
Map(s) 16

Abstract # 1152 - TE&L CO
P'ee: TEXAS EMIGRATION AND LAND
COMPANY
G'ee: TEXAS EMIGRATION AND LAND
COMPANY
T-Dt: -- --- -----
P-Dt: 07 Feb 1859
Dist/Class: Texas Emmigration and Land
Company
File#: 2720
Patent#: 478
Patent Vol.: 22
Certificate: 2720
Survey/Blk/Twp: 2720
Acres: 265
Map(s) 16, 24

Abstract # 1153 - TE&L CO
P'ee: TEXAS EMIGRATION AND LAND

COMPANY
G'ee: TEXAS EMIGRATION AND LAND
COMPANY
T-Dt: -- --- -----
P-Dt: 07 Feb 1859
Dist/Class: Texas Emmigration and Land
Company
File#: 2721
Patent#: 479
Patent Vol.: 22
Certificate: 2721
Survey/Blk/Twp: 2721
Acres: 265
Map(s) 24

Abstract # 1154 - TE&L CO
P'ee: TEXAS EMIGRATION AND LAND
COMPANY
G'ee: TEXAS EMIGRATION AND LAND
COMPANY
T-Dt: -- --- -----
P-Dt: 07 Feb 1859
Dist/Class: Texas Emmigration and Land
Company
File#: 2722
Patent#: 480
Patent Vol.: 22
Certificate: 2722
Survey/Blk/Twp: 2722
Acres: 265
Map(s) 24

Abstract # 1155 - TE&L CO
P'ee: TEXAS EMIGRATION AND LAND
COMPANY
G'ee: TEXAS EMIGRATION AND LAND
COMPANY
T-Dt: -- --- -----
P-Dt: 07 Feb 1859
Dist/Class: Texas Emmigration and Land
Company
File#: 2723
Patent#: 481
Patent Vol.: 22
Certificate: 2723
Survey/Blk/Twp: 2723
Acres: 265
Map(s) 24

Abstract # 1156 - TE&L CO
P'ee: TEXAS EMIGRATION AND LAND
COMPANY
G'ee: TEXAS EMIGRATION AND LAND
COMPANY
T-Dt: -- --- -----
P-Dt: 07 Feb 1859
Dist/Class: Texas Emmigration and Land
Company
File#: 2724
Patent#: 482
Patent Vol.: 22
Certificate: 2724
Survey/Blk/Twp: 2724
Acres: 265
Map(s) 24

Abstract # 1157 - TE&L CO
P'ee: TEXAS EMIGRATION AND LAND
COMPANY
G'ee: TEXAS EMIGRATION AND LAND
COMPANY
T-Dt: -- --- -----
P-Dt: 07 Feb 1859
Dist/Class: Texas Emmigration and Land
Company

File#: 2725
Patent#: 483
Patent Vol.: 22
Certificate: 2725
Survey/Blk/Twp: 2725
Acres: 265
Map(s) 24

Abstract # 1158 - TE&L CO
P'ee: TEXAS EMIGRATION AND LAND
COMPANY
G'ee: TEXAS EMIGRATION AND LAND
COMPANY
T-Dt: -- --- -----
P-Dt: 07 Feb 1859
Dist/Class: Texas Emmigration and Land
Company
File#: 2726
Patent#: 484
Patent Vol.: 22
Certificate: 2726
Survey/Blk/Twp: 2726
Acres: 265
Map(s) 24

Abstract # 1159 - TE&L CO
P'ee: TEXAS EMIGRATION AND LAND
COMPANY
G'ee: TEXAS EMIGRATION AND LAND
COMPANY
T-Dt: -- --- -----
P-Dt: 07 Feb 1859
Dist/Class: Texas Emmigration and Land
Company
File#: 2727
Patent#: 485
Patent Vol.: 22
Certificate: 2727
Survey/Blk/Twp: 2727
Acres: 265
Map(s) 24

Abstract # 1160 - TE&L CO
P'ee: TEXAS EMIGRATION AND LAND
COMPANY
G'ee: TEXAS EMIGRATION AND LAND
COMPANY
T-Dt: -- --- -----
P-Dt: 07 Feb 1859
Dist/Class: Texas Emmigration and Land
Company
File#: 2728
Patent#: 486
Patent Vol.: 22
Certificate: 2728
Survey/Blk/Twp: 2728
Acres: 265
Map(s) 24

Abstract # 1161 - TE&L CO
P'ee: TEXAS EMIGRATION AND LAND
COMPANY
G'ee: TEXAS EMIGRATION AND LAND
COMPANY
T-Dt: -- --- -----
P-Dt: 07 Feb 1859
Dist/Class: Texas Emmigration and Land
Company
File#: 2729
Patent#: 487
Patent Vol.: 22
Certificate: 2729
Survey/Blk/Twp: 2729
Acres: 265
Map(s) 16, 24

Abstract # 1162 - TE&L CO
P'ee: TEXAS EMIGRATION AND LAND
COMPANY
G'ee: TEXAS EMIGRATION AND LAND
COMPANY
T-Dt: -- --- -----
P-Dt: 07 Feb 1859
Dist/Class: Texas Emmigration and Land
Company
File#: 2730
Patent#: 488
Patent Vol.: 22
Certificate: 2730
Survey/Blk/Twp: 2730
Acres: 265
Map(s) 16

Abstract # 1163 - TE&L CO
P'ee: TEXAS EMIGRATION AND LAND
COMPANY
G'ee: TEXAS EMIGRATION AND LAND
COMPANY
T-Dt: -- --- -----
P-Dt: 07 Feb 1859
Dist/Class: Texas Emmigration and Land
Company
File#: 2731
Patent#: 489
Patent Vol.: 22
Certificate: 2731
Survey/Blk/Twp: 2731
Acres: 265
Map(s) 16

Abstract # 1164 - TE&L CO
P'ee: TEXAS EMIGRATION AND LAND
COMPANY
G'ee: TEXAS EMIGRATION AND LAND
COMPANY
T-Dt: -- --- -----
P-Dt: 07 Feb 1859
Dist/Class: Texas Emmigration and Land
Company
File#: 2732
Patent#: 490
Patent Vol.: 22
Certificate: 2732
Survey/Blk/Twp: 2732
Acres: 265
Map(s) 16

Abstract # 1165 - TE&L CO
P'ee: TEXAS EMIGRATION AND LAND
COMPANY
G'ee: TEXAS EMIGRATION AND LAND
COMPANY
T-Dt: -- --- -----
P-Dt: 11 Feb 1859
Dist/Class: Texas Emmigration and Land
Company
File#: 2791
Patent#: 549
Patent Vol.: 22
Certificate: 2791
Survey/Blk/Twp: 2791
Acres: 265
Map(s) 16

Abstract # 1166 - TE&L CO
P'ee: TEXAS EMIGRATION AND LAND
COMPANY
G'ee: TEXAS EMIGRATION AND LAND
COMPANY
T-Dt: -- --- -----
P-Dt: 11 Feb 1859

Dist/Class: Texas Emmigration and Land
Company
File#: 2792
Patent#: 550
Patent Vol.: 22
Certificate: 2792
Survey/Blk/Twp: 2792
Acres: 265
Map(s) 16

Abstract # 1167 - TE&L CO
P'ee: TEXAS EMIGRATION AND LAND
COMPANY
G'ee: TEXAS EMIGRATION AND LAND
COMPANY
T-Dt: -- --- -----
P-Dt: 11 Feb 1859
Dist/Class: Texas Emmigration and Land
Company
File#: 2793
Patent#: 551
Patent Vol.: 22
Certificate: 2793
Survey/Blk/Twp: 2793
Acres: 265
Map(s) 16

Abstract # 1168 - TE&L CO
P'ee: TEXAS EMIGRATION AND LAND
COMPANY
G'ee: TEXAS EMIGRATION AND LAND
COMPANY
T-Dt: -- --- -----
P-Dt: 11 Feb 1859
Dist/Class: Texas Emmigration and Land
Company
File#: 2794
Patent#: 552
Patent Vol.: 22
Certificate: 2794
Survey/Blk/Twp: 2794
Acres: 265
Map(s) 16

Abstract # 1169 - TE&L CO
P'ee: TEXAS EMIGRATION AND LAND
COMPANY
G'ee: TEXAS EMIGRATION AND LAND
COMPANY
T-Dt: -- --- -----
P-Dt: 11 Feb 1859
Dist/Class: Texas Emmigration and Land
Company
File#: 2795
Patent#: 553
Patent Vol.: 22
Certificate: 2795
Survey/Blk/Twp: 2795
Acres: 265
Map(s) 16

Abstract # 1170 - TE&L CO
P'ee: TEXAS EMIGRATION AND LAND
COMPANY
G'ee: TEXAS EMIGRATION AND LAND
COMPANY
T-Dt: -- --- -----
P-Dt: 19 Oct 1858
Dist/Class: Texas Emmigration and Land
Company
File#: 2901
Patent#: 90
Patent Vol.: 23
Certificate: 2901
Survey/Blk/Twp: 2901

Acres: 320
Map(s) 25, 26

Abstract # 1171 - TE&L CO
P'ee: TEXAS EMIGRATION AND LAND
COMPANY
G'ee: TEXAS EMIGRATION AND LAND
COMPANY
T-Dt: -- --- -----
P-Dt: 19 Oct 1858
Dist/Class: Texas Emmigration and Land
Company
File#: 2400
Patent#: 188
Patent Vol.: 22
Certificate: 2400
Survey/Blk/Twp: 2400
Acres: 320
Map(s) 25, 26

Abstract # 1172 - TE&L CO
P'ee: TEXAS EMIGRATION AND LAND
COMPANY
G'ee: TEXAS EMIGRATION AND LAND
COMPANY
T-Dt: -- --- -----
P-Dt: 19 Oct 1858
Dist/Class: Texas Emmigration and Land
Company
File#: 2902
Patent#: 91
Patent Vol.: 23
Certificate: 2902
Survey/Blk/Twp: 2902
Acres: 320
Map(s) 26

Abstract # 1173 - TE&L CO
P'ee: TEXAS EMIGRATION AND LAND
COMPANY
G'ee: TEXAS EMIGRATION AND LAND
COMPANY
T-Dt: -- --- -----
P-Dt: 19 Oct 1858
Dist/Class: Texas Emmigration and Land
Company
File#: 2903
Patent#: 92
Patent Vol.: 23
Certificate: 2903
Survey/Blk/Twp: 2903
Acres: 320
Map(s) 26

Abstract # 1174 - TE&L CO
P'ee: TEXAS EMIGRATION AND LAND
COMPANY
G'ee: TEXAS EMIGRATION AND LAND
COMPANY
T-Dt: -- --- -----
P-Dt: 20 Oct 1858
Dist/Class: Texas Emmigration and Land
Company
File#: 2904
Patent#: 93
Patent Vol.: 23
Certificate: 2904
Survey/Blk/Twp: 2904
Acres: 320
Map(s) 26

Abstract # 1175 - TE&L CO
P'ee: TEXAS EMIGRATION AND LAND
COMPANY
G'ee: TEXAS EMIGRATION AND LAND

COMPANY
T-Dt: -- --- -----
P-Dt: 20 Oct 1858
Dist/Class: Texas Emmigration and Land
Company
File#: 2905
Patent#: 94
Patent Vol.: 23
Certificate: 2905
Survey/Blk/Twp: 2905
Acres: 320
Map(s) 26

Abstract # 1176 - TE&L CO
P'ee: TEXAS EMIGRATION AND LAND
COMPANY
G'ee: TEXAS EMIGRATION AND LAND
COMPANY
T-Dt: -- --- -----
P-Dt: 20 Oct 1858
Dist/Class: Texas Emmigration and Land
Company
File#: 2906
Patent#: 95
Patent Vol.: 23
Certificate: 2906
Survey/Blk/Twp: 2906
Acres: 320
Map(s) 26

Abstract # 1177 - TE&L CO
P'ee: TEXAS EMIGRATION AND LAND
COMPANY
G'ee: TEXAS EMIGRATION AND LAND
COMPANY
T-Dt: -- --- -----
P-Dt: 20 Oct 1858
Dist/Class: Texas Emmigration and Land
Company
File#: 2907
Patent#: 96
Patent Vol.: 23
Certificate: 2907
Survey/Blk/Twp: 2907
Acres: 320
Map(s) 26

Abstract # 1178 - TE&L CO
P'ee: TEXAS EMIGRATION AND LAND
COMPANY
G'ee: TEXAS EMIGRATION AND LAND
COMPANY
T-Dt: -- --- -----
P-Dt: 20 Oct 1858
Dist/Class: Texas Emmigration and Land
Company
File#: 2908
Patent#: 97
Patent Vol.: 23
Certificate: 2908
Survey/Blk/Twp: 2908
Acres: 320
Map(s) 26

Abstract # 1179 - TE&L CO
P'ee: TEXAS EMIGRATION AND LAND
COMPANY
G'ee: TEXAS EMIGRATION AND LAND
COMPANY
T-Dt: -- --- -----
P-Dt: 20 Oct 1858
Dist/Class: Texas Emmigration and Land
Company
File#: 2909
Patent#: 98

Patent Vol.: 23
Certificate: 2909
Survey/Blk/Twp: 2909
Acres: 320
Map(s) 26

Abstract # 1180 - TE&L CO
P'ee: TEXAS EMIGRATION AND LAND
COMPANY
G'ee: TEXAS EMIGRATION AND LAND
COMPANY
T-Dt: -- --- -----
P-Dt: 20 Oct 1858
Dist/Class: Texas Emmigration and Land
Company
File#: 2910
Patent#: 99
Patent Vol.: 23
Certificate: 2910
Survey/Blk/Twp: 2910
Acres: 320
Map(s) 26

Abstract # 1181 - TE&L CO
P'ee: TEXAS EMIGRATION AND LAND
COMPANY
G'ee: TEXAS EMIGRATION AND LAND
COMPANY
T-Dt: -- --- -----
P-Dt: 20 Oct 1858
Dist/Class: Texas Emmigration and Land
Company
File#: 2911
Patent#: 100
Patent Vol.: 23
Certificate: 2911
Survey/Blk/Twp: 2911
Acres: 320
Map(s) 26

Abstract # 1182 - TE&L CO
P'ee: TEXAS EMIGRATION AND LAND
COMPANY
G'ee: TEXAS EMIGRATION AND LAND
COMPANY
T-Dt: -- --- -----
P-Dt: 20 Oct 1858
Dist/Class: Texas Emmigration and Land
Company
File#: 2912
Patent#: 101
Patent Vol.: 23
Certificate: 2912
Survey/Blk/Twp: 2912
Acres: 320
Map(s) 26

Abstract # 1183 - TE&L CO
P'ee: TEXAS EMIGRATION AND LAND
COMPANY
G'ee: TEXAS EMIGRATION AND LAND
COMPANY
T-Dt: -- --- -----
P-Dt: 20 Oct 1858
Dist/Class: Texas Emmigration and Land
Company
File#: 2913
Patent#: 102
Patent Vol.: 23
Certificate: 2913
Survey/Blk/Twp: 2913
Acres: 320
Map(s) 26

Abstract # 1184 - TE&L CO

P'ee: TEXAS EMIGRATION AND LAND
COMPANY
G'ee: TEXAS EMIGRATION AND LAND
COMPANY
T-Dt: -- --- -----
P-Dt: 20 Oct 1858
Dist/Class: Texas Emmigration and Land
Company
File#: 2914
Patent#: 103
Patent Vol.: 23
Certificate: 2914
Survey/Blk/Twp: 2914
Acres: 320
Map(s) 18

Abstract # 1185 - TE&L CO
P'ee: TEXAS EMIGRATION AND LAND
COMPANY
G'ee: TEXAS EMIGRATION AND LAND
COMPANY
T-Dt: -- --- -----
P-Dt: 20 Oct 1858
Dist/Class: Texas Emmigration and Land
Company
File#: 2915
Patent#: 104
Patent Vol.: 23
Certificate: 2915
Survey/Blk/Twp: 2915
Acres: 320
Map(s) 18, 26

Abstract # 1186 - TE&L CO
P'ee: TEXAS EMIGRATION AND LAND
COMPANY
G'ee: TEXAS EMIGRATION AND LAND
COMPANY
T-Dt: -- --- -----
P-Dt: 20 Oct 1858
Dist/Class: Texas Emmigration and Land
Company
File#: 2916
Patent#: 105
Patent Vol.: 23
Certificate: 2916
Survey/Blk/Twp: 2916
Acres: 320
Map(s) 26

Abstract # 1187 - TE&L CO
P'ee: TEXAS EMIGRATION AND LAND
COMPANY
G'ee: TEXAS EMIGRATION AND LAND
COMPANY
T-Dt: -- --- -----
P-Dt: 21 Oct 1858
Dist/Class: Texas Emmigration and Land
Company
File#: 2917
Patent#: 106
Patent Vol.: 23
Certificate: 2917
Survey/Blk/Twp: 2917
Acres: 320
Map(s) 26

Abstract # 1188 - TE&L CO
P'ee: TEXAS EMIGRATION AND LAND
COMPANY
G'ee: TEXAS EMIGRATION AND LAND
COMPANY
T-Dt: -- --- -----
P-Dt: 21 Oct 1858
Dist/Class: Texas Emmigration and Land

Company
File#: 2918
Patent#: 107
Patent Vol.: 23
Certificate: 2918
Survey/Blk/Twp: 2918
Acres: 320
Map(s) 26

Abstract # 1189 - TE&L CO
P'ee: TEXAS EMIGRATION AND LAND
COMPANY
G'ee: TEXAS EMIGRATION AND LAND
COMPANY
T-Dt: -- --- -----
P-Dt: 21 Oct 1858
Dist/Class: Texas Emmigration and Land
Company
File#: 2919
Patent#: 108
Patent Vol.: 23
Certificate: 2919
Survey/Blk/Twp: 2919
Acres: 320
Map(s) 26

Abstract # 1190 - TE&L CO
P'ee: TEXAS EMIGRATION AND LAND
COMPANY
G'ee: TEXAS EMIGRATION AND LAND
COMPANY
T-Dt: -- --- -----
P-Dt: 21 Oct 1858
Dist/Class: Texas Emmigration and Land
Company
File#: 2920
Patent#: 109
Patent Vol.: 23
Certificate: 2920
Survey/Blk/Twp: 2920
Acres: 320
Map(s) 26

Abstract # 1191 - TE&L CO
P'ee: TEXAS EMIGRATION AND LAND
COMPANY
G'ee: TEXAS EMIGRATION AND LAND
COMPANY
T-Dt: -- --- -----
P-Dt: 21 Oct 1858
Dist/Class: Texas Emmigration and Land
Company
File#: 2921
Patent#: 110
Patent Vol.: 23
Certificate: 2921
Survey/Blk/Twp: 2921
Acres: 320
Map(s) 26

Abstract # 1192 - TE&L CO
P'ee: TEXAS EMIGRATION AND LAND
COMPANY
G'ee: TEXAS EMIGRATION AND LAND
COMPANY
T-Dt: -- --- -----
P-Dt: 21 Oct 1858
Dist/Class: Texas Emmigration and Land
Company
File#: 2922
Patent#: 111
Patent Vol.: 23
Certificate: 2922
Survey/Blk/Twp: 2922
Acres: 320

Map(s) 26

Abstract # 1193 - TE&L CO
P'ee: TEXAS EMIGRATION AND LAND
COMPANY
G'ee: TEXAS EMIGRATION AND LAND
COMPANY
T-Dt: -- --- -----
P-Dt: 21 Oct 1858
Dist/Class: Texas Emmigration and Land
Company
File#: 2923
Patent#: 112
Patent Vol.: 23
Certificate: 2923
Survey/Blk/Twp: 2923
Acres: 320
Map(s) 26

Abstract # 1194 - TE&L CO
P'ee: TEXAS EMIGRATION AND LAND
COMPANY
G'ee: TEXAS EMIGRATION AND LAND
COMPANY
T-Dt: -- --- -----
P-Dt: 22 Oct 1858
Dist/Class: Texas Emmigration and Land
Company
File#: 2924
Patent#: 113
Patent Vol.: 23
Certificate: 2924
Survey/Blk/Twp: 2924
Acres: 320
Map(s) 18, 26

Abstract # 1195 - TE&L CO
P'ee: TEXAS EMIGRATION AND LAND
COMPANY
G'ee: TEXAS EMIGRATION AND LAND
COMPANY
T-Dt: -- --- -----
P-Dt: 22 Oct 1858
Dist/Class: Texas Emmigration and Land
Company
File#: 2925
Patent#: 114
Patent Vol.: 23
Certificate: 2925
Survey/Blk/Twp: 2925
Acres: 320
Map(s) 18

Abstract # 1196 - TE&L CO
P'ee: TEXAS EMIGRATION AND LAND
COMPANY
G'ee: TEXAS EMIGRATION AND LAND
COMPANY
T-Dt: -- --- -----
P-Dt: 22 Oct 1858
Dist/Class: Texas Emmigration and Land
Company
File#: 2926
Patent#: 115
Patent Vol.: 23
Certificate: 2926
Survey/Blk/Twp: 2926
Acres: 320
Map(s) 18

Abstract # 1197 - TE&L CO
P'ee: TEXAS EMIGRATION AND LAND
COMPANY
G'ee: TEXAS EMIGRATION AND LAND
COMPANY

T-Dt: -- --- -----
P-Dt: 22 Oct 1858
Dist/Class: Texas Emmigration and Land
Company
File#: 2927
Patent#: 116
Patent Vol.: 23
Certificate: 2927
Survey/Blk/Twp: 2927
Acres: 320
Map(s) 18

Abstract # 1198 - TE&L CO
P'ee: TEXAS EMIGRATION AND LAND
COMPANY
G'ee: TEXAS EMIGRATION AND LAND
COMPANY
T-Dt: -- --- -----
P-Dt: 22 Oct 1858
Dist/Class: Texas Emmigration and Land
Company
File#: 2928
Patent#: 117
Patent Vol.: 23
Certificate: 2928
Survey/Blk/Twp: 2928
Acres: 320
Map(s) 18

Abstract # 1199 - TE&L CO
P'ee: TEXAS EMIGRATION AND LAND
COMPANY
G'ee: TEXAS EMIGRATION AND LAND
COMPANY
T-Dt: -- --- -----
P-Dt: 22 Oct 1858
Dist/Class: Texas Emmigration and Land
Company
File#: 2929
Patent#: 118
Patent Vol.: 23
Certificate: 2929
Survey/Blk/Twp: 2929
Acres: 320
Map(s) 18, 26

Abstract # 1200 - TE&L CO
P'ee: TEXAS EMIGRATION AND LAND
COMPANY
G'ee: TEXAS EMIGRATION AND LAND
COMPANY
T-Dt: -- --- -----
P-Dt: 22 Oct 1858
Dist/Class: Texas Emmigration and Land
Company
File#: 2930
Patent#: 119
Patent Vol.: 23
Certificate: 2930
Survey/Blk/Twp: 2930
Acres: 320
Map(s) 26

Abstract # 1201 - TE&L CO
P'ee: TEXAS EMIGRATION AND LAND
COMPANY
G'ee: TEXAS EMIGRATION AND LAND
COMPANY
T-Dt: -- --- -----
P-Dt: 22 Oct 1858
Dist/Class: Texas Emmigration and Land
Company
File#: 2931
Patent#: 120
Patent Vol.: 23

Certificate: 2931
Survey/Blk/Twp: 2931
Acres: 320
Map(s) 26

Abstract # 1202 - TE&L CO
P'ee: TEXAS EMIGRATION AND LAND
COMPANY
G'ee: TEXAS EMIGRATION AND LAND
COMPANY
T-Dt: -- --- -----
P-Dt: 22 Oct 1858
Dist/Class: Texas Emmigration and Land
Company
File#: 2932
Patent#: 121
Patent Vol.: 23
Certificate: 2932
Survey/Blk/Twp: 2932
Acres: 320
Map(s) 26

Abstract # 1203 - TE&L CO
P'ee: TEXAS EMIGRATION AND LAND
COMPANY
G'ee: TEXAS EMIGRATION AND LAND
COMPANY
T-Dt: -- --- -----
P-Dt: 22 Oct 1858
Dist/Class: Texas Emmigration and Land
Company
File#: 2933
Patent#: 122
Patent Vol.: 23
Certificate: 2933
Survey/Blk/Twp: 2933
Acres: 320
Map(s) 26

Abstract # 1204 - TE&L CO
P'ee: TEXAS EMIGRATION AND LAND
COMPANY
G'ee: TEXAS EMIGRATION AND LAND
COMPANY
T-Dt: -- --- -----
P-Dt: 16 Jun 1858
Dist/Class: Texas Emmigration and Land
Company
File#: 2934
Patent#: 66
Patent Vol.: 21
Certificate: 2934
Survey/Blk/Twp: 2934
Acres: 320
Map(s) 26, 27

Abstract # 1205 - TE&L CO
P'ee: TEXAS EMIGRATION AND LAND
COMPANY
G'ee: TEXAS EMIGRATION AND LAND
COMPANY
T-Dt: -- --- -----
P-Dt: 16 Jun 1858
Dist/Class: Texas Emmigration and Land
Company
File#: 2935
Patent#: 67
Patent Vol.: 21
Certificate: 2935
Survey/Blk/Twp: 2935
Acres: 320
Map(s) 26, 27

Abstract # 1206 - TE&L CO
P'ee: TEXAS EMIGRATION AND LAND

COMPANY
G'ee: TEXAS EMIGRATION AND LAND
COMPANY
T-Dt: -- --- -----
P-Dt: 22 Oct 1858
Dist/Class: Texas Emmigration and Land
Company
File#: 2936
Patent#: 123
Patent Vol.: 23
Certificate: 2936
Survey/Blk/Twp: 2936
Acres: 320
Map(s) 26, 27

Abstract # 1207 - TE&L CO
P'ee: TEXAS EMIGRATION AND LAND
COMPANY
G'ee: TEXAS EMIGRATION AND LAND
COMPANY
T-Dt: -- --- -----
P-Dt: 22 Oct 1858
Dist/Class: Texas Emmigration and Land
Company
File#: 2937
Patent#: 124
Patent Vol.: 23
Certificate: 2937
Survey/Blk/Twp: 2937
Acres: 320
Map(s) 18, 19, 26, 27

Abstract # 1208 - TE&L CO
P'ee: TEXAS EMIGRATION AND LAND
COMPANY
G'ee: TEXAS EMIGRATION AND LAND
COMPANY
T-Dt: -- --- -----
P-Dt: 22 Oct 1858
Dist/Class: Texas Emmigration and Land
Company
File#: 2938
Patent#: 125
Patent Vol.: 23
Certificate: 2938
Survey/Blk/Twp: 2938
Acres: 320
Map(s) 18, 19

Abstract # 1209 - TE&L CO
P'ee: TEXAS EMIGRATION AND LAND
COMPANY
G'ee: TEXAS EMIGRATION AND LAND
COMPANY
T-Dt: -- --- -----
P-Dt: 22 Oct 1858
Dist/Class: Texas Emmigration and Land
Company
File#: 2939
Patent#: 126
Patent Vol.: 23
Certificate: 2939
Survey/Blk/Twp: 2939
Acres: 320
Map(s) 18, 19

Abstract # 1210 - TE&L CO
P'ee: TEXAS EMIGRATION AND LAND
COMPANY
G'ee: TEXAS EMIGRATION AND LAND
COMPANY
T-Dt: -- --- -----
P-Dt: 22 Oct 1858
Dist/Class: Texas Emmigration and Land
Company

File#: 2940
Patent#: 127
Patent Vol.: 23
Certificate: 2940
Survey/Blk/Twp: 2940
Acres: 320
Map(s) 19

Abstract # 1211 - TE&L CO
P'ee: TEXAS EMIGRATION AND LAND
COMPANY
G'ee: TEXAS EMIGRATION AND LAND
COMPANY
T-Dt: -- --- -----
P-Dt: 22 Oct 1858
Dist/Class: Texas Emmigration and Land
Company
File#: 2941
Patent#: 128
Patent Vol.: 23
Certificate: 2941
Survey/Blk/Twp: 2941
Acres: 320
Map(s) 19

Abstract # 1212 - TE&L CO
P'ee: TEXAS EMIGRATION AND LAND
COMPANY
G'ee: TEXAS EMIGRATION AND LAND
COMPANY
T-Dt: -- --- -----
P-Dt: 23 Oct 1858
Dist/Class: Texas Emmigration and Land
Company
File#: 2942
Patent#: 129
Patent Vol.: 23
Certificate: 2942
Survey/Blk/Twp: 2942
Acres: 320
Map(s) 19, 27

Abstract # 1213 - TE&L CO
P'ee: TEXAS EMIGRATION AND LAND
COMPANY
G'ee: TEXAS EMIGRATION AND LAND
COMPANY
T-Dt: -- --- -----
P-Dt: 23 Oct 1858
Dist/Class: Texas Emmigration and Land
Company
File#: 2943
Patent#: 130
Patent Vol.: 23
Certificate: 2943
Survey/Blk/Twp: 2943
Acres: 320
Map(s) 27

Abstract # 1214 - TE&L CO
P'ee: TEXAS EMIGRATION AND LAND
COMPANY
G'ee: TEXAS EMIGRATION AND LAND
COMPANY
T-Dt: -- --- -----
P-Dt: 23 Oct 1858
Dist/Class: Texas Emmigration and Land
Company
File#: 2944
Patent#: 131
Patent Vol.: 23
Certificate: 2944
Survey/Blk/Twp: 2944
Acres: 320
Map(s) 27

Abstract # 1215 - TE&L CO
P'ee: TEXAS EMIGRATION AND LAND
COMPANY
G'ee: TEXAS EMIGRATION AND LAND
COMPANY
T-Dt: -- --- -----
P-Dt: 23 Oct 1858
Dist/Class: Texas Emmigration and Land
Company
File#: 2945
Patent#: 132
Patent Vol.: 23
Certificate: 2945
Survey/Blk/Twp: 2945
Acres: 320
Map(s) 27

Abstract # 1216 - TE&L CO
P'ee: TEXAS EMIGRATION AND LAND
COMPANY
G'ee: TEXAS EMIGRATION AND LAND
COMPANY
T-Dt: -- --- -----
P-Dt: 20 Nov 1858
Dist/Class: Texas Emmigration and Land
Company
File#: 2946
Patent#: 133
Patent Vol.: 23
Certificate: 2946
Survey/Blk/Twp: 2946
Acres: 320
Map(s) 18, 19

Abstract # 1217 - TE&L CO
P'ee: TEXAS EMIGRATION AND LAND
COMPANY
G'ee: TEXAS EMIGRATION AND LAND
COMPANY
T-Dt: -- --- -----
P-Dt: 20 Nov 1858
Dist/Class: Texas Emmigration and Land
Company
File#: 2947
Patent#: 134
Patent Vol.: 23
Certificate: 2947
Survey/Blk/Twp: 2947
Acres: 320
Map(s) 18, 19

Abstract # 1218 - TE&L CO
P'ee: TEXAS EMIGRATION AND LAND
COMPANY
G'ee: TEXAS EMIGRATION AND LAND
COMPANY
T-Dt: -- --- -----
P-Dt: 23 Oct 1858
Dist/Class: Texas Emmigration and Land
Company
File#: 2948
Patent#: 135
Patent Vol.: 23
Certificate: 2948
Survey/Blk/Twp: 2948
Acres: 320
Map(s) 19

Abstract # 1219 - TE&L CO
P'ee: TEXAS EMIGRATION AND LAND
COMPANY
G'ee: TEXAS EMIGRATION AND LAND
COMPANY
T-Dt: -- --- -----
P-Dt: 23 Oct 1858

Dist/Class: Texas Emmigration and Land
Company
File#: 2949
Patent#: 136
Patent Vol.: 23
Certificate: 2949
Survey/Blk/Twp: 2949
Acres: 320
Map(s) 19

Abstract # 1220 - TE&L CO
P'ee: TEXAS EMIGRATION AND LAND
COMPANY
G'ee: TEXAS EMIGRATION AND LAND
COMPANY
T-Dt: -- --- -----
P-Dt: 23 Oct 1858
Dist/Class: Texas Emmigration and Land
Company
File#: 2950
Patent#: 137
Patent Vol.: 23
Certificate: 2950
Survey/Blk/Twp: 2950
Acres: 320
Map(s) 19

Abstract # 1221 - TE&L CO
P'ee: TEXAS EMIGRATION AND LAND
COMPANY
G'ee: TEXAS EMIGRATION AND LAND
COMPANY
T-Dt: -- --- -----
P-Dt: 07 Mar 1859
Dist/Class: Texas Emmigration and Land
Company
File#: 3401
Patent#: 1110
Patent Vol.: 14
Survey/Blk/Twp: 3401
Acres: 3385
Map(s) 4, 5, 6

Abstract # 1222 - TE&L CO
P'ee: TEXAS EMIGRATION AND LAND
COMPANY
G'ee: TEXAS EMIGRATION AND LAND
COMPANY
T-Dt: -- --- -----
P-Dt: 07 Mar 1859
Dist/Class: Texas Emmigration and Land
Company
File#: 3402
Patent#: 1111
Patent Vol.: 14
Certificate: 1957
Survey/Blk/Twp: 3402
Acres: 77
Map(s) 13

Abstract # 1223 - TE&L CO
P'ee: TEXAS EMIGRATION AND LAND
COMPANY
G'ee: TEXAS EMIGRATION AND LAND
COMPANY
T-Dt: -- --- -----
P-Dt: 08 Mar 1859
Dist/Class: Texas Emmigration and Land
Company
File#: 3403
Patent#: 1112
Patent Vol.: 14
Survey/Blk/Twp: 3403
Acres: 532
Map(s) 5, 13

Abstract # 1224 - TE&L CO
P'ee: TEXAS EMIGRATION AND LAND
COMPANY
G'ee: TEXAS EMIGRATION AND LAND
COMPANY
T-Dt: -- --- -----
P-Dt: 08 Mar 1859
Dist/Class: Texas Emmigration and Land
Company
File#: 3404
Patent#: 1113
Patent Vol.: 14
Survey/Blk/Twp: 3404
Acres: 505
Map(s) 14

Abstract # 1225 - TE&L CO
P'ee: TEXAS EMIGRATION AND LAND
COMPANY
G'ee: TEXAS EMIGRATION AND LAND
COMPANY
T-Dt: -- --- -----
P-Dt: 08 Mar 1859
Dist/Class: Texas Emmigration and Land
Company
File#: 3405
Patent#: 1114
Patent Vol.: 14
Survey/Blk/Twp: 3405
Acres: 593
Map(s) 14

Abstract # 1226 - TE&L CO
P'ee: TEXAS EMIGRATION AND LAND
COMPANY
G'ee: TEXAS EMIGRATION AND LAND
COMPANY
T-Dt: -- --- -----
P-Dt: 08 Mar 1859
Dist/Class: Texas Emmigration and Land
Company
File#: 3406
Patent#: 1115
Patent Vol.: 14
Survey/Blk/Twp: 3406
Acres: 385
Map(s) 22

Abstract # 1227 - TE&L CO
P'ee: TEXAS EMIGRATION AND LAND
COMPANY
G'ee: TEXAS EMIGRATION AND LAND
COMPANY
T-Dt: -- --- -----
P-Dt: 08 Mar 1859
Dist/Class: Texas Emmigration and Land
Company
File#: 3407
Patent#: 1116
Patent Vol.: 14
Survey/Blk/Twp: 3407
Acres: 880
Map(s) 23

Abstract # 1228 - TE&L CO
P'ee: TEXAS EMIGRATION AND LAND
COMPANY
G'ee: TEXAS EMIGRATION AND LAND
COMPANY
T-Dt: -- --- -----
P-Dt: 08 Mar 1859
Dist/Class: Texas Emmigration and Land
Company
File#: 3408
Patent#: 1117

Patent Vol.: 14
Survey/Blk/Twp: 3408
Acres: 1430
Map(s) 22

Abstract # 1229 - TE&L CO
P'ee: TEXAS EMIGRATION AND LAND
COMPANY
G'ee: TEXAS EMIGRATION AND LAND
COMPANY
T-Dt: -- --- -----
P-Dt: 09 Mar 1859
Dist/Class: Texas Emmigration and Land
Company
File#: 3409
Patent#: 1118
Patent Vol.: 14
Survey/Blk/Twp: 3409
Acres: 1980
Map(s) 26

Abstract # 1230 - TE&L CO
P'ee: TEXAS EMIGRATION AND LAND
COMPANY
G'ee: TEXAS EMIGRATION AND LAND
COMPANY
T-Dt: -- --- -----
P-Dt: 10 Mar 1859
Dist/Class: Texas Emmigration and Land
Company
File#: 3410
Patent#: 1119
Patent Vol.: 14
Survey/Blk/Twp: 3410
Acres: 10318
Map(s) 26, 27, 34, 35

Abstract # 1231 - TE&L CO
P'ee: TEXAS EMIGRATION AND LAND
COMPANY
G'ee: TEXAS EMIGRATION AND LAND
COMPANY
T-Dt: -- --- -----
P-Dt: 07 Apr 1859
Dist/Class: Texas Emmigration and Land
Company
File#: 3411
Patent#: 1135
Patent Vol.: 14
Survey/Blk/Twp: 3411
Acres: 1540
Map(s) 20, 21, 28, 29

Abstract # 1232 - TE&L CO
P'ee: TEXAS EMIGRATION AND LAND
COMPANY
G'ee: TEXAS EMIGRATION AND LAND
COMPANY
T-Dt: -- --- -----
P-Dt: 10 Mar 1859
Dist/Class: Texas Emmigration and Land
Company
File#: 3412
Patent#: 1120
Patent Vol.: 14
Survey/Blk/Twp: 3412
Acres: 2200
Map(s) 23

Abstract # 1233 - TE&L CO
P'ee: TEXAS EMIGRATION AND LAND
COMPANY
G'ee: TEXAS EMIGRATION AND LAND
COMPANY
T-Dt: -- --- -----

P-Dt: 11 Mar 1859
Dist/Class: Texas Emmigration and Land
Company
File#: 3413
Patent#: 1121
Patent Vol.: 14
Survey/Blk/Twp: 3413
Acres: 1426
Map(s) 21, 22

Abstract # 1234 - TE&L CO
P'ee: MENG, CHARLES J
G'ee: TEXAS EMIGRATION AND LAND
COMPANY
T-Dt: -- --- -----
P-Dt: 30 Jan 1861
Dist/Class: Texas Emmigration and Land
Company
File#: 3415
Patent#: 1149
Patent Vol.: 14
Certificate: 1011/2250
Acres: 201.25
Map(s) 36

Abstract # 1235 - TE&L CO
P'ee: MENG, CHARLES J
G'ee: TEXAS EMIGRATION AND LAND
COMPANY
T-Dt: -- --- -----
P-Dt: 11 Feb 1861
Dist/Class: Texas Emmigration and Land
Company
File#: 3416
Patent#: 1156
Patent Vol.: 14
Certificate: 1011
Survey/Blk/Twp: 1011
Acres: 146
Map(s) 20

Abstract # 1236 - TE&L CO
P'ee: WILDER, JAMES B
G'ee: TEXAS EMIGRATION AND LAND
COMPANY
T-Dt: -- --- -----
P-Dt: 27 Dec 1865
Dist/Class: Texas Emmigration and Land
Company
File#: 3417
Patent#: 485
Patent Vol.: 33
Certificate: 1007
Survey/Blk/Twp: 1007
Acres: 320
Map(s) 36

Abstract # 1237 - TE&L CO
P'ee: MERRY, CHARLES J
G'ee: TEXAS EMIGRATION AND LAND
COMPANY
T-Dt: -- --- -----
P-Dt: 05 Feb 1861
Dist/Class: Texas Emmigration and Land
Company
File#: 3418
Patent#: 1155
Patent Vol.: 14
Certificate: 1103
Survey/Blk/Twp: 1103
Acres: 320
Map(s) 36

Abstract # 1239 - TE&L CO
P'ee: TEXAS EMIGRATION AND LAND

COMPANY
G'ee: TEXAS EMIGRATION AND LAND
COMPANY
T-Dt: -- --- -----
P-Dt: 25 Feb 1859
Dist/Class: Texas Emmigration and Land
Company
File#: 1211
Patent#: 505
Patent Vol.: 20
Certificate: 1211
Survey/Blk/Twp: 1211
Acres: 320
Map(s) 35, 43

Abstract # 1240 - TE&L CO
P'ee: TEXAS EMIGRATION AND LAND
COMPANY
G'ee: TEXAS EMIGRATION AND LAND
COMPANY
T-Dt: -- --- -----
P-Dt: 14 Mar 1859
Dist/Class: Texas Emmigration and Land
Company
File#: 1116
Patent#: 506
Patent Vol.: 20
Certificate: 1116
Survey/Blk/Twp: 1116
Acres: 320
Map(s) 36, 44

Abstract # 1241 - TE&L CO
P'ee: TEXAS EMIGRATION AND LAND
COMPANY
G'ee: TEXAS EMIGRATION AND LAND
COMPANY
T-Dt: -- --- -----
P-Dt: 04 Aug 1858
Dist/Class: Texas Emmigration and Land
Company
File#: 1212
Patent#: 116
Patent Vol.: 20
Certificate: 1212
Survey/Blk/Twp: 1212
Acres: 320
Map(s) 34, 35, 42, 43

Abstract # 1242 - TE&L CO
P'ee: HEDGECOXE, OLIVER
G'ee: TEXAS EMIGRATION AND LAND
COMPANY
T-Dt: -- --- -----
P-Dt: 11 Jan 1858
Dist/Class: Texas Emmigration and Land
Company
File#: 2251&4
Patent#: 304
Patent Vol.: 14
Certificate: 4
Survey/Blk/Twp: 2250
Acres: 320
Map(s) 11, 12, 19, 20

Abstract # 1243 - TAYLOR, J N
P'ee: BARNARD, CHARLES E
G'ee: TAYLOR, JOHN N
T-Dt: -- --- -----
P-Dt: 03 Jan 1859
Dist/Class: Fannin Bounty
File#: 650
Patent#: 142
Patent Vol.: 9
Certificate: 4205/4306

Acres: 960
Map(s) 28, 36

Abstract # 1244 - T&NO RR CO
P'ee: WOOLFOLK, R H
G'ee: TEXAS AND NEW ORLEANS
RAILROAD COMPANY
T-Dt: -- --- -----
P-Dt: 04 Sep 1873
Dist/Class: Fannin Scrip
File#: 3725
Patent#: 370
Patent Vol.: 13
Certificate: 862
Survey/Blk/Twp: 7
Acres: 640
Map(s) 28, 29

Abstract # 1245 - T&NO RR CO
P'ee: WOOLFOLK, R H
G'ee: TEXAS AND NEW ORLEANS
RAILROAD COMPANY
T-Dt: -- --- -----
P-Dt: 03 Aug 1875
Dist/Class: Fannin Scrip
File#: 3726
Patent#: 136
Patent Vol.: 24
Certificate: 863
Survey/Blk/Twp: 9
Acres: 640
Map(s) 29

Abstract # 1246 - T&NO RR CO
P'ee: WOOLFOLK, R H
G'ee: TEXAS AND NEW ORLEANS
RAILROAD COMPANY
T-Dt: -- --- -----
P-Dt: 20 Jun 1873
Dist/Class: Fannin Scrip
File#: 4365
Patent#: 352
Patent Vol.: 13
Certificate: 861
Survey/Blk/Twp: 5
Acres: 640
Map(s) 29

Abstract # 1247 - T&NO RR CO
P'ee: WOOLFOLK, R H
G'ee: TEXAS AND NEW ORLEANS
RAILROAD COMPANY
T-Dt: -- --- -----
P-Dt: 14 Jun 1873
Dist/Class: Fannin Scrip
File#: 4366
Patent#: 349
Patent Vol.: 13
Certificate: 864
Survey/Blk/Twp: 1
Acres: 640
Map(s) 30, 31

Abstract # 1248 - T&NO RR CO
P'ee: WOOLFOLK, R H
G'ee: TEXAS AND NEW ORLEANS
RAILROAD COMPANY
T-Dt: -- --- -----
P-Dt: 20 Jun 1873
Dist/Class: Fannin Scrip
File#: 4367
Patent#: 351
Patent Vol.: 13
Certificate: 865
Survey/Blk/Twp: 3

Acres: 640
Map(s) 31

Abstract # 1254 - BACHEL, A
P'ee: TEXAS AND PACIFIC RAILROAD
COMPANY
G'ee: TEXAS AND PACIFIC RAILROAD
COMPANY
T-Dt: -- --- -----
P-Dt: 19 Mar 1877
Dist/Class: Fannin Scrip
File#: 9928
Patent#: 580
Patent Vol.: 33
Certificate: 2/497
Survey/Blk/Twp: 9
Acres: 17.50
Map(s) 29

Abstract # 1255 - TACKILL, P
P'ee: TACKITT, PLEASANT
G'ee: TACKITT, PLEASANT
T-Dt: -- --- -----
P-Dt: 31 Mar 1875
Dist/Class: Milam Scrip
File#: 483
Patent#: 39
Patent Vol.: 21
Acres: 160
Map(s) 35

Abstract # 1256 - TIMMONS, J S
P'ee: TIMMONS, J S
G'ee: TIMMONS, J S
T-Dt: -- --- -----
P-Dt: 21 Nov 1876
Dist/Class: Fannin Preemption
File#: 1425
Patent#: 93
Patent Vol.: 5
Acres: 160
Map(s) 37

Abstract # 1257 - TIMMONS, N J
P'ee: TIMMONS, N J
G'ee: TIMMONS, N J
T-Dt: -- --- -----
P-Dt: 21 Nov 1876
Dist/Class: Fannin Preemption
File#: 1436
Patent#: 91
Patent Vol.: 5
Acres: 160
Map(s) 37

Abstract # 1258 - TIMMONS, A
P'ee: TIMMONS, A
G'ee: TIMMONS, A
T-Dt: -- --- -----
P-Dt: 31 Oct 1876
Dist/Class: Fannin Preemption
File#: 1266
Patent#: 35
Patent Vol.: 5
Acres: 160
Map(s) 35, 36

Abstract # 1259 - THOMAS, F L
P'ee: THOMAS, F L
G'ee: THOMAS, FLOYD L
T-Dt: -- --- -----
P-Dt: 28 Jun 1876
Dist/Class: Fannin Preemption
File#: 1267
Patent#: 368

Patent Vol.: 4
Acres: 160
Map(s) 30, 38

Abstract # 1260 - TACKETT, A C
P'ee: BLACK, H M
G'ee: TACKITT, A C
T-Dt: -- --- -----
P-Dt: 03 Aug 1877
Dist/Class: Fannin Preemption
File#: 976
Patent#: 33
Patent Vol.: 6
Acres: 160
Map(s) 28, 36

Abstract # 1261 - TERRY, M L
P'ee: TERRY, M L
G'ee: TERRY, M L
T-Dt: -- --- -----
P-Dt: 19 Jun 1876
Dist/Class: Fannin Preemption
File#: 1178
Patent#: 349
Patent Vol.: 4
Acres: 160
Map(s) 31

Abstract # 1263 - UPHAM, E E
P'ee: UPHAM, ED E
G'ee: UPHAM, ED E
T-Dt: -- --- -----
P-Dt: 26 Sep 1876
Dist/Class: Fannin Preemption
File#: 1439
Patent#: 569
Patent Vol.: 4
Acres: 160
Map(s) 30, 38

Abstract # 1264 - UPHAM, L E
P'ee: BARRY, THOMAS
G'ee: UPHAM, L E
T-Dt: -- --- -----
P-Dt: 26 Sep 1876
Dist/Class: Fannin Preemption
File#: 1440
Patent#: 568
Patent Vol.: 4
Acres: 80
Map(s) 30

Abstract # 1265 - VIVEN, P
P'ee: STEWART, WILLIS
G'ee: VIREN, PHILIP
T-Dt: -- --- -----
P-Dt: 15 Jul 1859
Dist/Class: Fannin Bounty
File#: 662
Patent#: 20
Patent Vol.: 11
Certificate: 1394
Acres: 640
Map(s) 21, 22

Abstract # 1266 - WALTERS, M
P'ee: WALTERS, MOSES
G'ee: WALTERS, MOSES
T-Dt: -- --- -----
P-Dt: 25 Oct 1860
Dist/Class: Fannin 1st
File#: 930
Patent#: 300
Patent Vol.: 16
Certificate: 243/342

Acres: 49.69
Map(s) 19

Abstract # 1267 - WASH, S A
P'ee: STAPP, ANDREW
G'ee: WASH, SALLEY ANN
T-Dt: -- --- -----
P-Dt: 20 Dec 1855
Dist/Class: Fannin 3rd
File#: 995
Patent#: 33
Patent Vol.: 13
Certificate: 513
Acres: 320
Map(s) 19, 20

Abstract # 1268 - WASH, S A
P'ee: STAPP, ANDREW
G'ee: WASH, SALLEY ANN
T-Dt: -- --- -----
P-Dt: 20 Dec 1855
Dist/Class: Fannin 3rd
File#: 995
Patent#: 34
Patent Vol.: 13
Certificate: 513
Acres: 320
Map(s) 19, 20

Abstract # 1269 - WHITE, A
P'ee: STAPP, ANDREW
G'ee: WHITE, ARCHIBALD
T-Dt: -- --- -----
P-Dt: 29 Feb 1856
Dist/Class: Fannin 3rd
File#: 996
Patent#: 868
Patent Vol.: 12
Certificate: 61
Acres: 40
Map(s) 19

Abstract # 1270 - WHITE, A
P'ee: STAPP, ANDREW
G'ee: WHITE, ARCHIBALD
T-Dt: -- --- -----
P-Dt: 01 May 1854
Dist/Class: Fannin 3rd
File#: 996
Patent#: 149
Patent Vol.: 10
Certificate: 61
Acres: 600
Map(s) 19, 20

Abstract # 1271 - WOODRUFF, R W
P'ee: ABBOTT, EDWARD F
G'ee: WOODRUFF, R W
T-Dt: -- --- -----
P-Dt: 14 Apr 1856
Dist/Class: Fannin 3rd
File#: 1344
Patent#: 1307
Patent Vol.: 9
Certificate: 320
Acres: 320
Map(s) 20

Abstract # 1272 - WEEKLEY, G M
P'ee: BONARD, CHARLES E
G'ee: WEEKLEY, GEORGE M
T-Dt: -- --- -----
P-Dt: 02 Sep 1857
Dist/Class: Fannin 3rd
File#: 2200

Patent#: 1796
Patent Vol.: 9
Certificate: 29
Acres: 320
Map(s) 28

Abstract # 1273 - WILLIAMS, L L
P'ee: WILLIAMS, L L
G'ee: WILLIAMS, L L
T-Dt: -- --- -----
P-Dt: 15 May 1860
Dist/Class: Fannin 3rd
File#: 2665
Patent#: 87
Patent Vol.: 30
Acres: 280
Map(s) 28

Abstract # 1274 - WOOD, A
P'ee: WOOD, ANN
G'ee: WOOD, ANN
T-Dt: -- --- -----
P-Dt: 30 Oct 1874
Dist/Class: Fannin 3rd
File#: 4407
Patent#: 323
Patent Vol.: 42
Certificate: 572
Acres: 640
Map(s) 7

Abstract # 1275 - WILSON, R
P'ee: WILSON, JAMES T D
G'ee: WILSON, ROBERT
T-Dt: -- --- -----
P-Dt: 05 Oct 1855
Dist/Class: Fannin Donation
File#: 514
Patent#: 446
Patent Vol.: 2
Certificate: 584
Acres: 213
Map(s) 8

Abstract # 1276 - WILSON, R
P'ee: WILSON, JAMES T D
G'ee: WILSON, ROBERT
T-Dt: -- --- -----
P-Dt: 06 Jun 1856
Dist/Class: Fannin Donation
File#: 514
Patent#: 467
Patent Vol.: 2
Certificate: 584
Acres: 427
Map(s) 8

Abstract # 1277 - WHEELOCK, G R
P'ee: MILSAP, FULLER
G'ee: WHEELOCK, GEORGE R
T-Dt: -- --- -----
P-Dt: 06 Aug 1875
Dist/Class: Fannin Bounty
File#: 1481
Patent#: 200
Patent Vol.: 15
Certificate: 1840
Acres: 320
Map(s) 37, 38, 45, 46

Abstract # 1278 - WALKER, J B
P'ee: WALKER, J B
G'ee: WOOLFORK, R O
T-Dt: -- --- -----
P-Dt: 24 Jun 1861

Dist/Class: Fannin Scrip
File#: 1259
Patent#: 123
Patent Vol.: 9
Certificate: 166
Survey/Blk/Twp: 14
Acres: 320
Map(s) 39

Abstract # 1279 - WALKER, J B
P'ee: WALKER, J B
G'ee: WOOLFORK, R O
T-Dt: -- --- -----
P-Dt: 24 Jun 1861
Dist/Class: Fannin Scrip
File#: 1259
Patent#: 124
Patent Vol.: 9
Certificate: 166
Survey/Blk/Twp: 15
Acres: 320
Map(s) 39

Abstract # 1280 - WC RR CO
P'ee: MCINTYRE, H C
G'ee: WASHINGTON COUNTY RAIL-
ROAD COMPANY
T-Dt: -- --- -----
P-Dt: 05 Nov 1875
Dist/Class: Fannin Scrip
File#: 8494
Patent#: 172
Patent Vol.: 1
Certificate: 28/142
Survey/Blk/Twp: 1
Acres: 640
Map(s) 16

Abstract # 1281 - WATHON, J R
P'ee: WATHAN, J R
G'ee: WATHAN, J R
T-Dt: -- --- -----
P-Dt: 25 Jan 1877
Dist/Class: Fannin Preemption
File#: 1442
Patent#: 235
Patent Vol.: 5
Acres: 80
Map(s) 37

Abstract # 1282 - WHITTENBURG, J B
P'ee: WHITTENBURG, J B
G'ee: WHITTENBURG, J B
T-Dt: -- --- -----
P-Dt: 10 Jan 1877
Dist/Class: Fannin Preemption
File#: 1449
Patent#: 196
Patent Vol.: 5
Acres: 160
Map(s) 38

Abstract # 1283 - WOOLEY, W
P'ee: WOOLEY, WILLIAM
G'ee: WOOLEY, WILLIAM
T-Dt: -- --- -----
P-Dt: 09 Aug 1877
Dist/Class: Fannin Preemption
File#: 1450
Patent#: 57
Patent Vol.: 6
Acres: 80
Map(s) 29

Abstract # 1284 - YOUNG CSL

P'ee: YOUNG COUNTY SCHOOL
COMMISSION
G'ee: YOUNG COUNTY SCHOOL
LAND
T-Dt: -- --- -----
P-Dt: 24 Apr 1860
Dist/Class: Fannin 1st
File#: 1066
Patent#: 113
Patent Vol.: 15
Acres: 4478.40
Map(s) 8

Abstract # 1285 - YOUNG CSL
P'ee: YOUNG COUNTY SCHOOL
COMMISSION
G'ee: YOUNG COUNTY SCHOOL
LAND
T-Dt: -- --- -----
P-Dt: 31 Jul 1891
Dist/Class: Fannin 1st
File#: 1103
Patent#: 170
Patent Vol.: 25
Acres: 4111
Map(s) 25, 26, 33, 34

Abstract # 1286 - YOUNG, H F
P'ee: MATTHEWS, R H
G'ee: YOUNG, HUGH F
T-Dt: -- --- -----
P-Dt: 05 Sep 1860
Dist/Class: Fannin 3rd
File#: 1873
Patent#: 417
Patent Vol.: 30
Certificate: 160
Acres: 640
Map(s) 30

Abstract # 1287 - YOUNG, P
P'ee: MCCRAVEN, WILLIAM
G'ee: YOUNG, PHILIP
T-Dt: -- --- -----
P-Dt: 18 Jun 1874
Dist/Class: Fannin Bounty
File#: 348
Patent#: 564
Patent Vol.: 14
Certificate: 4050
Acres: 320
Map(s) 1

Abstract # 1288 - ASKEW, J M
P'ee: ASKEW, J M
G'ee: ASKEW, J M
T-Dt: -- --- -----
P-Dt: 07 Sep 1877
Dist/Class: Fannin Preemption
File#: 1287
Patent#: 134
Patent Vol.: 6
Acres: 80
Map(s) 29

Abstract # 1289 - AKINS, J A
P'ee: CULP, A S
G'ee: AKINS, JAMES A
T-Dt: -- --- -----
P-Dt: 30 Apr 1884
Dist/Class: Fannin Preemption
File#: 1705
Patent#: 399
Patent Vol.: 15
Acres: 160

Map(s) 34

Abstract # 1290 - BELLAMY, A F
P'ee: BELLAMY, A F
G'ee: BELLAMY, A F
T-Dt: -- --- -----
P-Dt: 30 Nov 1877
Dist/Class: Fannin Preemption
File#: 1296
Patent#: 318
Patent Vol.: 6
Acres: 160
Map(s) 30

Abstract # 1291 - BAKER, G W
P'ee: BAKER, G W
G'ee: BAKER, G W
T-Dt: -- --- -----
P-Dt: 18 Dec 1877
Dist/Class: Fannin Preemption
File#: 1291
Patent#: 369
Patent Vol.: 6
Acres: 160
Map(s) 38, 39

Abstract # 1292 - BUNGER, S
P'ee: GIVANS, JAMES
G'ee: BUNGER, SAMUEL
T-Dt: -- --- -----
P-Dt: 11 Jan 1878
Dist/Class: Fannin Preemption
File#: 1301
Patent#: 451
Patent Vol.: 6
Acres: 80
Map(s) 37, 38

Abstract # 1293 - BAKER, W A
P'ee: BAKER, W A
G'ee: BAKER, W A
T-Dt: -- --- -----
P-Dt: 18 Jan 1878
Dist/Class: Fannin Preemption
File#: 1290
Patent#: 496
Patent Vol.: 6
Acres: 160
Map(s) 38

Abstract # 1295 - BUTLER, E V
P'ee: LEDBETTER, F M
G'ee: BUTLER, E V
T-Dt: -- --- -----
P-Dt: 19 Dec 1878
Dist/Class: Fannin Preemption
File#: 1306
Patent#: 204
Patent Vol.: 8
Acres: 160
Map(s) 29

Abstract # 1296 - CAIRNES, J A
P'ee: CAIRNES, JOHN A
G'ee: CAIRNES, JOHN A
T-Dt: -- --- -----
P-Dt: 22 May 1878
Dist/Class: Fannin Preemption
File#: 1867
Patent#: 256
Patent Vol.: 7
Acres: 80
Map(s) 1

Abstract # 1297 - CRISWELL, S H

P'ee: CRISWELL, S H
G'ee: CRISWELL, S H
T-Dt: -- --- -----
P-Dt: 02 May 1878
Dist/Class: Fannin Preemption
File#: 1318
Patent#: 195
Patent Vol.: 7
Acres: 160
Map(s) 29

Abstract # 1298 - COMBS, T J
P'ee: BEARD, F J
G'ee: COMBS, T J
T-Dt: -- --- -----
P-Dt: 30 Nov 1878
Dist/Class: Fannin Preemption
File#: 1315
Patent#: 151
Patent Vol.: 8
Acres: 160
Map(s) 30

Abstract # 1299 - CROUCH, J R
P'ee: BOYD, RACHEL C
G'ee: CROUCH, J
T-Dt: -- --- -----
P-Dt: 01 Oct 1878
Dist/Class: Fannin Preemption
File#: 1319
Patent#: 567
Patent Vol.: 7
Acres: 160
Map(s) 30

Abstract # 1300 - CI CO
P'ee: WILLIAMSON, C C (MRS)
G'ee: CUDDRILLA IRRIGATION
COMPNAY
T-Dt: -- --- -----
P-Dt: 18 Feb 1878
Dist/Class: Fannin Scrip
File#: 11070
Patent#: 504
Patent Vol.: 29
Certificate: 6
Acres: 426.67
Map(s) 22, 30

Abstract # 1301 - CI CO
P'ee: DAVIS, H W
G'ee: CUDDRILLA IRRIGATION
COMPNAY
T-Dt: -- --- -----
P-Dt: 18 Feb 1878
Dist/Class: Fannin Scrip
File#: 11070
Patent#: 505
Patent Vol.: 29
Certificate: 6
Acres: 213.33
Map(s) 30

Abstract # 1302 - DECKER, J
P'ee: DECKER, JOSEPH
G'ee: DECKER, JOSEPH
T-Dt: -- --- -----
P-Dt: 07 Jan 1878
Dist/Class: Fannin Preemption
File#: 1323
Patent#: 426
Patent Vol.: 6
Acres: 160
Map(s) 29, 37

Abstract # 1303 - DAVIS, W J
P'ee: MAGILL, JOHN (HEIRS)
G'ee: DAVIS, W J
T-Dt: -- --- -----
P-Dt: 17 Apr 1878
Dist/Class: Fannin Preemption
File#: 1322
Patent#: 143
Patent Vol.: 7
Acres: 160
Map(s) 37

Abstract # 1306 - EVANS, S H
P'ee: EVANS, SAMUEL H
G'ee: EVANS, SAMUEL H
T-Dt: -- --- -----
P-Dt: 25 Aug 1896
Dist/Class: Fannin Preemption
File#: 1724
Patent#: 22
Patent Vol.: 29
Acres: 160
Map(s) 32

Abstract # 1307 - EL&RR RR CO
P'ee: GANT, A B
G'ee: EAST LINE AND RED RIVER
RAILROAD COMPANY
T-Dt: -- --- -----
P-Dt: 01 Jan 1879
Dist/Class: Fannin Scrip
File#: 11697
Patent#: 140
Patent Vol.: 45
Certificate: 554
Survey/Blk/Twp: 1
Acres: 640
Map(s) 29

Abstract # 1308 - FOSTER, S
P'ee: FOSTER, S
G'ee: FOSTER, S
T-Dt: -- --- -----
P-Dt: 28 Jan 1878
Dist/Class: Fannin Preemption
File#: 912
Patent#: 579
Patent Vol.: 6
Acres: 80
Map(s) 1

Abstract # 1309 - FORE, J S
P'ee: FORE, JOHN S
G'ee: FORE, JOHN S
T-Dt: -- --- -----
P-Dt: 17 Apr 1878
Dist/Class: Fannin Preemption
File#: 1337
Patent#: 141
Patent Vol.: 7
Acres: 80
Map(s) 38

Abstract # 1310 - FERGUSON, H H
P'ee: GLOVER, E D
G'ee: FERGUSON, H H
T-Dt: -- --- -----
P-Dt: 17 Jul 1878
Dist/Class: Fannin Preemption
File#: 1331
Patent#: 390
Patent Vol.: 7
Acres: 160
Map(s) 29, 37

Abstract # 1311 - FAIR, G F
P'ee: MCDERMIT, G B
G'ee: FAIR, G F
T-Dt: -- --- -----
P-Dt: 03 Aug 1883
Dist/Class: Fannin Preemption
File#: 1585
Patent#: 395
Patent Vol.: 14
Acres: 160
Map(s) 35

Abstract # 1312 - GOLDEN, P
P'ee: WILCOX, ROBERT M
G'ee: GOLDEN, PHILIP
T-Dt: -- --- -----
P-Dt: 06 May 1873
Dist/Class: Fannin 2nd
File#: 649
Patent#: 168
Patent Vol.: 9
Certificate: 518 6/544
Acres: 103.19
Map(s) 39

Abstract # 1313 - GILMORE, A C
P'ee: GILMORE, A C
G'ee: GILMORE, A C
T-Dt: -- --- -----
P-Dt: 17 Oct 1877
Dist/Class: Fannin Preemption
File#: 1344
Patent#: 236
Patent Vol.: 6
Acres: 80
Map(s) 39

Abstract # 1314 - GRIFFITH, B P
P'ee: GRIFFITH, B P
G'ee: GRIFFITH, B P
T-Dt: -- --- -----
P-Dt: 17 Apr 1878
Dist/Class: Fannin Preemption
File#: 1346
Patent#: 142
Patent Vol.: 7
Acres: 160
Map(s) 29

Abstract # 1315 - GOUDY, F H
P'ee: GOWDY, E L
G'ee: GOWDY, E L
T-Dt: -- --- -----
P-Dt: 06 Mar 1882
Dist/Class: Fannin Preemption
File#: 1707
Patent#: 161
Patent Vol.: 13
Acres: 80
Map(s) 34

Abstract # 1316 - GOUDY, F H
P'ee: GOWDY, F H
G'ee: GOWDY, F H
T-Dt: -- --- -----
P-Dt: 06 Mar 1882
Dist/Class: Fannin Preemption
File#: 1706
Patent#: 159
Patent Vol.: 13
Acres: 80
Map(s) 34

Abstract # 1317 - T&NO RR CO
S2: GOODE, W M

P'ee: GOODE, W M
G'ee: GOODE, W M
T-Dt: -- --- -----
P-Dt: 13 Oct 1886
Dist/Class: School
File#: 1468
Patent#: 206
Patent Vol.: 6
Certificate: 864
Survey/Blk/Twp: NE 1/4 2 T & NO-
Acres: 160
Map(s) 31

Abstract # 1319 - HORNER, J W
P'ee: HORNER, J W
G'ee: HORNER, J W
T-Dt: -- --- -----
P-Dt: 07 Jan 1878
Dist/Class: Fannin Preemption
File#: 1357
Patent#: 431
Patent Vol.: 6
Acres: 160
Map(s) 30

Abstract # 1320 - HAMMONS, B W
P'ee: HAMMONS, B W
G'ee: HAMMONS, B W
T-Dt: -- --- -----
P-Dt: 23 Apr 1878
Dist/Class: Fannin Preemption
File#: 1126
Patent#: 169
Patent Vol.: 7
Acres: 80
Map(s) 30

Abstract # 1321 - HAMILTON, R
P'ee: FRISBIE, H S (MRS)
G'ee: HAMILTON, ROBERT
T-Dt: -- --- -----
P-Dt: 18 Jul 1878
Dist/Class: Fannin Preemption
File#: 1347
Patent#: 391
Patent Vol.: 7
Acres: 160
Map(s) 29, 30

Abstract # 1323 - WC RR CO
S2: HUBER, B
P'ee: HUBER, BENHARD
G'ee: HUBER, BENHARD
T-Dt: -- --- -----
P-Dt: 18 Apr 1878
Dist/Class: School
File#: 1382
Patent#: 103
Patent Vol.: 1
Certificate: 28/142
Survey/Blk/Twp: NW 1/4 2 W.C.RR-
Acres: 160
Map(s) 16

Abstract # 1324 - I&GN RR CO
P'ee: HOUSTON AND GREAT NORTH-
ERN RAILROAD COMPANY
G'ee: HOUSTON AND GREAT
NORTHERN RAILROAD COMPANY
T-Dt: -- --- -----
P-Dt: 25 Sep 1877
Dist/Class: Fannin Scrip
File#: 11060
Patent#: 538
Patent Vol.: 36

Certificate: 33/171
Acres: 418.50
Map(s) 7

Abstract # 1325 - I&GN RR CO
P'ee: PIATT, HORACE A
G'ee: HOUSTON AND GREAT
NORTHERN RAILROAD COMPANY
T-Dt: -- --- -----
P-Dt: 13 Sep 1878
Dist/Class: Fannin Scrip
File#: 11253
Patent#: 383
Patent Vol.: 43
Certificate: 22/137
Acres: 131
Map(s) 36

Abstract # 1326 - I&GN RR CO
P'ee: GANT, A B
G'ee: HOUSTON AND GREAT
NORTHERN RAILROAD COMPANY
T-Dt: -- --- -----
P-Dt: 13 Sep 1878
Dist/Class: Fannin Scrip
File#: 11253
Patent#: 384
Patent Vol.: 43
Certificate: 22/137
Acres: 295
Map(s) 28

Abstract # 1327 - JAMES, J J
P'ee: JAMES, JOHN J
G'ee: JAMES, JOHN J
T-Dt: -- --- -----
P-Dt: 04 Sep 1877
Dist/Class: Fannin Preemption
File#: 1696
Patent#: 122
Patent Vol.: 6
Acres: 80
Map(s) 37

Abstract # 1328 - JONES, J E
P'ee: JONES, J E
G'ee: JONES, J E
T-Dt: -- --- -----
P-Dt: 11 Jun 1878
Dist/Class: Fannin Preemption
File#: 1586
Patent#: 296
Patent Vol.: 7
Acres: 160
Map(s) 31

Abstract # 1329 - JAMES, J M
P'ee: BURGESS, B E
G'ee: JAMES, J M
T-Dt: -- --- -----
P-Dt: 26 Mar 1879
Dist/Class: Fannin Preemption
File#: 1361
Patent#: 526
Patent Vol.: 8
Acres: 80
Map(s) 37

Abstract # 1330 - JOWELL, J A
P'ee: JOWELL, J A
G'ee: JOWELL, J A
T-Dt: -- --- -----
P-Dt: 20 Dec 1878
Dist/Class: Fannin Preemption
File#: 1364

Patent#: 209
Patent Vol.: 8
Acres: 160
Map(s) 38, 39

Abstract # 1331 - JOWELL, J R
P'ee: JOWELL, J R
G'ee: JOWELL, J R
T-Dt: -- --- -----
P-Dt: 20 Dec 1878
Dist/Class: Fannin Preemption
File#: 1365
Patent#: 210
Patent Vol.: 8
Acres: 160
Map(s) 38

Abstract # 1332 - JOWELL, J V
P'ee: JOWELL, J V (HEIRS)
G'ee: JOWELL, J V
T-Dt: -- --- -----
P-Dt: 20 Dec 1878
Dist/Class: Fannin Preemption
File#: 1363
Patent#: 211
Patent Vol.: 8
Acres: 80
Map(s) 38

Abstract # 1333 - KUTCH, B F
P'ee: KUTCH, B F
G'ee: KUTCH, B F
T-Dt: -- --- -----
P-Dt: 16 Apr 1878
Dist/Class: Fannin Preemption
File#: 1369
Patent#: 139
Patent Vol.: 7
Acres: 83.60
Map(s) 38

Abstract # 1334 - LYTLE, S
P'ee: LYTLE, SARAH
G'ee: LYTLE, SARAH
T-Dt: -- --- -----
P-Dt: 07 Dec 1877
Dist/Class: Fannin Preemption
File#: 1378
Patent#: 350
Patent Vol.: 6
Acres: 120.79
Map(s) 38

Abstract # 1335 - LAMAR, J T
P'ee: LAMAR, JAMES T
G'ee: LAMAR, JAMES T
T-Dt: -- --- -----
P-Dt: 20 Dec 1877
Dist/Class: Fannin Preemption
File#: 1372
Patent#: 383
Patent Vol.: 6
Acres: 160
Map(s) 29

Abstract # 1336 - LARD, W T
P'ee: LARD, W T
G'ee: LARD, W T
T-Dt: -- --- -----
P-Dt: 20 Dec 1877
Dist/Class: Fannin Preemption
File#: 1373
Patent#: 384
Patent Vol.: 6
Acres: 160

Map(s) 29, 30, 37, 38

Abstract # 1337 - LEDRICK, H
P'ee: LEDRICK, HENRY
G'ee: LEDRICK, HENRY
T-Dt: -- --- -----
P-Dt: 18 Jan 1878
Dist/Class: Fannin Preemption
File#: 1376
Patent#: 499
Patent Vol.: 6
Acres: 160
Map(s) 37, 38

Abstract # 1338 - MOSLEY, B J
P'ee: MOSELY, BENJAMIN SR
G'ee: MOSELY, BENJAMIN SR
T-Dt: -- --- -----
P-Dt: 17 Oct 1877
Dist/Class: Fannin Preemption
File#: 1398
Patent#: 239
Patent Vol.: 6
Acres: 160
Map(s) 30

Abstract # 1339 - MARSHALT, W H
P'ee: MARSHALL, W H
G'ee: MARSHALL, W H
T-Dt: -- --- -----
P-Dt: 08 Apr 1878
Dist/Class: Fannin Preemption
File#: 1382
Patent#: 124
Patent Vol.: 7
Acres: 160
Map(s) 29, 37

Abstract # 1340 - MCDERMITT, G B
P'ee: FISHER, J S
G'ee: MCDERMIT, G B
T-Dt: -- --- -----
P-Dt: 21 May 1878
Dist/Class: Fannin Preemption
File#: 1388
Patent#: 248
Patent Vol.: 7
Acres: 160
Map(s) 38

Abstract # 1341 - MUNNERLYN, W B
P'ee: MUNNERLYN, W B
G'ee: MUNNERLYN, W B
T-Dt: -- --- -----
P-Dt: 21 May 1878
Dist/Class: Fannin Preemption
File#: 1400
Patent#: 253
Patent Vol.: 7
Acres: 160
Map(s) 30

Abstract # 1343 - MERCER, J L
P'ee: MERCER, JAMES L
G'ee: MERCER, JAMES L
T-Dt: -- --- -----
P-Dt: 21 Sep 1878
Dist/Class: Fannin Preemption
File#: 1390
Patent#: 539
Patent Vol.: 7
Acres: 160
Map(s) 38

Abstract # 1344 - MCLAINE, J

P'ee: MCLAINE, JAMES
G'ee: MCLAINE, JAMES
T-Dt: -- --- -----
P-Dt: 23 Sep 1878
Dist/Class: Fannin Preemption
File#: 1385
Patent#: 560
Patent Vol.: 7
Acres: 80
Map(s) 30

Abstract # 1345 - POITEVENT, J
S2: MAHLER, H
P'ee: MAHLER, HENRY
G'ee: MAHLER, HENRY
T-Dt: -- --- -----
P-Dt: 22 Dec 1898
Dist/Class: School
File#: 1385
Patent#: 310
Patent Vol.: 17
Certificate: 2/164
Survey/Blk/Twp: E 1/4 4 J.POITEVENT-
Acres: 160
Map(s) 23

Abstract # 1347 - BRIR
S2: MILLER, A K
P'ee: BRIM, G P
G'ee: MILLER, A K
T-Dt: -- --- -----
P-Dt: 13 May 1879
Dist/Class: School
File#: 1467
Patent#: 194
Patent Vol.: 1
Survey/Blk/Twp: 1/4 106 BRIR-
Acres: 160
Map(s) 30

Abstract # 1348 - NEFF, A A
P'ee: NEFF, A A
G'ee: NEFF, A A
T-Dt: -- --- -----
P-Dt: 22 Feb 1878
Dist/Class: Fannin Preemption
File#: 1402
Patent#: 12
Patent Vol.: 7
Acres: 160
Map(s) 37, 38

Abstract # 1349 - NOBLE, J L
P'ee: NOBLE, J L
G'ee: NOBLE, J L
T-Dt: -- --- -----
P-Dt: 21 Nov 1878
Dist/Class: Fannin Preemption
File#: 1403
Patent#: 118
Patent Vol.: 8
Acres: 160
Map(s) 31

Abstract # 1350 - NELSON, P H
P'ee: NELSON, P H
G'ee: NELSON, P H
T-Dt: -- --- -----
P-Dt: 08 Jan 1890
Dist/Class: School
File#: 1387
Patent#: 612
Patent Vol.: 9
Certificate: 16/75
Survey/Blk/Twp: E 1/4 4 SP-

Acres: 160
Map(s) 35

Abstract # 1351 - HARMON, J
G'ee: POSERN, G ANTON
T-Dt: -- --- -----
P-Dt: -- --- -----
Dist/Class: School
File#: 1388
Certificate: 864
Survey/Blk/Twp: NW 1/4 2 T & NO-
Acres: 160
Map(s) 30, 31

Abstract # 1352 - ROSS, L W
P'ee: MOSELEY, WILLIAM
G'ee: ROSS, LEROY W
T-Dt: -- --- -----
P-Dt: 01 Jan 1879
Dist/Class: Fannin 1st
File#: 1858
Patent#: 579
Patent Vol.: 22
Acres: 415.97
Map(s) 7

Abstract # 1353 - RIBBLE, L J
P'ee: RIBBLE, E J
G'ee: RIBBLE, E J
T-Dt: -- --- -----
P-Dt: 11 Jun 1878
Dist/Class: Fannin Preemption
File#: 1417
Patent#: 294
Patent Vol.: 7
Acres: 160
Map(s) 38

Abstract # 1354 - REEDER , T P
P'ee: REEDER, T P
G'ee: REEDER, T P
T-Dt: -- --- -----
P-Dt: 14 Jun 1878
Dist/Class: Fannin Preemption
File#: 1413
Patent#: 306
Patent Vol.: 7
Acres: 80
Map(s) 39

Abstract # 1355 - SANDERSON, J
P'ee: MOSELEY, G W
G'ee: SANDERSON, JOHN
T-Dt: -- --- -----
P-Dt: 14 Nov 1878
Dist/Class: Fannin Preemption
File#: 1423
Patent#: 78
Patent Vol.: 8
Acres: 80
Map(s) 37

Abstract # 1356 - POITEVENT, J
S2: SCHLITTLER, J
P'ee: SCHLITTLER, JACOB
G'ee: SCHLITTLER, JACOB
T-Dt: -- --- -----
P-Dt: 05 Sep 1891
Dist/Class: School
File#: 1389
Patent#: 769
Patent Vol.: 12
Certificate: 2/163
Survey/Blk/Twp: N 1/4 2 J.POITEVENT-
Acres: 147

Map(s) 23

Abstract # 1357 - TE&L CO
P'ee: TEXAS EMIGRATION AND LAND
COMPANY
G'ee: TEXAS EMIGRATION AND LAND
COMPANY
T-Dt: -- --- -----
P-Dt: 18 Aug 1858
Dist/Class: Texas Emmigration and Land
Company
File#: 1393
Patent#: 240
Patent Vol.: 20
Certificate: 1393
Survey/Blk/Twp: 1393
Acres: 367
Map(s) 5, 6

Abstract # 1358 - TACKILL, J G
P'ee: SATCHELL, WILLIAM
G'ee: TACKITT, J G
T-Dt: -- --- -----
P-Dt: 01 Oct 1878
Dist/Class: Fannin Preemption
File#: 1431
Patent#: 568
Patent Vol.: 7
Acres: 160
Map(s) 30

Abstract # 1359 - WHITTENBURG, J C
P'ee: WHITTENBURG, J A
G'ee: WHITTENBURG, J C
T-Dt: -- --- -----
P-Dt: 25 Jun 1878
Dist/Class: Fannin Preemption
File#: 1448
Patent#: 326
Patent Vol.: 7
Acres: 80
Map(s) 38

Abstract # 1360 - ABERNATHY, J
P'ee: HUMPHRIES, CHARLES
G'ee: ABERNATHY, J
T-Dt: -- --- -----
P-Dt: 28 Feb 1879
Dist/Class: Fannin Preemption
File#: 2030
Patent#: 421
Patent Vol.: 8
Acres: 160
Map(s) 39

Abstract # 1361 - AKERS, N J
P'ee: STEWART, SARAH A
G'ee: AKERS, W J
T-Dt: -- --- -----
P-Dt: 21 Jun 1884
Dist/Class: Fannin Preemption
File#: 2017
Patent#: 619
Patent Vol.: 15
Acres: 160
Map(s) 22, 30

Abstract # 1362 - ADAMS, J P
P'ee: ADAMS, J P
G'ee: ADAMS, J P
T-Dt: -- --- -----
P-Dt: 26 Aug 1880
Dist/Class: Fannin Preemption
File#: 2003
Patent#: 155

Patent Vol.: 11
Acres: 160
Map(s) 16

Abstract # 1363 - AKERS, W A J
P'ee: TOWNSEND, J C
G'ee: AKERS, W A J
T-Dt: -- --- -----
P-Dt: 24 Apr 1880
Dist/Class: Fannin Preemption
File#: 2216
Patent#: 470
Patent Vol.: 10
Acres: 160
Map(s) 35, 36

Abstract # 1364 - ADAMS, W C
P'ee: ADAMS, W C
G'ee: ADAMS, W C
T-Dt: -- --- -----
P-Dt: 05 Sep 1883
Dist/Class: Fannin Preemption
File#: 1804
Patent#: 571
Patent Vol.: 14
Acres: 160
Map(s) 8

Abstract # 1365 - ANDERSON, R G
P'ee: ANDERSON, R G
G'ee: ANDERSON, R G
T-Dt: -- --- -----
P-Dt: 28 Mar 1881
Dist/Class: Fannin Preemption
File#: 1912
Patent#: 130
Patent Vol.: 12
Acres: 80
Map(s) 33

Abstract # 1366 - BRIR
S2: ASH, G H
P'ee: ASH, G H
G'ee: ASH, G H
T-Dt: -- --- -----
P-Dt: 02 Dec 1882
Dist/Class: Fannin Preemption
File#: 2039
Patent#: 53
Patent Vol.: 14
Survey/Blk/Twp: 121 BRIR-
Acres: 160
Map(s) 29

Abstract # 1367 - BRIR
S2: ALLEN, J B
P'ee: HEATH, GENEVA J (MRS)
G'ee: ALLEN, J B
T-Dt: -- --- -----
P-Dt: 26 Aug 1881
Dist/Class: Fannin Preemption
File#: 2038
Patent#: 456
Patent Vol.: 12
Survey/Blk/Twp: 105 BRIR-
Acres: 160
Map(s) 30

Abstract # 1368 - ADAMS, M V B
P'ee: RICHARDSON, JAMES R
G'ee: ADAMS, MARTIN V B
T-Dt: -- --- -----
P-Dt: 24 Dec 1879
Dist/Class: Fannin Preemption
File#: 1579

Patent#: 130
Patent Vol.: 10
Acres: 160
Map(s) 7

Abstract # 1369 - AB&M
P'ee: SHANAFELT, H C AND MILLS, C H
G'ee: ADAMS, BEATY AND MOULTON
T-Dt: -- --- -----
P-Dt: 15 May 1879
Dist/Class: Fannin Scrip
File#: 11043
Patent#: 641
Patent Vol.: 31
Certificate: 798
Survey/Blk/Twp: 11
Acres: 320
Map(s) 24, 32

Abstract # 1370 - AB&M
P'ee: GANT, A B
G'ee: ADAMS, BEATY AND MOULTON
T-Dt: -- --- -----
P-Dt: 08 May 1918
Dist/Class: Fannin Scrip
File#: 11043
Patent#: 174
Patent Vol.: 39
Certificate: 798
Survey/Blk/Twp: 7
Acres: 320
Map(s) 23, 24, 32

Abstract # 1371 - BRADLEY, HRS J
P'ee: BRADLEY, JAMES (HEIRS)
G'ee: BRADLEY, JAMES (HEIRS OF)
T-Dt: -- --- -----
P-Dt: 12 Apr 1880
Dist/Class: Fannin Bounty
File#: 1536
Patent#: 126
Patent Vol.: 16
Certificate: 29/235
Acres: 160
Map(s) 34

Abstract # 1374 - BRIR
S2: BYRD, W B
P'ee: BYRD, W E
G'ee: BYRD, W E
T-Dt: -- --- -----
P-Dt: 14 Jul 1879
Dist/Class: Fannin Preemption
File#: 2041
Patent#: 200
Patent Vol.: 9
Survey/Blk/Twp: 63
Acres: 80
Map(s) 37

Abstract # 1375 - BUNGER, S
P'ee: BECKHAM, CHARLES
G'ee: BURGER, SAMUEL
T-Dt: -- --- -----
P-Dt: 23 Dec 1901
Dist/Class: Fannin Preemption
File#: 2006
Patent#: 187
Patent Vol.: 32
Acres: 122.50
Map(s) 9

Abstract # 1376 - BAKER, W H
P'ee: BAKER, JOHN W

G'ee: BAKER, W H
T-Dt: -- --- -----
P-Dt: 22 Jan 1887
Dist/Class: Fannin Preemption
File#: 2005
Patent#: 254
Patent Vol.: 19
Acres: 160
Map(s) 28

Abstract # 1377 - BAKER, J W
P'ee: BAKER, T J
G'ee: BAKER, J W
T-Dt: -- --- -----
P-Dt: 15 Jan 1886
Dist/Class: Fannin Preemption
File#: 2004
Patent#: 27
Patent Vol.: 18
Acres: 150
Map(s) 28, 29

Abstract # 1378 - BLACKWOOD, J L
P'ee: BEACKWOOD, J L
G'ee: BEACKWOOD, J L
T-Dt: -- --- -----
P-Dt: 30 Jan 1882
Dist/Class: Fannin Preemption
File#: 2130
Patent#: 100
Patent Vol.: 13
Acres: 114
Map(s) 28, 29, 37

Abstract # 1379 - BEMUN, J S
P'ee: BEEMAN, J S
G'ee: BEEMAN, J S
T-Dt: -- --- -----
P-Dt: 18 Oct 1887
Dist/Class: Fannin Preemption
File#: 2129
Patent#: 230
Patent Vol.: 20
Acres: 62.75
Map(s) 33

Abstract # 1380 - BRAGG, G B
P'ee: BRAGG, GEORGE
G'ee: BRAGG, GEORGE
T-Dt: -- --- -----
P-Dt: 09 Apr 1881
Dist/Class: Fannin Preemption
File#: 2217
Patent#: 162
Patent Vol.: 12
Acres: 160
Map(s) 34, 42

Abstract # 1381 - BURNET, J W
P'ee: BURNETT, J W
G'ee: BURNETT, J W
T-Dt: -- --- -----
P-Dt: 18 Nov 1885
Dist/Class: Fannin Preemption
File#: 2279
Patent#: 540
Patent Vol.: 17
Acres: 160
Map(s) 27, 35

Abstract # 1382 - BLAINE, R A
P'ee: BLAINE, R A (HEIRS)
G'ee: BLAINE, R A
T-Dt: -- --- -----
P-Dt: 21 Dec 1880

Dist/Class: Fannin Preemption
File#: 1913
Patent#: 471
Patent Vol.: 11
Acres: 80
Map(s) 28, 36

Abstract # 1383 - BRIR
S2: BYRD, W A
P'ee: BYRD, WILLIAM A
G'ee: BYRD, WILLIAM A
T-Dt: -- --- -----
P-Dt: 12 Feb 1880
Dist/Class: Fannin Preemption
File#: 2040
Patent#: 254
Patent Vol.: 10
Survey/Blk/Twp: 53 BRIR-
Acres: 160
Map(s) 38

Abstract # 1384 - BUSSELL, B F
P'ee: SUMMERS, R M
G'ee: BUSSELL, B F
T-Dt: -- --- -----
P-Dt: 09 Dec 1879
Dist/Class: Fannin Preemption
File#: 1304
Patent#: 71
Patent Vol.: 10
Acres: 80
Map(s) 29

Abstract # 1385 - BBB&C RR CO
S2: BLAKEY, W C
P'ee: HOLT, J A
G'ee: BLAKEY, W C
T-Dt: -- --- -----
P-Dt: 20 Nov 1907
Dist/Class: School
File#: 1774
Patent#: 294
Patent Vol.: 35
Certificate: 683
Survey/Blk/Twp: SE 1/4 2 BBB & C-
Acres: 160
Map(s) 15

Abstract # 1386 - BBB&C RR CO
S2: BLAKEY, C B
P'ee: HAWKINS, L B
G'ee: BLAKEY, C B
T-Dt: -- --- -----
P-Dt: 11 Jun 1924
Dist/Class: School
File#: 1773
Patent#: 30
Patent Vol.: 23A
Certificate: 683
Survey/Blk/Twp: E 1/2 OF SW 1/4 2 BBB & C-
Acres: 80
Map(s) 15

Abstract # 1389 - CUNNINGHAM, R A
P'ee: CARTWRIGHT, MONROE
G'ee: CUNNINGHAM, R A
T-Dt: -- --- -----
P-Dt: 09 Apr 1879
Dist/Class: Fannin Preemption
File#: 1320
Patent#: 561
Patent Vol.: 8
Acres: 80
Map(s) 37

Abstract # 1390 - COLTHARP, E S
P'ee: COLTHARP, E S
G'ee: COLTHARP, E S
T-Dt: -- --- -----
P-Dt: 26 May 1879
Dist/Class: Fannin Preemption
File#: 1312
Patent#: 64
Patent Vol.: 9
Acres: 160
Map(s) 29

Abstract # 1391 - CRUMPTON, W A
P'ee: MANN, B F
G'ee: CRUMPTON, W A
T-Dt: -- --- -----
P-Dt: 20 Jun 1879
Dist/Class: Fannin Preemption
File#: 1019
Patent#: 149
Patent Vol.: 9
Acres: 160
Map(s) 39, 40

Abstract # 1392 - CHILDRESS, W
P'ee: ROBINSON, E AND ROBINSON, S A
G'ee: CHILDRESS, W
T-Dt: -- --- -----
P-Dt: 14 Mar 1884
Dist/Class: Fannin Preemption
File#: 2008
Patent#: 314
Patent Vol.: 15
Acres: 82
Map(s) 40

Abstract # 1393 - CANTWELL, W
P'ee: CANTWELL, WILLIAM
G'ee: CANTWELL, WILLIAM
T-Dt: -- --- -----
P-Dt: 02 Jan 1880
Dist/Class: Fannin Preemption
File#: 2007
Patent#: 137
Patent Vol.: 10
Acres: 160
Map(s) 7

Abstract # 1395 - CRISWELL, C T
P'ee: CRISWELL, O T (HEIRS)
G'ee: CRISWELL, O T
T-Dt: -- --- -----
P-Dt: 31 Mar 1879
Dist/Class: Fannin Preemption
File#: 2133
Patent#: 534
Patent Vol.: 8
Acres: 160
Map(s) 38, 39

Abstract # 1396 - COX, J
P'ee: COX, JESSE
G'ee: COX, JESSE
T-Dt: -- --- -----
P-Dt: 28 Mar 1881
Dist/Class: Fannin Preemption
File#: 2132
Patent#: 129
Patent Vol.: 12
Acres: 160
Map(s) 33

Abstract # 1397 - CRYSP, G
P'ee: WILLIAMS, NANCY

G'ee: CRYSP, GREEN
T-Dt: -- --- -----
P-Dt: 29 Apr 1884
Dist/Class: Fannin Preemption
File#: 2141
Patent#: 395
Patent Vol.: 15
Acres: 80
Map(s) 33, 41

Abstract # 1398 - CATES, J
P'ee: MCCAN, J S
G'ee: CATES, JOHN
T-Dt: -- --- -----
P-Dt: 10 Oct 1888
Dist/Class: Fannin Preemption
File#: 2218
Patent#: 280
Patent Vol.: 21
Acres: 80
Map(s) 27

Abstract # 1399 - CHILDRESS, W
P'ee: BROWN, L A AND BROWN, J C
G'ee: CHILDRESS, W
T-Dt: -- --- -----
P-Dt: 27 Mar 1884
Dist/Class: Fannin Preemption
File#: 1805
Patent#: 353
Patent Vol.: 15
Acres: 138
Map(s) 40

Abstract # 1400 - COTHRAN, J C
P'ee: RUSSELL, F G
G'ee: COTHRAN, JOHN
T-Dt: -- --- -----
P-Dt: 10 May 1880
Dist/Class: Fannin Preemption
File#: 1914
Patent#: 517
Patent Vol.: 10
Acres: 160
Map(s) 34

Abstract # 1401 - COTHRAN, G
P'ee: COTHRAN, GEORGE
G'ee: COTHRAN, GEORGE
T-Dt: -- --- -----
P-Dt: 21 May 1881
Dist/Class: Fannin Preemption
File#: 1980
Patent#: 270
Patent Vol.: 12
Acres: 160
Map(s) 36

Abstract # 1402 - CASE, MRS M
P'ee: TIDWELL, W J
G'ee: CASE, M (MRS)
T-Dt: -- --- -----
P-Dt: 26 May 1880
Dist/Class: Fannin Preemption
File#: 1967
Patent#: 555
Patent Vol.: 10
Acres: 160
Map(s) 31

Abstract # 1403 - COCKRELL, T J
P'ee: DUNLAP, JOHN Q
G'ee: COCKRELL, T J
T-Dt: -- --- -----
P-Dt: 08 Dec 1879

Dist/Class: Fannin Preemption
File#: 1309
Patent#: 65
Patent Vol.: 10
Acres: 80
Map(s) 29, 30

Abstract # 1404 - COFFMAN, E M
P'ee: COFFMAN, E M
G'ee: COFFMAN, E M
T-Dt: -- --- -----
P-Dt: 17 Dec 1879
Dist/Class: Fannin Preemption
File#: 1311
Patent#: 104
Patent Vol.: 10
Acres: 80
Map(s) 37

Abstract # 1405 - COOK, J R
P'ee: CROUCH, E H
G'ee: COOKE, J R
T-Dt: -- --- -----
P-Dt: 08 Oct 1880
Dist/Class: Fannin Preemption
File#: 2131
Patent#: 291
Patent Vol.: 11
Acres: 153
Map(s) 7

Abstract # 1406 - DUDNEY, B F
P'ee: DUDNEY, B F
G'ee: DUDNEY, B F
T-Dt: -- --- -----
P-Dt: 19 Mar 1879
Dist/Class: Fannin Preemption
File#: 1600
Patent#: 489
Patent Vol.: 8
Acres: 160
Map(s) 30

Abstract # 1410 - BRIR
S2: DAUGHERTY, W
P'ee: STAFFORD, W E
G'ee: DAUGHERTY, WILLIAM
T-Dt: -- --- -----
P-Dt: 26 Mar 1884
Dist/Class: Fannin Preemption
File#: 2135
Patent#: 350
Patent Vol.: 15
Survey/Blk/Twp: 9 BRIR-
Acres: 160
Map(s) 37

Abstract # 1412 - DEWITT, M
P'ee: HARRIS, DAVID
G'ee: DEWITT, MATILDA
T-Dt: -- --- -----
P-Dt: 05 Nov 1883
Dist/Class: Fannin Preemption
File#: 2220
Patent#: 29
Patent Vol.: 15
Acres: 160
Map(s) 34

Abstract # 1413 - DANIEL, S N
P'ee: HUMPHREYS, J A
G'ee: DANIEL, S N
T-Dt: -- --- -----
P-Dt: 23 Jun 1884
Dist/Class: Fannin Preemption

File#: 2219
Patent#: 625
Patent Vol.: 15
Acres: 160
Map(s) 34, 42

Abstract # 1415 - DANIEL, M L
P'ee: DANIEL, M L
G'ee: DANIEL, M L
T-Dt: -- --- -----
P-Dt: 21 Feb 1884
Dist/Class: Fannin Preemption
File#: 1915
Patent#: 272
Patent Vol.: 15
Acres: 160
Map(s) 34

Abstract # 1416 - BRIR
S2: DOBBS, M
P'ee: DOBBS, M
G'ee: DOBBS, M
T-Dt: -- --- -----
P-Dt: 09 Jun 1880
Dist/Class: Fannin Preemption
File#: 2043
Patent#: 579
Patent Vol.: 10
Survey/Blk/Twp: 109 BRIR-
Acres: 150.60
Map(s) 29, 30

Abstract # 1417 - BRIR
S2: DIEW, F M
P'ee: NEWBY, JOHN H
G'ee: DIEW, F M
T-Dt: -- --- -----
P-Dt: 03 Mar 1879
Dist/Class: Fannin Preemption
File#: 2042
Patent#: 426
Patent Vol.: 8
Survey/Blk/Twp: 3 BRIR-
Acres: 160
Map(s) 38, 46

Abstract # 1418 - AB&M
S2: DAVIDSON, J H
P'ee: ANDERSON, R M
G'ee: DAVIDSON, J H
T-Dt: -- --- -----
P-Dt: 24 Sep 1884
Dist/Class: School
File#: 1907
Patent#: 146
Patent Vol.: 4
Certificate: 417
Survey/Blk/Twp: SW 1/4 2 AB & M-
Acres: 160
Map(s) 40

Abstract # 1419 - ELDER, MRS C
P'ee: MAGILL, GEORGE W
G'ee: ELDER, CHRISTIANA (MRS)
T-Dt: -- --- -----
P-Dt: 24 Apr 1879
Dist/Class: Fannin Preemption
File#: 1328
Patent#: 610
Patent Vol.: 8
Acres: 160
Map(s) 37

Abstract # 1420 - EDDLEMAN, R C
P'ee: EDDLEMAN, R C

G'ee: EDDLEMAN, R C
T-Dt: -- --- -----
P-Dt: 10 Jun 1879
Dist/Class: Fannin Preemption
File#: 1327
Patent#: 113
Patent Vol.: 9
Acres: 160
Map(s) 37, 38

Abstract # 1421 - ELMORE, J L
P'ee: ELMORE, J L
G'ee: ELMORE, J L
T-Dt: -- --- -----
P-Dt: 05 Dec 1881
Dist/Class: Fannin Preemption
File#: 2138
Patent#: 13
Patent Vol.: 13
Acres: 160
Map(s) 7

Abstract # 1422 - EDWARDS, W W
P'ee: EDWARDS, W W
G'ee: EDWARDS, W W
T-Dt: -- --- -----
P-Dt: 08 Feb 1886
Dist/Class: Fannin Preemption
File#: 2137
Patent#: 99
Patent Vol.: 18
Acres: 160
Map(s) 36

Abstract # 1423 - EWING, G
P'ee: WILLIAMS, IRA E M
G'ee: EWING, GRAFFUS
T-Dt: -- --- -----
P-Dt: 23 Jun 1879
Dist/Class: Fannin Preemption
File#: 2299
Patent#: 147
Patent Vol.: 9
Acres: 80
Map(s) 32

Abstract # 1424 - EL&RR RR CO
P'ee: WILLIAMS, LUKE
G'ee: EAST LINE AND RED RIVER
RAILROAD COMPANY
T-Dt: -- --- -----
P-Dt: 21 Aug 1879
Dist/Class: Fannin Scrip
File#: 12808
Patent#: 604
Patent Vol.: 45
Certificate: 162
Survey/Blk/Twp: 1
Acres: 226.20
Map(s) 6

Abstract # 1425 - FRANKLIN, D D
P'ee: THOMAS, D P
G'ee: FRANKLIN, D D
T-Dt: -- --- -----
P-Dt: 05 May 1879
Dist/Class: Fannin Preemption
File#: 1339
Patent#: 6
Patent Vol.: 9
Acres: 160
Map(s) 29

Abstract # 1426 - FULLER, M A
P'ee: FULLER, M A

G'ee: FULLER, M A
T-Dt: -- --- -----
P-Dt: 07 Jun 1879
Dist/Class: Fannin Preemption
File#: 1496
Patent#: 107
Patent Vol.: 9
Acres: 160
Map(s) 28

Abstract # 1427 - FOWLER, T
P'ee: FOWLER, TONEY
G'ee: FOWLER, TONEY
T-Dt: -- --- -----
P-Dt: 21 May 1879
Dist/Class: Fannin Preemption
File#: 1020
Patent#: 58
Patent Vol.: 9
Acres: 160
Map(s) 39

Abstract # 1428 - FREEMAN, W H
P'ee: FREEMAN, W H
G'ee: FREEMAN, W H
T-Dt: -- --- -----
P-Dt: 19 Jun 1880
Dist/Class: Fannin Preemption
File#: 2013
Patent#: 629
Patent Vol.: 10
Acres: 160
Map(s) 39

Abstract # 1429 - FRANKLIN, J B
P'ee: HODGES, W J
G'ee: FRANKLIN, J B
T-Dt: -- --- -----
P-Dt: 08 Sep 1883
Dist/Class: Fannin Preemption
File#: 2011
Patent#: 592
Patent Vol.: 14
Acres: 80
Map(s) 7

Abstract # 1430 - BRIR
S2: FITCHETT, W H
P'ee: FITCHETT, W H
G'ee: FITCHETT, W H
T-Dt: -- --- -----
P-Dt: 16 Jul 1895
Dist/Class: Fannin Preemption
File#: 2044
Patent#: 558
Patent Vol.: 27
Survey/Blk/Twp: 65 BRIR-
Acres: 145.6
Map(s) 37

Abstract # 1431 - FIELDS, J
P'ee: JONES, W P
G'ee: FIELDS, JOSEPH
T-Dt: -- --- -----
P-Dt: 21 Sep 1883
Dist/Class: Fannin Preemption
File#: 1983
Patent#: 621
Patent Vol.: 14
Acres: 160
Map(s) 35

Abstract # 1432 - FITCHETT, W W
P'ee: FITCHETT, W H
G'ee: FITCHETT, W H

T-Dt: -- --- -----
P-Dt: 05 Jan 1884
Dist/Class: Fannin Preemption
File#: 2260
Patent#: 170
Patent Vol.: 15
Acres: 160
Map(s) 7

Abstract # 1433 - FOSTER, MRS E
P'ee: FOSTER, ELIZABETH (MRS)
G'ee: FOSTER, ELIZABETH (MRS)
T-Dt: -- --- -----
P-Dt: 08 Aug 1883
Dist/Class: Fannin Preemption
File#: 2139
Patent#: 424
Patent Vol.: 14
Acres: 160
Map(s) 34

Abstract # 1434 - GLASGOW, G W
P'ee: GLASGOW, GEORGE W
G'ee: GLASGOW, GEORGE W
T-Dt: -- --- -----
P-Dt: 03 Mar 1879
Dist/Class: Fannin Preemption
File#: 1664
Patent#: 430
Patent Vol.: 8
Acres: 160
Map(s) 21

Abstract # 1435 - GOORL, H A
P'ee: WOOD, G O
G'ee: GOURLEY, HENRY A
T-Dt: -- --- -----
P-Dt: 05 May 1885
Dist/Class: Fannin Preemption
File#: 2140
Patent#: 163
Patent Vol.: 17
Acres: 160
Map(s) 34

Abstract # 1436 - GOLDEN, E
P'ee: GOLDEN, E
G'ee: GOLDEN, E
T-Dt: -- --- -----
P-Dt: 21 Dec 1880
Dist/Class: Fannin Preemption
File#: 1934
Patent#: 472
Patent Vol.: 11
Acres: 160
Map(s) 31

Abstract # 1437 - GLASS, T J
P'ee: GLASS, T J
G'ee: GLASS, T J
T-Dt: -- --- -----
P-Dt: 13 Nov 1977
Dist/Class: Fannin Preemption
File#: 1918
Patent#: 272
Patent Vol.: 43-B
Acres: 160.00
Map(s) 33, 41

Abstract # 1438 - GLASS, H K
P'ee: GLASS, H K
G'ee: GLASS, H K
T-Dt: -- --- -----
P-Dt: 28 Mar 1881
Dist/Class: Fannin Preemption

File#: 1917
Patent#: 134
Patent Vol.: 12
Acres: 160
Map(s) 33

Abstract # 1439 - GILFOIL, J
P'ee: GILFOIL, JOHN SR
G'ee: GILFOIL, JOHN SR
T-Dt: -- --- -----
P-Dt: 12 Jan 1880
Dist/Class: Fannin Preemption
File#: 1916
Patent#: 179
Patent Vol.: 10
Acres: 160
Map(s) 34

Abstract # 1440 - BRIR
S2: GASS, R B
P'ee: BIRDWELL, J M
G'ee: GASS, R B
T-Dt: -- --- -----
P-Dt: 15 Oct 1886
Dist/Class: Fannin Preemption
File#: 2045
Patent#: 15
Patent Vol.: 19
Survey/Blk/Twp: 91 BRIR-
Acres: 160
Map(s) 31

Abstract # 1442 - HARKNESS, J A
P'ee: OWEN, ALBERT
G'ee: HARKNESS, J A
T-Dt: -- --- -----
P-Dt: 10 Jun 1879
Dist/Class: Fannin Preemption
File#: 1350
Patent#: 112
Patent Vol.: 9
Acres: 160
Map(s) 37, 38

Abstract # 1443 - HART, S A
P'ee: HART, GABRIEL
G'ee: HART, STEPHEN A
T-Dt: -- --- -----
P-Dt: 26 Jun 1879
Dist/Class: Fannin Preemption
File#: 1919
Patent#: 160
Patent Vol.: 9
Acres: 160
Map(s) 34

Abstract # 1444 - HILL, G W
P'ee: REID, BENJAMIN F
G'ee: HILL, GEORGE W
T-Dt: -- --- -----
P-Dt: 25 Jun 1879
Dist/Class: Fannin Preemption
File#: 1826
Patent#: 157
Patent Vol.: 9
Acres: 160
Map(s) 35, 36

Abstract # 1445 - HUBER, B
P'ee: HUBER, BERNHARD
G'ee: HUBER, BERNHARD
T-Dt: -- --- -----
P-Dt: 01 May 1880
Dist/Class: Fannin Preemption
File#: 2015

Patent#: 480
Patent Vol.: 10
Acres: 160
Map(s) 16

Abstract # 1446 - HARMON, M
P'ee: LYLES, R H
G'ee: HARMON, MARTIN
T-Dt: -- --- -----
P-Dt: 30 Aug 1884
Dist/Class: Fannin Preemption
File#: 2014
Patent#: 203
Patent Vol.: 16
Acres: 80
Map(s) 6

Abstract # 1447 - HUGHES, W J
P'ee: HUGHES, W J
G'ee: HUGHES, W J
T-Dt: -- --- -----
P-Dt: 16 Sep 1881
Dist/Class: Fannin Preemption
File#: 2148
Patent#: 507
Patent Vol.: 12
Acres: 160
Map(s) 34, 42

Abstract # 1448 - HOWARD, H J
P'ee: YANCY, C D
G'ee: HOWARD, H J
T-Dt: -- --- -----
P-Dt: 22 Oct 1888
Dist/Class: Fannin Preemption
File#: 2147
Patent#: 313
Patent Vol.: 21
Acres: 70.80
Map(s) 35, 43

Abstract # 1450 - HENDERSON, H T
P'ee: HENDERSON, H T
G'ee: HENDERSON, H T
T-Dt: -- --- -----
P-Dt: 04 May 1880
Dist/Class: Fannin Preemption
File#: 2145
Patent#: 495
Patent Vol.: 10
Acres: 160
Map(s) 33, 41

Abstract # 1452 - BRIR
S2: HALL, W R
P'ee: HALL, W R
G'ee: HALL, W R
T-Dt: -- --- -----
P-Dt: 13 May 1885
Dist/Class: Fannin Preemption
File#: 2143
Patent#: 180
Patent Vol.: 17
Survey/Blk/Twp: 5 BRIR-
Acres: 160
Map(s) 38, 46

Abstract # 1453 - BRIR
S2: HALL, M
P'ee: HALL, MARGARET (MRS)
G'ee: HALL, MARGARET (MRS)
T-Dt: -- --- -----
P-Dt: 25 Apr 1922
Dist/Class: Fannin Preemption
File#: 2142

Patent#: 443
Patent Vol.: 13A
Survey/Blk/Twp: 37 BRIR-
Acres: 211.27
Map(s) 37, 38

Abstract # 1454 - HEWITT, R
P'ee: HEWITT, ROBERT
G'ee: HEWITT, ROBERT
T-Dt: -- --- -----
P-Dt: 23 Jun 1884
Dist/Class: Fannin Preemption
File#: 2222
Patent#: 630
Patent Vol.: 15
Acres: 148.67
Map(s) 33, 41

Abstract # 1455 - BRIR
S2: HARMON, C
P'ee: HARMON, CALVIN
G'ee: HARMON, CALVIN
T-Dt: -- --- -----
P-Dt: 26 Mar 1879
Dist/Class: Fannin Preemption
File#: 2046
Patent#: 525
Patent Vol.: 8
Survey/Blk/Twp: 95 BRIR-
Acres: 160
Map(s) 30, 31

Abstract # 1456 - BBB&C RR CO
S2: HUNT, I
P'ee: HUNT, IRA
G'ee: HUNT, IRA
T-Dt: -- --- -----
P-Dt: 28 May 1912
Dist/Class: School
File#: 1798
Patent#: 262
Patent Vol.: 44
Certificate: 683
Survey/Blk/Twp: NE 1/4 2 BBB & CRR-
Acres: 160
Map(s) 15

Abstract # 1457 - T&NO RR CO
S2: HODGES, W J
P'ee: KNIGHT, F M
G'ee: HODGES, W J
T-Dt: -- --- -----
P-Dt: 14 Nov 1906
Dist/Class: School
File#: 1808
Patent#: 627
Patent Vol.: 32
Certificate: 861
Survey/Blk/Twp: SE 1/4 6 T & NO-
Acres: 160
Map(s) 29

Abstract # 1458 - I&GN RR CO
P'ee: GANT, A B
G'ee: HOUSTON AND GREAT
NORTHERN RAILROAD COMPANY
T-Dt: -- --- -----
P-Dt: 23 Nov 1881
Dist/Class: Fannin Scrip
File#: 12184
Patent#: 327
Patent Vol.: 66
Certificate: 1703
Survey/Blk/Twp: 99
Acres: 32.50

Map(s) 39, 47

Abstract # 1459 - I&GN RR CO
P'ee: GANT, A B
G'ee: HOUSTON AND GREAT
NORTHERN RAILROAD COMPANY
T-Dt: -- --- -----
P-Dt: 08 Feb 1887
Dist/Class: Fannin Scrip
File#: 12184
Patent#: 341
Patent Vol.: 93
Certificate: 1703
Survey/Blk/Twp: 101
Acres: 192.50
Map(s) 36

Abstract # 1460 - I&GN RR CO
P'ee: GRAHAM, G A
G'ee: HOUSTON AND GREAT
NORTHERN RAILROAD COMPANY
T-Dt: -- --- -----
P-Dt: 23 Nov 1881
Dist/Class: Fannin Scrip
File#: 12019
Patent#: 328
Patent Vol.: 66
Certificate: 1703
Acres: 400
Map(s) 29, 30

Abstract # 1461 - I&GN RR CO
P'ee: JONES, MORGAN
G'ee: HOUSTON AND GREAT
NORTHERN RAILROAD COMPANY
T-Dt: -- --- -----
P-Dt: 05 Oct 1893
Dist/Class: Fannin Scrip
File#: 12018
Patent#: 14
Patent Vol.: 112
Certificate: 174
Acres: 274
Map(s) 22, 29, 30

Abstract # 1462 - I&GN RR CO
P'ee: JONES, MORGAN
G'ee: HOUSTON AND GREAT
NORTHERN RAILROAD COMPANY
T-Dt: -- --- -----
P-Dt: 03 Dec 1879
Dist/Class: Fannin Scrip
File#: 12018
Patent#: 28
Patent Vol.: 54
Certificate: 174
Acres: 216
Map(s) 20

Abstract # 1463 - JEFFERY, S R
P'ee: TAYLOR, ANDREW
G'ee: JEFFREY, SIDNEY R
T-Dt: -- --- -----
P-Dt: 03 Feb 1879
Dist/Class: Fannin Preemption
File#: 1018
Patent#: 320
Patent Vol.: 8
Acres: 80
Map(s) 21

Abstract # 1464 - JACKSON, J D
P'ee: CLELLEN, ROBERT
G'ee: JACKSON, J D
T-Dt: -- --- -----

P-Dt: 15 Aug 1879
Dist/Class: Fannin Preemption
File#: 1588
Patent#: 309
Patent Vol.: 9
Acres: 160
Map(s) 35

Abstract # 1465 - JAMES, S H
P'ee: JAMES, S H
G'ee: JAMES, S H
T-Dt: -- --- -----
P-Dt: 28 Mar 1881
Dist/Class: Fannin Preemption
File#: 2016
Patent#: 133
Patent Vol.: 12
Acres: 160
Map(s) 39

Abstract # 1466 - JORDAN, T J
P'ee: DOZIER, SEABORN
G'ee: JORDAN, THOMAS J
T-Dt: -- --- -----
P-Dt: 24 Mar 1882
Dist/Class: Fannin Preemption
File#: 2149
Patent#: 220
Patent Vol.: 13
Acres: 140.7
Map(s) 28

Abstract # 1467 - JONES, J
P'ee: JAMES, JOHN
G'ee: JAMES, JOHN
T-Dt: -- --- -----
P-Dt: 18 Feb 1884
Dist/Class: Fannin Preemption
File#: 2223
Patent#: 247
Patent Vol.: 15
Acres: 160
Map(s) 34, 42

Abstract # 1468 - JONES, J H B
P'ee: JONES, J H B
G'ee: JONES, J H B
T-Dt: -- --- -----
P-Dt: 26 Aug 1879
Dist/Class: Fannin Preemption
File#: 1615
Patent#: 342
Patent Vol.: 9
Acres: 80
Map(s) 20

Abstract # 1469 - JONES, R G
P'ee: DAVIDSON, J W
G'ee: JONES, R G
T-Dt: -- --- -----
P-Dt: 27 Feb 1880
Dist/Class: Fannin Preemption
File#: 1809
Patent#: 300
Patent Vol.: 10
Acres: 80
Map(s) 6

Abstract # 1470 - KING, B C
P'ee: KING, B C
G'ee: KING, B C
T-Dt: -- --- -----
P-Dt: 27 Jul 1883
Dist/Class: Fannin Preemption
File#: 2150

Patent#: 351
Patent Vol.: 14
Acres: 160
Map(s) 16

Abstract # 1471 - BRIR
S2: KIRKPATRICK, R
P'ee: JONES, I H
G'ee: KIRKPATRICK, REID
T-Dt: -- --- -----
P-Dt: 06 Jan 1880
Dist/Class: Fannin Preemption
File#: 2103
Patent#: 162
Patent Vol.: 10
Survey/Blk/Twp: 61 BRIR-
Acres: 90.6
Map(s) 37

Abstract # 1472 - KEMBLE, J H
P'ee: KEMBLE, J H
G'ee: KEMBLE, J H
T-Dt: -- --- -----
P-Dt: 02 Jan 1880
Dist/Class: Fannin Preemption
File#: 1810
Patent#: 131
Patent Vol.: 10
Acres: 160
Map(s) 6, 7

Abstract # 1473 - KIMMEL, E C
P'ee: STEVENS, GEORGE B
G'ee: KIMMEL, E C
T-Dt: -- --- -----
P-Dt: 30 Mar 1880
Dist/Class: Fannin Preemption
File#: 1935
Patent#: 405
Patent Vol.: 10
Acres: 60.73
Map(s) 22

Abstract # 1474 - KEARBY, W C
P'ee: EDDLEMAN, W H
G'ee: KEARBY, W C
T-Dt: -- --- -----
P-Dt: 03 Mar 1882
Dist/Class: Fannin Preemption
File#: 2047
Patent#: 151
Patent Vol.: 13
Survey/Blk/Twp: -BRIR-
Acres: 40
Map(s) 38

Abstract # 1475 - KRAMER, D
P'ee: GAY, A T
G'ee: KRAMER, DAVID
T-Dt: -- --- -----
P-Dt: 15 Feb 1879
Dist/Class: Fannin Preemption
File#: 1368
Patent#: 375
Patent Vol.: 8
Acres: 160
Map(s) 29, 30

Abstract # 1476 - T&NO RR CO
S2: KELLY, D
P'ee: KELLEY, DAVID
G'ee: KELLEY, DAVID
T-Dt: -- --- -----
P-Dt: 15 Aug 1881
Dist/Class: School

File#: 1775
Patent#: 497
Patent Vol.: 1
Survey/Blk/Twp: NW 1/4 6 T & NO-
Acres: 160
Map(s) 28, 29

Abstract # 1477 - LEMONS, W H
P'ee: LEMONS, W H
G'ee: LEMONS, W H
T-Dt: -- --- -----
P-Dt: 08 Dec 1879
Dist/Class: Fannin Preemption
File#: 1811
Patent#: 64
Patent Vol.: 10
Acres: 160
Map(s) 6

Abstract # 1478 - LEE, J C
P'ee: WININGER, JAMES N
G'ee: LEE, J C
T-Dt: -- --- -----
P-Dt: 12 May 1880
Dist/Class: Fannin Preemption
File#: 1936
Patent#: 527
Patent Vol.: 10
Acres: 160
Map(s) 31

Abstract # 1480 - BS&F
S2: LOONEY, A
P'ee: LOONEY, A (HEIRS)
G'ee: LOONEY, A
T-Dt: -- --- -----
P-Dt: 06 Feb 1902
Dist/Class: School
File#: 1776
Patent#: 367
Patent Vol.: 22
Certificate: 1/264
Survey/Blk/Twp: NE 1/4 2 BS & F-
Acres: 160
Map(s) 15

Abstract # 1481 - MCLEOND, W
P'ee: MCLEOUD, WILLIAM
G'ee: MCLEOUD, WILLIAM
T-Dt: -- --- -----
P-Dt: 03 Apr 1879
Dist/Class: Fannin Preemption
File#: 1387
Patent#: 541
Patent Vol.: 8
Acres: 160
Map(s) 30

Abstract # 1482 - MATHIS, L J
P'ee: MATHIS, L J
G'ee: MATHIS, L J
T-Dt: -- --- -----
P-Dt: 30 Sep 1879
Dist/Class: Fannin Preemption
File#: 2019
Patent#: 427
Patent Vol.: 9
Acres: 80
Map(s) 39

Abstract # 1483 - MAUPIN, J G
P'ee: EATON, A
G'ee: MAUPIN, J G
T-Dt: -- --- -----
P-Dt: 26 Oct 1881

Dist/Class: Fannin Preemption
File#: 2018
Patent#: 587
Patent Vol.: 12
Acres: 160
Map(s) 7

Abstract # 1484 - MATTHEWS, W
P'ee: MATTHEWS, WILLIAM
G'ee: MATTHEWS, WILLIAM
T-Dt: -- --- -----
P-Dt: 26 Aug 1881
Dist/Class: Fannin Preemption
File#: 2185
Patent#: 457
Patent Vol.: 12
Acres: 160
Map(s) 7

Abstract # 1485 - MONTGOMERY, J
P'ee: MONTGOMERY, JOHN
G'ee: MONTGOMERY, JOHN
T-Dt: -- --- -----
P-Dt: 01 Aug 1884
Dist/Class: Fannin Preemption
File#: 2154
Patent#: 103
Patent Vol.: 16
Acres: 160
Map(s) 40

Abstract # 1486 - MCDOWELL, W M
P'ee: PARROTT, W G
G'ee: MCDOWELL, W M
T-Dt: -- --- -----
P-Dt: 08 Jan 1894
Dist/Class: Fannin Preemption
File#: 2153
Patent#: 209
Patent Vol.: 26
Acres: 109.70
Map(s) 35, 43

Abstract # 1488 - MCCARLY, W M
P'ee: MCCARTY, WILLIAM M
G'ee: MCCARTY, WILLIAM M
T-Dt: -- --- -----
P-Dt: 21 May 1881
Dist/Class: Fannin Preemption
File#: 2151
Patent#: 271
Patent Vol.: 12
Acres: 160
Map(s) 4

Abstract # 1489 - MEADORS, E
P'ee: BRAGG, WILLIAM AND BRAGG,
FANNIE
G'ee: MEADOWS, E
T-Dt: -- --- -----
P-Dt: 02 Dec 1884
Dist/Class: Fannin Preemption
File#: 2225
Patent#: 467
Patent Vol.: 16
Acres: 160
Map(s) 34, 41, 42

Abstract # 1491 - MEADOWS, A T
P'ee: ROUNTREE, REUBEN
G'ee: MEADOWS, A T
T-Dt: -- --- -----
P-Dt: 16 Jan 1880
Dist/Class: Fannin Preemption
File#: 1924

Patent#: 202
Patent Vol.: 10
Acres: 160
Map(s) 34

Abstract # 1492 - MEADOWS, MRS S
P'ee: MEADOWS, SARAH (MRS)
G'ee: MEADOWS, SARAH
T-Dt: -- --- -----
P-Dt: 20 Nov 1880
Dist/Class: Fannin Preemption
File#: 1923
Patent#: 385
Patent Vol.: 11
Acres: 160
Map(s) 33, 34

Abstract # 1493 - MAYES, R K
P'ee: MAYES, R K
G'ee: MAYES, R K
T-Dt: -- --- -----
P-Dt: 28 Mar 1881
Dist/Class: Fannin Preemption
File#: 1922
Patent#: 131
Patent Vol.: 12
Acres: 160
Map(s) 26

Abstract # 1494 - MAYES, W W
P'ee: MAYES, W W
G'ee: MAYES, W W
T-Dt: -- --- -----
P-Dt: 20 Jan 1881
Dist/Class: Fannin Preemption
File#: 1921
Patent#: 549
Patent Vol.: 11
Acres: 80
Map(s) 26, 34

Abstract # 1495 - MORRIS, W M
P'ee: MORRIS, W M
G'ee: MORRIS, W M
T-Dt: -- --- -----
P-Dt: 03 May 1884
Dist/Class: Fannin Preemption
File#: 2031
Patent#: 427
Patent Vol.: 15
Acres: 160
Map(s) 39

Abstract # 1496 - POITEVENT, J
S2: MCCANN, A J
P'ee: HUNT, MARGARET S
G'ee: MCCANN, A J
T-Dt: -- --- -----
P-Dt: 27 Feb 1895
Dist/Class: School
File#: 1868
Patent#: 526
Patent Vol.: 14
Certificate: 2/157
Survey/Blk/Twp: SW 1/4 2 J.POITEVENT-
Acres: 160
Map(s) 27, 28

Abstract # 1498 - NEWTON, S G
P'ee: RUGGLES, DANIEL
G'ee: NEWTON, S G
T-Dt: -- --- -----
P-Dt: 23 Apr 1875
Dist/Class: Milam 3rd
File#: 1112

Patent#: 375
Patent Vol.: 15
Certificate: 12
Acres: 280
Map(s) 28

Abstract # 1499 - NICHOLS, J
P'ee: NICHOLS, JACOB
G'ee: NICHOLS, JACOB
T-Dt: -- --- -----
P-Dt: 28 Jul 1881
Dist/Class: Fannin Preemption
File#: 2020
Patent#: 401
Patent Vol.: 12
Acres: 160
Map(s) 31

Abstract # 1500 - BRIR
S2: SHELBY, J
P'ee: RICE, M M (MRS)
G'ee: NEWBY, JOHN
T-Dt: -- --- -----
P-Dt: 12 Feb 1880
Dist/Class: Fannin Preemption
File#: 2155
Patent#: 256
Patent Vol.: 10
Survey/Blk/Twp: 31 BRIR-
Acres: 160
Map(s) 38, 39

Abstract # 1502 - NEWBOLDS, W
P'ee: NEWBOLDS, WILLIAM
G'ee: NEWBOLDS, WILLIAM
T-Dt: -- --- -----
P-Dt: 28 Jul 1881
Dist/Class: Fannin Preemption
File#: 2156
Patent#: 399
Patent Vol.: 12
Acres: 160
Map(s) 33, 34

Abstract # 1503 - OXFORD, J G
P'ee: HOLLY, R S
G'ee: OXFORD, JOHN G
T-Dt: -- --- -----
P-Dt: 04 Feb 1879
Dist/Class: Fannin Preemption
File#: 1405
Patent#: 329
Patent Vol.: 8
Acres: 160
Map(s) 38, 39

Abstract # 1504 - O
P'ee: O"HARROW, W W
G'ee: O"HARROW, W W
T-Dt: -- --- -----
P-Dt: 24 Nov 1879
Dist/Class: Fannin Preemption
File#: 2024
Patent#: 15
Patent Vol.: 10
Acres: 80
Map(s) 9

Abstract # 1505 - O
P'ee: O"HARROW, J H
G'ee: O"HARROW, J H
T-Dt: -- --- -----
P-Dt: 24 Nov 1879
Dist/Class: Fannin Preemption
File#: 2023

Patent#: 19
Patent Vol.: 10
Acres: 80
Map(s) 9

Abstract # 1507 - ORR, E
P'ee: DELANEY, T C AND DELANEY, CAROLINA
G'ee: ORR, ELISHA
T-Dt: -- --- -----
P-Dt: 29 Nov 1881
Dist/Class: Fannin Preemption
File#: 1925
Patent#: 640
Patent Vol.: 12
Acres: 160
Map(s) 33

Abstract # 1508 - POITEVENT, J
P'ee: POITEVENT, J
G'ee: POITEVENT, J
T-Dt: -- --- -----
P-Dt: 16 Apr 1879
Dist/Class: Fannin Scrip
File#: 11044
Patent#: 608
Patent Vol.: 31
Certificate: 2/165
Survey/Blk/Twp: 5
Acres: 640
Map(s) 22, 23, 31

Abstract # 1509 - POITEVENT, J
P'ee: POITEVENT, J
G'ee: POITEVENT, J
T-Dt: -- --- -----
P-Dt: 22 Dec 1884
Dist/Class: Fannin Scrip
File#: 12580
Patent#: 259
Patent Vol.: 35
Certificate: 2/159
Survey/Blk/Twp: 17
Acres: 640
Map(s) 24

Abstract # 1510 - PALMER, J
P'ee: RIDGELY, REBECCA C
G'ee: PALMER, JOHN
T-Dt: -- --- -----
P-Dt: 29 Jul 1879
Dist/Class: Fannin Preemption
File#: 2318
Patent#: 263
Patent Vol.: 9
Acres: 80
Map(s) 29, 37

Abstract # 1511 - PEACOCK, W
P'ee: PEACOCK, WILLIAM
G'ee: PEACOCK, WILLIAM
T-Dt: -- --- -----
P-Dt: 04 Feb 1879
Dist/Class: Fannin Preemption
File#: 1812
Patent#: 341
Patent Vol.: 8
Acres: 160
Map(s) 33

Abstract # 1512 - POTTER, G N
P'ee: WELCH, J A
G'ee: POTTER, GEORGE N
T-Dt: -- --- -----
P-Dt: 24 Jun 1879

Dist/Class: Fannin Preemption
File#: 1937
Patent#: 151
Patent Vol.: 9
Acres: 160
Map(s) 31

Abstract # 1513 - PARKER, G W
P'ee: PARKER, GEORGE W
G'ee: PARKER, GEORGE W
T-Dt: -- --- -----
P-Dt: 28 Mar 1881
Dist/Class: Fannin Preemption
File#: 2127
Patent#: 126
Patent Vol.: 12
Acres: 160
Map(s) 30

Abstract # 1514 - PAYNE, J A
P'ee: BAKER, W H
G'ee: PAYNE, I A
T-Dt: -- --- -----
P-Dt: 21 May 1881
Dist/Class: Fannin Preemption
File#: 2186
Patent#: 272
Patent Vol.: 12
Acres: 80
Map(s) 4

Abstract # 1515 - PAYNE, F G
P'ee: WARD, J M
G'ee: PAYNE, F G
T-Dt: -- --- -----
P-Dt: 13 Sep 1880
Dist/Class: Fannin Preemption
File#: 2158
Patent#: 204
Patent Vol.: 11
Acres: 160
Map(s) 39

Abstract # 1516 - PRUITT, D H
P'ee: GILLFOIL, J J
G'ee: PRUITT, D H
T-Dt: -- --- -----
P-Dt: 18 Apr 1888
Dist/Class: Fannin Preemption
File#: 2227
Patent#: 634
Patent Vol.: 20
Acres: 80
Map(s) 34

Abstract # 1518 - PROFFITT, C M
P'ee: TANKERSLEY, W L
G'ee: PRIFFITT, C M
T-Dt: -- --- -----
P-Dt: 27 Jul 1881
Dist/Class: Fannin Preemption
File#: 1969
Patent#: 397
Patent Vol.: 12
Acres: 56
Map(s) 17

Abstract # 1519 - BRIR
S2: PARHAN, A
P'ee: PARHAM, ALLEN
G'ee: PARHAM, ALLEN
T-Dt: -- --- -----
P-Dt: 04 Sep 1879
Dist/Class: School
File#: 1777

Patent#: 215
Patent Vol.: 1
Survey/Blk/Twp: 1/4 24 BRIR-
Acres: 160
Map(s) 38

Abstract # 1520 - ROBINSON, J J
P'ee: ROBINSON, JOHN J
G'ee: ROBINSON, JOHN J
T-Dt: -- --- -----
P-Dt: 27 May 1879
Dist/Class: Fannin Preemption
File#: 1419
Patent#: 68
Patent Vol.: 9
Acres: 160
Map(s) 38, 39

Abstract # 1521 - ROBINSON, E
P'ee: SHARP, W A
G'ee: ROBINSON, E
T-Dt: -- --- -----
P-Dt: 11 Oct 1881
Dist/Class: Fannin Preemption
File#: 2187
Patent#: 543
Patent Vol.: 12
Acres: 160
Map(s) 40

Abstract # 1523 - RHOADS, M
P'ee: WILHELM, J M
G'ee: RHOADS, MOSES
T-Dt: -- --- -----
P-Dt: 13 Mar 1880
Dist/Class: Fannin Preemption
File#: 1813
Patent#: 332
Patent Vol.: 10
Acres: 160
Map(s) 8

Abstract # 1525 - BBB&C RR CO
S2: RICHARDSON, R M
P'ee: RICHARDSON, R M
G'ee: RICHARDSON, R M
T-Dt: -- --- -----
P-Dt: 07 May 1919
Dist/Class: School
File#: 1810
Patent#: 414
Patent Vol.: 2A
Certificate: 683
Survey/Blk/Twp: NW 1/4 2 BBB & CRR-
Acres: 160
Map(s) 15

Abstract # 1526 - SMOOT, J
P'ee: GEGG, NICHOLAS
G'ee: SMOOT, JOHN
T-Dt: -- --- -----
P-Dt: 21 Aug 1880
Dist/Class: Fannin Preemption
File#: 2025
Patent#: 142
Patent Vol.: 11
Acres: 160
Map(s) 16

Abstract # 1527 - SMITH, J C
P'ee: SMITH, J C
G'ee: SMITH, J C
T-Dt: -- --- -----
P-Dt: 25 Sep 1879
Dist/Class: Fannin Preemption

File#: 2161
Patent#: 418
Patent Vol.: 9
Acres: 160
Map(s) 7

Abstract # 1528 - STAPLES, R S
P'ee: STAPLES, R S
G'ee: STAPLES, R S
T-Dt: -- --- -----
P-Dt: 18 Aug 1880
Dist/Class: Fannin Preemption
File#: 2160
Patent#: 129
Patent Vol.: 11
Acres: 80
Map(s) 7

Abstract # 1529 - STINNETT, J D
P'ee: STINNETT, JAMES D
G'ee: STINNETT, JAMES D
T-Dt: -- --- -----
P-Dt: 11 Oct 1881
Dist/Class: Fannin Preemption
File#: 2231
Patent#: 550
Patent Vol.: 12
Acres: 160
Map(s) 35

Abstract # 1531 - STINNETT, W
P'ee: STINNETT, WILLIAM
G'ee: STINNETT, WILLIAM
T-Dt: -- --- -----
P-Dt: 12 Jul 1882
Dist/Class: Fannin Preemption
File#: 2229
Patent#: 429
Patent Vol.: 13
Acres: 160
Map(s) 35

Abstract # 1532 - SHELTON, J C
P'ee: GORDON, GEORGE
G'ee: SHELTON, J C
T-Dt: -- --- -----
P-Dt: 30 Dec 1886
Dist/Class: Fannin Preemption
File#: 2228
Patent#: 191
Patent Vol.: 19
Acres: 160
Map(s) 35

Abstract # 1533 - STAFFORD, MRS M B
P'ee: MOSS, WILLIAM AND MOSS, NANNIE
G'ee: STAFFORD, MELVIN B
T-Dt: -- --- -----
P-Dt: 14 Jun 1886
Dist/Class: Fannin Preemption
File#: 2280
Patent#: 407
Patent Vol.: 18
Acres: 101
Map(s) 22

Abstract # 1534 - BRIR
S2: SHERMAN, W
P'ee: WHITE, A C
G'ee: SHERMAN, WELLS
T-Dt: -- --- -----
P-Dt: 11 Dec 1880
Dist/Class: Fannin Preemption
File#: 2050

Patent#: 445
Patent Vol.: 11
Survey/Blk/Twp: 101 BRIR-
Acres: 160
Map(s) 30

Abstract # 1536 - SMITH, M M
P'ee: RICE, D R
G'ee: SMITH, H M
T-Dt: -- --- -----
P-Dt: 08 Dec 1879
Dist/Class: Fannin Preemption
File#: 1427
Patent#: 66
Patent Vol.: 10
Acres: 160
Map(s) 37

Abstract # 1539 - JERRY, I
P'ee: TERRY, ISAAC
G'ee: TERRY, ISAAC
T-Dt: -- --- -----
P-Dt: 10 May 1879
Dist/Class: Fannin Preemption
File#: 876
Patent#: 26
Patent Vol.: 9
Acres: 160
Map(s) 30, 31

Abstract # 1541 - BRIR
S2: TAYLOR, J M
P'ee: CASEY, J W
G'ee: TAYLOR, J M
T-Dt: -- --- -----
P-Dt: 10 May 1880
Dist/Class: Fannin Preemption
File#: 2051
Patent#: 515
Patent Vol.: 10
Survey/Blk/Twp: 51 BRIR-
Acres: 160
Map(s) 37, 38

Abstract # 1542 - BRIR
S2: TAYLOR, R
P'ee: TAYLOR, R
G'ee: TAYLOR, R
T-Dt: -- --- -----
P-Dt: 04 Nov 1879
Dist/Class: Fannin Preemption
File#: 2163
Patent#: 562
Patent Vol.: 9
Survey/Blk/Twp: 97 BRIR-
Acres: 160
Map(s) 31

Abstract # 1543 - TAYLOR, J C
P'ee: TAYLOR, J C
G'ee: TAYLOR, J C
T-Dt: -- --- -----
P-Dt: 28 Mar 1881
Dist/Class: Fannin Preemption
File#: 1926
Patent#: 132
Patent Vol.: 12
Acres: 80
Map(s) 33

Abstract # 1544 - TERRY, J W
P'ee: ALLEN, CATHERINE (MRS)
G'ee: TERRY, JAMES W
T-Dt: -- --- -----
P-Dt: 07 Feb 1879

Dist/Class: Fannin Preemption
File#: 1911
Patent#: 337
Patent Vol.: 8
Acres: 160
Map(s) 30

Abstract # 1545 - TANKERSLEY, W L
P'ee: TANKERSLEY, W L
G'ee: TANKERSLEY, W L
T-Dt: -- --- -----
P-Dt: 21 May 1881
Dist/Class: Fannin Preemption
File#: 1970
Patent#: 274
Patent Vol.: 12
Acres: 56
Map(s) 17

Abstract # 1546 - TAYLOR, B F
P'ee: TAYLOR, B F
G'ee: TAYLOR, B F
T-Dt: -- --- -----
P-Dt: 09 Jun 1880
Dist/Class: Fannin Preemption
File#: 2034
Patent#: 578
Patent Vol.: 10
Acres: 160
Map(s) 33

Abstract # 1547 - TT RR CO
P'ee: GANT, A B
G'ee: TYLER TAP RAILROAD COM-
PANY
T-Dt: -- --- -----
P-Dt: 07 May 1879
Dist/Class: Fannin Scrip
File#: 11910
Patent#: 488
Patent Vol.: 35
Certificate: 606
Survey/Blk/Twp: 15
Acres: 640
Map(s) 32

Abstract # 1548 - POITEVENT, J
S2: TIMMONS, J S
P'ee: STEADHAM, W T
G'ee: TIMMONS, J S
T-Dt: -- --- -----
P-Dt: 24 Nov 1908
Dist/Class: School
File#: 1677
Patent#: 34
Patent Vol.: 37
Certificate: 2/157
Survey/Blk/Twp: NE 1/4 2 J.POITEVENT-
Acres: 151.59
Map(s) 28

Abstract # 1549 - VAN SICKLES, J H
P'ee: VAN SICKLES, J H
G'ee: VAN SICKLES, J H
T-Dt: -- --- -----
P-Dt: 25 Sep 1880
Dist/Class: Fannin Preemption
File#: 2028
Patent#: 243
Patent Vol.: 11
Acres: 160
Map(s) 15, 16

Abstract # 1550 - WILCOX, T A
P'ee: WILCOX, THOMAS A

G'ee: WILCOX, THOMAS A
T-Dt: -- --- -----
P-Dt: 08 Aug 1879
Dist/Class: Fannin Preemption
File#: 2192
Patent#: 294
Patent Vol.: 9
Acres: 80
Map(s) 32

Abstract # 1551 - WARD, G
P'ee: KEEN, W H
G'ee: WARD, GEORGE
T-Dt: -- --- -----
P-Dt: 19 Jul 1879
Dist/Class: Fannin Preemption
File#: 2165
Patent#: 228
Patent Vol.: 9
Acres: 160
Map(s) 9

Abstract # 1552 - WALSH, G W
P'ee: WALSH, GEORGE W
G'ee: WALSH, GEORGE W
T-Dt: -- --- -----
P-Dt: 24 Jan 1893
Dist/Class: Fannin Preemption
File#: 2168
Patent#: 213
Patent Vol.: 25
Acres: 63
Map(s) 25

Abstract # 1553 - WALSH, J W
P'ee: WALSH, JOHN W
G'ee: WALSH, JOHN W
T-Dt: -- --- -----
P-Dt: 05 Jul 1888
Dist/Class: Fannin Preemption
File#: 2169
Patent#: 112
Patent Vol.: 21
Acres: 80
Map(s) 25

Abstract # 1554 - WALSH, M F
P'ee: WALSH, MARY F
G'ee: WALSH, MARY F
T-Dt: -- --- -----
P-Dt: 20 Oct 1887
Dist/Class: Fannin Preemption
File#: 2167
Patent#: 244
Patent Vol.: 20
Acres: 160
Map(s) 25

Abstract # 1555 - WILLIAMS, J H
P'ee: WILLIAMS, J H
G'ee: WILLIAMS, J H
T-Dt: -- --- -----
P-Dt: 26 Mar 1884
Dist/Class: Fannin Preemption
File#: 2166
Patent#: 339
Patent Vol.: 15
Acres: 160
Map(s) 33

Abstract # 1556 - BRIR
S2: WALTERS, J T
P'ee: NEWBY, JOHN H
G'ee: WALTERS, J T
T-Dt: -- --- -----

P-Dt: 02 Dec 1886
Dist/Class: Fannin Preemption
File#: 2164
Patent#: 124
Patent Vol.: 19
Survey/Blk/Twp: 25 BRIR-
Acres: 160
Map(s) 38

Abstract # 1557 - BRIR
S2: WAYNE, T A
P'ee: WERTS, JACOB
G'ee: WAYNE, T A
T-Dt: -- --- -----
P-Dt: 01 Sep 1880
Dist/Class: Fannin Preemption
File#: 1816
Patent#: 174
Patent Vol.: 11
Survey/Blk/Twp: 59 BRIR-
Acres: 160
Map(s) 37

Abstract # 1558 - WINBOURNE, E
P'ee: WINBORNE, E
G'ee: WINBORNE, E
T-Dt: -- --- -----
P-Dt: 18 Oct 1881
Dist/Class: Fannin Preemption
File#: 1814
Patent#: 562
Patent Vol.: 12
Acres: 160
Map(s) 40

Abstract # 1559 - WILSON, M A
P'ee: WILSON, M A
G'ee: WILSON, M A
T-Dt: -- --- -----
P-Dt: 07 Sep 1882
Dist/Class: Fannin Preemption
File#: 1929
Patent#: 507
Patent Vol.: 13
Acres: 160
Map(s) 36

Abstract # 1562 - WALLACE, M D
P'ee: WALLACE, M D
G'ee: WALLACE, M D
T-Dt: -- --- -----
P-Dt: 14 Jul 1884
Dist/Class: Fannin Preemption
File#: 1971
Patent#: 29
Patent Vol.: 16
Acres: 160
Map(s) 36

Abstract # 1564 - BRIR
S2: WELCH, G T
P'ee: WELCH, GEORGE T
G'ee: WELCH, GEORGE T
T-Dt: -- --- -----
P-Dt: 24 Aug 1886
Dist/Class: School
File#: 1866
Patent#: 117
Patent Vol.: 6
Survey/Blk/Twp: 56 BRIR-
Acres: 112
Map(s) 37

Abstract # 1565 - ZINN, C M
P'ee: PRESTON, J L

G'ee: ZINN, C M
T-Dt: -- --- -----
P-Dt: 28 Mar 1881
Dist/Class: Fannin Preemption
File#: 2037
Patent#: 138
Patent Vol.: 12
Survey/Blk/Twp: 56
Acres: 80
Map(s) 6

Abstract # 1566 - ZINN, S H
P'ee: PRESTON, J L
G'ee: ZINN, S H
T-Dt: -- --- -----
P-Dt: 05 Jan 1881
Dist/Class: Fannin Preemption
File#: 2036
Patent#: 493
Patent Vol.: 11
Acres: 80
Map(s) 6

Abstract # 1567 - ABERNATHY, J
P'ee: PIERCE, A Q
G'ee: ABERNATHY, JESSE
T-Dt: -- --- -----
P-Dt: 09 Oct 1882
Dist/Class: Fannin Preemption
File#: 2448
Patent#: 588
Patent Vol.: 13
Acres: 137
Map(s) 39, 40

Abstract # 1568 - BIRDWELL, J M
P'ee: BIRDWELL, J M
G'ee: BIRDWELL, J M
T-Dt: -- --- -----
P-Dt: 20 Feb 1880
Dist/Class: Fannin Preemption
File#: 2386
Patent#: 283
Patent Vol.: 10
Acres: 160
Map(s) 31, 39

Abstract # 1569 - BENSON, C P
P'ee: PAYNE, B H
G'ee: BENSON, C P
T-Dt: -- --- -----
P-Dt: 21 Oct 1879
Dist/Class: Fannin Preemption
File#: 1298
Patent#: 516
Patent Vol.: 9
Acres: 160
Map(s) 37

Abstract # 1570 - BUSE, J
P'ee: BUSE, JAMES
G'ee: BUSE, JAMES
T-Dt: -- --- -----
P-Dt: 17 Nov 1879
Dist/Class: Fannin Preemption
File#: 1122
Patent#: 618
Patent Vol.: 9
Acres: 160
Map(s) 29, 36, 37

Abstract # 1571 - BASS, C F
P'ee: BASS, C F
G'ee: BASS, C F
T-Dt: -- --- -----

P-Dt: 19 Nov 1879
Dist/Class: Fannin Preemption
File#: 1295
Patent#: 629
Patent Vol.: 9
Acres: 160
Map(s) 37

Abstract # 1572 - BAKER, M W
P'ee: MATHEWS, JACOB
G'ee: BAKER, MARION W
T-Dt: -- --- -----
P-Dt: 02 Aug 1880
Dist/Class: Fannin Preemption
File#: 1059
Patent#: 77
Patent Vol.: 11
Acres: 160
Map(s) 40

Abstract # 1573 - BELLUH, G
P'ee: BELLAH, GEORGE
G'ee: BELLAH, GEORGE
T-Dt: -- --- -----
P-Dt: 26 Aug 1880
Dist/Class: Fannin Preemption
File#: 2184
Patent#: 153
Patent Vol.: 11
Acres: 96
Map(s) 35, 43

Abstract # 1574 - BELLAMY, J N
P'ee: BELLAMY, J N
G'ee: BELLAMY, J N
T-Dt: -- --- -----
P-Dt: 26 Aug 1880
Dist/Class: Fannin Preemption
File#: 1297
Patent#: 160
Patent Vol.: 11
Acres: 160
Map(s) 37

Abstract # 1575 - BUSSELL, J
P'ee: FRANKLIN, HIRAM
G'ee: BUSSELL, JAMES
T-Dt: -- --- -----
P-Dt: 11 Dec 1880
Dist/Class: Fannin Preemption
File#: 1303
Patent#: 444
Patent Vol.: 11
Acres: 80
Map(s) 29

Abstract # 1576 - BLACK, S
P'ee: BLACK, SAMUEL
G'ee: BLACK, SAMUEL
T-Dt: -- --- -----
P-Dt: 27 Jun 1882
Dist/Class: Fannin Preemption
File#: 2295
Patent#: 406
Patent Vol.: 13
Acres: 80
Map(s) 28, 36

Abstract # 1577 - BENNETT, J
P'ee: HODGES, E L
G'ee: BENNETT, J
T-Dt: -- --- -----
P-Dt: 10 Dec 1888
Dist/Class: Fannin Preemption
File#: 2408

Patent#: 396
Patent Vol.: 21
Acres: 96.50
Map(s) 7

Abstract # 1578 - BURCH, F P
P'ee: BURCH, F P
G'ee: BURCH, F P
T-Dt: -- --- -----
P-Dt: 24 May 1890
Dist/Class: Fannin Preemption
File#: 2455
Patent#: 97
Patent Vol.: 23
Acres: 155.25
Map(s) 21, 29

Abstract # 1579 - BRIR
S2: BUIE, L B
P'ee: BUIE, L B
G'ee: BUIE, L B
T-Dt: -- --- -----
P-Dt: 30 May 1881
Dist/Class: Fannin Preemption
File#: 2451
Patent#: 288
Patent Vol.: 12
Survey/Blk/Twp: 103
Acres: 160
Map(s) 30

Abstract # 1580 - BRIR
S2: BARNETT, S
P'ee: NORRIS, J B
G'ee: BARNETT, S
T-Dt: -- --- -----
P-Dt: 16 Feb 1898
Dist/Class: School
File#: 1960
Patent#: 507
Patent Vol.: 16
Survey/Blk/Twp: 1/4 110 BRIR-
Acres: 160
Map(s) 29, 30

Abstract # 1581 - COLTHARP, J
P'ee: FITCHETT, JOSEPH
G'ee: COLTHARP, JOHN
T-Dt: -- --- -----
P-Dt: 13 Nov 1879
Dist/Class: Fannin Preemption
File#: 1314
Patent#: 607
Patent Vol.: 9
Acres: 160
Map(s) 37

Abstract # 1582 - COLTHARP, H
P'ee: WOOLEY, THOMAS
G'ee: COLTHARP, H
T-Dt: -- --- -----
P-Dt: 11 Dec 1880
Dist/Class: Fannin Preemption
File#: 1313
Patent#: 447
Patent Vol.: 11
Acres: 80
Map(s) 29

Abstract # 1583 - CONNELLY, W A
P'ee: CONNELLY, W A
G'ee: CONNELLY, W A
T-Dt: -- --- -----
P-Dt: 20 Nov 1880
Dist/Class: Fannin Preemption

File#: 1316
Patent#: 383
Patent Vol.: 11
Acres: 160
Map(s) 30

Abstract # 1584 - CURTIS, V E
P'ee: CURTIS, V E
G'ee: CURTIS, V E
T-Dt: -- --- -----
P-Dt: 14 Nov 1881
Dist/Class: Fannin Preemption
File#: 2344
Patent#: 623
Patent Vol.: 12
Acres: 160
Map(s) 34, 35

Abstract # 1585 - BRIR
S2: CALHOUN, J H
P'ee: CALHOUN, J H (HEIRS)
G'ee: CALHOUN, J H
T-Dt: -- --- -----
P-Dt: 24 Jan 1887
Dist/Class: Fannin Preemption
File#: 2363
Patent#: 255
Patent Vol.: 19
Survey/Blk/Twp: 115 BRIR-
Acres: 160
Map(s) 29, 30

Abstract # 1586 - CANTWELL, J J
P'ee: CANTWELL, JAMES J
G'ee: CANTWELL, JAMES J
T-Dt: -- --- -----
P-Dt: 18 Jan 1882
Dist/Class: Fannin Preemption
File#: 2411 1/2
Patent#: 83
Patent Vol.: 13
Acres: 160
Map(s) 7

Abstract # 1587 - EDDLEMAN, I F
P'ee: RHEA, J F
G'ee: DOUGLAS, J E
T-Dt: -- --- -----
P-Dt: 05 Jan 1880
Dist/Class: Fannin Preemption
File#: 1325
Patent#: 152
Patent Vol.: 10
Acres: 124.33
Map(s) 37

Abstract # 1588 - DONNELL, W L
P'ee: DONNELL, W L
G'ee: DONNELL, W L
T-Dt: -- --- -----
P-Dt: 28 Apr 1880
Dist/Class: Fannin Preemption
File#: 2465
Patent#: 478
Patent Vol.: 10
Acres: 160
Map(s) 35, 43

Abstract # 1589 - DEISTER, J T
P'ee: DEISTER, J T
G'ee: DEISTER, J T
T-Dt: -- --- -----
P-Dt: 02 Jun 1882
Dist/Class: Fannin Preemption
File#: 2361

Patent#: 362
Patent Vol.: 13
Acres: 80
Map(s) 6, 7

Abstract # 1590 - BRIR
S2: DRIVER, J
P'ee: DRIVER, JOHN
G'ee: DRIVER, JOHN
T-Dt: -- --- -----
P-Dt: 29 May 1884
Dist/Class: Fannin Preemption
File#: 2499
Patent#: 534
Patent Vol.: 15
Survey/Blk/Twp: 13 BRIR-
Acres: 160
Map(s) 38, 46

Abstract # 1592 - DAVIDSON, J H
P'ee: BACHELDOR, O B
G'ee: DAVIDSON, J H
T-Dt: -- --- -----
P-Dt: 11 Nov 1880
Dist/Class: Fannin Preemption
File#: 1807
Patent#: 368
Patent Vol.: 11
Acres: 160
Map(s) 6

Abstract # 1593 - DAVIS, S D
P'ee: DAVIS, S D
G'ee: DAVIS, S D
T-Dt: -- --- -----
P-Dt: 05 Feb 1883
Dist/Class: Fannin Preemption
File#: 2364
Patent#: 75
Patent Vol.: 14
Acres: 160
Map(s) 34, 35, 43

Abstract # 1594 - POITEVENT, J
S2: DAVIS, W
P'ee: DONNELL, J M
G'ee: DAVIS, WILLIAM
T-Dt: -- --- -----
P-Dt: 14 Jul 1899
Dist/Class: School
File#: 1985
Patent#: 563
Patent Vol.: 17
Certificate: 1/129
Survey/Blk/Twp: SE 1/4 2 J.POITEVENT-
Acres: 160
Map(s) 4

Abstract # 1595 - POITEVENT, J
S2: DEE, A N
P'ee: ALLEN, ISAAC
G'ee: DEES, A N
T-Dt: -- --- -----
P-Dt: 21 Aug 1901
Dist/Class: School
File#: 2302
Patent#: 200
Patent Vol.: 21
Certificate: 2/165
Survey/Blk/Twp: E 1/4 6 J.POITEVENT-
Acres: 140.50
Map(s) 23

Abstract # 1597 - EDDLEMAN, W M
P'ee: EDDLEMAN, W H

G'ee: EDDLEMAN, W H
T-Dt: -- --- -----
P-Dt: 07 Jan 1881
Dist/Class: School
File#: 1984
Patent#: 382
Patent Vol.: 1
Survey/Blk/Twp: 124 BRIR-
Acres: 40
Map(s) 38

Abstract # 1598 - FISHER, J H
P'ee: FISHER, J H
G'ee: FISHER, J H
T-Dt: -- --- -----
P-Dt: 12 Jan 1880
Dist/Class: Fannin Preemption
File#: 1336
Patent#: 178
Patent Vol.: 10
Acres: 160
Map(s) 39

Abstract # 1599 - FRANKLIN, D D
P'ee: DAVIDSON, J H
G'ee: FRANKLIN, D D
T-Dt: -- --- -----
P-Dt: 07 Sep 1880
Dist/Class: Fannin Preemption
File#: 2012
Patent#: 193
Patent Vol.: 11
Acres: 160
Map(s) 7

Abstract # 1600 - HOWARD, J W
P'ee: GORRISSEN, V FREDRICK GUN-
THER
G'ee: HOWARD, J W
T-Dt: -- --- -----
P-Dt: 23 Sep 1879
Dist/Class: Fannin Preemption
File#: 1356
Patent#: 412
Patent Vol.: 9
Acres: 160
Map(s) 38

Abstract # 1601 - HOLLY, T J
P'ee: CLIFTON, G W
G'ee: HOLLY, T J
T-Dt: -- --- -----
P-Dt: 21 Oct 1879
Dist/Class: Fannin Preemption
File#: 1352
Patent#: 512
Patent Vol.: 9
Acres: 160
Map(s) 38

Abstract # 1602 - HOLLY, J C
P'ee: HOLLY, J C
G'ee: HOLLY, J C
T-Dt: -- --- -----
P-Dt: 17 Nov 1879
Dist/Class: Fannin Preemption
File#: 1353
Patent#: 617
Patent Vol.: 9
Acres: 160
Map(s) 37

Abstract # 1603 - HOWETH, F A
P'ee: VANHOOSER, JAKE
G'ee: HOWETH, F A

T-Dt: -- --- -----
P-Dt: 06 Oct 1884
Dist/Class: Fannin Preemption
File#: 2383
Patent#: 302
Patent Vol.: 16
Acres: 160
Map(s) 32

Abstract # 1604 - BRIR
S2: HOWARD, J W
P'ee: BROWN, JAMES H
G'ee: HOWARD, J W
T-Dt: -- --- -----
P-Dt: 17 May 1884
Dist/Class: Fannin Preemption
File#: 2419
Patent#: 479
Patent Vol.: 15
Survey/Blk/Twp: 43 BRIR-
Acres: 160
Map(s) 38

Abstract # 1605 - HOLMES, R
P'ee: HOLMES, REBECCA
G'ee: HOLMES, REBECCA
T-Dt: -- --- -----
P-Dt: 27 Jul 1881
Dist/Class: Fannin Preemption
File#: 2478
Patent#: 394
Patent Vol.: 12
Acres: 160
Map(s) 24

Abstract # 1606 - HARVEY, H
P'ee: LEE, M A
G'ee: HARVEY, HENRY
T-Dt: -- --- -----
P-Dt: 13 Oct 1880
Dist/Class: Fannin Preemption
File#: 1348
Patent#: 301
Patent Vol.: 11
Acres: 160
Map(s) 29

Abstract # 1608 - T&NO RR CO
S2: HOLLY, B
P'ee: HOLLY, B
G'ee: HOLLY, B
T-Dt: -- --- -----
P-Dt: 20 Apr 1901
Dist/Class: School
File#: 2580
Patent#: 46
Patent Vol.: 20
Certificate: 865
Survey/Blk/Twp: NE 1/4 4 T & NO-
Acres: 160
Map(s) 31

Abstract # 1609 - JONES, W R
P'ee: JONES, W R
G'ee: JONES, W R
T-Dt: -- --- -----
P-Dt: 03 Mar 1880
Dist/Class: Fannin Preemption
File#: 2337
Patent#: 311
Patent Vol.: 10
Acres: 160
Map(s) 20, 28

Abstract # 1610 - JAMES, W F

P'ee: JAMES, W F
G'ee: JAMES, W F
T-Dt: -- --- -----
P-Dt: 25 Sep 1879
Dist/Class: Fannin Preemption
File#: 1360
Patent#: 410
Patent Vol.: 9
Acres: 160
Map(s) 38

Abstract # 1611 - JACKSON, J L
P'ee: JACKSON, J L
G'ee: JACKSON, J L
T-Dt: -- --- -----
P-Dt: 20 Oct 1887
Dist/Class: Fannin Preemption
File#: 2446
Patent#: 245
Patent Vol.: 20
Acres: 160
Map(s) 32

Abstract # 1612 - JONES, H M
P'ee: BARRETT, J M
G'ee: JONES, H M
T-Dt: -- --- -----
P-Dt: 02 Aug 1883
Dist/Class: Fannin Preemption
File#: 2456
Patent#: 387
Patent Vol.: 14
Acres: 160
Map(s) 35

Abstract # 1613 - BRIR
S2: KIRK, J
P'ee: KIRK, JAMES
G'ee: KIRK, JAMES
T-Dt: -- --- -----
P-Dt: 24 Jun 1884
Dist/Class: Fannin Preemption
File#: 2497
Patent#: 633
Patent Vol.: 15
Survey/Blk/Twp: 67 BRIR-
Acres: 111
Map(s) 29

Abstract # 1614 - KELLY, E M
P'ee: CUNNINGHAM, J H
G'ee: KELLY, E M
T-Dt: -- --- -----
P-Dt: 21 Oct 1879
Dist/Class: Fannin Preemption
File#: 1366
Patent#: 515
Patent Vol.: 9
Acres: 160
Map(s) 38

Abstract # 1615 - MOSS, S
P'ee: GILMORE, JAMES
G'ee: MOSS, SAMUEL
T-Dt: -- --- -----
P-Dt: 03 Mar 1880
Dist/Class: Fannin Preemption
File#: 1397
Patent#: 313
Patent Vol.: 10
Acres: 80
Map(s) 39

Abstract # 1616 - MASSEY, E J
P'ee: DUNHAM, E

G'ee: MASSEY, E J
T-Dt: -- --- -----
P-Dt: 01 May 1880
Dist/Class: Fannin Preemption
File#: 1613
Patent#: 482
Patent Vol.: 10
Acres: 160
Map(s) 20

Abstract # 1618 - MURRAY, J J
P'ee: CARMACK, A S
G'ee: MURRAY, J J
T-Dt: -- --- -----
P-Dt: 24 Feb 1886
Dist/Class: Fannin Preemption
File#: 2296
Patent#: 142
Patent Vol.: 18
Acres: 37.80
Map(s) 26

Abstract # 1619 - MILLER, B B
P'ee: TAYLOR, MARY
G'ee: MILLER, B B
T-Dt: -- --- -----
P-Dt: 23 Dec 1884
Dist/Class: Fannin Preemption
File#: 2378
Patent#: 532
Patent Vol.: 16
Acres: 117.75
Map(s) 15

Abstract # 1620 - MCDOWELL, W M
P'ee: MCDOWELL, W M
G'ee: MCDOWELL, W M
T-Dt: -- --- -----
P-Dt: 05 Dec 1881
Dist/Class: Fannin Preemption
File#: 2464
Patent#: 10
Patent Vol.: 13
Acres: 160
Map(s) 31

Abstract # 1621 - MCDOWELL, W J
P'ee: TIDWELL, W F
G'ee: MCDOWELL, W J A
T-Dt: -- --- -----
P-Dt: 25 Mar 1882
Dist/Class: Fannin Preemption
File#: 2512
Patent#: 228
Patent Vol.: 13
Acres: 75
Map(s) 31

Abstract # 1622 - POITEVENT, J
S2: MELLINGER, D S
P'ee: HUNT, W C
G'ee: MELLINGER, D S
T-Dt: -- --- -----
P-Dt: 27 Sep 1901
Dist/Class: School
File#: 2485
Patent#: 440
Patent Vol.: 21
Certificate: 2/159
Survey/Blk/Twp: W 1/4 18 J.POITEVENT-
Acres: 137
Map(s) 24

Abstract # 1623 - BRIR
S2: MCCLENDON, D F

P'ee: MCCLENDON, D F
G'ee: MCCLENDON, D F
T-Dt: -- --- -----
P-Dt: 10 Dec 1885
Dist/Class: School
File#: 3376
Patent#: 192
Patent Vol.: 5
Survey/Blk/Twp: 12 BRIR-
Acres: 160
Map(s) 38

Abstract # 1624 - NELSON, J A
P'ee: NELSON, JOHN A
G'ee: NELSON, JOHN A
T-Dt: -- --- -----
P-Dt: 02 Aug 1880
Dist/Class: Fannin Preemption
File#: 1060
Patent#: 76
Patent Vol.: 11
Acres: 160
Map(s) 40

Abstract # 1625 - PADDOCK, J W V
P'ee: PADDOCK, J W V
G'ee: PADDOCK, J W V
T-Dt: -- --- -----
P-Dt: 19 Nov 1879
Dist/Class: Fannin Preemption
File#: 1270
Patent#: 624
Patent Vol.: 9
Acres: 160
Map(s) 7

Abstract # 1626 - PRICE, T
P'ee: PRICE, THOMAS
G'ee: PRICE, THOMAS
T-Dt: -- --- -----
P-Dt: 12 Mar 1880
Dist/Class: Fannin Preemption
File#: 1584
Patent#: 327
Patent Vol.: 10
Acres: 160
Map(s) 26

Abstract # 1627 - REED, G W
P'ee: PADGETT, I B
G'ee: REED, G W
T-Dt: -- --- -----
P-Dt: 27 Apr 1880
Dist/Class: Fannin Preemption
File#: 1414
Patent#: 474
Patent Vol.: 10
Acres: 80
Map(s) 30, 31

Abstract # 1628 - RAY, J
P'ee: RAY, JAMES
G'ee: RAY, JAMES
T-Dt: -- --- -----
P-Dt: 16 Sep 1879
Dist/Class: Fannin Preemption
File#: 1411
Patent#: 398
Patent Vol.: 9
Acres: 160
Map(s) 37

Abstract # 1629 - RODGERS, J E
P'ee: MCCLENDON, D F
G'ee: RODGERS, J E

T-Dt: -- --- -----
P-Dt: 28 Oct 1879
Dist/Class: Fannin Preemption
File#: 2033
Patent#: 546
Patent Vol.: 9
Acres: 160
Map(s) 38

Abstract # 1630 - RICE, J D
P'ee: RICE, J D
G'ee: RICE, J D
T-Dt: -- --- -----
P-Dt: 17 Nov 1879
Dist/Class: Fannin Preemption
File#: 2382
Patent#: 615
Patent Vol.: 9
Acres: 80
Map(s) 37

Abstract # 1631 - REYNOLDS, MRS N J
P'ee: REYNOLDS, N J (MRS)
G'ee: REYNOLDS, N J (MRS)
T-Dt: -- --- -----
P-Dt: 04 Dec 1884
Dist/Class: Fannin Preemption
File#: 2362
Patent#: 492
Patent Vol.: 16
Acres: 160
Map(s) 31

Abstract # 1632 - BRIR
S2: RODGERS, J
P'ee: MCCALL, J L L
G'ee: RODGERS, JAMES
T-Dt: -- --- -----
P-Dt: 27 Apr 1886
Dist/Class: Fannin Preemption
File#: 2412
Patent#: 292
Patent Vol.: 18
Survey/Blk/Twp: 89 BRIR-
Acres: 160
Map(s) 31

Abstract # 1633 - ROSE, T
P'ee: DRUM, W R
G'ee: ROSE, TAYLOR
T-Dt: -- --- -----
P-Dt: 06 Feb 1885
Dist/Class: Fannin Preemption
File#: 2473
Patent#: 617
Patent Vol.: 16
Acres: 120.60
Map(s) 6, 7

Abstract # 1634 - SMITH, C
P'ee: SMITH, CLARK
G'ee: SMITH, CLARK
T-Dt: -- --- -----
P-Dt: 29 Mar 1880
Dist/Class: Fannin Preemption
File#: 1429
Patent#: 395
Patent Vol.: 10
Acres: 160
Map(s) 37

Abstract # 1635 - SHAW, R
P'ee: SHAW, ROBERT
G'ee: SHAW, ROBERT
T-Dt: -- --- -----

P-Dt: 28 Oct 1879
Dist/Class: Fannin Preemption
File#: 1498
Patent#: 546 1/2
Patent Vol.: 9
Acres: 160
Map(s) 33

Abstract # 1637 - BRIR
S2: STEGALL, J H
P'ee: HOLLEY, J W
G'ee: STEGALL, J H
T-Dt: -- --- -----
P-Dt: 01 Aug 1881
Dist/Class: Fannin Preemption
File#: 2513
Patent#: 411
Patent Vol.: 12
Survey/Blk/Twp: 107
Acres: 156
Map(s) 29

Abstract # 1638 - BS&F
S2: SMITH, JP
P'ee: SIMPKINS, MACON (HEIRS)
G'ee: SMITH, J D
T-Dt: -- --- -----
P-Dt: 06 May 1901
Dist/Class: School
File#: 3312
Patent#: 147
Patent Vol.: 20
Certificate: 1/266
Survey/Blk/Twp: NE 1/4 4 BS & F-
Acres: 160
Map(s) 40

Abstract # 1639 - TRACY, N F
P'ee: TRACY, N F
G'ee: TRACY, N F
T-Dt: -- --- -----
P-Dt: 16 Sep 1879
Dist/Class: Fannin Preemption
File#: 1433
Patent#: 399
Patent Vol.: 9
Acres: 160
Map(s) 38

Abstract # 1640 - BRIR
S2: TREUE, J A
P'ee: TREUE, JOHN A
G'ee: TREUE, JOHN A
T-Dt: -- --- -----
P-Dt: 13 Nov 1879
Dist/Class: Fannin Preemption
File#: 1437
Patent#: 608
Patent Vol.: 9
Survey/Blk/Twp: 99
Acres: 160
Map(s) 31

Abstract # 1641 - TOWNSEND, J O
P'ee: TOWNSEND, J D
G'ee: TOWNSEND, J D
T-Dt: -- --- -----
P-Dt: 01 Nov 1883
Dist/Class: Fannin Preemption
File#: 2311
Patent#: 19
Patent Vol.: 15
Acres: 80
Map(s) 35, 36

Abstract # 1642 - TOWNSEND, C W
P'ee: PARHAM, JAMES
G'ee: TOWNSEND, C W
T-Dt: -- --- -----
P-Dt: 06 Aug 1883
Dist/Class: Fannin Preemption
File#: 2310
Patent#: 417
Patent Vol.: 14
Acres: 160
Map(s) 35, 36

Abstract # 1643 - TACKETT, W A
P'ee: TACKETT, W A
G'ee: TACKETT, W A
T-Dt: -- --- -----
P-Dt: 01 Sep 1885
Dist/Class: Fannin Preemption
File#: 2298
Patent#: 409
Patent Vol.: 17
Acres: 160
Map(s) 35

Abstract # 1644 - TYSON, D B
P'ee: FOUNTON, D F
G'ee: TYSON, D B
T-Dt: -- --- -----
P-Dt: 13 Jun 1885
Dist/Class: Fannin Preemption
File#: 2398
Patent#: 246
Patent Vol.: 17
Acres: 160
Map(s) 47

Abstract # 1645 - TOWNSEND, J T
P'ee: TOWNSEND, J T
G'ee: TOWNSEND, J T
T-Dt: -- --- -----
P-Dt: 20 Jun 1884
Dist/Class: Fannin Preemption
File#: 2352
Patent#: 579
Patent Vol.: 15
Acres: 80
Map(s) 35

Abstract # 1646 - BRIR
S2: THOMAS, S A
P'ee: DOWDLE, T E
G'ee: THOMAS, S A
T-Dt: -- --- -----
P-Dt: 05 Jun 1882
Dist/Class: Fannin Preemption
File#: 2447
Patent#: 376
Patent Vol.: 13
Acres: 119
Map(s) 37

Abstract # 1648 - VAN HOOSER, J C
P'ee: KING, J H
G'ee: VANHOOSER, JOHN C
T-Dt: -- --- -----
P-Dt: 05 Dec 1881
Dist/Class: Fannin Preemption
File#: 2466
Patent#: 11
Patent Vol.: 13
Acres: 160
Map(s) 32

Abstract # 1650 - WOOD, S
P'ee: WOOD, SAMUEL

G'ee: WOOD, SAMUEL
T-Dt: -- --- -----
P-Dt: 12 Feb 1880
Dist/Class: Fannin Preemption
File#: 1621
Patent#: 258
Patent Vol.: 10
Acres: 160
Map(s) 36

Abstract # 1651 - WHITTENBURG, J N
P'ee: BICE, JAMES
G'ee: WHITTENBURG, J A
T-Dt: -- --- -----
P-Dt: 03 Mar 1880
Dist/Class: Fannin Preemption
File#: 1446
Patent#: 314
Patent Vol.: 10
Acres: 80
Map(s) 38

Abstract # 1652 - WILLESS, J
P'ee: WILLESS, JAMES
G'ee: WILLESS, JAMES
T-Dt: -- --- -----
P-Dt: 01 May 1880
Dist/Class: Fannin Preemption
File#: 1091
Patent#: 481
Patent Vol.: 10
Acres: 160
Map(s) 39

Abstract # 1653 - WILSON, R M
P'ee: WILSON, R M
G'ee: WILSON, R M
T-Dt: -- --- -----
P-Dt: 02 Dec 1881
Dist/Class: Fannin Preemption
File#: 2312
Patent#: 5
Patent Vol.: 13
Acres: 160
Map(s) 7

Abstract # 1654 - WOOLLEY, T H
P'ee: WOOLLEY, T H
G'ee: WOOLLEY, T H
T-Dt: -- --- -----
P-Dt: 28 Mar 1918
Dist/Class: Fannin Preemption
File#: 2435
Patent#: 366
Patent Vol.: 33
Acres: 157.50
Map(s) 47

Abstract # 1655 - BRIR
S2: WOOD, J H
P'ee: WOOD, JOHN H
G'ee: WOOD, JOHN H
T-Dt: -- --- -----
P-Dt: 24 Aug 1881
Dist/Class: Fannin Preemption
File#: 2411
Patent#: 453
Patent Vol.: 12
Survey/Blk/Twp: 57 BRIR-
Acres: 160
Map(s) 37

Abstract # 1656 - WILSON, J E
P'ee: WILSON, J E
G'ee: WILSON, J E

T-Dt: -- --- -----
P-Dt: 26 Jul 1884
Dist/Class: Fannin Preemption
File#: 2498
Patent#: 86
Patent Vol.: 16
Acres: 160
Map(s) 31

Abstract # 1658 - BRIR
S2: WHITE, E
P'ee: WHITE, E
G'ee: WHITE, E
T-Dt: -- --- -----
P-Dt: 14 Dec 1883
Dist/Class: Fannin Preemption
File#: 2472
Patent#: 91
Patent Vol.: 15
Survey/Blk/Twp: 119 BRIR-
Acres: 158.50
Map(s) 29

Abstract # 1661 - ZINN, J A
P'ee: ZINN, J A
G'ee: ZINN, J A
T-Dt: -- --- -----
P-Dt: 09 Sep 1881
Dist/Class: Fannin Preemption
File#: 2365
Patent#: 496
Patent Vol.: 12
Acres: 160
Map(s) 6

Abstract # 1662 - ALLEN, J
P'ee: ALLEN, JOSEPH
G'ee: ALLEN, JOSEPH
T-Dt: -- --- -----
P-Dt: 14 Oct 1881
Dist/Class: Fannin Preemption
File#: 1620
Patent#: 556
Patent Vol.: 12
Acres: 160
Map(s) 36

Abstract # 1663 - AUBURG, C E F
P'ee: AUBURG, CHARLES E F
G'ee: AUBURG, CHARLES E F
T-Dt: -- --- -----
P-Dt: 20 Jan 1881
Dist/Class: Fannin Preemption
File#: 1288
Patent#: 550
Patent Vol.: 11
Acres: 160
Map(s) 38

Abstract # 1664 - BRADWELL, T M
P'ee: BOSKIN, JOHN C
G'ee: BRADWELL, T M
T-Dt: -- --- -----
P-Dt: 02 May 1881
Dist/Class: Fannin Preemption
File#: 1064
Patent#: 227
Patent Vol.: 12
Acres: 160
Map(s) 21

Abstract # 1667 - BRAY, W H
P'ee: BRAY, W H
G'ee: BRAY, W H
T-Dt: -- --- -----

P-Dt: 15 Apr 1887
Dist/Class: Fannin Preemption
File#: 2529
Patent#: 409
Patent Vol.: 19
Acres: 160
Map(s) 31

Abstract # 1668 - BARRY, T H
P'ee: BARRY, THOMAS H
G'ee: BARRY, THOMAS H
T-Dt: -- --- -----
P-Dt: 06 Sep 1886
Dist/Class: Fannin Preemption
File#: 2547
Patent#: 564
Patent Vol.: 18
Acres: 80
Map(s) 30, 38

Abstract # 1669 - SP RR CO
S2: BAKER, J M
P'ee: BAKER, J M
G'ee: BAKER, J M
T-Dt: -- --- -----
P-Dt: 20 Nov 1900
Dist/Class: School
File#: 4203
Patent#: 145
Patent Vol.: 19
Certificate: 16/69
Survey/Blk/Twp: SP
Acres: 199.50
Map(s) 24

Abstract # 1670 - BS&F
S2: BROWN, G F
P'ee: BROWN, G F
G'ee: BROWN, G F
T-Dt: -- --- -----
P-Dt: 04 Aug 1919
Dist/Class: School
File#: 4482
Patent#: 343
Patent Vol.: 3A
Survey/Blk/Twp: SW 1/4 2 BS & F-
Acres: 160
Map(s) 15

Abstract # 1672 - BRIR
S2: CASEY, J W
P'ee: DRIVER, A J
G'ee: CASEY, J W
T-Dt: -- --- -----
P-Dt: 29 Sep 1906
Dist/Class: School
File#: 4591
Patent#: 437
Patent Vol.: 32
Survey/Blk/Twp: 1/4 50 BRIR-
Acres: 172
Map(s) 38

Abstract # 1673 - T&NO RR CO
S2: CATES, J
P'ee: CATES, JOHN
G'ee: CATES, JOHN
T-Dt: -- --- -----
P-Dt: 22 Sep 1911
Dist/Class: School
File#: 4699
Patent#: 18
Patent Vol.: 43
Certificate: 861
Survey/Blk/Twp: SW 1/4 6 T & NO-

Acres: 160
Map(s) 28, 29

Abstract # 1674 - CURTIS, V E
P'ee: CURTIS, V E
G'ee: CURTIS, V E
T-Dt: -- --- -----
P-Dt: 13 Jul 1882
Dist/Class: Fannin Scrip
File#: 15139
Patent#: 45
Patent Vol.: 2
Acres: 78.33
Map(s) 34, 35

Abstract # 1675 - DE LONG, E
P'ee: DELONG, ELIAS
G'ee: DELONG, ELIAS
T-Dt: -- --- -----
P-Dt: 12 Feb 1881
Dist/Class: Milam Preemption
File#: 2716
Patent#: 627
Patent Vol.: 11
Acres: 160
Map(s) 43

Abstract # 1676 - DOOLEY, MRS F P
P'ee: DOOLEY, F P (MRS)
G'ee: DOOLEY, F P (MRS)
T-Dt: -- --- -----
P-Dt: 03 Aug 1885
Dist/Class: Fannin Preemption
File#: 2591
Patent#: 361
Patent Vol.: 17
Acres: 80
Map(s) 37

Abstract # 1678 - EVERETT, J P
P'ee: PHILLIPS, JOHN M
G'ee: EVERETT, J P
T-Dt: -- --- -----
P-Dt: 27 Mar 1884
Dist/Class: Fannin Preemption
File#: 2640
Patent#: 358
Patent Vol.: 15
Acres: 100.50
Map(s) 23, 31

Abstract # 1679 - FORD, B
P'ee: FORD, B
G'ee: FORD, B
T-Dt: -- --- -----
P-Dt: 02 Aug 1883
Dist/Class: Fannin Preemption
File#: 2623
Patent#: 388
Patent Vol.: 14
Acres: 80
Map(s) 32

Abstract # 1680 - HART, S F
P'ee: HART, S A
G'ee: HART, S A
T-Dt: -- --- -----
P-Dt: 28 Mar 1881
Dist/Class: Fannin Preemption
File#: 2221
Patent#: 135
Patent Vol.: 12
Acres: 160
Map(s) 34

Abstract # 1682 - HARDIN, L E
P'ee: HARDIN, L E (HEIRS)
G'ee: HARDIN, L E
T-Dt: -- --- -----
P-Dt: 03 Sep 1888
Dist/Class: Fannin Preemption
File#: 2553
Patent#: 209
Patent Vol.: 21
Acres: 131
Map(s) 6, 7

Abstract # 1684 - AB&M
S2: HARRIS, D
P'ee: MCCALLISTER, G W
G'ee: HARRIS, DAVID
T-Dt: -- --- -----
P-Dt: 01 May 1902
Dist/Class: School
File#: 4483
Patent#: 463
Patent Vol.: 23
Certificate: 16/63
Survey/Blk/Twp: E 1/2 OF SW 1/4 2 SPRR 2-
Acres: 80
Map(s) 35

Abstract # 1685 - BRIR
S2: JOHNSON, W
P'ee: JOHNSON, WILLIAM
G'ee: JOHNSON, WILLIAM
T-Dt: -- --- -----
P-Dt: 05 Sep 1883
Dist/Class: Fannin Preemption
File#: 2633
Patent#: 559
Patent Vol.: 14
Survey/Blk/Twp: 45 BRIR-
Acres: 160
Map(s) 38

Abstract # 1686 - G&BN CO
S2: JAMESON, A B
P'ee: JAMESON, A B
G'ee: JAMESON, A B
T-Dt: -- --- -----
P-Dt: 13 Dec 1884
Dist/Class: School
File#: 4290
Patent#: 277
Patent Vol.: 4
Survey/Blk/Twp: SW 1/4 1 G & BN CO.-
Acres: 160
Map(s) 6

Abstract # 1688 - KELLY, W
P'ee: KELLEY, WILLIAM
G'ee: KELLEY, WILLIAM
T-Dt: -- --- -----
P-Dt: 03 Jun 1886
Dist/Class: Fannin Preemption
File#: 2631
Patent#: 386
Patent Vol.: 18
Acres: 77.40
Map(s) 36, 37

Abstract # 1689 - BRIR
S2: LEDBETTER, A B
P'ee: LEDBETTER, A B
G'ee: LEDBETTER, A B
T-Dt: -- --- -----
P-Dt: 08 Sep 1883
Dist/Class: Fannin Preemption

File#: 2632
Patent#: 599
Patent Vol.: 14
Survey/Blk/Twp: 71 BRIR-
Acres: 160
Map(s) 38, 39

Abstract # 1690 - LOGAN, W
P'ee: LOGAN, WILLIAM
G'ee: LOGAN, WILLIAM
T-Dt: -- --- -----
P-Dt: 05 Nov 1891
Dist/Class: Fannin Preemption
File#: 2573
Patent#: 234
Patent Vol.: 24
Acres: 39
Map(s) 31

Abstract # 1691 - MOORE, A D
P'ee: FLEMING, R F
G'ee: MOORE, A D
T-Dt: -- --- -----
P-Dt: 28 Jul 1881
Dist/Class: Fannin Preemption
File#: 1393
Patent#: 400
Patent Vol.: 12
Acres: 160
Map(s) 29

Abstract # 1692 - MORRIS, W G
P'ee: MORRIS, W G
G'ee: MORRIS, W G
T-Dt: -- --- -----
P-Dt: 21 Aug 1890
Dist/Class: Fannin Preemption
File#: 2556
Patent#: 230
Patent Vol.: 23
Acres: 83.70
Map(s) 31

Abstract # 1693 - SP RR CO
S2: MEYER, J
P'ee: MEYER, JACOB
G'ee: MEYER, JACOB
T-Dt: -- --- -----
P-Dt: 01 May 1891
Dist/Class: School
File#: 3710
Patent#: 564
Patent Vol.: 11
Certificate: 16/129
Survey/Blk/Twp: NE 1/4 10 SPRR-
Acres: 160
Map(s) 23

Abstract # 1694 - BRIR
S2: MORRISON, J E
P'ee: FORE, J R
G'ee: MORRISON, J E
T-Dt: -- --- -----
P-Dt: 08 Mar 1901
Dist/Class: School
File#: 4615
Patent#: 459
Patent Vol.: 19
Survey/Blk/Twp: 54 BRIR-
Acres: 160
Map(s) 38

Abstract # 1695 - SP RR CO
S2: MCCOMBER, H A
P'ee: MCCOMBER, H A

G'ee: MCCOMBER, H A
T-Dt: -- --- -----
P-Dt: 03 Oct 1889
Dist/Class: School
File#: 4543
Patent#: 424
Patent Vol.: 9
Certificate: 16/69
Survey/Blk/Twp: E 1/2 6 SPRR-
Acres: 320
Map(s) 24, 32

Abstract # 1696 - NEFF, J
P'ee: PINKSTON, J B
G'ee: NEFF, J
T-Dt: -- --- -----
P-Dt: 16 Mar 1881
Dist/Class: Fannin Preemption
File#: 1401
Patent#: 67
Patent Vol.: 12
Acres: 80
Map(s) 37

Abstract # 1697 - NICHOLSON, W A
P'ee: DAVIDSON, J W
G'ee: NICHOLSON, W A
T-Dt: -- --- -----
P-Dt: 18 Feb 1884
Dist/Class: Fannin Preemption
File#: 2533
Patent#: 246
Patent Vol.: 15
Acres: 160
Map(s) 6, 7

Abstract # 1698 - PASSMORE, B
P'ee: LESLIE, JOHN T
G'ee: PASSMORE, BRYANT
T-Dt: -- --- -----
P-Dt: 13 Jul 1881
Dist/Class: Fannin Preemption
File#: 1499
Patent#: 369
Patent Vol.: 12
Acres: 160
Map(s) 33, 41

Abstract # 1700 - BBB&C RR CO
S2: PANKONIN, E
P'ee: PANKONIN, E
G'ee: PANKONIN, E
T-Dt: -- --- -----
P-Dt: 27 Feb 1901
Dist/Class: School
File#: 4249
Patent#: 432
Patent Vol.: 19
Certificate: 692
Survey/Blk/Twp: NE 1/4 4 BBB & CRR-
Acres: 160
Map(s) 3

Abstract # 1701 - BBB&C RR CO
S2: PANKKONIN, L
P'ee: PANKONIN, L
G'ee: PANKONIN, L
T-Dt: -- --- -----
P-Dt: 27 Feb 1901
Dist/Class: School
File#: 4248
Patent#: 431
Patent Vol.: 19
Certificate: 692
Survey/Blk/Twp: SE 1/4 4 BBB & CRR-

Acres: 160
Map(s) 3

Abstract # 1703 - ROW, W C
P'ee: ROW, E
G'ee: ROW, W C
T-Dt: -- --- -----
P-Dt: 05 May 1885
Dist/Class: Fannin Preemption
File#: 2613
Patent#: 162
Patent Vol.: 17
Acres: 95.50
Map(s) 7

Abstract # 1704 - REYNOLDS, J C
P'ee: REYNOLDS, J C
G'ee: REYNOLDS, J C
T-Dt: -- --- -----
P-Dt: 22 Jul 1936
Dist/Class: Fannin Scrip
File#: 14854
Patent#: 353
Patent Vol.: 62A
Acres: 132.80
Map(s) 9

Abstract # 1707 - STROUD, W W
P'ee: STROUD, W W
G'ee: STROUD, W W
T-Dt: -- --- -----
P-Dt: 23 Jan 1886
Dist/Class: Fannin Preemption
File#: 2555
Patent#: 67
Patent Vol.: 18
Acres: 160
Map(s) 6

Abstract # 1708 - SHARP, W A
P'ee: SHARP, W A
G'ee: SHARP, W A
T-Dt: -- --- -----
P-Dt: 22 Nov 1884
Dist/Class: Fannin Scrip
File#: 15228
Patent#: 135
Patent Vol.: 10
Acres: 49.82
Map(s) 40

Abstract # 1709 - BRIR
S2: SEDDON, S T
P'ee: SEDDON, S T
G'ee: SEDDON, S T
T-Dt: -- --- -----
P-Dt: 29 Aug 1884
Dist/Class: School
File#: 3870
Patent#: 102
Patent Vol.: 4
Survey/Blk/Twp: FRAC. 68 BRIR-
Acres: 111
Map(s) 29, 37

Abstract # 1711 - TT RR CO
S2: SCOTT, J E
P'ee: UPHAM, CHARLES
G'ee: SCOTT, J E
T-Dt: -- --- -----
P-Dt: 25 Jul 1917
Dist/Class: School
File#: 4481
Patent#: 289
Patent Vol.: 53

Certificate: 606
Survey/Blk/Twp: SW 1/4 16 TTRR-
Acres: 165
Map(s) 32

Abstract # 1713 - WILLIAMS, J H
P'ee: WILLIAMS, J H
G'ee: WILLIAMS, J H
T-Dt: -- --- -----
P-Dt: 19 Jan 1881
Dist/Class: Fannin Scrip
File#: 14862
Patent#: 134
Patent Vol.: 1
Acres: 160
Map(s) 33, 41

Abstract # 1714 - G&BN CO
S2: WANN, S M
P'ee: WANN, S M
G'ee: WANN, S M
T-Dt: -- --- -----
P-Dt: 21 Jul 1881
Dist/Class: School
File#: 3166
Patent#: 471
Patent Vol.: 1
Survey/Blk/Twp: NE 1/4 3 G & BN CO.-
Acres: 160
Map(s) 6, 7

Abstract # 1716 - AUTREY, T
P'ee: AUTREY, THOMAS
G'ee: AUTREY, THOMAS
T-Dt: -- --- -----
P-Dt: 13 Jun 1885
Dist/Class: Fannin Preemption
File#: 2664
Patent#: 247
Patent Vol.: 17
Acres: 80
Map(s) 33

Abstract # 1717 - BAILARD, P S
P'ee: BALLARD, P B
G'ee: BALLARD, P B
T-Dt: -- --- -----
P-Dt: 01 Aug 1887
Dist/Class: Fannin Preemption
File#: 2708
Patent#: 35
Patent Vol.: 20
Acres: 56.90
Map(s) 34, 42

Abstract # 1718 - BULLARD, J D
P'ee: BULLARD, L D
G'ee: BULLARD, L D
T-Dt: -- --- -----
P-Dt: 20 Jul 1886
Dist/Class: Fannin Preemption
File#: 2693
Patent#: 479
Patent Vol.: 18
Acres: 160
Map(s) 31

Abstract # 1719 - G&BN CO
S2: COMPERE, W T
P'ee: MANDEVILLE, M
G'ee: COMPERE, W T
T-Dt: -- --- -----
P-Dt: 26 Oct 1889
Dist/Class: School
File#: 5720

Patent#: 459
Patent Vol.: 9
Certificate: 29
Survey/Blk/Twp: NW 1/4 3 GB & N CO.-
Acres: 160
Map(s) 6

Abstract # 1720 - BBB&C RR CO
S2: CUNNINGHAM, J T
P'ee: LICHTE, FRITZ
G'ee: CUNNINGHAM, J T
T-Dt: -- --- -----
P-Dt: 03 Oct 1889
Dist/Class: School
File#: 6931
Patent#: 421
Patent Vol.: 9
Certificate: 681
Survey/Blk/Twp: SE 1/4 2 BBB & CRR-
Acres: 160
Map(s) 31, 32

Abstract # 1721 - BBB&C RR CO
S2: CLINGBERG, A
P'ee: CLINGBERG, AUGUST (HEIRS)
G'ee: CLINGBERG, AUGUST
T-Dt: -- --- -----
P-Dt: 20 Feb 1912
Dist/Class: School
File#: 7189
Patent#: 490
Patent Vol.: 43
Certificate: 682
Survey/Blk/Twp: SE 1/4 2 BBB & CRR-
Acres: 160
Map(s) 15, 16

Abstract # 1722 - COSBY, J
P'ee: KENDALL, JOSIAH
G'ee: COSBY, JAMES
T-Dt: -- --- -----
P-Dt: 29 Jan 1891
Dist/Class: School
File#: 7165
Patent#: 355
Patent Vol.: 11
Certificate: 1/269
Survey/Blk/Twp: 4 BS & F-
Acres: 610.9
Map(s) 35

Abstract # 1723 - BS&F
S2: COSBY, J
P'ee: KENDALL, JOSIAH
G'ee: COSBY, JAMES
T-Dt: -- --- -----
P-Dt: 16 Dec 1885
Dist/Class: School
File#: 7166
Patent#: 224
Patent Vol.: 5
Certificate: 1/270
Survey/Blk/Twp: 3/4 2 BS & F-
Acres: 480
Map(s) 34, 35

Abstract # 1725 - DEES, A N
P'ee: ALLEN, ISAAC
G'ee: DEES, A N
T-Dt: -- --- -----
P-Dt: 21 Aug 1901
Dist/Class: School
File#: 6051
Patent#: 201
Patent Vol.: 21

Certificate: 2/165
Survey/Blk/Twp: MID. 1/4 6
J.POITEVENT-
Acres: 160
Map(s) 23

Abstract # 1726 - SP RR CO
S2: DONNELL, W L
P'ee: DONNELL, W L
G'ee: DONNELL, W L
T-Dt: -- --- -----
P-Dt: 26 Jan 1899
Dist/Class: School
File#: 6343
Patent#: 435
Patent Vol.: 16
Certificate: 16/97
Survey/Blk/Twp: 2 SPRR-
Acres: 640
Map(s) 34, 35

Abstract # 1728 - EDDLEMAN, J
P'ee: EDDLEMAN, JOHN
G'ee: EDDLEMAN, JOHN
T-Dt: -- --- -----
P-Dt: 15 Sep 1882
Dist/Class: Fannin Preemption
File#: 1326
Patent#: 528
Patent Vol.: 13
Acres: 160
Map(s) 38

Abstract # 1730 - BRIR
S2: GILMORE, W J
P'ee: GILMORE, W J
G'ee: GILMORE, W J
T-Dt: -- --- -----
P-Dt: 14 Oct 1886
Dist/Class: Fannin Preemption
File#: 2648
Patent#: 629
Patent Vol.: 18
Acres: 160
Map(s) 38, 39

Abstract # 1731 - HULL, M
P'ee: HULL, MAJOR
G'ee: HULL, MAJOR
T-Dt: -- --- -----
P-Dt: 17 Dec 1885
Dist/Class: Fannin Preemption
File#: 2692
Patent#: 600
Patent Vol.: 17
Acres: 160
Map(s) 31

Abstract # 1732 - HARRINGTON, J
P'ee: HERRINGTON, JOHN
G'ee: HERRINGTON, JOHN
T-Dt: -- --- -----
P-Dt: 22 Apr 1884
Dist/Class: Fannin Preemption
File#: 2665
Patent#: 391
Patent Vol.: 15
Acres: 160
Map(s) 34, 42

Abstract # 1734 - AB&M
S2: HARRIS, D
P'ee: MCCALLISTER, G W
G'ee: HARRIS, DAVID
T-Dt: -- --- -----

P-Dt: 01 May 1902
Dist/Class: School
File#: 6373
Patent#: 464
Patent Vol.: 23
Certificate: 16/63
Survey/Blk/Twp: SE 1/4 2 SPRR 2-
Acres: 160
Map(s) 35

Abstract # 1735 - JONES, A
P'ee: JONES, ALBERT
G'ee: JONES, ALBERT
T-Dt: -- --- -----
P-Dt: 13 Sep 1884
Dist/Class: Fannin Preemption
File#: 2667
Patent#: 241
Patent Vol.: 16
Acres: 160
Map(s) 34, 42

Abstract # 1736 - KISER, J A
P'ee: KISER, J A
G'ee: KISER, J A
T-Dt: -- --- -----
P-Dt: 14 Apr 1876
Dist/Class: Fannin Preemption
File#: 2676
Patent#: 257
Patent Vol.: 18
Acres: 147
Map(s) 33

Abstract # 1737 - LAYNE, J L
P'ee: LAYNE, J L
G'ee: LAYNE, J L
T-Dt: -- --- -----
P-Dt: 05 May 1882
Dist/Class: Fannin Preemption
File#: 1375
Patent#: 305
Patent Vol.: 13
Acres: 160
Map(s) 37

Abstract # 1738 - BRIR
S2: LOVEJOY, J T
P'ee: MABRY, R E
G'ee: LOVEJOY, J T
T-Dt: -- --- -----
P-Dt: 21 Sep 1912
Dist/Class: School
File#: 6393
Patent#: 3
Patent Vol.: 45
Survey/Blk/Twp: E 1/2 77 BRIR-
Acres: 160
Map(s) 38

Abstract # 1739 - MORRIS, N
P'ee: MORRIS, N B (MRS)
G'ee: MORRIS, N B (MRS)
T-Dt: -- --- -----
P-Dt: 21 Jan 1886
Dist/Class: Fannin Preemption
File#: 2692 1/2
Patent#: 51
Patent Vol.: 18
Acres: 150.88
Map(s) 33

Abstract # 1740 - MAINES, W
P'ee: MORRISON, C B
G'ee: MAIMES, WILLIAM

T-Dt: -- --- -----
P-Dt: 25 Jul 1883
Dist/Class: Fannin Preemption
File#: 2694
Patent#: 338
Patent Vol.: 14
Acres: 113
Map(s) 30

Abstract # 1741 - MOSLEY, N S
P'ee: MOSLEY, N S
G'ee: MOSLEY, N S
T-Dt: -- --- -----
P-Dt: 24 Nov 1885
Dist/Class: Fannin Preemption
File#: 2685
Patent#: 566
Patent Vol.: 17
Acres: 160
Map(s) 39, 47

Abstract # 1742 - MULLINS, J B
P'ee: NORRIS, J B
G'ee: MULLINS, J B
T-Dt: -- --- -----
P-Dt: 17 Feb 1890
Dist/Class: Fannin Preemption
File#: 2653
Patent#: 507
Patent Vol.: 22
Acres: 160
Map(s) 32

Abstract # 1744 - MOONEY, J
P'ee: MOONEY, JAMES
G'ee: MOONEY, JAMES
T-Dt: -- --- -----
P-Dt: 27 Aug 1884
Dist/Class: Fannin Scrip
File#: 15841
Patent#: 6
Patent Vol.: 10
Acres: 190.50
Map(s) 33, 41

Abstract # 1745 - ORRELL, MRS S
P'ee: WEBSTER, J S
G'ee: ORRELL, SARAH (MRS)
T-Dt: -- --- -----
P-Dt: 20 Feb 1885
Dist/Class: Fannin Preemption
File#: 2669
Patent#: 21
Patent Vol.: 17
Acres: 150
Map(s) 38

Abstract # 1746 - POPE, W B
P'ee: POPE, W B
G'ee: POPE, W B
T-Dt: -- --- -----
P-Dt: 03 Mar 1882
Dist/Class: Fannin Preemption
File#: 1614
Patent#: 145
Patent Vol.: 13
Acres: 160
Map(s) 20

Abstract # 1748 - AB&M
S2: PARHAM, J
P'ee: PARHAM, JAMES (HEIRS)
G'ee: PARHAM, JAMES
T-Dt: -- --- -----
P-Dt: 09 May 1900

Dist/Class: School
File#: 6729
Patent#: 392
Patent Vol.: 18
Survey/Blk/Twp: NW 1/4 2 SPRR-
Acres: 160
Map(s) 35

Abstract # 1749 - ROGERS, T H
P'ee: ROGERS, T H
G'ee: ROGERS, T H
T-Dt: -- --- -----
P-Dt: 20 Oct 1887
Dist/Class: Fannin Preemption
File#: 2654
Patent#: 246
Patent Vol.: 20
Acres: 160
Map(s) 32

Abstract # 1750 - BS&F
S2: RUSSELL, D W
P'ee: RUSSELL, D W
G'ee: RUSSELL, D W
T-Dt: -- --- -----
P-Dt: 19 Sep 1888
Dist/Class: School
File#: 5776
Patent#: 416
Patent Vol.: 8
Certificate: 1/270
Survey/Blk/Twp: SW 1/4 2 BS & F-
Acres: 160
Map(s) 34

Abstract # 1751 - SP RR CO
S2: RODGERS, G
P'ee: WILLIS, PRUDENCE
G'ee: ROGERS, GEORGE
T-Dt: -- --- -----
P-Dt: 02 Jun 1920
Dist/Class: School
File#: 6492
Patent#: 331
Patent Vol.: 7A
Certificate: 16/115
Survey/Blk/Twp: SE 1/4 2 SPRR 3-
Acres: 204
Map(s) 31, 32

Abstract # 1752 - SMITH, W E
P'ee: CHISM, E M
G'ee: SMITH, W E
T-Dt: -- --- -----
P-Dt: 26 Jul 1882
Dist/Class: Fannin Preemption
File#: 1426
Patent#: 439
Patent Vol.: 13
Acres: 160
Map(s) 37

Abstract # 1753 - STINETT, J SR
P'ee: STINNETT, JAMES SR
G'ee: STINNETT, JAMES SR
T-Dt: -- --- -----
P-Dt: 16 Jul 1884
Dist/Class: Fannin Preemption
File#: 2678
Patent#: 44
Patent Vol.: 16
Acres: 160
Map(s) 35

Abstract # 1754 - STINETT, W M

P'ee: NELSON, P H
G'ee: STINNETT, WILLIAM
T-Dt: -- --- -----
P-Dt: 26 Dec 1895
Dist/Class: School
File#: 7717
Patent#: 210
Patent Vol.: 15
Certificate: 16/75
Survey/Blk/Twp: MID. 1/4 4 SPRR-
Acres: 160
Map(s) 35

Abstract # 1756 - STINNETT, W M
P'ee: PARROTT, R L
G'ee: STINNETT, W M
T-Dt: -- --- -----
P-Dt: 07 Feb 1895
Dist/Class: School
File#: 6086
Patent#: 502
Patent Vol.: 14
Certificate: 16/75
Survey/Blk/Twp: N.PT.4 SPRR-
Acres: 160
Map(s) 35

Abstract # 1757 - BBB&C RR CO
S2: UPHAM, C S
P'ee: UPHAM, CHARLES S
G'ee: UPHAM, CHARLES S
T-Dt: -- --- -----
P-Dt: 03 Apr 1890
Dist/Class: School
File#: 5822
Patent#: 296
Patent Vol.: 10
Certificate: 681
Survey/Blk/Twp: NE 1/4 2 BBB & CRR-
Acres: 160
Map(s) 31, 32

Abstract # 1758 - WILLIAMS, W
P'ee: WILLIAMS, WILLIAM
G'ee: WILLIAMS, WILLIAM
T-Dt: -- --- -----
P-Dt: 06 Mar 1882
Dist/Class: Fannin Preemption
File#: 1271
Patent#: 162
Patent Vol.: 13
Acres: 80
Map(s) 20

Abstract # 1759 - WILLIAMS, H D
P'ee: WILLIAMS, H D
G'ee: WILLIAMS, H D
T-Dt: -- --- -----
P-Dt: 06 Mar 1882
Dist/Class: Fannin Preemption
File#: 1268
Patent#: 163
Patent Vol.: 13
Acres: 160
Map(s) 20

Abstract # 1760 - WALKER, A F
P'ee: WALKER, A F
G'ee: WALKER, A F
T-Dt: -- --- -----
P-Dt: 16 Aug 1884
Dist/Class: Fannin Preemption
File#: 2690
Patent#: 138
Patent Vol.: 16

Acres: 160
Map(s) 34

Abstract # 1761 - WEST, A J
P'ee: WEST, A J
G'ee: WEST, A J
T-Dt: -- --- -----
P-Dt: 23 Nov 1883
Dist/Class: Fannin Preemption
File#: 2686
Patent#: 45
Patent Vol.: 15
Acres: 160
Map(s) 34

Abstract # 1763 - WOOD, Z F
P'ee: GRAHAM, E S
G'ee: WOOD, Z F
T-Dt: -- --- -----
P-Dt: 13 Oct 1888
Dist/Class: Fannin Preemption
File#: 2707
Patent#: 284
Patent Vol.: 21
Acres: 160
Map(s) 31

Abstract # 1766 - TT RR CO
S2: WOODS, B F
P'ee: WOODS, B F
G'ee: WOODS, B F
T-Dt: -- --- -----
P-Dt: 11 Sep 1896
Dist/Class: School
File#: 6612
Patent#: 518
Patent Vol.: 15
Certificate: 606
Survey/Blk/Twp: SE 1/4 16 TTRR-
Acres: 64
Map(s) 32

Abstract # 1767 - ALCORN, R
P'ee: ALCORN, ROBERT
G'ee: ALCORN, ROBERT
T-Dt: -- --- -----
P-Dt: 19 Jun 1883
Dist/Class: Fannin Preemption
File#: 2832
Patent#: 276
Patent Vol.: 14
Acres: 160
Map(s) 38

Abstract # 1768 - BIRDWELL, J
P'ee: BIRDWELL, JOSEPH
G'ee: BIRDWELL, JOSEPH
T-Dt: -- --- -----
P-Dt: 27 Mar 1884
Dist/Class: Fannin Preemption
File#: 2783
Patent#: 352
Patent Vol.: 15
Acres: 160
Map(s) 31, 32, 39, 40

Abstract # 1769 - BRAGG, B
P'ee: ELLIS, G W
G'ee: BRAGG, BENJAMIN
T-Dt: -- --- -----
P-Dt: 25 Apr 1887
Dist/Class: Fannin Preemption
File#: 2820
Patent#: 424
Patent Vol.: 19

Acres: 160
Map(s) 34

Abstract # 1770 - BURCH, T J
P'ee: BURCH, T J
G'ee: BURCH, T J
T-Dt: -- --- -----
P-Dt: 13 Sep 1887
Dist/Class: Fannin Scrip
File#: 19167
Patent#: 502
Patent Vol.: 10
Survey/Blk/Twp: 1
Acres: 73.25
Map(s) 21

Abstract # 1771 - BRIR
S2: BRIM, J F
P'ee: BRIM, JOHN F
G'ee: BRIM, JOHN F
T-Dt: -- --- -----
P-Dt: 24 Dec 1917
Dist/Class: School
File#: 9312
Patent#: 394
Patent Vol.: 54
Survey/Blk/Twp: SEC. 104 BRIR-
Acres: 200
Map(s) 30

Abstract # 1772 - CRISELL, MRS M E
P'ee: GRAHAM, E S
G'ee: CRISWELL, MARY E (MRS)
T-Dt: -- --- -----
P-Dt: 14 Aug 1884
Dist/Class: Fannin Donation
File#: 1569
Patent#: 535
Patent Vol.: 5
Certificate: 339
Acres: 1163.50
Map(s) 35

Abstract # 1773 - BRIR
S2: CUNNINGHAM, J H
P'ee: CUNNINGHAM, J H
G'ee: CUNNINGHAM, J H
T-Dt: -- --- -----
P-Dt: 27 Jun 1892
Dist/Class: School
File#: 7953
Patent#: 60
Patent Vol.: 13
Survey/Blk/Twp: 1/4 47 BRIR-
Acres: 157
Map(s) 38

Abstract # 1774 - POITEVENT, J
S2: COOK, L C
P'ee: SWINK, W T
G'ee: COOK, L C
T-Dt: -- --- -----
P-Dt: 24 May 1901
Dist/Class: School
File#: 8245
Patent#: 305
Patent Vol.: 20
Certificate: 2/159
Survey/Blk/Twp: 1/4 18 J.POITEVENT-
Acres: 137.5
Map(s) 24

Abstract # 1775 - DOZIER, H C
P'ee: DOZIER, H C
G'ee: DOZIER, H C

T-Dt: -- --- -----
P-Dt: 12 Dec 1883
Dist/Class: Fannin Preemption
File#: 2788
Patent#: 79
Patent Vol.: 15
Acres: 80
Map(s) 27

Abstract # 1776 - POITEVENT, J
S2: DAWSON, J T
P'ee: SMITH, J H
G'ee: DAWSON, J T
T-Dt: -- --- -----
P-Dt: 20 Mar 1924
Dist/Class: School
File#: 8247
Patent#: 177
Patent Vol.: 22A
Certificate: 2/159
Survey/Blk/Twp: E 1/2 18 J.POITEVENT-
Acres: 213.7
Map(s) 24

Abstract # 1777 - GUEST, M V
P'ee: CAMPBELL, JANE
G'ee: GUEST, M V
T-Dt: -- --- -----
P-Dt: 25 Sep 1884
Dist/Class: Fannin Preemption
File#: 2755
Patent#: 271
Patent Vol.: 16
Acres: 20.90
Map(s) 28

Abstract # 1778 - HUGHES, W J
P'ee: HUGHES, W J
G'ee: HUGHES, W J
T-Dt: -- --- -----
P-Dt: 21 Sep 1883
Dist/Class: Fannin Scrip
File#: 17197
Patent#: 332
Patent Vol.: 6
Acres: 45.90
Map(s) 42

Abstract # 1779 - T&NO RR CO
S2: IRVIN, A
P'ee: IRVIN, ANDREW
G'ee: IRVIN, ANDREW
T-Dt: -- --- -----
P-Dt: 24 May 1895
Dist/Class: School
File#: 9146
Patent#: 583
Patent Vol.: 14
Certificate: 863
Survey/Blk/Twp: SW 1/4 10 T & NO-
Acres: 160
Map(s) 29, 37

Abstract # 1781 - BRIR
S2: JOHNSON, C W & WILLIAMS, B F
P'ee: JOHNSON, C W
G'ee: JOHNSON, C W AND WILLIAMS, B F
T-Dt: -- --- -----
P-Dt: 09 Dec 1909
Dist/Class: School
File#: 9325
Patent#: 164
Patent Vol.: 39
Survey/Blk/Twp: 1/4 102 BRIR-

Acres: 160
Map(s) 30

Abstract # 1782 - KELLUM, MRS, E
P'ee: GRAHAM, E S
G'ee: KELLUM, EMILY (MRS)
T-Dt: -- --- -----
P-Dt: 17 Dec 1884
Dist/Class: Fannin Donation
File#: 1568
Patent#: 29
Patent Vol.: 6
Certificate: 657
Acres: 1280
Map(s) 31, 39

Abstract # 1783 - MCNEW, W
P'ee: HEFNER, J L
G'ee: MCNEW, ELI
T-Dt: -- --- -----
P-Dt: 27 Jan 1886
Dist/Class: Fannin Preemption
File#: 2754 1/2
Patent#: 76
Patent Vol.: 18
Acres: 160
Map(s) 35

Abstract # 1784 - MIERS, L
P'ee: MCALINEY, FRANCIS
G'ee: MIERS, LUCINDA
T-Dt: -- --- -----
P-Dt: 27 Nov 1886
Dist/Class: Fannin Preemption
File#: 2822
Patent#: 115
Patent Vol.: 19
Acres: 156.25
Map(s) 39

Abstract # 1785 - MITCHELL, MRS N A
P'ee: MITCHELL, N A (MRS)
G'ee: MITCHELL, N A (MRS)
T-Dt: -- --- -----
P-Dt: 01 Sep 1883
Dist/Class: Fannin Preemption
File#: 2468
Patent#: 521
Patent Vol.: 14
Acres: 160
Map(s) 32

Abstract # 1786 - O CONNER, P H
P'ee: DICK, W J
G'ee: O"CONNER, PATRICK H
T-Dt: -- --- -----
P-Dt: 03 Oct 1883
Dist/Class: Fannin Preemption
File#: 1649
Patent#: 5
Patent Vol.: 15
Acres: 160
Map(s) 8

Abstract # 1787 - PETERS, C
P'ee: PETERS, CARL
G'ee: PETERS, CARL
T-Dt: -- --- -----
P-Dt: 15 Apr 1887
Dist/Class: Milam Preemption
File#: 4125
Patent#: 407
Patent Vol.: 19
Acres: 80
Map(s) 44

Abstract # 1788 - RUSSELL, D W
P'ee: RUSSELL, D W
G'ee: RUSSELL, D W
T-Dt: -- --- -----
P-Dt: 25 Apr 1887
Dist/Class: Fannin Preemption
File#: 2819
Patent#: 423
Patent Vol.: 19
Acres: 160
Map(s) 34

Abstract # 1789 - RUSSELL, D C
P'ee: RUSSELL, D C
G'ee: RUSSELL, D C
T-Dt: -- --- -----
P-Dt: 26 May 1885
Dist/Class: Fannin Preemption
File#: 2789
Patent#: 210
Patent Vol.: 17
Acres: 160
Map(s) 34

Abstract # 1790 - SLADE, J T
P'ee: SLADE, J T
G'ee: SLADE, J T
T-Dt: -- --- -----
P-Dt: 06 Aug 1883
Dist/Class: Fannin Preemption
File#: 1269
Patent#: 416
Patent Vol.: 14
Acres: 160
Map(s) 8

Abstract # 1791 - SMITH, I N
P'ee: FICKLIN, THOMAS F
G'ee: SMITH, I N
T-Dt: -- --- -----
P-Dt: 07 Feb 1898
Dist/Class: Fannin Preemption
File#: 3064
Patent#: 622
Patent Vol.: 29
Acres: 160
Map(s) 36, 44

Abstract # 1794 - BRAY, S S
P'ee: BRYANT, R
G'ee: BRAY, S S
T-Dt: -- --- -----
P-Dt: 08 May 1888
Dist/Class: Fannin Preemption
File#: 2856
Patent#: 32
Patent Vol.: 21
Acres: 160
Map(s) 32

Abstract # 1795 - BRIR
S2: BUNGER, W T
P'ee: BUNGER, WILLIAM T
G'ee: BUNGER, WILLIAM T
T-Dt: -- --- -----
P-Dt: 26 May 1884
Dist/Class: School
File#: 2578
Patent#: 469
Patent Vol.: 3
Survey/Blk/Twp: 1/4 52 BRIR-
Acres: 160
Map(s) 37, 38

Abstract # 1796 - T&NO RR CO

S2: CLARK, T B
P'ee: HILL, J G
G'ee: CLARK, T B
T-Dt: -- --- -----
P-Dt: 29 Jun 1889
Dist/Class: School
File#: 10706
Patent#: 221
Patent Vol.: 9
Certificate: 865
Survey/Blk/Twp: SW 1/4 4 T & NO-
Acres: 160
Map(s) 31

Abstract # 1797 - DURHAM, J
P'ee: DURHAM, JAMES (HEIRS)
G'ee: DURHAM, JAMES
T-Dt: -- --- -----
P-Dt: 25 Apr 1887
Dist/Class: Fannin Preemption
File#: 2876
Patent#: 425
Patent Vol.: 19
Acres: 160
Map(s) 20, 21

Abstract # 1798 - FERGUSON, J C
P'ee: DAVIS, A P
G'ee: FERGUSON, JOHN C
T-Dt: -- --- -----
P-Dt: 12 Jun 1884
Dist/Class: Fannin Preemption
File#: 1333
Patent#: 557
Patent Vol.: 15
Acres: 80
Map(s) 29

Abstract # 1799 - GOSSETT, A E
P'ee: GRAHAM, E S
G'ee: GOSSETT, A E
T-Dt: -- --- -----
P-Dt: 18 Feb 1884
Dist/Class: Fannin Donation
File#: 1696
Patent#: 237
Patent Vol.: 5
Certificate: 716
Acres: 266
Map(s) 35, 36

Abstract # 1800 - GOSSETT, A E
P'ee: GRAHAM, E S
G'ee: GOSSETT, A E
T-Dt: -- --- -----
P-Dt: 18 Feb 1884
Dist/Class: Fannin Donation
File#: 1696
Patent#: 238
Patent Vol.: 5
Certificate: 716
Acres: 242
Map(s) 34, 42

Abstract # 1801 - GOSSETT, A E
T-Dt: -- --- -----
P-Dt: -- --- -----
Map(s) 27

Abstract # 1802 - GOSSETT, A E
P'ee: GRAHAM, E S
G'ee: GOSSETT, A E
T-Dt: -- --- -----
P-Dt: 05 Mar 1884
Dist/Class: Fannin Donation

File#: 1696
Patent#: 246
Patent Vol.: 5
Certificate: 716
Acres: 207.50
Map(s) 36

Abstract # 1804 - HOLDERNESS, S M
P'ee: GRAHAM, E S
G'ee: HOLDERNESS, S M
T-Dt: -- --- -----
P-Dt: 25 Apr 1895
Dist/Class: Fannin Donation
File#: 1694
Patent#: 199
Patent Vol.: 8
Certificate: 25/64
Acres: 243
Map(s) 35

Abstract # 1805 - HOLDERNESS, S M
P'ee: GRAHAM, E S
G'ee: HOLDERNESS, S M
T-Dt: -- --- -----
P-Dt: 22 Feb 1884
Dist/Class: Fannin Donation
File#: 1694
Patent#: 244
Patent Vol.: 5
Certificate: 25/64
Acres: 73
Map(s) 31

Abstract # 1806 - HOLDERNESS, S M
P'ee: GRAHAM, E S
G'ee: HOLDERNESS, S M
T-Dt: -- --- -----
P-Dt: 09 Apr 1884
Dist/Class: Fannin Donation
File#: 1694
Patent#: 370
Patent Vol.: 5
Certificate: 25/64
Acres: 178
Map(s) 31, 39

Abstract # 1807 - O
P'ee: REYNOLDS, J C
G'ee: HARROW, J P O
T-Dt: -- --- -----
P-Dt: 20 Jun 1884
Dist/Class: Fannin Preemption
File#: 2022
Patent#: 599
Patent Vol.: 15
Acres: 160
Map(s) 9

Abstract # 1808 - HUFFMACHER, A G
P'ee: WILLIAMS, B F
G'ee: HUFFMASTER, A G
T-Dt: -- --- -----
P-Dt: 05 May 1884
Dist/Class: Fannin Preemption
File#: 1358
Patent#: 436
Patent Vol.: 15
Acres: 192
Map(s) 30

Abstract # 1809 - HILL, J G
P'ee: HILL, J G
G'ee: HILL, J G
T-Dt: -- --- -----
P-Dt: 14 Oct 1886

Dist/Class: Fannin Preemption
File#: 2893
Patent#: 630
Patent Vol.: 18
Acres: 36.12
Map(s) 31

Abstract # 1811 - JONES, J C
P'ee: JONES, J C
G'ee: JONES, J C
T-Dt: -- --- -----
P-Dt: 23 Apr 1887
Dist/Class: Fannin Preemption
File#: 2963
Patent#: 422
Patent Vol.: 19
Acres: 160
Map(s) 34

Abstract # 1812 - BRIR
S2: JAMES, W W
P'ee: AYNESWORTH, G L
G'ee: JAMES, W W
T-Dt: -- --- -----
P-Dt: 18 Dec 1912
Dist/Class: School
File#: 11055
Patent#: 367
Patent Vol.: 45
Survey/Blk/Twp: 1/4 46 BRIR-
Acres: 160
Map(s) 38

Abstract # 1813 - KELLY, R J
P'ee: CAMPBELL, L H
G'ee: KELLY, R J
T-Dt: -- --- -----
P-Dt: 04 Oct 1884
Dist/Class: Fannin Preemption
File#: 1094
Patent#: 299
Patent Vol.: 16
Acres: 160
Map(s) 40

Abstract # 1814 - EL&RR RR CO
S2: KELLY, H
P'ee: NEWHOUS, CHARLES
G'ee: KELLY, HENRY
T-Dt: -- --- -----
P-Dt: 20 Oct 1905
Dist/Class: School
File#: 11701
Patent#: 396
Patent Vol.: 30
Certificate: 554
Survey/Blk/Twp: E 1/2 2 EL & RR-
Acres: 338.5
Map(s) 29

Abstract # 1817 - MORGAN, A
P'ee: MORGAN, I A
G'ee: MORGAN, I A
T-Dt: -- --- -----
P-Dt: 21 May 1884
Dist/Class: Fannin Preemption
File#: 2673
Patent#: 492
Patent Vol.: 15
Acres: 133.25
Map(s) 35, 43

Abstract # 1818 - BRIR
S2: MUNNERLYN, W B
P'ee: MUNNERLYN, W B

G'ee: MUNNERLYN, W B
T-Dt: -- --- -----
P-Dt: 30 Apr 1913
Dist/Class: School
File#: 10737
Patent#: 305
Patent Vol.: 46
Survey/Blk/Twp: FRAC.94 BRIR-
Acres: 106
Map(s) 30, 31

Abstract # 1820 - ROBINSON, G W
P'ee: GRAHAM, E S
G'ee: ROBINSON, G W
T-Dt: -- --- -----
P-Dt: 05 Mar 1884
Dist/Class: Fannin Donation
File#: 1695
Patent#: 247
Patent Vol.: 5
Certificate: 685
Acres: 579
Map(s) 32, 40

Abstract # 1821 - RI CO
P'ee: GIBSON, J W
G'ee: RUIDOSÁ IRRIGATION COM-
PANY
T-Dt: -- --- -----
P-Dt: 22 Mar 1886
Dist/Class: Fannin Scrip
File#: 19978
Patent#: 68
Patent Vol.: 36
Certificate: 24/208
Acres: 137
Map(s) 36, 37

Abstract # 1822 - SMITH, L W
P'ee: SMITH, L W
G'ee: SMITH, L W
T-Dt: -- --- -----
P-Dt: 05 Feb 1891
Dist/Class: Fannin Preemption
File#: 2993
Patent#: 470
Patent Vol.: 23
Acres: 160
Map(s) 16

Abstract # 1824 - STEEN, J L
P'ee: STEEN, J L
G'ee: STEEN, J L
T-Dt: -- --- -----
P-Dt: 08 May 1899
Dist/Class: School
File#: 10913
Patent#: 452
Patent Vol.: 17
Certificate: 162
Survey/Blk/Twp: 2 EL & RR CO.-
Acres: 226.20
Map(s) 6

Abstract # 1826 - T&NO RR CO
S2: AUSTIN, W W
P'ee: AUSTIN, ELLA V
G'ee: AUSTIN, W W
T-Dt: -- --- -----
P-Dt: 29 Jun 1920
Dist/Class: School
File#: 12582
Patent#: 12
Patent Vol.: 8A
Certificate: 863

Survey/Blk/Twp: SE 1/4 10 T & NO-
Acres: 187.5
Map(s) 29, 37

Abstract # 1828 - BRYANT, W H
P'ee: JACKSON, J I
G'ee: BRYANT, W H
T-Dt: -- --- -----
P-Dt: 27 Oct 1920
Dist/Class: Fannin Preemption
File#: 3062
Patent#: 94
Patent Vol.: 9A
Acres: 152.25
Map(s) 32

Abstract # 1830 - DONNELL, W L
P'ee: DONNELL, W L
G'ee: DONNELL, W L
T-Dt: -- --- -----
P-Dt: 15 Feb 1893
Dist/Class: School
File#: 14835
Patent#: 397
Patent Vol.: 13
Certificate: 16/75
Survey/Blk/Twp: SW 1/4 4 SPRR-
Acres: 160
Map(s) 35

Abstract # 1831 - DUTY, J W
P'ee: LOGAN, W H
G'ee: DUTY, J W
T-Dt: -- --- -----
P-Dt: 03 Jan 1897
Dist/Class: School
File#: 15249
Patent#: 620
Patent Vol.: 15
Certificate: 1/251
Survey/Blk/Twp: 2 J.POITEVENT-
Acres: 640
Map(s) 23, 24

Abstract # 1832 - EVANS, W P
P'ee: BENNETT, W A
G'ee: EVANS, W P
T-Dt: -- --- -----
P-Dt: 28 May 1890
Dist/Class: Fannin Preemption
File#: 3016
Patent#: 107
Patent Vol.: 23
Acres: 70.66
Map(s) 32

Abstract # 1833 - EADS, W A
P'ee: FOSTER, A E
G'ee: EADS, W A
T-Dt: -- --- -----
P-Dt: 18 Mar 1889
Dist/Class: Fannin Preemption
File#: 3124
Patent#: 631
Patent Vol.: 21
Acres: 160
Map(s) 39

Abstract # 1834 - FICKLIN, R G
P'ee: FICKLIN, R G
G'ee: FICKLIN, R G
T-Dt: -- --- -----
P-Dt: 06 Jul 1891
Dist/Class: Fannin Preemption
File#: 3054

Patent#: 90
Patent Vol.: 24
Acres: 160
Map(s) 36, 37

Abstract # 1835 - GIBSON, A J
P'ee: GIBSON, A J JR
G'ee: GIBSON, A J JR
T-Dt: -- --- -----
P-Dt: 01 Sep 1891
Dist/Class: Fannin Preemption
File#: 3074
Patent#: 149
Patent Vol.: 24
Acres: 145.20
Map(s) 37

Abstract # 1836 - BS&F
S2: HAWKINS, S J
P'ee: HAWKINS, S J
G'ee: HAWKINS, S J
T-Dt: -- --- -----
P-Dt: 04 Sep 1908
Dist/Class: School
File#: 13155
Patent#: 450
Patent Vol.: 36
Certificate: 1/264
Survey/Blk/Twp: W 1/2 OF NW 1/4 2 BS
& F-
Acres: 80
Map(s) 15

Abstract # 1837 - BRIR
S2: KIRBY, J M
P'ee: NEWBY, J H
G'ee: KERBY, JOHN M
T-Dt: -- --- -----
P-Dt: 13 Jul 1887
Dist/Class: Fannin Preemption
File#: 3065
Patent#: 637
Patent Vol.: 19
Survey/Blk/Twp: 27
Acres: 160
Map(s) 38, 39

Abstract # 1838 - BBB&C RR CO
S2: KUNKEL, H D
P'ee: BERNHARDT, WILLIAM
G'ee: KUNKEL, H D
T-Dt: -- --- -----
P-Dt: 05 Jan 1885
Dist/Class: School
File#: 3014
Patent#: 287
Patent Vol.: 4
Certificate: 692
Survey/Blk/Twp: W 1/2 4 BBB & CRR-
Acres: 320
Map(s) 3

Abstract # 1839 - LINDSEY, B F
P'ee: RHOMBERG, A L
G'ee: LINDSEY, B F
T-Dt: -- --- -----
P-Dt: 22 Mar 1887
Dist/Class: Fannin Donation
File#: 1860
Patent#: 411
Patent Vol.: 6
Certificate: 25/126
Acres: 540
Map(s) 34

Abstract # 1840 - BRIR
S2: LAMAR, R E
P'ee: NORRIS, J B
G'ee: LAMAR, R E
T-Dt: -- --- -----
P-Dt: 24 Apr 1888
Dist/Class: School
File#: 12641
Patent#: 276
Patent Vol.: 8
Survey/Blk/Twp: 1/4 114 BRIR-
Acres: 160
Map(s) 29, 30

Abstract # 1841 - MESSENGER, D
P'ee: MESSENGER, DANIEL
G'ee: MESSENGER, DANIEL
T-Dt: -- --- -----
P-Dt: 18 Jul 1885
Dist/Class: Fannin Preemption
File#: 1391
Patent#: 330
Patent Vol.: 17
Acres: 160
Map(s) 29

Abstract # 1842 - MCCONNELL, S M
P'ee: MCCONNELL, S M
G'ee: MCCONNELL, S M
T-Dt: -- --- -----
P-Dt: 17 Oct 1887
Dist/Class: Fannin Preemption
File#: 3078
Patent#: 224
Patent Vol.: 20
Acres: 114.25
Map(s) 33

Abstract # 1845 - MATHEWS, S M
P'ee: SPOTWOOD, M C
G'ee: MATHEWS, S M
T-Dt: -- --- -----
P-Dt: 17 Feb 1891
Dist/Class: Fannin Preemption
File#: 3130
Patent#: 527
Patent Vol.: 23
Acres: 102
Map(s) 34

Abstract # 1846 - BS&F
S2: MCCASLAND, A T
P'ee: MCCASLAND, A T
G'ee: MCCASLAND, A T
T-Dt: -- --- -----
P-Dt: 23 May 1941
Dist/Class: School
File#: 14874
Patent#: 477
Patent Vol.: 80A
Certificate: 1/264
Survey/Blk/Twp: SE 1/4 2 BS & F-
Acres: 160
Map(s) 15

Abstract # 1848 - BRIR
S2: MCBRAYER, J W
P'ee: MCBRAYER, J W (HEIRS)
G'ee: MCBRAYER, J W
T-Dt: -- --- -----
P-Dt: 08 Jan 1902
Dist/Class: School
File#: 15562
Patent#: 213
Patent Vol.: 22

Survey/Blk/Twp: FRAC. 1/4 58 BRIR-
Acres: 117.75
Map(s) 37

Abstract # 1852 - G&BN CO
S2: RICHARDSON, R L
P'ee: RICHARDSON, R L
G'ee: RICHARDSON, R L
T-Dt: -- --- -----
P-Dt: 12 Nov 1889
Dist/Class: School
File#: 14879
Patent#: 506
Patent Vol.: 9
Certificate: 91
Survey/Blk/Twp: NW 1/4 1 G & BN-
Acres: 160
Map(s) 15

Abstract # 1854 - THARP, D P
P'ee: MCCORKLE, R L
G'ee: THARP, D P
T-Dt: -- --- -----
P-Dt: 11 Dec 1888
Dist/Class: Fannin Preemption
File#: 3136
Patent#: 400
Patent Vol.: 21
Acres: 160
Map(s) 36

Abstract # 1855 - TOWNSEND, C W
P'ee: WILLIAMS, JAMES H
G'ee: TOWNSEND, C W
T-Dt: -- --- -----
P-Dt: 07 Aug 1888
Dist/Class: Fannin Preemption
File#: 3085
Patent#: 162
Patent Vol.: 21
Acres: 160
Map(s) 33, 41

Abstract # 1857 - BBB&C RR CO
S2: TURNER, M F
P'ee: TURNER, M F
G'ee: TURNER, M F
T-Dt: -- --- -----
P-Dt: 26 Feb 1919
Dist/Class: School
File#: 14158
Patent#: 537
Patent Vol.: 1A
Certificate: 681
Survey/Blk/Twp: NW 1/4 2 BBB & CRR-
Acres: 168.4
Map(s) 31

Abstract # 1858 - WHITE, N
P'ee: WHITE, N
G'ee: WHITE, N
T-Dt: -- --- -----
P-Dt: 19 Feb 1885
Dist/Class: Fannin Preemption
File#: 1444
Patent#: 16
Patent Vol.: 17
Acres: 160
Map(s) 30

Abstract # 1859 - WOOD, B G
P'ee: WOODS, B G
G'ee: WOODS, B G
T-Dt: -- --- -----
P-Dt: 17 Jul 1886

Dist/Class: Fannin Preemption
File#: 3028
Patent#: 477
Patent Vol.: 18
Acres: 11.33
Map(s) 30

Abstract # 1860 - BRIR
S2: WHITTENBURG, J
P'ee: WHITTENBURG, JACOB
G'ee: WHITTENBURG, JACOB
T-Dt: -- --- -----
P-Dt: 13 Jul 1891
Dist/Class: School
File#: 14359
Patent#: 162
Patent Vol.: 12
Survey/Blk/Twp: 1/4 8 BRIR-
Acres: 164.5
Map(s) 37, 38

Abstract # 1862 - G&BN CO
S2: ZINN, J A
P'ee: ZINN, J A SR
G'ee: ZINN, J A SR
T-Dt: -- --- -----
P-Dt: 17 Jun 1885
Dist/Class: School
File#: 2252
Patent#: 586
Patent Vol.: 4
Survey/Blk/Twp: NW 1/4 1 G & BN-
Acres: 160
Map(s) 6

Abstract # 1864 - BUTLER, M
P'ee: BUTLER, MOSES
G'ee: BUTLER, MOSES
T-Dt: -- --- -----
P-Dt: 03 Jun 1886
Dist/Class: Fannin Bounty
File#: 1363
Patent#: 391
Patent Vol.: 16
Certificate: 30/221
Acres: 382.60
Map(s) 36, 37, 44, 45

Abstract # 1865 - BROWN, W H
P'ee: BROWN, W H
G'ee: BROWN, W H
T-Dt: -- --- -----
P-Dt: 22 Oct 1888
Dist/Class: Fannin Preemption
File#: 3194
Patent#: 312
Patent Vol.: 21
Acres: 145
Map(s) 36

Abstract # 1866 - BRIR
S2: BROOKS, D C
P'ee: BROOKS, D C
G'ee: BROOKS, D C
T-Dt: -- --- -----
P-Dt: 08 Feb 1905
Dist/Class: School
File#: 16978
Patent#: 357
Patent Vol.: 29
Survey/Blk/Twp: 1/4 72 BRIR-
Acres: 163
Map(s) 39

Abstract # 1871 - HARGRAVE, J B

P'ee: HARGRAVE, J B
G'ee: HARGRAVE, J B
T-Dt: -- --- -----
P-Dt: 16 Mar 1896
Dist/Class: Fannin Preemption
File#: 3156
Patent#: 409
Patent Vol.: 28
Acres: 158.30
Map(s) 28, 29

Abstract # 1873 - BRIR
S2: MERCER, J L
P'ee: MERCER, J L
G'ee: MERCER, J L
T-Dt: -- --- -----
P-Dt: 05 Jul 1890
Dist/Class: School
File#: 16690
Patent#: 551
Patent Vol.: 10
Survey/Blk/Twp: 11 BRIR-
Acres: 241
Map(s) 38

Abstract # 1874 - POITEVENT, J
S2: NEELY, A C
P'ee: NEELEY, A C
G'ee: NEELEY, A C
T-Dt: -- --- -----
P-Dt: 24 Dec 1904
Dist/Class: School
File#: 16693
Patent#: 244
Patent Vol.: 29
Certificate: 1/129
Survey/Blk/Twp: W 1/2 2 J.POITEVENT
3-
Acres: 320
Map(s) 3, 4

Abstract # 1876 - PORTER, W W
P'ee: MATTHEWS, W M
G'ee: PORTER, W W
T-Dt: -- --- -----
P-Dt: 25 Nov 1890
Dist/Class: Fannin Preemption
File#: 3244
Patent#: 409
Patent Vol.: 23
Acres: 104.75
Map(s) 6

Abstract # 1877 - RIBBLE, E J
P'ee: RIBBLE, ED J
G'ee: RIBBLE, ED J
T-Dt: -- --- -----
P-Dt: 12 Dec 1906
Dist/Class: Fannin Preemption
File#: 3245
Patent#: 108
Patent Vol.: 33
Acres: 188.34
Map(s) 39, 47

Abstract # 1878 - SP RR CO
S2: RODGER, J M C
P'ee: ROGERS, J M C
G'ee: ROGERS, J M C
T-Dt: -- --- -----
P-Dt: 09 Nov 1889
Dist/Class: School
File#: 16687
Patent#: 501
Patent Vol.: 9

Certificate: 16/181
Survey/Blk/Twp: W 1/2 4 SPRR-
Acres: 320
Map(s) 32

Abstract # 1879 - SMITH, I N
P'ee: BRADDOCK, T J AND BRAD-
DOCK, EM
G'ee: SMITH, I N
T-Dt: -- --- -----
P-Dt: 20 Jul 1886
Dist/Class: Fannin Preemption
File#: 2849
Patent#: 478
Patent Vol.: 18
Acres: 157.70
Map(s) 36

Abstract # 1880 - STEWART, J C
P'ee: STEWART, J C
G'ee: STEWART, J C
T-Dt: -- --- -----
P-Dt: 07 Jun 1892
Dist/Class: Fannin Preemption
File#: 3195
Patent#: 499
Patent Vol.: 24
Acres: 154.25
Map(s) 35, 36

Abstract # 1883 - TWILLEGEAR, Y H
P'ee: VAUGHN, JOSEPH
G'ee: TWILLEGEAR, Y H
T-Dt: -- --- -----
P-Dt: 07 Oct 1889
Dist/Class: Fannin Preemption
File#: 3246
Patent#: 293
Patent Vol.: 22
Acres: 123.80
Map(s) 36

Abstract # 1886 - TT RR CO
S2: WILLIAMS, I E M
P'ee: WILLIAMS, IRA E M
G'ee: WILLIAMS, IRA E M
T-Dt: -- --- -----
P-Dt: 03 May 1886
Dist/Class: School
File#: 2209
Patent#: 582
Patent Vol.: 5
Survey/Blk/Twp: N 1/4 16 TTRR-
Acres: 160
Map(s) 32

Abstract # 1887 - BROOKS, S A
P'ee: BROOKS, S A
G'ee: BROOKS, S A
T-Dt: -- --- -----
P-Dt: 03 Oct 1887
Dist/Class: Fannin Preemption
File#: 1580
Patent#: 187
Patent Vol.: 20
Acres: 160
Map(s) 36, 37

Abstract # 1888 - BURCH, T J
P'ee: BURCH, T J
G'ee: BURCH, T J
T-Dt: -- --- -----
P-Dt: 07 Jun 1895
Dist/Class: Fannin Preemption
File#: 3369

Patent#: 464
Patent Vol.: 27
Acres: 76.70
Map(s) 21, 29

Abstract # 1889 - BUSSELL, C H
P'ee: FRANKLIN, HIRAM
G'ee: BUSSELL, C H
T-Dt: -- --- -----
P-Dt: 20 Jul 1887
Dist/Class: Fannin Preemption
File#: 1305
Patent#: 13
Patent Vol.: 20
Acres: 80
Map(s) 29

Abstract # 1890 - T&NO RR CO
S2: CORNELL, W L
P'ee: HILL, H
G'ee: CORNETT, W L
T-Dt: -- --- -----
P-Dt: 22 Mar 1920
Dist/Class: School
File#: 19521
Patent#: 340
Patent Vol.: 6A
Certificate: 862
Survey/Blk/Twp: SW 1/4 8 T & NO-
Acres: 165.2
Map(s) 29

Abstract # 1891 - DAVIS, H B L
P'ee: DAVIS, H B L
G'ee: DAVIS, H B L
T-Dt: -- --- -----
P-Dt: 16 May 1889
Dist/Class: Fannin Preemption
File#: 3367
Patent#: 73
Patent Vol.: 22
Acres: 79
Map(s) 34

Abstract # 1893 - FINCH, W T
P'ee: WALLACE, E M
G'ee: FINCH, W T
T-Dt: -- --- -----
P-Dt: 15 Feb 1890
Dist/Class: Fannin Preemption
File#: 3305
Patent#: 501
Patent Vol.: 22
Acres: 70
Map(s) 27, 28, 35, 36

Abstract # 1894 - FORTUNE, L
P'ee: FORTUNE, L
G'ee: FORTUNE, L
T-Dt: -- --- -----
P-Dt: 22 Sep 1887
Dist/Class: Fannin Preemption
File#: 1616
Patent#: 171
Patent Vol.: 20
Acres: 143.69
Map(s) 20

Abstract # 1896 - BRIR
S2: GREENWADE, R H
P'ee: LISLE, O D
G'ee: GREENWADE, R H
T-Dt: -- --- -----
P-Dt: 24 Nov 1891
Dist/Class: School

File#: 19650
Patent#: 352
Patent Vol.: 12
Survey/Blk/Twp: FRAC.6 BRIR-
Acres: 59.25
Map(s) 38, 46

Abstract # 1897 - HART, R A
P'ee: JONES, H M
G'ee: HART, R A
T-Dt: -- --- -----
P-Dt: 18 Jul 1887
Dist/Class: Fannin Preemption
File#: 2916
Patent#: 3
Patent Vol.: 20
Acres: 160
Map(s) 36

Abstract # 1898 - BRIR
S2: HERRON, F
P'ee: HERRON, F
G'ee: HERRON, F
T-Dt: -- --- -----
P-Dt: 30 Mar 1921
Dist/Class: School
File#: 21733
Patent#: 457
Patent Vol.: 10A
Survey/Blk/Twp: 1/4 29 BRIR-
Acres: 160
Map(s) 39

Abstract # 1899 - T&NO RR CO
S2: HILL, H
P'ee: HILL, H
G'ee: HILL, H
T-Dt: -- --- -----
P-Dt: 22 Mar 1920
Dist/Class: School
File#: 21581
Patent#: 342
Patent Vol.: 6A
Certificate: 862
Survey/Blk/Twp: NE 1/4 8 T & NO-
Acres: 172.5
Map(s) 29

Abstract # 1900 - BRIR
S2: HUDGIN, B A
P'ee: HUDGINS, B A
G'ee: HUDGINS, B A
T-Dt: -- --- -----
P-Dt: 03 Sep 1891
Dist/Class: School
File#: 3863
Patent#: 261
Patent Vol.: 12
Survey/Blk/Twp: FRAC.108 BRIR-
Acres: 156
Map(s) 29

Abstract # 1901 - POITEVENT, J
S2: HUNT, P B
P'ee: HUNT, P B
G'ee: HUNT, P B
T-Dt: -- --- -----
P-Dt: 11 Jul 1930
Dist/Class: School
File#: 22006
Patent#: 232
Patent Vol.: 47A
Certificate: 2/157
Survey/Blk/Twp: SE 1/4 2 J.POITEVENT-
Acres: 193

Map(s) 28

Abstract # 1902 - JONES, J Y
P'ee: JONES, J Y
G'ee: JONES, J Y
T-Dt: -- --- -----
P-Dt: 18 Jul 1887
Dist/Class: Fannin Preemption
File#: 2945
Patent#: 2
Patent Vol.: 20
Acres: 80
Map(s) 34, 42

Abstract # 1904 - MORROW, J G
P'ee: MORROW, J G
G'ee: MORROW, J G
T-Dt: -- --- -----
P-Dt: 07 Feb 1890
Dist/Class: Fannin Preemption
File#: 3368
Patent#: 485
Patent Vol.: 22
Acres: 160
Map(s) 32

Abstract # 1905 - MARR, J W
P'ee: SHEPARD, ROBERT L
G'ee: MARR, JOHN W
T-Dt: -- --- -----
P-Dt: 05 Jan 1922
Dist/Class: School
File#: 19278
Patent#: 428
Patent Vol.: 12A
Survey/Blk/Twp: 1/4 116 BRIR-
Acres: 189.62
Map(s) 29, 30

Abstract # 1908 - POITEVENT, J
S2: DAVIS, W
P'ee: PAYNE, E H
G'ee: PAYNE, E H
T-Dt: -- --- -----
P-Dt: 18 Oct 1906
Dist/Class: School
File#: 19523
Patent#: 541
Patent Vol.: 32
Certificate: 1/129
Survey/Blk/Twp: NE 1/4 2 J.POITEVENT-
Acres: 160
Map(s) 4

Abstract # 1909 - RIBBLE, S L
P'ee: RIBBLE, S L
G'ee: RIBBLE, S L
T-Dt: -- --- -----
P-Dt: 05 Apr 1900
Dist/Class: Fannin Preemption
File#: 3321
Patent#: 190
Patent Vol.: 30
Acres: 160
Map(s) 46, 47

Abstract # 1910 - T&NO RR CO
S2: SIMPSON, L C
P'ee: HILL, H
G'ee: SIMPSON, L C
T-Dt: -- --- -----
P-Dt: 22 Mar 1920
Dist/Class: School
File#: 19852
Patent#: 341

Patent Vol.: 6A
Certificate: 862
Survey/Blk/Twp: NW 1/4 8 T & NO-
Acres: 167.8
Map(s) 29

Abstract # 1912 - WADE, B J
P'ee: WADE, B J
G'ee: WADE, B J
T-Dt: -- --- -----
P-Dt: 18 Jul 1887
Dist/Class: Fannin Preemption
File#: 2944
Patent#: 4
Patent Vol.: 20
Acres: 80
Map(s) 42

Abstract # 1914 - ABERNATHY, M C
P'ee: ABERNATHY, M C
G'ee: ABERNATHY, M C
T-Dt: -- --- -----
P-Dt: 12 Jan 1892
Dist/Class: Fannin Preemption
File#: 3636
Patent#: 334
Patent Vol.: 24
Acres: 143
Map(s) 32, 40

Abstract # 1915 - BRIR
S2: AYNESWORTH, G L
P'ee: AYNESWORTH, G L
G'ee: AYNESWORTH, G L
T-Dt: -- --- -----
P-Dt: 18 Dec 1912
Dist/Class: School
File#: 23817
Patent#: 369
Patent Vol.: 45
Survey/Blk/Twp: 1/4 42 BRIR-
Acres: 160
Map(s) 38

Abstract # 1916 - BRIR
S2: AYNESWORTH, G L
P'ee: AYNESWORTH, G L
G'ee: AYNESWORTH, G L
T-Dt: -- --- -----
P-Dt: 18 Dec 1912
Dist/Class: School
File#: 23818
Patent#: 368
Patent Vol.: 45
Survey/Blk/Twp: 1/4 44 BRIR-
Acres: 161
Map(s) 38

Abstract # 1917 - BASS, A T
P'ee: BELLOMY, W D
G'ee: BASS, A T
T-Dt: -- --- -----
P-Dt: 07 Jun 1892
Dist/Class: Fannin Preemption
File#: 3464
Patent#: 502
Patent Vol.: 24
Acres: 160
Map(s) 27

Abstract # 1918 - CAMPBELL, A J
P'ee: CAMPBELL, A J
G'ee: CAMPBELL, A J
T-Dt: -- --- -----
P-Dt: 24 Nov 1890

Dist/Class: Fannin Preemption
File#: 3519
Patent#: 399
Patent Vol.: 23
Acres: 35.50
Map(s) 34

Abstract # 1919 - GATLIN, R A
P'ee: CATLIN, R A
G'ee: CATLIN, R A
T-Dt: -- --- -----
P-Dt: 26 Apr 1895
Dist/Class: Fannin Preemption
File#: 3540
Patent#: 393
Patent Vol.: 27
Acres: 93.60
Map(s) 22, 30

Abstract # 1920 - G&BN CO
S2: COX, E E
P'ee: COX, E E
G'ee: COX, E E
T-Dt: -- --- -----
P-Dt: 14 Jun 1920
Dist/Class: School
File#: 24458
Patent#: 424
Patent Vol.: 7A
Certificate: 91
Survey/Blk/Twp: N 1/2 OF SW 1/4 1 G &
BN CO.-
Acres: 81.8
Map(s) 15

Abstract # 1922 - DONNELL, J M
P'ee: DONNELL, J M
G'ee: DONNELL, J M
T-Dt: -- --- -----
P-Dt: 21 Jan 1901
Dist/Class: Fannin Preemption
File#: 3611
Patent#: 333
Patent Vol.: 31
Acres: 83
Map(s) 3, 4

Abstract # 1924 - GARDNER, J A
P'ee: DARDEN, J M
G'ee: GARDNER, J A
T-Dt: -- --- -----
P-Dt: 19 Apr 1907
Dist/Class: Fannin Preemption
File#: 3585
Patent#: 125
Patent Vol.: 33
Acres: 58
Map(s) 31

Abstract # 1927 - HIGGINS, W J
P'ee: HIGGINS, W J
G'ee: HIGGINS, W J
T-Dt: -- --- -----
P-Dt: 30 Jan 1893
Dist/Class: Fannin Preemption
File#: 3571
Patent#: 222
Patent Vol.: 25
Acres: 112. 33
Map(s) 34

Abstract # 1930 - JEFFERY, S R
P'ee: JEFFERY, S R
G'ee: JEFFERY, S R
T-Dt: -- --- -----

P-Dt: 18 Jun 1888
Dist/Class: Fannin Scrip
File#: 21289
Patent#: 15
Patent Vol.: 11
Acres: 164.50
Map(s) 21

Abstract # 1932 - KEEN, W H
P'ee: KEEN, W H
G'ee: KEEN, W H
T-Dt: -- --- -----
P-Dt: 24 Aug 1895
Dist/Class: Fannin Preemption
File#: 3583
Patent#: 639
Patent Vol.: 27
Acres: 83
Map(s) 3

Abstract # 1935 - BRIR
S2: KUYKENDALL, W H
P'ee: ROARK, A W
G'ee: KUYKENDALL, W H
T-Dt: -- --- -----
P-Dt: 27 Nov 1912
Dist/Class: School
File#: 23925
Patent#: 280
Patent Vol.: 45
Survey/Blk/Twp: 18 BRIR-
Acres: 160
Map(s) 39, 47

Abstract # 1936 - LASSITER, M L
P'ee: LASSITER, M L
G'ee: LASSITER, M L
T-Dt: -- --- -----
P-Dt: 03 Jan 1889
Dist/Class: Fannin Scrip
File#: 21764
Patent#: 114
Patent Vol.: 11
Acres: 13.40
Map(s) 39

Abstract # 1938 - BRIR
S2: LISLE, J N
P'ee: LISLE, J N
G'ee: LISLE, J N
T-Dt: -- --- -----
P-Dt: 18 Mar 1895
Dist/Class: School
File#: 16689
Patent#: 548
Patent Vol.: 14
Survey/Blk/Twp: 1/4 33 BRIR-
Acres: 167
Map(s) 38

Abstract # 1939 - MEADOR, R E
P'ee: WADE, L W
G'ee: MEADOR, R E
T-Dt: -- --- -----
P-Dt: 13 Jul 1891
Dist/Class: Fannin Preemption
File#: 3609
Patent#: 101
Patent Vol.: 24
Acres: 75
Map(s) 34

Abstract # 1941 - OTTS, P
P'ee: OTTS, POSEY
G'ee: OTTS, POSEY

T-Dt: -- --- -----
P-Dt: 14 Nov 1888
Dist/Class: Fannin Scrip
File#: 21775
Patent#: 101
Patent Vol.: 11
Acres: 16.80
Map(s) 33, 34

Abstract # 1942 - OLIVER, W P
P'ee: OLIVER, WILLIAM P
G'ee: OLIVER, WILLIAM P
T-Dt: -- --- -----
P-Dt: 21 Feb 1896
Dist/Class: Fannin Preemption
File#: 3549
Patent#: 352
Patent Vol.: 28
Acres: 114
Map(s) 33

Abstract # 1944 - RUSSELL, D M
P'ee: RUSSELL, D M
G'ee: RUSSELL, D M
T-Dt: -- --- -----
P-Dt: 06 Jun 1891
Dist/Class: Fannin Preemption
File#: 3572
Patent#: 53
Patent Vol.: 24
Acres: 160
Map(s) 34

Abstract # 1945 - SMITH, J N
P'ee: KIRBY, J M
G'ee: SMITH, J N
T-Dt: -- --- -----
P-Dt: 17 Apr 1888
Dist/Class: Fannin Preemption
File#: 1428
Patent#: 632
Patent Vol.: 20
Acres: 160
Map(s) 37

Abstract # 1947 - G&BN CO
S2: ADINGTON, I
P'ee: ADINGTON, THOMAS
G'ee: ADINGTON, THOMAS
T-Dt: -- --- -----
P-Dt: 28 Sep 1889
Dist/Class: School
File#: 2433
Patent#: 419
Patent Vol.: 9
Certificate: 91
Survey/Blk/Twp: NE 1/4 1 G & BN CO.-
Acres: 160
Map(s) 15

Abstract # 1948 - BRIR
S2: AYNESWORTH, G L
P'ee: DRIVER, J A AND DRIVER, A I
G'ee: AINSWORTH, G L
T-Dt: -- --- -----
P-Dt: 13 Aug 1913
Dist/Class: School
File#: 25075
Patent#: 3
Patent Vol.: 47
Survey/Blk/Twp: 1/4 49 BRIR-
Acres: 164
Map(s) 38

Abstract # 1949 - BRAY, J W

P'ee: BRAY, J W
G'ee: BRAY, J W
T-Dt: -- --- -----
P-Dt: 08 Feb 1892
Dist/Class: Fannin Preemption
File#: 3653
Patent#: 373
Patent Vol.: 24
Acres: 160
Map(s) 31

Abstract # 1950 - BRYANT, A
P'ee: BRYANT, ALEXANDER
G'ee: BRYANT, ALEXANDER
T-Dt: -- --- -----
P-Dt: 11 May 1892
Dist/Class: Fannin Preemption
File#: 3732
Patent#: 470
Patent Vol.: 24
Acres: 160
Map(s) 32

Abstract # 1951 - BULLARD, W A
P'ee: BULLARD, W A
G'ee: BULLARD, W A
T-Dt: -- --- -----
P-Dt: 22 Sep 1896
Dist/Class: Fannin Preemption
File#: 3744
Patent#: 69
Patent Vol.: 29
Acres: 80
Map(s) 31

Abstract # 1953 - CALLEN, S P
P'ee: CALLEN, S P
G'ee: CALLEN, S P
T-Dt: -- --- -----
P-Dt: 01 Nov 1889
Dist/Class: Fannin Scrip
File#: 21820
Patent#: 255
Patent Vol.: 11
Acres: 25.22
Map(s) 16

Abstract # 1954 - G&BN CO
S2: COMPERE, W T
P'ee: MANDEVILLE, M
G'ee: COMPERE, W T
T-Dt: -- --- -----
P-Dt: 26 Oct 1889
Dist/Class: School
File#: 8886
Patent#: 452
Patent Vol.: 9
Certificate: 29
Survey/Blk/Twp: SW 1/4 3 G & B NAV.
CO.-
Acres: 160
Map(s) 6

Abstract # 1955 - BRIR
S2: CUNNINGHAM, J H
P'ee: CUNNINGHAM, I H
G'ee: CUNNINGHAM, I H
T-Dt: -- --- -----
P-Dt: 14 Mar 1917
Dist/Class: School
File#: 25057
Patent#: 343
Patent Vol.: 52
Survey/Blk/Twp: FRAC.150 BRIR-
Acres: 98.5

Map(s) 38

Abstract # 1956 - EGGARS, C G
P'ee: SMITH, G T
G'ee: EGGARS, C G
T-Dt: -- --- -----
P-Dt: 19 Oct 1893
Dist/Class: Fannin Preemption
File#: 3678
Patent#: 67
Patent Vol.: 26
Acres: 160
Map(s) 16

Abstract # 1957 - ELKINS, W H
P'ee: ELKINS, W H
G'ee: ELKINS, W H
T-Dt: -- --- -----
P-Dt: 13 Jun 1912
Dist/Class: Fannin Preemption
File#: 3739
Patent#: 270
Patent Vol.: 33
Acres: 148.40
Map(s) 35

Abstract # 1959 - POITEVENT, J
S2: GUTHRIE, J
P'ee: GUTHRIE, JAMES
G'ee: GUTHRIE, JAMES
T-Dt: -- --- -----
P-Dt: 26 Oct 1889
Dist/Class: School
File#: 10090
Patent#: 460
Patent Vol.: 9
Certificate: 2/158
Survey/Blk/Twp: E 1/2 2 J.POITEVENT-
Acres: 210
Map(s) 39, 47

Abstract # 1961 - JONES, J C
P'ee: JONES, J C
G'ee: JONES, J C
T-Dt: -- --- -----
P-Dt: 26 Oct 1889
Dist/Class: Fannin Scrip
File#: 21807
Patent#: 252
Patent Vol.: 11
Acres: 22.80
Map(s) 34

Abstract # 1962 - LINDSEY, W P
P'ee: LINDSEY, W P
G'ee: LINDSEY, W P
T-Dt: -- --- -----
P-Dt: 16 Dec 1891
Dist/Class: Fannin Preemption
File#: 3684
Patent#: 304
Patent Vol.: 24
Acres: 160
Map(s) 34

Abstract # 1963 - G&BN CO
S2: LEFFEL, J W
P'ee: LEFFEL, J W
G'ee: LEFFEL, J W
T-Dt: -- --- -----
P-Dt: 16 Jul 1928
Dist/Class: School
File#: 25074
Patent#: 102
Patent Vol.: 40A

Certificate: 32
Survey/Blk/Twp: E.PT. 9 G & BN CO.-
Acres: 228.3
Map(s) 24

Abstract # 1964 - LASSITER, W S
P'ee: LASSITER, W S
G'ee: LASSITER, W S
T-Dt: -- --- -----
P-Dt: 17 Jun 1889
Dist/Class: Fannin Scrip
File#: 21764
Patent#: 169
Patent Vol.: 11
Acres: 11.50
Map(s) 39

Abstract # 1966 - MANDEVILLE, A
P'ee: PIEARCY, J A
G'ee: MANDEVILLE, A
T-Dt: -- --- -----
P-Dt: 12 Oct 1893
Dist/Class: Fannin Preemption
File#: 3679
Patent#: 47
Patent Vol.: 26
Acres: 160
Map(s) 16

Abstract # 1969 - PIERCE, R L
P'ee: CATES, J L
G'ee: PIERCE, R S
T-Dt: -- --- -----
P-Dt: 22 Jan 1889
Dist/Class: Fannin Preemption
File#: 1408
Patent#: 498
Patent Vol.: 21
Acres: 80
Map(s) 29

Abstract # 1970 - RAMSOURS, N
P'ee: OWENS, A P
G'ee: RAMSOURS, NANCY
T-Dt: -- --- -----
P-Dt: 15 Feb 1905
Dist/Class: Fannin Preemption
File#: 3731
Patent#: 603
Patent Vol.: 32
Acres: 160
Map(s) 39, 47

Abstract # 1972 - BRADLEY, HRS, J
G'ee: SLAUGHTER, W T
T-Dt: -- --- -----
P-Dt: -- --- -----
Dist/Class: School
File#: 24918
Certificate: 91
Survey/Blk/Twp: SE 1/4 1 G & BN CO.-
Acres: 160
Map(s) 33, 34

Abstract # 1973 - TAYLOR, B F
P'ee: TAYLOR, B F
G'ee: TAYLOR, B F
T-Dt: -- --- -----
P-Dt: 11 Jun 1889
Dist/Class: Fannin Scrip
File#: 21810
Patent#: 167
Patent Vol.: 11
Acres: 64.70
Map(s) 33

Abstract # 1974 - T&NO RR CO
S2: AHLERS, C
P'ee: SEYBOLD, J C
G'ee: AHLERS, CHARLES
T-Dt: -- --- -----
P-Dt: 10 May 1890
Dist/Class: School
File#: 394
Patent#: 401
Patent Vol.: 10
Certificate: 864
Survey/Blk/Twp: SE 1/4 2 T & NO-
Acres: 160
Map(s) 31

Abstract # 1975 - BARRICK, S
P'ee: BARRICK, SUSAN
G'ee: BARRICK, SUSAN (MRS)
T-Dt: -- --- -----
P-Dt: 21 Jan 1892
Dist/Class: Fannin Preemption
File#: 3769
Patent#: 350
Patent Vol.: 24
Acres: 160
Map(s) 22

Abstract # 1977 - CALLEN, A N
P'ee: COLSTON, J W
G'ee: CALLEN, A N
T-Dt: -- --- -----
P-Dt: 09 Oct 1894
Dist/Class: Fannin Preemption
File#: 3794
Patent#: 625
Patent Vol.: 26
Acres: 160
Map(s) 16

Abstract # 1978 - CHEEK, W C
P'ee: BRINKLEY, J W
G'ee: CHEEK, W C
T-Dt: -- --- -----
P-Dt: 05 Dec 1900
Dist/Class: Fannin Preemption
File#: 3816
Patent#: 235
Patent Vol.: 31
Acres: 58
Map(s) 7

Abstract # 1979 - DAVIS, J J
P'ee: DAWS, J J
G'ee: DAWS, J J
T-Dt: -- --- -----
P-Dt: 25 Sep 1895
Dist/Class: Fannin Scrip
File#: 21861
Patent#: 7
Patent Vol.: 13
Acres: 164.25
Map(s) 36

Abstract # 1980 - BRIR
S2: DRIVER, J A
P'ee: DRIVER, J A
G'ee: DRIVER, JOHN A
T-Dt: -- --- -----
P-Dt: 09 Feb 1921
Dist/Class: School
File#: 29693
Patent#: 184
Patent Vol.: 10A
Survey/Blk/Twp: 40 BRIR-
Acres: 182.25

Map(s) 38

Abstract # 1981 - WC RR CO
S2: EGGERS, G
P'ee: MORGAN, J W
G'ee: EGGERS, GUSTAV
T-Dt: -- --- -----
P-Dt: 31 Jul 1935
Dist/Class: School
File#: 27158
Patent#: 221
Patent Vol.: 59A
Certificate: 28/142
Survey/Blk/Twp: SE 1/4 2 WC-
Acres: 160
Map(s) 16

Abstract # 1982 - GARRETT, S
P'ee: GARRETT, SAMUEL
G'ee: GARRETT, SAMUEL
T-Dt: -- --- -----
P-Dt: 29 Jul 1895
Dist/Class: Fannin Preemption
File#: 3833
Patent#: 578
Patent Vol.: 27
Acres: 34.60
Map(s) 31

Abstract # 1983 - GHOLSON, MRS M A
P'ee: SHANNON, J W
G'ee: GHOLSON, MORGAN A (MRS)
T-Dt: -- --- -----
P-Dt: 17 Sep 1895
Dist/Class: Fannin Preemption
File#: 3947
Patent#: 41
Patent Vol.: 28
Acres: 160
Map(s) 32, 40

Abstract # 1984 - THOMAS, C H
G'ee: GARDNER, R H
T-Dt: -- --- -----
P-Dt: -- --- -----
Dist/Class: School
File#: 30068
Survey/Blk/Twp: W 1/2 4 SP-
Acres: 160
Map(s) 22

Abstract # 1985 - HILL, W
P'ee: FRAZIER, J S
G'ee: HILL, WILLIAM
T-Dt: -- --- -----
P-Dt: 09 Jun 1926
Dist/Class: Fannin Preemption
File#: 994
Patent#: 527
Patent Vol.: 29A
Acres: 160
Map(s) 24, 32

Abstract # 1991 - POITEVENT, J
S2: HUNT, P B
P'ee: HUNT, P B
G'ee: HUNT, P B
T-Dt: -- --- -----
P-Dt: 25 Jun 1930
Dist/Class: School
File#: 26929
Patent#: 233
Patent Vol.: 47A
Certificate: 2/157
Survey/Blk/Twp: NW 1/4 2

J.POITEVENT-
Acres: 188
Map(s) 27, 28

Abstract # 1994 - MARTIN, G J
P'ee: MCCAN, J S
G'ee: MARTIN, G J
T-Dt: -- --- -----
P-Dt: 26 Oct 1895
Dist/Class: Fannin Preemption
File#: 3782
Patent#: 104
Patent Vol.: 28
Acres: 80
Map(s) 27

Abstract # 1996 - RIBBLE, W
P'ee: RIBBLE, WILLIAM A
G'ee: RIBBLE, WILLIAM A
T-Dt: -- --- -----
P-Dt: 19 Feb 1891
Dist/Class: Fannin Scrip
File#: 21852
Patent#: 504
Patent Vol.: 11
Acres: 18
Map(s) 39

Abstract # 2010 - CRAWFORD, V T
P'ee: CRAWFORD, V T
G'ee: CRAWFORD, V T
T-Dt: -- --- -----
P-Dt: 26 Feb 1892
Dist/Class: Fannin Scrip
File#: 21881
Patent#: 657
Patent Vol.: 11
Acres: 18
Map(s) 28

Abstract # 2011 - BRIR
S2: COFFMAN, E M
P'ee: COFFMAN, E M
G'ee: COFFMAN, E M
T-Dt: -- --- -----
P-Dt: 21 May 1891
Dist/Class: School
File#: 4058
Patent#: 27
Patent Vol.: 12
Survey/Blk/Twp: FRAC.62 BRIR-
Acres: 90.60
Map(s) 37

Abstract # 2016 - JAYNE, B M
P'ee: JAYNE, B H
G'ee: JAYNE, B H
T-Dt: -- --- -----
P-Dt: 30 Jan 1898
Dist/Class: Fannin 3rd
File#: 4610
Patent#: 554
Patent Vol.: 46
Certificate: 29/72
Acres: 260
Map(s) 35, 36

Abstract # 2019 - MCKNIGHT, W N
P'ee: RIBBLE, E J
G'ee: MCKNIGHT, W N
T-Dt: -- --- -----
P-Dt: 23 Dec 1896
Dist/Class: Fannin Preemption
File#: 4056
Patent#: 202

Patent Vol.: 29
Acres: 160
Map(s) 39, 47

Abstract # 2021 - TE&L CO
P'ee: TEXAS EMIGRATION AND LAND
COMPANY
G'ee: TEXAS EMIGRATION AND LAND
COMPANY
T-Dt: -- --- -----
P-Dt: 05 Feb 1859
Dist/Class: Texas Emmigration and Land
Company
File#: 1171
Patent#: 498
Patent Vol.: 20
Certificate: 1171
Survey/Blk/Twp: 1171
Acres: 320
Map(s) 22

Abstract # 2022 - TIDWELL, W I
P'ee: TIDWELL, W I
G'ee: TIDWELL, W I
T-Dt: -- --- -----
P-Dt: 10 Sep 1891
Dist/Class: Fannin Scrip
File#: 21849
Patent#: 563
Patent Vol.: 11
Acres: 100
Map(s) 31

Abstract # 2023 - G&BN CO
S2: YOUNG, J
P'ee: YOUNG, JOSEPH
G'ee: YOUNG, JOSEPH
T-Dt: -- --- -----
P-Dt: 01 May 1929
Dist/Class: School
File#: 31198
Patent#: 86
Patent Vol.: 43A
Certificate: 91
Survey/Blk/Twp: SE 1/4 1 G & BN CO.-
Acres: 163
Map(s) 15

Abstract # 2026 - CASEY, A C
P'ee: CASEY, A C
G'ee: CASEY, A C
T-Dt: -- --- -----
P-Dt: 06 Oct 1893
Dist/Class: Fannin Scrip
File#: 21917
Patent#: 260
Patent Vol.: 12
Acres: 59
Map(s) 6

Abstract # 2028 - ELLIS, G W
P'ee: ELLIS, G W
G'ee: ELLIS, G W
T-Dt: -- --- -----
P-Dt: 11 Aug 1893
Dist/Class: Fannin Scrip
File#: 21897
Patent#: 241
Patent Vol.: 12
Acres: 65.50
Map(s) 34

Abstract # 2044 - MULANAX, J T M
P'ee: MULANAX, J T M
G'ee: MULANAX, J T M

T-Dt: -- --- -----
P-Dt: 06 Sep 1895
Dist/Class: Fannin Preemption
File#: 4157
Patent#: 22
Patent Vol.: 28
Acres: 151.60
Map(s) 36, 44

Abstract # 2049 - TE&L CO
P'ee: TEXAS EMIGRATION AND LAND
COMPANY
G'ee: TEXAS EMIGRATION AND LAND
COMPANY
T-Dt: -- --- -----
P-Dt: 08 Feb 1859
Dist/Class: Texas Emmigration and Land
Company
File#: 2735
Patent#: 493
Patent Vol.: 22
Certificate: 2735
Survey/Blk/Twp: 2735
Acres: 265
Map(s) 16

Abstract # 2050 - TE&L CO
P'ee: TEXAS EMIGRATION AND LAND
COMPANY
G'ee: TEXAS EMIGRATION AND LAND
COMPANY
T-Dt: -- --- -----
P-Dt: 08 Feb 1859
Dist/Class: Texas Emmigration and Land
Company
File#: 2736
Patent#: 494
Patent Vol.: 22
Certificate: 2736
Survey/Blk/Twp: 2736
Acres: 265
Map(s) 16

Abstract # 2051 - TE&L CO
P'ee: TEXAS EMIGRATION AND LAND
COMPANY
G'ee: TEXAS EMIGRATION AND LAND
COMPANY
T-Dt: -- --- -----
P-Dt: 08 Feb 1859
Dist/Class: Texas Emmigration and Land
Company
File#: 2737
Patent#: 495
Patent Vol.: 22
Certificate: 2737
Survey/Blk/Twp: 2737
Acres: 265
Map(s) 24

Abstract # 2052 - TE&L CO
P'ee: TEXAS EMIGRATION AND LAND
COMPANY
G'ee: TEXAS EMIGRATION AND LAND
COMPANY
T-Dt: -- --- -----
P-Dt: 08 Feb 1859
Dist/Class: Texas Emmigration and Land
Company
File#: 2738
Patent#: 496
Patent Vol.: 22
Certificate: 2738
Survey/Blk/Twp: 2738
Acres: 265

Map(s) 24

Abstract # 2053 - TE&L CO
P'ee: TEXAS EMMIGRATION AND LAND
COMPANY
G'ee: TEXAS EMMIGRATION AND LAND
COMPANY
T-Dt: -- --- -----
P-Dt: 12 Feb 1859
Dist/Class: Texas Emmigration and Land
Company
File#: 2798
Patent#: 556
Patent Vol.: 22
Certificate: 2798
Survey/Blk/Twp: 2798
Acres: 265
Map(s) 8

Abstract # 2055 - TE&L CO
P'ee: TEXAS EMMIGRATION AND LAND
COMPANY
G'ee: TEXAS EMMIGRATION AND LAND
COMPANY
T-Dt: -- --- -----
P-Dt: 11 Feb 1859
Dist/Class: Texas Emmigration and Land
Company
File#: 2788
Patent#: 546
Patent Vol.: 22
Certificate: 2788
Survey/Blk/Twp: 2788
Acres: 265
Map(s) 16

Abstract # 2056 - TE&L CO
P'ee: TEXAS EMMIGRATION AND LAND
COMPANY
G'ee: TEXAS EMMIGRATION AND LAND
COMPANY
T-Dt: -- --- -----
P-Dt: 11 Feb 1859
Dist/Class: Texas Emmigration and Land
Company
File#: 2789
Patent#: 547
Patent Vol.: 22
Certificate: 2789
Survey/Blk/Twp: 2789
Acres: 265
Map(s) 16

Abstract # 2057 - TE&L CO
P'ee: TEXAS EMMIGRATION AND LAND
COMPANY
G'ee: TEXAS EMMIGRATION AND LAND
COMPANY
T-Dt: -- --- -----
P-Dt: 11 Feb 1859
Dist/Class: Texas Emmigration and Land
Company
File#: 2786
Patent#: 544
Patent Vol.: 22
Certificate: 2786
Survey/Blk/Twp: 2786
Acres: 265
Map(s) 16

Abstract # 2058 - TE&L CO
P'ee: TEXAS EMMIGRATION AND LAND
COMPANY
G'ee: TEXAS EMMIGRATION AND LAND
COMPANY

T-Dt: -- --- -----
P-Dt: 11 Feb 1859
Dist/Class: Texas Emmigration and Land
Company
File#: 2787
Patent#: 545
Patent Vol.: 22
Certificate: 2787
Survey/Blk/Twp: 2787
Acres: 265
Map(s) 16

Abstract # 2059 - TE&L CO
P'ee: TEXAS EMMIGRATION AND LAND
COMPANY
G'ee: TEXAS EMMIGRATION AND LAND
COMPANY
T-Dt: -- --- -----
P-Dt: 11 Feb 1859
Dist/Class: Texas Emmigration and Land
Company
File#: 2796
Patent#: 554
Patent Vol.: 22
Certificate: 2796
Survey/Blk/Twp: 2796
Acres: 265
Map(s) 8, 16

Abstract # 2060 - TE&L CO
P'ee: TEXAS EMMIGRATION AND LAND
COMPANY
G'ee: TEXAS EMMIGRATION AND LAND
COMPANY
T-Dt: -- --- -----
P-Dt: 11 Feb 1859
Dist/Class: Texas Emmigration and Land
Company
File#: 2797
Patent#: 555
Patent Vol.: 22
Certificate: 2797
Survey/Blk/Twp: 2797
Acres: 265
Map(s) 8

Abstract # 2065 - TE&L CO
P'ee: TEXAS EMMIGRATION AND LAND
COMPANY
G'ee: TEXAS EMMIGRATION AND LAND
COMPANY
T-Dt: -- --- -----
P-Dt: 11 Feb 1859
Dist/Class: Texas Emmigration and Land
Company
File#: 2790
Patent#: 548
Patent Vol.: 22
Certificate: 2790
Survey/Blk/Twp: 2790
Acres: 265
Map(s) 16

Abstract # 2066 - TE&L CO
P'ee: TEXAS EMMIGRATION AND LAND
COMPANY
G'ee: TEXAS EMMIGRATION AND LAND
COMPANY
T-Dt: -- --- -----
P-Dt: 11 Feb 1859
Dist/Class: Texas Emmigration and Land
Company
File#: 2785
Patent#: 543
Patent Vol.: 22

Certificate: 2785
Survey/Blk/Twp: 2785
Acres: 265
Map(s) 8, 16

Abstract # 2067 - TE&L CO
P'ee: TEXAS EMMIGRATION AND LAND
COMPANY
G'ee: TEXAS EMMIGRATION AND LAND
COMPANY
T-Dt: -- --- -----
P-Dt: 08 Feb 1859
Dist/Class: Texas Emmigration and Land
Company
File#: 2733
Patent#: 491
Patent Vol.: 22
Certificate: 2733
Survey/Blk/Twp: 2733
Acres: 265
Map(s) 16

Abstract # 2068 - TE&L CO
P'ee: TEXAS EMMIGRATION AND LAND
COMPANY
G'ee: TEXAS EMMIGRATION AND LAND
COMPANY
T-Dt: -- --- -----
P-Dt: 08 Feb 1859
Dist/Class: Texas Emmigration and Land
Company
File#: 2734
Patent#: 492
Patent Vol.: 22
Certificate: 2734
Survey/Blk/Twp: 2734
Acres: 265
Map(s) 16

Abstract # 2071 - BRIR
S2: CRISWELL, T K
P'ee: HATFIELD, E R
G'ee: CRISWELL, T K
T-Dt: -- --- -----
P-Dt: 07 Jul 1906
Dist/Class: School
File#: 35736
Patent#: 141
Patent Vol.: 32
Survey/Blk/Twp: 69 BRIR-
Acres: 229
Map(s) 38, 39

Abstract # 2073 - BRIR
S2: DRIVER, J A
P'ee: DRIVER, J A
G'ee: DRIVER, JOHN A
T-Dt: -- --- -----
P-Dt: 09 Feb 1921
Dist/Class: School
File#: 35413
Patent#: 185
Patent Vol.: 10A
Survey/Blk/Twp: 41 BRIR-
Acres: 188.75
Map(s) 38

Abstract # 2074 - EVERETT, J P
P'ee: LOGAN, W H
G'ee: EVERETT, J P
T-Dt: -- --- -----
P-Dt: 04 Nov 1893
Dist/Class: School
File#: 2579
Patent#: 162

Patent Vol.: 14
Certificate: 2/165
Survey/Blk/Twp: SW 1/4 6 J.POITEVENT-
Acres: 160
Map(s) 23, 31

Abstract # 2075 - FINLAY, R
P'ee: FINLEY, ROWLAND
G'ee: FINLEY, ROWLAND
T-Dt: -- --- -----
P-Dt: 03 Jan 1893
Dist/Class: Fannin Preemption
File#: 1334
Patent#: 186
Patent Vol.: 25
Acres: 80
Map(s) 29

Abstract # 2078 - LAING, I
P'ee: BARNETT, W H
G'ee: LAING, ISAAC
T-Dt: -- --- -----
P-Dt: 11 Apr 1898
Dist/Class: Fannin Preemption
File#: 4302
Patent#: 63
Patent Vol.: 30
Acres: 80
Map(s) 27

Abstract # 2083 - TIMMONS, W S
P'ee: TIMMONS, W S
G'ee: TIMMONS, W S
T-Dt: -- --- -----
P-Dt: 11 Aug 1893
Dist/Class: Fannin Scrip
File#: 21929
Patent#: 239
Patent Vol.: 12
Acres: 71.50
Map(s) 29

Abstract # 2084 - GILCHREST, C
P'ee: OLIVER, LOUIS F
G'ee: GILCHRIST, CHARLES
T-Dt: -- --- -----
P-Dt: 22 Mar 1856
Dist/Class: Fannin 1st
File#: 468
Patent#: 19
Patent Vol.: 13
Certificate: 507
Acres: 177.10
Map(s) 1

Abstract # 2085 - MCKIMBS,S
P'ee: CARROLL, JOSEPH A
G'ee: MCKIMBS, SARAH
T-Dt: -- --- -----
P-Dt: 05 Dec 1883
Dist/Class: Fannin 1st
File#: 1914
Patent#: 134
Patent Vol.: 24
Certificate: 21/186
Acres: 535
Map(s) 8

Abstract # 2086 - HOPKINS, J A
P'ee: HOPKINS, JAMES A (HEIRS)
G'ee: HOPKINS, JAMES A
T-Dt: -- --- -----
P-Dt: 07 May 1875
Dist/Class: Fannin 3rd
File#: 4500

Patent#: 560
Patent Vol.: 42
Certificate: 45
Acres: 320
Map(s) 4

Abstract # 2087 - TE&L CO
P'ee: TEXAS EMIGRATION AND LAND
COMPANY
G'ee: TEXAS EMIGRATION AND LAND
COMPANY
T-Dt: -- --- -----
P-Dt: 07 Sep 1858
Dist/Class: Texas Emmigration and Land
Company
File#: 1576
Patent#: 320
Patent Vol.: 20
Certificate: 1576
Survey/Blk/Twp: 1576
Acres: 320
Map(s) 1

Abstract # 2088 - TE&L CO
P'ee: TEXAS EMIGRATION AND LAND
COMPANY
G'ee: TEXAS EMIGRATION AND LAND
COMPANY
T-Dt: -- --- -----
P-Dt: 27 Aug 1858
Dist/Class: Texas Emmigration and Land
Company
File#: 1578
Patent#: 322
Patent Vol.: 20
Certificate: 1578
Survey/Blk/Twp: 1578
Acres: 320
Map(s) 1

Abstract # 2089 - TE&L CO
P'ee: TEXAS EMIGRATION AND LAND
COMPANY
G'ee: TEXAS EMIGRATION AND LAND
COMPANY
T-Dt: -- --- -----
P-Dt: 08 Sep 1858
Dist/Class: Texas Emmigration and Land
Company
File#: 1584
Patent#: 328
Patent Vol.: 20
Certificate: 1584
Survey/Blk/Twp: 1584
Acres: 320
Map(s) 1

Abstract # 2090 - TE&L CO
P'ee: TEXAS EMIGRATION AND LAND
COMPANY
G'ee: TEXAS EMIGRATION AND LAND
COMPANY
T-Dt: -- --- -----
P-Dt: 16 Aug 1858
Dist/Class: Texas Emmigration and Land
Company
File#: 1373
Patent#: 221
Patent Vol.: 20
Certificate: 1373
Survey/Blk/Twp: 1373
Acres: 320
Map(s) 4

Abstract # 2091 - TE&L CO

P'ee: TEXAS EMIGRATION AND LAND
COMPANY
G'ee: TEXAS EMIGRATION AND LAND
COMPANY
T-Dt: -- --- -----
P-Dt: 17 Aug 1858
Dist/Class: Texas Emmigration and Land
Company
File#: 1377
Patent#: 225
Patent Vol.: 20
Certificate: 1377
Survey/Blk/Twp: 1377
Acres: 320
Map(s) 5

Abstract # 2092 - TE&L CO
P'ee: TEXAS EMIGRATION AND LAND
COMPANY
G'ee: TEXAS EMIGRATION AND LAND
COMPANY
T-Dt: -- --- -----
P-Dt: 18 Aug 1858
Dist/Class: Texas Emmigration and Land
Company
File#: 1383
Patent#: 230
Patent Vol.: 20
Certificate: 1383
Survey/Blk/Twp: 1383
Acres: 320
Map(s) 4, 5

Abstract # 2093 - TE&L CO
P'ee: TEXAS EMIGRATION AND LAND
COMPANY
G'ee: TEXAS EMIGRATION AND LAND
COMPANY
T-Dt: -- --- -----
P-Dt: 15 Jun 1858
Dist/Class: Texas Emmigration and Land
Company
File#: 785
Patent#: 785
Patent Vol.: 14
Certificate: 785
Survey/Blk/Twp: 785
Acres: 320
Map(s) 9

Abstract # 2094 - TE&L CO
P'ee: TEXAS EMIGRATION AND LAND
COMPANY
G'ee: TEXAS EMIGRATION AND LAND
COMPANY
T-Dt: -- --- -----
P-Dt: 18 Aug 1858
Dist/Class: Texas Emmigration and Land
Company
File#: 1389
Patent#: 236
Patent Vol.: 20
Certificate: 1389
Survey/Blk/Twp: 1389
Acres: 320
Map(s) 5

Abstract # 2095 - TE&L CO
P'ee: TEXAS EMIGRATION AND LAND
COMPANY
G'ee: TEXAS EMIGRATION AND LAND
COMPANY
T-Dt: -- --- -----
P-Dt: 19 Aug 1858
Dist/Class: Texas Emmigration and Land

Company
File#: 1397
Patent#: 244
Patent Vol.: 20
Certificate: 1397
Survey/Blk/Twp: 1397
Acres: 320
Map(s) 5

Abstract # 2096 - TE&L CO
P'ee: TEXAS EMIGRATION AND LAND COMPANY
G'ee: TEXAS EMIGRATION AND LAND COMPANY
T-Dt: -- --- -----
P-Dt: 19 Aug 1858
Dist/Class: Texas Emmigration and Land Company
File#: 1398
Patent#: 245
Patent Vol.: 20
Certificate: 1398
Survey/Blk/Twp: 1398
Acres: 320
Map(s) 5

Abstract # 2097 - TE&L CO
P'ee: TEXAS EMIGRATION AND LAND COMPANY
G'ee: TEXAS EMIGRATION AND LAND COMPANY
T-Dt: -- --- -----
P-Dt: 19 Aug 1858
Dist/Class: Texas Emmigration and Land Company
File#: 1399
Patent#: 246
Patent Vol.: 20
Certificate: 1399
Survey/Blk/Twp: 1399
Acres: 320
Map(s) 5, 6

Abstract # 2098 - TE&L CO
P'ee: TEXAS EMIGRATION AND LAND COMPANY
G'ee: TEXAS EMIGRATION AND LAND COMPANY
T-Dt: -- --- -----
P-Dt: 19 Aug 1858
Dist/Class: Texas Emmigration and Land Company
File#: 1400
Patent#: 247
Patent Vol.: 20
Certificate: 1400
Survey/Blk/Twp: 1400
Acres: 320
Map(s) 6

Abstract # 2099 - TE&L CO
P'ee: TEXAS EMIGRATION AND LAND COMPANY
G'ee: TEXAS EMIGRATION AND LAND COMPANY
T-Dt: -- --- -----
P-Dt: 08 Sep 1858
Dist/Class: Texas Emmigration and Land Company
File#: 1593
Patent#: 337
Patent Vol.: 20
Certificate: 1593
Survey/Blk/Twp: 1593
Acres: 320

Map(s) 2

Abstract # 2100 - TE&L CO
P'ee: TEXAS EMIGRATION AND LAND COMPANY
G'ee: TEXAS EMIGRATION AND LAND COMPANY
T-Dt: -- --- -----
P-Dt: 08 Sep 1858
Dist/Class: Texas Emmigration and Land Company
File#: 1594
Patent#: 338
Patent Vol.: 20
Certificate: 1594
Survey/Blk/Twp: 1594
Acres: 320
Map(s) 1, 2

Abstract # 2101 - TE&L CO
P'ee: TEXAS EMIGRATION AND LAND COMPANY
G'ee: TEXAS EMIGRATION AND LAND COMPANY
T-Dt: -- --- -----
P-Dt: 09 Sep 1858
Dist/Class: Texas Emmigration and Land Company
File#: 1595
Patent#: 339
Patent Vol.: 20
Certificate: 1595
Survey/Blk/Twp: 1595
Acres: 320
Map(s) 1

Abstract # 2102 - TE&L CO
P'ee: TEXAS EMIGRATION AND LAND COMPANY
G'ee: TEXAS EMIGRATION AND LAND COMPANY
T-Dt: -- --- -----
P-Dt: 09 Sep 1858
Dist/Class: Texas Emmigration and Land Company
File#: 1596
Patent#: 340
Patent Vol.: 20
Certificate: 1596
Survey/Blk/Twp: 1596
Acres: 320
Map(s) 1

Abstract # 2103 - TE&L CO
P'ee: TEXAS EMIGRATION AND LAND COMPANY
G'ee: TEXAS EMIGRATION AND LAND COMPANY
T-Dt: -- --- -----
P-Dt: 09 Sep 1858
Dist/Class: Texas Emmigration and Land Company
File#: 1597
Patent#: 341
Patent Vol.: 20
Certificate: 1597
Survey/Blk/Twp: 1597
Acres: 320
Map(s) 1

Abstract # 2104 - TE&L CO
P'ee: TEXAS EMIGRATION AND LAND COMPANY
G'ee: TEXAS EMIGRATION AND LAND COMPANY

T-Dt: -- --- -----
P-Dt: 05 Aug 1858
Dist/Class: Texas Emmigration and Land Company
File#: 1801
Patent#: 221
Patent Vol.: 21
Certificate: 1801
Survey/Blk/Twp: 1801
Acres: 320
Map(s) 6

Abstract # 2105 - TE&L CO
P'ee: TEXAS EMIGRATION AND LAND COMPANY
G'ee: TEXAS EMIGRATION AND LAND COMPANY
T-Dt: -- --- -----
P-Dt: 05 Aug 1858
Dist/Class: Texas Emmigration and Land Company
File#: 1802
Patent#: 14
Patent Vol.: 21
Certificate: 1802
Survey/Blk/Twp: 1802
Acres: 320
Map(s) 6

Abstract # 2106 - TE&L CO
P'ee: TEXAS EMIGRATION AND LAND COMPANY
G'ee: TEXAS EMIGRATION AND LAND COMPANY
T-Dt: -- --- -----
P-Dt: 05 Aug 1858
Dist/Class: Texas Emmigration and Land Company
File#: 1810
Patent#: 229
Patent Vol.: 21
Certificate: 1810
Survey/Blk/Twp: 1810
Acres: 320
Map(s) 4

Abstract # 2107 - TE&L CO
P'ee: TEXAS EMIGRATION AND LAND COMPANY
G'ee: TEXAS EMIGRATION AND LAND COMPANY
T-Dt: -- --- -----
P-Dt: 11 Aug 1858
Dist/Class: Texas Emmigration and Land Company
File#: 1856
Patent#: 273
Patent Vol.: 21
Certificate: 1856
Survey/Blk/Twp: 1856
Acres: 320
Map(s) 6

Abstract # 2109 - MCLYMAN, J B
P'ee: MCLYMAN, J B
G'ee: MCLYMAN, J B
T-Dt: -- --- -----
P-Dt: 16 Oct 1891
Dist/Class: Fannin Bounty
File#: 800
Patent#: 492
Patent Vol.: 16
Certificate: 120
Survey/Blk/Twp: 2
Acres: 240

Map(s) 4

Abstract # 2110 - NEWMAN, R D
P'ee: NEWMAN, R D
G'ee: NEWMAN, R D
T-Dt: -- --- -----
P-Dt: 01 Jul 1859
Dist/Class: Fannin Bounty
File#: 807
Patent#: 17
Patent Vol.: 12
Certificate: 125
Acres: 240
Map(s) 4

Abstract # 2111 - AKINS, J A
P'ee: BROGDEN, P H
G'ee: AKINS, J A
T-Dt: -- --- -----
P-Dt: 25 Oct 1879
Dist/Class: Fannin Preemption
File#: 1286
Patent#: 531
Patent Vol.: 9
Acres: 160
Map(s) 37

Abstract # 2115 - ANDERSON, A C
P'ee: ANDERSON, A C
G'ee: ANDERSON, A C
T-Dt: -- --- -----
P-Dt: 22 Sep 1894
Dist/Class: Fannin Scrip
File#: 21953
Patent#: 405
Patent Vol.: 12
Acres: 21.30
Map(s) 40

Abstract # 2116 - CROW, J G
P'ee: CROW, I G
G'ee: CROW, I G
T-Dt: -- --- -----
P-Dt: 15 Nov 1894
Dist/Class: Fannin Scrip
File#: 21959
Patent#: 426
Patent Vol.: 12
Acres: 36
Map(s) 40

Abstract # 2117 - MITCHELL, H L
P'ee: MITCHELL, H L
G'ee: MITCHELL, H L
T-Dt: -- --- -----
P-Dt: 04 Oct 1894
Dist/Class: Fannin Scrip
File#: 21951
Patent#: 410
Patent Vol.: 12
Acres: 8
Map(s) 37

Abstract # 2118 - SLATOR, J G
P'ee: SLATER, J G
G'ee: SLATER, J G
T-Dt: -- --- -----
P-Dt: 20 Jun 1894
Dist/Class: Fannin Scrip
File#: 21956
Patent#: 374
Patent Vol.: 12
Acres: 50
Map(s) 22

Abstract # 2119 - BRIR
S2: CHISM, M H
P'ee: CHISM, MATT H
G'ee: CHISM, MATT H
T-Dt: -- --- -----
P-Dt: 17 Nov 1919
Dist/Class: School
File#: 35905
Patent#: 329
Patent Vol.: 4A
Survey/Blk/Twp: 1/4 93 BRIR-
Acres: 122
Map(s) 31

Abstract # 2122 - TT RR CO
S2: BENNETT, W A
P'ee: BENNETT, W A
G'ee: BENNETT, W A
T-Dt: -- --- -----
P-Dt: 27 Mar 1917
Dist/Class: School
File#: 2484
Patent#: 392
Patent Vol.: 52
Certificate: 606
Survey/Blk/Twp: MID.PT. OF S.PT. SE 1/4 16 TTRR-
Acres: 160
Map(s) 32

Abstract # 2123 - BROGDON, M
P'ee: BROGDEN, M
G'ee: BROGDEN, M
T-Dt: -- --- -----
P-Dt: 29 Jan 1898
Dist/Class: Fannin Preemption
File#: 4513
Patent#: 614
Patent Vol.: 29
Acres: 62.80
Map(s) 29

Abstract # 2124 - CROW, T J
G'ee: CROW, T J
T-Dt: -- --- -----
P-Dt: -- --- -----
Dist/Class: Milam Preemption
File#: 5618
Acres: 76.60
Map(s) 48

Abstract # 2129 - SP RR CO
S2: RODGERS, G
P'ee: WILLIS, PRUDENCE
G'ee: ROGERS, GEORGE
T-Dt: -- --- -----
P-Dt: 02 Jun 1920
Dist/Class: School
File#: 2486
Patent#: 332
Patent Vol.: 7A
Certificate: 16/115
Survey/Blk/Twp: SW 1/4 2 SP 3-
Acres: 204
Map(s) 31

Abstract # 2131 - AB&M
S2: BELLOMY, W
P'ee: GRIFFIN, W W
G'ee: BELLOMY, W D
T-Dt: -- --- -----
P-Dt: 09 Jul 1919
Dist/Class: School
File#: 38501
Patent#: 240

Patent Vol.: 3A
Certificate: 16/63
Survey/Blk/Twp: NE 1/4 2 SP-
Acres: 160
Map(s) 35

Abstract # 2135 - BRIR
S2: GILMORE, J F
P'ee: GILMORE, W I
G'ee: GILMORE, J F
T-Dt: -- --- -----
P-Dt: 17 Jun 1907
Dist/Class: School
File#: 40109
Patent#: 285
Patent Vol.: 34
Survey/Blk/Twp: 76 BRIR-
Acres: 160
Map(s) 38

Abstract # 2136 - BRIR
S2: GREENWADE, J J
G'ee: GREENWADE, J J
T-Dt: -- --- -----
P-Dt: -- --- -----
Dist/Class: School
File#: 39373
Survey/Blk/Twp: 15 BRIR-
Acres: 160
Map(s) 38

Abstract # 2137 - SP RR CO
S2: HODGES, S G
P'ee: WILLIS, H M
G'ee: HODGES, S G
T-Dt: -- --- -----
P-Dt: 17 Jul 1914
Dist/Class: School
File#: 39221
Patent#: 434
Patent Vol.: 48
Certificate: 16/115
Survey/Blk/Twp: NE 1/4 2 SP 3-
Acres: 160
Map(s) 31, 32

Abstract # 2141 - MCCORKLE, R L
P'ee: HENDERSON, M
G'ee: MCCORKLE, R L
T-Dt: -- --- -----
P-Dt: 20 Aug 1906
Dist/Class: Fannin Preemption
File#: 4523
Patent#: 84
Patent Vol.: 33
Acres: 32
Map(s) 36

Abstract # 2142 - BRIR
S2: MCKNIGHT, W N
P'ee: RIBBLE, C M
G'ee: MCKNIGHT, WILLIAM
T-Dt: -- --- -----
P-Dt: 09 Aug 1917
Dist/Class: School
File#: 40696
Patent#: 339
Patent Vol.: 53
Survey/Blk/Twp: 2 BRIR-
Acres: 160
Map(s) 38, 46, 47

Abstract # 2143 - WC RR CO
S2: ROBINSON, J
P'ee: MORGAN, J W

G'ee: ROBINSON, JEP
T-Dt: -- --- -----
P-Dt: 31 Jul 1935
Dist/Class: School
File#: 40718
Patent#: 222
Patent Vol.: 59A
Certificate: 78/142
Survey/Blk/Twp: NE 1/4 2 WASH.CO.-
Acres: 160
Map(s) 16

Abstract # 2144 - BRIR
S2: SHANNON, W J
P'ee: SHANNON, W J
G'ee: SHANNON, W J
T-Dt: -- --- -----
P-Dt: 23 Mar 1937
Dist/Class: School
File#: 38362
Patent#: 500
Patent Vol.: 64A
Survey/Blk/Twp: 90 BRIR-
Acres: 158.8
Map(s) 31

Abstract # 2145 - I RR CO
S2: WRIGHT, A G
P'ee: WRIGHT, A G
G'ee: WRIGHT, A G
T-Dt: -- --- -----
P-Dt: 08 Feb 1927
Dist/Class: School
File#: 40285
Patent#: 351
Patent Vol.: 32A
Certificate: 16/161
Survey/Blk/Twp: NW 1/4 2 IND.RR-
Acres: 173
Map(s) 32

Abstract # 2146 - WOOD, F
P'ee: TURNER, WILLIAM
G'ee: WOOD, FRANKLIN
T-Dt: -- --- -----
P-Dt: 07 Oct 1896
Dist/Class: Fannin 3rd
File#: 4595
Patent#: 533
Patent Vol.: 46
Certificate: 20/185
Acres: 47
Map(s) 8

Abstract # 2147 - BRIR
S2: AINSWORTH, J A
P'ee: JOHNSON, C W
G'ee: AINSWORTH, J A
T-Dt: -- --- -----
P-Dt: 14 May 1920
Dist/Class: School
File#: 45006
Patent#: 197
Patent Vol.: 7A
Survey/Blk/Twp: 16 BRIR-
Acres: 160
Map(s) 38

Abstract # 2148 - BRIR
S2: AKIN, O W
P'ee: AKIN, JO W
G'ee: AKIN, JO W
T-Dt: -- --- -----
P-Dt: 25 Mar 1931
Dist/Class: School

File#: 43149
Patent#: 463
Patent Vol.: 49A
Survey/Blk/Twp: 1/4 92 BRIR-
Acres: 162.7
Map(s) 31

Abstract # 2149 - T&NO RR CO
S2: BLACKWOOD, L C
P'ee: BLACKWOOD, L C (HEIRS)
G'ee: BLACKWOOD, L C
T-Dt: -- --- -----
P-Dt: 04 Oct 1909
Dist/Class: School
File#: 48319
Patent#: 540
Patent Vol.: 38
Certificate: 863
Survey/Blk/Twp: NW 1/4 10 T & NO-
Acres: 210
Map(s) 29

Abstract # 2150 - BRIR
S2: BURCH, R
P'ee: BURCH, A
G'ee: BURCH, A
T-Dt: -- --- -----
P-Dt: 29 Dec 1919
Dist/Class: School
File#: 44167
Patent#: 93
Patent Vol.: 5A
Survey/Blk/Twp: 98 BRIR-
Acres: 162
Map(s) 31

Abstract # 2151 - SP RR CO
S2: BURK, J D
P'ee: BURK, J D
G'ee: BURK, J D
T-Dt: -- --- -----
P-Dt: 15 Jul 1947
Dist/Class: School
File#: 45721
Patent#: 22
Patent Vol.: 7-B
Certificate: 16/181
Survey/Blk/Twp: NE/4 4 S. P.-
Acres: 185.5
Map(s) 32

Abstract # 2152 - CT RR CO
S2: BUSSEY, J F
P'ee: BUSSEY, J F
G'ee: BUSSEY, J F
T-Dt: -- --- -----
P-Dt: 02 Apr 1917
Dist/Class: School
File#: 41238
Patent#: 423
Patent Vol.: 52
Certificate: 44
Survey/Blk/Twp: NE 1/4 2 CTRR-
Acres: 160
Map(s) 7, 8

Abstract # 2153 - COLE, J M
P'ee: COLE, J M
G'ee: COLE, J M
T-Dt: -- --- -----
P-Dt: 04 Jan 1897
Dist/Class: Fannin Scrip
File#: 21993
Patent#: 100
Patent Vol.: 13

Acres: 17.60
Map(s) 40

Abstract # 2154 - BRIR
S2: CUNNINGHAM, W H
P'ee: WHITTENBERG, R B
G'ee: CUNNINGHAM, W H
T-Dt: -- --- -----
P-Dt: 20 Nov 1907
Dist/Class: School
File#: 41637
Patent#: 297
Patent Vol.: 35
Survey/Blk/Twp: 35 BRIR-
Acres: 161
Map(s) 38

Abstract # 2155 - POITEVENT, J
S2: DOUGLASS, E L
P'ee: BURNS, W C
G'ee: DOUGLASS, E L
T-Dt: -- --- -----
P-Dt: 21 Sep 1900
Dist/Class: School
File#: 41395
Patent#: 59
Patent Vol.: 19
Certificate: 2/163
Survey/Blk/Twp: MID. 1/4 2
J.POITEVENT-
Acres: 160
Map(s) 23, 24

Abstract # 2156 - SP RR CO
S2: DOUGLASS, E L
P'ee: GOSS, W N
G'ee: DOUGLASS, E L
T-Dt: -- --- -----
P-Dt: 30 Jul 1909
Dist/Class: School
File#: 44702
Patent#: 309
Patent Vol.: 38
Certificate: 16/129
Survey/Blk/Twp: SW 1/4 10 SP-
Acres: 160
Map(s) 23

Abstract # 2157 - POITEVENT, J
S2: DOUGLASS, E L
P'ee: BURNS, W C
G'ee: DOUGLASS, E L
T-Dt: -- --- -----
P-Dt: 13 Oct 1902
Dist/Class: School
File#: 44703
Patent#: 230
Patent Vol.: 25
Certificate: 2/163
Survey/Blk/Twp: S 1/2 2 J.POITEVENT-
Acres: 320
Map(s) 23, 24

Abstract # 2158 - WC RR CO
S2: EGGERS, G
P'ee: EGGERS, GUSTAV
G'ee: EGGERS, GUSTAV
T-Dt: -- --- -----
P-Dt: 04 Apr 1903
Dist/Class: School
File#: 44238
Patent#: 266
Patent Vol.: 26
Certificate: 28/142
Survey/Blk/Twp: SW 1/4 2 WCRR-

Acres: 160
Map(s) 16

Abstract # 2160 - FOSTER, D L
P'ee: COSTELLO, E R AND COSTELLO, CON
G'ee: FOSTER, D L
T-Dt: -- --- -----
P-Dt: 24 Jan 1923
Dist/Class: School
File#: 48045
Patent#: 484
Patent Vol.: 16A
Certificate: 2/158
Survey/Blk/Twp: SW 1/4 2 J.POITEVENT-
Acres: 107.75
Map(s) 47

Abstract # 2161 - SP RR CO
S2: GACHTER, J A
P'ee: VICK, D G
G'ee: GACHTER, J A
T-Dt: -- --- -----
P-Dt: 10 Dec 1909
Dist/Class: School
File#: 44137
Patent#: 181
Patent Vol.: 39
Certificate: 16/129
Survey/Blk/Twp: SE 1/4 10 SPRR-
Acres: 160
Map(s) 23

Abstract # 2162 - SP RR CO
S2: HEIGHTON, J L
P'ee: MATTHEWS, T E
G'ee: HEIGHTON, J L
T-Dt: -- --- -----
P-Dt: 26 May 1920
Dist/Class: School
File#: 45005
Patent#: 281
Patent Vol.: 7A
Certificate: 16/129
Survey/Blk/Twp: NW 1/4 10 SPRR-
Acres: 160
Map(s) 23

Abstract # 2164 - SP RR CO
S2: HODGES, S G
P'ee: WILLIS, H M
G'ee: HODGES, S G
T-Dt: -- --- -----
P-Dt: 09 Sep 1914
Dist/Class: School
File#: 41027
Patent#: 526
Patent Vol.: 48
Certificate: 16/115
Survey/Blk/Twp: FRAC.NW PT.2 SPRR-
Acres: 196.5
Map(s) 31

Abstract # 2165 - T&NO RR CO
S2: HOLLEY, J L
P'ee: HOLLEY, J L
G'ee: HOLLEY, J L
T-Dt: -- --- -----
P-Dt: 03 Apr 1928
Dist/Class: School
File#: 41269
Patent#: 507
Patent Vol.: 38A
Certificate: 865
Survey/Blk/Twp: SE 1/4 4 T & NO-

Acres: 162.2
Map(s) 31

Abstract # 2166 - HYATT, J L E
P'ee: CULLERS, F M
G'ee: HYATT, J L E
T-Dt: -- --- -----
P-Dt: 11 Jun 1926
Dist/Class: School
File#: 41411
Patent#: 547
Patent Vol.: 29A
Certificate: 44
Survey/Blk/Twp: SE 1/4 2 CTRR-
Acres: 160
Map(s) 7, 8

Abstract # 2167 - T&NO RR CO
S2: KELLY, H
P'ee: KELLY, C A
G'ee: KELLY, HENRY
T-Dt: -- --- -----
P-Dt: 11 Dec 1951
Dist/Class: School
File#: 44978
Patent#: 215
Patent Vol.: 19-B
Certificate: 861
Survey/Blk/Twp: NE 1/4 6 T. & N. O.-
Acres: 175.3
Map(s) 29

Abstract # 2168 - AB&M
P'ee: MCCOMBER, H A
G'ee: MCCOMBER, H A
T-Dt: -- --- -----
P-Dt: 03 Oct 1889
Dist/Class: School
File#: 3555
Patent#: 423
Patent Vol.: 9
Certificate: 798
Survey/Blk/Twp: 1/2 SEC.12 AB & M-
Acres: 320
Map(s) 24, 32

Abstract # 2169 - AB&M
S2: PADGETT, MRS E C
P'ee: PADGETT, E C (MRS)
G'ee: PADGETT, E C (MRS)
T-Dt: -- --- -----
P-Dt: 07 Apr 1927
Dist/Class: School
File#: 41145
Patent#: 355
Patent Vol.: 33A
Certificate: 798
Survey/Blk/Twp: N 1/2 8 AB & M-
Acres: 136
Map(s) 31, 32

Abstract # 2170 - AB&M
S2: HARRIS, D
P'ee: PARHAM, JAMES (HEIRS)
G'ee: PARHAM, JAMES
T-Dt: -- --- -----
P-Dt: 27 Sep 1901
Dist/Class: School
File#: 40778
Patent#: 438
Patent Vol.: 21
Certificate: 16/63
Survey/Blk/Twp: W 1/2 OF SW 1/4 2 SP 2-
Acres: 80
Map(s) 35

Abstract # 2171 - T&NO RR CO
S2: POSERN, G A
P'ee: CHAMBERS, MATTIE (MRS)
G'ee: POSERN, G A
T-Dt: -- --- -----
P-Dt: 13 Mar 1914
Dist/Class: School
File#: 41392
Patent#: 74
Patent Vol.: 48
Certificate: 864
Survey/Blk/Twp: NW 1/4 2 T & NO-
Acres: 160
Map(s) 31

Abstract # 2172 - T&NO RR CO
S2: POSERN, E A
P'ee: CHAMBERS, V M
G'ee: POSERN, E A
T-Dt: -- --- -----
P-Dt: 28 Aug 1918
Dist/Class: School
File#: 44818
Patent#: 321
Patent Vol.: 56
Certificate: 864
Survey/Blk/Twp: SW 1/4 2 T & NO-
Acres: 160
Map(s) 31

Abstract # 2173 - BBB&C RR CO
S2: PRICE, W H
P'ee: PRICE, W H
G'ee: PRICE, W H
T-Dt: -- --- -----
P-Dt: 12 Sep 1921
Dist/Class: School
File#: 44385
Patent#: 531
Patent Vol.: 11A
Certificate: 682
Survey/Blk/Twp: N 1/2 & SW 1/4 2 BBB & CRR-
Acres: 480
Map(s) 15, 16

Abstract # 2174 - BS&F
S2: ROBERTSON, E
P'ee: VICK, JOHN H
G'ee: ROBERSON, E
T-Dt: -- --- -----
P-Dt: 31 May 1922
Dist/Class: School
File#: 47939
Patent#: 68
Patent Vol.: 14A
Certificate: 1/266
Survey/Blk/Twp: SW 1/4 4 BS & F 1-
Acres: 160
Map(s) 40

Abstract # 2175 - POITEVENT, J
S2: ROBERTSON, J H
P'ee: ROBERTSON, J H
G'ee: ROBERTSON, J H
T-Dt: -- --- -----
P-Dt: 10 Nov 1926
Dist/Class: School
File#: 41563
Patent#: 344
Patent Vol.: 31A
Certificate: 2/164
Survey/Blk/Twp: NW 1/2 4 J.POITEVENT-
Acres: 314

Map(s) 23

Abstract # 2176 - POITEVENT, J
S2: ROBERTSON, R J
P'ee: ROBERTSON, R J
G'ee: ROBERTSON, R J
T-Dt: -- --- -----
P-Dt: 09 Dec 1909
Dist/Class: School
File#: 41564
Patent#: 166
Patent Vol.: 39
Certificate: 2/164
Survey/Blk/Twp: S 1/4 4 J.POITEVENT-
Acres: 157.33
Map(s) 23

Abstract # 2177 - STINNETT, G U
P'ee: STINNETT, G U
G'ee: STINNETT, GEORGE U
T-Dt: -- --- -----
P-Dt: 28 Jul 1926
Dist/Class: School
File#: 44298
Patent#: 301
Patent Vol.: 30A
Certificate: 44
Survey/Blk/Twp: SW 1/4 2 CTRR-
Acres: 160
Map(s) 7

Abstract # 2178 - TE&L CO
P'ee: COLEMAN, THOMAS
G'ee: TEXAS EMIGRATION AND LAND
COMPANY
T-Dt: -- --- -----
P-Dt: 23 Feb 1858
Dist/Class: Texas Emmigration and Land
Company
File#: 1207
Patent#: 359
Patent Vol.: 14
Certificate: 1207
Survey/Blk/Twp: 1207
Acres: 320
Map(s) 35, 43

Abstract # 2179 - BRIR
S2: TIMMONS, J S
P'ee: TIMMONS, J S
G'ee: TIMMONS, J S
T-Dt: -- --- -----
P-Dt: 23 Apr 1919
Dist/Class: School
File#: 41253
Patent#: 352
Patent Vol.: 2A
Survey/Blk/Twp: 1/4 60 BRIR-
Acres: 160
Map(s) 37

Abstract # 2180 - BRIR
S2: TREUE, W C
P'ee: TREUE, W C
G'ee: TREUE, W C
T-Dt: -- --- -----
P-Dt: 17 Mar 1921
Dist/Class: School
File#: 41410
Patent#: 334
Patent Vol.: 10A
Survey/Blk/Twp: 96 BRIR-
Acres: 160
Map(s) 31

Abstract # 2181 - WHITFIELD, J M
P'ee: WHITFIELD, J M
G'ee: WHITFIELD, J M
T-Dt: -- --- -----
P-Dt: 27 May 1922
Dist/Class: School
File#: 45893
Patent#: 57
Patent Vol.: 14A
Certificate: 2/165
Survey/Blk/Twp: NW 1/4 6
J.POITEVENT-
Acres: 143.2
Map(s) 23

Abstract # 2183 - BRIR
S2: WOOD, J H
P'ee: WOOD, JOHN H
G'ee: WOOD, JOHN H
T-Dt: -- --- -----
P-Dt: 17 Feb 1920
Dist/Class: School
File#: 46095
Patent#: 21
Patent Vol.: 6A
Survey/Blk/Twp: 1/4 122 BRIR-
Acres: 160
Map(s) 29

Abstract # 2184 - SP RR CO
S2: BURK, J D
P'ee: BURK, J D
G'ee: BURK, J D
T-Dt: -- --- -----
P-Dt: 06 Jun 1923
Dist/Class: School
File#: 52127
Patent#: 476
Patent Vol.: 18A
Certificate: 16/181
Survey/Blk/Twp: SE 1/4 4 SPRR-
Acres: 160.9
Map(s) 32

Abstract # 2185 - BRIR
S2: COFFMAN, A W
P'ee: JONES, I H
G'ee: COFFMAN, A W
T-Dt: -- --- -----
P-Dt: 04 Jan 1905
Dist/Class: School
File#: 51262
Patent#: 255
Patent Vol.: 29
Survey/Blk/Twp: FRAC.64 BRIR-
Acres: 135.50
Map(s) 37

Abstract # 2186 - FOSTER, D L
P'ee: COSTELLO, E R AND COSTELLO,
CON
G'ee: FOSTER, D L
T-Dt: -- --- -----
P-Dt: 24 Jan 1923
Dist/Class: School
File#: 51728
Patent#: 485
Patent Vol.: 16A
Certificate: 2/158
Survey/Blk/Twp: NW 1/4 2
J.POITEVENT-
Acres: 107.75
Map(s) 39, 47

Abstract # 2187 - BS&F

S2: HARRISON, W A
P'ee: VICK, JOHN H
G'ee: HARRISON, W A
T-Dt: -- --- -----
P-Dt: 31 May 1922
Dist/Class: School
File#: 50912
Patent#: 69
Patent Vol.: 14A
Certificate: 1/266
Survey/Blk/Twp: NW 1/4 4 BS & F-
Acres: 160
Map(s) 40

Abstract # 2188 - JOHNSON, A S
P'ee: JOHNSTON, A SIDNEY
G'ee: JOHNSTON, A SIDNEY
T-Dt: -- --- -----
P-Dt: 23 Aug 1854
Dist/Class: Milam 1st
File#: 1030
Patent#: 168
Patent Vol.: 11
Acres: 3594
Map(s) 41

Abstract # 2189 - BRIR
S2: KILLION, D G
P'ee: KILLION, D G
G'ee: KILLION, D G
T-Dt: -- --- -----
P-Dt: 29 May 1919
Dist/Class: School
File#: 50870
Patent#: 6
Patent Vol.: 3A
Survey/Blk/Twp: 1/4 118 BRIR-
Acres: 131.8
Map(s) 29

Abstract # 2190 - I RR CO
S2: KIMBREL, L H
P'ee: HARGRAVE, J B
G'ee: KIMBREL, L H
T-Dt: -- --- -----
P-Dt: 09 Nov 1922
Dist/Class: School
File#: 52126
Patent#: 344
Patent Vol.: 15A
Certificate: 16/161
Survey/Blk/Twp: NE 1/4 2 IRR-
Acres: 172
Map(s) 32

Abstract # 2194 - TE&L CO
P'ee: COLEMAN, THOMAS
G'ee: TEXAS EMIGRATION AND LAND
COMPANY
T-Dt: -- --- -----
P-Dt: 23 Feb 1858
Dist/Class: Texas Emmigration and Land
Company
File#: 1208
Patent#: 360
Patent Vol.: 14
Certificate: 1208
Survey/Blk/Twp: 1208
Acres: 320
Map(s) 43

Abstract # 2197 - BRIR
S2: AINSWORTH, J A
P'ee: MILLER, J T
G'ee: AINSWORTH, J A

T-Dt: -- --- -----
P-Dt: 14 Mar 1917
Dist/Class: School
File#: 57042
Patent#: 344
Patent Vol.: 52
Survey/Blk/Twp: 1/4 21 BRIR-
Acres: 160
Map(s) 38

Abstract # 2198 - HURT, W C
G'ee: ARDIS, W H
T-Dt: -- --- -----
P-Dt: -- --- -----
Dist/Class: School
File#: 57577
Certificate: 2/160
Survey/Blk/Twp: 1/2 4 J.POITEVENT-
Acres: 320
Map(s) 24

Abstract # 2200 - BBB&C RR CO
S2: CLARK, J F
P'ee: TURNER, E C
G'ee: CLARK, J F
T-Dt: -- --- -----
P-Dt: 13 Apr 1909
Dist/Class: School
File#: 57140
Patent#: 567
Patent Vol.: 37
Certificate: 681
Survey/Blk/Twp: SW 1/4 2 BBB & CRR-
Acres: 160
Map(s) 31

Abstract # 2201 - BRIR
S2: GREEN, J W
P'ee: GREEN, J W
G'ee: CLARK, J F
T-Dt: -- --- -----
P-Dt: 31 Jan 1939
Dist/Class: School
File#: 57142
Patent#: 32
Patent Vol.: 71A
Survey/Blk/Twp: N.PT.32 BRIR-
Acres: 95.56
Map(s) 38

Abstract # 2202 - BRIR
S2: CLARK, J F
P'ee: CLARK, J F
G'ee: CLARK, J F
T-Dt: -- --- -----
P-Dt: 01 May 1939
Dist/Class: School
File#: 57141
Patent#: 138
Patent Vol.: 72A
Survey/Blk/Twp: 1/4 100 BRIR-
Acres: 149.7
Map(s) 31

Abstract # 2203 - BRIR
S2: GIBSON, P L
P'ee: GIBSON, P L
G'ee: GIBSON, P L
T-Dt: -- --- -----
P-Dt: 13 May 1910
Dist/Class: School
File#: 55934
Patent#: 309
Patent Vol.: 40
Survey/Blk/Twp: 78 BRIR-

Acres: 182
Map(s) 30

Abstract # 2204 - BRIR
S2: KNIGHT, J F
P'ee: KNIGHT, J F
G'ee: KNIGHT, J F
T-Dt: -- --- -----
P-Dt: 25 Oct 1938
Dist/Class: School
File#: 60234
Patent#: 489
Patent Vol.: 69A
Survey/Blk/Twp: 112 INDIAN RESERVA-
TION-
Acres: 105
Map(s) 30

Abstract # 2205 - BRIR
S2: MITCHELL, R F
P'ee: MITCHELL, R F
G'ee: MITCHELL, R F
T-Dt: -- --- -----
P-Dt: 14 Nov 1906
Dist/Class: School
File#: 60858
Patent#: 622
Patent Vol.: 32
Survey/Blk/Twp: 1/4 20 BRIR-
Acres: 160
Map(s) 38, 39

Abstract # 2206 - POITEVENT, J
S2: NEWHAUS, C
P'ee: NEWHOUS, CHARLES
G'ee: NEWHOUS, CHARLES
T-Dt: -- --- -----
P-Dt: 07 Jan 1913
Dist/Class: School
File#: 60378
Patent#: 486
Patent Vol.: 47
Certificate: 2/160
Survey/Blk/Twp: 2 J.POITEVENT-
Acres: 320
Map(s) 28

Abstract # 2207 - EL&RR RR CO
S2: NEWHAUS, C
P'ee: NEWHOUS, CHARLES
G'ee: NEWHOUS, CHARLES
T-Dt: -- --- -----
P-Dt: 06 Jan 1913
Dist/Class: School
File#: 60377
Patent#: 485
Patent Vol.: 47
Certificate: 554
Survey/Blk/Twp: W 1/2 2 EL & RR-
Acres: 339.8
Map(s) 28, 29

Abstract # 2208 - BRIR
S2: OLDHAM, M
P'ee: PRUITT, W A
G'ee: OLDHAM, MASON
T-Dt: -- --- -----
P-Dt: 12 Mar 1923
Dist/Class: School
File#: 59639
Patent#: 313
Patent Vol.: 17A
Survey/Blk/Twp: FRAC.30 BRIR-
Acres: 68.2
Map(s) 39

Abstract # 2209 - BRIR
S2: OLDHAM, S M
P'ee: NEWBY, W L
G'ee: OLDHAM, S M
T-Dt: -- --- -----
P-Dt: 31 Jul 1922
Dist/Class: School
File#: 60386
Patent#: 352
Patent Vol.: 14A
Survey/Blk/Twp: 28 BRIR-
Acres: 88.36
Map(s) 38, 39

Abstract # 2210 - SP RR CO
S2: WALKER, W T
P'ee: WALKER, W T
G'ee: WALKER, W T
T-Dt: -- --- -----
P-Dt: 14 Apr 1920
Dist/Class: School
File#: 58452
Patent#: 523
Patent Vol.: 6A
Certificate: 16/69
Survey/Blk/Twp: SW PT. OF SW 1/4 6
SPRR-
Acres: 47.6
Map(s) 32

Abstract # 2211 - BS&F
S2: ALFORD, J L
P'ee: ALFORD, J L
G'ee: ALFORD, J L
T-Dt: -- --- -----
P-Dt: 25 Jan 1945
Dist/Class: School
File#: 62889
Patent#: 365
Patent Vol.: 97A
Certificate: 1/268
Survey/Blk/Twp: W 1/2 & W 1/2 OF SE
1/4 2 B. S. & F.-
Acres: 400
Map(s) 32

Abstract # 2212 - BRIR
S2: CAPPS, W T
P'ee: CAPPS, W T
G'ee: CAPPS, W T
T-Dt: -- --- -----
P-Dt: 21 Nov 1941
Dist/Class: School
File#: 63338
Patent#: 387
Patent Vol.: 82A
Survey/Blk/Twp: W 1/2 OF 117 BRIR-
Acres: 88
Map(s) 29

Abstract # 2213 - I RR CO
S2: DAVIS, F M
P'ee: DAVIS, F M
G'ee: DAVIS, F M
T-Dt: -- --- -----
P-Dt: 19 Apr 1920
Dist/Class: School
File#: 62019
Patent#: 36
Patent Vol.: 7A
Certificate: 16/161
Survey/Blk/Twp: S 1/2 2 IND. R.R.-
Acres: 363.4
Map(s) 32

Abstract # 2214 - DAVIS, F M
P'ee: COSTELLO, E P AND COSTELLO,
CON
G'ee: DAVIS, F M
T-Dt: -- --- -----
P-Dt: 16 Aug 1928
Dist/Class: School
File#: 62020
Patent#: 182
Patent Vol.: 40A
Certificate: 32
Survey/Blk/Twp: 1/2 2 WACO MFG.CO.-
Acres: 256.2
Map(s) 47, 48

Abstract # 2215 - BRIR
S2: DOWDLE, J E
P'ee: DOWDLE, J E
G'ee: DOWDLE, J E
T-Dt: -- --- -----
P-Dt: 23 Apr 1913
Dist/Class: School
File#: 65764
Patent#: 271
Patent Vol.: 46
Survey/Blk/Twp: 1/4 39 BRIR-
Acres: 160
Map(s) 38

Abstract # 2216 - BRIR
S2: GREENWADE, J J
P'ee: GREENWADE, J J
G'ee: GREENWADE, J J
T-Dt: -- --- -----
P-Dt: 20 May 1921
Dist/Class: School
File#: 63037
Patent#: 138
Patent Vol.: 11A
Survey/Blk/Twp: S.PT.FRAC.14 BRIR-
Acres: 128.50
Map(s) 38

Abstract # 2217 - BRIR
S2: KING, H G
P'ee: BRENIZER, N O
G'ee: KING, H G
T-Dt: -- --- -----
P-Dt: 28 Nov 1919
Dist/Class: School
File#: 66604
Patent#: 403
Patent Vol.: 4A
Survey/Blk/Twp: 22 BRIR-
Acres: 145.7
Map(s) 38

Abstract # 2218 - BRIR
P'ee: KING, H G
G'ee: KING, H G
T-Dt: -- --- -----
P-Dt: 29 Aug 1917
Dist/Class: School
File#: 66605
Patent#: 391
Patent Vol.: 53
Survey/Blk/Twp: 70 BRIR-
Acres: 190
Map(s) 38

Abstract # 2219 - BRIR
S2: KING, H G
P'ee: KING, H G
G'ee: KING, H G
T-Dt: -- --- -----

P-Dt: 18 Dec 1912
Dist/Class: School
File#: 66606
Patent#: 370
Patent Vol.: 45
Survey/Blk/Twp: 48 BRIR-
Acres: 155.50
Map(s) 38

Abstract # 2221 - BRIR
S2: LISLE, O D
P'ee: SANTANGELO, O DE A
G'ee: LISLE, O D
T-Dt: -- --- -----
P-Dt: 05 Dec 1917
Dist/Class: School
File#: 63116
Patent#: 226
Patent Vol.: 54
Survey/Blk/Twp: 26 BRIR-
Acres: 82.8
Map(s) 38

Abstract # 2222 - BRIR
S2: MOSELEY, B G
P'ee: MOSELEY, B G
G'ee: MOSELEY, B G
T-Dt: -- --- -----
P-Dt: 14 Jul 1938
Dist/Class: School
File#: 63168
Patent#: 144
Patent Vol.: 69A
Certificate: 307
Survey/Blk/Twp: 113 BRIR-
Acres: 379
Map(s) 30

Abstract # 2224 - G&BN CO
S2: NICHOLSON, W A
P'ee: PRITCHETT, W A
G'ee: NICHOLSON, W A
T-Dt: -- --- -----
P-Dt: 06 Apr 1900
Dist/Class: School
File#: 2391
Patent#: 335
Patent Vol.: 18
Certificate: 29
Survey/Blk/Twp: SE 1/4 3 G & BN CO. A-
Acres: 160
Map(s) 6, 7

Abstract # 2225 - BRIR
S2: RIBBLE, S L
P'ee: RIBBLE, S L
G'ee: RIBBLE, S L
T-Dt: -- --- -----
P-Dt: 05 May 1921
Dist/Class: School
File#: 61723
Patent#: 94
Patent Vol.: 11A
Survey/Blk/Twp: 4 BRIR-
Acres: 170.50
Map(s) 38, 46

Abstract # 2226 - ROSS, L W
P'ee: URQUHART, ALLEN
G'ee: ROSS, LEROY W
T-Dt: -- --- -----
P-Dt: 21 Mar 1901
Dist/Class: Fannin 1st
File#: 1858
Patent#: 392

Patent Vol.: 25
Certificate: 1/4298
Acres: 102
Map(s) 20

Abstract # 2227 - ROSS, L W
P'ee: URQUHART, ALLEN
G'ee: ROSS, LEROY W
T-Dt: -- --- -----
P-Dt: 22 Mar 1901
Dist/Class: Fannin 1st
File#: 1858
Patent#: 393
Patent Vol.: 25
Certificate: 1/4298
Acres: 162
Map(s) 20

Abstract # 2228 - BRIR
S2: SHANNON, W J
P'ee: SHANNON, W J
G'ee: SHANNON, W J
T-Dt: -- --- -----
P-Dt: 23 Sep 1937
Dist/Class: School
File#: 65556
Patent#: 216
Patent Vol.: 66A
Survey/Blk/Twp: 126 BRIR-
Acres: 32
Map(s) 31

Abstract # 2230 - BRIR
S2: SMITH, T H
P'ee: SMITH, THOMAS H
G'ee: SMITH, THOMAS H
T-Dt: -- --- -----
P-Dt: 28 Jun 1907
Dist/Class: School
File#: 66634
Patent#: 362
Patent Vol.: 34
Survey/Blk/Twp: 19 BRIR-
Acres: 160
Map(s) 39

Abstract # 2231 - BRIR
S2: WADLEY, T H
P'ee: WADLEY, T C
G'ee: WADLEY, T C
T-Dt: -- --- -----
P-Dt: 26 Dec 1918
Dist/Class: School
File#: 64716
Patent#: 162
Patent Vol.: 1A
Survey/Blk/Twp: 66 BRIR-
Acres: 160
Map(s) 37

Abstract # 2233 - BRIR
S2: AKIN, D R
P'ee: AKIN, D R
G'ee: AKIN, D R
T-Dt: -- --- -----
P-Dt: 25 Mar 1931
Dist/Class: School
File#: 67377
Patent#: 464
Patent Vol.: 49A
Survey/Blk/Twp: 1/4 88 BRIR-
Acres: 160
Map(s) 31

Abstract # 2234 - BRIR

S2: AKIN, D R
P'ee: AKIN, J W
G'ee: AKIN, D R
T-Dt: -- --- -----
P-Dt: 23 Oct 1944
Dist/Class: School
File#: 67378
Patent#: 182
Patent Vol.: 96A
Survey/Blk/Twp: 1/4 85 B. R. I. R.-
Acres: 160
Map(s) 31

Abstract # 2235 - BRIR
S2: AKIN, D R
P'ee: AKIN, J W
G'ee: AKIN, D R
T-Dt: -- --- -----
P-Dt: 23 Oct 1944
Dist/Class: School
File#: 67379
Patent#: 183
Patent Vol.: 96A
Survey/Blk/Twp: 1/4 84 B. R. I. R.-
Acres: 160
Map(s) 31

Abstract # 2236 - BRIR
S2: AKIN, D R
P'ee: AKIN, J W
G'ee: AKIN, D R
T-Dt: -- --- -----
P-Dt: 23 Oct 1944
Dist/Class: School
File#: 67380
Patent#: 184
Patent Vol.: 96A
Survey/Blk/Twp: 1/4 83 B. R. I. R.-
Acres: 160
Map(s) 31

Abstract # 2237 - BRIR
S2: AKIN, D R
P'ee: AKIN, J W
G'ee: AKIN, D R
T-Dt: -- --- -----
P-Dt: 23 Oct 1944
Dist/Class: School
File#: 67381
Patent#: 185
Patent Vol.: 96A
Survey/Blk/Twp: 1/4 81 B. R. I. R.-
Acres: 160
Map(s) 31, 39

Abstract # 2238 - HAYNES, J R
P'ee: AKIN, J W
G'ee: AKIN, D R
T-Dt: -- --- -----
P-Dt: 23 Oct 1944
Dist/Class: School
File#: 68344
Patent#: 186
Patent Vol.: 96A
Survey/Blk/Twp: 1/8 2 J. R. HAYNES-
Acres: 80
Map(s) 30, 38

Abstract # 2239 - BRIR
S2: AKIN, D R
P'ee: AKIN, J W
G'ee: AKIN, D R
T-Dt: -- --- -----
P-Dt: 23 Oct 1944
Dist/Class: School

File#: 68345
Patent#: 187
Patent Vol.: 96A
Survey/Blk/Twp: 1/4 87 B. R. I. R.-
Acres: 160
Map(s) 30, 31

Abstract # 2240 - BRIR
S2: AKIN, D R
P'ee: AKIN, J W
G'ee: AKIN, D R
T-Dt: -- --- -----
P-Dt: 23 Oct 1944
Dist/Class: School
File#: 68570
Patent#: 188
Patent Vol.: 96A
Survey/Blk/Twp: PT 79 B. R. I. R.-
Acres: 491.59
Map(s) 30, 31, 38, 39

Abstract # 2241 - BRIR
S2: AKIN, D R
P'ee: AKIN, J W
G'ee: AKIN, D R
T-Dt: -- --- -----
P-Dt: 23 Oct 1944
Dist/Class: School
File#: 68645
Patent#: 189
Patent Vol.: 96A
Survey/Blk/Twp: PT 86 B. R. I. R.-
Acres: 260.6
Map(s) 30

Abstract # 2242 - ARNOLD, H
P'ee: ARNOLD, H G
G'ee: ARNOLD, H G
T-Dt: -- --- -----
P-Dt: 09 Sep 1901
Dist/Class: Scrap File
File#: 1297
Patent#: 229
Patent Vol.: 21
Survey/Blk/Twp: 126
Acres: 61.60
Map(s) 19, 27

Abstract # 2243 - BRIR
S2: GILMORE, J F
P'ee: BURCH, F P
G'ee: GILMORE, J F
T-Dt: -- --- -----
P-Dt: 14 Feb 1918
Dist/Class: School
File#: 67971
Patent#: 20
Patent Vol.: 55
Survey/Blk/Twp: 1/4 74 BRIR-
Acres: 157
Map(s) 39

Abstract # 2244 - BRIR
S2: MITCHELL, R F
P'ee: MITCHELL, R F
G'ee: MITCHELL, R F
T-Dt: -- --- -----
P-Dt: 14 Nov 1906
Dist/Class: School
File#: 70732
Patent#: 631
Patent Vol.: 32
Survey/Blk/Twp: 17 BRIR-
Acres: 160
Map(s) 38, 39, 46, 47

Abstract # 2245 - BRIR
S2: OWEN, R D
P'ee: OWEN, R D
G'ee: OWEN, R D
T-Dt: -- --- -----
P-Dt: 20 Oct 1919
Dist/Class: School
File#: 68814
Patent#: 269
Patent Vol.: 4A
Survey/Blk/Twp: 1/4 38 BRIR-
Acres: 160
Map(s) 38

Abstract # 2246 - AB&M
S2: RAGLAND, E R
P'ee: MILLER, C J
G'ee: RAGLAND, E R
T-Dt: -- --- -----
P-Dt: 03 Jan 1927
Dist/Class: School
File#: 69828
Patent#: 58
Patent Vol.: 32A
Certificate: 798
Survey/Blk/Twp: S 1/2 8 AB & M 8-
Acres: 147.50
Map(s) 31, 32

Abstract # 2247 - BRIR
S2: RIBBLE, C M
P'ee: RIBBLE, C M
G'ee: RIBBLE, C M
T-Dt: -- --- -----
P-Dt: 25 Feb 1916
Dist/Class: School
File#: 68821
Patent#: 342
Patent Vol.: 50
Survey/Blk/Twp: 1/4 1 BRIR-
Acres: 160
Map(s) 46, 47

Abstract # 2248 - BRIR
S2: TOWNSEND, C W
P'ee: JOHNSON, C W
G'ee: TOWNSEND, C W
T-Dt: -- --- -----
P-Dt: 05 Jun 1906
Dist/Class: School
File#: 68865
Patent#: 626
Patent Vol.: 31
Survey/Blk/Twp: NW 1/4 118 BRIR-
Acres: 80
Map(s) 29

Abstract # 2249 - BRIR
S2: AKIN, D R
P'ee: AKIN, J W
G'ee: AKIN, D R
T-Dt: -- --- -----
P-Dt: 23 Oct 1944
Dist/Class: School
File#: 73638
Patent#: 190
Patent Vol.: 96-A
Survey/Blk/Twp: 1/4 80 B. R. I. R.-
Acres: 160
Map(s) 30, 31, 38, 39

Abstract # 2250 - BRIR
S2: DOWDLE, J E
P'ee: GRIMSHAW, AMOS
G'ee: DOWDLE, J E

T-Dt: -- --- -----
P-Dt: 11 Sep 1913
Dist/Class: School
File#: 74717
Patent#: 92
Patent Vol.: 47
Survey/Blk/Twp: PT. 34 BRIR-
Acres: 199
Map(s) 38

Abstract # 2251 - BRIR
S2: GILMORE, J F
P'ee: BURCH, F P
G'ee: GILMORE, JOHN F
T-Dt: -- --- -----
P-Dt: 18 Jan 1917
Dist/Class: School
File#: 72614
Patent#: 141
Patent Vol.: 52
Survey/Blk/Twp: 1/4 73 BRIR-
Acres: 160
Map(s) 39

Abstract # 2252 - JOHNSON, C W
P'ee: JOHNSON, C W
G'ee: JOHNSON, C W
T-Dt: -- --- -----
P-Dt: 18 Apr 1903
Dist/Class: Scrap File
File#: 4594
Patent#: 321
Patent Vol.: 26
Survey/Blk/Twp: 125
Acres: 13.85
Map(s) 32

Abstract # 2253 - BRIR
S2: KILLION, D G
P'ee: KILLION, D G
G'ee: KILLION, D G
T-Dt: -- --- -----
P-Dt: 28 Dec 1918
Dist/Class: School
File#: 76219
Patent#: 185
Patent Vol.: 1A
Survey/Blk/Twp: 1/4 120 BRIR-
Acres: 160
Map(s) 29

Abstract # 2254 - BS&F
S2: SPIVY, W D
P'ee: VICK, JOHN H
G'ee: SPIVEY, W D
T-Dt: -- --- -----
P-Dt: 31 May 1922
Dist/Class: School
File#: 72804
Patent#: 70
Patent Vol.: 14A
Certificate: 1/266
Survey/Blk/Twp: SE 1/4 4 BS & F-
Acres: 160
Map(s) 40

Abstract # 2255 - BRIR
S2: WHITTENBURG, J B
P'ee: WHITTENBURG, J B (HEIRS)
G'ee: WHITTENBURG, J B
T-Dt: -- --- -----
P-Dt: 11 Sep 1907
Dist/Class: School
File#: 71204
Patent#: 633

Patent Vol.: 34
Survey/Blk/Twp: 1/4 36 BRIR-
Acres: 150
Map(s) 37, 38

Abstract # 2256 - WRIGHT, W
P'ee: WRIGHT, WILLIAM
G'ee: WRIGHT, WILLIAM
T-Dt: -- --- -----
P-Dt: 20 Apr 1903
Dist/Class: Scrap File
File#: 4409
Patent#: 328
Patent Vol.: 26
Survey/Blk/Twp: 129
Acres: 108.75
Map(s) 31, 39

Abstract # 2257 - JOHNSON, E W
P'ee: JOHNSON, C W
G'ee: JOHNSON, E W
T-Dt: -- --- -----
P-Dt: 22 Oct 1919
Dist/Class: School
File#: 76816
Patent#: 216
Patent Vol.: 4A
Certificate: 3426
Survey/Blk/Twp: 128 E.W.JOHNSON-
Acres: 19
Map(s) 30

Abstract # 2258 - KELLY, W S
P'ee: CAMPBELL, ALEXANDER
G'ee: KELLY, W S
T-Dt: -- --- -----
P-Dt: 04 Dec 1903
Dist/Class: Fannin Preemption
File#: 1095
Patent#: 448
Patent Vol.: 32
Acres: 160
Map(s) 40

Abstract # 2260 - T&NO RR CO
S2: JOHNSON, L A
P'ee: WATSON, J E
G'ee: JOHNSON, L A
T-Dt: -- --- -----
P-Dt: 14 Mar 1905
Dist/Class: School
File#: 2145
Patent#: 457
Patent Vol.: 29
Certificate: 862
Survey/Blk/Twp: SE 1/4 8 T & NO-
Acres: 160
Map(s) 29

Abstract # 2261 - BRIR
S2: DAVASHER, H W
P'ee: LEGRAND, G H
G'ee: DAVASHER, H W
T-Dt: -- --- -----
P-Dt: 02 May 1906
Dist/Class: School
File#: 2079
Patent#: 519
Patent Vol.: 31
Survey/Blk/Twp: N 1/4 82 BRIR-
Acres: 160
Map(s) 31, 39

Abstract # 2262 - FREEMAN, T F
P'ee: FREEMAN, T F

G'ee: FREEMAN, T F
T-Dt: -- --- -----
P-Dt: 21 Dec 1905
Dist/Class: Scrap File
File#: 7052
Patent#: 10
Patent Vol.: 31
Survey/Blk/Twp: 132
Acres: 40
Map(s) 20

Abstract # 2263 - T&NO RR CO
S2: MUNDELL, J A
P'ee: MUNDELL, J A
G'ee: MUNDELL, J A
T-Dt: -- --- -----
P-Dt: 08 Feb 1906
Dist/Class: School
File#: 82369
Patent#: 195
Patent Vol.: 31
Certificate: 863
Survey/Blk/Twp: NE 1/4 10 T & NO-
Acres: 183
Map(s) 29

Abstract # 2264 - DANIELS, H C
P'ee: DANIELS, H C
G'ee: DANIELS, H C
T-Dt: -- --- -----
P-Dt: 04 Feb 1907
Dist/Class: Scrap File
File#: 7629
Patent#: 278
Patent Vol.: 33
Survey/Blk/Twp: 133
Acres: 16.50
Map(s) 19

Abstract # 2265 - BS&F
S2: HOLT, J A
P'ee: HOLT, J A
G'ee: HOLT, J A
T-Dt: -- --- -----
P-Dt: 14 Sep 1908
Dist/Class: School
File#: 95708
Patent#: 467
Patent Vol.: 36
Certificate: 1/264
Survey/Blk/Twp: E 1/2 OF NW 1/4 2 BS
& F-
Acres: 80
Map(s) 15

Abstract # 2267 - TIMMONS, A A
P'ee: TIMMONS, A A
G'ee: TIMMONS, A A
T-Dt: -- --- -----
P-Dt: 11 Sep 1906
Dist/Class: Scrap File
File#: 6981
Patent#: 343
Patent Vol.: 32
Survey/Blk/Twp: 131 1-
Acres: 44
Map(s) 9

Abstract # 2268 - WRAY, H J
P'ee: WRAY, H J
G'ee: WRAY, H J
T-Dt: -- --- -----
P-Dt: 09 May 1907
Dist/Class: Scrap File
File#: 7822

Patent#: 89
Patent Vol.: 34
Survey/Blk/Twp: 134
Acres: 50
Map(s) 28

Abstract # 2270 - BURTON, E D
P'ee: BURTON, E D
G'ee: BURTON, E D
T-Dt: -- --- -----
P-Dt: 15 Jan 1908
Dist/Class: Scrap File
File#: 8321
Patent#: 485
Patent Vol.: 35
Survey/Blk/Twp: 152
Acres: 33
Map(s) 31

Abstract # 2271 - REYNOLDS, R A
P'ee: REYNOLDS, R A
G'ee: REYNOLDS, R A
T-Dt: -- --- -----
P-Dt: 04 Nov 1907
Dist/Class: Scrap File
File#: 7999
Patent#: 239
Patent Vol.: 35
Survey/Blk/Twp: 141
Acres: 37
Map(s) 9

Abstract # 2272 - ARNOLD, F T
P'ee: ARNOLD, F T
G'ee: ARNOLD, F T
T-Dt: -- --- -----
P-Dt: 07 Dec 1908
Dist/Class: Scrap File
File#: 8509
Patent#: 63
Patent Vol.: 37
Survey/Blk/Twp: 161
Acres: 44.50
Map(s) 19, 27

Abstract # 2274 - COOK, T M
P'ee: MARTIN, P A
G'ee: COOK, T M
T-Dt: -- --- -----
P-Dt: 25 Mar 1919
Dist/Class: School
File#: 112303
Patent#: 165
Patent Vol.: 2A
Certificate: SF9026
Survey/Blk/Twp: 173 T.M.COOK-
Acres: 130
Map(s) 40

Abstract # 2276 - BURKETT, F M
P'ee: MCLAREN, GEORGE H
G'ee: MCLAREN, GEORGE H
T-Dt: -- --- -----
P-Dt: 15 Oct 1909
Dist/Class: School
File#: 109732
Patent#: 593
Patent Vol.: 38
Survey/Blk/Twp: 149 J.C.GANNON-
Acres: 39.50
Map(s) 1

Abstract # 2278 - BENNETT, T S
P'ee: BENNETT, T S
G'ee: BENNETT, T S

T-Dt: -- --- -----
P-Dt: 07 Mar 1911
Dist/Class: Scrap File
File#: 8869
Patent#: 106
Patent Vol.: 42
Survey/Blk/Twp: 163
Acres: 34.50
Map(s) 19, 20

Abstract # 2279 - BURKETT, F M
P'ee: BURKETT, F M
G'ee: BURKETT, F M
T-Dt: -- --- -----
P-Dt: 16 May 1911
Dist/Class: Scrap File
File#: 10052
Patent#: 352
Patent Vol.: 42
Survey/Blk/Twp: 182
Acres: 17.50
Map(s) 37, 38

Abstract # 2280 - CHOATE, C S
P'ee: CHOATE, C S
G'ee: CHOATE, C S
T-Dt: -- --- -----
P-Dt: 07 Mar 1911
Dist/Class: Scrap File
File#: 9785
Patent#: 109
Patent Vol.: 42
Survey/Blk/Twp: 179
Acres: 59
Map(s) 36

Abstract # 2281 - DANIELS, MRS C E
P'ee: DANIELS, CHARLES B (MRS)
G'ee: DANIELS, CHARLES B (MRS)
T-Dt: -- --- -----
P-Dt: 12 Oct 1910
Dist/Class: Scrap File
File#: 8798
Patent#: 267
Patent Vol.: 41
Acres: 32
Map(s) 9

Abstract # 2282 - DICKSON, J
P'ee: DICKSON, J J
G'ee: DICKSON, J J
T-Dt: -- --- -----
P-Dt: 24 Jun 1911
Dist/Class: Scrap File
File#: 10098
Patent#: 450
Patent Vol.: 42
Survey/Blk/Twp: 183
Acres: 17
Map(s) 16

Abstract # 2283 - MEDLAN, E
P'ee: MEDLAN, ELIZABETH
G'ee: MEDLAN, ELIZABETH
T-Dt: -- --- -----
P-Dt: 09 Feb 1911
Dist/Class: Scrap File
File#: 9784
Patent#: 29
Patent Vol.: 42
Survey/Blk/Twp: 180
Acres: 26.75
Map(s) 28

Abstract # 2285 - CUSENBARRY, D D

P'ee: CUSENBARY, D D
G'ee: CUSENBARY, D D
T-Dt: -- --- -----
P-Dt: 20 Feb 1912
Dist/Class: Scrap File
File#: 10154
Patent#: 487
Patent Vol.: 43
Survey/Blk/Twp: 184
Acres: 47
Map(s) 30

Abstract # 2286 - KISSINGER, J
P'ee: KISINGER, JOHN
G'ee: KISINGER, JOHN
T-Dt: -- --- -----
P-Dt: 11 Dec 1911
Dist/Class: Scrap File
File#: 10247
Patent#: 237
Patent Vol.: 43
Survey/Blk/Twp: 187
Acres: 22.75
Map(s) 39

Abstract # 2287 - MABRY, R E
P'ee: MABRY, R E
G'ee: MABRY, R E
T-Dt: -- --- -----
P-Dt: 30 Jan 1920
Dist/Class: Scrap File
File#: 9699
Patent#: 396
Patent Vol.: 5A
Survey/Blk/Twp: 178
Acres: 198
Map(s) 30, 38

Abstract # 2288 - CT RR CO
S2: WILLIAMS, A
P'ee: WILLIAMS, ALLEN
G'ee: WILLIAMS, ALLEN
T-Dt: -- --- -----
P-Dt: 31 May 1912
Dist/Class: School
File#: 117263
Patent#: 269
Patent Vol.: 44
Certificate: 44
Survey/Blk/Twp: NW 1/4 2 CTRR-
Acres: 160
Map(s) 7

Abstract # 2290 - BRIR
S2: MILLER, J T
P'ee: MILLER, J T
G'ee: MILLER, J T
T-Dt: -- --- -----
P-Dt: 07 May 1913
Dist/Class: School
File#: 118919
Patent#: 317
Patent Vol.: 46
Survey/Blk/Twp: S.PT.32 BRIR-
Acres: 62
Map(s) 38

Abstract # 2291 - PINCKNEY, T F /
LONG, W R
P'ee: PINCKNEY, T F JR AND LONG,
W R
G'ee: PINCKNEY, T F JR AND LONG,
W R
T-Dt: -- --- -----
P-Dt: 19 Sep 1912

Dist/Class: Scrap File
File#: 10177
Patent#: 629
Patent Vol.: 44
Survey/Blk/Twp: 185
Acres: 85
Map(s) 32, 40

Abstract # 2292 - SAUNDERS, L O
P'ee: SAUNDERS, LUCY O"NEILL
G'ee: SAUNDERS, LUCY O"NEILL
T-Dt: -- --- -----
P-Dt: 06 Jun 1914
Dist/Class: School
File#: 119594
Patent#: 338
Patent Vol.: 48
Certificate: SF10569
Survey/Blk/Twp: 189 FRANK HERRON-
Acres: 12.75
Map(s) 39

Abstract # 2293 - NEWBY, L
P'ee: NEWBY, LOWE
G'ee: NEWBY, LOWE
T-Dt: -- --- -----
P-Dt: 04 Oct 1913
Dist/Class: Scrap File
File#: 10865
Patent#: 171
Patent Vol.: 47
Survey/Blk/Twp: 195
Acres: 11.25
Map(s) 39

Abstract # 2294 - PARSON, R W J
P'ee: PARSONS, R W J
G'ee: PARSONS, R W J
T-Dt: -- --- -----
P-Dt: 21 Nov 1913
Dist/Class: Scrap File
File#: 10880
Patent#: 319
Patent Vol.: 47
Survey/Blk/Twp: 196
Acres: 13
Map(s) 31

Abstract # 2297 - CAMPBELL, R
P'ee: CAMPBELL, RUTHY (HEIRS)
G'ee: CAMPBELL, RUTHY
T-Dt: -- --- -----
P-Dt: 22 Aug 1860
Dist/Class: Milam 1st
File#: 1508
Patent#: 262
Patent Vol.: 16
Certificate: 100
Survey/Blk/Twp: 1
Acres: 3033
Map(s) 44, 45

Abstract # 2298 - AB&M
S2: CROW, J T
P'ee: CROW, JOHN G
G'ee: CROW, JOHN G
T-Dt: -- --- -----
P-Dt: 24 May 1922
Dist/Class: School
File#: 44036
Patent#: 35
Patent Vol.: 14A
Certificate: 417
Survey/Blk/Twp: NW 1/4 2 AB & M-
Acres: 160.90

Map(s) 40

Abstract # 2299 - G&BN CO
S2: DANIEL, W H
P'ee: DANIEL, W H
G'ee: DANIEL, W H
T-Dt: -- --- -----
P-Dt: 11 Jun 1917
Dist/Class: School
File#: 126149
Patent#: 75
Patent Vol.: 53
Certificate: 91
Survey/Blk/Twp: S 1/2 OF SW 1/4 1 G &
BN CO.-
Acres: 80
Map(s) 15

Abstract # 2301 - SCOTT, B F
P'ee: SCOTT, B F
G'ee: SCOTT, B F
T-Dt: -- --- -----
P-Dt: 06 Mar 1922
Dist/Class: Scrap File
File#: 11696
Patent#: 174
Patent Vol.: 13A
Survey/Blk/Twp: 210
Acres: 15.16
Map(s) 36, 37

Abstract # 2302 - JOPLIN, G
P'ee: ATWOOD, W H
G'ee: ATWOOD, W H
T-Dt: -- --- -----
P-Dt: 27 Feb 1918
Dist/Class: School
File#: 126692
Patent#: 71
Patent Vol.: 55
Certificate: SF10862
Survey/Blk/Twp: 194 R.G.WALKER-
Acres: 23
Map(s) 8

Abstract # 2303 - COOK, W W
S2: ATWOOD, W H
P'ee: ATWOOD, W H
G'ee: ATWOOD, W H
T-Dt: -- --- -----
P-Dt: 27 Feb 1918
Dist/Class: School
File#: 126693
Patent#: 72
Patent Vol.: 55
Certificate: SF10713
Survey/Blk/Twp: 191 W.W.COOK-
Acres: 15.50
Map(s) 20, 21

Abstract # 2304 - BRIR
S2: BYNUM, H C
G'ee: BYNUM, H C JR
T-Dt: -- --- -----
P-Dt: -- --- -----
Dist/Class: School
File#: 126990
Survey/Blk/Twp: 10 BRIR-
Acres: 160
Map(s) 37

Abstract # 2305 - MOORE, J W
P'ee: MOORE, J W
G'ee: MOORE, J W
T-Dt: -- --- -----

P-Dt: 24 Jul 1918
Dist/Class: Scrap File
File#: 11954
Patent#: 157
Patent Vol.: 56
Acres: 34.75
Map(s) 28

Abstract # 2306 - BBB&C RR CO
S2: NEWMAN, J H
P'ee: HAWKINS, L B
G'ee: NEWMAN, J H
T-Dt: -- --- -----
P-Dt: 11 Jun 1924
Dist/Class: School
File#: 126542
Patent#: 31
Patent Vol.: 23A
Certificate: 683
Survey/Blk/Twp: W 1/2 OF SW 1/4 2 BBB
& CRR-
Acres: 80
Map(s) 15

Abstract # 2307 - REEVES, J R
P'ee: REEVES, JOHN R
G'ee: REEVES, JOHN R
T-Dt: -- --- -----
P-Dt: 02 Apr 1919
Dist/Class: School
File#: 127397
Patent#: 219
Patent Vol.: 2A
Certificate: SF11706
Survey/Blk/Twp: -E.K.LONGAN-
Acres: 18
Map(s) 37

Abstract # 2308 - STEWART, G D
P'ee: STEWART, GRAHAM P
G'ee: STEWART, GRAHAM P
T-Dt: -- --- -----
P-Dt: 09 Jul 1919
Dist/Class: Scrap File
File#: 12014
Patent#: 237
Patent Vol.: 3A
Survey/Blk/Twp: 104
Acres: 68.5
Map(s) 8

Abstract # 2309 - WADLEY, T C
P'ee: WADLEY, T C
G'ee: WADLEY, T C
T-Dt: -- --- -----
P-Dt: 21 Dec 1918
Dist/Class: Scrap File
File#: 12021
Patent#: 140
Patent Vol.: 1A
Survey/Blk/Twp: 63
Acres: 84.40
Map(s) 37

Abstract # 2310 - WHITTENBURG, R B
P'ee: WHITTENBURG, R B
G'ee: WHITTENBURG, R B
T-Dt: -- --- -----
P-Dt: 21 Dec 1918
Dist/Class: Scrap File
File#: 11944
Patent#: 139
Patent Vol.: 1A
Survey/Blk/Twp: 102
Acres: 30.50

Map(s) 37, 38

Abstract # 2311 - ANDERSON, J E
P'ee: ANDERSON, J E
G'ee: ANDERSON, J E
T-Dt: -- --- -----
P-Dt: 10 Jun 1920
Dist/Class: Scrap File
File#: 12250
Patent#: 399
Patent Vol.: 7A
Acres: 26
Map(s) 39

Abstract # 2312 - CHISUM, W C
P'ee: CHISUM, W C JR
G'ee: CHISUM, W C JR
T-Dt: -- --- -----
P-Dt: 05 Jan 1920
Dist/Class: School
File#: 127891
Patent#: 121
Patent Vol.: 5A
Certificate: SF11965
Survey/Blk/Twp: -C.G.WOOD-
Acres: 32.06
Map(s) 37

Abstract # 2313 - CHOATE, E L
P'ee: CHOATE, E L
G'ee: CHOATE, E L
T-Dt: -- --- -----
P-Dt: 03 Jan 1920
Dist/Class: Scrap File
File#: 12202
Patent#: 108
Patent Vol.: 5A
Acres: 20.90
Map(s) 32

Abstract # 2317 - LUCY, J E
P'ee: LUCY, JAMES E
G'ee: LUCY, JAMES E
T-Dt: -- --- -----
P-Dt: 22 Jul 1920
Dist/Class: School
File#: 129148
Patent#: 129
Patent Vol.: 8A
Survey/Blk/Twp: -C.W.THOMAS-
Acres: 24.80
Map(s) 33

Abstract # 2318 - NARRED, J L
P'ee: NARRED, J L
G'ee: NARRED, J L
T-Dt: -- --- -----
P-Dt: 05 Dec 1919
Dist/Class: Scrap File
File#: 12147
Patent#: 455
Patent Vol.: 4A
Acres: 17.50
Map(s) 22

Abstract # 2319 - WHITTENBURG, J C
S2: OSBORN, V H
P'ee: OSBORN, V H
G'ee: OSBORN, V H
T-Dt: -- --- -----
P-Dt: 17 Jun 1920
Dist/Class: School
File#: 129164
Patent#: 469
Patent Vol.: 7A

Survey/Blk/Twp: -J.C.WHITTENBURG-
Acres: 46.40
Map(s) 18, 19

Abstract # 2320 - OSWALT, R D
P'ee: OSWALT, ROBERT D
G'ee: OSWALT, ROBERT D
T-Dt: -- --- -----
P-Dt: 10 Jun 1920
Dist/Class: Scrap File
File#: 12297
Patent#: 403
Patent Vol.: 7A
Acres: 17.62
Map(s) 27, 28

Abstract # 2321 - ROBINSON, J W
P'ee: ROBINSON, J W
G'ee: ROBINSON, J W
T-Dt: -- --- -----
P-Dt: 23 Jun 1920
Dist/Class: Scrap File
File#: 12288
Patent#: 500
Patent Vol.: 7A
Acres: 13.60
Map(s) 21

Abstract # 2322 - ROBINSON, J W
P'ee: ROBINSON, J W
G'ee: ROBINSON, J W
T-Dt: -- --- -----
P-Dt: 23 Jun 1920
Dist/Class: Scrap File
File#: 12289
Patent#: 501
Patent Vol.: 7A
Acres: 32.28
Map(s) 27

Abstract # 2323 - ROBINSON, J W
P'ee: ROBINSON, J W
G'ee: ROBINSON, J W
T-Dt: -- --- -----
P-Dt: 23 Jun 1920
Dist/Class: Scrap File
File#: 12290
Patent#: 502
Patent Vol.: 7A
Acres: 31.9
Map(s) 47

Abstract # 2324 - ROBINSON, J W
P'ee: ROBINSON, J W
G'ee: ROBINSON, J W
T-Dt: -- --- -----
P-Dt: 10 Aug 1920
Dist/Class: Scrap File
File#: 12315
Patent#: 237
Patent Vol.: 8A
Acres: 48.50
Map(s) 28

Abstract # 2325 - ROBINSON, J W
P'ee: ROBINSON, J W
G'ee: ROBINSON, J W
T-Dt: -- --- -----
P-Dt: 10 Aug 1920
Dist/Class: Scrap File
File#: 12321
Patent#: 238
Patent Vol.: 8A
Acres: 2.23
Map(s) 24

Abstract # 2326 - ROBINSON, W A
P'ee: ROBINSON, J W
G'ee: ROBINSON, J W
T-Dt: -- --- -----
P-Dt: 10 Aug 1920
Dist/Class: Scrap File
File#: 12322
Patent#: 242
Patent Vol.: 8A
Acres: 47.20
Map(s) 32

Abstract # 2327 - TRIPLETT, C C
P'ee: TRIPLETT, CHARLES C
G'ee: TRIPLETT, CHARLES C
T-Dt: -- --- -----
P-Dt: 04 May 1920
Dist/Class: Scrap File
File#: 12272
Patent#: 140
Patent Vol.: 7A
Acres: 11.70
Map(s) 7

Abstract # 2328 - SP RR CO
S2: WALKER, W T
P'ee: WALKER, W T
G'ee: WALKER, W T
T-Dt: -- --- -----
P-Dt: 21 Feb 1920
Dist/Class: School
File#: 128917
Patent#: 78
Patent Vol.: 6A
Certificate: 16/69
Survey/Blk/Twp: N 1/2 & SE PT. OF SW
1/4 6 SPRR-
Acres: 160
Map(s) 24, 32

Abstract # 2329 - BRIR
S2: GREENWADE, J J
P'ee: GREENWADE, J J
G'ee: GREENWADE, J J
T-Dt: -- --- -----
P-Dt: 07 Jun 1921
Dist/Class: School
File#: 129671
Patent#: 201
Patent Vol.: 11A
Survey/Blk/Twp: N.PT. 14 BRIR-
Acres: 87
Map(s) 38

Abstract # 2331 - ROBINSON, J W
P'ee: ROBINSON, J W
G'ee: ROBINSON, J W
T-Dt: -- --- -----
P-Dt: 05 Jan 1921
Dist/Class: Scrap File
File#: 12374
Patent#: 525
Patent Vol.: 9A
Acres: 26.50
Map(s) 35

Abstract # 2332 - TRIPLETT, C C
P'ee: TRIPLETT, CHARLES C
G'ee: TRIPLETT, CHARLES C
T-Dt: -- --- -----
P-Dt: 13 Oct 1920
Dist/Class: Scrap File
File#: 12269
Patent#: 47
Patent Vol.: 9A

Acres: 15.45
Map(s) 28

Abstract # 2333 - JACKSON, W C JR
P'ee: JACKSON, W C JR
G'ee: JACKSON, W C JR
T-Dt: -- --- -----
P-Dt: 13 Jul 1922
Dist/Class: Scrap File
File#: 12510
Patent#: 266
Patent Vol.: 14A
Acres: 9.27
Map(s) 46

Abstract # 2336 - AB&M
S2: COLE, J M
P'ee: COLE, J M
G'ee: COLE, J M
T-Dt: -- --- -----
P-Dt: 26 Sep 1922
Dist/Class: School
File#: 47291
Patent#: 99
Patent Vol.: 15A
Certificate: 417
Survey/Blk/Twp: SE 1/4 2 AB & M-
Acres: 169
Map(s) 40

Abstract # 2337 - TYLER, J M
S2: CRAVENS, E P/SF 12559
P'ee: CRAVENS, E P
G'ee: CRAVENS, E P
T-Dt: -- --- -----
P-Dt: 13 Dec 1922
Dist/Class: Scrap File
File#: 12559
Patent#: 81
Patent Vol.: 16A
Survey/Blk/Twp: -JOHN H.TYLER-
Acres: 6.11
Map(s) 31

Abstract # 2339 - JOHNSTON, A W
P'ee: JOHNSTON, A W
G'ee: JOHNSTON, A W
T-Dt: -- --- -----
P-Dt: 23 Jan 1925
Dist/Class: Scrap File
File#: 12701
Patent#: 550
Patent Vol.: 24A
Acres: 68.73
Map(s) 40

Abstract # 2340 - JOHNSTON, A W
P'ee: JOHNSTON, A W
G'ee: JOHNSTON, A W
T-Dt: -- --- -----
P-Dt: 23 Jan 1925
Dist/Class: Scrap File
File#: 12702
Patent#: 1
Patent Vol.: 25A
Acres: 13.54
Map(s) 40

Abstract # 2341 - BRIR
S2: WOOD, J H
P'ee: WOOD, JOHN H
G'ee: WOOD, JOHN H
T-Dt: -- --- -----
P-Dt: 21 Dec 1923
Dist/Class: School

File#: 131369
Patent#: 50
Patent Vol.: 21A
Survey/Blk/Twp: E.PT. OF E 1/2 117
BRIR-
Acres: 51.60
Map(s) 29

Abstract # 2342 - JOHNSON, C W
P'ee: JOHNSON, C W
G'ee: JOHNSON, C W
T-Dt: -- --- -----
P-Dt: 18 Nov 1925
Dist/Class: Scrap File
File#: 12560
Patent#: 477
Patent Vol.: 27A
Acres: 9.74
Map(s) 28

Abstract # 2344 - G&BN CO
S2: LEFFEL, J W
P'ee: LEFFEL, J W
G'ee: LEFFEL, J W
T-Dt: -- --- -----
P-Dt: 26 Apr 1927
Dist/Class: School
File#: 144424
Patent#: 32
Patent Vol.: 34A
Certificate: 32
Survey/Blk/Twp: W 1/2 9 G & BN CO.-
Acres: 228.30
Map(s) 24

Abstract # 2346 - T&NO RR CO
S2: WILSON, J E
P'ee: WILSON, J E
G'ee: WILSON, J E
T-Dt: -- --- -----
P-Dt: 11 Mar 1927
Dist/Class: School
File#: 143540
Patent#: 55
Patent Vol.: 33A
Certificate: 865
Survey/Blk/Twp: S.PT. OF NW 1/4 4 T &
NO-
Acres: 100
Map(s) 31

Abstract # 2347 - EDDLEMAN, A B
P'ee: EDDLEMAN, A B
G'ee: EDDLEMAN, A B
T-Dt: -- --- -----
P-Dt: 29 Nov 1927
Dist/Class: Scrap File
File#: 13010
Patent#: 174
Patent Vol.: 37A
Acres: 19
Map(s) 30, 31

Abstract # 2348 - MEYER, J
S2: HOLCOMB, V
P'ee: HOLCOMB, V
G'ee: HOLCOMB, V
T-Dt: -- --- -----
P-Dt: 22 Feb 1931
Dist/Class: School
File#: 147130
Patent#: 72
Patent Vol.: 49A
Certificate: MF5553
Survey/Blk/Twp: -JOHN MEYER-

Acres: 14.80
Map(s) 31, 32

Abstract # 2349 - TE&L CO
P'ee: TEXAS EMIGRATION AND LAND
COMPANY
G'ee: TEXAS EMIGRATION AND LAND
COMPANY
T-Dt: -- --- -----
P-Dt: 11 Aug 1858
Dist/Class: Texas Emmigration and Land
Company
File#: 1859
Patent#: 276
Patent Vol.: 21
Certificate: 1859
Survey/Blk/Twp: 1859
Acres: 320
Map(s) 6

Abstract # 2350 - AB&M
P'ee: GUNTER AND MUNSON
G'ee: ADAMS, BEATY AND MOULTON
T-Dt: -- --- -----
P-Dt: 23 Oct 1875
Dist/Class: Milam Scrip
File#: 2024
Patent#: 441
Patent Vol.: 21
Certificate: 417
Acres: 640
Map(s) 40

Abstract # 2351 - CEPI&M CO
P'ee: MCADAMS, W C
G'ee: CONSOLIDATED EL PASO IR-
RIGATION AND MANUFACTURING
COMPANY
T-Dt: -- --- -----
P-Dt: 24 Mar 1877
Dist/Class: Milam Scrip
File#: 2625
Patent#: 507
Patent Vol.: 27
Certificate: 20
Acres: 109
Map(s) 40

Abstract # 2352 - PRUITT, D H
P'ee: PRUITT, DAVID H
G'ee: PRUITT, DAVID H
T-Dt: -- --- -----
P-Dt: 10 Jan 1883
Dist/Class: Milam Preemption
File#: 2932
Patent#: 67
Patent Vol.: 14
Acres: 160
Map(s) 42

Abstract # 2353 - SP RR CO
P'ee: PATILLO, T A
G'ee: SOUTHERN PACIFIC RAILROAD
COMPANY
T-Dt: -- --- -----
P-Dt: 12 Mar 1869
Dist/Class: Fannin Scrip
File#: 2912
Patent#: 402
Patent Vol.: 6
Certificate: 16/176
Acres: 640
Map(s) 8

Abstract # 2355 - SP RR CO

P'ee: PATILLO, T A
G'ee: SOUTHERN PACIFIC RAILROAD
COMPANY
T-Dt: -- --- -----
P-Dt: 09 Jul 1868
Dist/Class: Fannin Scrip
File#: 2908
Patent#: 388
Patent Vol.: 6
Certificate: 16/107
Survey/Blk/Twp: 1
Acres: 640
Map(s) 8

Abstract # 2356 - POITEVENT, J
S2: O
P'ee: ONEAL, BEN G
G'ee: ONEAL, BEN G
T-Dt: -- --- -----
P-Dt: 06 Feb 1947
Dist/Class: School
File#: 150185
Patent#: 391
Patent Vol.: 5-B
Certificate: 2/160
Survey/Blk/Twp: W 3/4 4 J. POITEVENT-
Acres: 219.2
Map(s) 35

Abstract # 2358 - CAMPBELL, M
P'ee: CAMPBELL, MARGUERITE
G'ee: CAMPBELL, MARGUERITE
T-Dt: -- --- -----
P-Dt: 30 Jul 1943
Dist/Class: Scrap File
File#: 14490
Patent#: 346
Patent Vol.: 90A
Acres: 27.5
Map(s) 26

Abstract # 2360 - BRIR
S2: MERCER, J L
P'ee: MERCER, J L
G'ee: MERCER, J L
T-Dt: -- --- -----
P-Dt: 05 Jul 1890
Dist/Class: School
File#: 16690
Patent#: 551
Patent Vol.: 10
Survey/Blk/Twp: BRIR
Acres: 241.00
Map(s) 37, 38

Abstract # 2361 - TE&L CO
P'ee: PICKARD, E B AND CANTWELL,
A J
G'ee: PICKARD, E B AND CANTWELL,
A J
T-Dt: -- --- -----
P-Dt: 10 Jan 1949
Dist/Class: Scrap File
File#: 14943
Patent#: 48
Patent Vol.: 12-B
Acres: 33.66
Map(s) 43

Abstract # 2364 - G&BN CO
T-Dt: -- --- -----
P-Dt: -- --- -----
Map(s) 24

Abstract # 2482 - AB&M

S2: WILLIAMS, S D
T-Dt: -- --- -----
P-Dt: -- --- -----
Map(s) 40

Abstract # ?1 - TE&L CO
T-Dt: -- --- -----
P-Dt: -- --- -----
Map(s) 1

Abstract # ?2 - LORD, J W
T-Dt: -- --- -----
P-Dt: -- --- -----
Map(s) 8

Abstract # ?3 - SP RR CO
T-Dt: -- --- -----
P-Dt: -- --- -----
Map(s) 8

Abstract # ?4 - THOMPSON, J C & W F
T-Dt: -- --- -----
P-Dt: -- --- -----
Map(s) 8

Abstract # ?5 - ALLEN, J
T-Dt: -- --- -----
P-Dt: -- --- -----
Map(s) 8

Abstract # ?6 - MCNEILL, J B
T-Dt: -- --- -----
P-Dt: -- --- -----
Map(s) 8

Abstract # ?7 -
T-Dt: -- --- -----
P-Dt: -- --- -----
Map(s) 7

Abstract # ?8 - COLSTON, J W
T-Dt: -- --- -----
P-Dt: -- --- -----
Map(s) 8

Abstract # ?9 - MCLAREN & TANKERS-
LEY
T-Dt: -- --- -----
P-Dt: -- --- -----
Map(s) 1

Abstract # ?10 - SAN AUGUSTINE UNIV
T-Dt: -- --- -----
P-Dt: -- --- -----
Map(s) 9

Abstract # ?11 - TE&L CO
T-Dt: -- --- -----
P-Dt: -- --- -----
Map(s) 9

Abstract # ?12 - TE&L CO
T-Dt: -- --- -----
P-Dt: -- --- -----
Map(s) 9

Abstract # ?13 -
T-Dt: -- --- -----
P-Dt: -- --- -----
Map(s) 9

Abstract # ?14 - TE&L CO
T-Dt: -- --- -----
P-Dt: -- --- -----
Map(s) 9

Abstract # ?15 - TE&L CO
T-Dt: -- --- -----
P-Dt: -- --- -----
Map(s) 9

Abstract # ?16 -
T-Dt: -- --- -----
P-Dt: -- --- -----
Map(s) 9

Abstract # ?17 - TE&L CO
T-Dt: -- --- -----
P-Dt: -- --- -----
Map(s) 9

Abstract # ?18 - TE&L CO
T-Dt: -- --- -----
P-Dt: -- --- -----
Map(s) 9, 17

Abstract # ?19 - JORDAN, F
T-Dt: -- --- -----
P-Dt: -- --- -----
Map(s) 19

Abstract # ?20 - TE&L CO
T-Dt: -- --- -----
P-Dt: -- --- -----
Map(s) 19

Abstract # ?21 - SNODGRASS, J F
T-Dt: -- --- -----
P-Dt: -- --- -----
Map(s) 31

Abstract # ?22 - STANTON, R R
T-Dt: -- --- -----
P-Dt: -- --- -----
Map(s) 32

Abstract # ?23 - FARLEY, M
T-Dt: -- --- -----
P-Dt: -- --- -----
Map(s) 32

Abstract # ?24 - COE, J G
T-Dt: -- --- -----
P-Dt: -- --- -----
Map(s) 32

Abstract # ?26 -
T-Dt: -- --- -----
P-Dt: -- --- -----
Map(s) 32

Abstract # ?27 -
T-Dt: -- --- -----
P-Dt: -- --- -----
Map(s) 31

Abstract # ?29 - STATE OF TEXAS
T-Dt: -- --- -----
P-Dt: -- --- -----
Map(s) 33, 34

Abstract # ?30 -
T-Dt: -- --- -----
P-Dt: -- --- -----
Map(s) 34, 35

Abstract # ?31 - STATE OF TEXAS
T-Dt: -- --- -----
P-Dt: -- --- -----
Map(s) 35, 36

Abstract # ?32 -
T-Dt: -- --- -----
P-Dt: -- --- -----
Map(s) 40

Abstract # ?33 -
T-Dt: -- --- -----
P-Dt: -- --- -----
Map(s) 39, 47

Abstract # ?34 - BLICK, W W
T-Dt: -- --- -----
P-Dt: -- --- -----
Map(s) 47

Abstract # ?35 - ROHNS, HRS J P
T-Dt: -- --- -----
P-Dt: -- --- -----
Map(s) 47

Abstract # ?36 - WM CO
T-Dt: -- --- -----
P-Dt: -- --- -----
Map(s) 47, 48

Abstract # ?37 - LUCKEY, M W
T-Dt: -- --- -----
P-Dt: -- --- -----
Map(s) 48

Abstract # ?38 - PEPPER, S T
T-Dt: -- --- -----
P-Dt: -- --- -----
Map(s) 41

– Part II –

Land Survey Maps

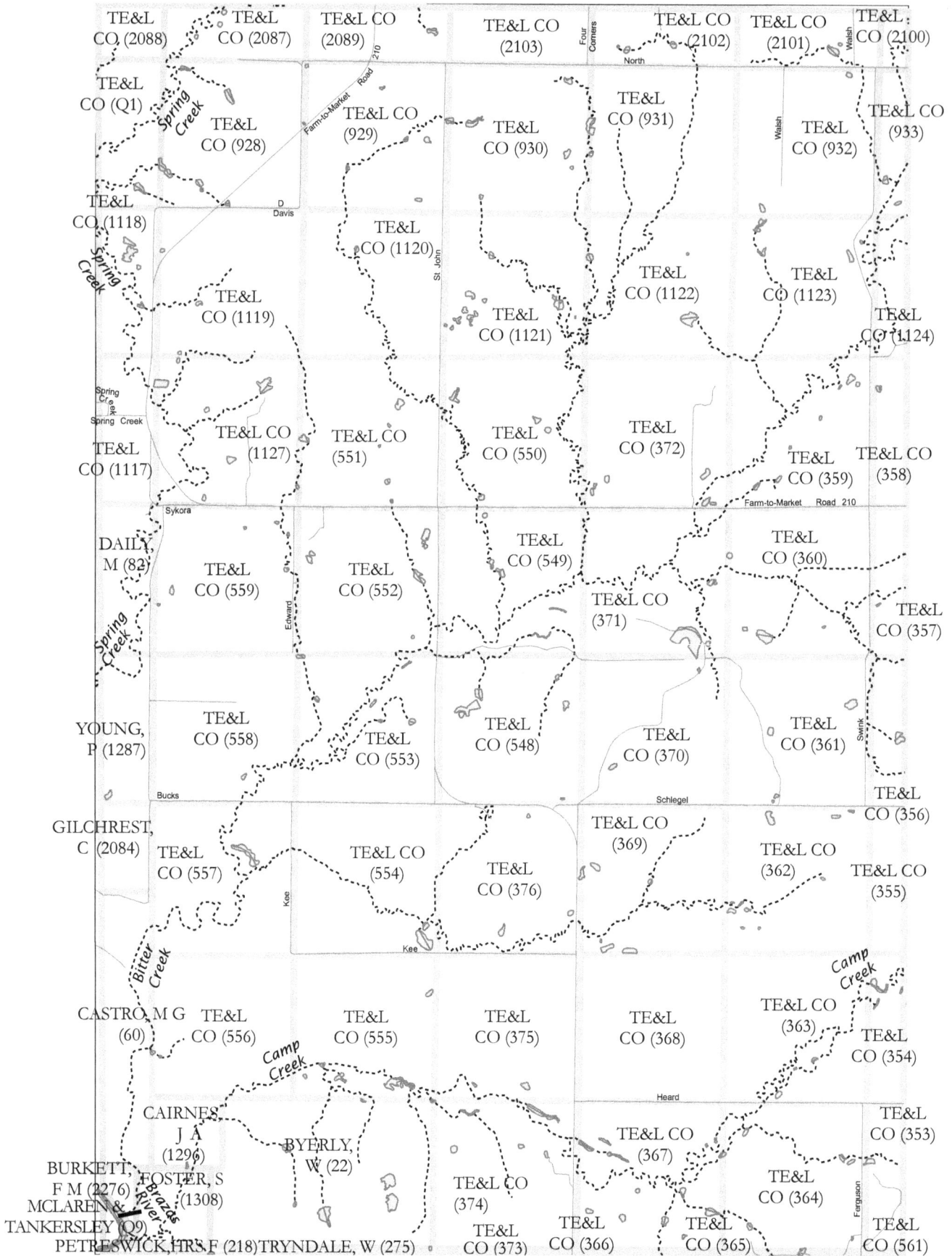

TE&L
CO (2088)

TE&L
CO (2087)

TE&L CO
(2089)

TE&L CO
(2103)

Four
Corners
North

TE&L CO
(2102)

TE&L CO
(2101)

Walsh

TE&L
CO (2100)

TE&L
CO (Q1)

Spring Creek

TE&L
CO (928)

Farm-to-Market Road 210

TE&L CO
(929)

TE&L
CO (930)

TE&L
CO (931)

Walsh

TE&L
CO (932)

TE&L CO
(933)

TE&L
CO (1118)

Spring Creek

D
Davis

TE&L
CO (1120)

St. John

TE&L
CO (1122)

TE&L
CO (1123)

TE&L
CO (933)

TE&L
CO (1119)

TE&L
CO (1121)

TE&L
CO (1124)

Spring
Creek

Spring Creek

TE&L
CO (1117)

TE&L CO
(1127)

TE&L CO
(551)

TE&L
CO (550)

TE&L
CO (372)

TE&L
CO (359)

TE&L CO
(358)

Sykora

Farm-to-Market Road 210

DAILY,
M (82)

TE&L
CO (559)

TE&L
CO (552)

TE&L
CO (549)

TE&L
CO (360)

Spring
Creek

TE&L CO
(371)

TE&L
CO (357)

YOUNG,
P (1287)

Edward

TE&L
CO (558)

TE&L
CO (553)

TE&L
CO (548)

TE&L
CO (370)

TE&L
CO (361)

Swink

Bucks

Schlegel

TE&L
CO (356)

GILCHREST,
C (2084)

TE&L
CO (557)

Kee

TE&L CO
(554)

TE&L
CO (376)

TE&L CO
(369)

TE&L CO
(362)

TE&L CO
(355)

Bitter Creek

Kee

Camp
Creek

CASTRO, M G
(60)

TE&L
CO (556)

Camp
Creek

TE&L
CO (555)

TE&L
CO (375)

TE&L
CO (368)

TE&L CO
(363)

TE&L
CO (354)

Heard

CAIRNES,
J A
(1296)

BYERLY,
W (22)

TE&L
CO (353)

BURKETT,
F M (2276)

FOSTER, S
(1308)

Brazos River

TE&L CO
(367)

TE&L
CO (364)

Ferguson

MCLAREN &
TANKERSLEY (Q9)

TE&L CO
(374)

TE&L
CO (366)

TE&L
CO (365)

TE&L
CO (561)

PETRESWICK, HRS F (218)

TRYNDALE, W (275)

TE&L
CO (373)

BURKETT, F M
Abs # 2276
15-Oct-1909

BYERLY, W
Abs # 22
09-Jul-1875

CAIRNES, J A
Abs # 1296
22-May-1878

CASTRO, M G
Abs # 60
19-Nov-1875

DAILY, M
Abs # 82
23-Feb-1859

FOSTER, S
Abs # 1308
28-Jan-1878

GILCHREST, C
Abs # 2084
22-Mar-1856

MCLAREN & TANKERSLEY
Abs # ?9

PETRESWICK,HRS F
Abs # 218
02-Oct-1875
see also, Map 9

TE&L CO
Abs # 1117
22-Oct-1858

TE&L CO
Abs # 1118
22-Oct-1858

TE&L CO
Abs # 1119
21-Oct-1858

TE&L CO
Abs # 1120
21-Oct-1858

TE&L CO
Abs # 1121
21-Oct-1858

TE&L CO
Abs # 1122
21-Oct-1858

TE&L CO
Abs # 1123
21-Oct-1858

TE&L CO
Abs # 1124
21-May-1858
see also, Map 2

TE&L CO
Abs # 1127
22-Oct-1858

TE&L CO
Abs # 2087
07-Sep-1858

TE&L CO
Abs # 2088
27-Aug-1858

TE&L CO
Abs # 2089
08-Sep-1858

TE&L CO
Abs # 2100
08-Sep-1858
see also, Map 2

TE&L CO
Abs # 2101
09-Sep-1858

TE&L CO
Abs # 2102
09-Sep-1858

TE&L CO
Abs # 2103

09-Sep-1858

TE&L CO
Abs # 353
14-Sep-1857
see also, Map 2

TE&L CO
Abs # 354
15-Sep-1857
see also, Map 2

TE&L CO
Abs # 355
15-Sep-1857
see also, Map 2

TE&L CO
Abs # 356
15-Sep-1857
see also, Map 2

TE&L CO
Abs # 357
15-Sep-1857
see also, Map 2

TE&L CO
Abs # 358
15-Sep-1857
see also, Map 2

TE&L CO
Abs # 359
15-Sep-1857

TE&L CO
Abs # 360
15-Sep-1857

TE&L CO
Abs # 361
15-Sep-1857

TE&L CO
Abs # 362
15-Sep-1857

TE&L CO
Abs # 363
16-Sep-1857

TE&L CO
Abs # 364
16-Sep-1857

TE&L CO
Abs # 365
16-Sep-1857
see also, Map 9

TE&L CO
Abs # 366
16-Sep-1857
see also, Map 9

TE&L CO
Abs # 367
16-Sep-1857

TE&L CO
Abs # 368
17-Sep-1857

TE&L CO
Abs # 369
17-Sep-1857

TE&L CO
Abs # 370
17-Sep-1857

TE&L CO
Abs # 371
17-Sep-1857

TE&L CO
Abs # 372
17-Sep-1857

TE&L CO
Abs # 373
17-Sep-1857
see also, Map 9

TE&L CO
Abs # 374
18-Sep-1857

TE&L CO

Abs # 375
18-Sep-1857

TE&L CO
Abs # 376
18-Sep-1857

TE&L CO
Abs # 548
09-Jan-1858

TE&L CO
Abs # 549
09-Jan-1858

TE&L CO
Abs # 550
09-Jan-1858

TE&L CO
Abs # 551
11-Jan-1858

TE&L CO
Abs # 552
11-Jan-1858

TE&L CO
Abs # 553
11-Jan-1858

TE&L CO
Abs # 554
12-Jan-1858

TE&L CO
Abs # 555
12-Jan-1858

TE&L CO
Abs # 556
12-Jan-1858

TE&L CO
Abs # 557
12-Jan-1858

TE&L CO
Abs # 558
13-Jan-1858

TE&L CO
Abs # 559
13-Jan-1858

TE&L CO
Abs # 561
13-Jan-1858
see also, Maps 2, 9, 10

TE&L CO
Abs # 928
08-Sep-1858

TE&L CO
Abs # 929
08-Sep-1858

TE&L CO
Abs # 930
08-Sep-1858

TE&L CO
Abs # 931
08-Sep-1858

TE&L CO
Abs # 932
08-Sep-1858

TE&L CO
Abs # 933
08-Sep-1858
see also, Map 2

TE&L CO
Abs # ?1

TRYNDALE, W
Abs # 275
05-Feb-1862
see also, Map 9

YOUNG, P
Abs # 1287
18-Jun-1874

Populated Places

None

Cemeteries

None

Water (larger bodies)

None

Other Water

Bitter Creek
Brazos River
Camp Creek
Spring Creek

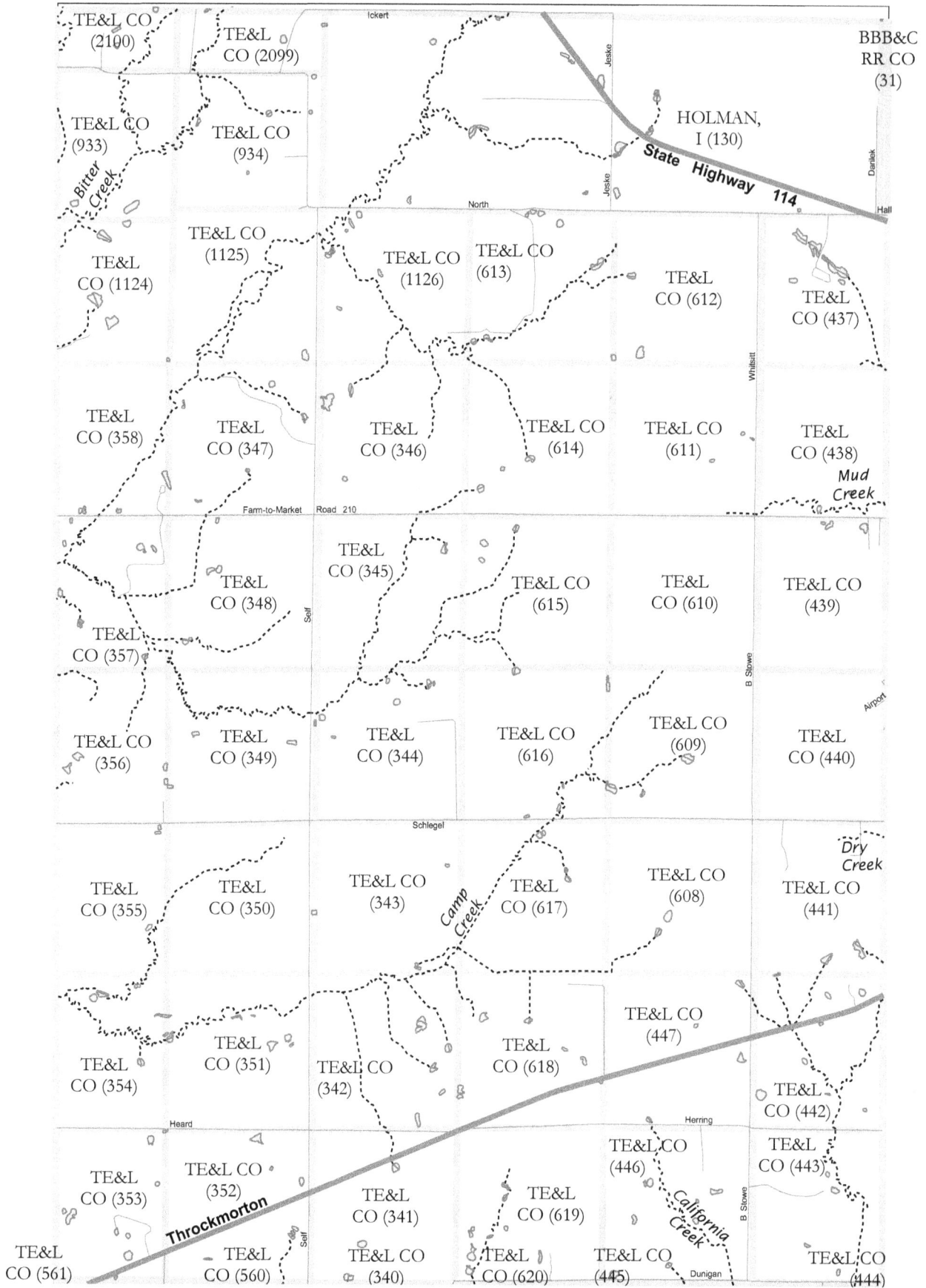

TE&L CO (2100)

TE&L CO (2099)

Ickert

Jeske

BBB&C RR CO (31)

TE&L CO (933)

TE&L CO (934)

Bitter Creek

HOLMAN, I (130)

State Highway 114

Darlek

Hall

Jeske

North

TE&L CO (1125)

TE&L CO (1126)

TE&L CO (613)

TE&L CO (612)

TE&L CO (437)

TE&L CO (1124)

Whitsit

TE&L CO (358)

TE&L CO (347)

TE&L CO (346)

TE&L CO (614)

TE&L CO (611)

TE&L CO (438)

Mud Creek

Farm-to-Market Road 210

TE&L CO (348)

TE&L CO (345)

TE&L CO (615)

TE&L CO (610)

TE&L CO (439)

Self

TE&L CO (357)

B Stowe

Airport

TE&L CO (356)

TE&L CO (349)

TE&L CO (344)

TE&L CO (616)

TE&L CO (609)

TE&L CO (440)

Schlegel

Dry Creek

TE&L CO (355)

TE&L CO (350)

TE&L CO (343)

Camp Creek

TE&L CO (617)

TE&L CO (608)

TE&L CO (441)

TE&L CO (354)

TE&L CO (351)

TE&L CO (342)

TE&L CO (618)

TE&L CO (447)

TE&L CO (442)

Heard

Herring

TE&L CO (353)

TE&L CO (352)

Throckmorton

TE&L CO (341)

TE&L CO (619)

TE&L CO (446)

TE&L CO (443)

California Creek

B Stowe

Self

TE&L CO (561)

TE&L CO (560)

TE&L CO (340)

TE&L CO (620)

TE&L CO (445)

Dunigan

TE&L CO (444)

BBB&C RR CO
Abs # 31
28-Oct-1873
see also, Map 3

HOLMAN, I
Abs # 130
15-Feb-1873

TE&L CO
Abs # 1124
21-May-1858
see also, Map 1

TE&L CO
Abs # 1125
21-May-1858

TE&L CO
Abs # 1126
22-Oct-1858

TE&L CO
Abs # 2099
08-Sep-1858

TE&L CO
Abs # 2100
08-Sep-1858
see also, Map 1

TE&L CO
Abs # 340
11-Sep-1857
see also, Map 10

TE&L CO
Abs # 341
12-Sep-1857

TE&L CO
Abs # 342
12-Sep-1857

TE&L CO
Abs # 343
12-Sep-1857

TE&L CO
Abs # 344
12-Sep-1857

TE&L CO
Abs # 345
12-Sep-1857

TE&L CO
Abs # 346
14-Sep-1857

TE&L CO
Abs # 347
14-Sep-1857

TE&L CO
Abs # 348
14-Sep-1857

TE&L CO
Abs # 349
14-Sep-1857

TE&L CO
Abs # 350
14-Sep-1857

TE&L CO
Abs # 351
14-Sep-1857

TE&L CO
Abs # 352
14-Sep-1857

TE&L CO
Abs # 353
14-Sep-1857
see also, Map 1

TE&L CO
Abs # 354
15-Sep-1857
see also, Map 1

TE&L CO
Abs # 355
15-Sep-1857
see also, Map 1

TE&L CO

Abs # 356
15-Sep-1857
see also, Map 1

TE&L CO
Abs # 357
15-Sep-1857
see also, Map 1

TE&L CO
Abs # 358
15-Sep-1857
see also, Map 1

TE&L CO
Abs # 437
13-Nov-1857
see also, Map 3

TE&L CO
Abs # 438
13-Nov-1857
see also, Map 3

TE&L CO
Abs # 439
13-Nov-1857
see also, Map 3

TE&L CO
Abs # 440
13-Nov-1857
see also, Map 3

TE&L CO
Abs # 441
16-Nov-1857
see also, Map 3

TE&L CO
Abs # 442
16-Nov-1857
see also, Map 3

TE&L CO
Abs # 443
16-Nov-1857
see also, Map 3

TE&L CO
Abs # 444
16-Nov-1857
see also, Maps 3, 10, 11

TE&L CO
Abs # 445
16-Nov-1857
see also, Map 10

TE&L CO
Abs # 446
16-Nov-1857

TE&L CO
Abs # 447
16-Nov-1857

TE&L CO
Abs # 560
13-Jan-1858
see also, Map 10

TE&L CO
Abs # 561
13-Jan-1858
see also, Maps 1, 9, 10

TE&L CO
Abs # 608
19-Mar-1858

TE&L CO
Abs # 609
19-Mar-1858

TE&L CO
Abs # 610
19-Mar-1858

TE&L CO
Abs # 611
19-Mar-1858

TE&L CO
Abs # 612
19-Mar-1858

TE&L CO
Abs # 613
19-Mar-1858

TE&L CO
Abs # 614
20-Mar-1858

TE&L CO
Abs # 615
20-Mar-1858

TE&L CO
Abs # 616
20-Mar-1858

TE&L CO
Abs # 617
20-Mar-1858

TE&L CO
Abs # 618
20-Mar-1858

TE&L CO
Abs # 619
22-Mar-1858

TE&L CO
Abs # 620
22-Mar-1858
see also, Map 10

TE&L CO
Abs # 933
08-Sep-1858
see also, Map 1

TE&L CO
Abs # 934
08-Sep-1858

Populated Places	
None	

Cemeteries	
None	

Water (larger bodies)	
None	

Other Water	
Bitter Creek	
California Creek	
Camp Creek	
Dry Creek	
Mud Creek	

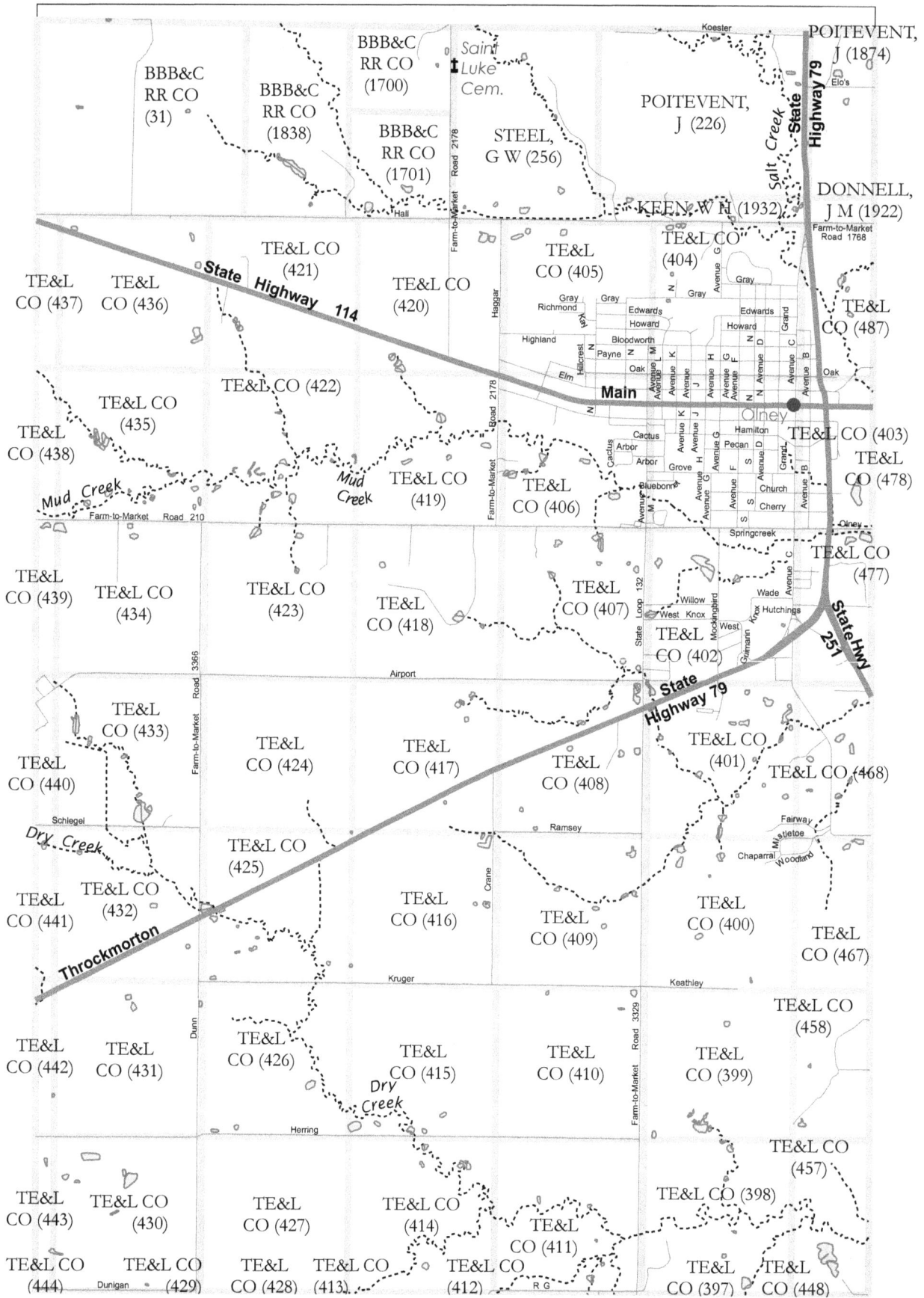

BBB&C RR CO (31)

BBB&C RR CO (1838)

BBB&C RR CO (1700)

BBB&C RR CO (1701)

Saint Luke Cem.

STEEL, G W (256)

POITEVENT, J (226)

Koester

POITEVENT, J (1874)

Elo's

State Highway 79

Salt Creek

KEEN, W H (1932)

DONNELL, J M (1922)

Farm-to-Market Road 1768

TE&L CO (421)

TE&L CO (420)

TE&L CO (405)

TE&L CO (404)

TE&L CO (437)

TE&L CO (436)

State Highway 114

Farm-to-Market Road 2178

Hall

TE&L CO (487)

Gray
Richmond
Gray
Gray
Gray
Edwards
Edwards
Highland
Howard
Howard
Bloodworth
Hillcrest
Payne
Highland
Oak
Elm
Main
Oak
Olney

TE&L CO (422)

TE&L CO (435)

TE&L CO (438)

Haggar
Kirk

Road 2178

TE&L CO (419)

Mud Creek

TE&L CO (406)

Cactus
Arbor
Cactus
Arbor
Grove
Bluebonnet

Hamilton
Pedan
Church
Cherry

Hutchings

TE&L CO (403)

TE&L CO (478)

Mud Creek

Farm-to-Market Road 210

Mud Creek

Farm-to-Market Road

Springcreek
Olney

TE&L CO (477)

TE&L CO (439)

TE&L CO (434)

TE&L CO (423)

TE&L CO (418)

TE&L CO (407)

State Loop 132

Willow
West Knox
West
Knox

Wade

TE&L CO (402)

State Hwy 251

Airport

TE&L CO (433)

TE&L CO (440)

TE&L CO (424)

TE&L CO (417)

State Highway 79

TE&L CO (408)

TE&L CO (401)

TE&L CO (468)

Farm-to-Market Road 3366

Schlegel

Dry Creek

Ramsey

Fairway
Mistletoe
Chaparral
Woodland

TE&L CO (425)

TE&L CO (441)

TE&L CO (432)

Throckmorton

TE&L CO (416)

Crane

TE&L CO (409)

TE&L CO (400)

TE&L CO (467)

Dunn

Kruger

Keathley

Farm-to-Market Road 3329

TE&L CO (458)

TE&L CO (442)

TE&L CO (431)

TE&L CO (426)

Dry Creek

TE&L CO (415)

TE&L CO (410)

TE&L CO (399)

Herring

TE&L CO (457)

TE&L CO (443)

TE&L CO (430)

TE&L CO (427)

TE&L CO (414)

TE&L CO (411)

TE&L CO (398)

TE&L CO (444)

Dunigan

TE&L CO (429)

TE&L CO (428)

TE&L CO (413)

TE&L CO (412)

R G

TE&L CO (397)

TE&L CO (448)

BBB&C RR CO
Abs # 1700
Survey2: PANKONIN, E
27-Feb-1901

BBB&C RR CO
Abs # 1701
Survey2: PANKKONIN, L
27-Feb-1901

BBB&C RR CO
Abs # 1838
Survey2: KUNKEL, H D
05-Jan-1885

BBB&C RR CO
Abs # 31
28-Oct-1873
see also, Map 2

DONNELL, J M
Abs # 1922
21-Jan-1901
see also, Map 4

KEEN, W H
Abs # 1932
24-Aug-1895

POITEVENT, J
Abs # 1874
Survey2: NEELY, A C
24-Dec-1904
see also, Map 4

POITEVENT, J
Abs # 226
03-Mar-1875

STEEL, G W
Abs # 256
07-May-1875

TE&L CO
Abs # 397
26-Oct-1857
see also, Map 11

TE&L CO
Abs # 398
26-Oct-1857

TE&L CO
Abs # 399
27-Oct-1857

TE&L CO
Abs # 400
27-Oct-1857

TE&L CO
Abs # 401
27-Oct-1857

TE&L CO
Abs # 402
27-Oct-1857

TE&L CO
Abs # 403
27-Oct-1857

TE&L CO
Abs # 404
27-Oct-1857

TE&L CO
Abs # 405
27-Oct-1857

TE&L CO
Abs # 406
28-Oct-1857

TE&L CO
Abs # 407
28-Oct-1857

TE&L CO
Abs # 408
28-Oct-1857

TE&L CO
Abs # 409
28-Oct-1857

TE&L CO
Abs # 410
28-Oct-1857

TE&L CO
Abs # 411
28-Oct-1857

TE&L CO
Abs # 412
28-Oct-1857
see also, Map 11

TE&L CO
Abs # 413
28-Oct-1857
see also, Map 11

TE&L CO
Abs # 414
28-Oct-1857

TE&L CO
Abs # 415
31-Oct-1857

TE&L CO
Abs # 416
31-Oct-1857

TE&L CO
Abs # 417
31-Oct-1857

TE&L CO
Abs # 418
31-Oct-1857

TE&L CO
Abs # 419
31-Oct-1857

TE&L CO
Abs # 420
20-Oct-1857

TE&L CO
Abs # 421
31-Oct-1857

TE&L CO
Abs # 422
31-Oct-1857

TE&L CO
Abs # 423
31-Oct-1857

TE&L CO
Abs # 424
31-Oct-1857

TE&L CO
Abs # 425
31-Oct-1857

TE&L CO
Abs # 426
31-Oct-1857

TE&L CO
Abs # 427
10-Nov-1857

TE&L CO
Abs # 428
11-Nov-1857
see also, Map 11

TE&L CO
Abs # 429
11-Nov-1857
see also, Map 11

TE&L CO
Abs # 430
11-Nov-1857

TE&L CO
Abs # 431
11-Nov-1857

TE&L CO
Abs # 432
17-Dec-1857

TE&L CO
Abs # 433
18-Dec-1857

TE&L CO
Abs # 434
18-Dec-1857

TE&L CO
Abs # 435
12-Nov-1857

TE&L CO
Abs # 436
13-Nov-1857

TE&L CO
Abs # 437
13-Nov-1857
see also, Map 2

TE&L CO
Abs # 438
13-Nov-1857
see also, Map 2

TE&L CO
Abs # 439
13-Nov-1857
see also, Map 2

TE&L CO
Abs # 440
13-Nov-1857
see also, Map 2

TE&L CO
Abs # 441
16-Nov-1857
see also, Map 2

TE&L CO
Abs # 442
16-Nov-1857
see also, Map 2

TE&L CO
Abs # 443
16-Nov-1857
see also, Map 2

TE&L CO
Abs # 444
16-Nov-1857
see also, Maps 2, 10, 11

TE&L CO
Abs # 448
19-Nov-1857
see also, Maps 4, 11, 12

TE&L CO
Abs # 457
23-Nov-1857
see also, Map 4

TE&L CO
Abs # 458
23-Nov-1857
see also, Map 4

TE&L CO
Abs # 467
24-Nov-1857
see also, Map 4

TE&L CO
Abs # 468
25-Nov-1857
see also, Map 4

TE&L CO
Abs # 477
28-Nov-1857
see also, Map 4

TE&L CO
Abs # 478
28-Nov-1857
see also, Map 4

TE&L CO
Abs # 487
01-Dec-1857
see also, Map 4

Populated Places
Olney

Cemeteries
Saint Luke Cemetery

Water (larger bodies)
None

Other Water
Dry Creek
Mud Creek
Salt Creek

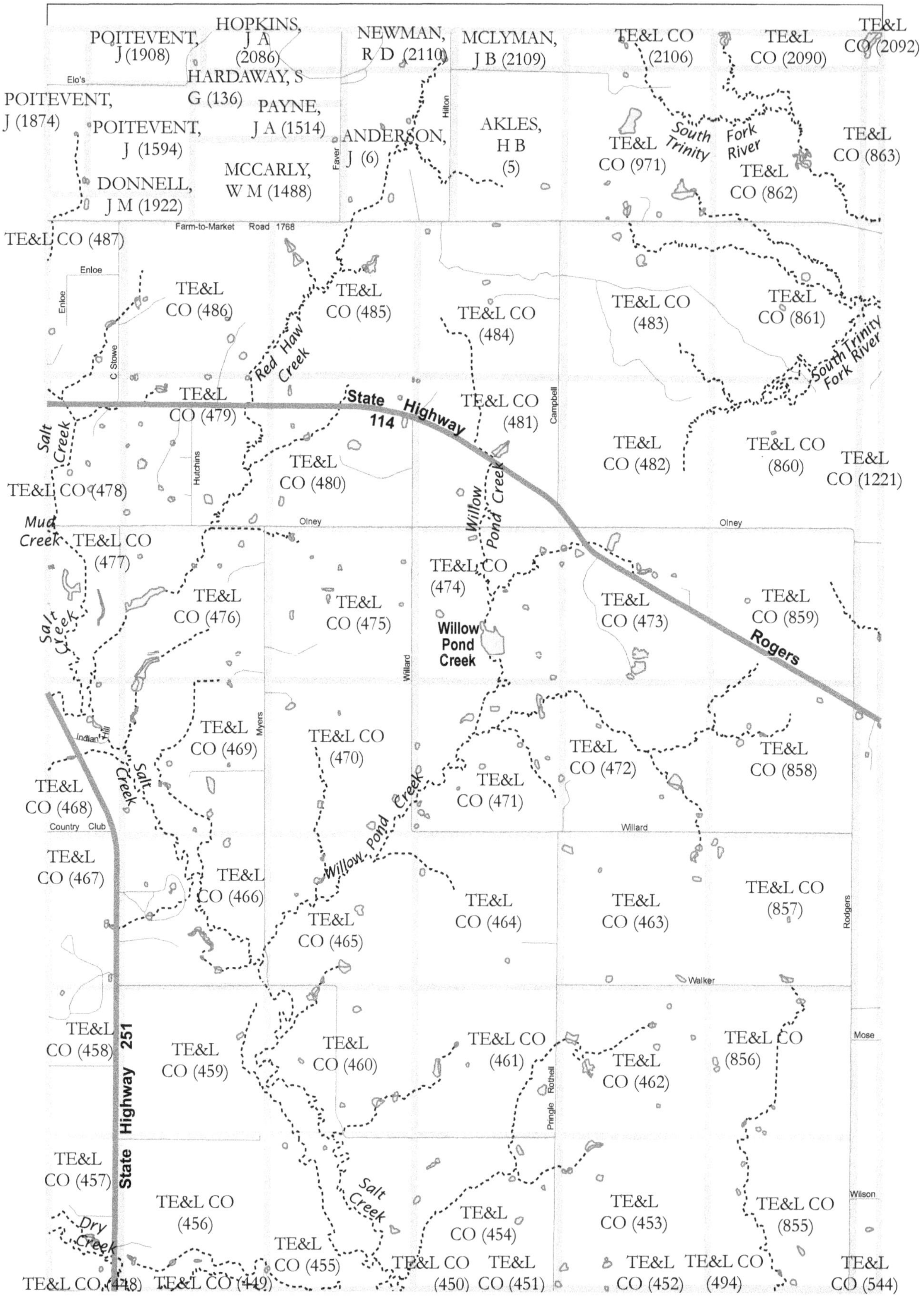

POITEVENT, J (1908)

HOPKINS, J A (2086)

NEWMAN, R D (2110)

MCLYMAN, J B (2109)

TE&L CO (2106)

TE&L CO (2090)

TE&L CO (2092)

Elo's

HARDAWAY, S G (136)

POITEVENT, J (1874)

POITEVENT, J (1594)

PAYNE, J A (1514)

ANDERSON, J (6)

AKLES, H B (5)

TE&L CO (971)

South Trinity Fork River

TE&L CO (862)

TE&L CO (863)

MCCARLY, W M (1488)

DONNELL, J M (1922)

Favor

Hilton

TE&L CO (487)

Farm-to-Market Road 1768

Enloe

Enloe

C Stowe

TE&L CO (486)

Red Haw Creek

TE&L CO (485)

TE&L CO (484)

TE&L CO (483)

TE&L CO (861)

South Trinity Fork River

Salt Creek

TE&L CO (479)

State Highway 114

TE&L CO (481)

Campbell

TE&L CO (478)

Hutchins

TE&L CO (480)

TE&L CO (482)

TE&L CO (860)

TE&L CO (1221)

Mud Creek

TE&L CO (477)

Olney

Willow Pond Creek

TE&L CO (474)

Olney

TE&L CO (476)

TE&L CO (475)

Willow Pond Creek

TE&L CO (473)

TE&L CO (859)

Rogers

Salt Creek

TE&L CO (469)

Myers

TE&L CO (470)

Willard

TE&L CO (471)

TE&L CO (472)

TE&L CO (858)

Indian

Salt Creek

TE&L CO (468)

Country Club

TE&L CO (467)

TE&L CO (466)

Willow Pond Creek

TE&L CO (465)

TE&L CO (464)

TE&L CO (463)

Willard

TE&L CO (857)

Rodgers

State Highway 251

TE&L CO (458)

TE&L CO (459)

TE&L CO (460)

TE&L CO (461)

Rothell

TE&L CO (462)

TE&L CO (856)

Mose

Pringle

TE&L CO (457)

Wilson

Dry Creek

TE&L CO (456)

Salt Creek

TE&L CO (454)

TE&L CO (453)

TE&L CO (855)

TE&L CO (455)

TE&L CO (448)

TE&L CO (449)

TE&L CO (450)

TE&L CO (451)

TE&L CO (452)

TE&L CO (494)

TE&L CO (544)

AKLES, H B
Abs # 5
01-Jul-1859

ANDERSON, J
Abs # 6
02-Jul-1859

DONNELL, J M
Abs # 1922
21-Jan-1901
see also, Map 3

HARDAWAY, S G
Abs # 136
20-Aug-1877

HOPKINS, J A
Abs # 2086
07-May-1875

MCCARLY, W M
Abs # 1488
21-May-1881

MCLYMAN, J B
Abs # 2109
16-Oct-1891

NEWMAN, R D
Abs # 2110
01-Jul-1859

PAYNE, J A
Abs # 1514
21-May-1881

POITEVENT, J
Abs # 1594
Survey2: DAVIS, W
14-Jul-1899

POITEVENT, J
Abs # 1874
Survey2: NEELY, A C
24-Dec-1904
see also, Map 3

POITEVENT, J
Abs # 1908
Survey2: DAVIS, W
18-Oct-1906

TE&L CO
Abs # 1221
07-Mar-1859
see also, Maps 5, 6

TE&L CO
Abs # 2090
16-Aug-1858

TE&L CO
Abs # 2092
18-Aug-1858
see also, Map 5

TE&L CO
Abs # 2106
05-Aug-1858

TE&L CO
Abs # 448
19-Nov-1857
see also, Maps 3, 11, 12

TE&L CO
Abs # 449
19-Nov-1857
see also, Map 12

TE&L CO
Abs # 450
19-Nov-1857
see also, Map 12

TE&L CO
Abs # 451
28-Sep-1953
see also, Map 12

TE&L CO
Abs # 452
23-Nov-1857
see also, Map 12

TE&L CO
Abs # 453
23-Nov-1857

TE&L CO
Abs # 454
23-Nov-1857

TE&L CO
Abs # 455
23-Nov-1857

TE&L CO
Abs # 456
23-Nov-1857

TE&L CO
Abs # 457
23-Nov-1857
see also, Map 3

TE&L CO
Abs # 458
23-Nov-1857
see also, Map 3

TE&L CO
Abs # 459
24-Nov-1857

TE&L CO
Abs # 460
24-Nov-1857

TE&L CO
Abs # 461
24-Nov-1857

TE&L CO
Abs # 462
24-Nov-1857

TE&L CO
Abs # 463
18-May-1858

TE&L CO
Abs # 464
24-Nov-1857

TE&L CO
Abs # 465
24-Nov-1857

TE&L CO
Abs # 466
24-Nov-1857

TE&L CO
Abs # 467
24-Nov-1857
see also, Map 3

TE&L CO
Abs # 468
25-Nov-1857
see also, Map 3

TE&L CO
Abs # 469
25-Nov-1857

TE&L CO
Abs # 470
25-Nov-1857

TE&L CO
Abs # 471
25-Nov-1857

TE&L CO
Abs # 472
25-Nov-1857

TE&L CO
Abs # 473
25-Nov-1857

TE&L CO
Abs # 474
25-Nov-1857

TE&L CO
Abs # 475
27-Nov-1857

TE&L CO
Abs # 476
28-Nov-1857

TE&L CO
Abs # 477
28-Nov-1857
see also, Map 3

TE&L CO
Abs # 478
28-Nov-1857
see also, Map 3

TE&L CO
Abs # 479
30-Nov-1857

TE&L CO
Abs # 480
30-Nov-1857

TE&L CO
Abs # 481
30-Nov-1857

TE&L CO
Abs # 482
01-Dec-1857

TE&L CO
Abs # 483
01-Dec-1857

TE&L CO
Abs # 484
01-Dec-1857

TE&L CO
Abs # 485
01-Dec-1857

TE&L CO
Abs # 486
01-Dec-1857

TE&L CO
Abs # 487
01-Dec-1857
see also, Map 3

TE&L CO
Abs # 494
03-Dec-1857
see also, Map 12

TE&L CO
Abs # 544
02-Jan-1858
see also, Maps 5, 12, 13

TE&L CO
Abs # 855
13-Aug-1858

TE&L CO
Abs # 856
13-Aug-1858

TE&L CO
Abs # 857
13-Aug-1858

TE&L CO
Abs # 858
13-Aug-1858

TE&L CO
Abs # 859
13-Aug-1858

TE&L CO
Abs # 860
13-Aug-1858

TE&L CO
Abs # 861
13-Aug-1858

TE&L CO
Abs # 862
13-Aug-1858

TE&L CO
Abs # 863
17-Aug-1858
see also, Map 5

TE&L CO
Abs # 971
05-Aug-1858

Populated Places
None

Cemeteries
None

Water (larger bodies)
Willow Pond Creek

Other Water
Dry Creek
Mud Creek
Red Haw Creek
Salt Creek
South Fork Trinity River
Willow Pond Creek

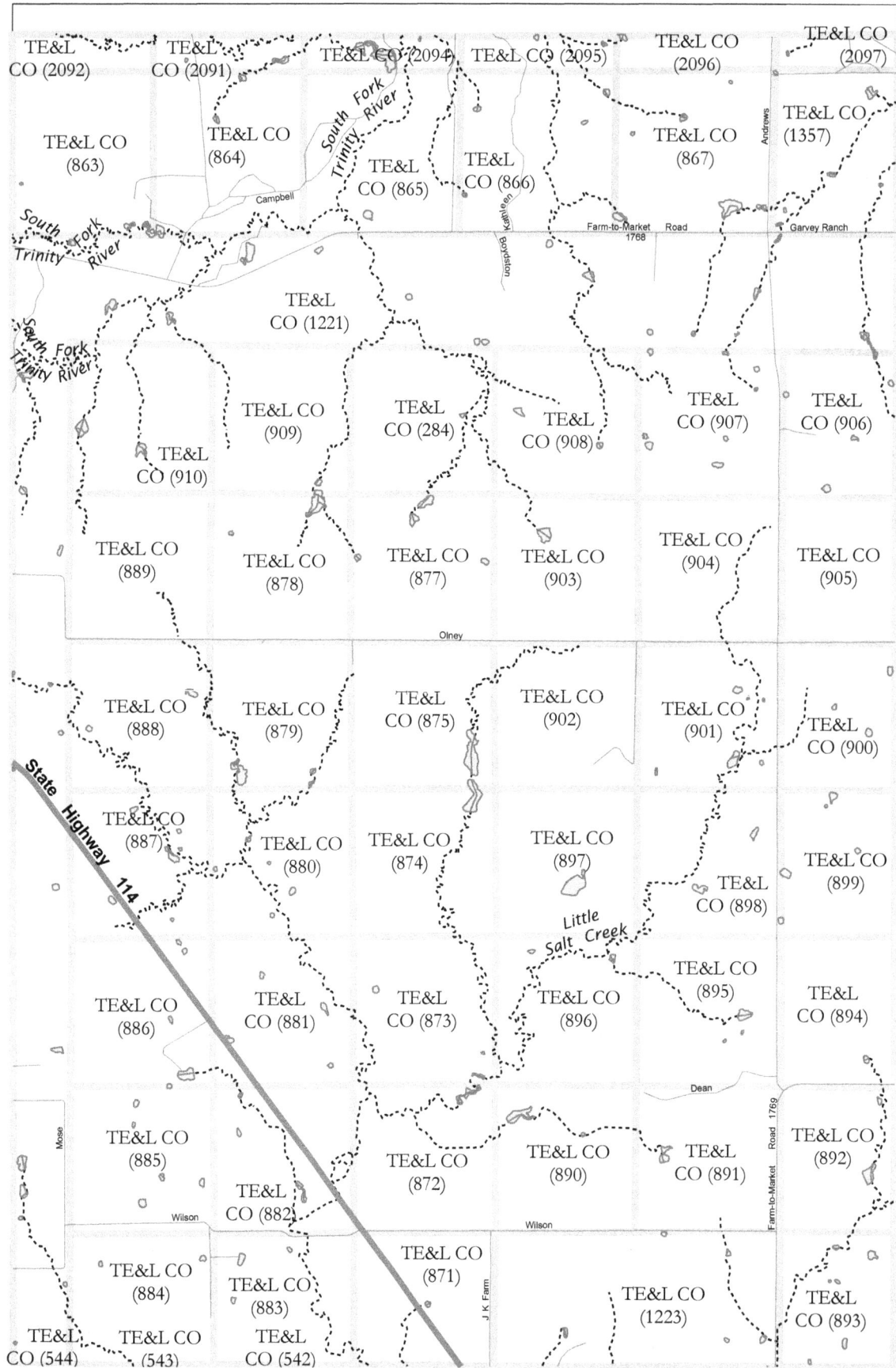

TE&L
CO (2092)

TE&L
CO (2091)

TE&L CO (2094)

TE&L CO (2095)

TE&L CO
(2096)

TE&L CO
(2097)

TE&L CO
(863)

TE&L CO
(864)

South Fork Trinity River

TE&L
CO (865)

TE&L
CO (866)

TE&L CO
(867)

TE&L CO
(1357)

Campbell

South Fork Trinity River

Karleen

Boydston

Andrews

Farm-to-Market Road
1768

Garvey Ranch

TE&L
CO (1221)

South Fork Trinity River

TE&L CO
(909)

TE&L
CO (284)

TE&L
CO (908)

TE&L
CO (907)

TE&L
CO (906)

TE&L
CO (910)

TE&L CO
(889)

TE&L CO
(878)

TE&L CO
(877)

TE&L CO
(903)

TE&L CO
(904)

TE&L CO
(905)

Olney

TE&L CO
(888)

TE&L CO
(879)

TE&L
CO (875)

TE&L CO
(902)

TE&L CO
(901)

TE&L
CO (900)

State Highway 114

TE&L CO
(887)

TE&L CO
(880)

TE&L CO
(874)

TE&L CO
(897)

TE&L
CO (898)

TE&L CO
(899)

Little Salt Creek

TE&L CO
(895)

TE&L CO
(886)

TE&L
CO (881)

TE&L
CO (873)

TE&L CO
(896)

TE&L
CO (894)

Dean

Mose

TE&L CO
(885)

TE&L
CO (882)

TE&L CO
(872)

TE&L CO
(890)

TE&L
CO (891)

Farm-to-Market Road 1769

TE&L CO
(892)

Wilson

Wilson

TE&L CO
(884)

TE&L CO
(883)

TE&L CO
(871)

J K Farm

TE&L CO
(1223)

TE&L
CO (893)

TE&L
CO (544)

TE&L CO
(543)

TE&L
CO (542)

TE&L CO
Abs # 1221
07-Mar-1859
see also, Maps 4, 6

TE&L CO
Abs # 1223
08-Mar-1859
see also, Map 13

TE&L CO
Abs # 1357
18-Aug-1858
see also, Map 6

TE&L CO
Abs # 2091
17-Aug-1858

TE&L CO
Abs # 2092
18-Aug-1858
see also, Map 4

TE&L CO
Abs # 2094
18-Aug-1858

TE&L CO
Abs # 2095
19-Aug-1858

TE&L CO
Abs # 2096
19-Aug-1858

TE&L CO
Abs # 2097
19-Aug-1858
see also, Map 6

TE&L CO
Abs # 284
24-Dec-1858

TE&L CO
Abs # 542
02-Jan-1858
see also, Map 13

TE&L CO
Abs # 543
02-Jan-1858
see also, Map 13

TE&L CO
Abs # 544
02-Jan-1858
see also, Maps 4, 12, 13

TE&L CO
Abs # 863
17-Aug-1858
see also, Map 4

TE&L CO
Abs # 864
17-Aug-1858

TE&L CO
Abs # 865
18-Aug-1858

TE&L CO
Abs # 866
18-Aug-1858

TE&L CO
Abs # 867
18-Aug-1858

TE&L CO
Abs # 871
17-Jan-1859
see also, Map 13

TE&L CO
Abs # 872
25-Jan-1859

TE&L CO
Abs # 873
26-Jan-1859

TE&L CO
Abs # 874
26-Jan-1859

TE&L CO
Abs # 875

26-Jan-1859

TE&L CO
Abs # 877
23-Oct-1858

TE&L CO
Abs # 878
17-Jan-1859

TE&L CO
Abs # 879
18-Jan-1859

TE&L CO
Abs # 880
20-Jan-1859

TE&L CO
Abs # 881
20-Jan-1859

TE&L CO
Abs # 882
20-Jan-1859

TE&L CO
Abs # 883
20-Jan-1859

TE&L CO
Abs # 884
20-Jan-1859

TE&L CO
Abs # 885
20-Jan-1859

TE&L CO
Abs # 886
19-Jan-1859

TE&L CO
Abs # 887
19-Jan-1859

TE&L CO
Abs # 888
19-Jan-1859

TE&L CO
Abs # 889
19-Jan-1859

TE&L CO
Abs # 890
19-Jan-1859

TE&L CO
Abs # 891
19-Jan-1859

TE&L CO
Abs # 892
19-Jan-1859
see also, Map 6

TE&L CO
Abs # 893
19-Jan-1859
see also, Maps 6, 13, 14

TE&L CO
Abs # 894
18-Jan-1859
see also, Map 6

TE&L CO
Abs # 895
19-Jan-1859

TE&L CO
Abs # 896
19-Jan-1859

TE&L CO
Abs # 897
19-Jan-1859

TE&L CO
Abs # 898
20-Jan-1859

TE&L CO
Abs # 899
20-Jan-1859
see also, Map 6

TE&L CO
Abs # 900

18-Jan-1859
see also, Map 6

TE&L CO
Abs # 901
18-Jan-1859

TE&L CO
Abs # 902
19-Jan-1859

TE&L CO
Abs # 903
20-Jan-1859

TE&L CO
Abs # 904
19-Jan-1859

TE&L CO
Abs # 905
19-Jan-1859
see also, Map 6

TE&L CO
Abs # 906
17-Jan-1859
see also, Map 6

TE&L CO
Abs # 907
17-Jan-1859

TE&L CO
Abs # 908
17-Jan-1859

TE&L CO
Abs # 909
17-Jan-1859

TE&L CO
Abs # 910
17-Jan-1859

Populated Places
None

Cemeteries
None

Water (larger bodies)
None

Other Water
Little Salt Creek
South Fork Trinity River

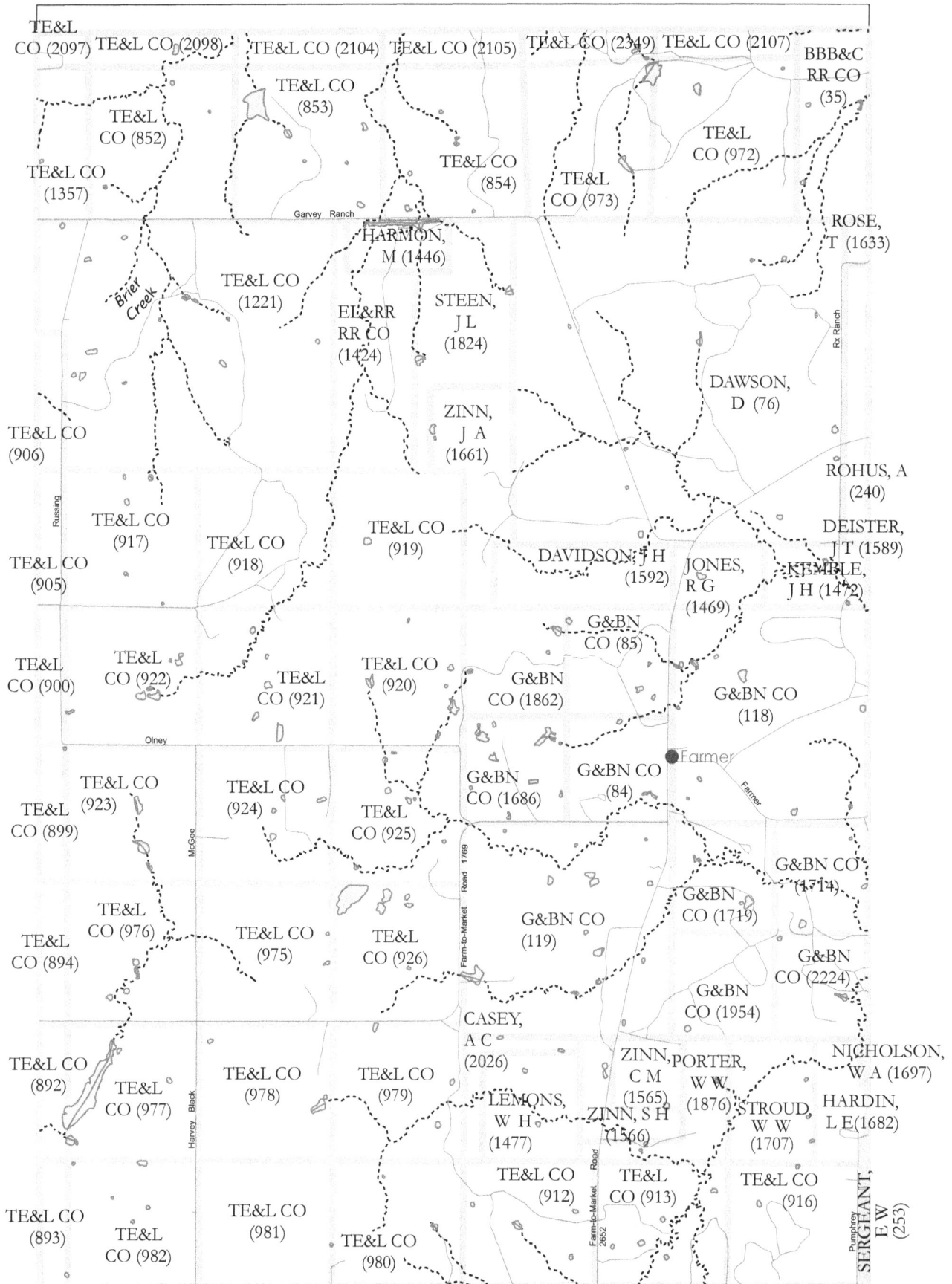

TE&L CO (2097) TE&L CO (2098) TE&L CO (2104) TE&L CO (2105) TE&L CO (2349) TE&L CO (2107)

BBB&C RR CO (35)

TE&L CO (852)

TE&L CO (853)

TE&L CO (972)

TE&L CO (1357)

TE&L CO (854)

TE&L CO (973)

Garvey Ranch

HARMON, M (1446)

ROSE, T (1633)

Brier Creek

TE&L CO (1221)

EL&RR RR CO (1424)

STEEN, J L (1824)

DAWSON, D (76)

Rx Ranch

ZINN, J A (1661)

ROHUS, A (240)

TE&L CO (906)

Russing

DEISTER, J T (1589)

TE&L CO (917)

TE&L CO (918)

TE&L CO (919)

DAVIDSON, J H (1592)

JONES, R G (1469)

KEMBLE, J H (1472)

TE&L CO (905)

G&BN CO (85)

TE&L CO (900)

TE&L CO (922)

TE&L CO (921)

TE&L CO (920)

G&BN CO (1862)

G&BN CO (118)

Olney

Farmer

TE&L CO (923)

TE&L CO (924)

G&BN CO (1686)

G&BN CO (84)

Farmer

TE&L CO (899)

McGee

TE&L CO (925)

G&BN CO (1719)

G&BN CO (1714)

TE&L CO (976)

TE&L CO (975)

TE&L CO (926)

Farm-to-Market Road 1769

G&BN CO (119)

G&BN CO (2224)

TE&L CO (894)

G&BN CO (1954)

CASEY, A C (2026)

TE&L CO (892)

TE&L CO (977)

Harvey Black

TE&L CO (978)

TE&L CO (979)

LEMONS, W H (1477)

ZINN, C M (1565)

ZINN, S H (1566)

PORTER, W W (1876)

STROUD, W W (1707)

NICHOLSON, W A (1697)

HARDIN, L E (1682)

TE&L CO (893)

TE&L CO (982)

TE&L CO (981)

TE&L CO (980)

TE&L CO (912)

TE&L CO (913)

Farm-to-Market Road 2652

TE&L CO (916)

Pumphrey Road

SERGEANT, E W (253)

BBB&C RR CO
Abs # 35
21-Oct-1873
see also, Map 7

CASEY, A C
Abs # 2026
06-Oct-1893

DAVIDSON, J H
Abs # 1592
11-Nov-1880

DAWSON, D
Abs # 76
14-Dec-1874

DEISTER, J T
Abs # 1589
02-Jun-1882
see also, Map 7

EL&RR RR CO
Abs # 1424
21-Aug-1879

G&BN CO
Abs # 118
04-Aug-1873
see also, Map 7

G&BN CO
Abs # 119
04-Aug-1873

G&BN CO
Abs # 1686
Survey2: JAMESON, A B
13-Dec-1884

G&BN CO
Abs # 1714
Survey2: WANN, S M
21-Jul-1881
see also, Map 7

G&BN CO
Abs # 1719
Survey2: COMPERE, W T
26-Oct-1889

G&BN CO
Abs # 1862
Survey2: ZINN, J A
17-Jun-1885

G&BN CO
Abs # 1954
Survey2: COMPERE, W T
26-Oct-1889

G&BN CO
Abs # 2224
Survey2: NICHOLSON, W A
06-Apr-1900
see also, Map 7

G&BN CO
Abs # 84
Survey2: DAVIDSON, S
05-Oct-1885

G&BN CO
Abs # 85
Survey2: DAVIDSON, J H
13-Jan-1880

HARDIN, L E
Abs # 1682
03-Sep-1888
see also, Map 7

HARMON, M
Abs # 1446
30-Aug-1884

JONES, R G
Abs # 1469
27-Feb-1880

KEMBLE, J H
Abs # 1472
02-Jan-1880
see also, Map 7

LEMONS, W H
Abs # 1477
08-Dec-1879

NICHOLSON, W A

Abs # 1697
18-Feb-1884
see also, Map 7

PORTER, W W
Abs # 1876
25-Nov-1890

ROHUS, A
Abs # 240
03-Aug-1875
see also, Maps 7, 8

ROSE, T
Abs # 1633
06-Feb-1885
see also, Map 7

SERGEANT, E W
Abs # 253
01-Jun-1859
see also, Maps 7, 14, 15

STEEN, J L
Abs # 1824
08-May-1899

STROUD, W W
Abs # 1707
23-Jan-1886

TE&L CO
Abs # 1221
07-Mar-1859
see also, Maps 4, 5

TE&L CO
Abs # 1357
18-Aug-1858
see also, Map 5

TE&L CO
Abs # 2097
19-Aug-1858
see also, Map 5

TE&L CO
Abs # 2098
19-Aug-1858

TE&L CO
Abs # 2104
05-Aug-1858

TE&L CO
Abs # 2105
05-Aug-1858

TE&L CO
Abs # 2107
11-Aug-1858

TE&L CO
Abs # 2349
11-Aug-1858

TE&L CO
Abs # 852
18-Aug-1858

TE&L CO
Abs # 853
19-Aug-1858

TE&L CO
Abs # 854
19-Aug-1858

TE&L CO
Abs # 892
19-Jan-1859
see also, Map 5

TE&L CO
Abs # 893
19-Jan-1859
see also, Maps 5, 13, 14

TE&L CO
Abs # 894
18-Jan-1859
see also, Map 5

TE&L CO
Abs # 899
20-Jan-1859
see also, Map 5

TE&L CO
Abs # 900

18-Jan-1859
see also, Map 5

TE&L CO
Abs # 905
19-Jan-1859
see also, Map 5

TE&L CO
Abs # 906
17-Jan-1859
see also, Map 5

TE&L CO
Abs # 912
18-Jan-1859
see also, Map 14

TE&L CO
Abs # 913
18-Jan-1859
see also, Map 14

TE&L CO
Abs # 916
18-Jan-1859
see also, Map 14

TE&L CO
Abs # 917
18-Jan-1859

TE&L CO
Abs # 918
14-Jan-1859

TE&L CO
Abs # 919
14-Jan-1859

TE&L CO
Abs # 920
14-Jan-1859

TE&L CO
Abs # 921
14-Jan-1859

TE&L CO
Abs # 922
18-Jan-1859

TE&L CO
Abs # 923
18-Jan-1859

TE&L CO
Abs # 924
17-Jan-1859

TE&L CO
Abs # 925
17-Jan-1859

TE&L CO
Abs # 926
26-Jan-1859

TE&L CO
Abs # 972
11-Aug-1858

TE&L CO
Abs # 973
11-Aug-1858

TE&L CO
Abs # 975
25-Jan-1859

TE&L CO
Abs # 976
25-Jan-1859

TE&L CO
Abs # 977
25-Jan-1859

TE&L CO
Abs # 978
29-Jan-1859

TE&L CO
Abs # 979
29-Jan-1859

TE&L CO
Abs # 980
27-Jan-1859
see also, Map 14

TE&L CO
Abs # 981
27-Jan-1859
see also, Map 14

TE&L CO
Abs # 982
28-Jan-1859
see also, Map 14

ZINN, C M
Abs # 1565
28-Mar-1881

ZINN, J A
Abs # 1661
09-Sep-1881

ZINN, S H
Abs # 1566
05-Jan-1881

Populated Places
Farmer

Cemeteries
None

Water (larger bodies)
None

Other Water
Brier Creek

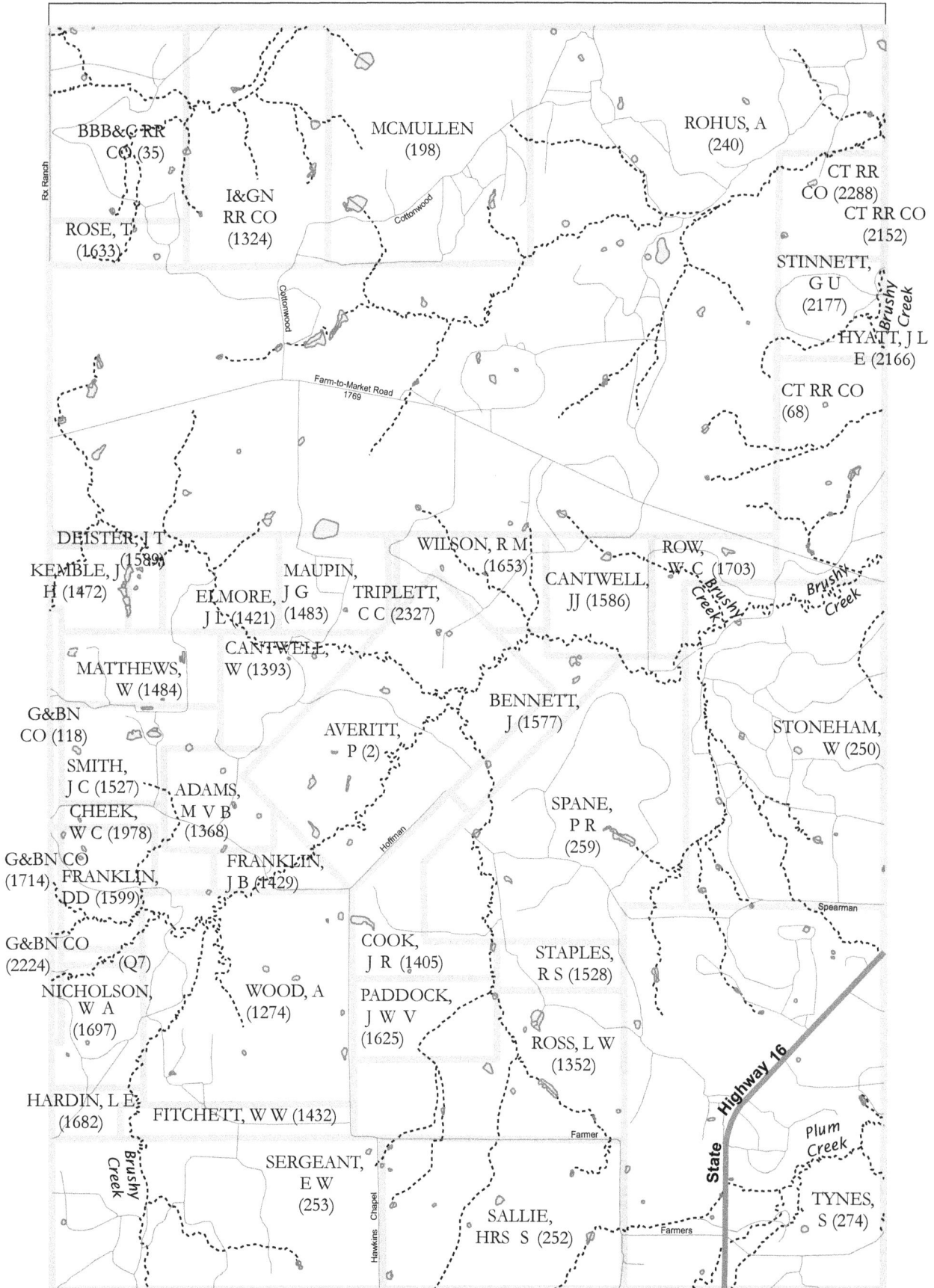

BBB&C RR
CO (35)

MCMULLEN
(198)

ROHUS, A
(240)

Rx Ranch

I&GN
RR CO
(1324)

CT RR
CO (2288)

CT RR CO
(2152)

ROSE, T
(1633)

Cottonwood

STINNETT,
G U
(2177)

Brushy Creek

Cottonwood

HYATT, J L
E (2166)

Farm-to-Market Road
1769

CT RR CO
(68)

DEISTER, J T
(1589)

WILSON, R M
(1653)

ROW,
W C (1703)

Brushy
Creek

KEMBLE, J
H (1472)

MAUPIN,
J G
(1483)

CANTWELL,
JJ (1586)

ELMORE,
J L (1421)

TRIPLETT,
C C (2327)

Brushy
Creek

CANTWELL,
W (1393)

MATTHEWS,
W (1484)

BENNETT,
J (1577)

STONEHAM,
W (250)

G&BN
CO (118)

AVERITT,
P (2)

SMITH,
J C (1527)

ADAMS,
M V B
(1368)

SPANE,
P R
(259)

CHEEK,
W C (1978)

G&BN CO
(1714)

FRANKLIN,
J B (1429)

FRANKLIN,
DD (1599)

Hoffman

Spearman

G&BN CO
(2224)

(Q7)

COOK,
J R (1405)

STAPLES,
R S (1528)

NICHOLSON,
W A
(1697)

WOOD, A
(1274)

PADDOCK,
J W V
(1625)

State Highway 16

ROSS, L W
(1352)

HARDIN, L E
(1682)

FITCHETT, W W (1432)

Plum
Creek

Brushy
Creek

SERGEANT,
E W
(253)

Farmer

TYNES,
S (274)

Hawkins Chapel

SALLIE,
HRS S (252)

Farmers

ADAMS, M V B
Abs # 1368
24-Dec-1879

AVERITT, P
Abs # 2
17-Oct-1859

BBB&C RR CO
Abs # 35
21-Oct-1873
see also, Map 6

BENNETT, J
Abs # 1577
10-Dec-1888

CANTWELL, J J
Abs # 1586
18-Jan-1882

CANTWELL, W
Abs # 1393
02-Jan-1880

CHEEK, W C
Abs # 1978
05-Dec-1900

COOK, J R
Abs # 1405
08-Oct-1880

CT RR CO
Abs # 2152
Survey2: BUSSEY, J F
02-Apr-1917
see also, Map 8

CT RR CO
Abs # 2288
Survey2: WILLIAMS, A
31-May-1912

CT RR CO
Abs # 68
01-Aug-1873
see also, Map 8

DEISTER, J T
Abs # 1589
02-Jun-1882
see also, Map 6

ELMORE, J L
Abs # 1421
05-Dec-1881

FITCHETT, W W
Abs # 1432
05-Jan-1884

FRANKLIN, D D
Abs # 1599
07-Sep-1880

FRANKLIN, J B
Abs # 1429
08-Sep-1883

G&BN CO
Abs # 118
04-Aug-1873
see also, Map 6

G&BN CO
Abs # 1714
Survey2: WANN, S M
21-Jul-1881
see also, Map 6

G&BN CO
Abs # 2224
Survey2: NICHOLSON, W A
06-Apr-1900
see also, Map 6

HARDIN, L E
Abs # 1682
03-Sep-1888
see also, Map 6

HYATT, J L E
Abs # 2166
11-Jun-1926
see also, Map 8

I&GN RR CO
Abs # 1324
25-Sep-1877

KEMBLE, J H
Abs # 1472
02-Jan-1880
see also, Map 6

MATTHEWS, W
Abs # 1484
26-Aug-1881

MAUPIN, J G
Abs # 1483
26-Oct-1881

MCMULLEN
Abs # 198
15-May-1854

NICHOLSON, W A
Abs # 1697
18-Feb-1884
see also, Map 6

PADDOCK, J W V
Abs # 1625
19-Nov-1879

ROHUS, A
Abs # 240
03-Aug-1875
see also, Maps 6, 8

ROSE, T
Abs # 1633
06-Feb-1885
see also, Map 6

ROSS, L W
Abs # 1352
01-Jan-1879

ROW, W C
Abs # 1703
05-May-1885

SALLIE, HRS S
Abs # 252
31-Jul-1877
see also, Map 15

SERGEANT, E W
Abs # 253
01-Jun-1859
see also, Maps 6, 14, 15

SMITH, J C
Abs # 1527
25-Sep-1879

SPANE, P R
Abs # 259
19-Dec-1860

STAPLES, R S
Abs # 1528
18-Aug-1880

STINNETT, G U
Abs # 2177
28-Jul-1926

STONEHAM, W
Abs # 250
08-Mar-1861
see also, Map 8

TRIPLETT, C C
Abs # 2327
04-May-1920

TYNES, S
Abs # 274
10-Mar-1879
see also, Maps 8, 15, 16

WILSON, R M
Abs # 1653
02-Dec-1881

WOOD, A
Abs # 1274
30-Oct-1874

Abs # ?7

Populated Places
None

Cemeteries
None

Water (larger bodies)
None

Other Water
Brushy Creek
Plum Creek

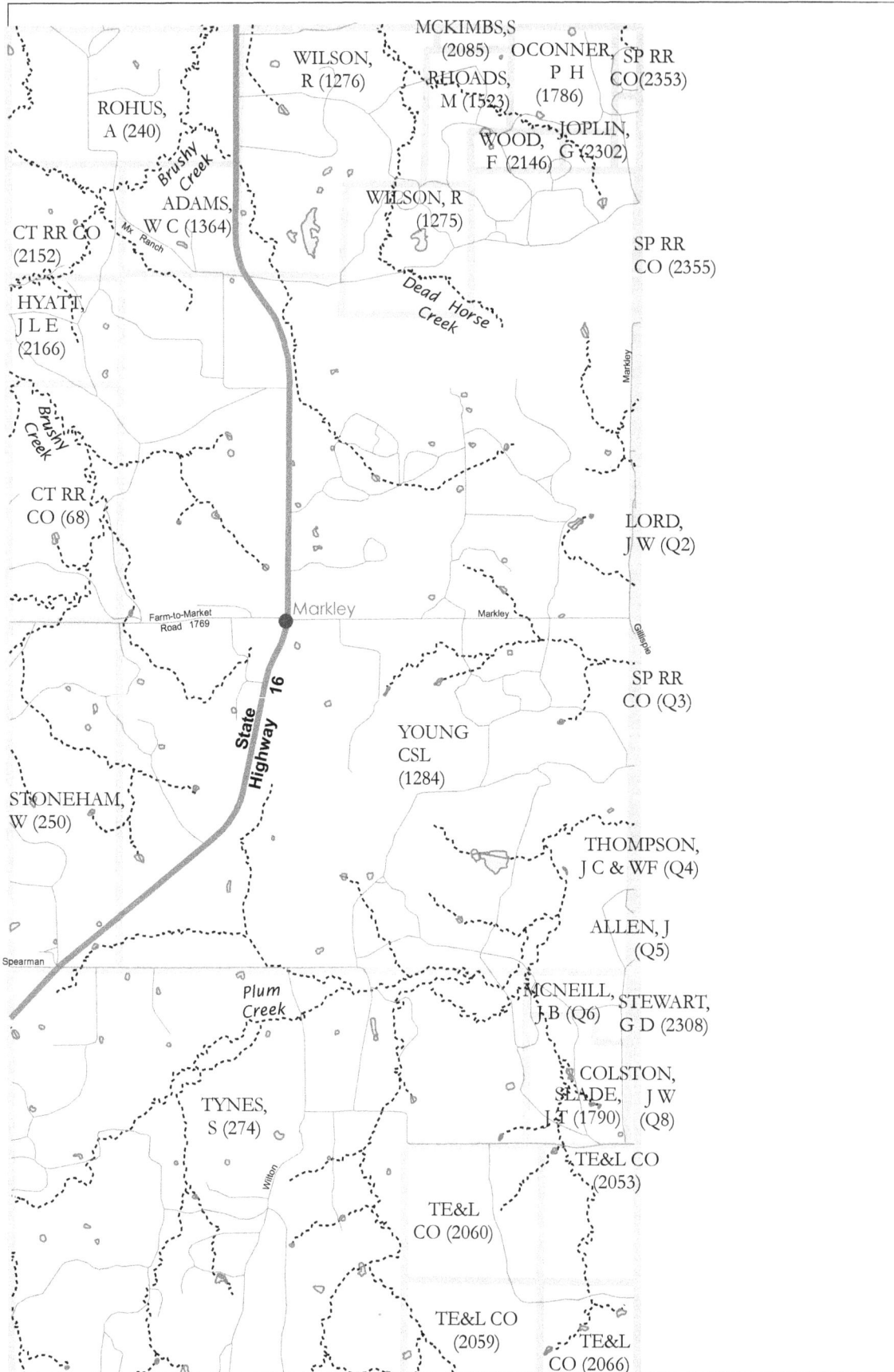

ADAMS, W C
Abs # 1364
05-Sep-1883

ALLEN, J
Abs # ?5

CT RR CO
Abs # 2152
Survey2: BUSSEY, J F
02-Apr-1917
see also, Map 7

COLSTON, J W
Abs # ?8

CT RR CO
Abs # 68
01-Aug-1873
see also, Map 7

HYATT, J L E
Abs # 2166
11-Jun-1926
see also, Map 7

JOPLIN, G
Abs # 2302
27-Feb-1918

MCKIMBS,S
Abs # 2085
05-Dec-1883

MCNEIL, J B
Abs # ?6

O CONNER, P H
Abs # 1786
03-Oct-1883

RHOADS, M
Abs # 1523
13-Mar-1880

ROHUS, A
Abs # 240
03-Aug-1875
see also, Maps 6, 7

SLADE, J T
Abs # 1790
06-Aug-1883

SP RR CO
Abs # 2353
12-Mar-1869

SP RR CO
Abs # 2355
09-Jul-1868

SP RR CO
Abs # ?3

STEWART, G D
Abs # 2308
09-Jul-1919

STONEHAM, W
Abs # 250
08-Mar-1861
see also, Map 7

TE&L CO
Abs # 2053
12-Feb-1859

TE&L CO
Abs # 2059
11-Feb-1859
see also, Map 16

TE&L CO
Abs # 2060
11-Feb-1859

TE&L CO
Abs # 2066
11-Feb-1859
see also, Map 16

THOMPSON, J C & W F
Abs # ?4

TYNES, S
Abs # 274
10-Mar-1879
see also, Maps 7, 15, 16

WILSON, R
Abs # 1275
05-Oct-1855

WILSON, R
Abs # 1276
06-Jun-1856

WOOD, F
Abs # 2146
07-Oct-1896

YOUNG CSL
Abs # 1284
24-Apr-1860

Populated Places
Markley

Cemeteries
None

Water (larger bodies)
None

Other Water
Brushy Creek
Dead Horse Creek
Plum Creek

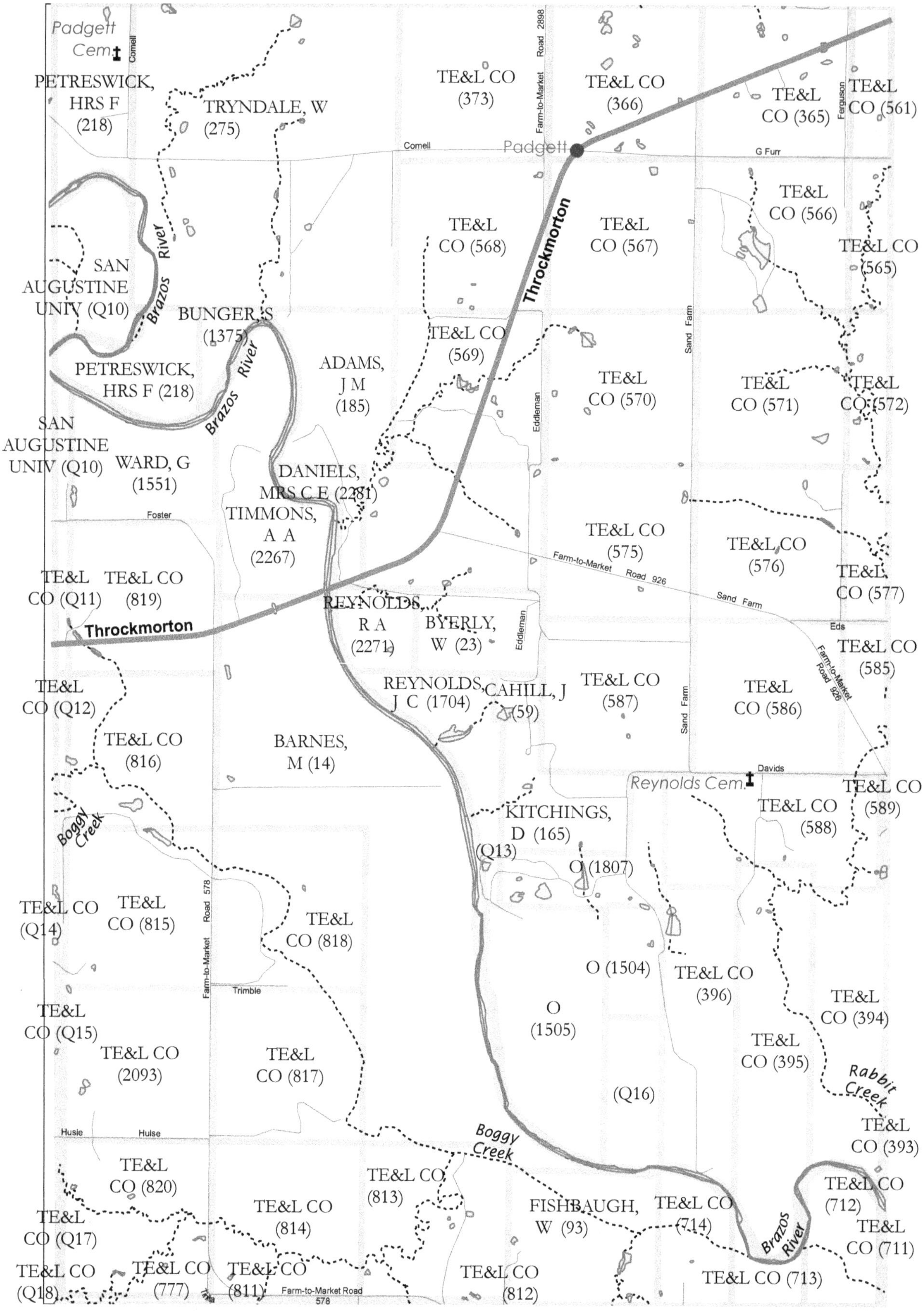

Padgett
Cem.

PETRESWICK,
HRS F
(218)

TRYNDALE, W
(275)

Comell

TE&L CO
(373)

TE&L CO
(366)

Road 2898

TE&L
CO (365)

TE&L
CO (561)

Comell

Padgett

G Furr

Ferguson

Brazos River

SAN
AUGUSTINE
UNIV (Q10)

BUNGER, S
(1375)

Throckmorton

TE&L
CO (568)

TE&L
CO (567)

TE&L
CO (566)

TE&L CO
(565)

PETRESWICK,
HRS F (218)

Brazos River

ADAMS,
J M
(185)

TE&L CO
(569)

TE&L
CO (570)

Eddleman

TE&L
CO (571)

TE&L
CO (572)

Sand Farm

SAN
AUGUSTINE
UNIV (Q10)

WARD, G
(1551)

DANIELS,
MRS C E (2281)

Foster

TIMMONS,
A A
(2267)

TE&L CO
(575)

TE&L CO
(576)

Sand Farm

TE&L
CO (577)

TE&L
CO (Q11)

TE&L CO
(819)

Throckmorton

REYNOLDS,
R A
(2271)

BYERLY,
W (23)

Eddleman

Farm-to-Market Road 926

Eds

TE&L CO
(585)

Farm-to-Market Road 926

TE&L
CO (Q12)

REYNOLDS,
J C (1704)

CAHILL, J
(59)

TE&L CO
(587)

TE&L
CO (586)

TE&L CO
(816)

BARNES,
M (14)

Davids

Reynolds Cem.

TE&L CO
(588)

TE&L CO
(589)

Boggy Creek

TE&L CO
(Q14)

TE&L
CO (815)

Road 578

TE&L
CO (818)

Trimble

KITCHINGS,
D (165)
(Q13)

O (1807)

O (1504)

TE&L CO
(396)

TE&L
CO (394)

TE&L
CO (Q15)

TE&L CO
(2093)

TE&L
CO (817)

Farm-to-Market Road

O
(1505)

(Q16)

TE&L
CO (395)

Rabbit
Creek

TE&L
CO (393)

Husie

Hulse

Boggy
Creek

TE&L CO
(820)

TE&L CO
(813)

FISHBAUGH,
W (93)

TE&L CO
(714)

Brazos River

TE&L CO
(712)

TE&L
CO (711)

TE&L
CO (Q17)

TE&L CO
(814)

TE&L CO
(Q18)

TE&L CO
(777)

TE&L CO
(811)

Farm-to-Market Road 578

TE&L CO
(812)

TE&L CO (713)

ADAMS, J M
Abs # 185
03-May-1875

BARNES, M
Abs # 14
27-Apr-1859

BUNGER, S
Abs # 1375
23-Dec-1901

BYERLY, W
Abs # 23
09-Jul-1875

CAHILL, J
Abs # 59
05-Feb-1862

DANIELS, MRS C E
Abs # 2281
12-Oct-1910

FISHBAUGH, W
Abs # 93
25-Mar-1856
see also, Map 17

KITCHINGS, D
Abs # 165
05-Feb-1862

O
Abs # 1504
24-Nov-1879

O
Abs # 1505
24-Nov-1879

O
Abs # 1807
20-Jun-1884

PETRESWICK, HRS F
Abs # 218
02-Oct-1875
see also, Map 1

REYNOLDS, J C
Abs # 1704
22-Jul-1936

REYNOLDS, R A
Abs # 2271
04-Nov-1907

SAN AGUSTINE UNIV
Abs # 10

TE&L CO
Abs # 2093
15-Jun-1858

TE&L CO
Abs # 365
16-Sep-1857
see also, Map 1

TE&L CO
Abs # 366
16-Sep-1857
see also, Map 1

TE&L CO
Abs # 373
17-Sep-1857
see also, Map 1

TE&L CO
Abs # 393
06-Oct-1857
see also, Map 10

TE&L CO
Abs # 394
06-Oct-1857
see also, Map 10

TE&L CO
Abs # 395
06-Oct-1857

TE&L CO
Abs # 396
07-Oct-1857

TE&L CO
Abs # 561

13-Jan-1858
see also, Maps 1, 2, 10

TE&L CO
Abs # 565
15-Jan-1858
see also, Map 10

TE&L CO
Abs # 566
15-Jan-1858

TE&L CO
Abs # 567
15-Jan-1858

TE&L CO
Abs # 568
15-Jan-1858

TE&L CO
Abs # 569
15-Jan-1858

TE&L CO
Abs # 570
15-Jan-1858

TE&L CO
Abs # 571
16-Jan-1858

TE&L CO
Abs # 572
16-Jan-1858
see also, Map 10

TE&L CO
Abs # 575
22-Jan-1858

TE&L CO
Abs # 576
22-Jan-1858

TE&L CO
Abs # 577
22-Jan-1858
see also, Map 10

TE&L CO
Abs # 585
25-Jan-1858
see also, Map 10

TE&L CO
Abs # 586
25-Jan-1858

TE&L CO
Abs # 587
25-Jan-1858

TE&L CO
Abs # 588
27-Jan-1858

TE&L CO
Abs # 589
27-Jan-1858
see also, Map 10

TE&L CO
Abs # 711
31-May-1858
see also, Maps 10, 17, 18

TE&L CO
Abs # 712
31-May-1858
see also, Map 17

TE&L CO
Abs # 713
31-May-1858
see also, Map 17

TE&L CO
Abs # 714
01-Jun-1858
see also, Map 17

TE&L CO
Abs # 777
12-Jun-1858
see also, Map 17

TE&L CO
Abs # 811
14-Jun-1858

see also, Map 17

TE&L CO
Abs # 812
14-Jun-1858
see also, Map 17

TE&L CO
Abs # 813
14-Jun-1858

TE&L CO
Abs # 814
14-Jun-1858

TE&L CO
Abs # 815
15-Jun-1858

TE&L CO
Abs # 816
15-Jun-1858

TE&L CO
Abs # 817
15-Jun-1858

TE&L CO
Abs # 818
17-Jun-1858

TE&L CO
Abs # 819
16-Jun-1858

TE&L CO
Abs # 820
14-Jun-1858

TE&L CO
Abs # ?11

TE&L CO
Abs # ?12

TE&L CO
Abs # ?14

TE&L CO
Abs # ?15

TE&L CO
Abs # ?17

TE&L CO
Abs # ?18
see also, Map 17

TIMMONS, A A
Abs # 2267
11-Sep-1906

TRYNDALE, W
Abs # 275
05-Feb-1862
see also, Map 1

WARD, G
Abs # 1551
19-Jul-1879

Abs # ?13

Abs # ?16

Populated Places
Padgett

Cemeteries
Padgett Cemetery
Reynolds Cemetery

Water (larger bodies)
None

Other Water
Boggy Creek
Brazos River
Rabbit Creek

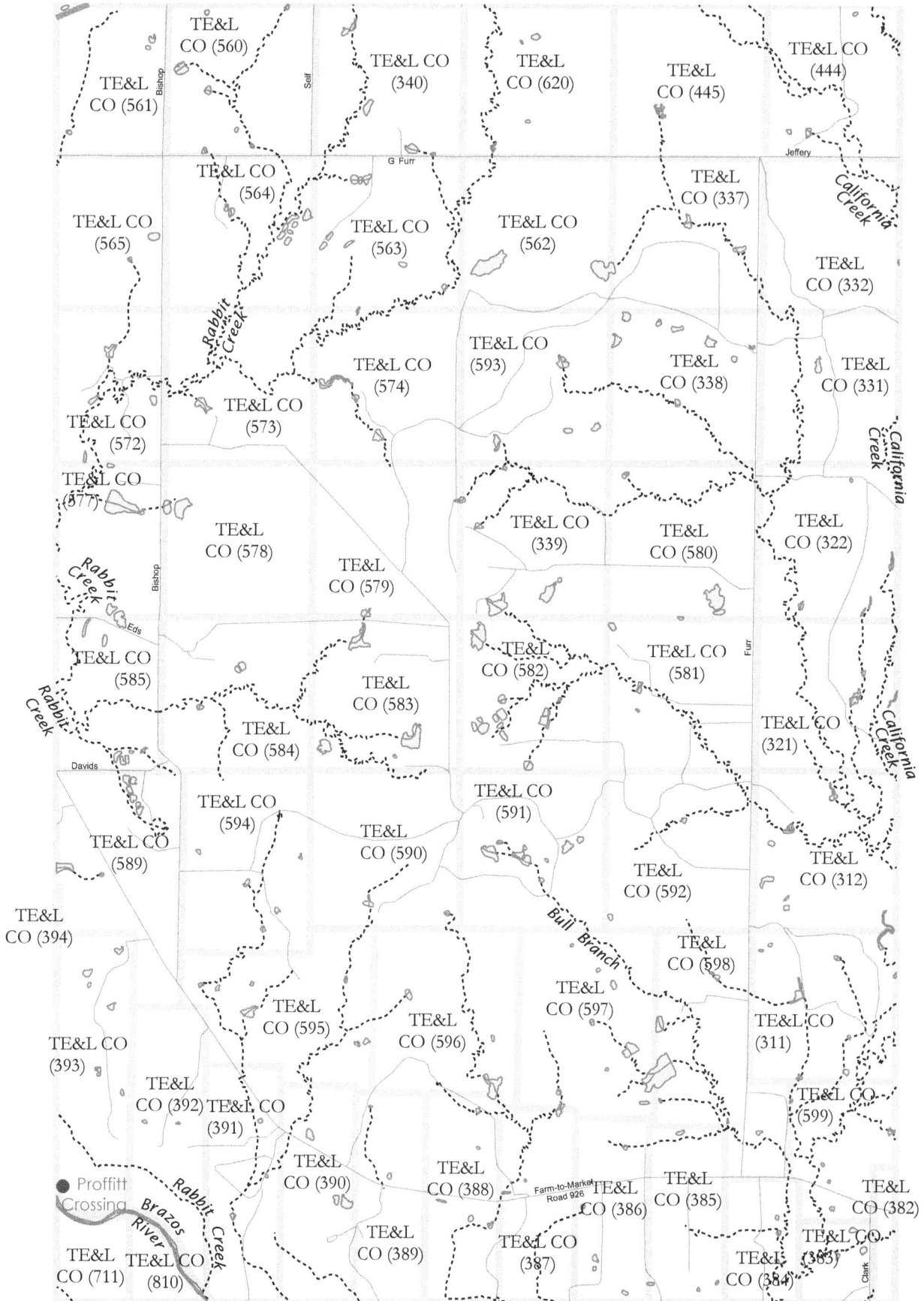

TE&L CO (560)

TE&L CO (561)

Bishop

Self

TE&L CO (340)

TE&L CO (620)

TE&L CO (445)

TE&L CO (444)

Jeffery

G Furr

TE&L CO (564)

TE&L CO (337)

California Creek

TE&L CO (565)

TE&L CO (563)

TE&L CO (562)

TE&L CO (332)

Rabbit Creek

TE&L CO (593)

TE&L CO (338)

TE&L CO (331)

California Creek

TE&L CO (574)

TE&L CO (572)

TE&L CO (573)

TE&L CO (577)

Bishop

TE&L CO (578)

TE&L CO (339)

TE&L CO (580)

TE&L CO (322)

California Creek

Rabbit Creek

TE&L CO (579)

Eds

TE&L CO (585)

TE&L CO (582)

TE&L CO (581)

Furr

TE&L CO (321)

California Creek

Rabbit Creek

TE&L CO (583)

TE&L CO (584)

Davids

TE&L CO (594)

TE&L CO (591)

TE&L CO (589)

TE&L CO (590)

TE&L CO (592)

TE&L CO (312)

TE&L CO (394)

Bull Branch

TE&L CO (598)

TE&L CO (597)

TE&L CO (595)

TE&L CO (596)

TE&L CO (311)

TE&L CO (393)

TE&L CO (392)

TE&L CO (391)

TE&L CO (599)

Proffitt Crossing

Rabbit Creek

Brazos River

TE&L CO (390)

TE&L CO (388)

Farm-to-Market Road 926

TE&L CO (386)

TE&L CO (385)

TE&L CO (382)

TE&L CO (711)

TE&L CO (810)

TE&L CO (389)

TE&L CO (387)

TE&L CO (384)

TE&L CO (383)

Clark

TE&L CO
Abs # 311
18-Aug-1857
see also, Map 11

TE&L CO
Abs # 312
18-Aug-1857
see also, Map 11

TE&L CO
Abs # 321
07-Sep-1857
see also, Map 11

TE&L CO
Abs # 322
07-Sep-1857
see also, Map 11

TE&L CO
Abs # 331
09-Sep-1857
see also, Map 11

TE&L CO
Abs # 332
09-Sep-1857
see also, Map 11

TE&L CO
Abs # 337
10-Sep-1857

TE&L CO
Abs # 338
10-Sep-1857

TE&L CO
Abs # 339
10-Sep-1857

TE&L CO
Abs # 340
11-Sep-1857
see also, Map 2

TE&L CO
Abs # 382
23-Sep-1857
see also, Maps 11, 18, 19

TE&L CO
Abs # 383
23-Sep-1857
see also, Map 18

TE&L CO
Abs # 384
24-Sep-1857
see also, Map 18

TE&L CO
Abs # 385
24-Sep-1857
see also, Map 18

TE&L CO
Abs # 386
24-Sep-1857
see also, Map 18

TE&L CO
Abs # 387
24-Sep-1857
see also, Map 18

TE&L CO
Abs # 388
24-Sep-1857
see also, Map 18

TE&L CO
Abs # 389
05-Oct-1857
see also, Map 18

TE&L CO
Abs # 390
05-Oct-1857
see also, Map 18

TE&L CO
Abs # 391
06-Oct-1857
see also, Map 18

TE&L CO
Abs # 392
06-Oct-1857

TE&L CO
Abs # 393
06-Oct-1857
see also, Map 9

TE&L CO
Abs # 394
06-Oct-1857
see also, Map 9

TE&L CO
Abs # 444
16-Nov-1857
see also, Maps 2, 3, 11

TE&L CO
Abs # 445
16-Nov-1857
see also, Map 2

TE&L CO
Abs # 560
13-Jan-1858
see also, Map 2

TE&L CO
Abs # 561
13-Jan-1858
see also, Maps 1, 2, 9

TE&L CO
Abs # 562
13-Jan-1858

TE&L CO
Abs # 563
14-Jan-1858

TE&L CO
Abs # 564
15-Jan-1858

TE&L CO
Abs # 565
15-Jan-1858
see also, Map 9

TE&L CO
Abs # 572
16-Jan-1858
see also, Map 9

TE&L CO
Abs # 573
22-Jan-1858

TE&L CO
Abs # 574
22-Jan-1858

TE&L CO
Abs # 577
22-Jan-1858
see also, Map 9

TE&L CO
Abs # 578
22-Jan-1858

TE&L CO
Abs # 579
22-Jan-1858

TE&L CO
Abs # 580
23-Jan-1858

TE&L CO
Abs # 581
25-Jan-1858

TE&L CO
Abs # 582
23-Jan-1858

TE&L CO
Abs # 583
25-Jan-1858

TE&L CO
Abs # 584
25-Jan-1858

TE&L CO
Abs # 585
25-Jan-1858
see also, Map 9

TE&L CO
Abs # 589

27-Jan-1858
see also, Map 9

TE&L CO
Abs # 590
27-Jan-1858

TE&L CO
Abs # 591
27-Jan-1858

TE&L CO
Abs # 592
28-Jan-1858

TE&L CO
Abs # 593
28-Jan-1858

TE&L CO
Abs # 594
28-Jan-1858

TE&L CO
Abs # 595
28-Jan-1858

TE&L CO
Abs # 596
28-Jan-1858

TE&L CO
Abs # 597
28-Jan-1858

TE&L CO
Abs # 598
19-Feb-1858

TE&L CO
Abs # 599
19-Feb-1858
see also, Map 11

TE&L CO
Abs # 620
22-Mar-1858
see also, Map 2

TE&L CO
Abs # 711
31-May-1858
see also, Maps 9, 17, 18

TE&L CO
Abs # 810
31-May-1858
see also, Map 18

Populated Places
Proffitt Crossing

Cemeteries
None

Water (larger bodies)
None

Other Water
Brazos River
Bull Branch
California Creek
Rabbit Creek

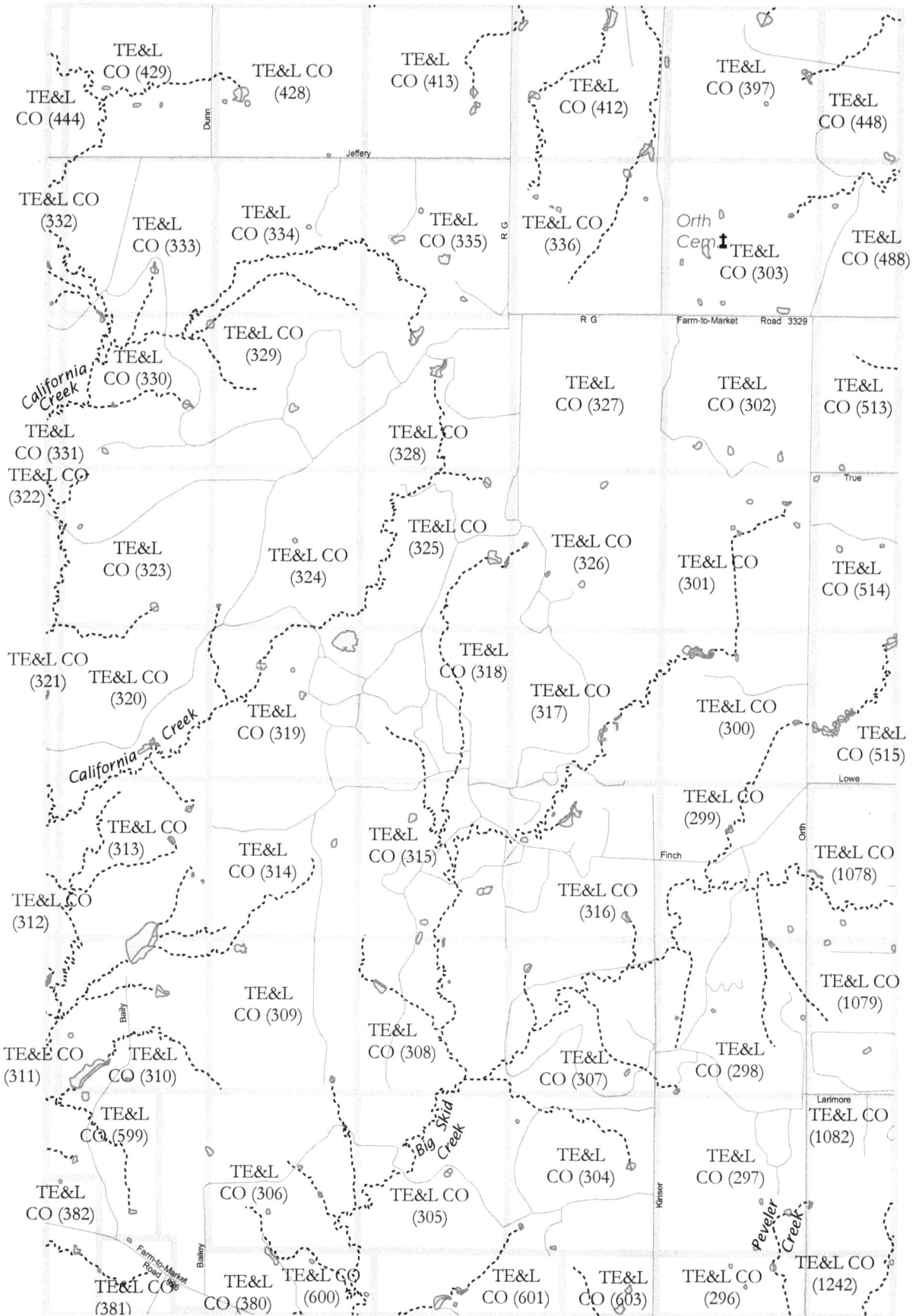

TE&L CO (429)

TE&L CO (428)

TE&L CO (413)

TE&L CO (412)

TE&L CO (397)

TE&L CO (444)

TE&L CO (448)

Dunn

Jeffery

TE&L CO (332)

TE&L CO (333)

TE&L CO (334)

TE&L CO (335)

R G

TE&L CO (336)

Orth Cem.

TE&L CO (303)

TE&L CO (488)

R G

Farm-to-Market Road 3329

TE&L CO (329)

TE&L CO (330)

California Creek

TE&L CO (327)

TE&L CO (302)

TE&L CO (513)

TE&L CO (331)

TE&L CO (328)

True

TE&L CO (322)

TE&L CO (323)

TE&L CO (324)

TE&L CO (325)

TE&L CO (326)

TE&L CO (301)

TE&L CO (514)

TE&L CO (321)

TE&L CO (320)

TE&L CO (319)

California Creek

TE&L CO (318)

TE&L CO (317)

TE&L CO (300)

TE&L CO (515)

Lowe

TE&L CO (313)

TE&L CO (314)

TE&L CO (315)

TE&L CO (299)

Finch

Orth

TE&L CO (1078)

TE&L CO (312)

TE&L CO (316)

TE&L CO (309)

TE&L CO (1079)

Baily

TE&L CO (311)

TE&L CO (310)

TE&L CO (308)

TE&L CO (307)

TE&L CO (298)

Larimore

TE&L CO (1082)

TE&L CO (599)

TE&L CO (382)

Big Skid Creek

TE&L CO (304)

TE&L CO (297)

Kinser

Peveler Creek

Farm-to-Market Road

Bailey

TE&L CO (306)

TE&L CO (305)

TE&L CO (296)

TE&L CO (1242)

TE&L CO (381)

TE&L CO (380)

TE&L CO (600)

TE&L CO (601)

TE&L CO (603)

TE&L CO
Abs # 1078
04-Oct-1858
see also, Map 12

TE&L CO
Abs # 1079
04-Oct-1858
see also, Map 12

TE&L CO
Abs # 1082
04-Oct-1858
see also, Map 12

TE&L CO
Abs # 1242
11-Jan-1858
see also, Maps 12, 19, 20

TE&L CO
Abs # 296
15-Aug-1857
see also, Map 19

TE&L CO
Abs # 297
15-Aug-1857

TE&L CO
Abs # 298
15-Aug-1857

TE&L CO
Abs # 299
15-Aug-1857

TE&L CO
Abs # 300
17-Aug-1857

TE&L CO
Abs # 301
17-Aug-1857

TE&L CO
Abs # 302
17-Aug-1857

TE&L CO
Abs # 303
17-Aug-1857

TE&L CO
Abs # 304
17-Aug-1857

TE&L CO
Abs # 305
17-Aug-1857

TE&L CO
Abs # 306
17-Aug-1857

TE&L CO
Abs # 307
18-Aug-1857

TE&L CO
Abs # 308
18-Aug-1857

TE&L CO
Abs # 309
18-Aug-1857

TE&L CO
Abs # 310
18-Aug-1857

TE&L CO
Abs # 311
18-Aug-1857
see also, Map 10

TE&L CO
Abs # 312
18-Aug-1857
see also, Map 10

TE&L CO
Abs # 313
19-Aug-1857

TE&L CO
Abs # 314
25-Aug-1857

TE&L CO

TE&L CO
Abs # 315
19-Aug-1857

TE&L CO
Abs # 316
25-Aug-1857

TE&L CO
Abs # 317
07-Sep-1857

TE&L CO
Abs # 318
07-Sep-1857

TE&L CO
Abs # 319
07-Sep-1857

TE&L CO
Abs # 320
07-Sep-1857

TE&L CO
Abs # 321
07-Sep-1857
see also, Map 10

TE&L CO
Abs # 322
07-Sep-1857
see also, Map 10

TE&L CO
Abs # 323
07-Sep-1857

TE&L CO
Abs # 324
07-Sep-1857

TE&L CO
Abs # 325
07-Sep-1857

TE&L CO
Abs # 326
08-Sep-1857

TE&L CO
Abs # 327
08-Sep-1857

TE&L CO
Abs # 328
09-Sep-1857

TE&L CO
Abs # 329
09-Sep-1857

TE&L CO
Abs # 330
09-Sep-1857

TE&L CO
Abs # 331
09-Sep-1857
see also, Map 10

TE&L CO
Abs # 332
09-Sep-1857
see also, Map 10

TE&L CO
Abs # 333
09-Sep-1857

TE&L CO
Abs # 334
09-Sep-1857

TE&L CO
Abs # 335
09-Sep-1857

TE&L CO
Abs # 336
10-Sep-1857

TE&L CO
Abs # 380
23-Sep-1857
see also, Map 19

TE&L CO
Abs # 381
23-Sep-1857
see also, Map 19

TE&L CO
Abs # 382
23-Sep-1857
see also, Maps 10, 18, 19

TE&L CO
Abs # 397
26-Oct-1857
see also, Map 3

TE&L CO
Abs # 412
28-Oct-1857
see also, Map 3

TE&L CO
Abs # 413
28-Oct-1857
see also, Map 3

TE&L CO
Abs # 428
11-Nov-1857
see also, Map 3

TE&L CO
Abs # 429
11-Nov-1857
see also, Map 3

TE&L CO
Abs # 444
16-Nov-1857
see also, Maps 2, 3, 10

TE&L CO
Abs # 448
19-Nov-1857
see also, Maps 3, 4, 12

TE&L CO
Abs # 488
02-Dec-1857
see also, Map 12

TE&L CO
Abs # 513
15-Dec-1857
see also, Map 12

TE&L CO
Abs # 514
15-Dec-1857
see also, Map 12

TE&L CO
Abs # 515
15-Dec-1857
see also, Map 12

TE&L CO
Abs # 599
19-Feb-1858
see also, Map 10

TE&L CO
Abs # 600
19-Feb-1858
see also, Map 19

TE&L CO
Abs # 601
19-Feb-1858
see also, Map 19

TE&L CO
Abs # 603
20-Feb-1858
see also, Map 19

Populated Places
None

Cemeteries
Orth Cemetery

Water (larger bodies)
None

Other Water
Big Skid Creek
California Creek
Peveler Creek

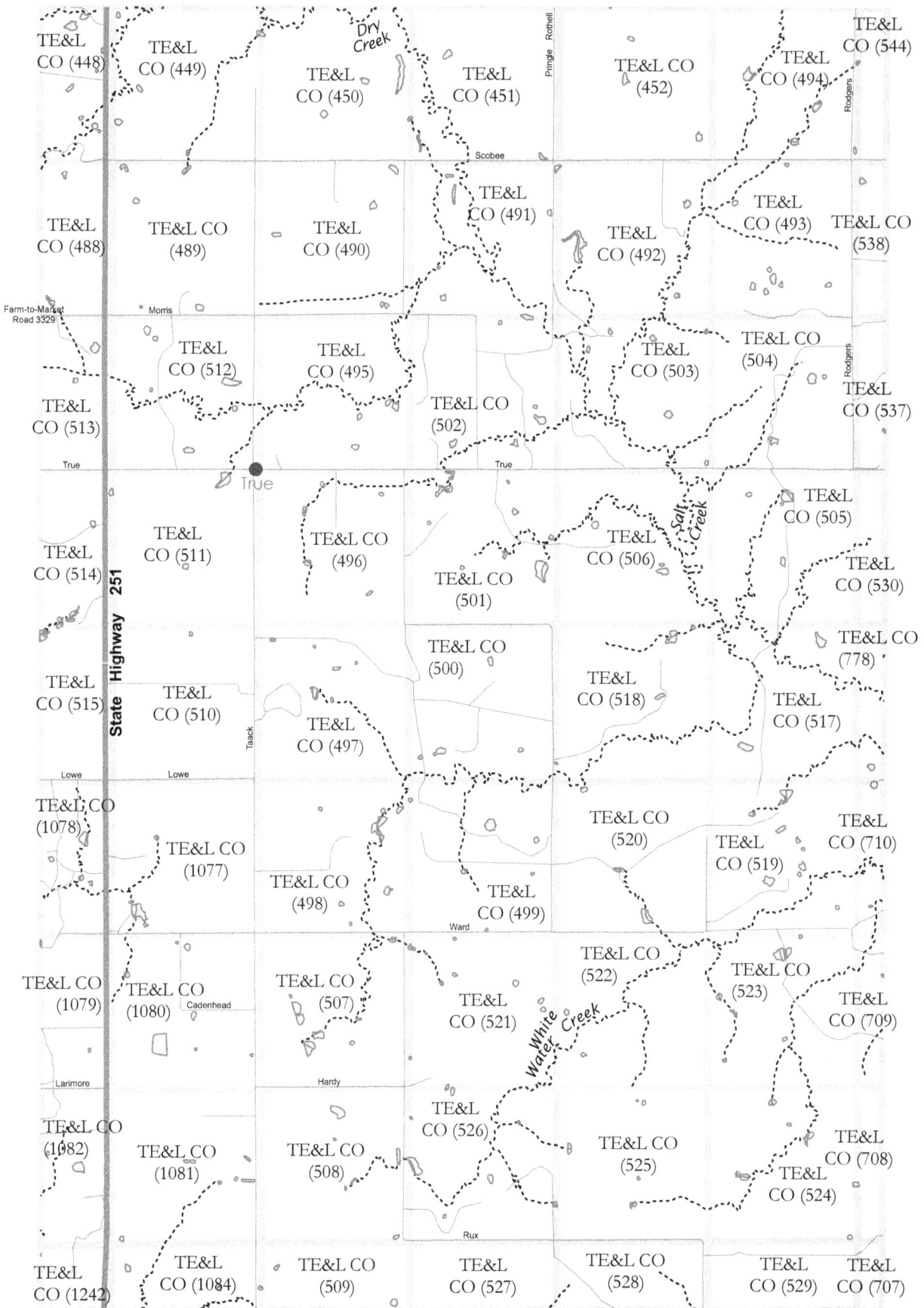

TE&L CO (448)

TE&L CO (449)

Dry Creek

TE&L CO (450)

TE&L CO (451)

Pringle Rothell

TE&L CO (452)

TE&L CO (494)

TE&L CO (544)

Rodgers

Scobee

TE&L CO (488)

TE&L CO (489)

TE&L CO (490)

TE&L CO (491)

TE&L CO (492)

TE&L CO (493)

TE&L CO (538)

Farm-to-Market Road 3329

Morris

TE&L CO (512)

TE&L CO (495)

TE&L CO (503)

TE&L CO (504)

Rodgers

TE&L CO (513)

TE&L CO (502)

TE&L CO (537)

True

True

True

TE&L CO (505)

Salt Creek

TE&L CO (514)

State Highway 251

TE&L CO (511)

TE&L CO (496)

TE&L CO (506)

TE&L CO (530)

TE&L CO (501)

TE&L CO (500)

TE&L CO (778)

TE&L CO (515)

TE&L CO (510)

Taack

TE&L CO (497)

TE&L CO (518)

TE&L CO (517)

Lowe

Lowe

TE&L CO (1078)

TE&L CO (1077)

TE&L CO (520)

TE&L CO (519)

TE&L CO (710)

TE&L CO (498)

TE&L CO (499)

Ward

TE&L CO (1079)

TE&L CO (1080)

Cadenhead

TE&L CO (507)

TE&L CO (521)

TE&L CO (522)

TE&L CO (523)

White Water Creek

TE&L CO (709)

Larimore

Hardy

TE&L CO (1082)

TE&L CO (1081)

TE&L CO (508)

TE&L CO (526)

TE&L CO (525)

TE&L CO (524)

TE&L CO (708)

Rux

TE&L CO (1242)

TE&L CO (1084)

TE&L CO (509)

TE&L CO (527)

TE&L CO (528)

TE&L CO (529)

TE&L CO (707)

TE&L CO
Abs # 1077
04-Oct-1858

TE&L CO
Abs # 1078
04-Oct-1858
see also, Map 11

TE&L CO
Abs # 1079
04-Oct-1858
see also, Map 11

TE&L CO
Abs # 1080
04-Oct-1858

TE&L CO
Abs # 1081
04-Oct-1858

TE&L CO
Abs # 1082
04-Oct-1858
see also, Map 11

TE&L CO
Abs # 1084
18-Mar-1858
see also, Map 20

TE&L CO
Abs # 1242
11-Jan-1858
see also, Maps 11, 19, 20

TE&L CO
Abs # 448
19-Nov-1857
see also, Maps 3, 4, 11

TE&L CO
Abs # 449
19-Nov-1857
see also, Map 4

TE&L CO
Abs # 450
19-Nov-1857
see also, Map 4

TE&L CO
Abs # 451
28-Sep-1953
see also, Map 4

TE&L CO
Abs # 452
23-Nov-1857
see also, Map 4

TE&L CO
Abs # 488
02-Dec-1857
see also, Map 11

TE&L CO
Abs # 489
02-Dec-1857

TE&L CO
Abs # 490
03-Dec-1857

TE&L CO
Abs # 491
03-Dec-1857

TE&L CO
Abs # 492
03-Dec-1857

TE&L CO
Abs # 493
03-Dec-1857

TE&L CO
Abs # 494
03-Dec-1857
see also, Map 4

TE&L CO
Abs # 495
03-Dec-1857

TE&L CO
Abs # 496
04-Dec-1857

TE&L CO
Abs # 497
04-Dec-1857

TE&L CO
Abs # 498
04-Dec-1857

TE&L CO
Abs # 499
04-Dec-1857

TE&L CO
Abs # 500
04-Dec-1857

TE&L CO
Abs # 501
04-Dec-1857

TE&L CO
Abs # 502
07-Dec-1857

TE&L CO
Abs # 503
09-Dec-1857

TE&L CO
Abs # 504
09-Dec-1857

TE&L CO
Abs # 505
10-Dec-1857

TE&L CO
Abs # 506
10-Dec-1857

TE&L CO
Abs # 507
10-Dec-1857

TE&L CO
Abs # 508
11-Dec-1857

TE&L CO
Abs # 509
12-Dec-1857
see also, Map 20

TE&L CO
Abs # 510
12-Dec-1857

TE&L CO
Abs # 511
12-Dec-1857

TE&L CO
Abs # 512
12-Dec-1857

TE&L CO
Abs # 513
15-Dec-1857
see also, Map 11

TE&L CO
Abs # 514
15-Dec-1857
see also, Map 11

TE&L CO
Abs # 515
15-Dec-1857
see also, Map 11

TE&L CO
Abs # 517
15-Dec-1857

TE&L CO
Abs # 518
17-Dec-1857

TE&L CO
Abs # 519
27-May-1858

TE&L CO
Abs # 520
17-Dec-1857

TE&L CO
Abs # 521
17-Dec-1857

TE&L CO
Abs # 522
17-Dec-1857

TE&L CO
Abs # 523
18-Dec-1857

TE&L CO
Abs # 524
18-Dec-1857

TE&L CO
Abs # 525
19-Dec-1857

TE&L CO
Abs # 526
19-Dec-1857

TE&L CO
Abs # 527
03-Apr-1858
see also, Map 20

TE&L CO
Abs # 528
05-Apr-1858
see also, Map 20

TE&L CO
Abs # 529
29-Dec-1857
see also, Map 20

TE&L CO
Abs # 530
29-Dec-1857
see also, Map 13

TE&L CO
Abs # 537
31-Dec-1857
see also, Map 13

TE&L CO
Abs # 538
31-Dec-1857
see also, Map 13

TE&L CO
Abs # 544
02-Jan-1858
see also, Maps 4, 5, 13

TE&L CO
Abs # 707
12-May-1858
see also, Maps 13, 20, 21

TE&L CO
Abs # 708
13-May-1858
see also, Map 13

TE&L CO
Abs # 709
13-May-1858
see also, Map 13

TE&L CO
Abs # 710
13-May-1858
see also, Map 13

TE&L CO
Abs # 778
13-May-1858
see also, Map 13

Populated Places
True

Cemeteries
None

Water (larger bodies)
None

Other Water
Dry Creek
Salt Creek
White Water Creek

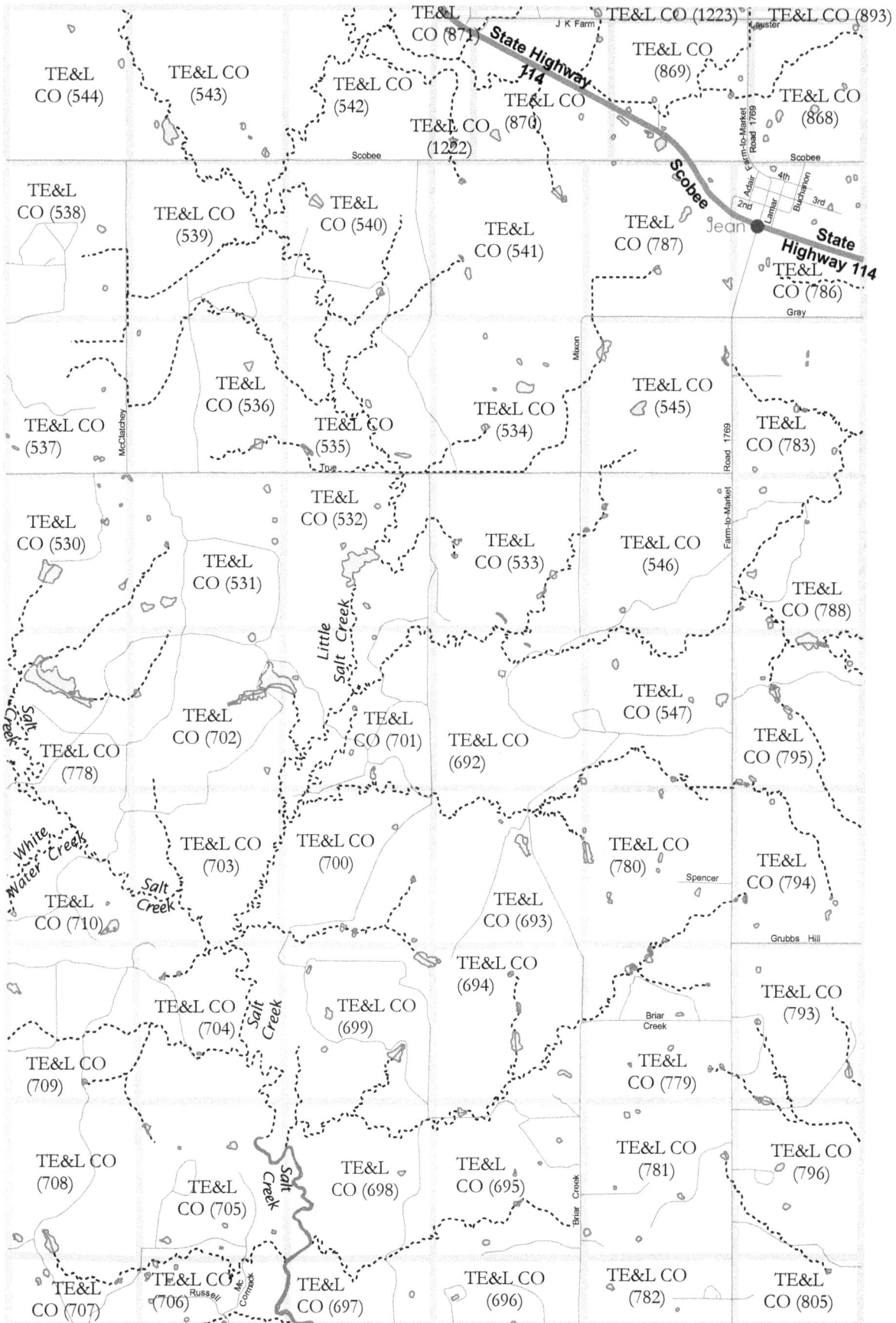

TE&L CO (544)

TE&L CO (543)

TE&L CO (542)

TE&L CO (871)

State Highway 114

J K Farm

TE&L CO (1223)

Lawster

TE&L CO (893)

TE&L CO (869)

TE&L CO (870)

TE&L CO (1222)

TE&L CO (868)

Scobee

Scobee

TE&L CO (538)

TE&L CO (539)

TE&L CO (540)

TE&L CO (541)

TE&L CO (787)

Jean

Scobee

4th

Buchanan

Adair

2nd

Lamar

3rd

Farm-to-Market Road 1769

State Highway 114

TE&L CO (786)

Gray

TE&L CO (536)

TE&L CO (537)

McClatchey

TE&L CO (535)

Tice

TE&L CO (534)

Mixon

TE&L CO (545)

Road 1769

TE&L CO (783)

TE&L CO (530)

TE&L CO (531)

TE&L CO (532)

TE&L CO (533)

Little Salt Creek

TE&L CO (546)

Farm-to-Market

TE&L CO (788)

TE&L CO (778)

Salt Creek

TE&L CO (702)

TE&L CO (701)

TE&L CO (692)

TE&L CO (547)

TE&L CO (795)

White Water Creek

TE&L CO (710)

Salt Creek

TE&L CO (703)

TE&L CO (700)

TE&L CO (693)

TE&L CO (780)

Spencer

TE&L CO (794)

Grubbs Hill

TE&L CO (704)

Salt Creek

TE&L CO (699)

TE&L CO (694)

Briar Creek

TE&L CO (793)

TE&L CO (709)

TE&L CO (779)

TE&L CO (708)

TE&L CO (705)

Salt Creek

TE&L CO (698)

TE&L CO (695)

Briar Creek

TE&L CO (781)

TE&L CO (796)

TE&L CO (707)

TE&L CO (706)

Russell

Mc Cormack

TE&L CO (697)

TE&L CO (696)

TE&L CO (782)

TE&L CO (805)

TE&L CO
Abs # 1222
07-Mar-1859

TE&L CO
Abs # 1223
08-Mar-1859
see also, Map 5

TE&L CO
Abs # 530
29-Dec-1857
see also, Map 12

TE&L CO
Abs # 531
29-Dec-1857

TE&L CO
Abs # 532
30-Dec-1857

TE&L CO
Abs # 533
31-Dec-1857

TE&L CO
Abs # 534
31-Dec-1857

TE&L CO
Abs # 535
31-Dec-1857

TE&L CO
Abs # 536
31-Dec-1857

TE&L CO
Abs # 537
31-Dec-1857
see also, Map 12

TE&L CO
Abs # 538
31-Dec-1857
see also, Map 12

TE&L CO
Abs # 539
31-Dec-1857

TE&L CO
Abs # 540
01-Jan-1858

TE&L CO
Abs # 541
02-Jan-1858

TE&L CO
Abs # 542
02-Jan-1858
see also, Map 5

TE&L CO
Abs # 543
02-Jan-1858
see also, Map 5

TE&L CO
Abs # 544
02-Jan-1858
see also, Maps 4, 5, 12

TE&L CO
Abs # 545
02-Jan-1858

TE&L CO
Abs # 546
04-Jan-1858

TE&L CO
Abs # 547
04-Jan-1858

TE&L CO
Abs # 692
10-May-1858

TE&L CO
Abs # 693
10-May-1858

TE&L CO
Abs # 694
10-May-1858

TE&L CO

Abs # 695
10-May-1858

TE&L CO
Abs # 696
10-May-1858
see also, Map 21

TE&L CO
Abs # 697
11-May-1858
see also, Map 21

TE&L CO
Abs # 698
11-May-1858

TE&L CO
Abs # 699
11-May-1858

TE&L CO
Abs # 700
11-May-1858

TE&L CO
Abs # 701
28-May-1858

TE&L CO
Abs # 702
11-May-1858

TE&L CO
Abs # 703
12-May-1858

TE&L CO
Abs # 704
12-May-1858

TE&L CO
Abs # 705
12-May-1858

TE&L CO
Abs # 706
12-May-1858
see also, Map 21

TE&L CO
Abs # 707
12-May-1858
see also, Maps 12, 20, 21

TE&L CO
Abs # 708
13-May-1858
see also, Map 12

TE&L CO
Abs # 709
13-May-1858
see also, Map 12

TE&L CO
Abs # 710
13-May-1858
see also, Map 12

TE&L CO
Abs # 778
13-May-1858
see also, Map 12

TE&L CO
Abs # 779
13-May-1858

TE&L CO
Abs # 780
13-May-1858

TE&L CO
Abs # 781
13-May-1858

TE&L CO
Abs # 782
13-May-1858
see also, Map 21

TE&L CO
Abs # 783
14-May-1858
see also, Map 14

TE&L CO
Abs # 786
14-May-1858

see also, Map 14

TE&L CO
Abs # 787
14-May-1858

TE&L CO
Abs # 788
14-May-1858
see also, Map 14

TE&L CO
Abs # 793
15-May-1858
see also, Map 14

TE&L CO
Abs # 794
17-May-1858
see also, Map 14

TE&L CO
Abs # 795
17-May-1858
see also, Map 14

TE&L CO
Abs # 796
17-May-1858
see also, Map 14

TE&L CO
Abs # 805
18-May-1858
see also, Maps 14, 21, 22

TE&L CO
Abs # 868
24-Jan-1859
see also, Map 14

TE&L CO
Abs # 869
25-Jan-1859

TE&L CO
Abs # 870
17-Jan-1859

TE&L CO
Abs # 871
17-Jan-1859
see also, Map 5

TE&L CO
Abs # 893
19-Jan-1859
see also, Maps 5, 6, 14

<u>Populated Places</u>
Jean

<u>Cemeteries</u>
None

<u>Water</u> (larger bodies)
None

<u>Other Water</u>
Little Salt Creek
Salt Creek
White Water Creek

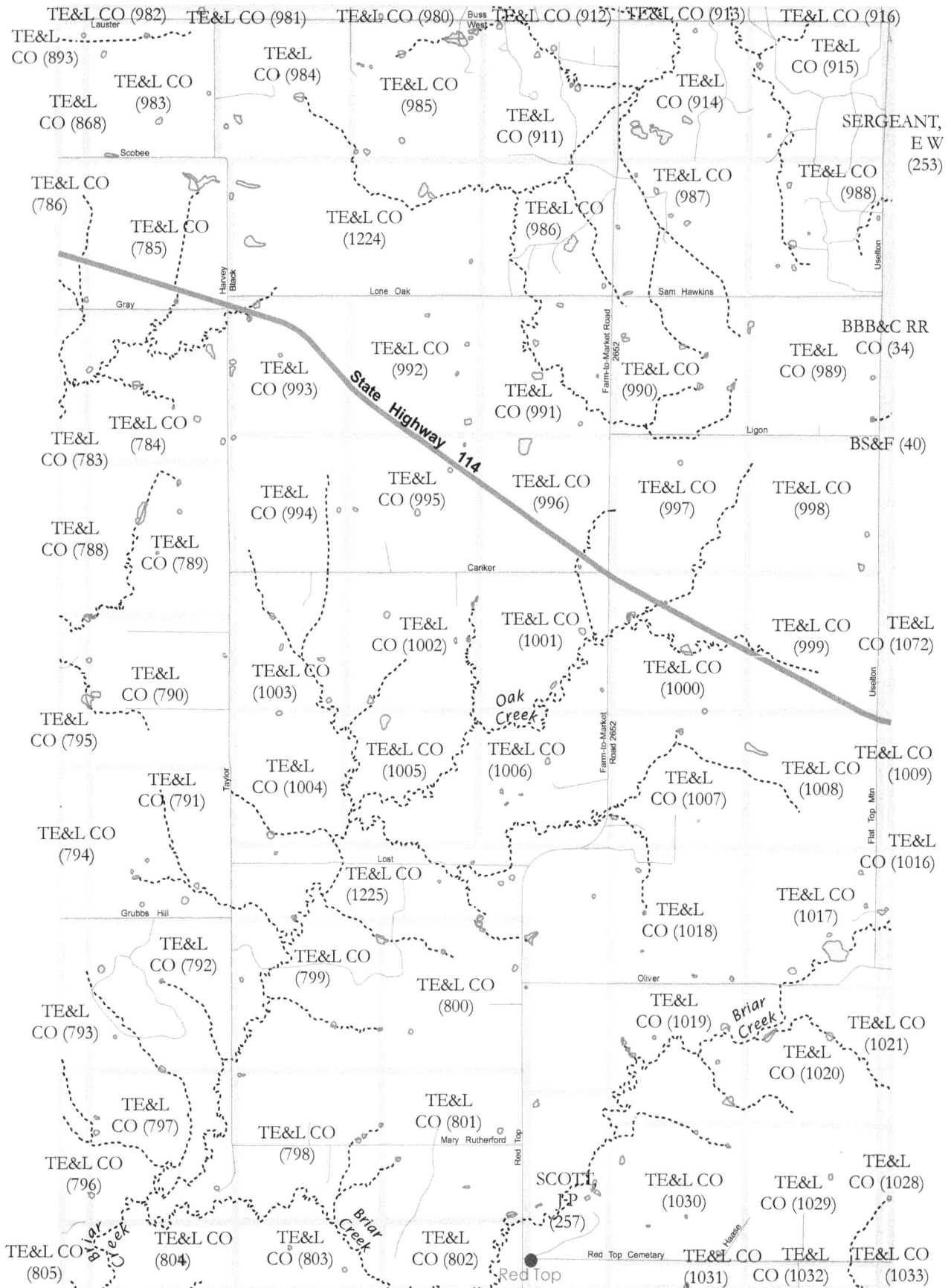

TE&L CO (982)
Lauster
TE&L CO (981)
TE&L CO (980)
Buss West
TE&L CO (912)
TE&L CO (913)
TE&L CO (916)

TE&L CO (893)

TE&L CO (984)

TE&L CO (985)

TE&L CO (911)

TE&L CO (914)

TE&L CO (915)

TE&L CO (983)

TE&L CO (868)

SERGEANT, E W (253)

Scobee

TE&L CO (786)

TE&L CO (785)

TE&L CO (1224)

TE&L CO (986)

TE&L CO (987)

TE&L CO (988)

Uselton

Harvey Black

Gray

Lone Oak

Sam Hawkins

TE&L CO (783)

TE&L CO (784)

TE&L CO (993)

TE&L CO (992)

TE&L CO (991)

Farm-to-Market Road 2652

TE&L CO (990)

TE&L CO (989)

BBB&C RR CO (34)

Ligon

BS&F (40)

TE&L CO (788)

TE&L CO (789)

TE&L CO (994)

TE&L CO (995)

TE&L CO (996)

TE&L CO (997)

TE&L CO (998)

State Highway 114

Cariker

TE&L CO (795)

TE&L CO (790)

TE&L CO (1003)

TE&L CO (1002)

TE&L CO (1001)

TE&L CO (1000)

TE&L CO (999)

TE&L CO (1072)

Oak Creek

Uselton

TE&L CO (791)

Taylor

TE&L CO (1004)

TE&L CO (1005)

TE&L CO (1006)

Farm-to-Market Road 2652

TE&L CO (1007)

TE&L CO (1008)

TE&L CO (1009)

TE&L CO (794)

Lost

Flat Top Mtn

TE&L CO (1016)

TE&L CO (1225)

TE&L CO (1018)

TE&L CO (1017)

Grubbs Hill

TE&L CO (792)

TE&L CO (799)

TE&L CO (800)

Oliver

TE&L CO (1019)

Briar Creek

TE&L CO (1021)

TE&L CO (793)

TE&L CO (1020)

TE&L CO (797)

TE&L CO (801)

TE&L CO (1030)

TE&L CO (1029)

TE&L CO (1028)

TE&L CO (798)

Mary Rutherford

Red Top

SCOTT, J P (257)

TE&L CO (796)

Briar Creek

TE&L CO (804)

TE&L CO (803)

TE&L CO (802)

Red Top Cemetary

Hasse

TE&L CO (1031)

TE&L CO (1032)

TE&L CO (1033)

TE&L CO (805)

Briar Creek

Red Top

BBB&C RR CO
Abs # 34
21-Oct-1873
see also, Map 15

BS&F
Abs # 40
07-Jul-1875
see also, Map 15

SCOTT, J P
Abs # 257
08-Jun-1860
see also, Map 22

SERGEANT, E W
Abs # 253
01-Jun-1859
see also, Maps 6, 7, 15

TE&L CO
Abs # 1000
28-Jan-1859

TE&L CO
Abs # 1001
28-Jan-1859

TE&L CO
Abs # 1002
28-Jan-1859

TE&L CO
Abs # 1003
29-Jan-1859

TE&L CO
Abs # 1004
29-Jan-1859

TE&L CO
Abs # 1005
29-Jan-1859

TE&L CO
Abs # 1006
29-Jan-1859

TE&L CO
Abs # 1007
29-Jan-1859

TE&L CO
Abs # 1008
29-Jan-1859

TE&L CO
Abs # 1009
29-Jan-1859
see also, Map 15

TE&L CO
Abs # 1016
31-Jan-1859
see also, Map 15

TE&L CO
Abs # 1017
31-Jan-1859

TE&L CO
Abs # 1018
31-Jan-1859

TE&L CO
Abs # 1019
31-Jan-1859

TE&L CO
Abs # 1020
31-Jan-1859

TE&L CO
Abs # 1021
31-Jan-1859
see also, Map 15

TE&L CO
Abs # 1028
01-Feb-1859
see also, Map 15

TE&L CO
Abs # 1029
01-Feb-1859

TE&L CO
Abs # 1030
01-Feb-1859

TE&L CO
Abs # 1031
01-Feb-1859
see also, Map 22

TE&L CO
Abs # 1032
01-Feb-1859
see also, Map 22

TE&L CO
Abs # 1033
01-Feb-1859
see also, Maps 15, 22, 23

TE&L CO
Abs # 1072
14-Feb-1859
see also, Map 15

TE&L CO
Abs # 1224
08-Mar-1859

TE&L CO
Abs # 1225
08-Mar-1859

TE&L CO
Abs # 783
14-May-1858
see also, Map 13

TE&L CO
Abs # 784
14-May-1858

TE&L CO
Abs # 785
14-May-1858

TE&L CO
Abs # 786
14-May-1858
see also, Map 13

TE&L CO
Abs # 788
14-May-1858
see also, Map 13

TE&L CO
Abs # 789
15-May-1858

TE&L CO
Abs # 790
15-May-1858

TE&L CO
Abs # 791
15-Apr-1858

TE&L CO
Abs # 792
15-Apr-1858

TE&L CO
Abs # 793
15-May-1858
see also, Map 13

TE&L CO
Abs # 794
17-May-1858
see also, Map 13

TE&L CO
Abs # 795
17-May-1858
see also, Map 13

TE&L CO
Abs # 796
17-May-1858
see also, Map 13

TE&L CO
Abs # 797
17-May-1858

TE&L CO
Abs # 798
17-May-1858

TE&L CO
Abs # 799
17-May-1858

TE&L CO

TE&L CO
Abs # 800
17-May-1858

TE&L CO
Abs # 801
17-May-1858

TE&L CO
Abs # 802
18-May-1858
see also, Map 22

TE&L CO
Abs # 803
18-May-1858
see also, Map 22

TE&L CO
Abs # 804
21-Sep-1857
see also, Map 22

TE&L CO
Abs # 805
18-May-1858
see also, Maps 13, 21, 22

TE&L CO
Abs # 868
24-Jan-1859
see also, Map 13

TE&L CO
Abs # 893
19-Jan-1859
see also, Maps 5, 6, 13

TE&L CO
Abs # 911
17-Jan-1859

TE&L CO
Abs # 912
18-Jan-1859
see also, Map 6

TE&L CO
Abs # 913
18-Jan-1859
see also, Map 6

TE&L CO
Abs # 914
18-Jan-1859

TE&L CO
Abs # 915
18-Jan-1859

TE&L CO
Abs # 916
18-Jan-1859
see also, Map 6

TE&L CO
Abs # 980
27-Jan-1859
see also, Map 6

TE&L CO
Abs # 981
27-Jan-1859
see also, Map 6

TE&L CO
Abs # 982
28-Jan-1859
see also, Map 6

TE&L CO
Abs # 983
28-Jan-1859

TE&L CO
Abs # 984
28-Jan-1859

TE&L CO
Abs # 985
28-Jan-1859

TE&L CO
Abs # 986
28-Jan-1859

TE&L CO
Abs # 987
28-Jan-1859

TE&L CO

TE&L CO
Abs # 988
26-Jan-1859

TE&L CO
Abs # 989
26-Jan-1859

TE&L CO
Abs # 990
26-Jan-1859

TE&L CO
Abs # 991
26-Jan-1859

TE&L CO
Abs # 992
26-Jan-1859

TE&L CO
Abs # 993
26-Jan-1859

TE&L CO
Abs # 994
27-Jan-1859

TE&L CO
Abs # 995
27-Jan-1859

TE&L CO
Abs # 996
28-Jan-1859

TE&L CO
Abs # 997
28-Jan-1859

TE&L CO
Abs # 998
28-Jan-1859

TE&L CO
Abs # 999
28-Jan-1859

Populated Places
Red Top

Cemeteries
None

Water (larger bodies)
None

Other Water
Briar Creek
Oak Creek

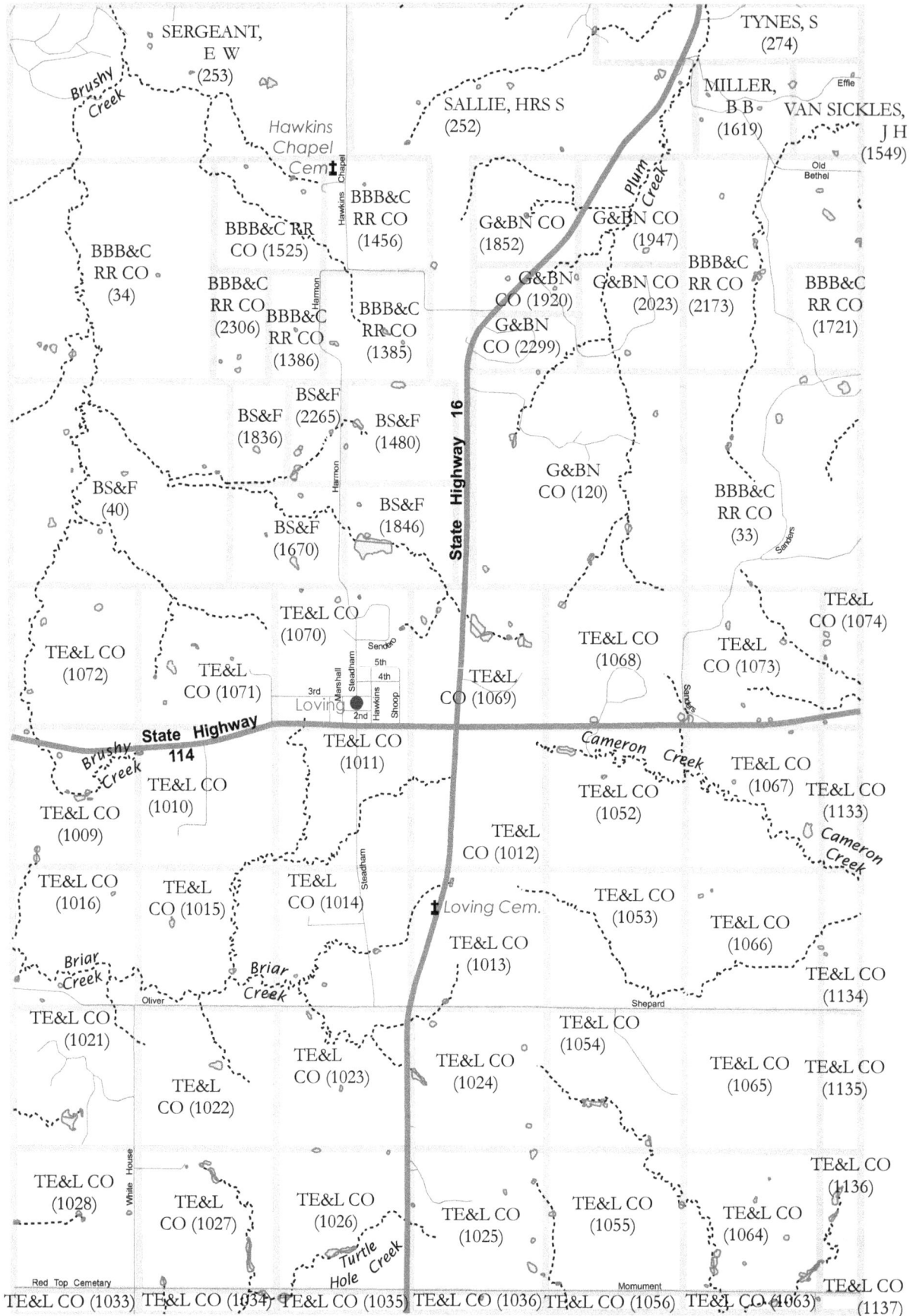

SERGEANT,
E W
(253)

Brushy Creek

Hawkins Chapel Cem

TYNES, S
(274)

MILLER,
B B
(1619)

VAN SICKLES,
J H
(1549)

Effie

SALLIE, HRS S
(252)

Old Bethel

BBB&C
RR CO
(1456)

BBB&C RR
CO (1525)

Plum Creek

G&BN CO
(1852)

G&BN CO
(1947)

BBB&C
RR CO
(34)

BBB&C
RR CO
(2306)

BBB&C
RR CO
(1386)

BBB&C
RR CO
(1385)

G&BN
CO (1920)

G&BN CO
(2023)

BBB&C
RR CO
(2173)

BBB&C
RR CO
(1721)

G&BN
CO (2299)

BS&F
(2265)

BS&F
(1836)

BS&F
(1480)

G&BN
CO (120)

BBB&C
RR CO
(33)

BS&F
(40)

BS&F
(1670)

BS&F
(1846)

Sanders

TE&L CO
(1070)

Sendero

TE&L
CO (1074)

TE&L CO
(1072)

TE&L
CO (1071)

Steadham
Marshall

3rd
5th
4th

Loving
2nd

Hawkins
Shoop

TE&L
CO (1069)

TE&L CO
(1068)

TE&L
CO (1073)

Sanders

State Highway 16

Brushy Creek

State Highway 114

TE&L CO
(1009)

TE&L CO
(1010)

TE&L CO
(1011)

Cameron Creek

TE&L CO
(1052)

TE&L CO
(1067)

TE&L CO
(1133)

Cameron Creek

TE&L CO
(1016)

TE&L
CO (1015)

TE&L
CO (1014)

Steadham

TE&L
CO (1012)

Loving Cem.

TE&L CO
(1053)

TE&L CO
(1066)

Briar Creek

Briar Creek

Oliver

TE&L CO
(1013)

Shepard

TE&L CO
(1134)

TE&L CO
(1021)

TE&L
CO (1022)

TE&L
CO (1023)

TE&L CO
(1024)

TE&L CO
(1054)

TE&L CO
(1065)

TE&L CO
(1135)

White House

TE&L CO
(1028)

TE&L
CO (1027)

TE&L CO
(1026)

TE&L CO
(1025)

TE&L CO
(1055)

TE&L CO
(1064)

TE&L CO
(1136)

Turtle Hole Creek

Red Top Cemetary

Momument

TE&L CO (1033)   TE&L CO (1034)   TE&L CO (1035)   TE&L CO (1036)   TE&L CO (1056)   TE&L CO (1063)   TE&L CO
(1137)

BBB&C RR CO
Abs # 1385
Survey2: BLAKEY, W C
20-Nov-1907

BBB&C RR CO
Abs # 1386
Survey2: BLAKEY, C B
11-Jun-1924

BBB&C RR CO
Abs # 1456
Survey2: HUNT, I
28-May-1912

BBB&C RR CO
Abs # 1525
Survey2: RICHARDSON, R M
07-May-1919

BBB&C RR CO
Abs # 1721
Survey2: CLINGBERG, A
20-Feb-1912
see also, Map 16

BBB&C RR CO
Abs # 2173
Survey2: PRICE, W H
12-Sep-1921
see also, Map 16

BBB&C RR CO
Abs # 2306
Survey2: NEWMAN, J H
11-Jun-1924

BBB&C RR CO
Abs # 33
22-Oct-1873
see also, Map 16

BBB&C RR CO
Abs # 34
21-Oct-1873
see also, Map 14

BS&F
Abs # 1480
Survey2: LOONEY, A
06-Feb-1902

BS&F
Abs # 1670
Survey2: BROWN, G F
04-Aug-1919

BS&F
Abs # 1836
Survey2: HAWKINS, S J
04-Sep-1908

BS&F
Abs # 1846
Survey2: MCCASLAND, A T
23-May-1941

BS&F
Abs # 2265
Survey2: HOLT, J A
14-Sep-1908

BS&F
Abs # 40
07-Jul-1875
see also, Map 14

G&BN CO
Abs # 120
07-Dec-1874

G&BN CO
Abs # 1852
Survey2: RICHARDSON, R L
12-Nov-1889

G&BN CO
Abs # 1920
Survey2: COX, E E
14-Jun-1920

G&BN CO
Abs # 1947
Survey2: ADINGTON, I
28-Sep-1889

G&BN CO
Abs # 2023
Survey2: YOUNG, J
01-May-1929

G&BN CO
Abs # 2299
Survey2: DANIEL, W H
11-Jun-1917

MILLER, B B
Abs # 1619
23-Dec-1884

SALLIE, HRS S
Abs # 252
31-Jul-1877
see also, Map 7

SERGEANT, E W
Abs # 253
01-Jun-1859
see also, Maps 6, 7, 14

TE&L CO
Abs # 1009
29-Jan-1859
see also, Map 14

TE&L CO
Abs # 1010
31-Jan-1859

TE&L CO
Abs # 1011
31-Jan-1859

TE&L CO
Abs # 1012
31-Jan-1859

TE&L CO
Abs # 1013
31-Jan-1859

TE&L CO
Abs # 1014
31-Jan-1859

TE&L CO
Abs # 1015
31-Jan-1859

TE&L CO
Abs # 1016
31-Jan-1859
see also, Map 14

TE&L CO
Abs # 1021
31-Jan-1859
see also, Map 14

TE&L CO
Abs # 1022
31-Jan-1859

TE&L CO
Abs # 1023
31-Jan-1859

TE&L CO
Abs # 1024
01-Feb-1859

TE&L CO
Abs # 1025
01-Feb-1859

TE&L CO
Abs # 1026
01-Feb-1859

TE&L CO
Abs # 1027
01-Feb-1859

TE&L CO
Abs # 1028
01-Feb-1859
see also, Map 14

TE&L CO
Abs # 1033
01-Feb-1859
see also, Maps 14, 22, 23

TE&L CO
Abs # 1034
01-Feb-1859
see also, Map 23

TE&L CO
Abs # 1035
01-Feb-1859

see also, Map 23

TE&L CO
Abs # 1036
01-Feb-1859
see also, Map 23

TE&L CO
Abs # 1052
02-Feb-1859

TE&L CO
Abs # 1053
02-Feb-1859

TE&L CO
Abs # 1054
02-Feb-1859

TE&L CO
Abs # 1055
02-Feb-1859

TE&L CO
Abs # 1056
03-Feb-1859
see also, Map 23

TE&L CO
Abs # 1063
12-Feb-1859
see also, Map 23

TE&L CO
Abs # 1064
14-Feb-1859

TE&L CO
Abs # 1065
14-Feb-1859

TE&L CO
Abs # 1066
14-Feb-1859

TE&L CO
Abs # 1067
14-Feb-1859

TE&L CO
Abs # 1068
14-Feb-1859

TE&L CO
Abs # 1069
14-Feb-1859

TE&L CO
Abs # 1070
14-Feb-1859

TE&L CO
Abs # 1071
14-Feb-1859

TE&L CO
Abs # 1072
14-Feb-1859
see also, Map 14

TE&L CO
Abs # 1073
14-Feb-1859

TE&L CO
Abs # 1074
14-Feb-1859
see also, Map 16

TE&L CO
Abs # 1133
04-Feb-1859
see also, Map 16

TE&L CO
Abs # 1134
04-Feb-1859
see also, Map 16

TE&L CO
Abs # 1135
04-Feb-1859
see also, Map 16

TE&L CO
Abs # 1136
04-Feb-1859
see also, Map 16

TE&L CO

Abs # 1137
04-Feb-1859
see also, Maps 16, 23, 24

TYNES, S
Abs # 274
10-Mar-1879
see also, Maps 7, 8, 16

VAN SICKLES, J H
Abs # 1549
25-Sep-1880
see also, Map 16

Populated Places
Loving

Cemeteries
Hawkins Chapel Cemetery
Loving Cemetery

Water (larger bodies)
None

Other Water
Briar Creek
Brushy Creek
Cameron Creek
Plum Creek
Turtle Hole Creek

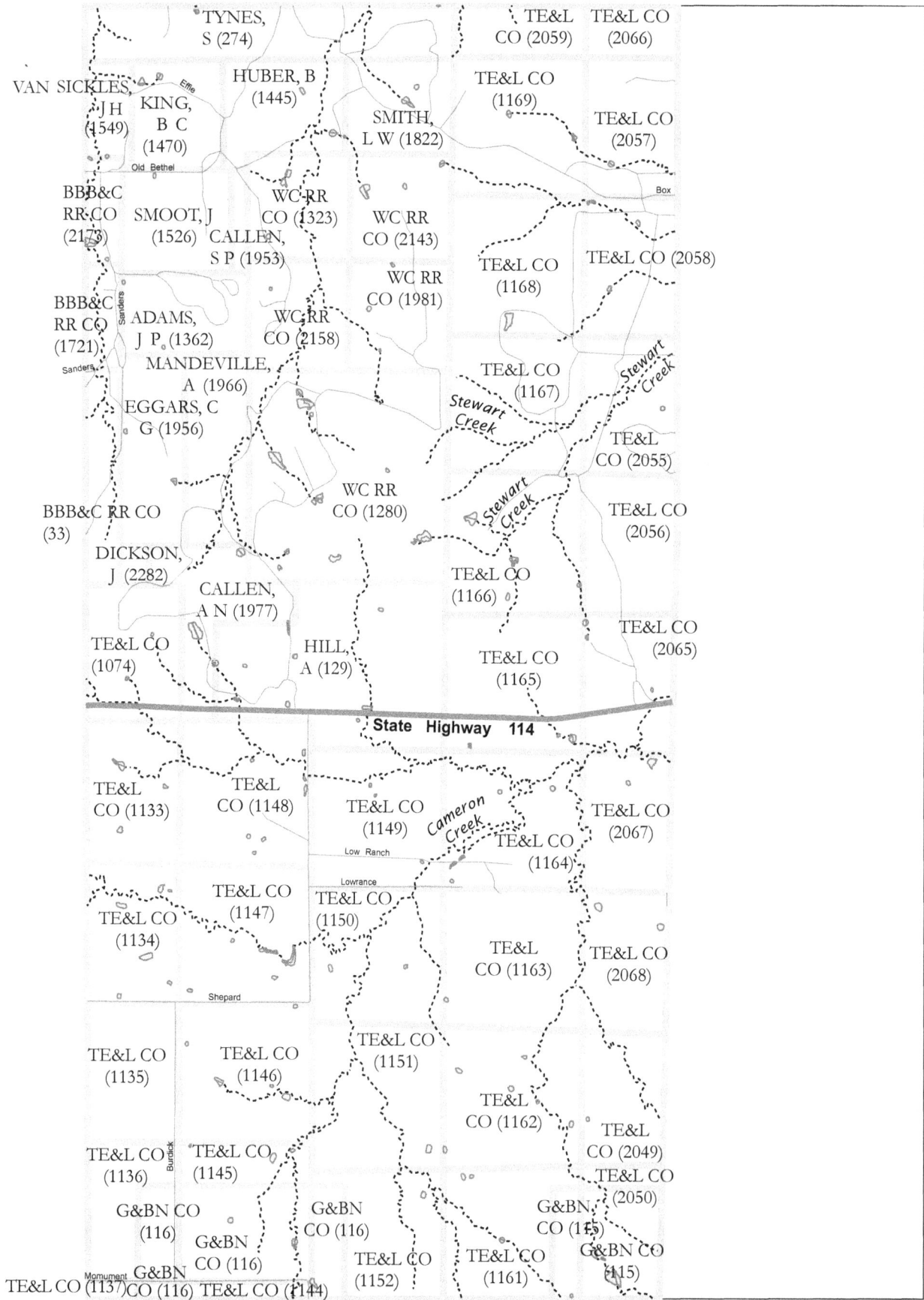

TYNES,
S (274)

VAN SICKLES,
J H
(1549)

KING,
B C
(1470)

HUBER, B
(1445)

TE&L
CO (2059)

TE&L CO
(2066)

TE&L CO
(1169)

SMITH,
L W (1822)

TE&L CO
(2057)

Old Bethel

Effie

BBB&C
RR CO
(2173)

SMOOT, J
(1526)

WC RR
CO (1323)

CALLEN,
S P (1953)

WC RR
CO (2143)

Box

TE&L CO
(1168)

TE&L CO (2058)

WC RR
CO (1981)

Sanders

BBB&C
RR CO
(1721)

ADAMS,
J P (1362)

WC RR
CO (2158)

MANDEVILLE,
A (1966)

EGGARS, C
G (1956)

TE&L CO
(1167)

Stewart
Creek

Stewart
Creek

TE&L
CO (2055)

Sanders

WC RR
CO (1280)

BBB&C RR CO
(33)

DICKSON,
J (2282)

CALLEN,
A N (1977)

TE&L CO
(1166)

Stewart
Creek

TE&L CO
(2056)

TE&L CO
(2065)

TE&L CO
(1074)

HILL,
A (129)

TE&L CO
(1165)

State Highway 114

TE&L
CO (1133)

TE&L
CO (1148)

TE&L CO
(1149)

Cameron
Creek

TE&L CO
(2067)

TE&L CO
(1164)

Low Ranch

Lowrance

TE&L CO
(1134)

TE&L CO
(1147)

TE&L CO
(1150)

TE&L
CO (1163)

TE&L CO
(2068)

Shepard

TE&L CO
(1135)

TE&L CO
(1146)

TE&L CO
(1151)

TE&L
CO (1162)

TE&L
CO (2049)

Burdick

TE&L CO
(1136)

TE&L CO
(1145)

TE&L CO
(2050)

G&BN CO
(116)

G&BN
CO (116)

G&BN
CO (116)

TE&L CO
(1152)

TE&L CO
(1161)

G&BN
CO (115)

G&BN CO
(115)

Monument

TE&L CO (1137)

G&BN
CO (116)

TE&L CO (1144)

ADAMS, J P
Abs # 1362
26-Aug-1880

BBB&C RR CO
Abs # 1721
Survey2: CLINGBERG, A
20-Feb-1912
see also, Map 15

BBB&C RR CO
Abs # 2173
Survey2: PRICE, W H
12-Sep-1921
see also, Map 15

BBB&C RR CO
Abs # 33
22-Oct-1873
see also, Map 15

CALLEN, A N
Abs # 1977
09-Oct-1894

CALLEN, S P
Abs # 1953
01-Nov-1889

DICKSON, J
Abs # 2282
24-Jun-1911

EGGARS, C G
Abs # 1956
19-Oct-1893

G&BN CO
Abs # 115
05-Aug-1873
see also, Map 24

G&BN CO
Abs # 116
01-Aug-1873
see also, Map 24

HILL, A
Abs # 129
09-Nov-1885

HUBER, B
Abs # 1445
01-May-1880

KING, B C
Abs # 1470
27-Jul-1883

MANDEVILLE, A
Abs # 1966
12-Oct-1893

SMITH, L W
Abs # 1822
05-Feb-1891

SMOOT, J
Abs # 1526
21-Aug-1880

TE&L CO
Abs # 1074
14-Feb-1859
see also, Map 15

TE&L CO
Abs # 1133
04-Feb-1859
see also, Map 15

TE&L CO
Abs # 1134
04-Feb-1859
see also, Map 15

TE&L CO
Abs # 1135
04-Feb-1859
see also, Map 15

TE&L CO
Abs # 1136
04-Feb-1859
see also, Map 15

TE&L CO
Abs # 1137
04-Feb-1859
see also, Maps 15, 23, 24

TE&L CO
Abs # 1144
05-Feb-1859
see also, Map 24

TE&L CO
Abs # 1145
05-Feb-1859

TE&L CO
Abs # 1146
05-Feb-1859

TE&L CO
Abs # 1147
05-Feb-1859

TE&L CO
Abs # 1148
05-Feb-1859

TE&L CO
Abs # 1149
05-Feb-1859

TE&L CO
Abs # 1150
05-Feb-1859

TE&L CO
Abs # 1151
07-Feb-1859

TE&L CO
Abs # 1152
07-Feb-1859
see also, Map 24

TE&L CO
Abs # 1161
07-Feb-1859
see also, Map 24

TE&L CO
Abs # 1162
07-Feb-1859

TE&L CO
Abs # 1163
07-Feb-1859

TE&L CO
Abs # 1164
07-Feb-1859

TE&L CO
Abs # 1165
11-Feb-1859

TE&L CO
Abs # 1166
11-Feb-1859

TE&L CO
Abs # 1167
11-Feb-1859

TE&L CO
Abs # 1168
11-Feb-1859

TE&L CO
Abs # 1169
11-Feb-1859

TE&L CO
Abs # 2049
08-Feb-1859

TE&L CO
Abs # 2050
08-Feb-1859

TE&L CO
Abs # 2055
11-Feb-1859

TE&L CO
Abs # 2056
11-Feb-1859

TE&L CO
Abs # 2057
11-Feb-1859

TE&L CO
Abs # 2058
11-Feb-1859

TE&L CO

Abs # 2059
11-Feb-1859
see also, Map 8

TE&L CO
Abs # 2065
11-Feb-1859

TE&L CO
Abs # 2066
11-Feb-1859
see also, Map 8

TE&L CO
Abs # 2067
08-Feb-1859

TE&L CO
Abs # 2068
08-Feb-1859

TYNES, S
Abs # 274
10-Mar-1879
see also, Maps 7, 8, 15

VAN SICKLES, J H
Abs # 1549
25-Sep-1880
see also, Map 15

WC RR CO
Abs # 1280
05-Nov-1875

WC RR CO
Abs # 1323
Survey2: HUBER, B
18-Apr-1878

WC RR CO
Abs # 1981
Survey2: EGGERS, G
31-Jul-1935

WC RR CO
Abs # 2143
Survey2: ROBINSON, J
31-Jul-1935

WC RR CO
Abs # 2158
Survey2: EGGERS, G
04-Apr-1903

Populated Places
None

Cemeteries
None

Water (larger bodies)
None

Other Water
Cameron Creek
Stewart Creek

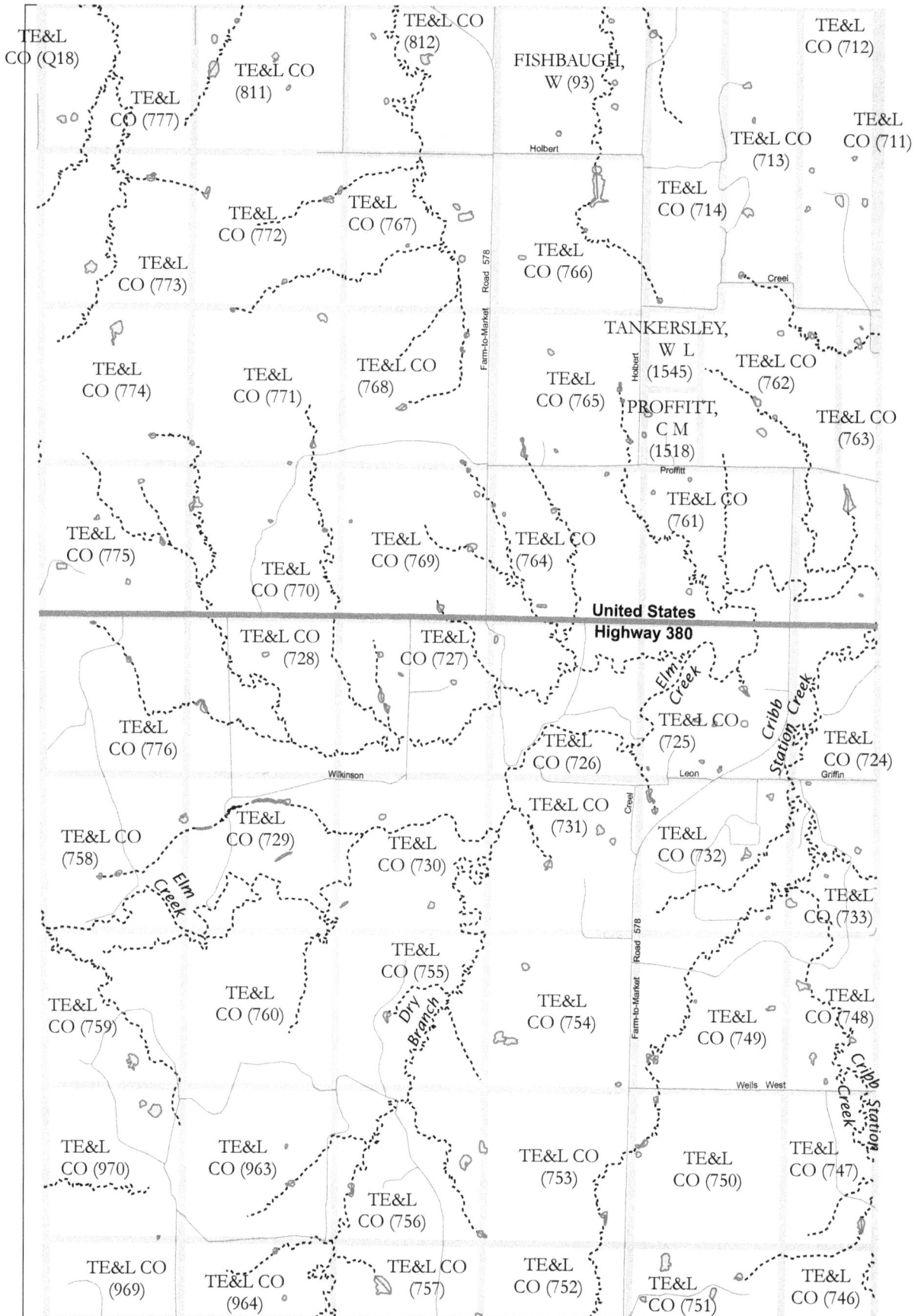

TE&L CO (Q18)

TE&L CO (777)

TE&L CO (811)

TE&L CO (812)

FISHBAUGH, W (93)

TE&L CO (712)

Holbert

TE&L CO (713)

TE&L CO (711)

TE&L CO (772)

TE&L CO (767)

TE&L CO (714)

TE&L CO (773)

TE&L CO (766)

Creel

TANKERSLEY, W L (1545)

TE&L CO (762)

TE&L CO (774)

TE&L CO (771)

TE&L CO (768)

TE&L CO (765)

PROFFITT, C M (1518)

TE&L CO (763)

Holbert

Road 578

Farm-to-Market

Proffitt

TE&L CO (775)

TE&L CO (770)

TE&L CO (769)

TE&L CO (764)

TE&L CO (761)

United States Highway 380

TE&L CO (728)

TE&L CO (727)

Elm Creek

Cribb Station Creek

TE&L CO (776)

TE&L CO (725)

TE&L CO (724)

Wilkinson

TE&L CO (726)

Leon

Griffin

TE&L CO (758)

TE&L CO (729)

TE&L CO (731)

Creel

TE&L CO (732)

Elm Creek

TE&L CO (730)

TE&L CO (733)

TE&L CO (755)

TE&L CO (759)

TE&L CO (760)

Dry Branch

TE&L CO (754)

Road 578

Farm-to-Market

TE&L CO (749)

TE&L CO (748)

Cribb Station Creek

Wells West

TE&L CO (970)

TE&L CO (963)

TE&L CO (753)

TE&L CO (750)

TE&L CO (747)

TE&L CO (756)

TE&L CO (969)

TE&L CO (964)

TE&L CO (757)

TE&L CO (752)

TE&L CO (751)

TE&L CO (746)

FISHBAUGH, W
Abs # 93
25-Mar-1856
see also, Map 9

PROFFITT, C M
Abs # 1518
27-Jul-1881

TANKERSLEY, W L
Abs # 1545
21-May-1881

TE&L CO
Abs # 711
31-May-1858
see also, Maps 9, 10, 18

TE&L CO
Abs # 712
31-May-1858
see also, Map 9

TE&L CO
Abs # 713
31-May-1858
see also, Map 9

TE&L CO
Abs # 714
01-Jun-1858
see also, Map 9

TE&L CO
Abs # 724
02-Jun-1858
see also, Map 18

TE&L CO
Abs # 725
02-Jun-1858

TE&L CO
Abs # 726
02-Jun-1858

TE&L CO
Abs # 727
03-Jun-1858

TE&L CO
Abs # 728
03-Jun-1858

TE&L CO
Abs # 729
03-Jun-1858

TE&L CO
Abs # 730
03-Jun-1858

TE&L CO
Abs # 731
03-Jun-1858

TE&L CO
Abs # 732
04-Jun-1858

TE&L CO
Abs # 733
04-Jun-1858
see also, Map 18

TE&L CO
Abs # 746
13-Mar-1911
see also, Maps 18, 25, 26

TE&L CO
Abs # 747
07-Jun-1858
see also, Map 18

TE&L CO
Abs # 748
07-Jun-1858
see also, Map 18

TE&L CO
Abs # 749
07-Jun-1858

TE&L CO
Abs # 750
08-Jun-1858

TE&L CO
Abs # 751

08-Jun-1858
see also, Map 25

TE&L CO
Abs # 752
08-Jun-1858
see also, Map 25

TE&L CO
Abs # 753
08-Jun-1858

TE&L CO
Abs # 754
08-Jun-1858

TE&L CO
Abs # 755
08-Jun-1858

TE&L CO
Abs # 756
08-Jun-1858

TE&L CO
Abs # 757
09-Jun-1858
see also, Map 25

TE&L CO
Abs # 758
09-Jun-1858

TE&L CO
Abs # 759
09-Jun-1858

TE&L CO
Abs # 760
09-Jun-1858

TE&L CO
Abs # 761
09-May-1858

TE&L CO
Abs # 762
09-Jun-1858

TE&L CO
Abs # 763
09-Jun-1858
see also, Map 18

TE&L CO
Abs # 764
10-Jun-1858

TE&L CO
Abs # 765
10-Jun-1858

TE&L CO
Abs # 766
10-Jun-1858

TE&L CO
Abs # 767
10-Jun-1858

TE&L CO
Abs # 768
10-Jun-1858

TE&L CO
Abs # 769
10-Jun-1858

TE&L CO
Abs # 770
10-Jun-1858

TE&L CO
Abs # 771
10-Jun-1858

TE&L CO
Abs # 772
11-Jun-1858

TE&L CO
Abs # 773
11-Jun-1858

TE&L CO
Abs # 774
11-Jun-1858

TE&L CO
Abs # 775

11-Jun-1858

TE&L CO
Abs # 776
11-Jun-1858

TE&L CO
Abs # 777
12-Jun-1858
see also, Map 9

TE&L CO
Abs # 811
14-Jun-1858
see also, Map 9

TE&L CO
Abs # 812
14-Jun-1858
see also, Map 9

TE&L CO
Abs # 963
12-Jun-1858

TE&L CO
Abs # 964
12-Jun-1858
see also, Map 25

TE&L CO
Abs # 969
17-Jul-1858
see also, Map 25

TE&L CO
Abs # 970
17-Jul-1858

TE&L CO
Abs # ?18
see also, Map 9

Populated Places
None

Cemeteries
None

Water (larger bodies)
None

Other Water
Cribb Station Creek
Dry Branch
Elm Creek

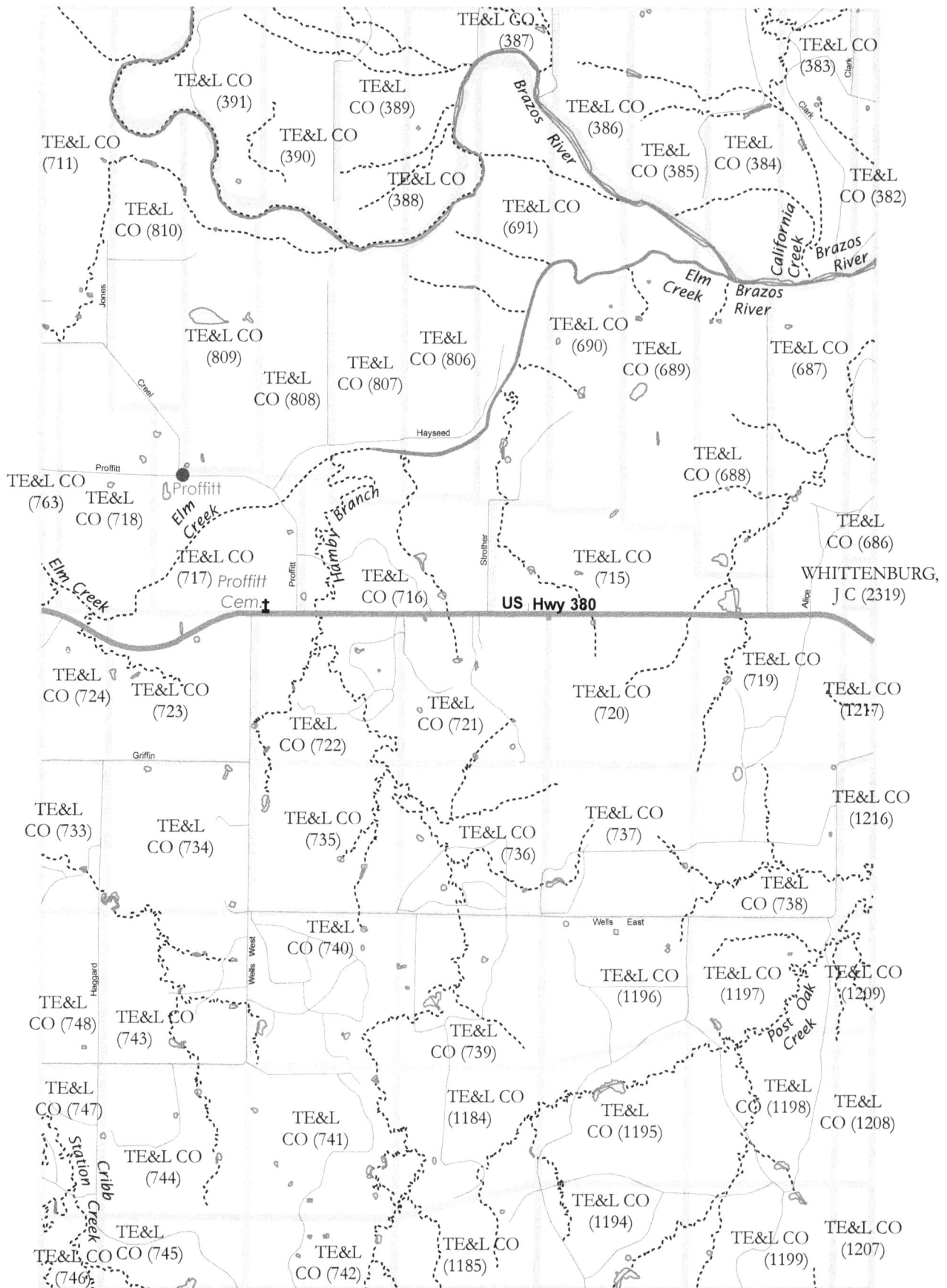

TE&L CO (387)

TE&L CO (391)

TE&L CO (389)

Brazos River

TE&L CO (386)

TE&L CO (383)

Clark

Clark

TE&L CO (711)

TE&L CO (390)

TE&L CO (388)

TE&L CO (385)

TE&L CO (384)

TE&L CO (382)

TE&L CO (810)

TE&L CO (691)

California Creek

Brazos River

Jones

Creek

Elm Creek

Brazos River

TE&L CO (809)

TE&L CO (806)

TE&L CO (690)

TE&L CO (689)

TE&L CO (687)

TE&L CO (808)

TE&L CO (807)

Hayseed

TE&L CO (688)

Proffitt

TE&L CO (763)

TE&L CO (718)

Proffitt

Elm Creek

TE&L CO (686)

Hamby Branch

Proffitt

Strother

Alice

TE&L CO (717)

Proffitt Cem.

TE&L CO (716)

TE&L CO (715)

WHITTENBURG, J C (2319)

Elm Creek

US Hwy 380

TE&L CO (724)

TE&L CO (723)

TE&L CO (721)

TE&L CO (720)

TE&L CO (719)

TE&L CO (1217)

Griffin

TE&L CO (722)

TE&L CO (1216)

TE&L CO (733)

TE&L CO (734)

TE&L CO (735)

TE&L CO (736)

TE&L CO (737)

TE&L CO (738)

Wells East

Wells West

Haggard

TE&L CO (740)

TE&L CO (1196)

TE&L CO (1197)

TE&L CO (1209)

Post Oak Creek

TE&L CO (748)

TE&L CO (743)

TE&L CO (739)

TE&L CO (747)

Station

Cribb Creek

TE&L CO (741)

TE&L CO (1184)

TE&L CO (1195)

TE&L CO (1198)

TE&L CO (1208)

TE&L CO (744)

TE&L CO (1194)

TE&L CO (746)

TE&L CO (745)

TE&L CO (742)

TE&L CO (1185)

TE&L CO (1199)

TE&L CO (1207)

TE&L CO
Abs # 1184
20-Oct-1858

TE&L CO
Abs # 1185
20-Oct-1858
see also, Map 26

TE&L CO
Abs # 1194
22-Oct-1858
see also, Map 26

TE&L CO
Abs # 1195
22-Oct-1858

TE&L CO
Abs # 1196
22-Oct-1858

TE&L CO
Abs # 1197
22-Oct-1858

TE&L CO
Abs # 1198
22-Oct-1858

TE&L CO
Abs # 1199
22-Oct-1858
see also, Map 26

TE&L CO
Abs # 1207
22-Oct-1858
see also, Maps 19, 26, 27

TE&L CO
Abs # 1208
22-Oct-1858
see also, Map 19

TE&L CO
Abs # 1209
22-Oct-1858
see also, Map 19

TE&L CO
Abs # 1216
20-Nov-1858
see also, Map 19

TE&L CO
Abs # 1217
20-Nov-1858
see also, Map 19

TE&L CO
Abs # 382
23-Sep-1857
see also, Maps 10, 11, 19

TE&L CO
Abs # 383
23-Sep-1857
see also, Map 10

TE&L CO
Abs # 384
24-Sep-1857
see also, Map 10

TE&L CO
Abs # 385
24-Sep-1857
see also, Map 10

TE&L CO
Abs # 386
24-Sep-1857
see also, Map 10

TE&L CO
Abs # 387
24-Sep-1857
see also, Map 10

TE&L CO
Abs # 388
24-Sep-1857
see also, Map 10

TE&L CO
Abs # 389
05-Oct-1857
see also, Map 10

TE&L CO
Abs # 390
05-Oct-1857
see also, Map 10

TE&L CO
Abs # 391
06-Oct-1857
see also, Map 10

TE&L CO
Abs # 686
10-Apr-1858
see also, Map 19

TE&L CO
Abs # 687
10-Apr-1858

TE&L CO
Abs # 688
19-Mar-1859

TE&L CO
Abs # 689
10-Apr-1858

TE&L CO
Abs # 690
12-Apr-1858

TE&L CO
Abs # 691
13-Apr-1858

TE&L CO
Abs # 711
31-May-1858
see also, Maps 9, 10, 17

TE&L CO
Abs # 715
01-Jun-1858

TE&L CO
Abs # 716
01-Jun-1858

TE&L CO
Abs # 717
01-Jun-1858

TE&L CO
Abs # 718
01-Jun-1858

TE&L CO
Abs # 719
01-Jun-1858

TE&L CO
Abs # 720
02-Jun-1858

TE&L CO
Abs # 721
02-Jun-1858

TE&L CO
Abs # 722
02-Jun-1858

TE&L CO
Abs # 723
02-Jun-1858

TE&L CO
Abs # 724
02-Jun-1858
see also, Map 17

TE&L CO
Abs # 733
04-Jun-1858
see also, Map 17

TE&L CO
Abs # 734
04-Jun-1858

TE&L CO
Abs # 735
04-Jun-1858

TE&L CO
Abs # 736
04-Jun-1858

TE&L CO
Abs # 737
04-Jun-1858

TE&L CO
Abs # 738
04-Jun-1858

TE&L CO
Abs # 739
05-Jun-1858

TE&L CO
Abs # 740
05-Jun-1858

TE&L CO
Abs # 741
05-Jun-1858

TE&L CO
Abs # 742
05-Jun-1858
see also, Map 26

TE&L CO
Abs # 743
05-Jun-1858

TE&L CO
Abs # 744
07-Jun-1858

TE&L CO
Abs # 745
07-Jun-1858
see also, Map 26

TE&L CO
Abs # 746
13-Mar-1911
see also, Maps 17, 25, 26

TE&L CO
Abs # 747
07-Jun-1858
see also, Map 17

TE&L CO
Abs # 748
07-Jun-1858
see also, Map 17

TE&L CO
Abs # 763
09-Jun-1858
see also, Map 17

TE&L CO
Abs # 806
28-May-1858

TE&L CO
Abs # 807
31-May-1858

TE&L CO
Abs # 808
31-May-1858

TE&L CO
Abs # 809
31-May-1858

TE&L CO
Abs # 810
31-May-1858
see also, Map 10

WHITTENBURG, J C
Abs # 2319
Survey2: OSBORN, V H
17-Jun-1920
see also, Map 19

Populated Places
Proffitt

Cemeteries
Proffitt Cemetery

Water (larger bodies)
None

Other Water
Brazos River
California Creek
Cribb Station Creek
Elm Creek
Hamby Branch
Post Oak Creek

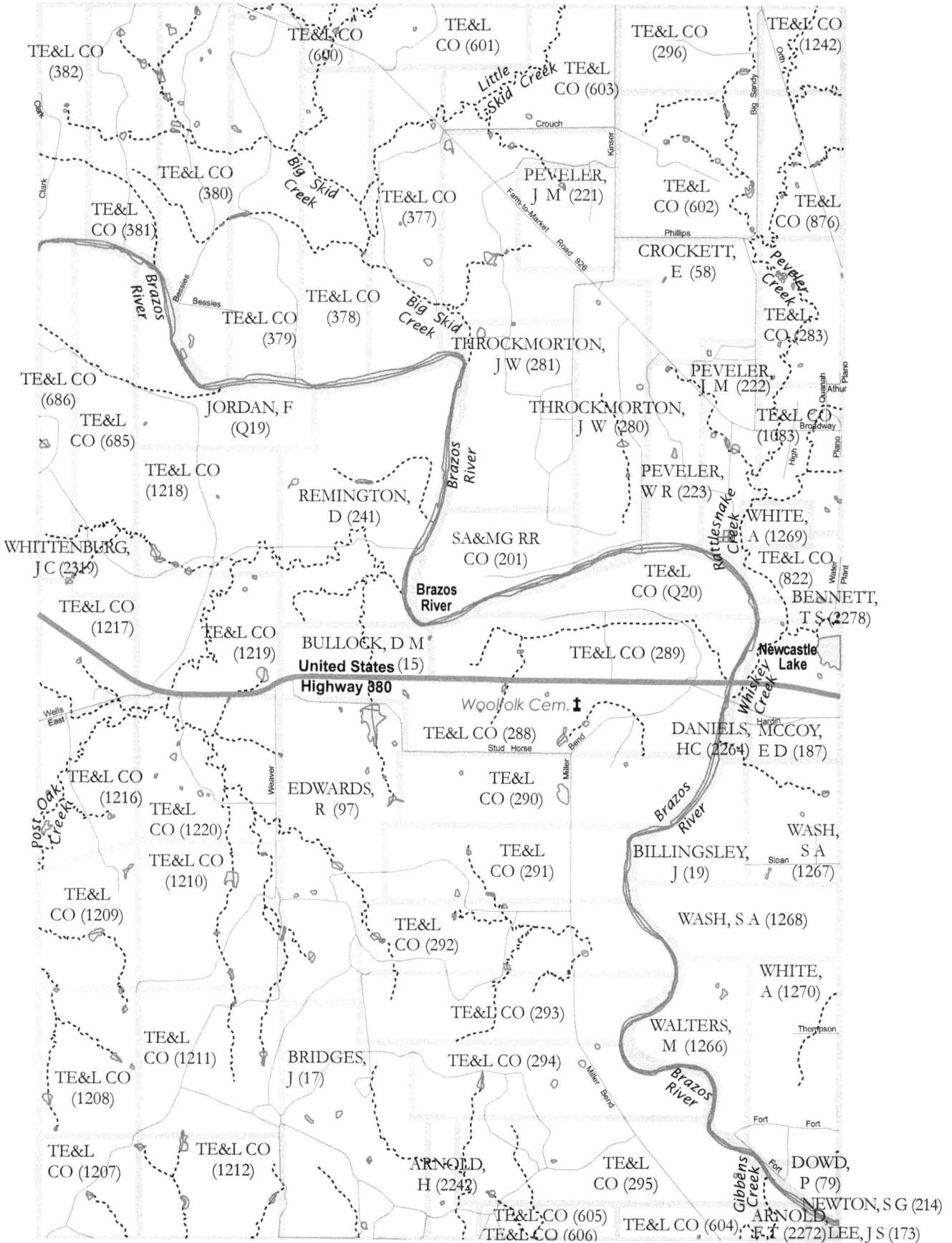

TE&L CO
(382)

TE&L CO
(600)

TE&L
CO (601)

TE&L CO
(296)

TE&L CO
(1242)

Little Skid Creek

TE&L
CO (603)

Crouch

Kinser

Big Sandy

Orin

TE&L CO
(380)

Big Skid Creek

TE&L CO
(377)

PEVELER,
J M (221)

TE&L
CO (602)

TE&L
CO (876)

Farm-to-Market Road 926

TE&L
CO (381)

Clark

Clark

Brazos River

Bessies

Bessies

TE&L CO
(378)

Big Skid Creek

Phillips

CROCKETT,
E (58)

Peveler Creek

TE&L CO
(379)

THROCKMORTON,
J W (281)

TE&L
CO (283)

TE&L CO
(686)

JORDAN, F
(Q19)

THROCKMORTON,
J W (280)

PEVELER,
J M (222)

Quanah

Arthur

Plano

TE&L
CO (685)

TE&L CO
(1083)

Broadway

High

Plano

TE&L CO
(1218)

REMINGTON,
D (241)

PEVELER,
W R (223)

Rattlesnake Creek

WHITE,
A (1269)

WHITTENBURG,
J C (2319)

SA&MG RR
CO (201)

TE&L CO.
(822)

Water Plant

Brazos
River

TE&L
CO (Q20)

BENNETT,
T S (2278)

TE&L CO
(1217)

TE&L CO
(1219)

BULLOCK, D M
(15)
United States
Highway 380

TE&L CO (289)

Newcastle
Lake

Whiskey Creek

Wells East

Woolfolk Cem. ✝

DANIELS,
HC (2264)

MCCOY,
E D (187)

Hardin

TE&L CO
(1216)

Post Oak Creek

Weaver

EDWARDS,
R (97)

TE&L CO (288)

Stud Horse

TE&L
CO (290)

Miller Bend

Brazos River

BILLINGSLEY,
J (19)

Sloan

WASH,
S A
(1267)

TE&L CO
(1220)

TE&L CO
(1210)

TE&L
CO (291)

WASH, S A (1268)

TE&L
CO (1209)

WHITE,
A (1270)

Thompson

TE&L
CO (1211)

TE&L CO (292)

TE&L CO (293)

WALTERS,
M (1266)

TE&L CO
(1208)

BRIDGES,
J (17)

TE&L CO (294)

Miller Bend

Brazos River

Fort

Fort

TE&L CO
(1207)

TE&L CO
(1212)

ARNOLD,
H (2242)

TE&L
CO (295)

Gibbens Creek

Fort

DOWD,
P (79)

NEWTON, S G (214)

TE&L CO (605)
TE&L CO (606)

TE&L CO (604)

ARNOLD,
E T (2272) LEE, J S (173)

ARNOLD, F T
Abs # 2272
07-Dec-1908
see also, Map 27

ARNOLD, H
Abs # 2242
09-Sep-1901
see also, Map 27

BENNETT, T S
Abs # 2278
07-Mar-1911
see also, Map 20

BILLINGSLEY, J
Abs # 19
02-Apr-1861

BRIDGES, J
Abs # 17
15-May-1857
see also, Map 27

BULLOCK, D M
Abs # 15
28-Jan-1858

CROCKETT, E
Abs # 58
01-May-1861

DANIELS, H C
Abs # 2264
04-Feb-1907

DOWD, P
Abs # 79
24-Jul-1861
see also, Maps 20, 28

EDWARDS, R
Abs # 97
21-Oct-1873

LEE, J S
Abs # 173
25-Oct-1860
see also, Maps 20, 27, 28

MCCOY, E D
Abs # 187
02-Feb-1856
see also, Map 20

NEWTON, S G
Abs # 214
23-Apr-1857
see also, Map 27

PEVELER, J M
Abs # 221
03-Nov-1859

PEVELER, J M
Abs # 222
09-Dec-1859

PEVELER, W R
Abs # 223
24-Apr-1860

REMINGTON, D
Abs # 241
07-Sep-1857

SA&MG RR CO
Abs # 201

TE&L CO
Abs # 1083
05-Mar-1859
see also, Map 20

TE&L CO
Abs # 1207
22-Oct-1858
see also, Maps 18, 26, 27

TE&L CO
Abs # 1208
22-Oct-1858
see also, Map 18

TE&L CO
Abs # 1209
22-Oct-1858
see also, Map 18

TE&L CO

Abs # 1210
22-Oct-1858

TE&L CO
Abs # 1211
22-Oct-1858

TE&L CO
Abs # 1212
23-Oct-1858
see also, Map 27

TE&L CO
Abs # 1216
20-Nov-1858
see also, Map 18

TE&L CO
Abs # 1217
20-Nov-1858
see also, Map 18

TE&L CO
Abs # 1218
23-Oct-1858

TE&L CO
Abs # 1219
23-Oct-1858

TE&L CO
Abs # 1220
23-Oct-1858

TE&L CO
Abs # 1242
11-Jan-1858
see also, Maps 11, 12, 20

TE&L CO
Abs # 283
26-May-1859
see also, Map 20

TE&L CO
Abs # 288
28-Feb-1856

TE&L CO
Abs # 289
01-Apr-1859

TE&L CO
Abs # 290
28-Feb-1856

TE&L CO
Abs # 291
28-Feb-1856

TE&L CO
Abs # 292
28-Feb-1856

TE&L CO
Abs # 293
28-Feb-1856

TE&L CO
Abs # 294
29-Feb-1856

TE&L CO
Abs # 295
15-Aug-1857

TE&L CO
Abs # 296
15-Aug-1857
see also, Map 11

TE&L CO
Abs # 377
21-Sep-1857

TE&L CO
Abs # 378
11-Mar-1859

TE&L CO
Abs # 379
11-Mar-1859

TE&L CO
Abs # 380
23-Sep-1857
see also, Map 11

TE&L CO
Abs # 381

23-Sep-1857
see also, Map 11

TE&L CO
Abs # 382
23-Sep-1857
see also, Maps 10, 11, 18

TE&L CO
Abs # 600
19-Feb-1858
see also, Map 11

TE&L CO
Abs # 601
19-Feb-1858
see also, Map 11

TE&L CO
Abs # 602
19-Feb-1858

TE&L CO
Abs # 603
20-Feb-1858
see also, Map 11

TE&L CO
Abs # 604
23-Feb-1858
see also, Map 27

TE&L CO
Abs # 605
23-Feb-1858
see also, Map 27

TE&L CO
Abs # 606
11-Jan-1858
see also, Map 27

TE&L CO
Abs # 685
06-Apr-1858

TE&L CO
Abs # 686
10-Apr-1858
see also, Map 18

TE&L CO
Abs # 822
03-Aug-1858
see also, Map 20

TE&L CO
Abs # 876
21-Oct-1858
see also, Map 20T

TE&L CO
Abs # ?20

THROCKMORTON, J W
Abs # 280
15-Apr-1857

THROCKMORTON, J W
Abs # 281
15-Feb-1858

WALTERS, M
Abs # 1266
25-Oct-1860

WASH, S A
Abs # 1267
20-Dec-1855
see also, Map 20

WASH, S A
Abs # 1268
20-Dec-1855
see also, Map 20

WHITE, A
Abs # 1269
29-Feb-1856

WHITE, A
Abs # 1270
01-May-1854
see also, Map 20

WHITTENBURG, J C
Abs # 2319
Survey2: OSBORN, V H
17-Jun-1920
see also, Map 18

Populated Places
None

Cemeteries
Woolfolk Cemetery

Water (larger bodies)
Brazos River
Newcastle Lake

Other Water
Big Skid Creek
Brazos River
Gibbens Creek
Little Skid Creek
Peveler Creek
Post Oak Creek
Rattlesnake Creek
Whiskey Creek

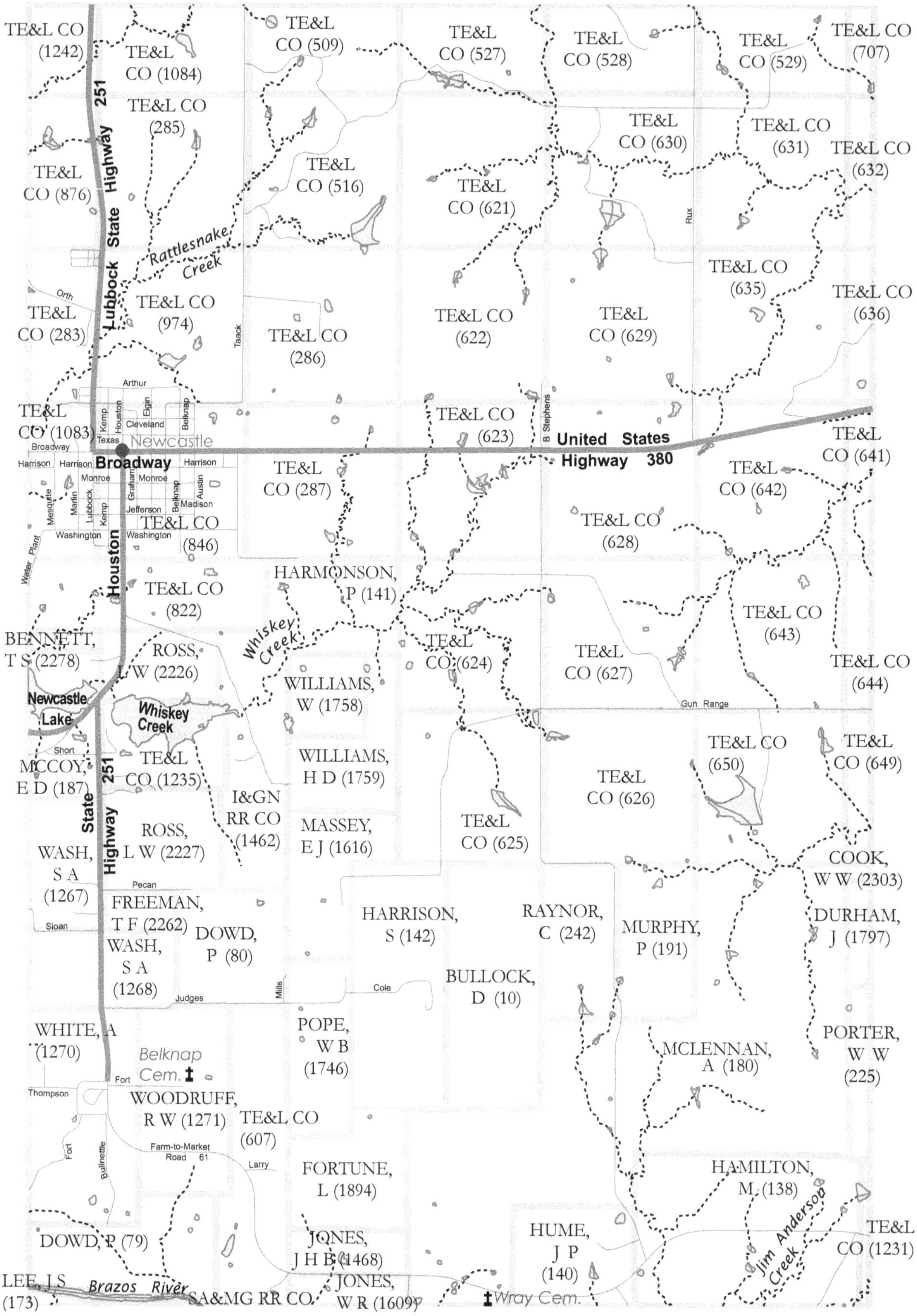

TE&L CO (1242)

TE&L CO (1084)

TE&L CO (509)

TE&L CO (527)

TE&L CO (528)

TE&L CO (529)

TE&L CO (707)

State Highway 251

TE&L CO (285)

TE&L CO (876)

TE&L CO (516)

TE&L CO (630)

TE&L CO (631)

TE&L CO (632)

Rattlesnake Creek

Rux

TE&L CO (283)

Orth

TE&L CO (974)

Taack

TE&L CO (286)

TE&L CO (621)

TE&L CO (622)

TE&L CO (629)

TE&L CO (635)

TE&L CO (636)

TE&L CO (1083)

Arthur

Houston Elgin Cleveland Belknap Kemp

Newcastle

TE&L CO (623)

B. Stephens

United States Highway 380

TE&L CO (641)

Broadway

Harrison Harrison **Broadway** Harrison

Monroe Monroe

TE&L CO (287)

TE&L CO (628)

TE&L CO (642)

Martin Mesquite Lubbock Kemp Graham Jefferson Belknap Austin Madison

Washington Washington Washington

TE&L CO (846)

TE&L CO (822)

Water Plant

HARMONSON, P (141)

Whiskey Creek

TE&L CO (624)

TE&L CO (643)

BENNETT, T S (2278)

ROSS, L W (2226)

WILLIAMS, W (1758)

TE&L CO (627)

Newcastle Lake

Whiskey Creek

Short

MCCOY, E D (187)

TE&L CO (1235)

WILLIAMS, H D (1759)

TE&L CO (650)

TE&L CO (649)

State Highway 251

I&GN RR CO (1462)

MASSEY, E J (1616)

TE&L CO (626)

ROSS, L W (2227)

TE&L CO (625)

COOK, W W (2303)

Gun Range

WASH, S A (1267)

Pecan

FREEMAN, T F (2262)

HARRISON, S (142)

RAYNOR, C (242)

MURPHY, P (191)

DURHAM, J (1797)

Sloan

DOWD, P (80)

WASH, S A (1268)

Judges

Mills

Cole

BULLOCK, D (10)

MCLENNAN, A (180)

WHITE, A (1270)

Belknap Cem.

Fort

POPE, W B (1746)

PORTER, W W (225)

Thompson

WOODRUFF, R W (1271)

TE&L CO (607)

Fort Bullnettle

Farm-to-Market Road 61

Larry

FORTUNE, L (1894)

HAMILTON, M (138)

DOWD, P (79)

JONES, J H B (1468)

HUME, J P (140)

Jim Anderson Creek

TE&L CO (1231)

LEE, J S (173)

Brazos River

SA&MG RR CO

JONES, W R (1609)

Wray Cem.

BENNETT, T S
Abs # 2278
07-Mar-1911
see also, Map 19

BULLOCK, D
Abs # 10
29-Apr-1861

COOK, W W
Abs # 2303
Survey2: ATWOOD, W H
27-Feb-1918
see also, Map 21

DOWD, P
Abs # 79
24-Jul-1861
see also, Maps 19, 28

DOWD, P
Abs # 80
24-Jul-1861

DURHAM, J
Abs # 1797
25-Apr-1887
see also, Map 21

FORTUNE, L
Abs # 1894
22-Sep-1887

FREEMAN, T F
Abs # 2262
21-Dec-1905

HAMILTON, M
Abs # 138
24-May-1860
see also, Map 28

HARMONSON, P
Abs # 141
07-Mar-1861

HARRISON, S
Abs # 142
30-Sep-1857

HUME, J P
Abs # 140
23-Jul-1856
see also, Map 28

I&GN RR CO
Abs # 1462
03-Dec-1879

JONES, J H B
Abs # 1468
26-Aug-1879

JONES, W R
Abs # 1609
03-Mar-1880
see also, Map 28

LEE, J S
Abs # 173
25-Oct-1860
see also, Maps 19, 27, 28

MASSEY, E J
Abs # 1616
01-May-1880

MCCOY, E D
Abs # 187
02-Feb-1856
see also, Map 19

MCLENNAN, A
Abs # 180
12-Oct-1855
see also, Map 28

MURPHY, P
Abs # 191
02-Dec-1859

POPE, W B
Abs # 1746
03-Mar-1882

PORTER, W W
Abs # 225
08-Jan-1862
see also, Map 21

RAYNOR, C
Abs # 242
02-Dec-1859

ROSS, L W
Abs # 2226
21-Mar-1901

ROSS, L W
Abs # 2227
22-Mar-1901

SA&MG RR CO
Abs # 262
11-Dec-1860
see also, Map 28

TE&L CO
Abs # 1083
05-Mar-1859
see also, Map 19

TE&L CO
Abs # 1084
18-Mar-1858
see also, Map 12

TE&L CO
Abs # 1231
07-Apr-1859
see also, Maps 21, 28, 29

TE&L CO
Abs # 1235
11-Feb-1861

TE&L CO
Abs # 1242
11-Jan-1858
see also, Maps 11, 12, 19

TE&L CO
Abs # 283
26-May-1859
see also, Map 19

TE&L CO
Abs # 285
11-Aug-1857

TE&L CO
Abs # 286
11-Aug-1857

TE&L CO
Abs # 287
11-Aug-1857

TE&L CO
Abs # 509
12-Dec-1857
see also, Map 12

TE&L CO
Abs # 516
15-Dec-1857

TE&L CO
Abs # 527
03-Apr-1858
see also, Map 12

TE&L CO
Abs # 528
05-Apr-1858
see also, Map 12

TE&L CO
Abs # 529
29-Dec-1857
see also, Map 12

TE&L CO
Abs # 607
24-Feb-1858
see also, Map 28

TE&L CO
Abs # 621
22-Mar-1858

TE&L CO
Abs # 622
22-Mar-1858

TE&L CO
Abs # 623
22-Mar-1858

TE&L CO

Abs # 624
22-Mar-1858

TE&L CO
Abs # 625
22-Mar-1858

TE&L CO
Abs # 626
22-Mar-1858

TE&L CO
Abs # 627
22-Mar-1858

TE&L CO
Abs # 628
23-Mar-1858

TE&L CO
Abs # 629
23-Mar-1858

TE&L CO
Abs # 630
23-Mar-1858

TE&L CO
Abs # 631
23-Mar-1858

TE&L CO
Abs # 632
23-Mar-1858
see also, Map 21

TE&L CO
Abs # 635
24-Mar-1858

TE&L CO
Abs # 636
24-Mar-1858
see also, Map 21

TE&L CO
Abs # 641
24-Mar-1858
see also, Map 21

TE&L CO
Abs # 642
24-Mar-1858

TE&L CO
Abs # 643
24-Mar-1858

TE&L CO
Abs # 644
27-Jun-1951
see also, Map 21

TE&L CO
Abs # 649
25-Mar-1858
see also, Map 21

TE&L CO
Abs # 650
25-Mar-1858

TE&L CO
Abs # 707
12-May-1858
see also, Maps 12, 13, 21

TE&L CO
Abs # 822
03-Aug-1858
see also, Map 19

TE&L CO
Abs # 846
03-Aug-1858

TE&L CO
Abs # 876
21-Oct-1858
see also, Map 19

TE&L CO
Abs # 974
12-Aug-1858

WASH, S A
Abs # 1267
20-Dec-1855
see also, Map 19

WASH, S A
Abs # 1268
20-Dec-1855
see also, Map 19

WHITE, A
Abs # 1270
01-May-1854
see also, Map 19

WILLIAMS, H D
Abs # 1759
06-Mar-1882

WILLIAMS, W
Abs # 1758
06-Mar-1882

WOODRUFF, R W
Abs # 1271
14-Apr-1856

Populated Places
Newcastle

Cemeteries
Belknap Cemetery
Wray Cemetery

Water (larger bodies)
Newcastle Lake
Whiskey Creek

Other Water
Brazos River
Jim Anderson Creek
Rattlesnake Creek
Whiskey Creek

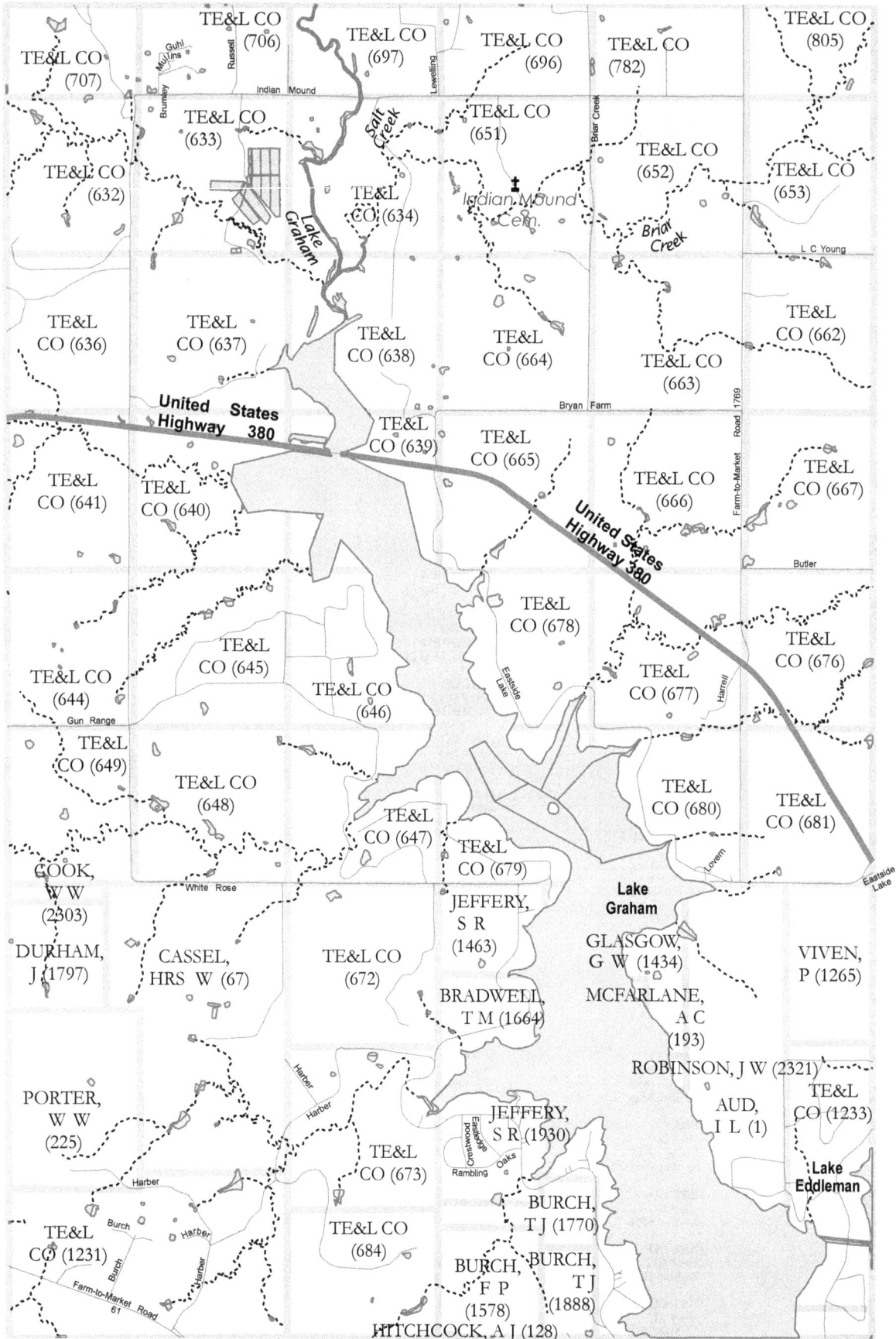

TE&L CO
(707)

TE&L CO
(706)

TE&L CO
(697)

TE&L CO
(696)

TE&L CO
(782)

TE&L CO
(805)

Guhl

Mullins

Russell

Brumley

Indian Mound

TE&L CO
(633)

TE&L CO
(651)

TE&L CO
(652)

TE&L CO
(653)

TE&L CO
(632)

Salt Creek

TE&L
CO (634)

Indian Mound
Cem.

Briar Creek

Briar Creek

L C Young

Lake Graham

TE&L
CO (636)

TE&L
CO (637)

TE&L
CO (638)

TE&L
CO (664)

TE&L CO
(663)

TE&L
CO (662)

Bryan Farm

Farm-to-Market Road 1769

United States
Highway 380

TE&L
CO (639)

TE&L
CO (665)

TE&L CO
(666)

TE&L
CO (667)

TE&L
CO (641)

TE&L
CO (640)

United States
Highway 380

Butler

TE&L
CO (678)

TE&L
CO (676)

TE&L
CO (645)

Eastside Lake

TE&L
CO (677)

Harrell

TE&L CO
(644)

TE&L CO
(646)

Gun Range

TE&L
CO (649)

TE&L CO
(648)

TE&L
CO (680)

TE&L
CO (681)

TE&L
CO (647)

Lovern

Eastside Lake

White Rose

TE&L
CO (679)

COOK,
W W
(2303)

JEFFERY,
S R
(1463)

Lake
Graham

VIVEN,
P (1265)

DURHAM,
J (1797)

CASSEL,
HRS W (67)

TE&L CO
(672)

GLASGOW,
G W (1434)

BRADWELL,
T M (1664)

MCFARLANE,
A C
(193)

ROBINSON, J W (2321)

AUD,
I L (1)

TE&L
CO (1233)

PORTER,
W W
(225)

Harber

Harber

JEFFERY,
S R (1930)

Eastside

Oaks

Rambling

Lake
Eddleman

TE&L
CO (673)

Harber

BURCH,
T J (1770)

Burch

TE&L
CO (1231)

Burch

Harber

Harber

TE&L CO
(684)

BURCH,
F P
(1578)

BURCH,
T J
(1888)

Farm-to-Market
Road 61

HITCHCOCK, A J (128)

AUD, I L
Abs # 1
16-Nov-1860
see also, Maps 22, 29, 30

BRADWELL, T M
Abs # 1664
02-May-1881

BURCH, F P
Abs # 1578
24-May-1890
see also, Map 29

BURCH, T J
Abs # 1770
13-Sep-1887

BURCH, T J
Abs # 1888
07-Jun-1895
see also, Map 29

CASSEL, HRS W
Abs # 67
20-Dec-1876

COOK, W W
Abs # 2303
Survey2: ATWOOD, W H
27-Feb-1918
see also, Map 20

DURHAM, J
Abs # 1797
25-Apr-1887
see also, Map 20

GLASGOW, G W
Abs # 1434
03-Mar-1879

HITCHCOCK, A J
Abs # 128
22-Aug-1873
see also, Map 29

JEFFERY, S R
Abs # 1463
03-Feb-1879

JEFFERY, S R
Abs # 1930
18-Jun-1888

MCFARLANE, A C
Abs # 193
07-Mar-1878

PORTER, W W
Abs # 225
08-Jan-1862
see also, Map 20

ROBINSON, J W
Abs # 2321
23-Jun-1920

TE&L CO
Abs # 1231
07-Apr-1859
see also, Maps 20, 28, 29

TE&L CO
Abs # 1233
11-Mar-1859
see also, Map 22

TE&L CO
Abs # 632
23-Mar-1858
see also, Map 20

TE&L CO
Abs # 633
24-Sep-1857

TE&L CO
Abs # 634
24-Sep-1857

TE&L CO
Abs # 636
24-Mar-1858
see also, Map 20

TE&L CO
Abs # 637
25-Sep-1857

TE&L CO
Abs # 638
25-Sep-1857

TE&L CO
Abs # 639
24-Mar-1858

TE&L CO
Abs # 640
24-Mar-1858

TE&L CO
Abs # 641
24-Mar-1858
see also, Map 20

TE&L CO
Abs # 644
27-Jun-1951
see also, Map 20

TE&L CO
Abs # 645
25-Mar-1858

TE&L CO
Abs # 646
25-Mar-1858

TE&L CO
Abs # 647
25-Mar-1858

TE&L CO
Abs # 648
25-Mar-1858

TE&L CO
Abs # 649
25-Mar-1858
see also, Map 20

TE&L CO
Abs # 651
25-Mar-1858

TE&L CO
Abs # 652
25-Mar-1858

TE&L CO
Abs # 653
25-Sep-1857
see also, Map 22

TE&L CO
Abs # 662
29-Mar-1858
see also, Map 22

TE&L CO
Abs # 663
29-Mar-1858

TE&L CO
Abs # 664
29-Mar-1858

TE&L CO
Abs # 665
30-Mar-1858

TE&L CO
Abs # 666
30-Mar-1858

TE&L CO
Abs # 667
30-Mar-1858
see also, Map 22

TE&L CO
Abs # 672
30-Mar-1858

TE&L CO
Abs # 673
31-Mar-1858

TE&L CO
Abs # 676
31-Mar-1858
see also, Map 22

TE&L CO
Abs # 677
31-Mar-1858

TE&L CO

Abs # 678
31-Mar-1858

TE&L CO
Abs # 679
31-Mar-1858

TE&L CO
Abs # 680
01-Apr-1858

TE&L CO
Abs # 681
01-Apr-1858
see also, Map 22

TE&L CO
Abs # 684
01-Apr-1858
see also, Map 29

TE&L CO
Abs # 696
10-May-1858
see also, Map 13

TE&L CO
Abs # 697
11-May-1858
see also, Map 13

TE&L CO
Abs # 706
12-May-1858
see also, Map 13

TE&L CO
Abs # 707
12-May-1858
see also, Maps 12, 13, 20

TE&L CO
Abs # 782
13-May-1858
see also, Map 13

TE&L CO
Abs # 805
18-May-1858
see also, Maps 13, 14, 22

VIVEN, P
Abs # 1265
15-Jul-1859
see also, Map 22

Populated Places

None

Cemeteries

Indian Mound Cemetery

Water (larger bodies)

Lake Eddleman
Lake Graham

Other Water

Briar Creek
Lake Graham
Salt Creek

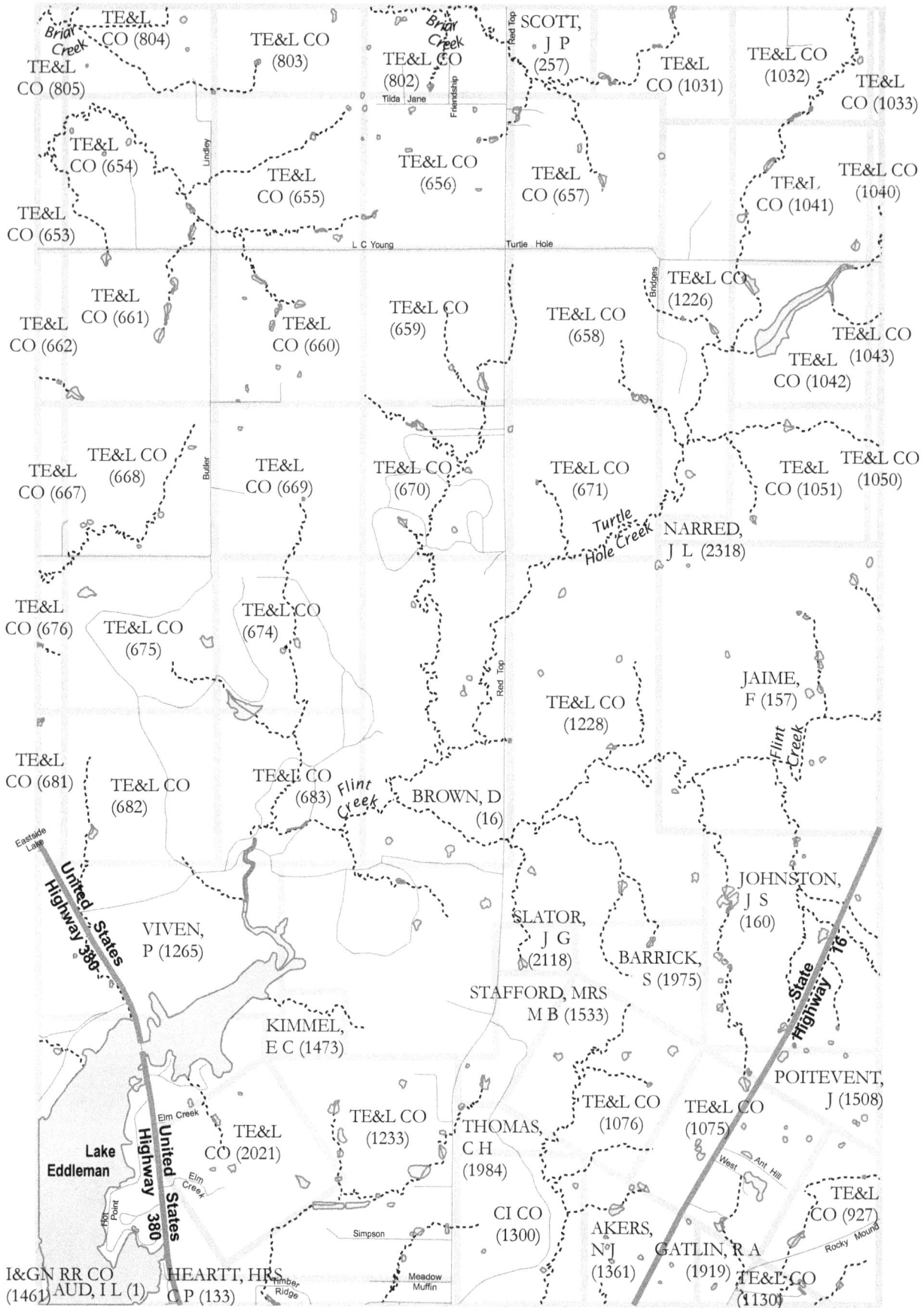

TE&L CO (804)

Briar Creek

TE&L CO (805)

TE&L CO (803)

Briar Creek

TE&L CO (802)

Tilda Jane

Friendship

SCOTT, J P (257)

TE&L CO (1031)

TE&L CO (1032)

TE&L CO (1033)

Lindley

TE&L CO (654)

TE&L CO (655)

TE&L CO (656)

TE&L CO (657)

TE&L CO (1041)

TE&L CO (1040)

TE&L CO (653)

L C Young

Turtle Hole

TE&L CO (661)

TE&L CO (662)

TE&L CO (660)

TE&L CO (659)

TE&L CO (658)

Bridges

TE&L CO (1226)

TE&L CO (1042)

TE&L CO (1043)

TE&L CO (667)

TE&L CO (668)

Butler

TE&L CO (669)

TE&L CO (670)

TE&L CO (671)

TE&L CO (1051)

TE&L CO (1050)

Turtle Hole Creek

NARRED, J L (2318)

TE&L CO (676)

TE&L CO (675)

TE&L CO (674)

Red Top

JAIME, F (157)

Flint Creek

TE&L CO (1228)

TE&L CO (681)

TE&L CO (682)

TE&L CO (683)

Flint Creek

BROWN, D (16)

Eastside Lake

United States Highway 380

VIVEN, P (1265)

SLATOR, J G (2118)

JOHNSTON, J S (160)

BARRICK, S (1975)

State Highway 16

STAFFORD, MRS M B (1533)

KIMMEL, E C (1473)

POITEVENT, J (1508)

Elm Creek

TE&L CO (2021)

Elm Creek

Lake Eddleman

Holt Point

TE&L CO (1233)

THOMAS, C H (1984)

TE&L CO (1076)

TE&L CO (1075)

West

Ant Hill

TE&L CO (927)

Simpson

CI CO (1300)

AKERS, N J (1361)

GATLIN, R A (1919)

Rocky Mound

I&GN RR CO (1461)

AUD, I L (1)

HEARTT, HRS C P (133)

Timber Ridge

Meadow Muffin

TE&L CO (1130)

AKERS, N J
Abs # 1361
21-Jun-1884
see also, Map 30

AUD, I L
Abs # 1
16-Nov-1860
see also, Maps 21, 29, 30

BARRICK, S
Abs # 1975
21-Jan-1892

BROWN, D
Abs # 16
22-Dec-1857

CI CO
Abs # 1300
18-Feb-1878
see also, Map 30

GATLIN, R A
Abs # 1919
26-Apr-1895
see also, Map 30

HEARTT, HRS C P
Abs # 133
05-Nov-1889
see also, Map 30

I&GN RR CO
Abs # 1461
05-Oct-1893
see also, Maps 29, 30

JAIME, F
Abs # 157
20-Mar-1873
see also, Map 23

JOHNSTON, J S
Abs # 160
28-Jan-1858
see also, Map 23

KIMMEL, E C
Abs # 1473
30-Mar-1880

NARRED, J L
Abs # 2318
05-Dec-1919

POITEVENT, J
Abs # 1508
16-Apr-1879
see also, Maps 23, 31

SCOTT, J P
Abs # 257
08-Jun-1860
see also, Map 14

SLATOR, J G
Abs # 2118
20-Jun-1894

STAFFORD, MRS M B
Abs # 1533
14-Jun-1886

TE&L CO
Abs # 1031
01-Feb-1859
see also, Map 14

TE&L CO
Abs # 1032
01-Feb-1859
see also, Map 14

TE&L CO
Abs # 1033
01-Feb-1859
see also, Maps 14, 15, 23

TE&L CO
Abs # 1040
02-Feb-1859
see also, Map 23

TE&L CO
Abs # 1041
02-Feb-1859

TE&L CO
Abs # 1042

02-Feb-1859

TE&L CO
Abs # 1043
02-Feb-1859
see also, Map 23

TE&L CO
Abs # 1050
02-Feb-1859
see also, Map 23

TE&L CO
Abs # 1051
02-Feb-1859

TE&L CO
Abs # 1075
25-Aug-1858

TE&L CO
Abs # 1076
31-Aug-1858

TE&L CO
Abs # 1130
19-Nov-1858
see also, Maps 30, 31

TE&L CO
Abs # 1226
08-Mar-1859

TE&L CO
Abs # 1228
08-Mar-1859

TE&L CO
Abs # 1233
11-Mar-1859
see also, Map 21

TE&L CO
Abs # 2021
05-Feb-1859

TE&L CO
Abs # 653
25-Sep-1857
see also, Map 21

TE&L CO
Abs # 654
21-Sep-1857

TE&L CO
Abs # 655
26-Mar-1858

TE&L CO
Abs # 656
26-Mar-1858

TE&L CO
Abs # 657
26-Mar-1858

TE&L CO
Abs # 658
29-Mar-1858

TE&L CO
Abs # 659
29-Mar-1858

TE&L CO
Abs # 660
29-Mar-1858

TE&L CO
Abs # 661
29-Mar-1858

TE&L CO
Abs # 662
29-Mar-1858
see also, Map 21

TE&L CO
Abs # 667
30-Mar-1858
see also, Map 21

TE&L CO
Abs # 668
30-Mar-1858

TE&L CO
Abs # 669
30-Mar-1858

TE&L CO
Abs # 670
30-Mar-1858

TE&L CO
Abs # 671
30-Mar-1858

TE&L CO
Abs # 674
31-Mar-1858

TE&L CO
Abs # 675
31-Mar-1858

TE&L CO
Abs # 676
31-Mar-1858
see also, Map 21

TE&L CO
Abs # 681
01-Apr-1858
see also, Map 21

TE&L CO
Abs # 682
01-Apr-1858

TE&L CO
Abs # 683
01-Apr-1858

TE&L CO
Abs # 802
18-May-1858
see also, Map 14

TE&L CO
Abs # 803
18-May-1858
see also, Map 14

TE&L CO
Abs # 804
21-Sep-1857
see also, Map 14

TE&L CO
Abs # 805
18-May-1858
see also, Maps 13, 14, 21

TE&L CO
Abs # 927
07-Sep-1858
see also, Maps 23, 30, 31

THOMAS, C H
Abs # 1984

VIVEN, P
Abs # 1265
15-Jul-1859
see also, Map 21

Populated Places
None

Cemeteries
None

Water (larger bodies)
Lake Eddleman

Other Water
Briar Creek
Flint Creek
Turtle Hole Creek

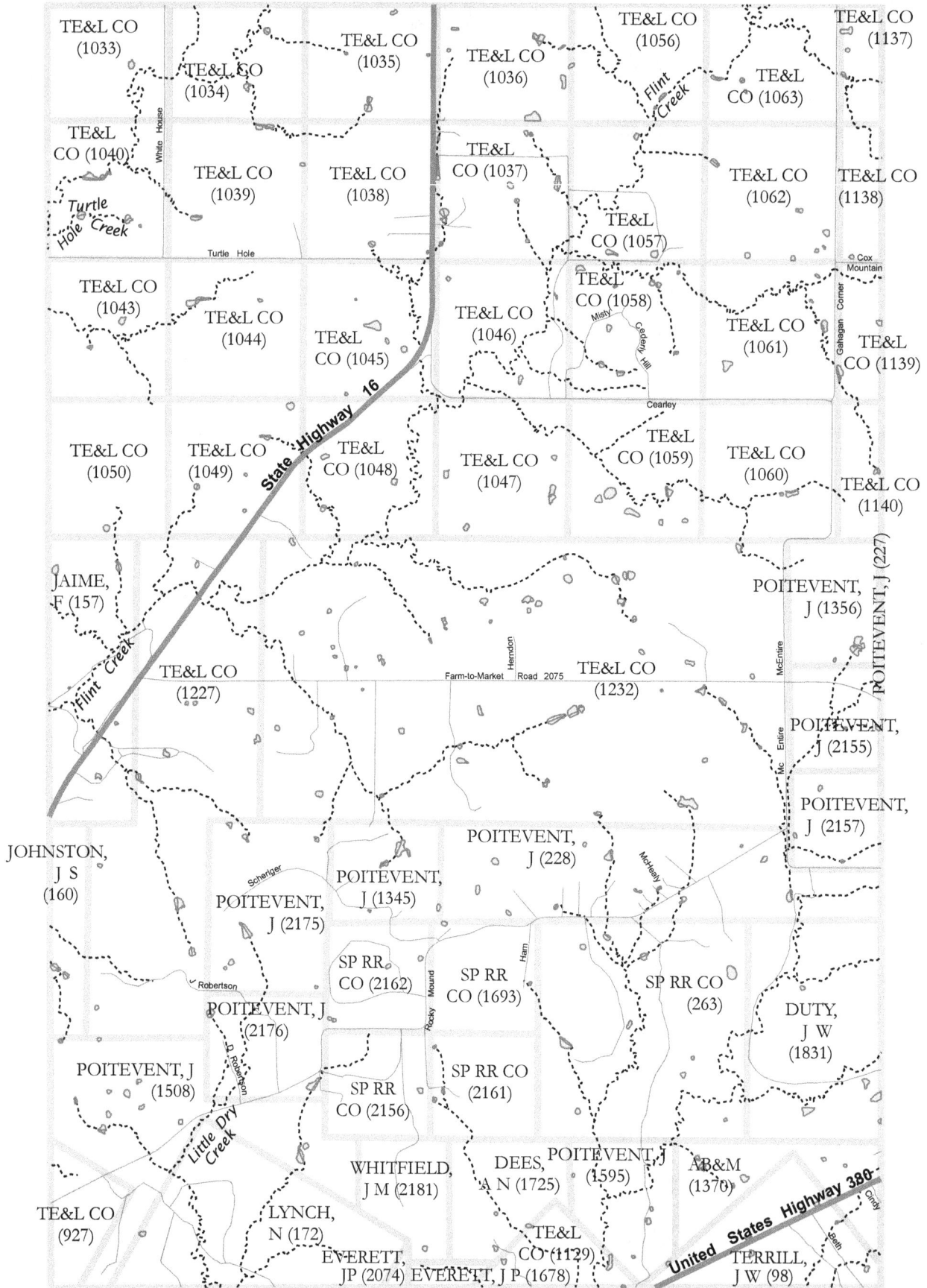

TE&L CO
(1033)

TE&L CO
(1034)

TE&L CO
(1035)

TE&L CO
(1036)

TE&L CO
(1056)

TE&L CO
(1137)

Flint Creek

TE&L
CO (1063)

TE&L
CO (1040)

White House

TE&L CO
(1039)

TE&L CO
(1038)

TE&L
CO (1037)

TE&L CO
(1062)

TE&L CO
(1138)

Turtle
Hole Creek

Turtle Hole

TE&L
CO (1057)

Cox
Mountain

TE&L CO
(1043)

TE&L CO
(1044)

TE&L
CO (1045)

TE&L CO
(1046)

TE&L
CO (1058)

Misty

Cearley Hill

TE&L CO
(1061)

TE&L
CO (1139)

Gahagan Corner

State Highway 16

Cearley

TE&L CO
(1050)

TE&L CO
(1049)

TE&L
CO (1048)

TE&L CO
(1047)

TE&L
CO (1059)

TE&L CO
(1060)

TE&L CO
(1140)

JAIME,
F (157)

POITEVENT,
J (1356)

POITEVENT, J (227)

Flint Creek

TE&L CO
(1227)

Herndon

Farm-to-Market Road 2075

TE&L CO
(1232)

McEntire

POITEVENT,
J (2155)

Mc Entire

POITEVENT,
J (2157)

JOHNSTON,
J S
(160)

Scheriger

POITEVENT,
J (1345)

POITEVENT,
J (228)

POITEVENT,
J (2175)

McHealy

Robertson

SP RR
CO (2162)

Rocky Mound

SP RR
CO (1693)

Ham

SP RR CO
(263)

DUTY,
J W
(1831)

POITEVENT, J
(2176)

Robertson

SP RR CO
(2161)

POITEVENT, J
(1508)

SP RR
CO (2156)

Little Dry Creek

WHITFIELD,
J M (2181)

DEES,
A N (1725)

POITEVENT, J
(1595)

AB&M
(1370)

United States Highway 380

Cindy

TE&L CO
(927)

LYNCH,
N (172)

TE&L
CO (1129)

TERRILL,
J W (98)

Beth

EVERETT,
JP (2074)

EVERETT, J P (1678)

AB&M
Abs # 1370
08-May-1918
see also, Maps 24, 32

DEES, A N
Abs # 1725
21-Aug-1901

DUTY, J W
Abs # 1831
03-Jan-1897
see also, Map 24

EVERETT, J P
Abs # 1678
27-Mar-1884
see also, Map 31

EVERETT, J P
Abs # 2074
04-Nov-1893
see also, Map 31

JAIME, F
Abs # 157
20-Mar-1873
see also, Map 22

JOHNSTON, J S
Abs # 160
28-Jan-1858
see also, Map 22

LYNCH, N
Abs # 172
30-Mar-1875
see also, Map 31

POITEVENT, J
Abs # 1345
Survey2: MAHLER, H
22-Dec-1898

POITEVENT, J
Abs # 1356
Survey2: SCHLITTLER, J
05-Sep-1891

POITEVENT, J
Abs # 1508
16-Apr-1879
see also, Maps 22, 31

POITEVENT, J
Abs # 1595
Survey2: DEE, A N
21-Aug-1901

POITEVENT, J
Abs # 2155
Survey2: DOUGLASS, E L
21-Sep-1900
see also, Map 24

POITEVENT, J
Abs # 2157
Survey2: DOUGLASS, E L
13-Oct-1902
see also, Map 24

POITEVENT, J
Abs # 2175
Survey2: ROBERTSON, J H
10-Nov-1926

POITEVENT, J
Abs # 2176
Survey2: ROBERTSON, R J
09-Dec-1909

POITEVENT, J
Abs # 227
21-Jan-1878
see also, Map 24

POITEVENT, J
Abs # 228
22-Jan-1878
see also, Map 24

SP RR CO
Abs # 1693
Survey2: MEYER, J
01-May-1891

SP RR CO
Abs # 2156
Survey2: DOUGLASS, E L
30-Jul-1909

SP RR CO
Abs # 2161
Survey2: GACHTER, J A
10-Dec-1909

SP RR CO
Abs # 2162
Survey2: HEIGHTON, J L
26-May-1920

SP RR CO
Abs # 263
29-May-1875

TE&L CO
Abs # 1033
01-Feb-1859
see also, Maps 14, 15, 22

TE&L CO
Abs # 1034
01-Feb-1859
see also, Map 15

TE&L CO
Abs # 1035
01-Feb-1859
see also, Map 15

TE&L CO
Abs # 1036
01-Feb-1859
see also, Map 15

TE&L CO
Abs # 1037
02-Feb-1859

TE&L CO
Abs # 1038
02-Feb-1859

TE&L CO
Abs # 1039
02-Feb-1859

TE&L CO
Abs # 1040
02-Feb-1859
see also, Map 22

TE&L CO
Abs # 1043
02-Feb-1859
see also, Map 22

TE&L CO
Abs # 1044
01-Feb-1860

TE&L CO
Abs # 1045
02-Feb-1860

TE&L CO
Abs # 1046
02-Feb-1859

TE&L CO
Abs # 1047
02-Feb-1859

TE&L CO
Abs # 1048
21-Mar-1859

TE&L CO
Abs # 1049
24-Jan-1859

TE&L CO
Abs # 1050
02-Feb-1859
see also, Map 22

TE&L CO
Abs # 1056
03-Feb-1859
see also, Map 15

TE&L CO
Abs # 1057
03-Feb-1859

TE&L CO
Abs # 1058
12-Feb-1859

TE&L CO
Abs # 1059
12-Feb-1859

TE&L CO
Abs # 1060
12-Feb-1859

TE&L CO
Abs # 1061
12-Feb-1859

TE&L CO
Abs # 1062
12-Feb-1859

TE&L CO
Abs # 1063
12-Feb-1859
see also, Map 15

TE&L CO
Abs # 1129
18-Nov-1858
see also, Map 31

TE&L CO
Abs # 1137
04-Feb-1859
see also, Maps 15, 16, 24

TE&L CO
Abs # 1138
04-Feb-1859
see also, Map 24

TE&L CO
Abs # 1139
04-Feb-1859
see also, Map 24

TE&L CO
Abs # 1140
04-Feb-1859
see also, Map 24

TE&L CO
Abs # 1227
08-Mar-1859

TE&L CO
Abs # 1232
10-Mar-1859

TE&L CO
Abs # 927
07-Sep-1858
see also, Maps 22, 30, 31

TERRILL, J W
Abs # 98
22-Dec-1873
see also, Maps 24, 31, 32

WHITFIELD, J M
Abs # 2181
27-May-1922

Populated Places
None

Cemeteries
None

Water (larger bodies)
None

Other Water
Flint Creek
Little Dry Creek
Turtle Hole Creek

213

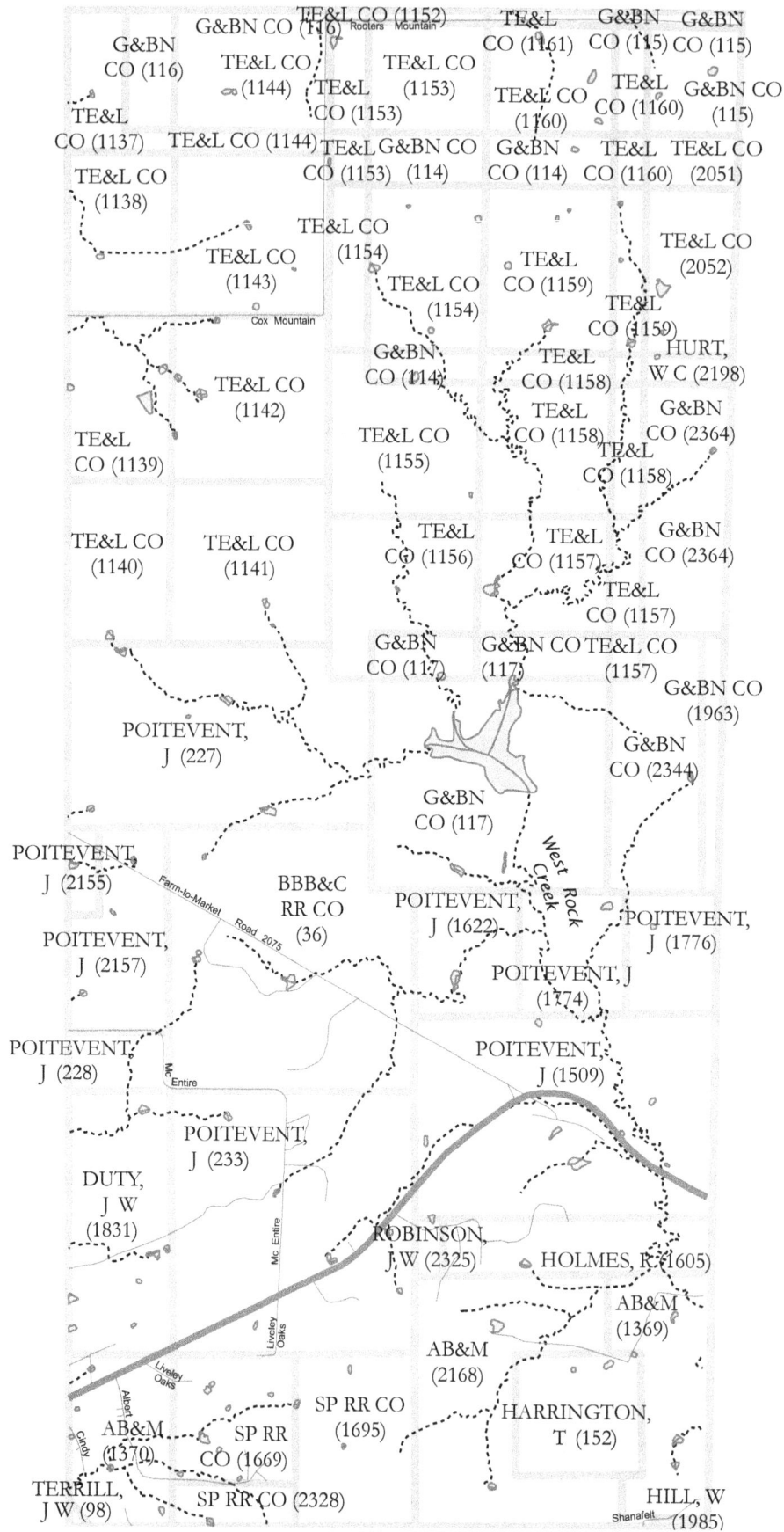

G&BN
CO (116)

G&BN CO (116)

TE&L CO (1152)
Rooters Mountain

TE&L
CO (1161)

G&BN
CO (115)

G&BN
CO (115)

TE&L CO
(1144)

TE&L CO
(1153)

TE&L
CO (1160)

TE&L
CO (1160)

TE&L
CO (1137)

TE&L
CO (1153)

G&BN CO
(115)

TE&L CO (1144)

TE&L
CO (1153)

G&BN CO
(114)

G&BN
CO (114)

TE&L
CO (1160)

TE&L CO
(2051)

TE&L CO
(1138)

TE&L CO
(1154)

TE&L CO
(2052)

TE&L CO
(1143)

TE&L CO
(1154)

TE&L
CO (1159)

TE&L
CO (1159)

Cox Mountain

HURT,
W C (2198)

TE&L CO
(1142)

G&BN
CO (114)

TE&L
CO (1158)

G&BN
CO (2364)

TE&L
CO (1139)

TE&L CO
(1155)

TE&L
CO (1158)

TE&L
CO (1158)

TE&L CO
(1140)

TE&L CO
(1141)

TE&L
CO (1156)

TE&L
CO (1157)

G&BN
CO (2364)

TE&L
CO (1157)

G&BN
CO (117)

G&BN CO
(117)

TE&L CO
(1157)

G&BN CO
(1963)

POITEVENT,
J (227)

G&BN
CO (117)

G&BN
CO (2344)

POITEVENT,
J (2155)

BBB&C
RR CO
(36)

POITEVENT,
J (1622)

West Rock Creek

POITEVENT,
J (1776)

Farm-to-Market Road 2075

POITEVENT,
J (2157)

POITEVENT, J
(1774)

POITEVENT,
J (228)

POITEVENT,
J (1509)

Mc Entire

POITEVENT,
J (233)

DUTY,
J W
(1831)

Mc Entire

ROBINSON,
J W (2325)

HOLMES, R (1605)

AB&M
(1369)

Liveley Oaks

AB&M
(2168)

Liveley
Oaks

SP RR CO
(1695)

HARRINGTON,
T (152)

Albert

AB&M
(1370)

SP RR
CO (1669)

Cindy

TERRILL,
J W (98)

SP RR CO (2328)

HILL, W
(1985)

Shanafelt

AB&M
  Abs # 1369
  15-May-1879
  see also, Map 32

AB&M
  Abs # 1370
  08-May-1918
  see also, Maps 23, 32

AB&M
  Abs # 2168
  03-Oct-1889
  see also, Map 32

BBB&C RR CO
  Abs # 36
  09-Oct-1876

DUTY, J W
  Abs # 1831
  03-Jan-1897
  see also, Map 23

G&BN CO
  Abs # 114
  02-Aug-1873

G&BN CO
  Abs # 115
  05-Aug-1873
  see also, Map 16

G&BN CO
  Abs # 116
  01-Aug-1873
  see also, Map 16

G&BN CO
  Abs # 117
  31-Jul-1873

G&BN CO
  Abs # 1963
  Survey2: LEFFEL, J W
  16-Jul-1928

G&BN CO
  Abs # 2344
  Survey2: LEFFEL, J W
  26-Apr-1927

G&BN CO
  Abs # 2364

HARRINGTON, T
  Abs # 152
  12-Sep-1876

HILL, W
  Abs # 1985
  09-Jun-1926
  see also, Map 32

HOLMES, R
  Abs # 1605
  27-Jul-1881

HURT, W C
  Abs # 2198

POITEVENT, J
  Abs # 1509
  22-Dec-1884

POITEVENT, J
  Abs # 1622
  Survey2: MELLINGER, D S
  27-Sep-1901

POITEVENT, J
  Abs # 1774
  Survey2: COOK, L C
  24-May-1901

POITEVENT, J
  Abs # 1776
  Survey2: DAWSON, J T
  20-Mar-1924

POITEVENT, J
  Abs # 2155
  Survey2: DOUGLASS, E L
  21-Sep-1900
  see also, Map 23

POITEVENT, J
  Abs # 2157
  Survey2: DOUGLASS, E L
  13-Oct-1902

  see also, Map 23

POITEVENT, J
  Abs # 227
  21-Jan-1878
  see also, Map 23

POITEVENT, J
  Abs # 228
  22-Jan-1878
  see also, Map 23

POITEVENT, J
  Abs # 233
  04-Aug-1875

ROBINSON, J W
  Abs # 2325
  10-Aug-1920

SP RR CO
  Abs # 1669
  Survey2: BAKER, J M
  20-Nov-1900

SP RR CO
  Abs # 1695
  Survey2: MCCOMBER, H A
  03-Oct-1889
  see also, Map 32

SP RR CO
  Abs # 2328
  Survey2: WALKER, W T
  21-Feb-1920
  see also, Map 32

TE&L CO
  Abs # 1137
  04-Feb-1859
  see also, Maps 15, 16, 23

TE&L CO
  Abs # 1138
  04-Feb-1859
  see also, Map 23

TE&L CO
  Abs # 1139
  04-Feb-1859
  see also, Map 23

TE&L CO
  Abs # 1140
  04-Feb-1859
  see also, Map 23

TE&L CO
  Abs # 1141
  04-Feb-1859

TE&L CO
  Abs # 1142
  05-Feb-1859

TE&L CO
  Abs # 1143
  05-Feb-1859

TE&L CO
  Abs # 1144
  05-Feb-1859
  see also, Map 16

TE&L CO
  Abs # 1152
  07-Feb-1859
  see also, Map 16

TE&L CO
  Abs # 1153
  07-Feb-1859

TE&L CO
  Abs # 1154
  07-Feb-1859

TE&L CO
  Abs # 1155
  07-Feb-1859

TE&L CO
  Abs # 1156
  07-Feb-1859

TE&L CO
  Abs # 1157
  07-Feb-1859

TE&L CO

  Abs # 1158
  07-Feb-1859

TE&L CO
  Abs # 1159
  07-Feb-1859

TE&L CO
  Abs # 1160
  07-Feb-1859

TE&L CO
  Abs # 1161
  07-Feb-1859
  see also, Map 16

TE&L CO
  Abs # 2051
  08-Feb-1859

TE&L CO
  Abs # 2052
  08-Feb-1859

TERRILL, J W
  Abs # 98
  22-Dec-1873
  see also, Maps 23, 31, 32

Populated Places
None

Cemeteries
None

Water (larger bodies)
None

Other Water
West Rock Creek

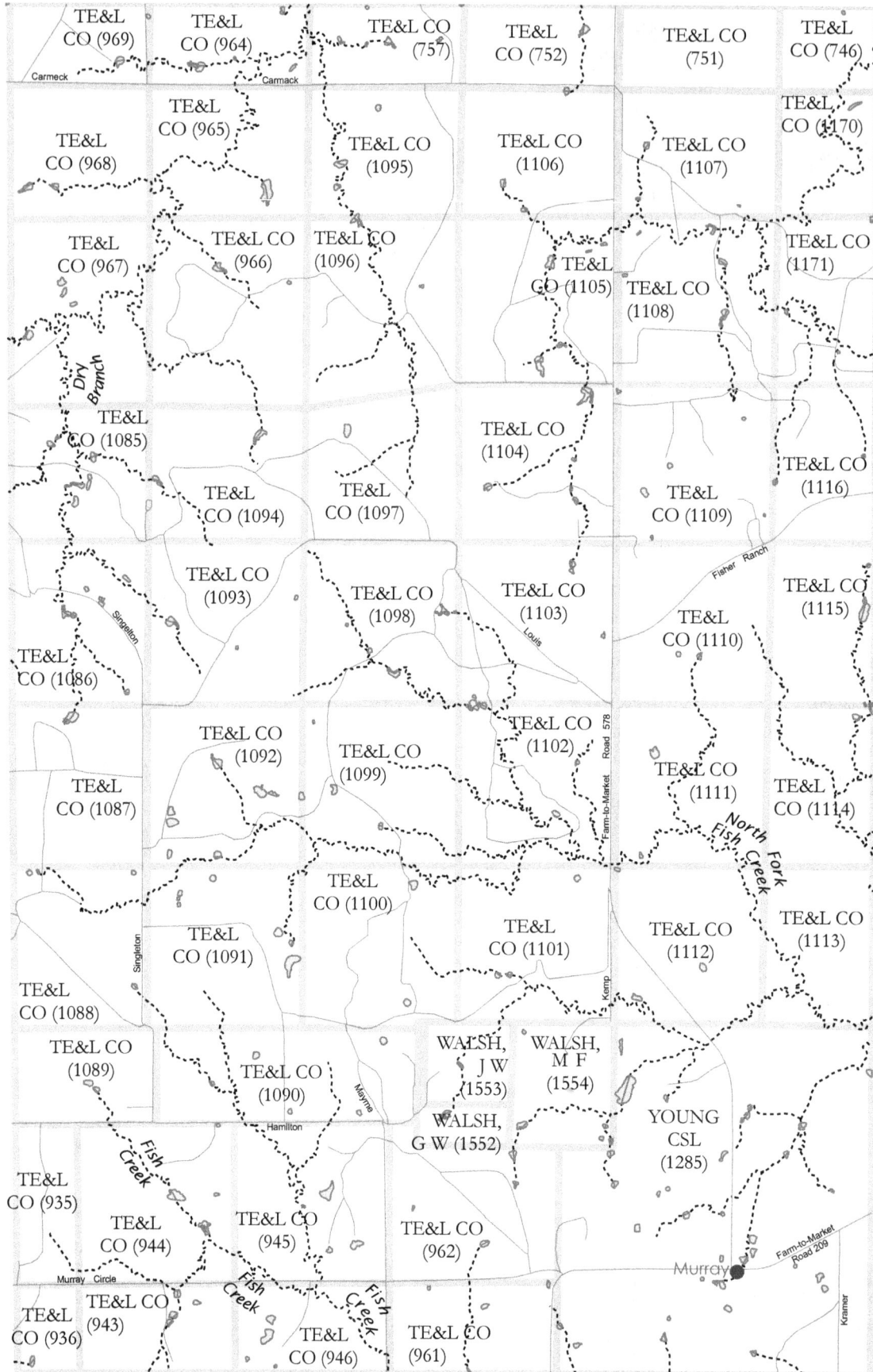

TE&L CO (969)

TE&L CO (964)

TE&L CO (757)

TE&L CO (752)

TE&L CO (751)

TE&L CO (746)

Carmeck

Carmack

TE&L CO (965)

TE&L CO (968)

TE&L CO (1095)

TE&L CO (1106)

TE&L CO (1107)

TE&L CO (1170)

TE&L CO (967)

TE&L CO (966)

TE&L CO (1096)

TE&L CO (1105)

TE&L CO (1108)

TE&L CO (1171)

Dry Branch

TE&L CO (1085)

TE&L CO (1104)

TE&L CO (1109)

TE&L CO (1116)

TE&L CO (1094)

TE&L CO (1097)

Fisher Ranch

TE&L CO (1093)

TE&L CO (1098)

TE&L CO (1103)

Louis

TE&L CO (1110)

TE&L CO (1115)

Singleton

TE&L CO (1086)

TE&L CO (1092)

TE&L CO (1099)

TE&L CO (1102)

Farm-to-Market Road 578

TE&L CO (1111)

TE&L CO (1114)

North Fork Fish Creek

TE&L CO (1087)

TE&L CO (1100)

TE&L CO (1091)

TE&L CO (1101)

TE&L CO (1112)

TE&L CO (1113)

Singleton

Kemp

TE&L CO (1088)

TE&L CO (1089)

TE&L CO (1090)

Mayne

WALSH, J W (1553)

WALSH, M F (1554)

WALSH, G W (1552)

YOUNG CSL (1285)

Hamilton

Fish Creek

TE&L CO (935)

TE&L CO (944)

TE&L CO (945)

TE&L CO (962)

Murray

Farm-to-Market Road 209

Murray Circle

Fish Creek

Fish Creek

Kramer

TE&L CO (936)

TE&L CO (943)

TE&L CO (946)

TE&L CO (961)

TE&L CO
Abs # 1085
15-Oct-1858

TE&L CO
Abs # 1086
15-Oct-1858

TE&L CO
Abs # 1087
16-Oct-1858

TE&L CO
Abs # 1088
16-Oct-1858

TE&L CO
Abs # 1089
16-Oct-1858

TE&L CO
Abs # 1090
16-Oct-1858

TE&L CO
Abs # 1091
16-Oct-1858

TE&L CO
Abs # 1092
16-Oct-1858

TE&L CO
Abs # 1093
16-Oct-1858

TE&L CO
Abs # 1094
16-Oct-1858

TE&L CO
Abs # 1095
16-Oct-1858

TE&L CO
Abs # 1096
18-Oct-1858

TE&L CO
Abs # 1097
18-Oct-1858

TE&L CO
Abs # 1098
18-Oct-1858

TE&L CO
Abs # 1099
18-Oct-1858

TE&L CO
Abs # 1100
18-Oct-1858

TE&L CO
Abs # 1101
18-Oct-1858

TE&L CO
Abs # 1102
18-Oct-1858

TE&L CO
Abs # 1103
18-Oct-1858

TE&L CO
Abs # 1104
18-Oct-1858

TE&L CO
Abs # 1105
18-Oct-1858

TE&L CO
Abs # 1106
18-Oct-1858

TE&L CO
Abs # 1107
18-Oct-1858

TE&L CO
Abs # 1108
18-Oct-1858

TE&L CO
Abs # 1109
18-Oct-1858

TE&L CO
Abs # 1110
18-Oct-1858

TE&L CO
Abs # 1111
19-Oct-1858

TE&L CO
Abs # 1112
19-Oct-1858

TE&L CO
Abs # 1113
19-Oct-1858
see also, Map 26

TE&L CO
Abs # 1114
19-Oct-1858
see also, Map 26

TE&L CO
Abs # 1115
19-Oct-1858
see also, Map 26

TE&L CO
Abs # 1116
19-Oct-1858
see also, Map 26

TE&L CO
Abs # 1170
19-Oct-1858
see also, Map 26

TE&L CO
Abs # 1171
19-Oct-1858
see also, Map 26

TE&L CO
Abs # 746
13-Mar-1911
see also, Maps 17, 18, 26

TE&L CO
Abs # 751
08-Jun-1858
see also, Map 17

TE&L CO
Abs # 752
08-Jun-1858
see also, Map 17

TE&L CO
Abs # 757
09-Jun-1858
see also, Map 17

TE&L CO
Abs # 935
23-Sep-1858

TE&L CO
Abs # 936
23-Sep-1858
see also, Map 33

TE&L CO
Abs # 943
12-Jun-1858
see also, Map 33

TE&L CO
Abs # 944
12-Jun-1858

TE&L CO
Abs # 945
13-Jul-1858

TE&L CO
Abs # 946
13-Jul-1858
see also, Map 33

TE&L CO
Abs # 961
16-Jul-1858
see also, Map 33

TE&L CO
Abs # 962
16-Jul-1858

TE&L CO
Abs # 964

12-Jun-1858
see also, Map 17

TE&L CO
Abs # 965
16-Jul-1858

TE&L CO
Abs # 966
16-Jul-1858

TE&L CO
Abs # 967
16-Jul-1858

TE&L CO
Abs # 968
16-Jul-1858

TE&L CO
Abs # 969
17-Jul-1858
see also, Map 17

WALSH, G W
Abs # 1552
24-Jan-1893

WALSH, J W
Abs # 1553
05-Jul-1888

WALSH, M F
Abs # 1554
20-Oct-1887

YOUNG CSL
Abs # 1285
31-Jul-1891
see also, Maps 26, 33, 34

Populated Places
Murray

Cemeteries
None

Water (larger bodies)
None

Other Water
Dry Branch
Fish Creek
North Fork Fish Creek

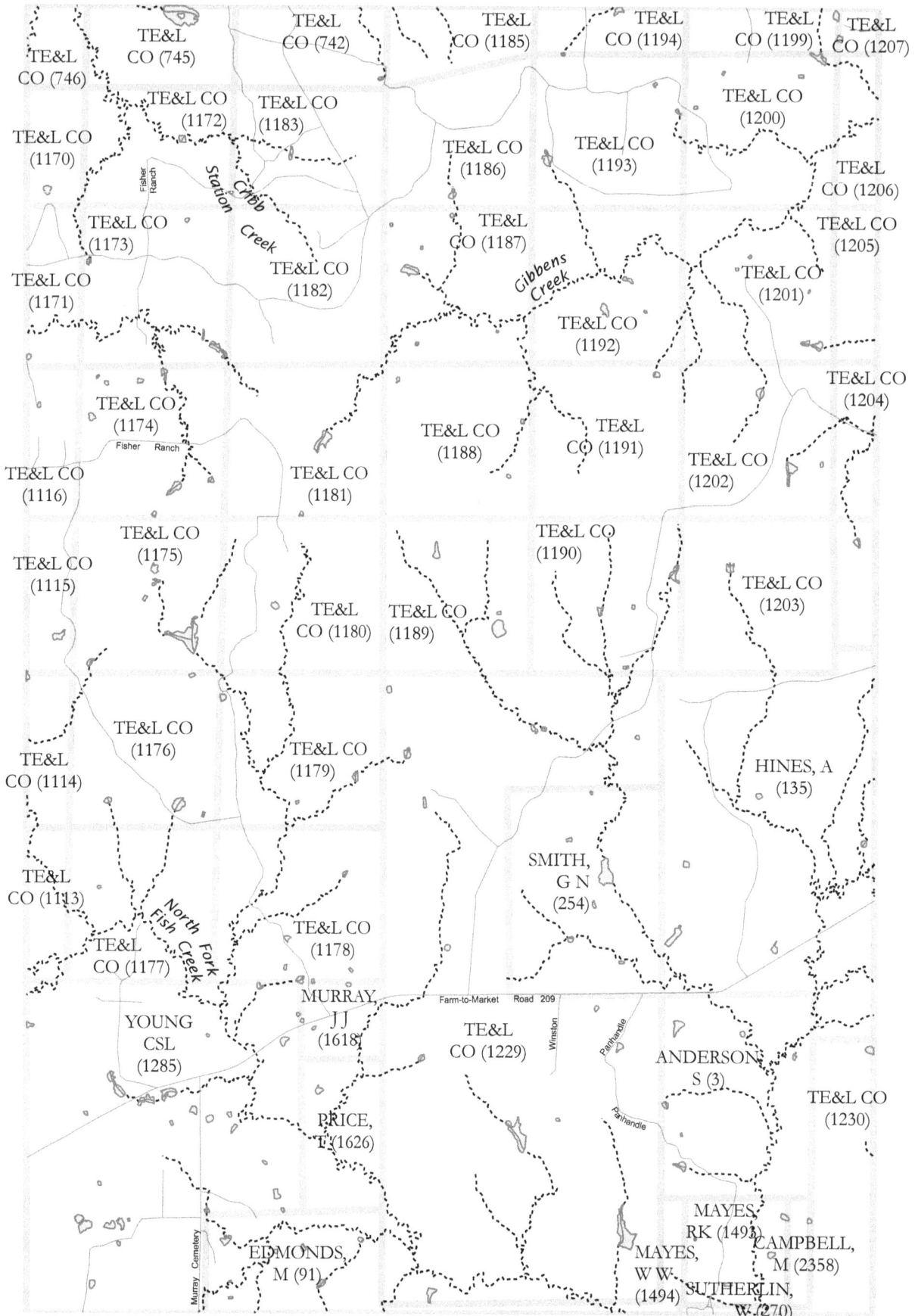

TE&L
CO (746)

TE&L
CO (745)

TE&L
CO (742)

TE&L
CO (1185)

TE&L
CO (1194)

TE&L
CO (1199)

TE&L
CO (1207)

TE&L CO
(1172)

TE&L CO
(1183)

TE&L CO
(1170)

Fisher
Ranch

Chibb
Station Creek

TE&L CO
(1186)

TE&L CO
(1193)

TE&L CO
(1200)

TE&L
CO (1206)

TE&L CO
(1173)

TE&L
CO (1187)

TE&L CO
(1205)

TE&L CO
(1171)

TE&L CO
(1182)

Gibbens
Creek

TE&L CO
(1201)

TE&L CO
(1192)

TE&L CO
(1204)

TE&L CO
(1174)

Fisher   Ranch

TE&L CO
(1188)

TE&L
CO (1191)

TE&L CO
(1202)

TE&L CO
(1116)

TE&L CO
(1181)

TE&L CO
(1175)

TE&L CO
(1190)

TE&L CO
(1203)

TE&L CO
(1115)

TE&L
CO (1180)

TE&L CO
(1189)

TE&L CO
(1176)

TE&L CO
(1179)

HINES, A
(135)

TE&L
CO (1114)

SMITH,
G N
(254)

TE&L
CO (1113)

North Fork
Fish Creek

TE&L
CO (1177)

TE&L CO
(1178)

MURRAY
J J
(1618)

Farm-to-Market   Road   209

YOUNG
CSL
(1285)

TE&L
CO 1229)

Winston

Panhandle

ANDERSON
S (3)

TE&L CO
(1230)

PRICE,
T (1626)

Panhandle

MAYES
RK (1493)

CAMPBELL,
M (2358)

Murray Cemetery

EDMONDS,
M (91)

MAYES,
W W
(1494)

SUTHERLIN,
W (270)

ANDERSON, S
Abs # 3
07-Dec-1860

CAMPBELL, M
Abs # 2358
30-Jul-1943

EDMONDS, M
Abs # 91
21-Feb-1862
see also, Map 34

HINES, A
Abs # 135
23-Nov-1866
see also, Map 27

MAYES, R K
Abs # 1493
28-Mar-1881

MAYES, W W
Abs # 1494
20-Jan-1881
see also, Map 34

MURRAY, J J
Abs # 1618
24-Feb-1886

PRICE, T
Abs # 1626
12-Mar-1880

SMITH, G N
Abs # 254
27-Sep-1860

SUTHERLIN, W
Abs # 270
08-Sep-1863
see also, Map 34

TE&L CO
Abs # 1113
19-Oct-1858
see also, Map 25

TE&L CO
Abs # 1114
19-Oct-1858
see also, Map 25

TE&L CO
Abs # 1115
19-Oct-1858
see also, Map 25

TE&L CO
Abs # 1116
19-Oct-1858
see also, Map 25

TE&L CO
Abs # 1170
19-Oct-1858
see also, Map 25

TE&L CO
Abs # 1171
19-Oct-1858
see also, Map 25

TE&L CO
Abs # 1172
19-Oct-1858

TE&L CO
Abs # 1173
19-Oct-1858

TE&L CO
Abs # 1174
20-Oct-1858

TE&L CO
Abs # 1175
20-Oct-1858

TE&L CO
Abs # 1176
20-Oct-1858

TE&L CO
Abs # 1177
20-Oct-1858

TE&L CO
Abs # 1178
20-Oct-1858

TE&L CO
Abs # 1179
20-Oct-1858

TE&L CO
Abs # 1180
20-Oct-1858

TE&L CO
Abs # 1181
20-Oct-1858

TE&L CO
Abs # 1182
20-Oct-1858

TE&L CO
Abs # 1183
20-Oct-1858

TE&L CO
Abs # 1185
20-Oct-1858
see also, Map 18

TE&L CO
Abs # 1186
20-Oct-1858

TE&L CO
Abs # 1187
21-Oct-1858

TE&L CO
Abs # 1188
21-Oct-1858

TE&L CO
Abs # 1189
21-Oct-1858

TE&L CO
Abs # 1190
21-Oct-1858

TE&L CO
Abs # 1191
21-Oct-1858

TE&L CO
Abs # 1192
21-Oct-1858

TE&L CO
Abs # 1193
21-Oct-1858

TE&L CO
Abs # 1194
22-Oct-1858
see also, Map 18

TE&L CO
Abs # 1199
22-Oct-1858
see also, Map 18

TE&L CO
Abs # 1200
22-Oct-1858

TE&L CO
Abs # 1201
22-Oct-1858

TE&L CO
Abs # 1202
22-Oct-1858

TE&L CO
Abs # 1203
22-Oct-1858

TE&L CO
Abs # 1204
16-Jun-1858
see also, Map 27

TE&L CO
Abs # 1205
16-Jun-1858
see also, Map 27

TE&L CO
Abs # 1206
22-Oct-1858
see also, Map 27

TE&L CO
Abs # 1207
22-Oct-1858
see also, Maps 18, 19, 27

TE&L CO
Abs # 1229
09-Mar-1859

TE&L CO
Abs # 1230
10-Mar-1859
see also, Maps 27, 34, 35

TE&L CO
Abs # 742
05-Jun-1858
see also, Map 18

TE&L CO
Abs # 745
07-Jun-1858
see also, Map 18

TE&L CO
Abs # 746
13-Mar-1911
see also, Maps 17, 18, 25

YOUNG CSL
Abs # 1285
31-Jul-1891
see also, Maps 25, 33, 34

Populated Places

None

Cemeteries

None

Water (larger bodies)

None

Other Water

Cribb Station Creek
Gibbens Creek
North Fork Fish Creek

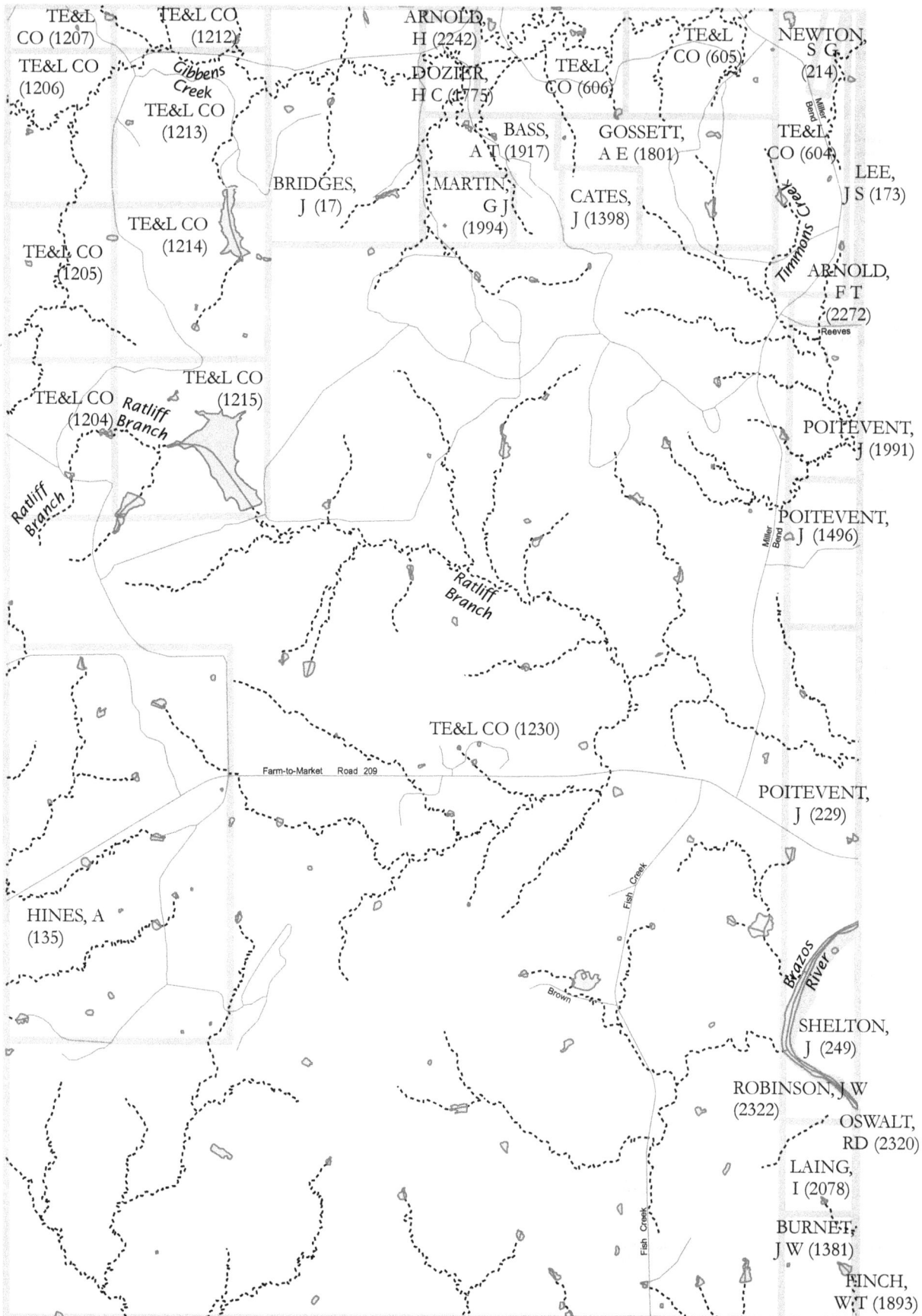

TE&L
CO (1207)

TE&L CO
(1212)

ARNOLD,
H (2242)

TE&L
CO (605)

NEWTON,
S G
(214)

TE&L CO
(1206)

Gibbens
Creek

DOZIER,
H C (1775)

TE&L
CO (606)

TE&L CO
(1213)

BASS,
A T (1917)

GOSSETT,
A E (1801)

TE&L
CO (604)

LEE,
J S (173)

BRIDGES,
J (17)

MARTIN,
G J
(1994)

CATES,
J (1398)

Timmons Creek

ARNOLD,
F T
(2272)

TE&L CO
(1214)

Reeves

TE&L CO
(1205)

POITEVENT,
J (1991)

TE&L CO
(1204)

Ratliff
Branch

TE&L CO
(1215)

POITEVENT,
J (1496)

Ratliff
Branch

Miller
Bend

Ratliff
Branch

TE&L CO (1230)

Farm-to-Market   Road 209

POITEVENT,
J (229)

Fish   Creek

HINES, A
(135)

Brazos
River

Brown

SHELTON,
J (249)

ROBINSON, J W
(2322)

OSWALT,
RD (2320)

LAING,
I (2078)

Fish Creek

BURNET,
J W (1381)

FINCH,
W T (1893)

ARNOLD, F T
Abs # 2272
07-Dec-1908
see also, Map 19

ARNOLD, H
Abs # 2242
09-Sep-1901
see also, Map 19

BASS, A T
Abs # 1917
07-Jun-1892

BRIDGES, J
Abs # 17
15-May-1857
see also, Map 19

BURNET, J W
Abs # 1381
18-Nov-1885
see also, Map 35

CATES, J
Abs # 1398
10-Oct-1888

DOZIER, H C
Abs # 1775
12-Dec-1883

FINCH, W T
Abs # 1893
15-Feb-1890
see also, Maps 28, 35, 36

GOSSETT, A E
Abs # 1801

HINES, A
Abs # 135
23-Nov-1866
see also, Map 26

LAING, I
Abs # 2078
11-Apr-1898

LEE, J S
Abs # 173
25-Oct-1860
see also, Maps 19, 20, 28

MARTIN, G J
Abs # 1994
26-Oct-1895

NEWTON, S G
Abs # 214
23-Apr-1857
see also, Map 19

OSWALT, R D
Abs # 2320
10-Jun-1920
see also, Map 28

POITEVENT, J
Abs # 1496
Survey2: MCCANN, A J
27-Feb-1895
see also, Map 28

POITEVENT, J
Abs # 1991
Survey2: HUNT, P B
25-Jun-1930
see also, Map 28

POITEVENT, J
Abs # 229
22-Jan-1878
see also, Map 28

ROBINSON, J W
Abs # 2322
23-Jun-1920

SHELTON, J
Abs # 249
19-Sep-1855
see also, Map 28

TE&L CO
Abs # 1204
16-Jun-1858
see also, Map 26

TE&L CO

Abs # 1205
16-Jun-1858
see also, Map 26

TE&L CO
Abs # 1206
22-Oct-1858
see also, Map 26

TE&L CO
Abs # 1207
22-Oct-1858
see also, Maps 18, 19, 26

TE&L CO
Abs # 1212
23-Oct-1858
see also, Map 19

TE&L CO
Abs # 1213
23-Oct-1858

TE&L CO
Abs # 1214
23-Oct-1858

TE&L CO
Abs # 1215
23-Oct-1858

TE&L CO
Abs # 1230
10-Mar-1859
see also, Maps 26, 34, 35

TE&L CO
Abs # 604
23-Feb-1858
see also, Map 19

TE&L CO
Abs # 605
23-Feb-1858
see also, Map 19

TE&L CO
Abs # 606
11-Jan-1858
see also, Map 19

Populated Places
None

Cemeteries
None

Water (larger bodies)
None

Other Water
Brazos River
Gibbens Creek
Ratliff Branch
Timmons Creek

DOWD, P (79)

TE&L CO. (607)

JONES, W R (1609)

MCLENNAN, A (180)

HAMILTON, M (138)

TE&L CO (1231)

SA&MG RR CO (262)

Jim Anderson Creek

POITEVENT, J (2206)

LEE, J S (173)

CRAWFORD, V I (2010)

FULLER, M A (1426)

HUME, J P (140)

POITEVENT, J (230)

Clark

GUEST M V (1777)

HUGHES, C (139)

Brazos River

NEWTON, S G (1498)

JORDAN, T J (1466)

EL&RR RR CO (2207)

WRAY, H J (2268)

Brazos River

POITEVENT, J (1548)

Reeves

HEARTT, HRS C P (131)

RECTOR, E G (239)

CARSON, R (71)

POITEVENT, J (1991)

I&GN RR CO (1326)

MOORE, J W (2305)

T&NO RR CO (1476)

POITEVENT, J (1901)

Brazos River

FISHER, R J (95)

Phillip George Branch

CARSON, R (69)

T&NO RR CO (1673)

POITEVENT, J (1496)

Timmons Creek

WILLIAMS, L L (1273)

Holcomb

Holcomb

HARGRAVE, J B (1871)

ROBINSON, J W (2324)

TRIPLETT, C C (2332)

GEORGE, P S (109)

T&NO RR CO (1244)

Ratliff Branch

Brazos River

GARRETT, J (107)

BROWN, J C (39)

RATLIFF, A (244)

Farm-to-Market Rd 209

MCLENNAN A (195)

HILL, I L (126)

Fitzgerald

CAUFMAN, J (63)

POITEVENT, J (229)

Brooks Cem.

Pink Brooks

Medlan Chapel

JOHNSON, C W (2342)

MCKISSICK, S (184)

SHELTON, J (249)

MCLENNAN, A (194)

Place

KUYKENDALL, T P (167)

WEEKLEY, G M (1272)

Upper Tonk Valley

BAKER, J W (1377)

OSWALT, R D (2320)

Brazos River

TAYLOR, J N (1243)

MOSES, D (179)

BAKER, W H (1376)

BLACKWOOD, J L (1378)

FINCH, W T (1893)

Medlan Branch

MEDLAN, E (2283)

MARLIN, J (199)

BLACK, S (1576)

TACKETT, A C (1260)

MEDLAN, DUNN, A B (189) W (83)

BLAINE, R A (1382)

MARLIN, W N P (190)

BAKER, J W
Abs # 1377
15-Jan-1886
see also, Map 29

BAKER, W H
Abs # 1376
22-Jan-1887

BLACK, S
Abs # 1576
27-Jun-1882
see also, Map 36

BLACKWOOD, J L
Abs # 1378
30-Jan-1882
see also, Maps 29, 37

BLAINE, R A
Abs # 1382
21-Dec-1880
see also, Map 36

BROWN, J C
Abs # 39
31-Jul-1875
see also, Map 29

CARSON, R
Abs # 69
04-Aug-1875

CARSON, R
Abs # 71
04-Aug-1875

CAUFMAN, J
Abs # 63
05-Jun-1875
see also, Map 29

CRAWFORD, V T
Abs # 2010
26-Feb-1892

DOWD, P
Abs # 79
24-Jul-1861
see also, Maps 19, 20

DUNN, W
Abs # 83
24-Nov-1871
see also, Map 36

EL&RR RR CO
Abs # 2207
Survey2: NEWHAUS, C
06-Jan-1913
see also, Map 29

FINCH, W T
Abs # 1893
15-Feb-1890
see also, Maps 27, 35, 36

FISHER, R J
Abs # 95
19-Sep-1855

FULLER, M A
Abs # 1426
07-Jun-1879

GARRETT, J
Abs # 107
01-Jun-1875

GEORGE, P S
Abs # 109
15-May-1860

GUEST, M V
Abs # 1777
25-Sep-1884

HAMILTON, M
Abs # 138
24-May-1860
see also, Map 20

HARGRAVE, J B
Abs # 1871
16-Mar-1896
see also, Map 29

HEARTT, HRS C P
Abs # 131
20-Sep-1878

HILL, I L
Abs # 126
19-Nov-1856

HUGHES, C
Abs # 139
15-May-1861

HUME, J P
Abs # 140
23-Jul-1856
see also, Map 20

I&GN RR CO
Abs # 1326
13-Sep-1878

JOHNSON, C W
Abs # 2342
18-Nov-1925

JONES, W R
Abs # 1609
03-Mar-1880
see also, Map 20

JORDAN, T J
Abs # 1466
24-Mar-1882

KUYKENDALL, T P
Abs # 167
26-Feb-1890
see also, Map 29

LEE, J S
Abs # 173
25-Oct-1860
see also, Maps 19, 20, 27

MARLIN, J
Abs # 199
24-Oct-1857
see also, Maps 29, 36, 37

MARLIN, W N P
Abs # 190
15-Aug-1859
see also, Map 36

MCKISSICK, S
Abs # 184
16-Jun-1873
see also, Map 29

MCLENNAN, A
Abs # 180
12-Oct-1855
see also, Map 20

MCLENNAN, A
Abs # 194
10-Oct-1855

MCLENNAN, A
Abs # 195
10-Oct-1855

MEDLAN, A B
Abs # 189
25-Feb-1860
see also, Map 36

MEDLAN, E
Abs # 2283
09-Feb-1911

MOORE, J W
Abs # 2305
24-Jul-1918

MOSES, D
Abs # 179
16-Aug-1855
see also, Map 36

NEWTON, S G
Abs # 1498
23-Apr-1875

OSWALT, R D
Abs # 2320
10-Jun-1920
see also, Map 27

POITEVENT, J
Abs # 1496
Survey2: MCCANN, A J
27-Feb-1895
see also, Map 27

POITEVENT, J
Abs # 1548
Survey2: TIMMONS, J S
24-Nov-1908

POITEVENT, J
Abs # 1901
Survey2: HUNT, P B
11-Jul-1930

POITEVENT, J
Abs # 1991
Survey2: HUNT, P B
25-Jun-1930
see also, Map 27

POITEVENT, J
Abs # 2206
Survey2: NEWHAUS, C
07-Jan-1913

POITEVENT, J
Abs # 229
22-Jan-1878
see also, Map 27

POITEVENT, J
Abs # 230
22-Jan-1878

RATLIFF, A
Abs # 244
24-Jul-1860

RECTOR, E G
Abs # 239
19-Sep-1876

ROBINSON, J W
Abs # 2324
10-Aug-1920

SA&MG RR CO
Abs # 262
11-Dec-1860
see also, Map 20

SHELTON, J
Abs # 249
19-Sep-1855
see also, Map 27

T&NO RR CO
Abs # 1244
04-Sep-1873
see also, Map 29

T&NO RR CO
Abs # 1476
Survey2: KELLY, D
15-Aug-1881
see also, Map 29

T&NO RR CO
Abs # 1673
Survey2: CATES, J
22-Sep-1911
see also, Map 29

TACKETT, A C
Abs # 1260
03-Aug-1877
see also, Map 36

TAYLOR, J N
Abs # 1243
03-Jan-1859
see also, Map 36

TE&L CO
Abs # 1231
07-Apr-1859
see also, Maps 20, 21, 29

TE&L CO
Abs # 607
24-Feb-1858
see also, Map 20

TRIPLETT, C C
Abs # 2332
13-Oct-1920

WEEKLEY, G M
Abs # 1272
02-Sep-1857

WILLIAMS, L L
Abs # 1273
15-May-1860

WRAY, H J
Abs # 2268
09-May-1907

Populated Places

None

Cemeteries

Brooks Cemetery

Water (larger bodies)

None

Other Water

Brazos River
Jim Anderson Creek
Medlan Branch
Phillip George Branch
Ratliff Branch
Timmons Creek

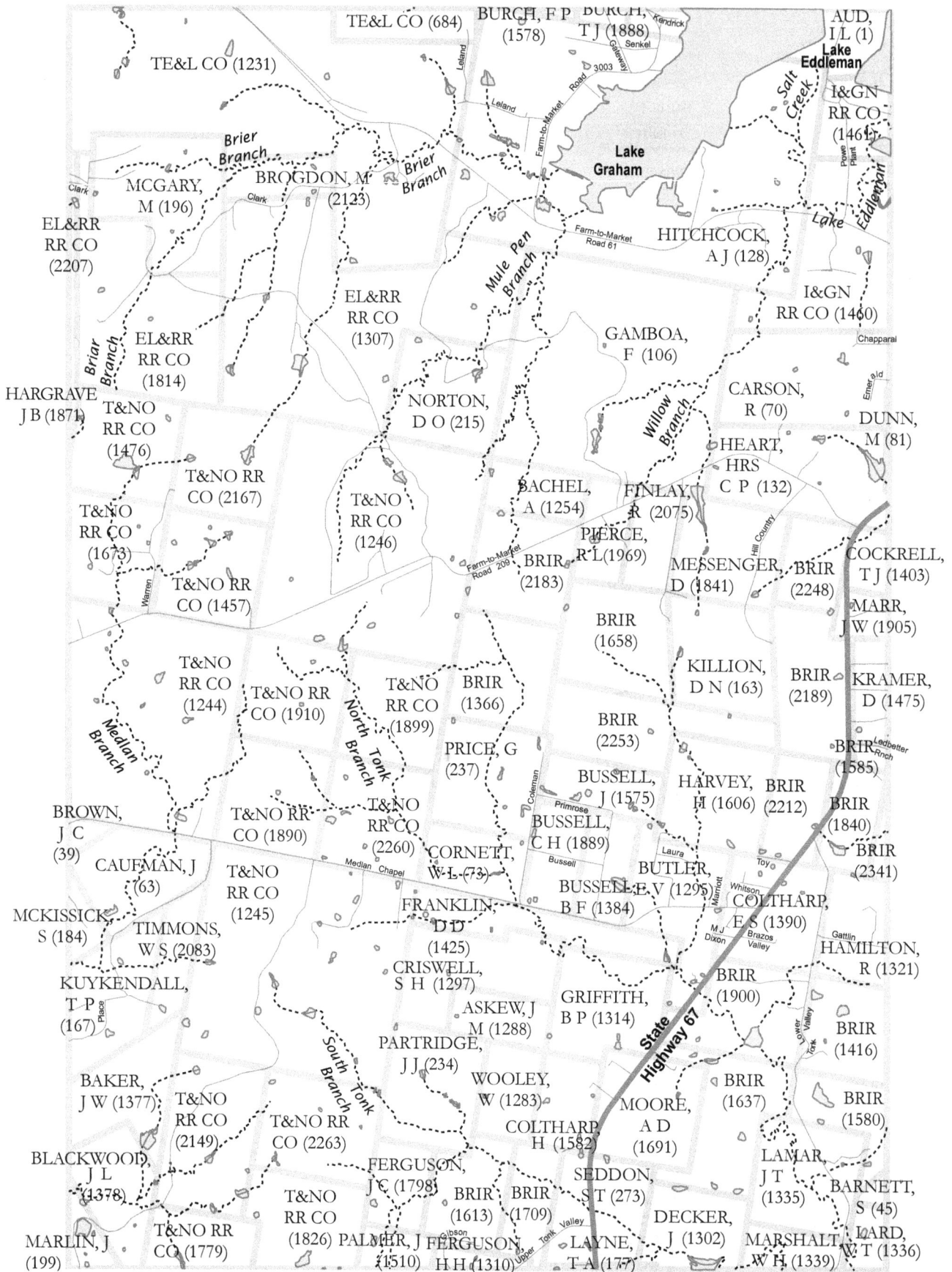

TE&L CO (684)

BURCH, F P (1578)

BURCH, T J (1888)

AUD, I L (1)

Lake Eddleman

TE&L CO (1231)

Leland

3003

Kendrick

Senkel

Galloway

Salt Creek

I&GN RR CO (1461)

Brier Branch

MCGARY, M (196)

Clark

BROGDON, M (2123)

Brier Branch

Clark

Lake Graham

Road

Farm-to-Market

Lake Eddleman

Power Plant

EL&RR RR CO (2207)

Mule Pen Branch

Farm-to-Market Road 61

HITCHCOCK, A J (128)

Briar Branch

EL&RR RR CO (1814)

EL&RR RR CO (1307)

GAMBOA, F (106)

I&GN RR CO (1460)

Chapparal

HARGRAVE J B (1871)

T&NO RR CO (1476)

NORTON, D O (215)

Willow Branch

CARSON, R (70)

Emerald

DUNN, M (81)

T&NO RR CO (2167)

HEART, HRS C P (132)

T&NO RR CO (1673)

BACHEL, A (1254)

FINLAY, R (2075)

Hill Country

T&NO RR CO (1246)

PIERCE, R L (1969)

MESSENGER, D (1841)

COCKRELL, T J (1403)

T&NO RR CO (1457)

Farm-to-Market Road 209

BRIR (2183)

BRIR (2248)

MARR, J W (1905)

Warren

BRIR (1658)

T&NO RR CO (1244)

T&NO RR CO (1910)

North Tonk Branch

T&NO RR CO (1899)

BRIR (1366)

KILLION, D N (163)

BRIR (2189)

KRAMER, D (1475)

BRIR (2253)

Ledbetter Rnch

BRIR (1585)

Medlan Branch

PRICE, G (237)

BRIR (1840)

BROWN, J C (39)

T&NO RR CO (1890)

T&NO RR CO (2260)

Coleman

BUSSELL, J (1575)

HARVEY, H (1606)

BRIR (2212)

BRIR (2341)

Primrose

CAUFMAN, J (63)

CORNETT, W L (73)

BUSSELL, C H (1889)

Laura

Bussell

BUTLER, (1295)

Toy

COLTHARP, E S (1390)

T&NO RR CO (1245)

Medlan Chapel

BUSSELL, B F (1384)

Marriott

Whitson

M J Dixon

Brazos Valley

MCKISSICK, S (184)

TIMMONS, W S (2083)

FRANKLIN, D D (1425)

HAMILTON, R (1321)

Gattlin

KUYKENDALL, T P (167)

Place

CRISWELL, S H (1297)

GRIFFITH, B P (1314)

BRIR (1900)

Lower Valley

York

BRIR (1416)

ASKEW, J M (1288)

State Highway 67

PARTRIDGE, J J (234)

South Tonk Branch

WOOLEY, W (1283)

MOORE, A D (1691)

BRIR (1637)

BRIR (1580)

BAKER, J W (1377)

T&NO RR CO (2149)

T&NO RR CO (2263)

COLTHARP, H (1582)

BLACKWOOD, J L (1378)

FERGUSON, J C (1798)

BRIR (1613)

BRIR (1709)

SEDDON, S T (273)

LAMAR, J T (1335)

BARNETT, S (45)

DECKER, J (1302)

MARLIN, J (199)

T&NO RR CO (1779)

T&NO RR CO (1826)

PALMER, J (1510)

Gibson

FERGUSON, H H (1310)

Upper Tonk Valley

LAYNE, T A (177)

MARSHALL, W H (1339)

LARD, W T (1336)

ASKEW, J M
Abs # 1288
07-Sep-1877

AUD, I L
Abs # 1
16-Nov-1860
see also, Maps 21, 22, 30

BACHEL, A
Abs # 1254
19-Mar-1877

BAKER, J W
Abs # 1377
15-Jan-1886
see also, Map 28

BARNETT, S
Abs # 45
06-Jul-1877
see also, Map 30

BLACKWOOD, J L
Abs # 1378
30-Jan-1882
see also, Maps 28, 37

BRIR
Abs # 1366
Survey2: ASH, G H
02-Dec-1882

BRIR
Abs # 1416
Survey2: DOBBS, M
09-Jun-1880
see also, Map 30

BRIR
Abs # 1580
Survey2: BARNETT, S
16-Feb-1898
see also, Map 30

BRIR
Abs # 1585
Survey2: CALHOUN, J H
24-Jan-1887
see also, Map 30

BRIR
Abs # 1613
Survey2: KIRK, J
24-Jun 1884

BRIR
Abs # 1637
Survey2: STEGALL, J H
01-Aug-1881

BRIR
Abs # 1658
Survey2: WHITE, E
14-Dec-1883

BRIR
Abs # 1709
Survey2: SEDDON, S T
29-Aug-1884
see also, Map 37

BRIR
Abs # 1840
Survey2: LAMAR, R E
24-Apr-1888
see also, Map 30

BRIR
Abs # 1900
Survey2: HUDGIN, B A
03-Sep-1891

BRIR
Abs # 2183
Survey2: WOOD, J H
17-Feb-1920

BRIR
Abs # 2189
Survey2: KILLION, D G
29-May-1919

BRIR
Abs # 2212
Survey2: CAPPS, W T
21-Nov-1941

BRIR
Abs # 2248

Survey2: TOWNSEND, C W
05-Jun-1906

BRIR
Abs # 2253
Survey2: KILLION, D G
28-Dec-1918

BRIR
Abs # 2341
Survey2: WOOD, J H
21-Dec-1923

BROGDON, M
Abs # 2123
29-Jan-1898

BROWN, J C
Abs # 39
31-Jul-1875
see also, Map 28

BURCH, F P
Abs # 1578
24-May-1890
see also, Map 21

BURCH, T J
Abs # 1888
07-Jun-1895
see also, Map 21

BUSE, J
Abs # 1570
17-Nov-1879
see also, Maps 36, 37

BUSSELL, B F
Abs # 1384
09-Dec-1879

BUSSELL, C H
Abs # 1889
20-Jul-1887

BUSSELL, J
Abs # 1575
11-Dec-1880

BUTLER, E V
Abs # 1295
19-Dec-1878

CARSON, R
Abs # 70
25-Oct-1876
see also, Map 30

CAUFMAN, J
Abs # 63
05-Jun-1875
see also, Map 28

COCKRELL, T J
Abs # 1403
08-Dec-1879
see also, Map 30

COLTHARP, E S
Abs # 1390
26-May-1879

COLTHARP, H
Abs # 1582
11-Dec-1880

CORNETT, W L
Abs # 73
03-Aug-1877

CRISWELL, S H
Abs # 1297
02-May-1878

DECKER, J
Abs # 1302
07-Jan-1878
see also, Map 37

DUNN, M
Abs # 81
16-Jun-1868
see also, Map 30

EL&RR RR CO
Abs # 1307
01-Jan-1879

EL&RR RR CO
Abs # 1814

Survey2: KELLY, H
20-Oct-1905

EL&RR RR CO
Abs # 2207
Survey2: NEWHAUS, C
06-Jan-1913
see also, Map 28

FERGUSON, H H
Abs # 1310
17-Jul-1878
see also, Map 37

FERGUSON, J C
Abs # 1798
12-Jun-1884

FINLAY, R
Abs # 2075
03-Jan-1893

FRANKLIN, D D
Abs # 1425
05-May-1879

GAMBOA, F
Abs # 106
26-May-1859

GRIFFITH, B P
Abs # 1314
17-Apr-1878

HAMILTON, R
Abs # 1321
18-Jul-1878
see also, Map 30

HARGRAVE, J B
Abs # 1871
16-Mar-1896
see also, Map 28

HARVEY, H
Abs # 1606
13-Oct-1880

HEART, HRS C P
Abs # 132
06-Oct-1880
see also, Map 30

HITCHCOCK, A J
Abs # 128
22-Aug-1873
see also, Map 21

I&GN RR CO
Abs # 1460
23-Nov-1881
see also, Map 30

I&GN RR CO
Abs # 1461
05-Oct-1893
see also, Maps 22, 30

KILLION, D N
Abs # 163
31-May-1876

KRAMER, D
Abs # 1475
15-Feb-1879
see also, Map 30

KUYKENDALL, T P
Abs # 167
26-Feb-1890
see also, Map 28

LAMAR, J T
Abs # 1335
20-Dec-1877

LARD, W T
Abs # 1336
20-Dec-1877
see also, Maps 30, 37, 38

LAYNE, T A
Abs # 177
26-Aug-1876
see also, Map 37

MARLIN, J
Abs # 199
24-Oct-1857
see also, Maps 28, 36, 37

MARR, J W
Abs # 1905
05-Jan-1922
see also, Map 30

MARSHALT, W H
Abs # 1339
08-Apr-1878
see also, Map 37

MCGARY, M
Abs # 196
12-Sep-1857

MCKISSICK, S
Abs # 184
16-Jun-1873
see also, Map 28

MESSENGER, D
Abs # 1841
18-Jul-1885

MOORE, A D
Abs # 1691
28-Jul-1881

NORTON, D O
Abs # 215
13-Jun-1873

PALMER, J
Abs # 1510
29-Jul-1879
see also, Map 37

PARTRIDGE, J J
Abs # 234
28-Aug-1877

PIERCE, R L
Abs # 1969
22-Jan-1889

PRICE, G
Abs # 237
25-Aug-1877

SEDDON, S T
Abs # 273
28-Aug-1877

T&NO RR CO
Abs # 1244
04-Sep-1873
see also, Map 28

T&NO RR CO
Abs # 1245
03-Aug-1875

T&NO RR CO
Abs # 1246
20-Jun-1873

T&NO RR CO
Abs # 1457
Survey2: HODGES, W J
14-Nov-1906

T&NO RR CO
Abs # 1476
Survey2: KELLY, D
15-Aug-1881
see also, Map 28

T&NO RR CO
Abs # 1673
Survey2: CATES, J
22-Sep-1911
see also, Map 28

T&NO RR CO
Abs # 1779
Survey2: IRVIN, A
24-May-1895
see also, Map 37

T&NO RR CO
Abs # 1826
Survey2: AUSTIN, W W
29-Jun-1920
see also, Map 37

T&NO RR CO
Abs # 1890
Survey2: CORNELL, W L
22-Mar-1920

T&NO RR CO
Abs # 1899
Survey2: HILL, H
22-Mar-1920

T&NO RR CO
Abs # 1910
Survey2: SIMPSON, L C
22-Mar-1920

T&NO RR CO
Abs # 2149
Survey2: BLACKWOOD, L C
04-Oct-1909

T&NO RR CO
Abs # 2167
Survey2: KELLY, H
11-Dec-1951

T&NO RR CO
Abs # 2260
Survey2: JOHNSON, L A
14-Mar-1905

T&NO RR CO
Abs # 2263
Survey2: MUNDELL, J A
08-Feb-1906

TE&L CO
Abs # 1231
07-Apr-1859
see also, Maps 20, 21, 28

TE&L CO
Abs # 684
01-Apr-1858
see also, Map 21

TIMMONS, W S
Abs # 2083
11-Aug-1893

WOOLEY, W
Abs # 1283
09-Aug-1877

Populated Places
None

Cemeteries
None

Water (larger bodies)
Lake Eddleman
Lake Graham

Other Water
Briar Branch
Brier Branch
Lake Eddleman
Medlan Branch
Mule Pen Branch
North Tonk Branch
Salt Creek
South Tonk Branch
Willow Branch

Lake
Eddleman

Rathmell
Timber Ridge
Timber Ridge
Boat Ramp
Billy Doc
Edwards
Wards
Maudlin

HEARTT,
HRS
C P (133)

CI CO
(1300)

GATLIN,
R A (1919)

TE&L
CO (927)

MANNING,
J W (188)

CI CO
(1301)

TE&L
CO (1130)

State Highway 16

Seaberry

Rocky Mound

I&GN RR
CO (1461)

Boat Ramp

Salt
Creek

TANNER, J
R (276)

Calhoun
Bale

Farmers
Branch

Young
Hall
Victory
Dixie
Pine

PIER,
P (219)

Red Top

CI CO
(1301)

TE&L
CO (1131)

Craig
Industrial
Industrial

LYNCH,
N (171)

Fawn

Lincoln

Victory
Powell
Cliff

HAMMONS,
B W
(1320)

Ohio

Avenue F

TE&L
CO (1132)

Woody Graham East
Carol
Craig

Eastpark

Wolf

I&GN
RR CO
(1460)

Farm-to-Market Road 61

Fawn

United States Highway 380

Avenue D

JOHNSON,
E W (2257)

TERRY,
J W (1544)

Dara

ROSS,
MRS E H (246)

Chapparal

CARSON,
R (70)

Emerald

Cherry
7th

States Highway 380
Avenue C
Avenue B
Avenue A

Gleese
Ragland
Summit
Ohio
Colorado

Old Jacksboro

SHERILL,
E (271)

Berry

JERRY,
I (1539)

MCGARY,
M (197)

7th Oak United
6th Supply
Grove
Cem.
5th
5th

North
Virginia Smith
Tennessee

McBrayer
Florea
Gleese
Johnnie
Remington
Biewett

Ohio
Ohio
Pennsylvania

JONES,
J E (164)

Rodeo

EDDLEMAN, A B (2347)

DUNN,
M (81)

Pecan
Echo

Twin
4th
Mountains

Summit
Ohio
Ohio

4th

WOOD,
B G (1859)

Dry Creek

St Hwy 67

Graham
West
3rd
2nd

4th
Elm
HILL,
B (137)
2nd

Indiana

Pioneer Cem.

2nd

T&NO
RR CO (1247)

HEART,
HRS C P
(132)

COY, G
(64)

Oak
1st
Short
Grove
South
Southview
Brazos
Shawnee

Plum
East
Cherry

South

Carolina
Moringside

Kentucky
Brazos

Texas

Tennessee

Fairview
Rolling
Hills

Cliff

FERGUSON,
S (96)

Finis

COCKRELL,
T J (1403)

MARR,
J W (1905)

Sewer Plant

Shawnee

Calaveras
Shawnee

Oak
Scenic
Thompson
Hills
Rogers
Fiesta

BRIR (1781)

Flat
Rock

KRAMER, D
(1475)

WHITE,
N (1858)

Park
Gregory

Woodlawn

MCLEOND,
W (1481)

Quail
Roanoke
Red Bud

HUFFMACHER,
A G (1808)

Dry Creek

BRIR
(1585)

Lake
Eddleman

DUDNEY,
B F
(1406)

Austin

Royal
Lovers

Corto
Morado
Fairview
Green

BRIR
(1534) HARMON, J
(1351)

BELLAMY
A F
(1290)

Ledbetter

Rush

Normandy

Catalina
Circle
Pine
Tree

Pine Tree

Dakota

Randy
Thomas

Forest

Oak
Arapaho

CUSENBARRY,
D D (2285)

BRIR
(1455)

BRIR
(1840)

BRIR
(2222)

MOSLEY,
B J (1338)

Old Burger
Bunger

MCLAINE,
J (1344)

Melssa

BRIR
(1367)

YOUNG,
H F (1286)

REED, G W
(1627)

Keen
Mack
Birdwell

Nesez

Terry
Gravel

BRIR
(1347)

Mars

Alford
Bobby
Christi

MUNNERLYN,
W B (1341)

HAMILTON, R
(1321)

Gatlin

PARKER,
G W
(1513)

Stoffer

State Hwy 16

Moody
Dresser
Medra
Allison
Lindy
Louis
Crawford
Lindy
Jap

BRIR
(1771)

Birdwell

BRIR
(1818)

BRIR (2204)
BRIR
(1416)

MAINES, W
(1740)

Dry Creek

Salt Creek

HILL,
B (144)

CROUCH,
J R (1299)

COMBS,
T J
(1298)

BRIR
(2239)

BRIR
(1580)

CONNELLY,
W A (1583)

Old
Bunger

Heather

BRIR
(1579)

BRIR
(2203)

Flatrock Creek

BRIR
(2241)

BARNETT,
D (46)

TACKILL,
J G (1358)

Salt Creek

Farm-to-Market Road 1287

Deck

BRIR
(2240)

Theresa

BARNETT,
S (45)

Tonk Branch

Brazos
River

HORNER,
J W (1319)

CUNNINGHAM,
D (74)

UPHAM,
LE (1264)

GREGORY
L M
(121)

MABRY,
R E
(2287)

Canyon
Old Hwy 16

HAYNES,
J R
(2238)

BRIR
(2249)

LARD, W T (1336)

THOMAS, F L (1259)

UPHAM,
E E (1263)

BARRY,
T H (1668)

AKERS, N J
Abs # 1361
21-Jun-1884
see also, Map 22

AUD, I L
Abs # 1
16-Nov-1860
see also, Maps 21, 22, 29

BARNETT, D
Abs # 46
06-Jul-1877

BARNETT, S
Abs # 45
06-Jul-1877
see also, Map 29

BARRY, T H
Abs # 1668
06-Sep-1886
see also, Map 38

BELLAMY, A F
Abs # 1290
30-Nov-1877

BRIR
Abs # 1347
Survey2: MILLER, A K
13-May-1879

BRIR
Abs # 1367
Survey2: ALLEN, J B
26-Aug-1881

BRIR
Abs # 1416
Survey2: DOBBS, M
09-Jun-1880
see also, Map 29

BRIR
Abs # 1455
Survey2: HARMON, C
26-Mar-1879
see also, Map 31

BRIR
Abs # 1534
Survey2: SHERMAN, W
11-Dec-1880

BRIR
Abs # 1579
Survey2: BUIE, L B
30-May-1881

BRIR
Abs # 1580
Survey2: BARNETT, S
16-Feb-1898
see also, Map 29

BRIR
Abs # 1585
Survey2: CALHOUN, J H
24-Jan-1887
see also, Map 29

BRIR
Abs # 1771
Survey2: BRIM, J F
24-Dec-1917

BRIR
Abs # 1781
Survey2: JOHNSON, C W & WIL-
LIAMS, B F
09-Dec-1909

BRIR
Abs # 1818
Survey2: MUNNERLYN, W B
30-Apr-1913
see also, Map 31

BRIR
Abs # 1840
Survey2: LAMAR, R E
24-Apr-1888
see also, Map 29

BRIR
Abs # 2203
Survey2: GIBSON, P L
13-May-1910

BRIR
Abs # 2204
Survey2: KNIGHT, J F
25-Oct-1938

BRIR
Abs # 2222
Survey2: MOSELEY, B G
14-Jul-1938

BRIR
Abs # 2239
Survey2: AKIN, D R
23-Oct-1944
see also, Map 31

BRIR
Abs # 2240
Survey2: AKIN, D R
23-Oct-1944
see also, Maps 31, 38, 39

BRIR
Abs # 2241
Survey2: AKIN, D R
23-Oct-1944

BRIR
Abs # 2249
Survey2: AKIN, D R
23-Oct-1944
see also, Maps 31, 38, 39

CARSON, R
Abs # 70
25-Oct-1876
see also, Map 29

CI CO
Abs # 1300
18-Feb-1878
see also, Map 22

CI CO
Abs # 1301
18-Feb-1878

COCKRELL, T J
Abs # 1403
08-Dec-1879
see also, Map 29

COMBS, T J
Abs # 1298
30-Nov-1878

CONNELLY, W A
Abs # 1583
20-Nov-1880

COY, G
Abs # 64
21-Mar-1857

CROUCH, J R
Abs # 1299
01-Oct-1878

CUNNINGHAM, D
Abs # 74
06-Jul-1877

CUSENBARRY, D D
Abs # 2285
20-Feb-1912

DUDNEY, B F
Abs # 1406
19-Mar-1879

DUNN, M
Abs # 81
16-Jun-1868
see also, Map 29

EDDLEMAN, A B
Abs # 2347
29-Nov-1927
see also, Map 31

FERGUSON, S
Abs # 96
16-Jun-1873

GATLIN, R A
Abs # 1919
26-Apr-1895
see also, Map 22

GREGORY, L M

Abs # 121
27-Nov-1876
see also, Map 38

HAMILTON, R
Abs # 1321
18-Jul-1878
see also, Map 29

HAMMONS, B W
Abs # 1320
23-Apr-1878

HARMON, J
Abs # 1351
see also, Map 31

HAYNES, J R
Abs # 2238
23-Oct-1944
see also, Map 38

HEART, HRS C P
Abs # 132
06-Oct-1880
see also, Map 29

HEARTT, HRS C P
Abs # 133
05-Nov-1889
see also, Map 22

HILL, B
Abs # 137
05-Sep-1860

HILL, B
Abs # 144
07-Sep-1860

HORNER, J W
Abs # 1319
07-Jan-1878

HUFFMACHER, A G
Abs # 1808
05-May-1884

I&GN RR CO
Abs # 1460
23-Nov-1881
see also, Map 29

I&GN RR CO
Abs # 1461
05-Oct-1893
see also, Maps 22, 29

JERRY, I
Abs # 1539
10-May-1879
see also, Map 31

JOHNSON, E W
Abs # 2257
22-Oct-1919

JONES, J E
Abs # 164
05-Jun-1875

KRAMER, D
Abs # 1475
15-Feb-1879
see also, Map 29

LARD, W T
Abs # 1336
20-Dec-1877
see also, Maps 29, 37, 38

LYNCH, N
Abs # 171
30-Mar-1875
see also, Map 31

MABRY, R E
Abs # 2287
30-Jan-1920
see also, Map 38

MAINES, W
Abs # 1740
25-Jul-1883

MANNING, J W
Abs # 188
20-Feb-1860

MARR, J W

Abs # 1905
05-Jan-1922
see also, Map 29

MCGARY, M
Abs # 197
12-Sep-1857

MCLAINE, J
Abs # 1344
23-Sep-1878

MCLEOND, W
Abs # 1481
03-Apr-1879

MOSLEY, B J
Abs # 1338
17-Oct-1877

MUNNERLYN, W B
Abs # 1341
21-May-1878

PARKER, G W
Abs # 1513
28-Mar-1881

PIER, P
Abs # 219
11-Jun-1873

REED, G W
Abs # 1627
27-Apr-1880
see also, Map 31

ROSS, MRS E H
Abs # 246
15-Jun-1876
see also, Map 31

SHERILL, E
Abs # 271
07-Feb-1876

T&NO RR CO
Abs # 1247
14-Jun-1873
see also, Map 31

TACKILL, J G
Abs # 1358
01-Oct-1878

TANNER, J R
Abs # 276
21-Oct-1871

TE&L CO
Abs # 1130
19-Nov-1858
see also, Maps 22, 31

TE&L CO
Abs # 1131
19-Nov-1858
see also, Map 31

TE&L CO
Abs # 1132
20-Nov-1858

TE&L CO
Abs # 927
07-Sep-1858
see also, Maps 22, 23, 31

TERRY, J W
Abs # 1544
07-Feb-1879

THOMAS, F L
Abs # 1259
28-Jun-1876
see also, Map 38

UPHAM, E E
Abs # 1263
26-Sep-1876
see also, Map 38

UPHAM, L E
Abs # 1264
26-Sep-1876

WHITE, N
Abs # 1858
19-Feb-1885

WOOD, B G
Abs # 1859
17-Jul-1886

YOUNG, H F
Abs # 1286
05-Sep-1860

Populated Places
Graham
Twin Mountains

Cemeteries
Oak Grove Cemetery
Pioneer Cemetery

Water (larger bodies)
Brazos River
Lake Eddleman

Other Water
Dry Creek
Farmers Branch
Flatrock Creek
Lake Eddleman
Salt Creek
Tonk Branch

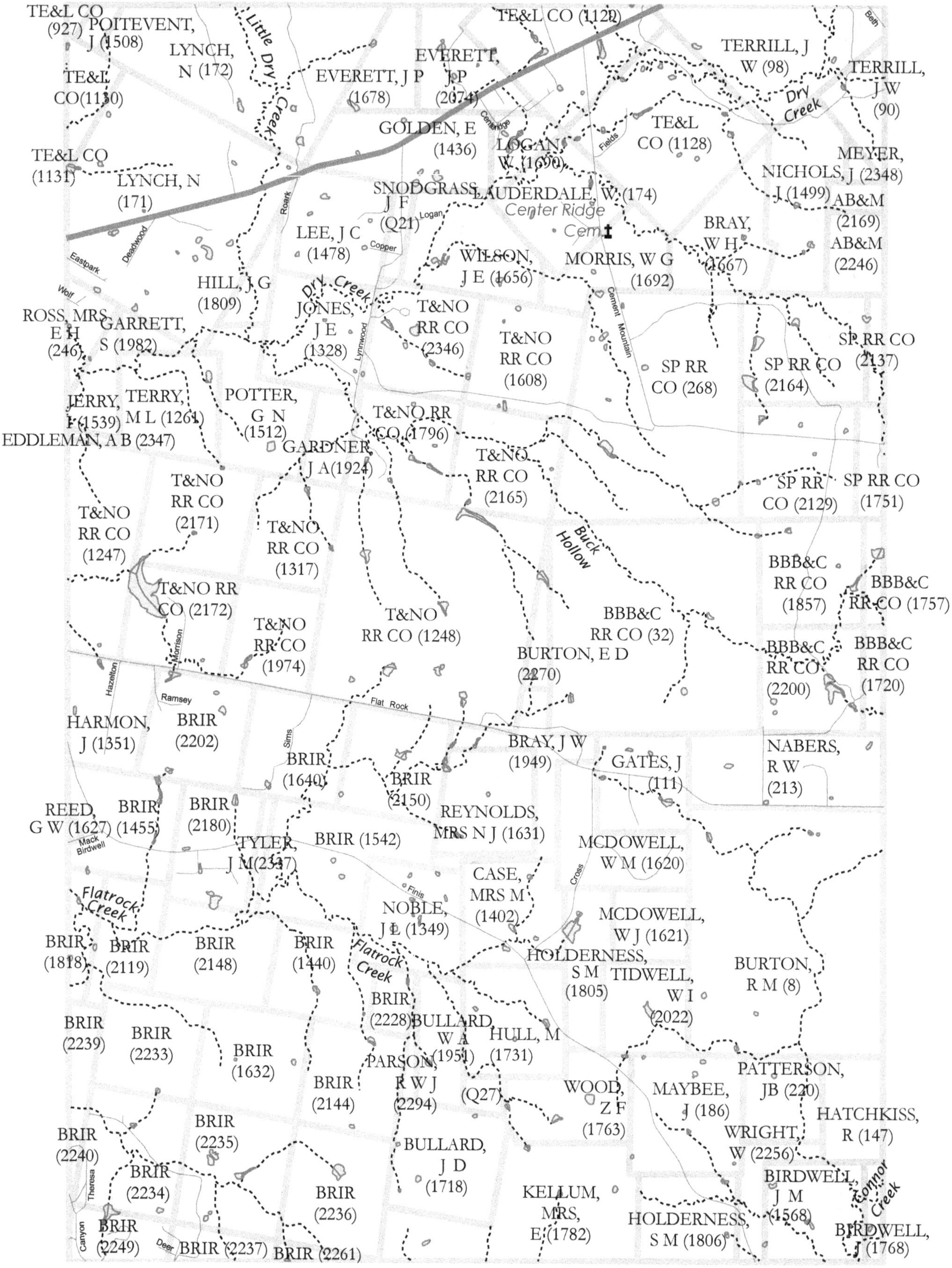

TE&L CO (927)
POITEVENT, J (1508)
LYNCH, N (172)
TE&L CO(1130)
EVERETT, J P (1678)
EVERETT, J P (2074)
TE&L CO (1120)
TERRILL, J W (98)
TERRILL, J W (90)

Little Dry Creek

GOLDEN, E (1436)
LOGAN, W (1090)
TE&L CO (1128)
Dry Creek

TE&L CO (1131)
LYNCH, N (171)
Roark
Deadwood
Eastpark

SNODGRASS, J F (Q21)
LAUDERDALE, W (174)
Center Ridge Cem
Logan
Copper

MEYER, J (1499)
NICHOLS, J (2348)
AB&M (2169)
AB&M (2246)

LEE, J C (1478)
WILSON, J E (1656)
MORRIS, W G (1692)
BRAY, W H (1667)

Wolf
ROSS, MRS E H (246)
GARRETT, S (1982)
HILL, J G (1809)
Dry Creek
JONES, J E (1328)
Lynnwood
T&NO RR CO (2346)
T&NO RR CO (1608)
Fields
Cement Mountain
SP RR CO (268)
SP RR CO (2164)
SP RR CO (2137)

JERRY, F (1539)
TERRY, M L (1261)
POTTER, G N (1512)
T&NO RR CO (1796)
GARDNER, J A (1924)
T&NO RR CO (2165)
SP RR CO (2129)
SP RR CO (1751)

EDDLEMAN, A B (2347)

T&NO RR CO (2171)
T&NO RR CO (1247)
T&NO RR CO (1317)
Buck Hollow
BBB&C RR CO (1857)
BBB&C RR CO (1757)

T&NO RR CO (2172)
Morrison
T&NO RR CO (1974)
T&NO RR CO (1248)
BBB&C RR CO (32)
BURTON, E D (2270)
BBB&C RR CO (2200)
BBB&C RR CO (1720)

Hazelton
Ramsey
Flat Rock

HARMON, J (1351)
BRIR (2202)
Sims
BRIR (1640)
BRIR (2150)
BRAY, J W (1949)
GATES, J (111)
NABERS, R W (213)

REED, G W (1627)
BRIR (1455)
BRIR (2180)
BRIR (1542)
REYNOLDS, MRS N J (1631)
MCDOWELL, W M (1620)

Mack Birdwell
TYLER, J M (2347)
CASE, MRS M (1402)
Cross

Flatrock Creek
NOBLE, J L (1349)
MCDOWELL, W J (1621)
BURTON, R M (8)

BRIR (1818)
BRIR (2119)
BRIR (2148)
BRIR (1440)
Flatrock Creek
HOLDERNESS, S M (1805)
TIDWELL, W I (2022)

BRIR (2228)
BULLARD, W A (1951)
HULL, M (1731)

BRIR (2239)
BRIR (2233)
BRIR (1632)
BRIR (2144)
PARSON, R W J (2294)
(Q27)
WOOD, Z F (1763)
MAYBEE, J (186)
PATTERSON, J B (220)

BRIR (2240)
BRIR (2235)
BULLARD, J D (1718)
WRIGHT, W (2256)
HATCHKISS, R (147)

Theresa
BRIR (2234)
Canyon
KELLUM, MRS, E (1782)
BIRDWELL, J M (1568)
Connor Creek

BRIR (2249)
Deer
BRIR (2237)
BRIR (2236)
BRIR (2261)
HOLDERNESS, S M (1806)
BIRDWELL, J (1768)

AB&M
Abs # 2169
Survey2: PADGETT, MRS E C
07-Apr-1927
see also, Map 32

AB&M
Abs # 2246
Survey2: RAGLAND, E R
03-Jan-1927
see also, Map 32

BBB&C RR CO
Abs # 1720
Survey2: CUNNINGHAM, J T
03-Oct-1889
see also, Map 32

BBB&C RR CO
Abs # 1757
Survey2: UPHAM, C S
03-Apr-1890
see also, Map 32

BBB&C RR CO
Abs # 1857
Survey2: TURNER, M F
26-Feb-1919

BBB&C RR CO
Abs # 2200
Survey2: CLARK, J F
13-Apr-1909

BBB&C RR CO
Abs # 32
21-May-1941

BIRDWELL, J
Abs # 1768
27-Mar-1884
see also, Maps 32, 39, 40

BIRDWELL, J M
Abs # 1568
20-Feb-1880
see also, Map 39

BRAY, J W
Abs # 1949
08-Feb-1892

BRAY, W H
Abs # 1667
15-Apr-1887

BRIR
Abs # 1440
Survey2: GASS, R B
15-Oct-1886

BRIR
Abs # 1455
Survey2: HARMON, C
26-Mar-1879
see also, Map 30

BRIR
Abs # 1542
Survey2: TAYLOR, R
04-Nov-1879

BRIR
Abs # 1632
Survey2: RODGERS, J
27-Apr-1886

BRIR
Abs # 1640
Survey2: TREUE, J A
13-Nov-1879

BRIR
Abs # 1818
Survey2: MUNNERLYN, W B
30-Apr-1913
see also, Map 30

BRIR
Abs # 2119
Survey2: CHISM, M H
17-Nov-1919

BRIR
Abs # 2144
Survey2: SHANNON, W J
23-Mar-1937

BRIR
Abs # 2148

Survey2: AKIN, O W
25-Mar-1931

BRIR
Abs # 2150
Survey2: BURCH, R
29-Dec-1919

BRIR
Abs # 2180
Survey2: TREUE, W C
17-Mar-1921

BRIR
Abs # 2202
Survey2: CLARK, J F
01-May-1939

BRIR
Abs # 2228
Survey2: SHANNON, W J
23-Sep-1937

BRIR
Abs # 2233
Survey2: AKIN, D R
25-Mar-1931

BRIR
Abs # 2234
Survey2: AKIN, D R
23-Oct-1944

BRIR
Abs # 2235
Survey2: AKIN, D R
23-Oct-1944

BRIR
Abs # 2236
Survey2: AKIN, D R
23-Oct-1944

BRIR
Abs # 2237
Survey2: AKIN, D R
23-Oct-1944
see also, Map 39

BRIR
Abs # 2239
Survey2: AKIN, D R
23-Oct-1944
see also, Map 30

BRIR
Abs # 2240
Survey2: AKIN, D R
23-Oct-1944
see also, Maps 30, 38, 39

BRIR
Abs # 2249
Survey2: AKIN, D R
23-Oct-1944
see also, Maps 30, 38, 39

BRIR
Abs # 2261
Survey2: DAVASHER, H W
02-May-1906
see also, Map 39

BULLARD, J D
Abs # 1718
20-Jul-1886

BULLARD, W A
Abs # 1951
22-Sep-1896

BURTON, E D
Abs # 2270
15-Jan-1908

BURTON, R M
Abs # 8
05-Apr-1883
see also, Map 32

CASE, MRS M
Abs # 1402
26-May-1880

EDDLEMAN, A B
Abs # 2347
29-Nov-1927
see also, Map 30

EVERETT, J P

Abs # 1678
27-Mar-1884
see also, Map 23

EVERETT, J P
Abs # 2074
04-Nov-1893
see also, Map 23

GARDNER, J A
Abs # 1924
19-Apr-1907

GARRETT, S
Abs # 1982
29-Jul-1895

GATES, J
Abs # 111
17-Mar-1876

GOLDEN, E
Abs # 1436
21-Dec-1880

HARMON, J
Abs # 1351
see also, Map 30

HATCHKISS, R
Abs # 147
03-Jul-1875
see also, Map 32

HILL, J G
Abs # 1809
14-Oct-1886

HOLDERNESS, S M
Abs # 1805
22-Feb-1884

HOLDERNESS, S M
Abs # 1806
09-Apr-1884
see also, Map 39

HULL, M
Abs # 1731
17-Dec-1885

JERRY, I
Abs # 1539
10-May-1879
see also, Map 30

JONES, J E
Abs # 1328
11-Jun-1878

KELLUM, MRS, E
Abs # 1782
17-Dec-1884
see also, Map 39

LAUDERDALE, W
Abs # 174
17-Jul-1874

LEE, J C
Abs # 1478
12-May-1880

LOGAN, W
Abs # 1690
05-Nov-1891

LYNCH, N
Abs # 171
30-Mar-1875
see also, Map 30

LYNCH, N
Abs # 172
30-Mar-1875
see also, Map 23

MAYBEE, J
Abs # 186
08-Jul-1875

MCDOWELL, W J
Abs # 1621
25-Mar-1882

MCDOWELL, W M
Abs # 1620
05-Dec-1881

MEYER, J

Abs # 2348
Survey2: HOLCOMB, V
22-Feb-1931
see also, Map 32

MORRIS, W G
Abs # 1692
21-Aug-1890

NABERS, R W
Abs # 213
31-Mar-1879
see also, Map 32

NICHOLS, J
Abs # 1499
28-Jul-1881

NOBLE, J L
Abs # 1349
21-Nov-1878

PARSON, R W J
Abs # 2294
21-Nov-1913

PATTERSON, J B
Abs # 220
05-Jul-1875

POITEVENT, J
Abs # 1508
16-Apr-1879
see also, Maps 22, 23

POTTER, G N
Abs # 1512
24-Jun-1879

REED, G W
Abs # 1627
27-Apr-1880
see also, Map 30

REYNOLDS, MRS N J
Abs # 1631
04-Dec-1884

ROSS, MRS E H
Abs # 246
15-Jun-1876
see also, Map 30

SNODGRASS, J F
Abs # ?21

SP RR CO
Abs # 1751
Survey2: RODGERS, G
02-Jun-1920
see also, Map 32

SP RR CO
Abs # 2129
Survey2: RODGERS, G
02-Jun-1920

SP RR CO
Abs # 2137
Survey2: HODGES, S G
17-Jul-1914
see also, Map 32

SP RR CO
Abs # 2164
Survey2: HODGES, S G
09-Sep-1914

SP RR CO
Abs # 268
29-May-1875

T&NO RR CO
Abs # 1247
14-Jun-1873
see also, Map 30

T&NO RR CO
Abs # 1248
20-Jun-1873

T&NO RR CO
Abs # 1317
Survey2: GOODE, W M
13-Oct-1886

T&NO RR CO
Abs # 1608
Survey2: HOLLY, B
20-Apr-1901

T&NO RR CO
Abs # 1796
Survey2: CLARK, T B
29-Jun-1889

T&NO RR CO
Abs # 1974
Survey2: AHLERS, C
10-May-1890

T&NO RR CO
Abs # 2165
Survey2: HOLLEY, J L
03-Apr-1928

T&NO RR CO
Abs # 2171
Survey2: POSERN, G A
13-Mar-1914

T&NO RR CO
Abs # 2172
Survey2: POSERN, E A
28-Aug-1918

T&NO RR CO
Abs # 2346
Survey2: WILSON, J E
11-Mar-1927

TE&L CO
Abs # 1128
18-Nov-1858

TE&L CO
Abs # 1129
18-Nov-1858
see also, Map 23

TE&L CO
Abs # 1130
19-Nov-1858
see also, Maps 22, 30

TE&L CO
Abs # 1131
19-Nov-1858
see also, Map 30

TE&L CO
Abs # 927
07-Sep-1858
see also, Maps 22, 23, 30

Populated Places
None

Cemeteries
Center Ridge Cemetery

Water (larger bodies)
None

Other Water
Buck Hollow
Connor Creek
Dry Creek
Flatrock Creek
Little Dry Creek

TERRILL, J W
Abs # 90
06-Apr-1858
see also, Map 32

TERRILL, J W
Abs # 98
22-Dec-1873
see also, Maps 23, 24, 32

TERRY, M L
Abs # 1261
19-Jun-1876

TIDWELL, W I
Abs # 2022
10-Sep-1891

TYLER, J M
Abs # 2337
Survey2: CRAVENS, E P/SF 12559
13-Dec-1922

WILSON, J E
Abs # 1656
26-Jul-1884

WOOD, Z F
Abs # 1763
13-Oct-1888

WRIGHT, W
Abs # 2256
20-Apr-1903
see also, Map 39

Abs # ?27

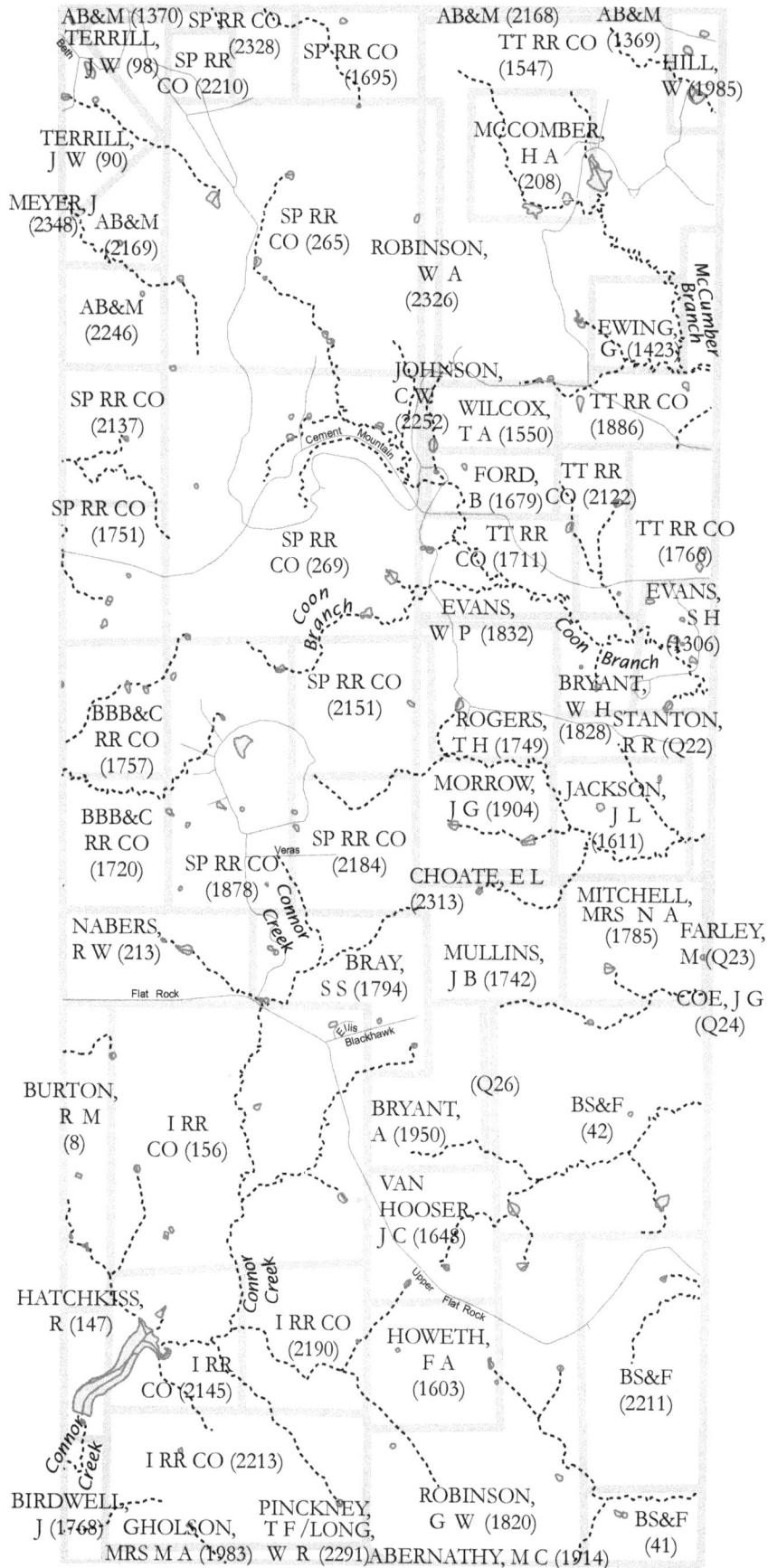

AB&M (1370) SP RR CO
TERRILL,
J W (98)   SP RR
CO (2210)   SP RR CO
(1695)

AB&M (2168)   AB&M
TT RR CO (1369)
(1547)   HILL,
W (1985)

TERRILL,
J W (90)

MCCOMBER,
H A
(208)

MEYER, J
(2348)   AB&M
(2169)

SP RR
CO (265)   ROBINSON,
W A
(2326)

AB&M
(2246)

EWING,
G (1423)

SP RR CO
(2137)

JOHNSON,
C W
(2252)   WILCOX,
T A (1550)   TT RR CO
(1886)

SP RR CO
(1751)

FORD,
B (1679)   TT RR
CO (2122)

SP RR
CO (269)   TT RR
CO (1711)   TT RR CO
(1766)

EVANS,
S H
(2306)

Coon
Branch   EVANS,
W P (1832)   Coon
Branch

SP RR CO
(2151)   BRYANT,
W H
(1828)   STANTON,
R R (Q22)

BBB&C
RR CO
(1757)   ROGERS,
T H (1749)

BBB&C
RR CO
(1720)   SP RR CO
(2184)   MORROW,
J G (1904)   JACKSON,
J L
(1611)

SP RR CO
(1878)   Veras
Connor Creek   CHOATE, E L
(2313)   MITCHELL,
MRS N A
(1785)   FARLEY,
M (Q23)

NABERS,
R W (213)   BRAY,
S S (1794)   MULLINS,
J B (1742)   COE, J G
(Q24)

Flat Rock

Ellis
Blackhawk

BURTON,
R M
(8)   I RR
CO (156)   BRYANT,
A (1950)   (Q26)   BS&F
(42)

VAN
HOOSER,
J C (1648)

Connor
Creek   Upper Flat Rock

HATCHKISS,
R (147)   I RR CO
(2190)   HOWETH,
F A
(1603)   BS&F
(2211)

I RR
CO (2145)

Connor Creek

I RR CO (2213)

BIRDWELL,
J (1768)   GHOLSON,
MRS M A (1983)   PINCKNEY,
T F /LONG,
W R (2291)   ROBINSON,
G W (1820)   BS&F
(41)

ABERNATHY, M C (1914)

AB&M
Abs # 1369
15-May-1879
see also, Map 24

AB&M
Abs # 1370
08-May-1918
see also, Maps 23, 24

AB&M
Abs # 2168
03-Oct-1889
see also, Map 24

AB&M
Abs # 2169
Survey2: PADGETT, MRS E C
07-Apr-1927
see also, Map 31

AB&M
Abs # 2246
Survey2: RAGLAND, E R
03-Jan-1927
see also, Map 31

ABERNATHY, M C
Abs # 1914
12-Jan-1892
see also, Map 40

BBB&C RR CO
Abs # 1720
Survey2: CUNNINGHAM, J T
03-Oct-1889
see also, Map 31

BBB&C RR CO
Abs # 1757
Survey2: UPHAM, C S
03-Apr-1890
see also, Map 31

BIRDWELL, J
Abs # 1768
27-Mar-1884
see also, Maps 31, 39, 40

BRAY, S S
Abs # 1794
08-May-1888

BRYANT, A
Abs # 1950
11-May-1892

BRYANT, W H
Abs # 1828
27-Oct-1920

BS&F
Abs # 2211
Survey2: ALFORD, J L
25-Jan-1945

BS&F
Abs # 41
07-Jul-1875
see also, Map 40

BS&F
Abs # 42
07-Jul-1875

BURTON, R M
Abs # 8
05-Apr-1883
see also, Map 31

CHOATE, E L
Abs # 2313
03-Jan-1920

COE, J G
Abs # ?24

EVANS, S H
Abs # 1306
25-Aug-1896

EVANS, W P
Abs # 1832
28-May-1890

EWING, G
Abs # 1423
23-Jun-1879

FORD, B

Abs # 1679
02-Aug-1883

GHOLSON, MRS M A
Abs # 1983
17-Sep-1895
see also, Map 40

HATCHKISS, R
Abs # 147
03-Jul-1875
see also, Map 31

HILL, W
Abs # 1985
09-Jun-1926
see also, Map 24

HOWETH, F A
Abs # 1603
06-Oct-1884

I RR CO
Abs # 156
07-Jul-1875

I RR CO
Abs # 2145
Survey2: WRIGHT, A G
08-Feb-1927

I RR CO
Abs # 2190
Survey2: KIMBREL, L H
09-Nov-1922

I RR CO
Abs # 2213
Survey2: DAVIS, F M
19-Apr-1920

JACKSON, J L
Abs # 1611
20-Oct-1887

JOHNSON, C W
Abs # 2252
18-Apr-1903

MCCOMBER, H A
Abs # 208
05-Aug-1876

MEYER, J
Abs # 2348
Survey2: HOLCOMB, V
22-Feb-1931
see also, Map 31

MITCHELL, MRS N A
Abs # 1785
01-Sep-1883

MORROW, J G
Abs # 1904
07-Feb-1890

MULLINS, J B
Abs # 1742
17-Feb-1890

NABERS, R W
Abs # 213
31-Mar-1879
see also, Map 31

PINCKNEY, T F / LONG, W R
Abs # 2291
19-Sep-1912
see also, Map 40

ROBINSON, G W
Abs # 1820
05-Mar-1884
see also, Map 40

ROBINSON, W A
Abs # 2326
10-Aug-1920

ROGERS, T H
Abs # 1749
20-Oct-1887

SP RR CO
Abs # 1695
Survey2: MCCOMBER, H A
03-Oct-1889
see also, Map 24

SP RR CO
Abs # 1751
Survey2: RODGERS, G
02-Jun-1920
see also, Map 31

SP RR CO
Abs # 1878
Survey2: RODGER, J M C
09-Nov-1889

SP RR CO
Abs # 2137
Survey2: HODGES, S G
17-Jul-1914
see also, Map 31

SP RR CO
Abs # 2151
Survey2: BURK, J D
15-Jul-1947

SP RR CO
Abs # 2184
Survey2: BURK, J D
06-Jun-1923

SP RR CO
Abs # 2210
Survey2: WALKER, W T
14-Apr-1920

SP RR CO
Abs # 2328
Survey2: WALKER, W T
21-Feb-1920
see also, Map 24

SP RR CO
Abs # 265
31-Jul-1875

SP RR CO
Abs # 269
29-May-1875

TERRILL, J W
Abs # 90
06-Apr-1858
see also, Map 31

TERRILL, J W
Abs # 98
22-Dec-1873
see also, Maps 23, 24, 31

TT RR CO
Abs # 1547
07-May-1879

TT RR CO
Abs # 1711
Survey2: SCOTT, J E
25-Jul-1917

TT RR CO
Abs # 1766
Survey2: WOODS, B F
11-Sep-1896

TT RR CO
Abs # 1886
Survey2: WILLIAMS, I E M
03-May-1886

TT RR CO
Abs # 2122
Survey2: BENNETT, W A
27-Mar-1917

VAN HOOSER, J C
Abs # 1648
05-Dec-1881

WILCOX, T A
Abs # 1550
08-Aug-1879

Abs # ?26

Populated Places
None

Cemeteries
None

Water (larger bodies)
None

Other Water
Connor Creek
Coon Branch
McCumber Branch

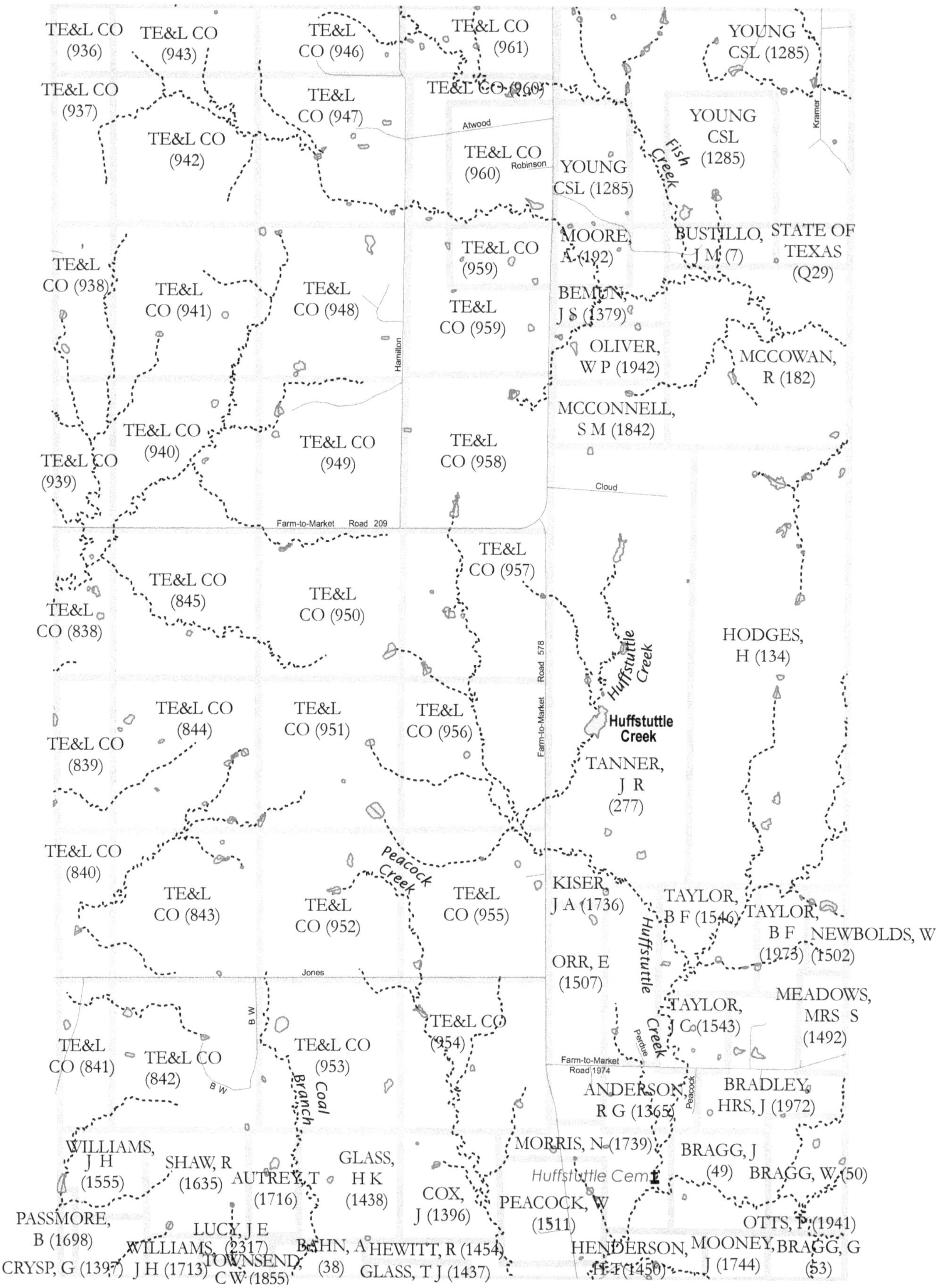

TE&L CO (936)

TE&L CO (943)

TE&L CO (946)

TE&L CO (961)

YOUNG CSL (1285)

TE&L CO (937)

TE&L CO (942)

TE&L CO (947)

TE&L CO (960)

Atwood

YOUNG CSL (1285)

Fish Creek

Kramer

TE&L CO (960)

Robinson

YOUNG CSL (1285)

MOORE, A (192)

BUSTILLO, J M (7)

STATE OF TEXAS (Q29)

TE&L CO (938)

TE&L CO (941)

TE&L CO (948)

TE&L CO (959)

TE&L CO (959)

BEMEN, J S (1379)

OLIVER, W P (1942)

MCCOWAN, R (182)

Hamilton

MCCONNELL, S M (1842)

TE&L CO (940)

TE&L CO (939)

TE&L CO (949)

TE&L CO (958)

Cloud

Farm-to-Market Road 209

TE&L CO (957)

TE&L CO (845)

TE&L CO (838)

TE&L CO (950)

HODGES, H (134)

Farm-to-Market Road 578

Huffstuttle Creek

TE&L CO (844)

TE&L CO (951)

TE&L CO (956)

TE&L CO (839)

Huffstuttle Creek

TANNER, J R (277)

TE&L CO (840)

TE&L CO (843)

TE&L CO (952)

Peacock Creek

TE&L CO (955)

KISER, J A (1736)

TAYLOR, B F (1546)

TAYLOR, B F (1973)

NEWBOLDS, W (1502)

Huffstuttle Creek

ORR, E (1507)

TAYLOR, J C (1543)

MEADOWS, MRS S (1492)

Jones

B W

TE&L CO (841)

TE&L CO (842)

B W

TE&L CO (953)

Coal Branch

TE&L CO (954)

Farm-to-Market Road 1974

Perdue

ANDERSON, R G (1365)

Peacock

BRADLEY, HRS, J (1972)

WILLIAMS, J H (1555)

SHAW, R (1635)

AUTREY, T (1716)

GLASS, H K (1438)

COX, J (1396)

MORRIS, N (1739)

PEACOCK, W (1511)

Huffstuttle Cem

BRAGG, J (49)

BRAGG, W (50)

PASSMORE, B (1698)

LUCY, J E (2317)

WILLIAMS, J H (1713)

TOWNSEND, C W (1855)

BAHN, A (38)

HEWITT, R (1454)

OTTS, P (1941)

CRYSP, G (1397)

GLASS, T J (1437)

HENDERSON, H T (1450)

MOONEY, J (1744)

BRAGG, G (53)

234

ANDERSON, R G
Abs # 1365
28-Mar-1881

AUTREY, T
Abs # 1716
13-Jun-1885

BAHN, A
Abs # 38
20-Nov-1875
see also, Map 41

BEMUN, J S
Abs # 1379
18-Oct-1887

BRADLEY, HRS, J
Abs # 1972
see also, Map 34

BRAGG, G
Abs # 53
08-Jan-1879
see also, Maps 34, 41, 42

BRAGG, J
Abs # 49
07-May-1877

BRAGG, W
Abs # 50
01-Jun-1878
see also, Map 34

BUSTILLO, J M
Abs # 7
23-Aug-1876

COX, J
Abs # 1396
28-Mar-1881

CRYSP, G
Abs # 1397
29-Apr-1884
see also, Map 41

GLASS, H K
Abs # 1438
28-Mar-1881

GLASS, T J
Abs # 1437
13-Nov-1977
see also, Map 41

HENDERSON, H T
Abs # 1450
04-May-1880
see also, Map 41

HEWITT, R
Abs # 1454
23-Jun-1884
see also, Map 41

HODGES, H
Abs # 134
24-May-1875
see also, Map 34

KISER, J A
Abs # 1736
14-Apr-1876

LUCY, J E
Abs # 2317
22-Jul-1920

MCCONNELL, S M
Abs # 1842
17-Oct-1887

MCCOWAN, R
Abs # 182
09-Oct-1874
see also, Map 34

MEADOWS, MRS S
Abs # 1492
20-Nov-1880
see also, Map 34

MOONEY, J
Abs # 1744
27-Aug-1884
see also, Map 41

MOORE, A

Abs # 192
20-Sep-1872

MORRIS, N
Abs # 1739
21-Jan-1886

NEWBOLDS, W
Abs # 1502
28-Jul-1881
see also, Map 34

OLIVER, W P
Abs # 1942
21-Feb-1896

ORR, E
Abs # 1507
29-Nov-1881

OTTS, P
Abs # 1941
14-Nov-1888
see also, Map 34

PASSMORE, B
Abs # 1698
13-Jul-1881
see also, Map 41

PEACOCK, W
Abs # 1511
04-Feb-1879

SHAW, R
Abs # 1635
28-Oct-1879

STATE OF TEXAS
Abs # ?29
see also, Map 34

TANNER, J R
Abs # 277
08-Jun-1875

TAYLOR, B F
Abs # 1546
09-Jun-1880

TAYLOR, B F
Abs # 1973
11-Jun-1889

TAYLOR, J C
Abs # 1543
28-Mar-1881

TE&L CO
Abs # 838
14-Jul-1858

TE&L CO
Abs # 839
14-Jul-1858

TE&L CO
Abs # 840
15-Jul-1858

TE&L CO
Abs # 841
15-Jul-1858

TE&L CO
Abs # 842
15-Jul-1858

TE&L CO
Abs # 843
16-Jul-1858

TE&L CO
Abs # 844
16-Jul-1858

TE&L CO
Abs # 845
16-Jul-1858

TE&L CO
Abs # 936
23-Sep-1858
see also, Map 25

TE&L CO
Abs # 937
10-Jul-1858

TE&L CO

Abs # 938
12-Jul-1858

TE&L CO
Abs # 939
12-Jul-1858

TE&L CO
Abs # 940
12-Jul-1858

TE&L CO
Abs # 941
13-Jul-1858

TE&L CO
Abs # 942
13-Jul-1858

TE&L CO
Abs # 943
12-Jun-1858
see also, Map 25

TE&L CO
Abs # 946
13-Jul-1858
see also, Map 25

TE&L CO
Abs # 947
13-Jul-1858

TE&L CO
Abs # 948
13-Jul-1858

TE&L CO
Abs # 949
14-Jul-1858

TE&L CO
Abs # 950
14-Jul-1858

TE&L CO
Abs # 951
14-Jul-1858

TE&L CO
Abs # 952
14-Jul-1858

TE&L CO
Abs # 953
14-Jul-1858

TE&L CO
Abs # 954
14-Jul-1858

TE&L CO
Abs # 955
15-Jul-1858

TE&L CO
Abs # 956
15-Jul-1858

TE&L CO
Abs # 957
15-Jul-1858

TE&L CO
Abs # 958
15-Jul-1858

TE&L CO
Abs # 959
15-Jul-1858

TE&L CO
Abs # 960
15-Jul-1858

TE&L CO
Abs # 961
16-Jul-1858
see also, Map 25

TOWNSEND, C W
Abs # 1855
07-Aug-1888
see also, Map 41

WILLIAMS, J H
Abs # 1555
26-Mar-1884

WILLIAMS, J H

Abs # 1713
19-Jan-1881
see also, Map 41

YOUNG CSL
Abs # 1285
31-Jul-1891
see also, Maps 25, 26, 34

Populated Places
None

Cemeteries
Huffstuttle Cemetery

Water (larger bodies)
Huffstuttle Creek

Other Water
Coal Branch
Fish Creek
Huffstuttle Creek
Peacock Creek

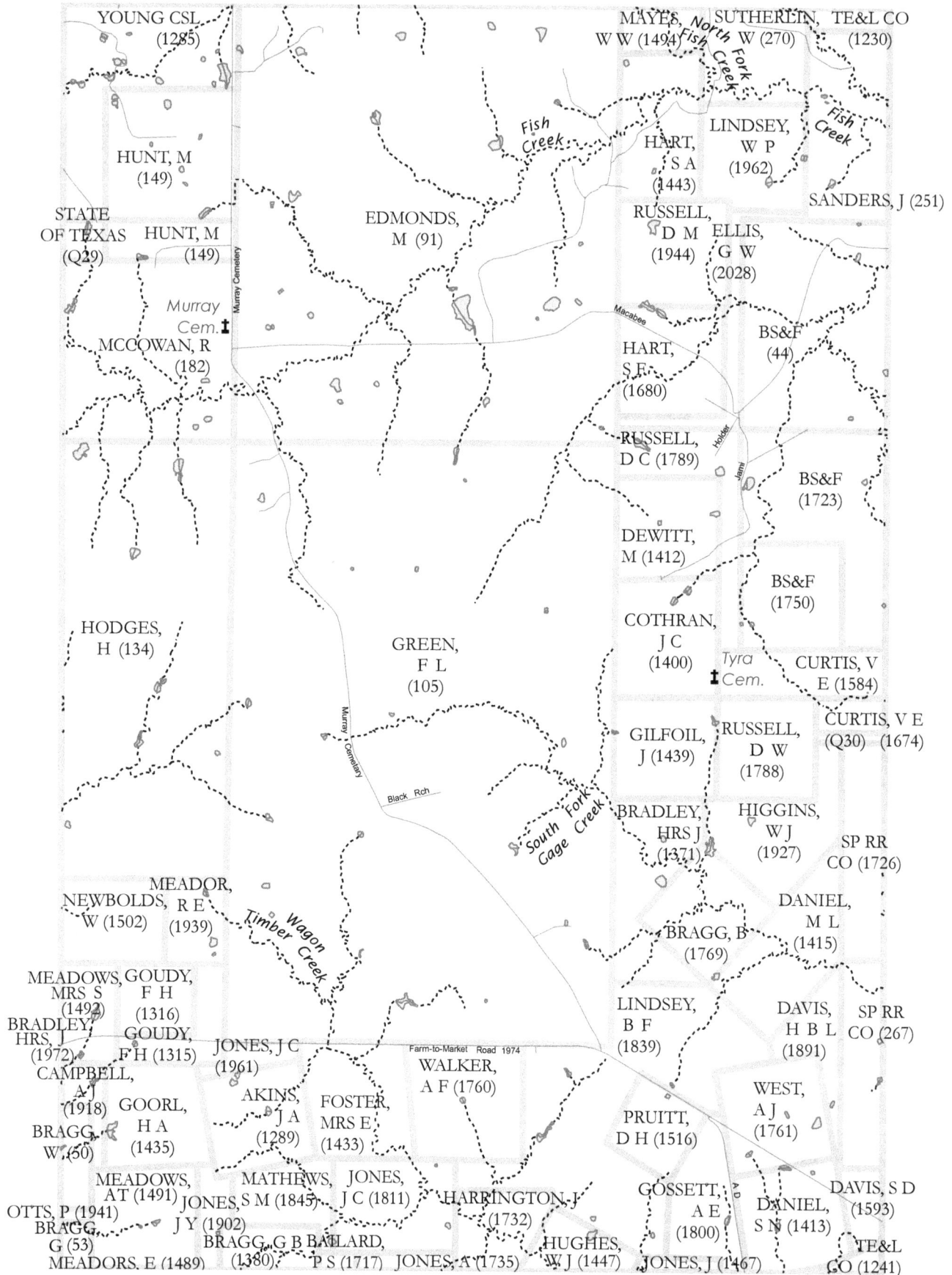

YOUNG CSL
(1285)

HUNT, M
(149)

STATE
OF TEXAS
(Q29)

HUNT, M
(149)

*Murray
Cem.*

MCCOWAN, R
(182)

EDMONDS,
M (91)

Murray Cemetery

MAYES,
W W (1494)

*North Fork
Fish Creek*

SUTHERLIN,
W (270)

TE&L CO
(1230)

*Fish
Creek*

HART,
S A
(1443)

LINDSEY,
W P
(1962)

*Fish
Creek*

SANDERS, J (251)

RUSSELL,
D M
(1944)

ELLIS,
G W
(2028)

Macabee

HART,
S E
(1680)

BS&F
(44)

Holder

Jam

RUSSELL,
D C (1789)

BS&F
(1723)

DEWITT,
M (1412)

BS&F
(1750)

HODGES,
H (134)

GREEN,
F L
(105)

COTHRAN,
J C
(1400)

*Tyra
Cem.*

BS&F
(1750)

CURTIS, V
E (1584)

Murray Cemetery

Black Rch

GILFOIL,
J (1439)

RUSSELL,
D W
(1788)

CURTIS, V E
(Q30)   (1674)

*South Fork
Gage Creek*

BRADLEY,
HRS J
(1371)

HIGGINS,
W J
(1927)

SP RR
CO (1726)

MEADOR,
R E
(1939)

NEWBOLDS,
W (1502)

*Wagon
Timber Creek*

DANIEL,
M L
(1415)

BRAGG, B
(1769)

MEADOWS,
MRS S
(1492)

GOUDY,
F H
(1316)

BRADLEY,
HRS, J
(1972)

GOUDY,
F H (1315)

JONES, J C
(1961)

Farm-to-Market Road 1974

LINDSEY,
B F
(1839)

DAVIS,
H B L
(1891)

SP RR
CO (267)

CAMPBELL,
A J
(1918)

GOORL,
H A
(1435)

AKINS,
J A
(1289)

FOSTER,
MRS E
(1433)

WALKER,
A F (1760)

WEST,
A J
(1761)

BRAGG,
W (50)

PRUITT,
D H (1516)

MEADOWS,
A T (1491)

JONES, S M (1845)

MATHEWS,
J Y (1902)

JONES,
J C (1811)

HARRINGTON, J
(1732)

GOSSETT,
A E
(1800)

DANIEL,
S N (1413)

DAVIS, S D
(1593)

OTTS, P (1941)

BRAGG,
G (53)

MEADORS, E (1489)

BRAGG, G B
(1380)

BALLARD,
P S (1717)

JONES, A (1735)

HUGHES,
W J (1447)

JONES, J (1467)

TE&L
CO (1241)

AKINS, J A
Abs # 1289
30-Apr-1884

BAILARD, P S
Abs # 1717
01-Aug-1887
see also, Map 42

BRADLEY, HRS J
Abs # 1371
12-Apr-1880

BRADLEY, HRS, J
Abs # 1972
see also, Map 33

BRAGG, B
Abs # 1769
25-Apr-1887

BRAGG, G
Abs # 53
08-Jan-1879
see also, Maps 33, 41, 42

BRAGG, G B
Abs # 1380
09-Apr-1881
see also, Map 42

BRAGG, W
Abs # 50
01-Jun-1878
see also, Map 33

BS&F
Abs # 1723
Survey2: COSBY, J
16-Dec-1885
see also, Map 35

BS&F
Abs # 1750
Survey2: RUSSELL, D W
19-Sep-1888

BS&F
Abs # 44
01-Jul-1881
see also, Map 35

CAMPBELL, A J
Abs # 1918
24-Nov-1890

COTHRAN, J C
Abs # 1400
10-May-1880

CURTIS, V E
Abs # 1584
14-Nov-1881
see also, Map 35

CURTIS, V E
Abs # 1674
13-Jul-1882
see also, Map 35

DANIEL, M L
Abs # 1415
21-Feb-1884

DANIEL, S N
Abs # 1413
23-Jun-1884
see also, Map 42

DAVIS, H B L
Abs # 1891
16-May-1889

DAVIS, S D
Abs # 1593
05-Feb-1883
see also, Maps 35, 43

DEWITT, M
Abs # 1412
05-Nov-1883

EDMONDS, M
Abs # 91
21-Feb-1862
see also, Map 26

ELLIS, G W
Abs # 2028
11-Aug-1893

FOSTER, MRS E
Abs # 1433
08-Aug-1883

GILFOIL, J
Abs # 1439
12-Jan-1880

GOORL, H A
Abs # 1435
05-May-1885

GOSSETT, A E
Abs # 1800
18-Feb-1884
see also, Map 42

GOUDY, F H
Abs # 1315
06-Mar-1882

GOUDY, F H
Abs # 1316
06-Mar-1882

GREEN, F L
Abs # 105
27-Aug-1859

HARRINGTON, J
Abs # 1732
22-Apr-1884
see also, Map 42

HART, S A
Abs # 1443
26-Jun-1879

HART, S F
Abs # 1680
28-Mar-1881

HIGGINS, W J
Abs # 1927
30-Jan-1893

HODGES, H
Abs # 134
24-May-1875
see also, Map 33

HUGHES, W J
Abs # 1447
16-Sep-1881
see also, Map 42

HUNT, M
Abs # 149
12-Nov-1874

JONES, A
Abs # 1735
13-Sep-1884
see also, Map 42

JONES, J
Abs # 1467
18-Feb-1884
see also, Map 42

JONES, J C
Abs # 1811
23-Apr-1887

JONES, J C
Abs # 1961
26-Oct-1889

JONES, J Y
Abs # 1902
18-Jul-1887
see also, Map 42

LINDSEY, B F
Abs # 1839
22-Mar-1887

LINDSEY, W P
Abs # 1962
16-Dec-1891

MATHEWS, S M
Abs # 1845
17-Feb-1891

MAYES, W W
Abs # 1494
20-Jan-1881
see also, Map 26

MCCOWAN, R
Abs # 182
09-Oct-1874
see also, Map 33

MEADOR, R E
Abs # 1939
13-Jul-1891

MEADORS, E
Abs # 1489
02-Dec-1884
see also, Maps 41, 42

MEADOWS, A T
Abs # 1491
16-Jan-1880

MEADOWS, MRS S
Abs # 1492
20-Nov-1880
see also, Map 33

NEWBOLDS, W
Abs # 1502
28-Jul-1881
see also, Map 33

OTTS, P
Abs # 1941
14-Nov-1888
see also, Map 33

PRUITT, D H
Abs # 1516
18-Apr-1888

RUSSELL, D C
Abs # 1789
26-May-1885

RUSSELL, D M
Abs # 1944
06-Jun-1891

RUSSELL, D W
Abs # 1788
25-Apr-1887

SANDERS, J
Abs # 251
05-Jul-1870
see also, Map 35

SP RR CO
Abs # 1726
Survey2: DONNELL, W L
26-Jan-1899
see also, Map 35

SP RR CO
Abs # 267
29-Apr-1874
see also, Map 35

STATE OF TEXAS
Abs # ?29
see also, Map 33

SUTHERLIN, W
Abs # 270
08-Sep-1863
see also, Map 26

TE&L CO
Abs # 1230
10-Mar-1859
see also, Maps 26, 27, 35

TE&L CO
Abs # 1241
04-Aug-1858
see also, Maps 35, 42, 43

WALKER, A F
Abs # 1760
16-Aug-1884

WEST, A J
Abs # 1761
23-Nov-1883

YOUNG CSL
Abs # 1285
31-Jul-1891
see also, Maps 25, 26, 33

Abs # ?30
see also, Map 35

Populated Places
None

Cemeteries
Murray Cemetery
Tyra Cemetery

Water (larger bodies)
None

Other Water
Fish Creek
North Fork Fish Creek
South Fork Gage Creek
Wagon Timber Creek

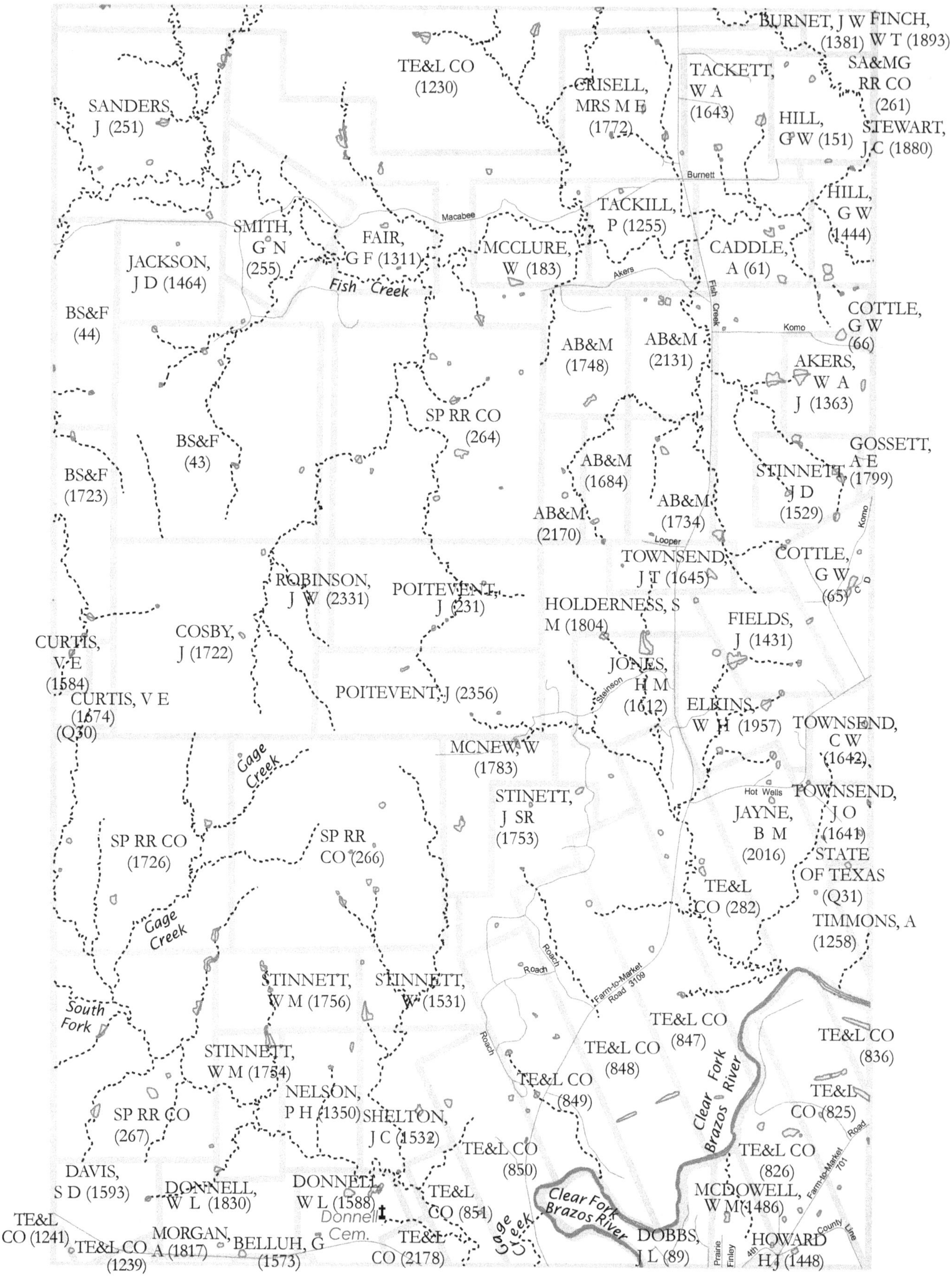

BURNET, J W FINCH,
(1381) W T (1893)

TE&L CO
(1230)

CRISELL,
MRS M E
(1772)

TACKETT,
W A
(1643)

SA&MG
RR CO
(261)

SANDERS
J (251)

HILL,
G W (151)

STEWART,
J C (1880)

SMITH,
G N
(255)

FAIR,
G F (1311)

TACKILL,
P (1255)

HILL,
G W
(1444)

JACKSON,
J D (1464)

MCCLURE,
W (183)

CADDLE,
A (61)

Fish Creek

COTTLE,
G W
(66)

BS&F
(44)

AB&M
(1748)

AB&M
(2131)

AKERS,
W A
J (1363)

BS&F
(43)

SP RR CO
(264)

AB&M
(1684)

STINNETT
J D
(1529)

GOSSETT,
A E
(1799)

BS&F
(1723)

AB&M
(2170)

AB&M
(1734)

COTTLE,
G W
(65)

ROBINSON,
J W (2331)

POITEVENT,
J (231)

TOWNSEND,
J T (1645)

CURTIS,
V E
(1584)

COSBY,
J (1722)

HOLDERNESS, S
M (1804)

FIELDS,
J (1431)

CURTIS, V E
(1674)
(Q30)

POITEVENT, J (2356)

JONES,
H M
(1612)

ELKINS,
W H (1957)

TOWNSEND,
C W
(1642)

Gage Creek

MCNEW, W
(1783)

STINETT,
J SR
(1753)

TOWNSEND,
J O
(1641)

SP RR CO
(1726)

SP RR
CO (266)

JAYNE,
B M
(2016)

STATE
OF TEXAS
(Q31)

*Gage
Creek*

TE&L
CO (282)

TIMMONS, A
(1258)

*South
Fork*

STINNETT,
W M (1756)

STINNETT,
W (1531)

TE&L CO
(847)

TE&L CO
(836)

STINNETT,
W M (1754)

TE&L CO
(848)

Clear Fork Brazos River

TE&L
CO (825)

NELSON,
P H (1350)

TE&L CO
(849)

SP RR CO
(267)

SHELTON,
J C (1532)

TE&L CO
(850)

TE&L CO
(826)

DAVIS,
S D (1593)

DONNELL,
W L (1830)

DONNELL,
W L (1588)

TE&L
CO (851)

*Clear Fork
Brazos River*

MCDOWELL,
W M (1486)

*Donnell
Cem.*

TE&L
CO (1241)

TE&L CO
(1239)

MORGAN,
A (1817)

BELLUH, G
(1573)

TE&L
CO (2178)

DOBBS,
J L (89)

HOWARD
H J (1448)

AB&M
Abs # 1684
Survey2: HARRIS, D
01-May-1902

AB&M
Abs # 1734
Survey2: HARRIS, D
01-May-1902

AB&M
Abs # 1748
Survey2: PARHAM, J
09-May-1900

AB&M
Abs # 2131
Survey2: BELLOMY, W
09-Jul-1919

AB&M
Abs # 2170
Survey2: HARRIS, D
27-Sep-1901

AKERS, W A J
Abs # 1363
24-Apr-1880
see also, Map 36

BELLUH, G
Abs # 1573
26-Aug-1880
see also, Map 43

BS&F
Abs # 1723
Survey2: COSBY, J
16-Dec-1885
see also, Map 34

BS&F
Abs # 43
07-Jul-1875

BS&F
Abs # 44
01-Jul-1881
see also, Map 34

BURNET, J W
Abs # 1381
18-Nov-1885
see also, Map 27

CADDLE, A
Abs # 61
09-Mar-1861

COSBY, J
Abs # 1722
29-Jan-1891

COTTLE, G W
Abs # 65
05-Apr-1877
see also, Map 36

COTTLE, G W
Abs # 66
05-Apr-1877
see also, Map 36

CRISELL, MRS M E
Abs # 1772
14-Aug-1884

CURTIS, V E
Abs # 1584
14-Nov-1881
see also, Map 34

CURTIS, V E
Abs # 1674
13-Jul-1882
see also, Map 34

DAVIS, S D
Abs # 1593
05-Feb-1883
see also, Maps 34, 43

DOBBS, J L
Abs # 89
12-Apr-1877
see also, Map 43

DONNELL, W L
Abs # 1588
28-Apr-1880

see also, Map 43

DONNELL, W L
Abs # 1830
15-Feb-1893

ELKINS, W H
Abs # 1957
13-Jun-1912

FAIR, G F
Abs # 1311
03-Aug-1883

FIELDS, J
Abs # 1431
21-Sep-1883

FINCH, W T
Abs # 1893
15-Feb-1890
see also, Maps 27, 28, 36

GOSSETT, A E
Abs # 1799
18-Feb-1884
see also, Map 36

HILL, G W
Abs # 1444
25-Jun-1879
see also, Map 36

HILL, G W
Abs # 151
16-Sep-1876

HOLDERNESS, S M
Abs # 1804
25-Apr-1895

HOWARD, H J
Abs # 1448
22-Oct-1888
see also, Map 43

JACKSON, J D
Abs # 1464
15-Aug-1879

JAYNE, B M
Abs # 2016
30-Jan-1898
see also, Map 36

JONES, H M
Abs # 1612
02-Aug-1883

MCCLURE, W
Abs # 183
02-Jun-1862

MCDOWELL, W M
Abs # 1486
08-Jan-1894
see also, Map 43

MCNEW, W
Abs # 1783
27-Jan-1886

MORGAN, A
Abs # 1817
21-May-1884
see also, Map 43

NELSON, P H
Abs # 1350
08-Jan-1890

POITEVENT, J
Abs # 231
22-Jan-1878

POITEVENT, J
Abs # 2356
Survey2: O
06-Feb-1947

ROBINSON, J W
Abs # 2331
05-Jan-1921

SA&MG RR CO
Abs # 261
11-Dec-1860
see also, Map 36

SANDERS, J

Abs # 251
05-Jul-1870
see also, Map 34

SHELTON, J C
Abs # 1532
30-Dec-1886

SMITH, G N
Abs # 255
27-Sep-1860

SP RR CO
Abs # 1726
Survey2: DONNELL, W L
26-Jan-1899
see also, Map 34

SP RR CO
Abs # 264
01-Jun-1875

SP RR CO
Abs # 266
01-Jun-1875

SP RR CO
Abs # 267
29-Apr-1874
see also, Map 34

STATE OF TEXAS
Abs # ?31
see also, Map 36

STEWART, J C
Abs # 1880
07-Jun-1892
see also, Map 36

STINETT, J SR
Abs # 1753
16-Jul-1884

STINNETT, J D
Abs # 1529
11-Oct-1881

STINNETT, W
Abs # 1531
12-Jul-1882

STINNETT, W M
Abs # 1754
26-Dec-1895

STINNETT, W M
Abs # 1756
07-Feb-1895

TACKETT, W A
Abs # 1643
01-Sep-1885

TACKILL, P
Abs # 1255
31-Mar-1875

TE&L CO
Abs # 1230
10-Mar-1859
see also, Maps 26, 27, 34

TE&L CO
Abs # 1239
25-Feb-1859
see also, Map 43

TE&L CO
Abs # 1241
04-Aug-1858
see also, Maps 34, 42, 43

TE&L CO
Abs # 2178
23-Feb-1858
see also, Map 43

TE&L CO
Abs # 282
24-May-1859

TE&L CO
Abs # 825
26-Aug-1858
see also, Maps 36, 43, 44

TE&L CO
Abs # 826
26-Aug-1858

see also, Maps 43, 44

TE&L CO
Abs # 836
29-Jul-1858
see also, Maps 36, 44

TE&L CO
Abs # 847
03-Aug-1858

TE&L CO
Abs # 848
31-May-1859

TE&L CO
Abs # 849
31-May-1859

TE&L CO
Abs # 850
11-Jun-1858
see also, Map 43

TE&L CO
Abs # 851
03-Aug-1858
see also, Map 43

TIMMONS, A
Abs # 1258
31-Oct-1876
see also, Map 36

TOWNSEND, C W
Abs # 1642
06-Aug-1883
see also, Map 36

TOWNSEND, J O
Abs # 1641
01-Nov-1883
see also, Map 36

TOWNSEND, J T
Abs # 1645
20-Jun-1884

Abs # ?30
see also, Map 34

Populated Places
None

Cemeteries
Donnell Cemetery

Water (larger bodies)
None

Other Water
Clear Fork Brazos River
Fish Creek
Gage Creek
South Fork

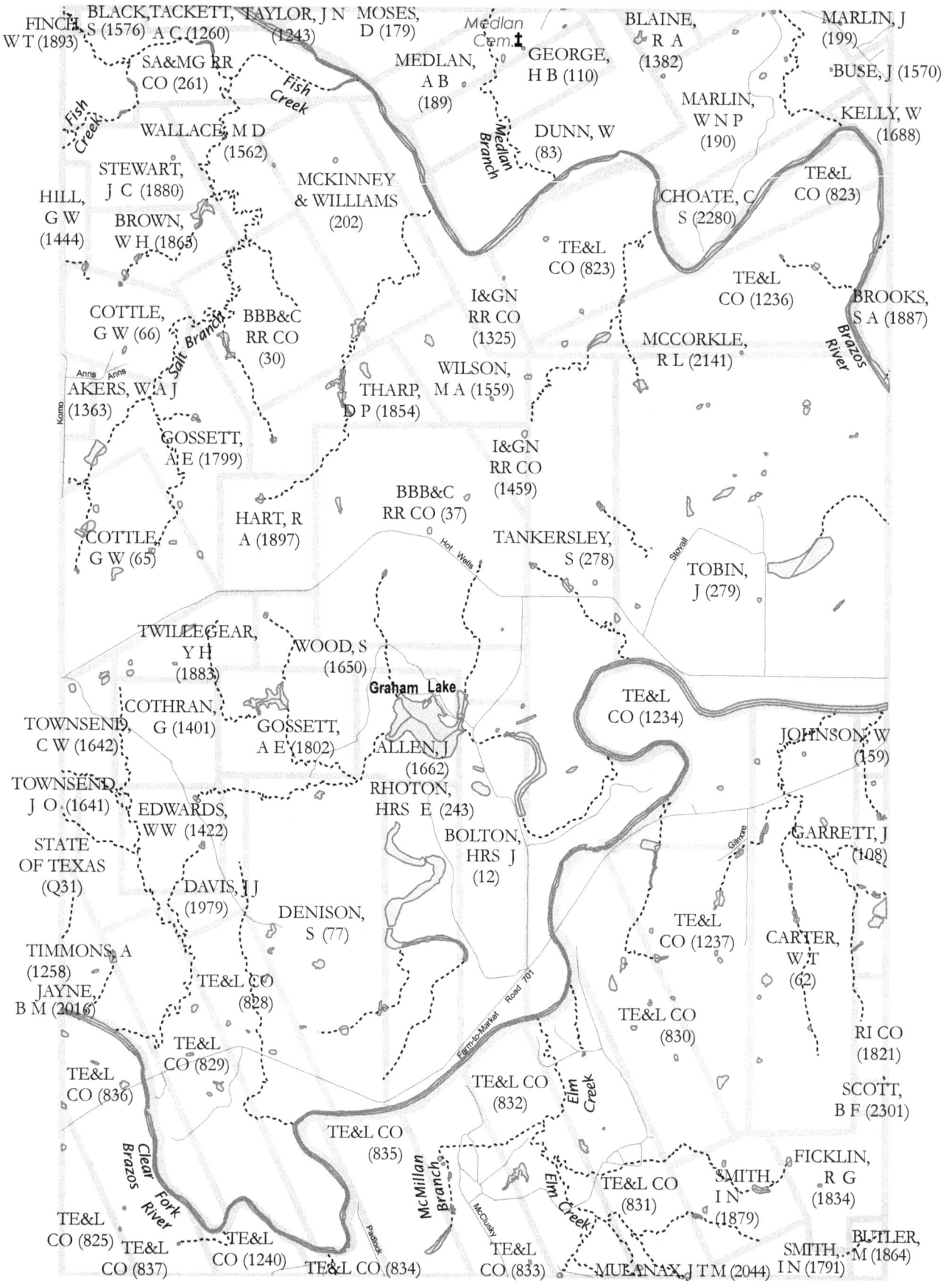

FINCH, W T (1893)

BLACK, S (1576)

TACKETT, A C (1260)

TAYLOR, J N (1243)

MOSES, D (179)

Medlan Cem.

BLAINE, R A (1382)

MARLIN, J (199)

SA&MG RR CO (261)

Fish Creek

MEDLAN, A B (189)

GEORGE, H B (110)

BUSE, J (1570)

Fish Creek

WALLACE M D (1562)

Medlan Branch

DUNN, W (83)

MARLIN, W N P (190)

KELLY, W (1688)

STEWART, J C (1880)

TE&L CO (823)

HILL, G W (1444)

BROWN, W H (1865)

MCKINNEY & WILLIAMS (202)

CHOATE, C S (2280)

COTTLE, G W (66)

Salt Branch

BBB&C RR CO (30)

TE&L CO (823)

TE&L CO (1236)

BROOKS, S A (1887)

Brazos River

I&GN RR CO (1325)

Anns Anns

AKERS, W A J (1363)

Komo

GOSSETT, A E (1799)

WILSON, M A (1559)

MCCORKLE, R L (2141)

THARP, D P (1854)

I&GN RR CO (1459)

COTTLE, G W (65)

HART, R A (1897)

BBB&C RR CO (37)

Hot Wells

TANKERSLEY, S (278)

Stovall

TOBIN, J (279)

TWILLEGEAR, Y H (1883)

WOOD, S (1650)

Graham Lake

TE&L CO (1234)

TOWNSEND, C W (1642)

COTHRAN, G (1401)

GOSSETT, A E (1802)

ALLEN, J (1662)

JOHNSON, W (159)

TOWNSEND, J O (1641)

EDWARDS, W W (1422)

RHOTON, HRS E (243)

Glmoe

GARRETT, J (108)

STATE OF TEXAS (Q31)

DAVIS, J J (1979)

BOLTON, HRS J (12)

TE&L CO (1237)

CARTER, W T (62)

DENISON, S (77)

TIMMONS, A (1258)

JAYNE, B M (2016)

TE&L CO (828)

Farm-to-Market Road 701

TE&L CO (830)

RI CO (1821)

TE&L CO (829)

TE&L CO (836)

TE&L CO (832)

Elm Creek

SCOTT, B F (2301)

TE&L CO (835)

McMillan Branch

McClusky

Elm Creek

TE&L CO (831)

SMITH, I N (1879)

FICKLIN, R G (1834)

Clear Brazos Fork River

TE&L CO (825)

TE&L CO (837)

TE&L CO (1240)

Paddock

TE&L CO (834)

TE&L CO (833)

MULANAX, J T M (2044)

SMITH, I N (1791)

SMITH, M (1864)

BUTLER, (...)

AKERS, W A J
Abs # 1363
24-Apr-1880
see also, Map 35

ALLEN, J
Abs # 1662
14-Oct-1881

BBB&C RR CO
Abs # 30
29-Oct-1861

BBB&C RR CO
Abs # 37
09-Oct-1876

BLACK, S
Abs # 1576
27-Jun-1882
see also, Map 28

BLAINE, R A
Abs # 1382
21-Dec-1880
see also, Map 28

BOLTON, HRS J
Abs # 12
31-Jul-1857

BROOKS, S A
Abs # 1887
03-Oct-1887
see also, Map 37

BROWN, W H
Abs # 1865
22-Oct-1888

BUSE, J
Abs # 1570
17-Nov-1879
see also, Maps 29, 37

BUTLER, M
Abs # 1864
03-Jun-1886
see also, Maps 37, 44, 45

CARTER, W T
Abs # 62
31-Jul-1857

CHOATE, C S
Abs # 2280
07-Mar-1911

COTHRAN, G
Abs # 1401
21-May-1881

COTTLE, G W
Abs # 65
05-Apr-1877
see also, Map 35

COTTLE, G W
Abs # 66
05-Apr-1877
see also, Map 35

DAVIS, J J
Abs # 1979
25-Sep-1895

DENISON, S
Abs # 77
04-Oct-1875

DUNN, W
Abs # 83
24-Nov-1871
see also, Map 28

EDWARDS, W W
Abs # 1422
08-Feb-1886

FICKLIN, R G
Abs # 1834
06-Jul-1891
see also, Map 37

FINCH, W T
Abs # 1893
15-Feb-1890
see also, Maps 27, 28, 35

GARRETT, J

Abs # 108
29-Aug-1884
see also, Map 37

GEORGE, H B
Abs # 110
24-Feb-1860

GOSSETT, A E
Abs # 1799
18-Feb-1884
see also, Map 35

GOSSETT, A E
Abs # 1802
05-Mar-1884

HART, R A
Abs # 1897
18-Jul-1887

HILL, G W
Abs # 1444
25-Jun-1879
see also, Map 35

I&GN RR CO
Abs # 1325
13-Sep-1878

I&GN RR CO
Abs # 1459
08-Feb-1887

JAYNE, B M
Abs # 2016
30-Jan-1898
see also, Map 35

JOHNSON, W
Abs # 159
31-Jul-1857
see also, Map 37

KELLY, W
Abs # 1688
03-Jun-1886
see also, Map 37

MARLIN, J
Abs # 199
24-Oct-1857
see also, Maps 28, 29, 37

MARLIN, W N P
Abs # 190
15-Aug-1859
see also, Map 28

MCCORKLE, R L
Abs # 2141
20-Aug-1906

MCKINNEY & WILLIAMS
Abs # 202
12-Mar-1861

MEDLAN, A B
Abs # 189
25-Feb-1860
see also, Map 28

MOSES, D
Abs # 179
16-Aug-1855
see also, Map 28

MULANAX, J T M
Abs # 2044
06-Sep-1895
see also, Map 44

RHOTON, HRS E
Abs # 243
15-Jul-1857

RI CO
Abs # 1821
22-Mar-1886
see also, Map 37

SA&MG RR CO
Abs # 261
11-Dec-1860
see also, Map 35

SCOTT, B F
Abs # 2301
06-Mar-1922
see also, Map 37

SMITH, I N
Abs # 1791
07-Feb-1898
see also, Map 44

SMITH, I N
Abs # 1879
20-Jul-1886

STATE OF TEXAS
Abs # ?31
see also, Map 35

STEWART, J C
Abs # 1880
07-Jun-1892
see also, Map 35

TACKETT, A C
Abs # 1260
03-Aug-1877
see also, Map 28

TANKERSLEY, S
Abs # 278
19-Mar-1867

TAYLOR, J N
Abs # 1243
03-Jan-1859
see also, Map 28

TE&L CO
Abs # 1234
30-Jan-1861

TE&L CO
Abs # 1236
27-Dec-1865

TE&L CO
Abs # 1237
05-Feb-1861

TE&L CO
Abs # 1240
14-Mar-1859
see also, Map 44

TE&L CO
Abs # 823
14-Mar-1859

TE&L CO
Abs # 825
26-Aug-1858
see also, Maps 35, 43, 44

TE&L CO
Abs # 828
25-May-1859

TE&L CO
Abs # 829
25-May-1859

TE&L CO
Abs # 830
24-Oct-1895

TE&L CO
Abs # 831
29-Jul-1858
see also, Map 44

TE&L CO
Abs # 832
29-Jul-1858
see also, Map 44

TE&L CO
Abs # 833
26-May-1859
see also, Map 44

TE&L CO
Abs # 834
29-Jul-1858
see also, Map 44

TE&L CO
Abs # 835
18-Mar-1859
see also, Map 44

TE&L CO
Abs # 836
29-Jul-1858
see also, Maps 35, 44

TE&L CO
Abs # 837
29-Jul-1858
see also, Map 44

THARP, D P
Abs # 1854
11-Dec-1888

TIMMONS, A
Abs # 1258
31-Oct-1876
see also, Map 35

TOBIN, J
Abs # 279
21-Jan-1858
see also, Map 37

TOWNSEND, C W
Abs # 1642
06-Aug-1883
see also, Map 35

TOWNSEND, J O
Abs # 1641
01-Nov-1883
see also, Map 35

TWILLEGEAR, Y H
Abs # 1883
07-Oct-1889

WALLACE, M D
Abs # 1562
14-Jul-1884

WILSON, M A
Abs # 1559
07-Sep-1882

WOOD, S
Abs # 1650
12-Feb-1880

Populated Places
None

Cemeteries
Medlan Cemetery

Water (larger bodies)
Graham Lake

Other Water
Brazos River
Clear Fork Brazos River
Elm Creek
Fish Creek
Mc Millan Branch
Medlan Branch
Salt Branch

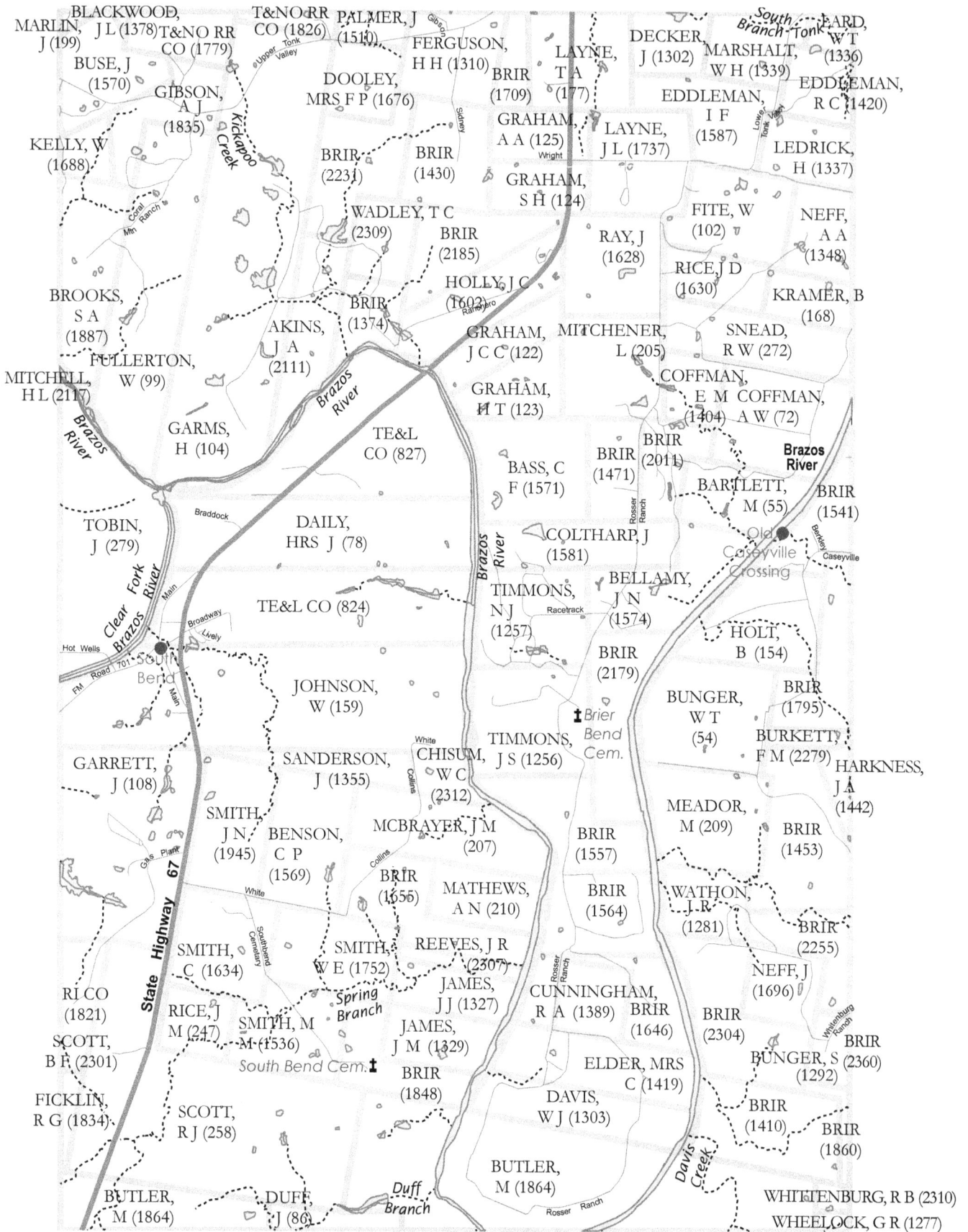

MARLIN, J (199)

BLACKWOOD, J L (1378)

T&NO RR CO (1779)

T&NO RR CO (1826)

PALMER, J (1510)

FERGUSON, H H (1310)

DECKER, J (1302)

MARSHALT, W H (1339)

EARD, W T (1336)

BUSE, J (1570)

GIBSON, A J (1835)

DOOLEY, MRS F P (1676)

BRIR (1709)

LAYNE, T A (177)

EDDLEMAN, I F (1587)

EDDLEMAN, R C (1420)

KELLY, W (1688)

BRIR (2231)

BRIR (1430)

GRAHAM, A A (125)

LAYNE, J L (1737)

LEDRICK, H (1337)

WADLEY, T C (2309)

BRIR (2185)

GRAHAM, S H (124)

FITE, W (102)

NEFF, A A (1348)

BROOKS, S A (1887)

BRIR (1374)

HOLLY, J C (1602)

RAY, J (1628)

RICE, J D (1630)

KRAMER, B (168)

AKINS, J A (2111)

GRAHAM, J C C (122)

MITCHENER, L (205)

SNEAD, R W (272)

FULLERTON, W (99)

MITCHELL, H L (2117)

GARMS, H (104)

Brazos River

TE&L CO (827)

GRAHAM, H T (123)

COFFMAN, E M (1404)

COFFMAN, A W (72)

BRIR (1471)

BRIR (2011)

Brazos River

BASS, C F (1571)

BARTLETT, M (55)

BRIR (1541)

TOBIN, J (279)

Braddock

DAILY, HRS J (78)

Brazos River

COLTHARP, J (1581)

Old Caseyville Crossing

Caseyville

Clear Fork Brazos River

TE&L CO (824)

TIMMONS, N J (1257)

BELLAMY, J N (1574)

Racetrack

HOLT, B (154)

Hot Wells

South Bend

Broadway

Lively

Main

JOHNSON, W (159)

BRIR (2179)

Brier Bend Cem.

BUNGER, W T (54)

BRIR (1795)

FM Road 701

GARRETT, J (108)

SANDERSON, J (1355)

CHISUM, W C (2312)

White

Collins

TIMMONS, J S (1256)

BRIR (2279)

BURKETT, F M (2279)

BRIR (1453)

HARKNESS, J A (1442)

SMITH, J N (1945)

BENSON, C P (1569)

MCBRAYER, J M (207)

MEADOR, M (209)

State Highway 67

Gas Plant

Collins

BRIR (1655)

MATHEWS, A N (210)

BRIR (1557)

BRIR (1564)

WATHON, J R (1281)

BRIR (2255)

White

SMITH, C (1634)

Southbend Cemetary

SMITH, W E (1752)

REEVES, J R (2307)

Rosser Ranch

NEFF, J (1696)

Whitenburg Ranch

RICO (1821)

RICE, J M (247)

SMITH, M M (1536)

Spring Branch

JAMES, J J (1327)

JAMES, J M (1329)

CUNNINGHAM, R A (1389)

BRIR (1646)

BRIR (2304)

BUNGER, S (1292)

BRIR (2360)

SCOTT, B F (2301)

South Bend Cem.

BRIR (1848)

ELDER, MRS C (1419)

DAVIS, W J (1303)

BRIR (1410)

BRIR (1860)

FICKLIN, R G (1834)

SCOTT, R J (258)

BUTLER, M (1864)

Davis Creek

BUTLER, M (1864)

DUFF, J (86)

Duff Branch

Rosser Ranch

WHITENBURG, R B (2310)

WHEELOCK, G R (1277)

AKINS, J A
Abs # 2111
25-Oct-1879

BARTLETT, M
Abs # 55
23-Jun-1887

BASS, C F
Abs # 1571
19-Nov-1879

BELLAMY, J N
Abs # 1574
26-Aug-1880

BENSON, C P
Abs # 1569
21-Oct-1879

BLACKWOOD, J L
Abs # 1378
30-Jan-1882
see also, Maps 28, 29

BRIR
Abs # 1374
Survey2: BYRD, W B
14-Jul-1879

BRIR
Abs # 1410
Survey2: DAUGHERTY, W
26-Mar-1884

BRIR
Abs # 1430
Survey2: FITCHETT, W H
16-Jul-1895

BRIR
Abs # 1453
Survey2: HALL, M
25-Apr-1922
see also, Map 38

BRIR
Abs # 1471
Survey2: KIRKPATRICK, R
06-Jan-1880

BRIR
Abs # 1541
Survey2: TAYLOR, J M
10-May-1880
see also, Map 38

BRIR
Abs # 1557
Survey2: WAYNE, T A
01-Sep-1880

BRIR
Abs # 1564
Survey2: WELCH, G T
24-Aug-1886

BRIR
Abs # 1646
Survey2: THOMAS, S A
05-Jun-1882

BRIR
Abs # 1655
Survey2: WOOD, J H
24-Aug-1881

BRIR
Abs # 1709
Survey2: SEDDON, S T
29-Aug-1884
see also, Map 29

BRIR
Abs # 1795
Survey2: BUNGER, W T
26-May-1884
see also, Map 38

BRIR
Abs # 1848
Survey2: MCBRAYER, J W
08-Jan-1902

BRIR
Abs # 1860
Survey2: WHITTENBURG, J
13-Jul-1891
see also, Map 38

BRIR
Abs # 2011
Survey2: COFFMAN, E M
21-May-1891

BRIR
Abs # 2179
Survey2: TIMMONS, J S
23-Apr-1919

BRIR
Abs # 2185
Survey2: COFFMAN, A W
04-Jan-1905

BRIR
Abs # 2231
Survey2: WADLEY, T H
26-Dec-1918

BRIR
Abs # 2255
Survey2: WHITTENBURG, J B
11-Sep-1907
see also, Map 38

BRIR
Abs # 2304
Survey2: BYNUM, H C

BRIR
Abs # 2360
Survey2: MERCER, J L
05-Jul-1890
see also, Map 38

BROOKS, S A
Abs # 1887
03-Oct-1887
see also, Map 36

BUNGER, S
Abs # 1292
11-Jan-1878
see also, Map 38

BUNGER, W T
Abs # 54
15-Dec-1876

BURKETT, F M
Abs # 2279
16-May-1911
see also, Map 38

BUSE, J
Abs # 1570
17-Nov-1879
see also, Maps 29, 36

BUTLER, M
Abs # 1864
03-Jun-1886
see also, Maps 36, 44, 45

CHISUM, W C
Abs # 2312
05-Jan-1920

COFFMAN, A W
Abs # 72
08-Jan-1877
see also, Map 38

COFFMAN, E M
Abs # 1404
17-Dec-1879

COLTHARP, J
Abs # 1581
13-Nov-1879

CUNNINGHAM, R A
Abs # 1389
09-Apr-1879

DAILY, HRS J
Abs # 78
15-Jul-1857

DAVIS, W J
Abs # 1303
17-Apr-1878

DECKER, J
Abs # 1302
07-Jan-1878
see also, Map 29

DOOLEY, MRS F P

Abs # 1676
03-Aug-1885

DUFF, J
Abs # 86
08-Oct-1917
see also, Map 45

EDDLEMAN, I F
Abs # 1587
05-Jan-1880

EDDLEMAN, R C
Abs # 1420
10-Jun-1879
see also, Map 38

ELDER, MRS C
Abs # 1419
24-Apr-1879

FERGUSON, H H
Abs # 1310
17-Jul-1878
see also, Map 29

FICKLIN, R G
Abs # 1834
06-Jul-1891
see also, Map 36

FITE, W
Abs # 102
09-Jul-1877

FULLERTON, W
Abs # 99
20-Feb-1861

GARMS, H
Abs # 104
20-Nov-1860

GARRETT, J
Abs # 108
29-Aug-1884
see also, Map 36

GIBSON, A J
Abs # 1835
01-Sep-1891

GRAHAM, A A
Abs # 125
10-Oct-1876

GRAHAM, H T
Abs # 123
11-Nov-1876

GRAHAM, J C C
Abs # 122
25-Sep-1876

GRAHAM, S H
Abs # 124
10-Oct-1876

HARKNESS, J A
Abs # 1442
10-Jun-1879
see also, Map 38

HOLLY, J C
Abs # 1602
17-Nov-1879

HOLT, B
Abs # 154
17-Aug-1877

JAMES, J J
Abs # 1327
04-Sep-1877

JAMES, J M
Abs # 1329
26-Mar-1879

JOHNSON, W
Abs # 159
31-Jul-1857
see also, Map 36

KELLY, W
Abs # 1688
03-Jun-1886
see also, Map 36

KRAMER, B

Abs # 168
22-Jan-1877
see also, Map 38

LARD, W T
Abs # 1336
20-Dec-1877
see also, Maps 29, 30, 38

LAYNE, J L
Abs # 1737
05-May-1882

LAYNE, T A
Abs # 177
26-Aug-1876
see also, Map 29

LEDRICK, H
Abs # 1337
18-Jan-1878
see also, Map 38

MARLIN, J
Abs # 199
24-Oct-1857
see also, Maps 28, 29, 36

MARSHALT, W H
Abs # 1339
08-Apr-1878
see also, Map 29

MATHEWS, A N
Abs # 210
13-Dec-1876

MCBRAYER, J M
Abs # 207
22-Jan-1877

MEADOR, M
Abs # 209
15-Dec-1876

MITCHELL, H L
Abs # 2117
04-Oct-1894

MITCHENER, L
Abs # 205
21-Mar-1877

NEFF, A A
Abs # 1348
22-Feb-1878
see also, Map 38

NEFF, J
Abs # 1696
16-Mar-1881

PALMER, J
Abs # 1510
29-Jul-1879
see also, Map 29

RAY, J
Abs # 1628
16-Sep-1879

REEVES, J R
Abs # 2307
02-Apr-1919

RI CO
Abs # 1821
22-Mar-1886
see also, Map 36

RICE, J D
Abs # 1630
17-Nov-1879

RICE, J M
Abs # 247
03-Aug-1877

SANDERSON, J
Abs # 1355
14-Nov-1878

SCOTT, B F
Abs # 2301
06-Mar-1922
see also, Map 36

SCOTT, R J
Abs # 258
08-Jun-1880

SMITH, C
Abs # 1634
29-Mar-1880

SMITH, J N
Abs # 1945
17-Apr-1888

SMITH, M M
Abs # 1536
08-Dec-1879

SMITH, W E
Abs # 1752
26-Jul-1882

SNEAD, R W
Abs # 272
23-Oct-1876
see also, Map 38

T&NO RR CO
Abs # 1779
Survey2: IRVIN, A
24-May-1895
see also, Map 29

T&NO RR CO
Abs # 1826
Survey2: AUSTIN, W W
29-Jun-1920
see also, Map 29

TE&L CO
Abs # 824
01-Feb-1860

TE&L CO
Abs # 827
01-Feb-1860

TIMMONS, J S
Abs # 1256
21-Nov-1876

TIMMONS, N J
Abs # 1257
21-Nov-1876

TOBIN, J
Abs # 279
21-Jan-1858
see also, Map 36

Populated Places
Old Caseyville Crossing
South Bend

Cemeteries
Brier Bend Cemetery
South Bend Cemetery

Water (larger bodies)
Brazos River

Other Water
Brazos River
Clear Fork Brazos River
Davis Creek
Duff Branch
Kickapoo Creek
North Tonk Branch
South Tonk Branch
Spring Branch
Tonk Branch

WADLEY, T C
Abs # 2309
21-Dec-1918

WATHON, J R
Abs # 1281
25-Jan-1877

WHEELOCK, G R
Abs # 1277
06-Aug-1875
see also, Maps 38, 45, 46

WHITTENBURG, R B
Abs # 2310
21-Dec-1918
see also, Map 38

LARD,
W T (1336)

THOMAS, F L (1259)

BARRY,
T H (1668)

GREGORY,
L M (121)

Pettus

HAYNES,
J R (2238)

Old Hwy
16

BRIR
(2249)

ERNEST, A
J (92)

Brazos
River

Forbus

Jarry

EDDLEMAN,
R C (1420)

Farmer
Cem.

Jarry

Farm to Market
Road 1287

UPHAM, E
E (1263)

MABRY, R E
(2287)

Salem

BRIR
(2240)

LEDRICK,
H (1337)

LOVEJOY,
J T (178)

WHITTENBURG,
J B
(1282)

BRIR
(1738)

BRIR
(2135)

BRIR
(1730)

NEFF,
A A (1348)

EDDLEMAN,
W M (1597)

Wiley

BAKER,
M W
(52)

BYRD,
R E (47)

KEARBY,
W C (1474)

BAKER,
W A
(1293)

FORE,
G W
(103)

JOWELL,
J R (1331)

JOWELL,
J V
(1332)

BAKER,
G W (1291)

Berry

Jeffery Farm

KRAMER,
B (168)

Gooseneck
Cem.

Gooseneck
Cemetery

ROBINSON,
J J (1520)

SNEAD,
R W (272)

BRIR
(1694)

MORRISON,
J E (212)

KUTCH, B F
(1333)

MCLAREN,
F M (211)

TRACY,
N F
(1639)

BRIR
(2218)

BRIR
(1689)

COFFMAN,
A W (72)

BRIR
(1383)

MORRISON,
J P
(206)

FORE,
J S (1309)

RIBBLE, W A
(248)

Jeffery
Farm

Burgess

JOWELL,
J A
(1330)

LAFFERTY,
J A (175)

Gooseneck Cemetery

LYTLE, S (1334)

Indian Springs

BAKER,
J R (56)

Bunger

EDDLEMAN,
J (1728)

LYTLE, W A (176)

FERGUSON,
J (100)

MCDERMITT,
G B
(1340)

Salem

BRIR
(1541)

HOWARD,
J W (1600)

BRIR
(1812)

BRIR
(2071)

Caseyville

BRIR
(1916)

BRIR
(1685)

Ming
Bend

KUTCH,
R M (169)

BRIR
(1795)

BRIR
(1672)

RIBBLE,
L J
(1353)

HOLLY,
T J
(1601)

BRIR
(2219)

CRISWELL,
C T (1395)

BRIR
(1948)

AUBURG,
C E F
(1663)

BRIR
(1773)

PIRTLE,
G P (236)

FULLERTON,
J (101)

BURKETT,
F M (2279)

BRIR
(1604)

BRIR
(1915)

KELLY,
E M (1614)

JAMES,
W F
(1610)

BRIR
(1500)

HARKNESS,
J A (1442)

BRIR
(2215)

BRIR (2201)

BRIR
(2245)

Oil City

Ranch

BRIR
(1980)

BRIR
(2073)

BRIR
(1955)

BRIR
(2290)

OXFORD,
W R (216)

OXFORD,
J G (1503)

BRIR
(1453)

Whitenburg

BRIR
(2154)

BRIR
(2250)

ORRELL,
MRS S (1745)

BRIR
(1556)

BRIR
(1837)

BRIR
(2255)

BRIR
(1938)

ALCORN,
R (1767)

BRIR
(1519)

BRIR
(2221)

BUNGER, S
(1292)

BRIR
(1623)

Pugh

Mountain Home

WHITTENBURG, J C (1359)

BRIR (2329)

BRIR
(2217)

BRIR
(2197)

BRIR (2209)

BRIR
(2360)

BRIR (2216)

BRIR
(2205)

BRIR
(1860)

BRIR
(1873)

Marvin Home

Hamilton

MERCER,
J L (1343)

Mountain Home Cem.

BRIR
(2136)

Cove
Creek

BRIR
(2147)

BRIR
(2244)

WHITTENBURG,
R B (2310)

Sunset

WHITTENBURG,
J N

Truesdell

RODGERS,
J E
(1629)

BRIR
(1590)

BRIR
(2225)

BRIR (1417)

BRIR
(2142)

WHEELOCK, G R (1277)

MORGAN,
C (200)

(1651)

BRIR (1896)

BRIR (1452)

ALCORN, R
Abs # 1767
19-Jun-1883

AUBURG, C E F
Abs # 1663
20-Jan-1881

BAKER, G W
Abs # 1291
18-Dec-1877
see also, Map 39

BAKER, J R
Abs # 56
23-Jun-1877

BAKER, M W
Abs # 52
12-Apr-1877

BAKER, W A
Abs # 1293
18-Jan-1878

BARRY, T H
Abs # 1668
06-Sep-1886
see also, Map 30

BRIR
Abs # 1383
Survey2: BYRD, W A
12-Feb-1880

BRIR
Abs # 1417
Survey2: DIEW, F M
03-Mar-1879
see also, Map 46

BRIR
Abs # 1452
Survey2: HALL, W R
13-May-1885
see also, Map 46

BRIR
Abs # 1453
Survey2: HALL, M
25-Apr-1922
see also, Map 37

BRIR
Abs # 1500
Survey2: SHELBY, J
12-Feb-1880
see also, Map 39

BRIR
Abs # 1519
Survey2: PARHAN, A
04-Sep-1879

BRIR
Abs # 1541
Survey2: TAYLOR, J M
10-May-1880
see also, Map 37

BRIR
Abs # 1556
Survey2: WALTERS, J T
02-Dec-1886

BRIR
Abs # 1590
Survey2: DRIVER, J
29-May-1884
see also, Map 46

BRIR
Abs # 1604
Survey2: HOWARD, J W
17-May-1884

BRIR
Abs # 1623
Survey2: MCCLENDON, D F
10-Dec-1885

BRIR
Abs # 1672
Survey2: CASEY, J W
29-Sep-1906

BRIR
Abs # 1685
Survey2: JOHNSON, W
05-Sep-1883

BRIR
Abs # 1689
Survey2: LEDBETTER, A B
08-Sep-1883
see also, Map 39

BRIR
Abs # 1694
Survey2: MORRISON, J E
08-Mar-1901

BRIR
Abs # 1730
Survey2: GILMORE, W J
14-Oct-1886
see also, Map 39

BRIR
Abs # 1738
Survey2: LOVEJOY, J T
21-Sep-1912

BRIR
Abs # 1773
Survey2: CUNNINGHAM, J H
27-Jun-1892

BRIR
Abs # 1795
Survey2: BUNGER, W T
26-May-1884
see also, Map 37

BRIR
Abs # 1812
Survey2: JAMES, W W
18-Dec-1912

BRIR
Abs # 1837
Survey2: KIRBY, J M
13-Jul-1887
see also, Map 39

BRIR
Abs # 1860
Survey2: WHITTENBURG, J
13-Jul-1891
see also, Map 37

BRIR
Abs # 1873
Survey2: MERCER, J L
05-Jul-1890

BRIR
Abs # 1896
Survey2: GREENWADE, R H
24-Nov-1891
see also, Map 46

BRIR
Abs # 1915
Survey2: AYNESWORTH, G L
18-Dec-1912

BRIR
Abs # 1916
Survey2: AYNESWORTH, G L
18-Dec-1912

BRIR
Abs # 1938
Survey2: LISLE, J N
18-Mar-1895

BRIR
Abs # 1948
Survey2: AYNESWORTH, G L
13-Aug-1913

BRIR
Abs # 1955
Survey2: CUNNINGHAM, J H
14-Mar-1917

BRIR
Abs # 1980
Survey2: DRIVER, J A
09-Feb-1921

BRIR
Abs # 2071
Survey2: CRISWELL, T K
07-Jul-1906
see also, Map 39

BRIR
Abs # 2073

Survey2: DRIVER, J A
09-Feb-1921

BRIR
Abs # 2135
Survey2: GILMORE, J F
17-Jun-1907

BRIR
Abs # 2136
Survey2: GREENWADE, J J

BRIR
Abs # 2142
Survey2: MCKNIGHT, W N
09-Aug-1917
see also, Maps 46, 47

BRIR
Abs # 2147
Survey2: AINSWORTH, J A
14-May-1920

BRIR
Abs # 2154
Survey2: CUNNINGHAM, W H
20-Nov-1907

BRIR
Abs # 2197
Survey2: AINSWORTH, J A
14-Mar-1917

BRIR
Abs # 2201
Survey2: GREEN, J W
31-Jan-1939

BRIR
Abs # 2205
Survey2: MITCHELL, R F
14-Nov-1906
see also, Map 39

BRIR
Abs # 2209
Survey2: OLDHAM, S M
31-Jul-1922
see also, Map 39

BRIR
Abs # 2215
Survey2: DOWDLE, J E
23-Apr-1913

BRIR
Abs # 2216
Survey2: GREENWADE, J J
20-May-1921

BRIR
Abs # 2217
Survey2: KING, H G
28-Nov-1919

BRIR
Abs # 2218
29-Aug-1917

BRIR
Abs # 2219
Survey2: KING, H G
18-Dec-1912

BRIR
Abs # 2221
Survey2: LISLE, O D
05-Dec-1917

BRIR
Abs # 2225
Survey2: RIBBLE, S L
05-May-1921
see also, Map 46

BRIR
Abs # 2240
Survey2: AKIN, D R
23-Oct-1944
see also, Maps 30, 31, 39

BRIR
Abs # 2244
Survey2: MITCHELL, R F
14-Nov-1906
see also, Maps 39, 46, 47

BRIR
Abs # 2245
Survey2: OWEN, R D

20-Oct-1919

BRIR
Abs # 2249
Survey2: AKIN, D R
23-Oct-1944
see also, Maps 30, 31, 39

BRIR
Abs # 2250
Survey2: DOWDLE, J E
11-Sep-1913

BRIR
Abs # 2255
Survey2: WHITTENBURG, J B
11-Sep-1907
see also, Map 37

BRIR
Abs # 2290
Survey2: MILLER, J T
07-May-1913

BRIR
Abs # 2329
Survey2: GREENWADE, J J
07-Jun-1921

BRIR
Abs # 2360
Survey2: MERCER, J L
05-Jul-1890
see also, Map 37

BUNGER, S
Abs # 1292
11-Jan-1878
see also, Map 37

BURKETT, F M
Abs # 2279
16-May-1911
see also, Map 37

BYRD, R E
Abs # 47
02-Feb-1877

COFFMAN, A W
Abs # 72
08-Jan-1877
see also, Map 37

CRISWELL, C T
Abs # 1395
31-Mar-1879
see also, Map 39

EDDLEMAN, J
Abs # 1728
15-Sep-1882

EDDLEMAN, R C
Abs # 1420
10-Jun-1879
see also, Map 37

EDDLEMAN, W M
Abs # 1597
07-Jan-1881

ERNEST, A J
Abs # 92
14-Oct-1876

FERGUSON, J
Abs # 100
10-Feb-1877

FORE, G W
Abs # 103
09-Jul-1877

FORE, J S
Abs # 1309
17-Apr-1878

FULLERTON, J
Abs # 101
20-Oct-1876
see also, Map 39

GREGORY, L M
Abs # 121
27-Nov-1876
see also, Map 30

HARKNESS, J A
Abs # 1442

10-Jun-1879
see also, Map 37

HAYNES, J R
Abs # 2238
23-Oct-1944
see also, Map 30

HOLLY, T J
Abs # 1601
21-Oct-1879

HOWARD, J W
Abs # 1600
23-Sep-1879

JAMES, W F
Abs # 1610
25-Sep-1879

JOWELL, J A
Abs # 1330
20-Dec-1878
see also, Map 39

JOWELL, J R
Abs # 1331
20-Dec-1878

JOWELL, J V
Abs # 1332
20-Dec-1878

KEARBY, W C
Abs # 1474
03-Mar-1882

KELLY, E M
Abs # 1614
21-Oct-1879

KRAMER, B
Abs # 168
22-Jan-1877
see also, Map 37

KUTCH, B F
Abs # 1333
16-Apr-1878

KUTCH, R M
Abs # 169
11-Nov-1876

Populated Places
Bunger

Cemeteries
Farmer Cemetery
Gooseneck Cemetery
Mountain Home Cemetery

Water (larger bodies)
Brazos River

Other Water
Cove Creek
Tonk Branch

LAFFERTY, J A
Abs # 175
28-Jul-1879

LARD, W T
Abs # 1336
20-Dec-1877
see also, Maps 29, 30, 37

LEDRICK, H
Abs # 1337
18-Jan-1878
see also, Map 37

LOVEJOY, J T
Abs # 178
01-Dec-1876

LYTLE, S
Abs # 1334
07-Dec-1877

LYTLE, W A
Abs # 176
25-Jan-1877

MABRY, R E
Abs # 2287
30-Jan-1920
see also, Map 30

MCDERMITT, G B
Abs # 1340
21-May-1878

MCLAREN, F M
Abs # 211
09-Aug-1877

MERCER, J L
Abs # 1343
21-Sep-1878

MORGAN, C
Abs # 200
28-May-1875
see also, Map 46

MORRISON, J E
Abs # 212
23-Jun-1877

MORRISON, J P
Abs # 206
23-Jun-1877

NEFF, A A
Abs # 1348
22-Feb-1878
see also, Map 37

ORRELL, MRS S
Abs # 1745
20-Feb-1885

OXFORD, J G
Abs # 1503
04-Feb-1879
see also, Map 39

OXFORD, W R
Abs # 216
25-Apr-1877

PIRTLE, G P
Abs # 236
20-Oct-1876

RIBBLE, L J
Abs # 1353
11-Jun-1878

RIBBLE, W A
Abs # 248
23-Jun-1877

ROBINSON, J J
Abs # 1520
27-May-1879
see also, Map 39

RODGERS, J E
Abs # 1629
28-Oct-1879

SNEAD, R W
Abs # 272
23-Oct-1876
see also, Map 37

THOMAS, F L
Abs # 1259
28-Jun-1876
see also, Map 30

TRACY, N F
Abs # 1639
16-Sep-1879

UPHAM, E E
Abs # 1263
26-Sep-1876
see also, Map 30

WHEELOCK, G R
Abs # 1277
06-Aug-1875
see also, Maps 37, 45, 46

WHITTENBURG, J B
Abs # 1282
10-Jan-1877

WHITTENBURG, J C
Abs # 1359
25-Jun-1878

WHITTENBURG, J N
Abs # 1651
03-Mar-1880

WHITTENBURG, R B
Abs # 2310
21-Dec-1918
see also, Map 37

BRIR
(2249)

Kaye
Leighln

BRIR
(2237)

BRIR
(2261)

HOLDERNESS, BIRDWELL, J M (1568)
S M (1806)

BRIR
(2240)

KELLUM,
MRS, E
(1782)

PAYNE
F G (1515)

WILLESS
J (1652)

BIRDWELL,
J (1768)

Finis

BRIR
(1730)

BRIR
(2243)

FOWLER,
T (1427)

CRUMPTON,
W A
(1391)

BRIR
(2251)

BARR,
R (9)

ABERNATHY, J
(1567)

BAKER,
G W
(1291)

Salem

Salem

PATTER,
H N
(224)

BBB&C
RR CO
(25)

ROBINSON,
J J (1520)

BRIR
(1689)

BRIR
(1866)

REEDER
, T P
(1354)

JOWELL,
J A
(1330)

BROOKS,
D C
(48)

State
Highway 16

Connor
Creek

CONNER,
J (57)

GILMORE,
A C (1313)

MOSS, S
(1615)

BBB&C
RR CO
(27)

BRIR
(2071)

HILL,
J A (127)

CRISWELL,
C T
(1395)

DENTON,
A L
(88)

Brazos
River

GOLDEN, P
(1312)

Indian Springs Indian

Indian

Connor
Creek

FARRIS,
E (94)

KISSINGER,
J (2286)

FULLERTON,
J (101)

HUMPHREYS,
P J (153)

MATHIS,
L J (1482)

WALKER,
J B
(1278)

ORRICK,
W J
(217)

BRIR
(1500)

Cove Creek

BRIR
(1898)

BRIR
(2208)

ABERNATHY,
(1360)

MORRIS,
W M (1495)

WALKER,
J B
(1279)

Country Meadows

GILLIAM,
R (112)

OXFORD,
J G
(1503)

SAUNDERS,
L O
(2292)

FISHER, J
H (1598)

JAMES,
S H (1465)

LASSITER,
M L
(1936)

BRIR
(1837)

NEWBY, L
(2293) FREEMAN,
W H (1428)

LASSITER,
W S (1964)

Ming
Bend
Cem.

Ming
Bend

JOHNSON,
J M (161)

BRIR
(2209)

ANDERSON, J
E (2311)

ROSE, HRS
J (245)

Perez

BRIR
(2230)

EADS,
W A (1833)

MIERS,
L (1784)

RIBBLE, W
(1996)

BRIR
2205)

MCKNIGHT,
W N (2019)

Possum
Kingdom
Lake

POITEVENT, J (232)

BROWN,
O T
(24)

BRIR
(2244)

BRIR
(1935)

RAMSOURS,
N (1970)

(Q33)

RIBBLE,
E J (1877)

KISINGER,
G (170)

MOSLEY,
N S (1741)

FOSTER,
D L (2186)

POITEVENT,
J (1959)

I&GN RR
CO (1458)

ABERNATHY, J
Abs # 1360
28-Feb-1879

ABERNATHY, J
Abs # 1567
09-Oct-1882
see also, Map 40

ANDERSON, J E
Abs # 2311
10-Jun-1920

BAKER, G W
Abs # 1291
18-Dec-1877
see also, Map 38

BARR, R
Abs # 9
03-Aug-1875

BBB&C RR CO
Abs # 25
23-Mar-1859
see also, Map 40

BBB&C RR CO
Abs # 27
24-Mar-1859
see also, Map 40

BIRDWELL, J
Abs # 1768
27-Mar-1884
see also, Maps 31, 32, 40

BIRDWELL, J M
Abs # 1568
20-Feb-1880
see also, Map 31

BRIR
Abs # 1500
Survey2: SHELBY, J
12-Feb-1880
see also, Map 38

BRIR
Abs # 1689
Survey2: LEDBETTER, A B
08-Sep-1883
see also, Map 38

BRIR
Abs # 1730
Survey2: GILMORE, W J
14-Oct-1886
see also, Map 38

BRIR
Abs # 1837
Survey2: KIRBY, J M
13-Jul-1887
see also, Map 38

BRIR
Abs # 1866
Survey2: BROOKS, D C
08-Feb-1905

BRIR
Abs # 1898
Survey2: HERRON, F
30-Mar-1921

BRIR
Abs # 1935
Survey2: KUYKENDALL, W H
27-Nov-1912
see also, Map 47

BRIR
Abs # 2071
Survey2: CRISWELL, T K
07-Jul-1906
see also, Map 38

BRIR
Abs # 2205
Survey2: MITCHELL, R F
14-Nov-1906
see also, Map 38

BRIR
Abs # 2208
Survey2: OLDHAM, M
12-Mar-1923

BRIR

Abs # 2209
Survey2: OLDHAM, S M
31-Jul-1922
see also, Map 38

BRIR
Abs # 2230
Survey2: SMITH, T H
28-Jun-1907

BRIR
Abs # 2237
Survey2: AKIN, D R
23-Oct-1944
see also, Map 31

BRIR
Abs # 2240
Survey2: AKIN, D R
23-Oct-1944
see also, Maps 30, 31, 38

BRIR
Abs # 2243
Survey2: GILMORE, J F
14-Feb-1918

BRIR
Abs # 2244
Survey2: MITCHELL, R F
14-Nov-1906
see also, Maps 38, 46, 47

BRIR
Abs # 2249
Survey2: AKIN, D R
23-Oct-1944
see also, Maps 30, 31, 38

BRIR
Abs # 2251
Survey2: GILMORE, J F
18-Jan-1917

BRIR
Abs # 2261
Survey2: DAVASHER, H W
02-May-1906
see also, Map 31

BROOKS, D C
Abs # 48
07-Aug-1877

BROWN, O T
Abs # 24
15-Mar-1878
see also, Maps 40, 47, 48

CONNER, J
Abs # 57
30-Oct-1857
see also, Map 40

CRISWELL, C T
Abs # 1395
31-Mar-1879
see also, Map 38

CRUMPTON, W A
Abs # 1391
20-Jun-1879
see also, Map 40

DENTON, A L
Abs # 88
10-Oct-1876

EADS, W A
Abs # 1833
18-Mar-1889

FARRIS, E
Abs # 94
31-Oct-1857

FISHER, J H
Abs # 1598
12-Jan-1880

FOSTER, D L
Abs # 2186
24-Jan-1923
see also, Map 47

FOWLER, T
Abs # 1427
21-May-1879

FREEMAN, W H

Abs # 1428
19-Jun-1880

FULLERTON, J
Abs # 101
20-Oct-1876
see also, Map 38

GILLIAM, R
Abs # 112
15-Mar-1878
see also, Map 40

GILMORE, A C
Abs # 1313
17-Oct-1877

GOLDEN, P
Abs # 1312
06-May-1873

HILL, J A
Abs # 127
02-May-1859

HOLDERNESS, S M
Abs # 1806
09-Apr-1884
see also, Map 31

HUMPHREYS, P J
Abs # 153
23-Oct-1876

I&GN RR CO
Abs # 1458
23-Nov-1881
see also, Map 47

JAMES, S H
Abs # 1465
28-Mar-1881

JOHNSON, J M
Abs # 161
31-May-1862
see also, Map 40

JOWELL, J A
Abs # 1330
20-Dec-1878
see also, Map 38

KELLUM, MRS, E
Abs # 1782
17-Dec-1884
see also, Map 31

KISINGER, G
Abs # 170
11-Aug-1877

KISSINGER, J
Abs # 2286
11-Dec-1911

LASSITER, M L
Abs # 1936
03-Jan-1889

LASSITER, W S
Abs # 1964
17-Jun-1889

MATHIS, L J
Abs # 1482
30-Sep-1879

MCKNIGHT, W N
Abs # 2019
23-Dec-1896
see also, Map 47

MIERS, L
Abs # 1784
27-Nov-1886

MORRIS, W M
Abs # 1495
03-May-1884

MOSLEY, N S
Abs # 1741
24-Nov-1885
see also, Map 47

MOSS, S
Abs # 1615
03-Mar-1880

NEWBY, L
Abs # 2293
04-Oct-1913

ORRICK, W J
Abs # 217
15-Mar-1878
see also, Map 40

OXFORD, J G
Abs # 1503
04-Feb-1879
see also, Map 38

PATTER, H N
Abs # 224
14-Apr-1860

PAYNE, F G
Abs # 1515
13-Sep-1880

POITEVENT, J
Abs # 1959
Survey2: GUTHRIE, J
26-Oct-1889
see also, Map 47

POITEVENT, J
Abs # 232
19-Feb-1878
see also, Map 40

RAMSOURS, N
Abs # 1970
15-Feb-1905
see also, Map 47

REEDER , T P
Abs # 1354
14-Jun-1878

RIBBLE, E J
Abs # 1877
12-Dec-1906
see also, Map 47

RIBBLE, W
Abs # 1996
19-Feb-1891

ROBINSON, J J
Abs # 1520
27-May-1879
see also, Map 38

ROSE, HRS J
Abs # 245
01-May-1862
see also, Map 40

SAUNDERS, L O
Abs # 2292
06-Jun-1914

WALKER, J B
Abs # 1278
24-Jun-1861

WALKER, J B
Abs # 1279
24-Jun-1861

WILLESS, J
Abs # 1652
01-May-1880

WRIGHT, W
Abs # 2256
20-Apr-1903
see also, Map 31

Abs # ?33
see also, Map 47

Populated Places
None

Cemeteries
Ming Bend Cemetery

Water (larger bodies)
Brazos River
Connor Creek
Possum Kingdom Lake

Other Water
Connor Creek
Cove Creek
Possum Kingdom Lake

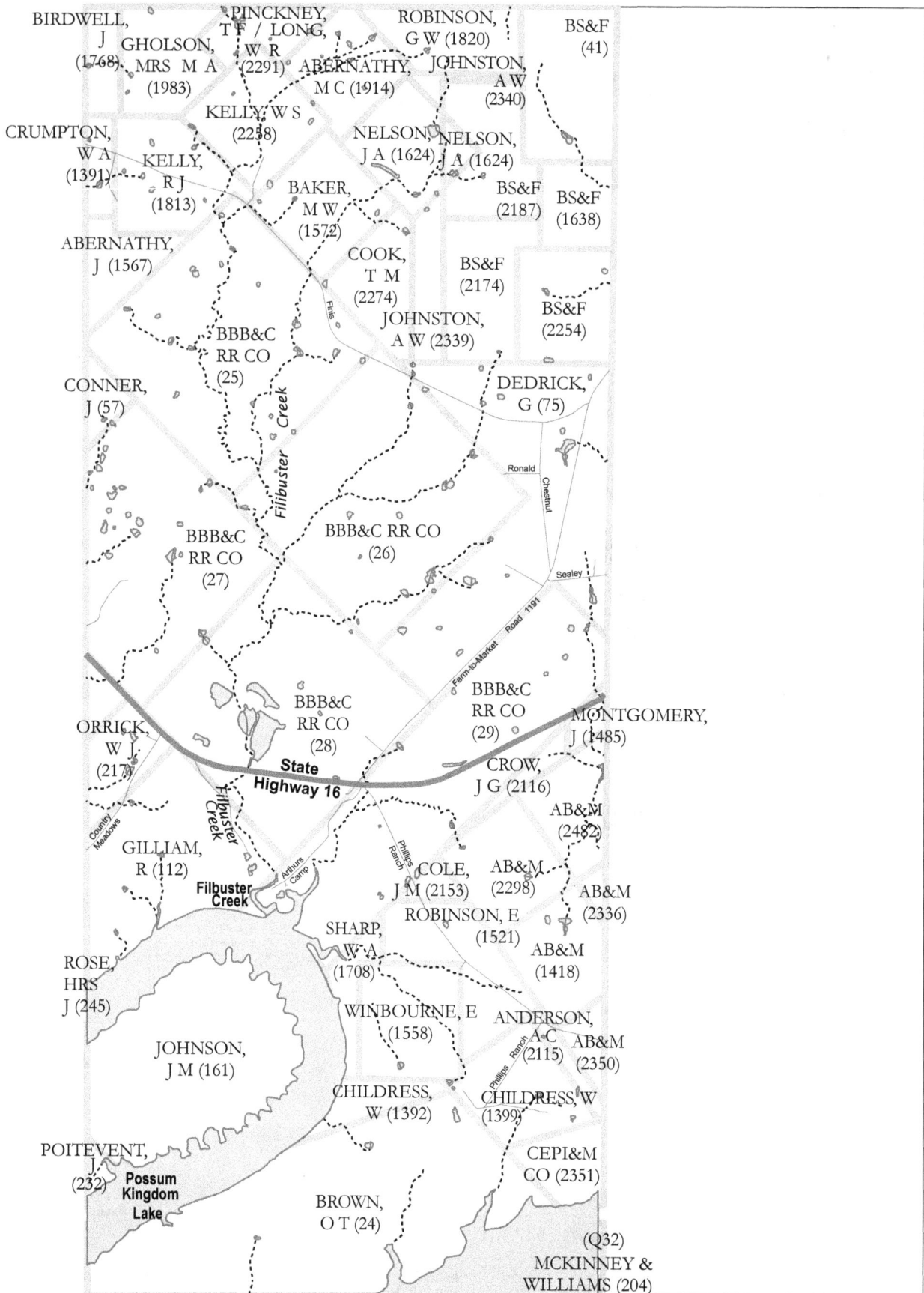

BIRDWELL,
J
(1768)

GHOLSON,
MRS M A
(1983)

PINCKNEY,
T F / LONG,
W R
(2291)

ABERNATHY,
M C (1914)

ROBINSON,
G W (1820)

BS&F
(41)

JOHNSTON,
A W
(2340)

KELLY, W S
(2238)

NELSON,
J A (1624)

NELSON,
J A (1624)

CRUMPTON,
W A
(1391)

KELLY,
R J
(1813)

BAKER,
M W
(1572)

BS&F
(2187)

BS&F
(1638)

ABERNATHY,
J (1567)

COOK,
T M
(2274)

BS&F
(2174)

BS&F
(2254)

JOHNSTON,
A W (2339)

BBB&C
RR CO
(25)

Finis

CONNER,
J (57)

DEDRICK,
G (75)

Filibuster Creek

Ronald

Chestnut

BBB&C
RR CO
(27)

BBB&C RR CO
(26)

Sealey

BBB&C
RR CO
(28)

BBB&C
RR CO
(29)

Farm-to-Market   Road 1191

MONTGOMERY,
J (1485)

ORRICK,
W J
(2170)

State
Highway 16

CROW,
J G (2116)

AB&M
(2482)

Country
Meadows

Filibuster
Creek

GILLIAM,
R (112)

Arthurs
Camp

Phillips
Ranch

COLE,
J M (2153)

AB&M
(2298)

AB&M
(2336)

Filibuster
Creek

ROBINSON, E
(1521)

AB&M
(1418)

ROSE,
HRS
J (245)

SHARP,
W A
(1708)

WINBOURNE, E
(1558)

ANDERSON,
A C
(2115)

AB&M
(2350)

JOHNSON,
J M (161)

Phillips Ranch

CHILDRESS,
W (1392)

CHILDRESS, W
(1399)

POITEVENT,
J,
(232)

Possum
Kingdom
Lake

BROWN,
O T (24)

CEPI&M
CO (2351)

(Q32)

MCKINNEY &
WILLIAMS (204)

Filibuster
Creek

AB&M
  Abs # 1418
  Survey2: DAVIDSON, J H
  24-Sep-1884

AB&M
  Abs # 2298
  Survey2: CROW, J T
  24-May-1922

AB&M
  Abs # 2336
  Survey2: COLE, J M
  26-Sep-1922

AB&M
  Abs # 2350
  23-Oct-1875

AB&M
  Abs # 2482
  Survey2: WILLIAMS, S D

ABERNATHY, J
  Abs # 1567
  09-Oct-1882
  see also, Map 39

ABERNATHY, M C
  Abs # 1914
  12-Jan-1892
  see also, Map 32

ANDERSON, A C
  Abs # 2115
  22-Sep-1894

BAKER, M W
  Abs # 1572
  02-Aug-1880

BBB&C RR CO
  Abs # 25
  23-Mar-1859
  see also, Map 39

BBB&C RR CO
  Abs # 26
  24-Mar-1859

BBB&C RR CO
  Abs # 27
  24-Mar-1859
  see also, Map 39

BBB&C RR CO
  Abs # 28
  24-Mar-1859

BBB&C RR CO
  Abs # 29
  21-Mar-1859

BIRDWELL, J
  Abs # 1768
  27-Mar-1884
  see also, Maps 31, 32, 39

BROWN, O T
  Abs # 24
  15-Mar-1878
  see also, Maps 39, 47, 48

BS&F
  Abs # 1638
  Survey2: SMITH, J P
  06-May-1901

BS&F
  Abs # 2174
  Survey2: ROBERTSON, E
  31-May-1922

BS&F
  Abs # 2187
  Survey2: HARRISON, W A
  31-May-1922

BS&F
  Abs # 2254
  Survey2: SPIVY, W D
  31-May-1922

BS&F
  Abs # 41
  07-Jul-1875
  see also, Map 32

CEPI&M CO
  Abs # 2351

24-Mar-1877

CHILDRESS, W
  Abs # 1392
  14-Mar-1884

CHILDRESS, W
  Abs # 1399
  27-Mar-1884

COLE, J M
  Abs # 2153
  04-Jan-1897

CONNER, J
  Abs # 57
  30-Oct-1857
  see also, Map 39

COOK, T M
  Abs # 2274
  25-Mar-1919

CROW, J G
  Abs # 2116
  15-Nov-1894

CRUMPTON, W A
  Abs # 1391
  20-Jun-1879
  see also, Map 39

DEDRICK, G
  Abs # 75
  24-Sep-1860

GHOLSON, MRS M A
  Abs # 1983
  17-Sep-1895
  see also, Map 32

GILLIAM, R
  Abs # 112
  15-Mar-1878
  see also, Map 39

JOHNSON, J M
  Abs # 161
  31-May-1862
  see also, Map 39

JOHNSTON, A W
  Abs # 2339
  23-Jan-1925

JOHNSTON, A W
  Abs # 2340
  23-Jan-1925

KELLY, R J
  Abs # 1813
  04-Oct-1884

KELLY, W S
  Abs # 2258
  04-Dec-1903

MCKINNEY & WILLIAMS
  Abs # 204
  28-Jan-1871
  see also, Map 48

MONTGOMERY, J
  Abs # 1485
  01-Aug-1884

NELSON, J A
  Abs # 1624
  02-Aug-1880

ORRICK, W J
  Abs # 217
  15-Mar-1878
  see also, Map 39

PINCKNEY, T F / LONG, W R
  Abs # 2291
  19-Sep-1912
  see also, Map 32

POITEVENT, J
  Abs # 232
  19-Feb-1878
  see also, Map 39

ROBINSON, E
  Abs # 1521
  11-Oct-1881

ROBINSON, G W

Abs # 1820
05-Mar-1884
see also, Map 32

ROSE, HRS J
  Abs # 245
  01-May-1862
  see also, Map 39

SHARP, W A
  Abs # 1708
  22-Nov-1884

WINBOURNE, E
  Abs # 1558
  18-Oct-1881

Abs # ?32

Populated Places
  None

Cemeteries
  None

Water (larger bodies)
  Filbuster Creek
  Possum Kingdom Lake

Other Water
  Filbuster Creek

PASSMORE, CRYSP, G   TOWNSEND,   BAHN,
B (1698)   (1397)   C W (1855)   A (38)   GLASS,   HEWITT, HEWITT, HENDERSON,   BRAGG, G
                                                     T J (1437)   R (1454)   R (150) H T (1450)   (53)
   WILLIAMS, J H (1713)   MOONEY, MEADORS,
   JOHNSON,   PEPPER,   J (1744)   E (1489)
   A S (2188)   S T (Q38)

Cox Branch

Kings Creek

Huffstuttle Creek

FM Road 578

BAHN, A
Abs # 38
20-Nov-1875
see also, Map 33

BRAGG, G
Abs # 53
08-Jan-1879
see also, Maps 33, 34, 42

CRYSP, G
Abs # 1397
29-Apr-1884
see also, Map 33

GLASS, T J
Abs # 1437
13-Nov-1977
see also, Map 33

HENDERSON, H T
Abs # 1450
04-May-1880
see also, Map 33

HEWITT, R
Abs # 1454
23-Jun-1884
see also, Map 33

HEWITT, R
Abs # 150
07-Aug-1876

JOHNSON, A S
Abs # 2188
23-Aug-1854

MEADORS, E
Abs # 1489
02-Dec-1884
see also, Maps 34, 42

MOONEY, J
Abs # 1744
27-Aug-1884
see also, Map 33

PASSMORE, B
Abs # 1698
13-Jul-1881
see also, Map 33

PEPPER, S T
Abs # ?38

TOWNSEND, C W
Abs # 1855
07-Aug-1888
see also, Map 33

WILLIAMS, J H
Abs # 1713
19-Jan-1881
see also, Map 33

Populated Places
None

Cemeteries
None

Water (larger bodies)
None

Other Water
Coal Branch
East Kings Creek
Huffstuttle Creek
Kings Creek

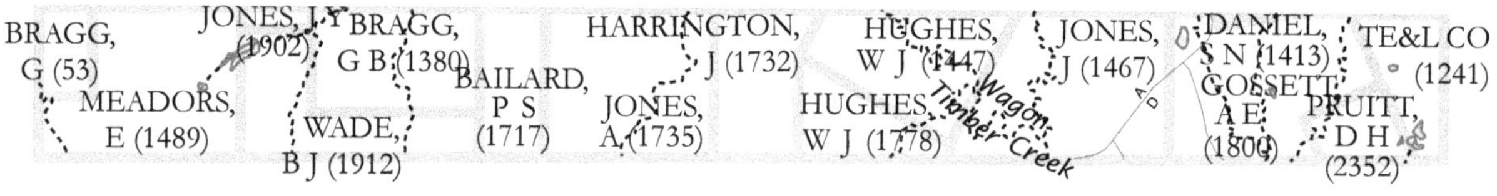

BRAGG,
G (53)

JONES, J
(1902)

BRAGG,
G B (1380)

BAILARD,
P S
(1717)

HARRINGTON,
J (1732)

HUGHES,
W J (1447)

JONES,
J (1467)

DANIEL,
S N (1413)

TE&L CO
(1241)

MEADORS,
E (1489)

WADE,
B J (1912)

JONES,
A (1735)

HUGHES,
W J (1778)

GOSSETT,
A E
(1800)

PRUITT,
D H
(2352)

Wagon

Timber Creek

BAILARD, P S
Abs # 1717
01-Aug-1887
see also, Map 34

BRAGG, G
Abs # 53
08-Jan-1879
see also, Maps 33, 34, 41

BRAGG, G B
Abs # 1380
09-Apr-1881
see also, Map 34

DANIEL, S N
Abs # 1413
23-Jun-1884
see also, Map 34

GOSSETT, A E
Abs # 1800
18-Feb-1884
see also, Map 34

HARRINGTON, J
Abs # 1732
22-Apr-1884
see also, Map 34

HUGHES, W J
Abs # 1447
16-Sep-1881
see also, Map 34

HUGHES, W J
Abs # 1778
21-Sep-1883

JONES, A
Abs # 1735
13-Sep-1884
see also, Map 34

JONES, J
Abs # 1467
18-Feb-1884
see also, Map 34

JONES, J Y
Abs # 1902
18-Jul-1887
see also, Map 34

MEADORS, E
Abs # 1489
02-Dec-1884
see also, Maps 34, 41

PRUITT, D H
Abs # 2352
10-Jan-1883

TE&L CO
Abs # 1241
04-Aug-1858
see also, Maps 34, 35, 43

WADE, B J
Abs # 1912
18-Jul-1887

Populated Places
None

Cemeteries
None

Water (larger bodies)
None

Other Water
Wagon Timber Creek

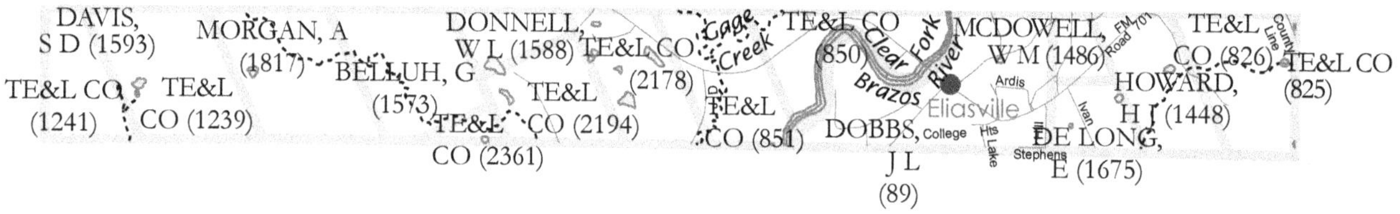
DAVIS, S D (1593)
MORGAN, A (1817)
TE&L CO (1241)
TE&L CO (1239)
BELL, H, G (1573)
DONNELL, W L (1588)
TE&L CO (2178)
TE&L CO (2194)
TE&L CO (2361)
Cage Creek
TE&L CO (850)
TE&L CO (851)
Clear Fork Brazos River
MCDOWELL, W M (1486)
Eliasville
Ardis
College
DOBBS, J L (89)
Hts Lake
Stephens
Ivan
FM Road 701
DE LONG, E (1675)
HOWARD, H J (1448)
TE&L CO (826)
TE&L CO (825)
County Line

BELLUH, G
Abs # 1573
26-Aug-1880
see also, Map 35

DAVIS, S D
Abs # 1593
05-Feb-1883
see also, Maps 34, 35

DE LONG, E
Abs # 1675
12-Feb-1881

DOBBS, J L
Abs # 89
12-Apr-1877
see also, Map 35

DONNELL, W L
Abs # 1588
28-Apr-1880
see also, Map 35

HOWARD, H J
Abs # 1448
22-Oct-1888
see also, Map 35

MCDOWELL, W M
Abs # 1486
08-Jan-1894
see also, Map 35

MORGAN, A
Abs # 1817
21-May-1884
see also, Map 35

TE&L CO
Abs # 1239
25-Feb-1859
see also, Map 35

TE&L CO
Abs # 1241
04-Aug-1858
see also, Maps 34, 35, 42

TE&L CO
Abs # 2178
23-Feb-1858
see also, Map 35

TE&L CO
Abs # 2194
23-Feb-1858

TE&L CO
Abs # 2361
10-Jan-1949

TE&L CO
Abs # 825
26-Aug-1858
see also, Maps 35, 36, 44

TE&L CO
Abs # 826
26-Aug-1858
see also, Maps 35, 44

TE&L CO
Abs # 850
11-Jun-1858
see also, Map 35

TE&L CO
Abs # 851
03-Aug-1858
see also, Map 35

<u>**Populated Places**</u>
Eliasville

<u>**Cemeteries**</u>
None

<u>**Water**</u> (larger bodies)
None

<u>**Other Water**</u>
Clear Fork Brazos River
Gage Creek

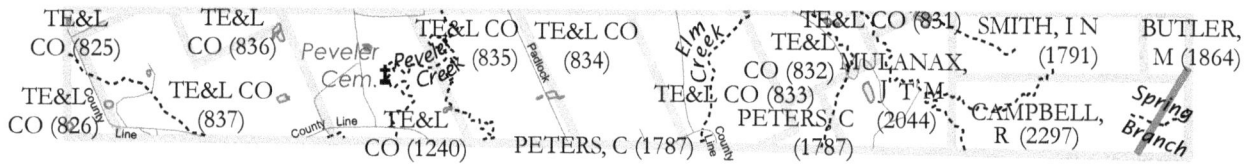

BUTLER, M
Abs # 1864
03-Jun-1886
see also, Maps 36, 37, 45

CAMPBELL, R
Abs # 2297
22-Aug-1860
see also, Map 45

MULANAX, J T M
Abs # 2044
06-Sep-1895
see also, Map 36

PETERS, C
Abs # 1787
15-Apr-1887

SMITH, I N
Abs # 1791
07-Feb-1898
see also, Map 36

TE&L CO
Abs # 1240
14-Mar-1859
see also, Map 36

TE&L CO
Abs # 825
26-Aug-1858
see also, Maps 35, 36, 43

TE&L CO
Abs # 826
26-Aug-1858
see also, Maps 35, 43

TE&L CO
Abs # 831
29-Jul-1858
see also, Map 36

TE&L CO
Abs # 832
29-Jul-1858
see also, Map 36

TE&L CO
Abs # 833
26-May-1859
see also, Map 36

TE&L CO
Abs # 834
29-Jul-1858
see also, Map 36

TE&L CO
Abs # 835
18-Mar-1859
see also, Map 36

TE&L CO
Abs # 836
29-Jul-1858
see also, Maps 35, 36

TE&L CO
Abs # 837
29-Jul-1858
see also, Map 36

Populated Places
None

Cemeteries
Peveler Cemetery

Water (larger bodies)
None

Other Water
Elm Creek
Peveler Creek
Spring Branch

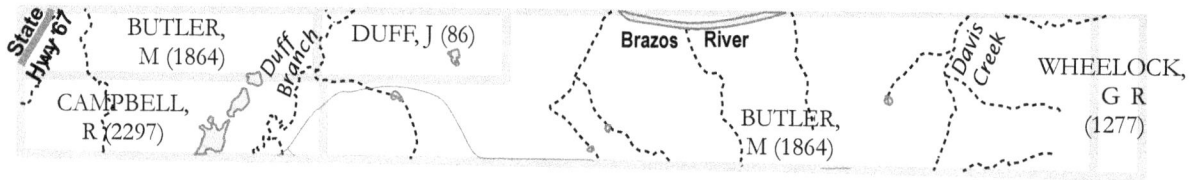

BUTLER, M
  Abs # 1864
  03-Jun-1886
  see also, Maps 36, 37, 44

CAMPBELL, R
  Abs # 2297
  22-Aug-1860
  see also, Map 44

DUFF, J
  Abs # 86
  08-Oct-1917
  see also, Map 37

WHEELOCK, G R
  Abs # 1277
  06-Aug-1875
  see also, Maps 37, 38, 46

Populated Places
None

Cemeteries
None

Water (larger bodies)
Brazos River

Other Water
Davis Creek
Duff Branch

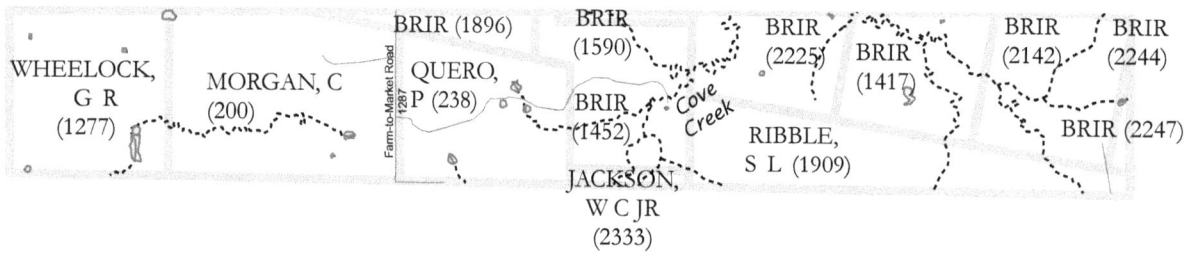

BRIR
Abs # 1417
Survey2: DIEW, F M
03-Mar-1879
see also, Map 38

BRIR
Abs # 1452
Survey2: HALL, W R
13-May-1885
see also, Map 38

BRIR
Abs # 1590
Survey2: DRIVER, J
29-May-1884
see also, Map 38

BRIR
Abs # 1896
Survey2: GREENWADE, R H
24-Nov-1891
see also, Map 38

BRIR
Abs # 2142
Survey2: MCKNIGHT, W N
09-Aug-1917
see also, Maps 38, 47

BRIR
Abs # 2225
Survey2: RIBBLE, S L
05-May-1921
see also, Map 38

BRIR
Abs # 2244
Survey2: MITCHELL, R F
14-Nov-1906
see also, Maps 38, 39, 47

BRIR
Abs # 2247
Survey2: RIBBLE, C M
25-Feb-1916
see also, Map 47

JACKSON, W C JR
Abs # 2333
13-Jul-1922

MORGAN, C
Abs # 200
28-May-1875
see also, Map 38

QUERO, P
Abs # 238
14-Jun-1875

RIBBLE, S L
Abs # 1909
05-Apr-1900
see also, Map 47

WHEELOCK, G R
Abs # 1277
06-Aug-1875
see also, Maps 37, 38, 45

Populated Places
None

Cemeteries
None

Water (larger bodies)
None

Other Water
Cove Creek

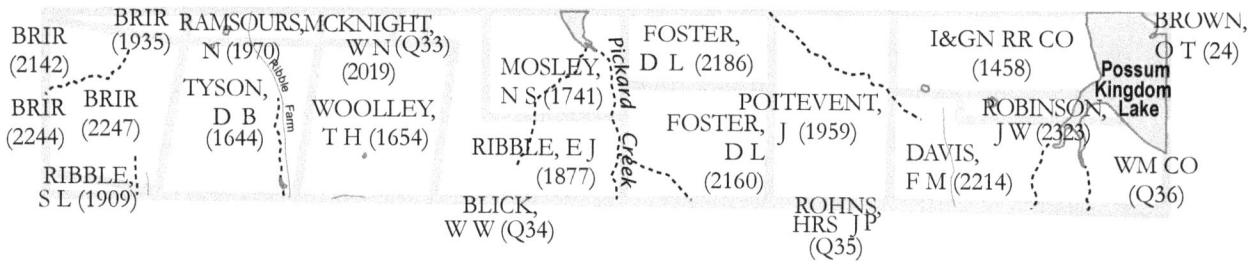

BLICK, W W
Abs # ?34

BRIR
Abs # 1935
Survey2: KUYKENDALL, W H
27-Nov-1912
see also, Map 39

BRIR
Abs # 2142
Survey2: MCKNIGHT, W N
09-Aug-1917
see also, Maps 38, 46

BRIR
Abs # 2244
Survey2: MITCHELL, R F
14-Nov-1906
see also, Maps 38, 39, 46

BRIR
Abs # 2247
Survey2: RIBBLE, C M
25-Feb-1916
see also, Map 46

BROWN, O T
Abs # 24
15-Mar-1878
see also, Maps 39, 40, 48

DAVIS, F M
Abs # 2214
16-Aug-1928
see also, Map 48

FOSTER, D L
Abs # 2160
24-Jan-1923

FOSTER, D L
Abs # 2186
24-Jan-1923
see also, Map 39

I&GN RR CO
Abs # 1458
23-Nov-1881
see also, Map 39

MCKNIGHT, W N
Abs # 2019
23-Dec-1896
see also, Map 39

MOSLEY, N S
Abs # 1741
24-Nov-1885
see also, Map 39

POITEVENT, J
Abs # 1959
Survey2: GUTHRIE, J
26-Oct-1889
see also, Map 39

RAMSOURS, N
Abs # 1970
15-Feb-1905
see also, Map 39

RIBBLE, E J
Abs # 1877
12-Dec-1906
see also, Map 39

RIBBLE, S L
Abs # 1909
05-Apr-1900
see also, Map 46

ROBINSON, J W
Abs # 2323
23-Jun-1920

ROHNS, HRS J P
Abs # ?35

TYSON, D B
Abs # 1644
13-Jun-1885

WM CO
Abs # ?36
see also, Map 48

WOOLLEY, T H
Abs # 1654
28-Mar-1918

Abs # ?33
see also, Map 39

Populated Places	
None	

Cemeteries	
None	

Water (larger bodies)	
Possum Kingdom Lake	

Other Water	
Pickard Creek	

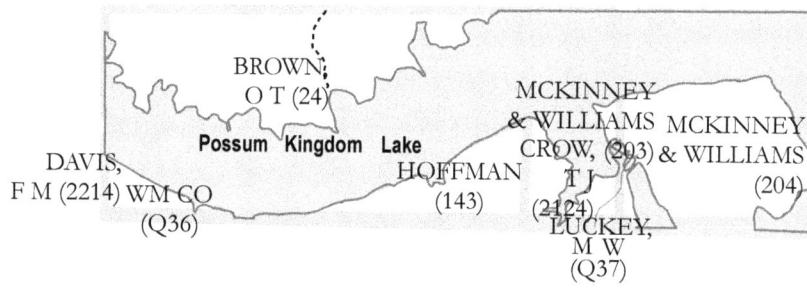

BROWN, O T
Abs # 24
15-Mar-1878
see also, Maps 39, 40, 47

CROW, T J
Abs # 2124

DAVIS, F M
Abs # 2214
16-Aug-1928
see also, Map 47

HOFFMAN
Abs # 143
10-Jul-1873

LUCKEY, M W
Abs # ?37

MCKINNEY & WILLIAMS
Abs # 203
21-Feb-1873

MCKINNEY & WILLIAMS
Abs # 204
28-Jan-1871
see also, Map 40

WM CO
Abs # ?36
see also, Map 47

Populated Places
None

Cemeteries
None

Water (larger bodies)
Possum Kingdom Lake

Other Water
None

This series and others like it are published and printed
in the U.S.A. by:

Arphax Publishing

please check out our hundreds of offerings

by phone . . .
1-800-681-5298

email . . .
info@arphax.com

or the web . . .
www.arphax.com

www.ingramcontent.com/pod-product-compliance
Lightning Source LLC
Chambersburg PA
CBHW080233270326
41926CB00020B/4222